INVESTMENT MANAGEMENT, STEWARDSHIP AND SUSTAINABILITY

This book brings together thought leadership from academia and leading figures in asset management in key global jurisdictions, to pool together insights regarding the transformative visions and challenges for modern investment management, as well as best practices that realise the policy objectives in regulation and soft law.

The world of investment management is being challenged by new legal, regulatory and soft law developments to demonstrate that their practices cohere with the long-term needs of the saving population as well as public interest needs in financing global sustainability and social development. The chapters in this book uniquely bring together the views of academia and practice on the key developments that can transform the law and practice of investment management, including the EU's new sustainable finance reform package, the UK Stewardship Code 2020, and developments in the US regarding the fit between fiduciary law for investment management and modern sustainability concerns.

The book brings together the best of both worlds – critical thoughtful perspectives from academia and qualitative insight from the investment management industry. It will be of interest to researchers in law, investment management, business and management, practitioners in the investment management industry and their legal advisers, and policy-makers in the EU, UK and beyond who are grappling with the appropriate governance paradigms for bringing about more sustainable outcomes globally.

CONTEMPORARY STUDIES IN CORPORATE LAW

Series editors: Marc Moore, Christopher Bruner

Corporate law scholarship has a relatively recent history despite the fact that corporations have existed and been subject to legal regulation for three centuries. The modern flourishing of corporate law scholarship has been matched by some broadening of the field of study to embrace insolvency, corporate finance, corporate governance and regulation of the financial markets. At the same time the intersection between other branches of law such as, for example, labour, contract, criminal law, competition, and intellectual property law and the introduction of new interdisciplinary methodologies affords new possibilities for studying the corporation. This series seeks to foster intellectually diverse approaches to thinking about the law and its role, scope and effectiveness in the context of corporate activity. In so doing the series aims to publish works of high intellectual content and theoretical rigour.

Titles in this series

Investment Management, Stewardship and Sustainability

Transformation and Challenges in Law and Regulation

Edited by

Iris H-Y Chiu

and

Hans-Christoph Hirt

·HART·

OXFORD · LONDON · NEW YORK · NEW DELHI · SYDNEY

HART PUBLISHING

Bloomsbury Publishing Plc

Kemp House, Chawley Park, Cumnor Hill, Oxford, OX2 9PH, UK

1385 Broadway, New York, NY 10018, USA

29 Earlsfort Terrace, Dublin 2, Ireland

HART PUBLISHING, the Hart/Stag logo, BLOOMSBURY and the Diana logo are
trademarks of Bloomsbury Publishing Plc

First published in Great Britain 2023

A catalogue record for this book is available from the British Library.

Library of Congress Cataloging-in-Publication data

Names: Chiu, Iris H.-Y., editor. | Hirt, Hans C. (Hans-Christoph), 1973- editor.

Title: Investment management, stewardship and sustainability : transformation and challenges in law
and regulation / edited by Iris H-Y Chiu and Hans-Christoph Hirt.

Description: Oxford ; New York,: Hart , 2023. | Series: Contemporary studies in corporate law | Includes bibliographical
references and index. | Summary: "This book brings together thought leadership from academia and leading figures in
asset management in key global jurisdictions, to pool together insights regarding the transformative visions and challenges
for modern investment management, as well as best practices that realise the policy objectives in regulation and soft law. The
world of investment management is being challenged by new legal, regulatory and soft law developments to demonstrate that
their practices cohere with the long-term needs of the saving population as well as public interest needs in financing global
sustainability and social development. The chapters in this book uniquely bring together the views of academia and practice on
the key developments that can transform the law and practice of investment management, including the EU's new sustainable
finance reform package, the UK Stewardship Code 2020, and developments in the US regarding the fit between fiduciary law for
investment management and modern sustainability concerns. The book brings together the best of both worlds-critical thoughtful
perspectives from academia and qualitative insight from the investment management industry. It will be of interest to researchers
in law, investment management, business and management, practitioners in the investment management industry and their legal
advisers, and policy-makers in the EU, UK and beyond who are grappling with the appropriate governance paradigms for bringing
about more sustainable outcomes globally"—Provided by publisher.

Identifiers: LCCN 2022046012 | ISBN 9781509953752 (hardback) | ISBN 9781509953790 (paperback) |
ISBN 9781509953776 (pdf) | ISBN 9781509953769 (Epub)

Subjects: LCSH: Social responsibility of business—Law and legislation. | Investments—Law and legislation.

Classification: LCC K1329.5 .I58 2022 | DDC 346/.0664—dc23/eng/20221201

LC record available at https://lccn.loc.gov/2022046012

ISBN:	HB:	978-1-50995-375-2
	ePDF:	978-1-50995-377-6
	ePub:	978-1-50995-376-9

Typeset by Compuscript Ltd, Shannon

To find out more about our authors and books visit www.hartpublishing.co.uk. Here you will find extracts, author information,
details of forthcoming events and the option to sign up for our newsletters.

Table of Contents

PART II
PRACTICAL REFLECTIONS ON INVESTMENT MANAGEMENT STEWARDSHIP AND SUSTAINABLE FINANCE

List of Contributors

Ken Bertsch

Ken Bertsch served as executive director of the Council of Institutional Investors from 2016 to 2020. Previously, he was a partner at CamberView Partners; president and CEO of the Society for Corporate Governance (then the Society of Corporate Secretaries and Governance Professionals); head of corporate governance at Morgan Stanley Investment Management; managing director for corporate governance analysis at Moody's Investors Service; director of governance engagement at TIAA-CREF; and in various roles at the Investor Responsibility Research Center. He currently serves as chair of the Legion Partners Asset Management Advisory Council, and a consultant to Broadridge Financial. He served as a member of the PJT/Camberview Advisory Council from 2020 to 2021. He holds a JD from Fordham University School of Law (2004) and an undergraduate degree from Williams College (1978).

Hanne S Birkmose

Hanne S Birkmose is a professor at the Department of Law, University of Southern Denmark. Her research areas include company law – in particular international company law and EU company law – and corporate governance, and she has written several national and international articles within these areas. In addition, she is the editor of several international volumes on company law topics. She is also the author of Danish books on UCITS and alternative investment funds. Recently, she has mainly worked with shareholder activism, the role of institutional shareholders, and sustainable finance. In 2014, she received a research grant from the Danish Independent Research Council for a project on 'Shareholders' Duties'. Hanne S Birkmose is an academic member of the ECGI, the Nordic Company Law Network and the Nordic Corporate Governance Network.

Iris H-Y Chiu

Iris Chiu is Professor of Corporate Law and Financial Regulation at University College London. She is Director of the UCL Centre of Ethics and Law and advances the public and stakeholder engagement of the Centre's agenda in relation to a wide range of issues in relation to law, regulation, governance and ethics in business and finance. She has published extensively in the areas of corporate governance and financial regulation, including *The Foundations and Anatomy of Shareholder Activism* (2010), *Investment Management and Corporate Governance* (2017), *The Legal Framework for Internal Control in Banks and Financial Institutions* (2015) and *Banking Law and Regulation* (2019). She has interests in financial regulation and governance, law and technology, corporate law and governance and the law and policy for business and finance generally. She is a Research Fellow of the European Corporate Governance Institute and, most recently, a Senior Scholar at the European Central Bank's Legal Research Programme.

Theodor F Cojoianu

Dr Cojoianu (PhD) is Associate Professor in Sustainable Finance and Director of Research at the Centre for Business, Climate Change and Sustainability at the University of Edinburgh Business School. He is a member of the EU's Platform on Sustainable Finance (PSF) and of the Green Taxonomy Advisory Group (GTAG) at HM Treasury (United Kingdom). Theodor is co-founder of RoSIF, academic-in-residence at Agent Green and at Sustainable Nation Ireland, and sits on the Executive Committee of the Global Network on Financial Geography.

George Dallas

George Dallas has served as Policy Director at the International Corporate Governance Network since 2014, where he coordinates ICGN's governance policies and committees, and leads ICGN's policy development and regulatory outreach on behalf of members, whose assets under management represent $70 trillion. George is also a Visiting Lecturer at Bayes (formerly Cass) Business School, University of London, where he teaches MSc and executive education courses in corporate governance. Previously, George served as Director of Corporate Governance at F&C Investments (now BMO Global Asset Management) in London, where he led F&C's global policies relating to corporate governance, including proxy voting and engagement matters. Prior to joining F&C George was a Managing Director at Standard & Poor's, where he held a range of managerial and analytical roles in New York and London. He is co-author of *Governance, Stewardship and Sustainability*, whose second edition will be published by Routledge in 2022.

Ola Peter K Gjessing

Ola Peter Krohn Gjessing is Lead Investment Stewardship Manager in Norges Bank Investment Management. Since he joined NBIM in 2005, he has focused on board-level engagement with major companies in the equity portfolio, governance policy and ownership strategies, and the interface with Norwegian authorities. He currently works with internal global investment teams covering the financial sector and basic industries. He monitors market practices for corporate governance in several European markets and oversees NBIM's global policies on executive remuneration. He is a Certified European Financial Analyst (EFFAS) and holds an MBA in Finance from the Norwegian School of Economics (NHH). Previously, he has been a journalist in Reuters' Oslo financial newsroom, covering equity, fixed income, foreign exchange and energy, and has been a political adviser to the chairman of the Conservative Party in Norway and the Oslo city government. He can be contacted via okg@nbim.no.

Virginia Harper Ho

Virginia Harper Ho is a Professor of Law at the City University of Hong Kong. Her research focuses on the intersections of corporate governance, finance, and securities regulation from a comparative perspective, and she has written recently on shareholder activism, ESG disclosure reform, and sustainable finance. Her work has been published in edited volumes and leading journals, and she has also recently contributed to ESG reform initiatives led by the of the Singapore Exchange (SGX), the Securities and Exchange Commission of Brazil (Comissão de Valores Mobiliários), and the US Securities and Exchange Commission. She received her JD from Harvard Law School.

David Hickey

David has been involved in equity portfolio management since 2006, and most recently worked at Lothian Pension Fund as a European equity portfolio manager and the firm's lead on responsible investment. His work at Lothian included ESG Integration across all asset classes, completing PRI, TCFD and Stewardship reports and setting overall RI policy. He has worked on major projects throughout the industry, contributing to TCFD guidance, acting as an engagement lead on two Climate Action 100+ engagements, running workshops for the Institutional Investor Group on Climate Change (IIGCC) and the CFA Society UK and running the industry leading podcast Talking Responsibly. He has been a CFA charterholder since 2010. He lives in Edinburgh with his wife Sandra and dog Zara, and he also teaches the martial art iaido, in which he holds a fifth degree black belt.

Hans-Christoph Hirt

Dr Hans-Christoph Hirt is a Trustee Director of the Hermes Group Pension Scheme (HGPS) in London. Until March 2022, he was Managing Director and a member of the Board of EOS at Federated Hermes, the leading provider of engagement and voting services representing more than $1.6 trillion of assets under advice (2021). EOS is part of Federated Hermes, Inc, the US-based fund manager with assets under management of more than $650 billion (2021). Before his time with EOS, Dr Hirt worked with the international law firm Ashurst and at the London School of Economics. In addition to his work in the financial services sector, Dr Hirt has been affiliated with the Law School at University College London (UCL) for many years. He has a multi-disciplinary background in business administration, law, accounting and auditing, asset management and climate science. He can be contacted at: hans-christoph.hirt@alumni.lse.ac.uk.

Chris Hodge

Chris Hodge is an independent adviser on corporate governance and regulation who assisted ICGN and the GISD Alliance with the revisions to the Model Mandate. Chris is currently an adviser to the UK's Institute of Directors, where he is responsible for the operations of its Centre for Corporate Governance. For ten years until 2014 Chris was the Director of Corporate Governance at the UK Financial Reporting Council, where he was responsible for overseeing the UK Corporate Governance Code and introducing the UK Stewardship Code for investors, the first code of its sort in the world.

Andreas GF Hoepner

Professor Hoepner (PhD) is Full Professor of Operational Risk, Banking & Finance at the Michael Smurfit Graduate Business School & the Lochlann Quinn School of Business of University College Dublin (UCD), Vice Principal for Equality, Diversity and Inclusion (EDI), and is a supervisor for UCD's SFI Centre for Research Training in Machine Learning. Professor Hoepner serves on the EU's Platform on Sustainable Finance (PSF) as independent member. Prior to PSF, Andreas served as independent member on the Technical Expert Group (TEG) on Sustainable Finance.

Andrew R Johnston

Andrew Johnston is Professor of Company Law and Corporate Governance in the School of Law at the University of Warwick. He is also a member of the Companies,

Markets and Sustainability Research Group at the University of Oslo; a research associate at the University of Cambridge Centre for Business Research; and a member of the GOODCORP Research Network. Recently he has been a visiting professor at Mines ParisTech and Queensland University of Technology. In the past, he has held positions at the Universities of Sheffield, Queensland, Cambridge and Warsaw. He has published widely on company law, corporate governance in the UK and EU (its history, its sustainability), takeovers, corporate social responsibility, stewardship and regulatory and policy responses to the financial crisis. Recently he has worked on informal finance in China and independent directors in Japan. Before joining academia, he practised law with Herbert Smith and the Treasury Solicitor in London.

Kenneth Khoo

Kenneth Khoo is a Lecturer at the NUS Faculty of Law. Kenneth graduated from NUS in 2014 with a Bachelor of Laws (First Class Honours) and a Bachelor of Social Sciences (Economics) (First Class Honours), from the London School of Economics and Political Science with a Master of Science in Economics in 2018, and from Yale Law School with a Master of Laws in 2019. He also received the Ministry of Trade and Industry (Economist Service) Prize for Best Thesis in Economics from NUS. Kenneth has research and teaching interests in hybrid areas where law and economics intersect, especially in commercial subjects like corporate law, mergers and acquisitions, securities regulations, and competition law. His work has been published (or is forthcoming) in international journals such as the *University of Pennsylvania Journal of Business Law*, the *Journal of Competition Law and Economics* and the *American Business Law Journal*.

Li-Wen Lin

Li-Wen Lin is an Associate Professor at the Allard School of Law, University of British Columbia. Her research and teaching interests include comparative corporate governance, corporate social responsibility, state capitalism, Chinese law, and law and economic sociology. She has written extensively on various legal innovations of corporate social responsibility (CSR), including codes of vendor conduct in global supply chains, sustainability reporting, and mandatory CSR legislation around the world. Professor Lin's research work has been published in a wide range of law and interdisciplinary journals, including the *American Journal of Comparative Law*, the *China Quarterly*, *Stanford Law Review*, the *World Trade Review*, *Columbia Business Law Review*, *Berkeley Journal of International Law*, *University of Pennsylvania Asian Law Review*, etc. Professor Lin holds LLM and JSD degrees from the University of Illinois at Urbana-Champaign and a PhD degree in Sociology from Columbia University, where she was appointed as a Paul F Lazarsfeld Fellow.

Yanan Lin

Dr Lin (PhD) is a case researcher at China Europe International Business School in Shanghai. She has three years of research experience in Sustainable Finance at UCD Michael Smurfit Business School in Dublin. Her research area is in corporate social performance and financial performance, and anti-greenwashing.

Catherine Malecki
Catherine Malecki is Professor of Private Law, Rennes 2 University, France. She is an Awardee of French Scholars Lectures Series at UBC, https://international.univ-rennes2. fr/article/rennes-2-professor-catherine-malecki-awardee-prestigious-french-scholar-lecture-series; http://www.idep.universite-paris-saclay.fr/equipe/malecki-catherine. She can be contacted at: catherine.malecki@univ-rennes2.fr.

Kate van der Merve
Kate is a freelance researcher with UCD, following completion of UCD's Renewable Energy & Environmental Finance Masters. A fellow of Chartered Accountants Ireland, she has extensive finance experience across accounting practice, MNCs, and NGOs. Kate sits on Chartered Accountants Ireland's Thought Leadership & Publishing committee and Sustainable Expert Working Group.

Andrew Parry
Andrew Parry is the Head of Investments at JO Hambro Capital Management and Regnan. He is responsible for overseeing the investment functions within these businesses, including sustainable and impact capabilities, and he also sits on the executive committee. Andrew is a highly respected investment expert with over 30 years' experience. He has held senior roles at a number of leading asset management companies, including Lazard, Barings and Hermes and was most recently, prior to joining JO Hambro, the Head of Sustainable Investment at Newton Investment Management. He is a member of a number of investment bodies, he sits on the CFA UK Society Committee on Diversity and Inclusion and is a Trustee Director of the Trafalgar House Pension Trust. He was a former co-chair of the UNEP FI Positive Impact Initiative.

Brian Tomlinson
Brian Tomlinson is an adviser, consultant and thought leader on ESG, long-termism, corporate purpose, and sustainability. Brian's work has been featured in leading journals and publications including the *Harvard Business Review*, *MIT Sloan Management Review*, and the *Journal of Applied Corporate Finance*. Brian is a former attorney with 20 years' experience across law, finance, public policy and sustainability. Brian has a Masters in Public Administration from Harvard Kennedy School and an undergraduate degree in Politics Philosophy and Economics from the University of Oxford.

Christoph Van der Elst
Christoph Van der Elst is Professor of Business Law and Economics at Tilburg University, the Netherlands, Professor at Ghent University, Belgium and is a European Corporate Governance Institute research associate. He has held/holds visiting professorships at Vanderbilt (US), IDC (Israel), UAMS (Belgium), TIAS (The Netherlands), European College (Belgium), Babeş-Bolyai University (Romania) and CLEI (Italy). He is also a member of the audit committee of the Ghent University Hospital and an independent director of Aphilion. He is a member of the Belgian Bar (Cottyn) and has advised many different government agencies at national and international level. His current research interests are corporate governance, corporate voting, company law and DLT, all topics on which he has published widely in academic and professional journals.

Anh Vu
Anh Vu is a PhD candidate in sustainable finance at Queen's University Belfast. Her research interests include sustainable finance policies and their impacts on the financial sector, especially investment banks and pension funds.

Faith Ward
Faith is currently Chief Responsible Investment Officer for Brunel Pension Partnership and Chair of the Institutional Investors Group on Climate Change (IIGCC). These roles enable her to advocate for better appreciation of systemic risk as well as design solutions that embed such risks, like climate change, into the operations of finance and investment, an industry she has served for over 25 years. Faith was one of the co-creators of the Transition Pathway Initiative and is currently a NED. Her other roles include member of the Ethics Investment Advisory Group for the Church of England National Investing Bodies; member of Investor Advisory Group for SASB (becoming ISSB); Member of the UK Green Taxonomy Advisory Group and Transition Plan Taskforce Delivery Group; and Climate Ambassador for the National Federation of Women's Institutes. She was also formerly the chair of the Reporting and Assessment Advisory Committee for the United Nations Principles for Responsible Investment (UNPRI).

Abbreviations and Acronyms

AGM	Annual General Meeting
AMF	Autorité des marchés financiers
AUM	assets under management
BRT	Business Roundtable
BWI	Business Watch Indonesia
CalPERs	California Public Employees' Retirement System
CEO	Chief Executive Officer
CFA	Certified Financial Analysts' Institute
CFTC	Commodity Futures Trading Commission
CSR	corporate social responsibility
CSRD	Corporate Sustainability Reporting Directive
DiD	difference-in-differences
DNSH	'do no significant harm' principle
DOL	Department of Labor (US)
E&S	environmental and social
EBSA	Employee Benefits Security Administration (US)
ECB	European Central Bank
EFAMA	European Fund and Asset Management Association
EFSI	European Fund for Strategic Investments
EIB	European Investment Bank
EIOPA	European Insurance and Occupational Pensions Authority
ERISA	Employee Retirement and Income Security Act of 1974 (US)
ESAs	European Supervisory Authorities
ESG	environmental, social and governance
ESMA	European Securities and Markets Authority
ETFs	exchange traded funds

EuGB	European Green Bond
FCA	Financial Conduct Authority
FRC	Financial Reporting Council
FSOC	Financial Stability Oversight Council
FTC	Federal Trade Commission
GHG	greenhouse gas
GICS	Global Industrial Classification System
GIIN	Global Impact Investing Network
GISD	Global Investors in Sustainable Development
GLM	generalised linear model
GPFG	Government Pension Fund Global (Norway)
GSIA	Global Sustainable Investment Alliance
GSP	Global Stewardship Principles
HLEG	High Level Expert Group
ICA	Investment Company Act of 1940 (US)
ICGN	International Corporate Governance Network
ICMA	International Capital Market Association
IFRS	International Financial Reporting Standards
IIGCC	Institutional Investors Group on Climate Change
IIs	institutional investors
ILO	International Labour Organization
IMA	investment management agreement
IORPs	Institutions for Occupational Retirement Provisions
IOSCO	International Organization of Securities Commissions
IPR	Inevitable Policy Response
ISC	Institutional Shareholders' Committee
ISSB	International Sustainability Standards Board
ITT	invitation to tender
KPIs	key performance indicators
LGIM	Legal & General Investment Management
NBIM	Norges Bank Investment Management

NFA	national financial authorities
NFRD	Non-Financial Reporting Directive
NGO	non-governmental organisation
NIC	National Intelligence Council (US)
NZAM	Net-Zero Asset Managers Initiative
NZAOA	Net-Zero Asset Owner Alliance
NZIF	Net-Zero Investment Framework
OECD	Organisation for Economic Co-operation and Development
PAI	Principal Adverse Impact
PAII	Paris Aligned Investment Initiative
PRI	Principles for Responsible Investment
SASB	Sustainability Accounting Standards Board
SC 2020	Stewardship Code 2020 (UK)
SDG	Sustainable Development Goals
SEC	Securities and Exchange Commission
SFDR	Sustainable Finance Disclosure Regulation
SOEs	state-owned enterprises
SRD II	Shareholder Rights Directive
SWF	sovereign wealth fund
TCFD	Taskforce on Climate-related Financial Disclosures
TEG	Technical Expert Group
TNFD	Task Force on Nature-related Financial Disclosure
TPI	Transition Pathway Initiative
UCITS	undertakings for the collective investment in transferable securities
UNEPFI	United Nations Environment Programme Finance Initiative
UNFCCC	United Nations Framework Convention on Climate Change
WBCSD	World Business Council for Sustainable Development

Introduction: Investment Management, Stewardship and Sustainability: Key Gaps and Challenges

IRIS H-Y CHIU AND HANS-CHRISTOPH HIRT

I. AIMS AND OBJECTIVES

THE PRACTICE OF investment management, though strongly rooted in the paradigms of private mandates and accountability to clients and beneficiaries, is increasingly scrutinised by and made accountable to policy-makers and society. Since the end of the global financial crisis 2007–2009, policy-makers in many different jurisdictions[1] have framed institutional investors' roles in capital markets as 'stewards', drawing inspiration from the UK's pioneering Stewardship Code. 'Stewards' are expected to play a key role in safeguarding not only the long-term financial interests of savers in society, but also to act as monitors and challengers of corporate behaviour, seemingly in the interests of society, in maintaining a healthy and accountable listed corporate sector.[2] As the global asset management industry has passed the US$100 trillion mark in 2020,[3] this profile inevitably attracts social and policy attention to its roles, influences and potential. The industry has developed markedly in terms of its bottom-up practices in investment management, integrating conventional financial fundamentals as well as an increasing array of non-financial issues, offering different forms of 'stewardship' for customers.

We observe the progression of policy for the investment management industry elevating from the soft law premises of 'stewardship' to harder regulatory policy, particularly in recent legislative reforms in the European Union regarding sustainable finance. This entanglement between the private mandates of financial intermediation and policy interest in the power of financial allocation is only going to persist.

---

[1] D Katelouzou and M Siems, 'The Global Diffusion of Stewardship Codes' (2020), http://ssrn.com/abstract_id=3616798.

[2] J Kay, *The Kay Review of UK Equity Markets and Long-term Decision Making* (Final Report, July 2012), https://assets.publishing.service.gov.uk/government/uploads/system/uploads/attachment_data/file/253454/bis-12-917-kay-review-of-equity-markets-final-report.pdf; IH-Y Chiu, 'Turning Institutional Investors into "Stewards" – Exploring the Meaning and Objectives in "Stewardship"' (2013) 66 *Current Legal Problems* 443.

[3] PwC, *Asset Management 2020, a Brave New World* (2020), https://www.pwc.com/gx/en/industries/financial-services/asset-management/publications/asset-management-2020-a-brave-new-world.html.

Progression towards regulatory 'hardening' can be viewed as a debate in theoretical terms, as the theoretical premises of the 'agency paradigm' (which also forms the basis of private law and regulatory duties governing investment managers' conduct vis-à-vis their clients) are being challenged by newer policy developments that require new theorisation of investment intermediaries' roles, such as in relation to public or social interest. However, this progression leads chiefly to practical implementational ramifications for the practitioners of investment management, as there may be changes to investment management practices as well as compliance obligations with new regulations and rules.

The 'sense-making' of the corpus of regulatory policy as a whole gives rise to practitioners' 'legal interpretive' roles[4] that shape the practice of investment management, as these new requirements intersect with already-growing initiatives in the industry. Sense-making at the theoretical level, often carried out by academics who wish to provide perspective for appraising new developments, is often observed to be at odds with the practice of investment management.[5] This observation has been made since the soft law of 'stewardship' has been introduced, and it remains to be seen how the more recent introduction of hard regulatory policy in sustainable finance may further affect this 'sense-making' gap regarding the roles of the investment management industry. It is also to be queried whether this 'sense-making' gap is in fact an expectations gap, ie a gap between the social and wider expectations of the industry's roles and achievements, and the industry's own perception of its roles and its achievements.

The editors of this volume have been intrigued by this gap. Hence we have curated a volume and commissioned leading academics and practitioners in investment management to discuss their respective takes, focusing on the mainstream investment management markets in the US, EU and UK. This book does not deal in detail with focused or more niche forms of investment management such as impact investing,[6] and acknowledges that the notion of 'responsible' investing remains ambiguously wedged between specific 'socially responsible' mandates[7] and the mainstream.[8] This is especially critiqued in Hickey's chapter in Part II of the book, which features practitioners' reflections.

The book is divided into two parts. The first part, 'The Conception, Policy and Expectations of Investment Management Stewardship and Sustainable Finance' features usually longer pieces of work contributed by academics, intending to unpack the notions of 'stewardship' and various shades of 'responsible', Environmental,

---

[4] M Lenglet, 'Ambivalence and Ambiguity: The Interpretive Role of Compliance Officers' in I Huault and C Richard (eds), *Finance: The Discreet Regulator* (Palgrave Macmillan, 2012) at 59.

[5] A Reisberg, 'The UK Stewardship Code: On the Road to Nowhere?' (2015) 15 *Journal of Corporate Law Studies* 217; SCY Wong, 'Is Institutional Investor Stewardship Still Elusive?' (2015) *Butterworths Journal of Banking and Financial Law* 508.

[6] O Weber, 'Impact Investing'; J Clifford and T Jung, 'Social Impact Bonds'; M Martin, 'Building The Impact Investing Market', R Tekula and A Shah, 'Impact Investing' and G Rexhepi, 'The Architecture of Social Finance' in OM Lehner (ed), *Routledge Handbook of Sustainable and Social Finance* (Routledge, 2016).

[7] Socially responsible investing, or SRI as specific mandates.

[8] Now that the EU Sustainable Disclosure Regulation 2019/2088 compels all investment intermediaries to disclose how they 'integrate' sustainability risks where material, Art 3.

Social and Governance ('ESG') or 'sustainable' investment, as well as normative expectations for the industry of investment management. There are also a couple of empirical pieces in this part that complement the exploration into normative expectations of investment managers' roles and achievements. The second part, 'Practical Reflections on Investment Management Stewardship and Sustainable Finance' offers practitioners' insights into the practice of stewardship, with particular focus on responsible, ESG or sustainable investment. These contributions are sourced from leading asset owners from a variety of walks, including pension as well sovereign wealth funds, and asset managers in mainstream investing faced with new opportunities and challenges in responsible, ESG or sustainable investment.

This editorial chapter takes stock of the key themes drawn out in the volume in order to determine whether an expectations gap exists between theoretical/policy commentators who have normative visions of the roles of the investment management industry and the perceptions of practitioners in the industry, and what the nature of such a gap may be.

First, we take stock of the debate between incentives for the investment management industry and socially-facing interests and to what extent they are reconcilable or otherwise. A number of academic chapters argue that incentives drive investment management purposes and objectives but regulatory policy has increasingly attempted to broaden the purposes and interests that ought to be served by the investment management industry. The industry is, however, caught between private law in terms of fiduciary framing, especially in the US, and increasingly socially-facing demands from society and policy-makers. In this landscape, are incentives changing or being infused with other purposes in practice? How are practitioners viewing these changes and challenges? This chapter draws out some of the narratives of normative expectations discussed in the academic chapters, in order to map out any expectations gaps.

If normative expectations are pitched at a high level, such as 'achieving sustainable behaviour on the part of the corporate sector' for example, these expectations would feed into framing the investment management industry's roles and achievements in a particular manner, such as seeing them as agents for change or gatekeepers of behaviour. In this manner, observed practice in investment management that is perceived to fall short of such roles could result in an expectations gap. Both academic and practitioner chapters in this volume address such expectations, and there are differences in the expectations articulated for the industry, which therefore lead to different views regarding whether there is an expectations gap and of what nature. Further, these differing views relate to different 'levels' of actions involved in the chain of investment intermediation entities acting as 'agents' for change or 'monitors'. As Ward's chapter shows, asset owners may pull their weight in decarbonising their assets in their recruitment and monitoring of asset managers, but this also means that 'agency' for influencing portfolio companies' behaviour would be on the part of asset managers. The different levels of actions and spheres of influence in the investment chain exacerbate the problem of an expectations gap between the investment management industry and society.

In this editorial, we suggest that the expectations gap between the investment management industry and its stakeholders or society should be understood in relation to three role perceptions for the industry. We discuss the nature of these role perceptions and consider the potential for them to conflict with each other, as well as how the interaction between law and industry practice shapes the interrelationships between these roles. To a larger or smaller extent, the three role perceptions for the investment management industry reflect forms of market-based regulation, and it is important to consider the achievements and limitations of market-based regulation, and what can be achieved by instituting a greater role for direct forms of regulatory steering. A number of chapters in both the academic and practitioner parts reflect on this broader issue which must ultimately be addressed with policy leadership.

II. METHODOLOGIES IN THE VOLUME

This volume showcases contributions that deploy a variety of methodologies in order to shed light on the perspectives and practice of investment management, in terms of its 'stewardship' and engagement with responsible, ESG or sustainable concerns. First, the 'law and policy' approach is used extensively in both academic and practitioner chapters. This approach focuses on the purposes, objectives and functions of the activity in question, ie investment management, and critically questions what 'stewardship' means in relation to: (a) self-regulatory practice; and (b) changes to self-regulatory practice with the introduction of both soft law and law. Next, although no chapter on its own undertakes comparative discussion, our curation and placement of contributors' chapters allow comparative insights to be drawn across both academic and practitioner chapters in relation to the UK, EU and US, as well as a few other selected jurisdictions. The positioning of the academic chapters on the development of 'stewardship' as soft law and regulatory policy for the investment management industry allows comparisons to be made between the UK, EU and US approaches. Such comparative insights also relate to practical implementation. In particular it is queried whether the Model Mandate initiative (see Chapter 14 by Dallas and Hodge) can act as a form of international convergence for investment managers based in different jurisdictions through increased standardisation or harmonisation of contractual mandates. Finally, empirical research methodologies are also used in a number of chapters to tease out topical gaps in knowledge in the practice of investment management. In this volume, we use the term 'empirical research' broadly, as our volume showcases quantitative, qualitative and case study-based findings.

First in terms of the 'law and policy' approach, the academic chapters – such as those by Johnston, Birkmose and Chiu – explore how policy-makers and society view the role of investment managers in a broader context beyond serving contractual mandates. These perspectives are by no means 'right' or 'absolute'. Translating into soft law, such as in Stewardship Codes and in the comply-or-explain regime for shareholder engagement in the European Shareholders' Rights Directive 2017, the expectations placed on the investment management industry can be critically questioned in terms of what can really be achieved for private and social outcomes. The practitioner chapters – such as those by Parry and Hirt – tease out how the industry has responded to broader policy and social demands, while navigating the needs of their private contractual mandates. The 'law and policy' approach in contributors' chapters most pertinently relate to the issue of the expectations gap which we discuss below shortly.

Next, in terms of comparative law insights, we see a transatlantic 'divide' in relation to: (a) the conception of 'stewardship' as a paradigm for framing investment management, as well as (b) the importance of 'ESG' issues to investment management. The chapters focused on the US – ie Harper Ho's chapter and Bertsch's chapter – clearly situate the law of investment management within fiduciary framing. There are some aspects of overlap between the fiduciary framing, such as the express need for institutional investors managing ERISA (Employment Retirement Income Security Act) plans to exercise their voting rights as part of fiduciary management, and the conception of 'stewardship' or 'engagement' in the meaning of the EU Shareholders' Rights Directive 2017. However the EU and UK diverge significantly from the US in terms of a positive and encouraging stance towards informal modes of corporate engagement that can be carried out in various ways. The US framing is less reliant on institutional investors as a force for governance, and even corporate governance,[9] than in the UK and EU. This may partly be due to the power of the business lobby in the form of the Business Roundtable and American jurisprudence that staunchly protects valid managerial discretion.[10] Further, informal modes of engagement can be associated with the less 'mainstream' tactics adopted by hedge fund activists, which are seen as adversarial forms of challenge for corporate Boards. The traditions of corporate law, which are beyond the scope of this book, may be the real context in which the difference in 'stewardship' framing is situated.

In terms of the engagement with 'ESG' concerns in investment management, Harper Ho's and Bertsch's chapters agree with each other in relation to the limitations for ESG considerations as non-financial considerations in conventional fiduciary investment management. Although the United Nations Environment Programme Finance Initiative (UNEPFI) report[11] argues that the fiduciary concept is of considerable elasticity, jurisdictional differences and limitations are acknowledged.[12] The risk aversion in American jurisprudence against 'straying' away from the core financial mandate is reflected in scepticism for integrating 'ESG' concerns. This is in contrast with the European approach, which leverages upon harmonised European policy and regulation to 'cut across' domestic law in order to compel investment intermediaries to explicitly 'integrate' material sustainability risk. This 'strong' regulatory approach is discussed in Birkmose's and Malecki's chapters, and very much reflects the pro-social policy tenor in European regulation that is aimed at constructing the Internal

---

[9] The differences between the UK and US for example in relation to the rhetoric of shareholder primacy is discussed extensively in C Bruner, *Corporate Governance in the Common-Law World: The Political Foundations of Shareholder Power* (Cambridge University Press, 2013).

[10] See generally D Kershaw, *The Foundations of Anglo-American Corporate Fiduciary Law* (Cambridge University Press, 2018).

[11] UNEPFI, *Fiduciary Duty in the 21st Century* (2019), https://www.unepfi.org/wordpress/wp-content/uploads/2019/10/Fiduciary-duty-21st-century-final-report.pdf.

[12] UNEPFI, Generation Foundation and PRI, *A Legal Framework for Impact* (2021), https://www.freshfields.com/en-gb/our-thinking/campaigns/a-legal-framework-for-impact/.

Market as an economic order that is also socially desirable.[13] Hence, at one level the comparative insights show the fragmented landscape which may cause difficulties and confusion for investment management practice that spans global markets, yet at another level such comparative insights reflect more entrenched differences in legal traditions and economic and social policy that may not be reconciled easily.

Finally, the volume showcases a variety of broadly-defined empirical research methodologies that shed novel light on the outcomes or effects of institutional shareholder stewardship. Cojoianu et al's chapter takes a qualitative approach and examines the voting records of asset owners who have signed up to the Net-Zero Asset Owner Alliance. The chapter is useful but somewhat depressing on the lack of conspicuous advance by NZAOA members in relation to pro-climate voting at corporate annual general meetings. This may shed some light on whether the expectations gaps perceived are real as opposed to merely differences in sense-making. Van der Elst's chapter combines quantitative and qualitative methodologies to discern whether institutional shareholders' preferences diverge from or cohere with retail investors, shedding light on the likely representative capacity of institutional shareholders for the 'beneficiary' society of pension and mutual fund savers. The divergence of interests gives rise to the need to further interrogate incentives, and policy makers may also at a broader level consider whether they assume too much that institutional shareholders take on a socially representative capacity. This chapter provides the first clues to help policy-makers consider more realistically what their expectations of institutional shareholders should be. Khoo's chapter on financial institutions' common ownership of the global corporate sector takes a quantitative approach and provides findings on an important issue, highlighted also in Johnson's chapter, which pinpoints passive common ownership as the major trend to watch in relation to the impact upon corporate behaviour and outcomes. This chapter finds that financial institution common owners have some but unremarkable impact upon the ESG performance of companies they own, based on the Refinitiv ESG scores. Although this is a quantitative study that relies on correlation analyses, it adds to questions whether the policy reliance on institutional shareholders as governance actors for global ESG outcomes is sound. Finally, Ward's chapter provides case study findings based on the Brunel Pension Partnership's policies as asset owner. The chapter highlights several practices on the part of the Partnership as asset owner in terms of recruitment and monitoring asset managers towards portfolio decarbonisation while being engaged in detailed and intense financial risk discussions in relation to climate change and impact on portfolio companies. These insights from practice add great value to the dynamics of the asset owner-asset manager relationship and how these contribute to broader discussions relating to perceived expectations gaps and market-based governance for sustainable goals.

---

[13] J Mulder, '(Re) Conceptualising a Social Market Economy for the EU Internal Market' (2019) 15 *Utretcht Law Review* 16; critically see C Joerges, 'The Overburdening of Law by Ordoliberalism and the Integration Project' in J Hien and C Joerges (eds), *Ordoliberalism, Law and the Rule of Economics* (Hart Publishing, 2017) ch 11.

III. IS THERE AN EXPECTATIONS GAP BASED ON THE IRRECONCILABILITY BETWEEN INCENTIVES FOR INVESTMENT MANAGEMENT AND BROADER HOPES FOR THE INDUSTRY'S ROLES?

A recurring theme in our volume is the 'expectations gap' for the role of the investment management industry. After the global financial crisis, expectations for the investment management industry were framed around securing the due monitoring of corporate management and the long-term viability and performance of corporations as engines of the economy. These expectations were consistent in the EU[14] and UK.[15] In recent years, the expectations are now framed around the investment management industry's role in influencing sustainable behaviour on the part of corporations, in relation primarily to climate change, but also more broadly to environmental and social objectives. In this manner, although the 'ESG' movement has been around for some time,[16] the expectations for the investment management industry arguably revolve around objectives 'external' to the corporation and would benefit society more broadly, as contrasted with 'governance' objectives that are more internal in nature to the corporation.

The expectations gap can be explained at two levels. First, the gap relates to what actions can be taken on the part of the investment management industry, that would translate into attainment of certain outcomes by corporations or the corporate sector more generally. In this manner, this is perhaps an outcomes-based gap, and relates to the role of the investment management sector as financiers of the corporate sector. As financiers and intermediaries that allocate financial resources and steward them as invested in the corporate sector, what levers can the investment management sector pull in order to affect outcomes say, in relation to environmental sustainability, pay equity or respect for human rights in supply chains?

It can be argued that this 'expectations' gap should not be regarded as a gap at all, as such expectations are unrealistic for the roles played by the investment management industry, ie asset owners and managers alike. The industry's core objective is to manage financial resources for the purposes of providing returns for purposes defined over different time horizons for different asset owners. In this volume, discussions feature different types of asset owners, such as pension asset owners discussed in Ward's chapter and sovereign wealth asset owners discussed in Gjessing's chapter. Long-term asset owners like these are private sector entities with mandates for their roles. Although they may contribute to broader societal goals such as sustainability and development, finance is one of a number of levers and arguably cannot be overly relied upon. Indeed elsewhere MacNeil and Esser[17] also argue for the essential limitations of the 'financial lever' and that a variety of regulatory tools for changing

---

[14] D Ahern, 'The Mythical Value of Voice and Stewardship in the EU Directive on Long-term Shareholder Engagement: Rights Do Not an Engaged Shareholder Make' (2018) 20 *Cambridge Yearbook of European Legal Studies* 88.

[15] Kay (n 2 above).

[16] IG MacNeil and I-M Esser, 'From a Financial to an Entity Model of ESG' (2022) 23 *European Business Organisations Law Review* 9.

[17] ibid.

corporate behaviour need to be explored besides the financial lever, such as corporate regulation, including the EU's proposed Corporate Due Diligence Directive[18] which would impose additional duties for companies and their management. This view is echoed in Tomlinson's chapter, which sees the need for corporate law to be rejuvenated with a broader purpose that encompasses consistency with social good and goals, very much in line with the recent 'corporate purpose' movement led by Colin Mayer.[19] It may be queried whether direct regulations to compel corporations to behave in a responsible manner would be effective. Lin's and Chiu's chapter reflects on broad corporate responsibility statutes, such as adopted in China and Indonesia, to discern their effects upon corporate behaviour. Surprisingly, broad and direct regulation of 'responsible behaviour' proves too vague to have much of an impact on corporations.

On the other hand, it may be argued that the financial lever is in many respects central to corporate behaviour, as listed corporations heed market signals which affect their cost of funding or their reputations. Decisions such as investment divestment, for example, can have an overall effect of reduction of funding for a particular sector,[20] and this may prompt shifts in strategy or support for new and greener businesses, therefore having an overall effect on climate change. Divestment, however, is not without other side effects.[21] The investment management industry can be regarded as simply not doing enough, as Cojoianu et al's empirical research chapter suggests, in relation to the stewardship and voting behaviour of Net Zero Alliance asset owners. This concern is echoed in Johnston's chapter regarding the importance of large passive asset managers and their outsized 'lack' of influence upon portfolio companies' behaviour. In particular, many passive asset managers have certain cross-cutting policies such as regarding sustainability or worker rights. Although they sound laudable in principle, their application at portfolio level may be uneven and uncertain, and may not translate into particular voting behaviour or any form of issuer-specific engagement. In this manner, it can be argued that regulation itself is needed to compel and steer investment intermediaries' behaviour, as they may rightly be perceived to be falling short of what is legitimately expected of the 'financial lever'. The EU has provided leading policy and regulatory reform in this area, in the EU sustainable finance reforms, ie the Taxonomy Regulation 2020, the Sustainable Financial Disclosure Regulation 2019 and accompanying proposed legislation such as the Green Bonds Regulation and amendments to other investment regulations such as the Markets in Financial Instruments Directive 2014, UCITs Directive 2009, Alternative Investment Fund Managers Directive 2011 and

---

[18] European Commission, *Proposal for a Directive on Corporate Sustainability Due Diligence* (23 February 2022), https://eur-lex.europa.eu/legal-content/EN/TXT/?uri=CELEX%3A52022PC0071.

[19] C Mayer, 'The Governance of Corporate Purpose' (2021), https://papers.ssrn.com/sol3/papers.cfm?abstract_id=3928613.

[20] TF Cojoianu et al, 'Does the Fossil Fuel Divestment Movement Impact New Oil and Gas Fundraising?' (2021) 21 *Journal of Economic Geography* 141; B McKibben, 'Divestment Works – and One Huge Bank Can Lead the Way' (*The Guardian*, 13 October 2019), https://www.theguardian.com/commentisfree/2019/oct/13/divestment-bank-european-investment-fossil-fuels. Also see Chapter 10 below by Hans-Christoph Hirt.

[21] Cojoianu et al (n 20).

Benchmarks Regulation 2017. These seem to represent a proactive approach to define and steer conventional financial intermediaries into sustainable finance, therefore coming closer to achieving actual sustainable outcomes. Malecki's chapter provides an introduction to this hub-and-spoke framework but raises doubts as to the nature of its market-based governance. Ultimately the framework works on the financial sector's incentives and does not intervene in an allocative manner. However, it arguably provides more accountability in order to bridge social scrutiny with financial sector allocations and decisions.

The other level at which an expectations gap arises pertains to the difference in perception between society and the investment management industry in relation to the industry's conduct. This expectations gap does not relate to 'what is sought to be achieved' via investment management, which is the subject matter of the expectations gap discussed above. However, this expectations gap fundamentally affects the one discussed above, as conflicting expectations of what is 'legitimate' conduct on the part of the industry and society result in different expectations of what outcomes ought to be achieved. From the industry's point of view, incentive-driven investment management may be regarded as the 'default' paradigm, incentives for example including the need for asset managers to capture market share, the need for asset managers to win mandates, the need for asset owners to achieve certain performance targets etc. These can be perceived as legitimate conduct for the industry based on their private, for-profit nature as well as based on contractual mandates. Broader society, however, may view the paradigm of incentive-driven investment management as being narrow or flawed. This expectations gap is discussed below.

A. Materiality and Incentives in Investment Management

The contributions to this book suggest that the two levels that explain the expectations gap revolve around incentives and limitations of asset managers as commercial entities operating within the constraints of the legal framework on the one hand and insufficient alignment of interests along the investment chain between ultimate beneficiaries, representing society, asset owners, and asset managers on the other.

i. Constraints and Limitations of the Investment Industry at the Systems and Practical Level

There are significant systems and practical constraints and limitations to the investment management industry's role in influencing behaviour on the part of investee companies in relation to broader environmental and social objectives, such as tackling the climate or biodiversity crises and inequality.

The contributions of practitioners, such as Hickey, Parry and Ward, suggest a realistic view on what the investment management industry can and cannot achieve in isolation and without supportive policy and regulation regarding systemic risks and corporate externalities. However, this is not the message that asset managers are typically leading their communications with when they are communicating in public. This is most likely driven by a desire to meet the expectations of society, as discussed above, and avoid triggering difficult discussions with clients around potential trade-offs.

The limitations are much more openly acknowledged by practitioners who have left the industry, such as the former chief investment officer for sustainable investing at BlackRock, who has become highly critical of sustainable investing ('a dangerous placebo that harms the public interest') and calls for regulation regarding corporate externalities, including carbon emissions.[22] A related question is, of course, whether addressing a systemic risk such as climate change should be left to investors through private sector initiatives, as there is a danger that this could delay necessary policy intervention.

As Ward highlights in her chapter, institutional investors need to deliver on their fiduciary duties and fulfil the expectations regarding the role of the investment management industry in facilitating a smooth transition towards a net-zero carbon economy. This, she highlights, will require changes by everyone and importantly a supportive regulatory framework that facilitates the channelling of finance within markets between private and public actors. This is because without unprecedented policy intervention – for example regarding infrastructure investment, R&D, incentives, such as subsidies and tax breaks, and targeted regulation all underpinned by a carbon pricing strategy – it is unlikely that all investments that are necessary for the transition can generate adequate financial returns.

Moreover, there is the question of whether addressing systemic risks should be left to investors. Are they capable and best placed to address issues such as the climate crisis? Or does the involvement of the private sector deflect responsibility from better placed actors, such as governments and regulators, thus delaying necessary policy intervention? Some might argue that the best contribution asset managers can make towards solving systemic issues, such as the climate crisis, is to highlight their own limitations to regulators and policy-makers.[23] Similarly, important ESG issues such as human and labour rights, as well as corporate taxation, can arguably be much more effectively addressed through policy and regulatory interventions.

ii. Costs and Benefits of Addressing Systemic Risks and the Legal Framework

Even assuming that asset managers could achieve meaningful change regarding systemic risks such as climate risks in the absence of a robust regulatory framework, there are questions around the costs and benefits of such activities and, related to this, contractual obligations and fiduciary duties of participants in the investment chain.

As many of the contributors to this book have highlighted, the dominating financial and legal framework of the investment industry creates significant constraints and limitations on its ability to drive wide-ranging environmental and social changes in the real world. This is true even though such issues may drive long-term returns for investors.

---

[22] T Fancy, 'The Secret Diary of a "Sustainable Investor"' (2021) https://d1va1lgf0ctsi4.cloudfront.net/pub/thumb/www/The%20Secret%20Diary%20of%20a%20Sustainable%20Investor%20-%20Tariq%20Fancy.pdf.

[23] M Tyrrell, 'Investors' Biodiversity Bandwagon ... Needs a Better Chassis' (April 2022), https://www.linkedin.com/pulse/investors-biodiversity-bandwagon-needs-better-chassis-mike-tyrrell.

It has been shown that market performance, driven by systematic (non-diversifiable) risk, or beta, rather than relative outperformance of a specific company or portfolio, or alpha, drives returns for well-diversified investors.[24] This has important implications for universal owners and their ESG investment and stewardship activities. Because the overall economic or market performance, driven by systematic risk, beta, will impact on the future value of the aggregate portfolios of universal owners more than alpha,[25] they should focus their activities much more on systemic risks, which are the risks to or arising from, environmental, social and financial systems.

The challenge with this conclusion is that asset managers will struggle to quantify the benefits which will arise indirectly and over multiple decades for their clients and ultimate beneficiaries or end investors. In contrast, the costs of addressing systemic risks are easy to ascertain at a time where there are significant cost pressures in the asset management industry. While asset owners and managers may agree that the focus on systemic risks and long-term market returns is correct from a theoretical perspective, they are constrained by the legal framework and, critically, the timelines within which they are operating.

Without regulatory intervention the argument that most ESG issues directly or indirectly and over the very long-term will have some financial materiality is insufficient to align the interests of wider society regarding environmental and social issues and commercially driven asset managers operating within the current legal framework.

The predominance of the private law framework and fiduciary duties of key participants in the investment chain constrain or at least focus ESG investment and stewardship practice on financially material issues at the investee level. As Harper Ho and Bertsch explain in their chapters focused on developments in the US, the scope for ESG investment and stewardship under existing regulation in this important market is particularly restricted. However, the underlying constraint is global: Depending on the jurisdiction and the ESG issue under consideration, without specific client instructions, the law creates limitations for asset managers to pursue wider societal objectives in investment and stewardship. At the same time, as Chiu argues in her chapter regarding the UK Stewardship Code, with increasing assets of the investment industry – and consequently significant influence over companies and wider capital allocation – come societal and public expectations. The question is whether and how these can be squared with the prevailing legal framework and the commercial nature of asset management. In this respect the EU's regulatory approach that seeks to integrate more public interest within the legal framework for asset managers, as discussed in Malecki's and Birkmose's chapters, should be empirically examined in a few years to ascertain the extent to which double materiality is really achieved.

---

[24] J Lukomnik and J Hawley, *Moving Beyond Modern Portfolio Theory – Investing That Matters* (Routledge, 2021) 32. Systematic market risk in the investment context is often created by systemic risks in the real world.
[25] ibid, 32–35.

iii. Incentives and Mandates of Asset Managers

Most asset managers are commercial entities and many of them are listed, or part of a listed company. Their key stakeholders include shareholders and their employees. They rely on how much they manage (assets under management) and, for active managers, how successfully their funds perform relative to a benchmark in the short- and medium term, as this attracts more funds and potentially generates performance fees. Staff costs are a main driver of profit margins in an increasingly competitive market environment for asset managers. This context drives the mainly financial incentives of the investment management industry.

Successfully addressing systemic risks, such as climate change, loss of biodiversity and inequality through ESG investment integration and stewardship activities may be critical when looking at market returns in the long term. However, neither the financial nor the non-financial benefits will directly benefit the asset manager or the fund that incurs the costs of doing so or may fall behind in terms of relative performance because of it.

Accordingly, in his chapter, Johnston argues that the stewardship activities of asset managers are primarily driven by their incentives and related time horizons and therefore limited in scope and effectiveness in addressing ESG issues. As soft law, such as the UK Stewardship Code, has had a disappointing effect, he concludes that regulatory intervention has become more likely.

However, as Hirt argues in his chapter, focusing exclusively on ESG issues that are material at the specific company and thus portfolio level in the short to medium term can contribute to relative outperformance, or alpha. This of course can be captured by an asset manager and from a financial perspective can directly benefit its clients, shareholders and employees. The challenge of ESG investment integration and stewardship thus seems largely about the financial materiality of the underlying issue for specific investments and critically related timeframes. Often, these aspects go together, as Fancy described in his analysis of the industry:

> the reality is that much of what matters to society simply doesn't affect the returns of a particular investment strategy. Often this is because of the timeline of the underlying investment: many strategies have a very short time horizon, meaning that longer-term ESG issues aren't particularly relevant.[26]

The chapter by Dallas and Hodge on the revised Model Mandate of the International Corporate Governance Network (ICGN), which aims to hardwire stewardship into investment management, highlights some of these challenges and outlines potential solutions, including around systemic risks and timeframes.

The underlying challenge is the commercial nature of fund management and the incentives for individual firms. To justify additional costs and differentiate their offering, asset managers will need to be able to demonstrate to clients how systematic ESG investment integration or stewardship activities add value to the main services they provide, namely investment management, and is aligned with the objectives of their

---

[26] Fancy (n 22 above).

clients, mainly asset owners. In this regard, there needs to be more reflection on the important topic of time horizons, which can be addressed in investment mandates.

iv. A Starting Point: Categorisation of ESG Issues and Materiality

Based on the contributions to this book, we argue that the ESG debate would benefit from more clarity on the nomenclature and better disclosure about the primary objectives of ESG investment integration and stewardship activities and the nature of the issues that are being addressed and their materiality. Not surprisingly given the current loose nomenclature, which Hickey discussed as a fundamental problem in his chapter, the evidence that ESG enhances investment performance is inconclusive. As Hirt argues in his chapter, there seem to be three distinct though overlapping and interdependent categories of ESG issues that can be addressed through investment strategies or stewardship activities, namely:

(1) investment level issues relating to opportunities and risks for a specific company/ portfolio and investment returns over a relatively short timeframe;
(2) real world issues relating to systemic or systems risks impacting market returns in the long term; and
(3) real world issues related to values and norms which may or may not contribute to investment returns.

A different way of looking at the categories is through the lens of materiality, where broadly issues falling into category 1 would be regarded as financially material in the conventional sense, whereas issues in categories 2 and 3 could be regarded as material regarding their impact on the real world, or double materiality. However, there are overlaps and interdependencies between the categories, for example regarding a company's response to climate change. As highlighted in a recent report by the UN-convened Net-Zero Asset Owner Alliance,[27] up to a certain point, a company's actions to decarbonise would fall into category 1, as long as there is a 'business case' for taking action. But requesting decarbonisation beyond this point, where further action is 'impractical, uneconomic or uncertain', given the current regulatory context and state of technology, would place the issue in category 2 (and may well have a negative performance effect at the company/portfolio level during a typical holding period). Similarly, an issue that on the face of it seems to fall within category 3, such as the right of freedom of association, could at the very minimum cause a reputational risk for a company, thus falling into category 1.

It is important to note that even advocates of a greater focus on systemic risks recognise that there can be real trade-offs between company and portfolio investment returns (in the short term) and market returns (in the long term), in addition to questions around the compatibility with fiduciary duty. Tomlinson discusses the inevitability of trade-offs specifically when taking a systems-level view in his

---

[27] Net-Zero Asset Owner Alliance, 'The Future of Investor Engagement: A Call for Systematic Stewardship to Address Systemic Climate Risk' (April 2022), https://www.unepfi.org/wordpress/wp-content/uploads/2022/03/NZAOA_The-future-of-investor-engagement.pdf.

chapter on corporate purpose as a bridge between corporate sustainability and ESG investment. A shareholder resolution presented at the 2022 shareholder meeting of BlackRock, which asks the asset manager to prioritise the financial performance of its clients' diversified portfolios over the financial performance of individual portfolio companies, has brought this topic into sharp focus.[28]

Regulators have the ability to influence the categories into which a particular ESG issue falls, for example by forcing an internalisation of externalities, such as carbon emissions, through the introduction of a market price. In effect, they can make real world outcomes financially material.

The practitioners from across the investment chain who contributed to this book are clear in their focus on financial materiality, though the nomenclature remains inconsistent. In describing the investment and stewardship activities of Norges Bank Investment Management (NBIM), Gjessing emphasises the importance of financial materiality and returns in the investment framework of one of the largest sovereign wealth funds in the world. This framework is complemented by the Finance Ministry of Norway which transparently restricts the investment universe of NBIM – on an explicitly ethical basis – to ensure legitimacy with the population. While focusing on maximising returns, the fund recognises the impact of negative externalities, such as carbon emissions, associated with the operations of investee companies that may arise over time and recognises their impact on long-term returns of the fund. As Gjessing describes, this recognition justifies NBIM's focus and significant work on carbon emissions and climate change. As such, given its unique ownership structure and governance, effectively eliminating the investment chain, NBIM seems to have found a way to operate across the three ESG categories we defined earlier.

From the perspective of an asset owner, Ward's chapter describes what the role of asset managers should be in working towards portfolio decarbonisation. She recognises the tensions between fiduciary duties and societal expectations in addressing climate change as a systemic risk and highlights the importance of change across the wider ecosystem in which the investment industry operates, including regarding policy and regulation.

The chapters by Parry and Hickey reinforce the importance of clarity about the materiality of ESG issues in an investment context. Parry describes the status quo of responsible investing and highlights some of the remaining challenges, including the lack of clear definitions around ESG, sustainable and impact investing. Hickey's chapter explains the meaning of terms such as ESG and sustainable investing and argues that even within the responsible investment industry, there are still two distinct groups – namely investment and sustainability professionals – that are divided by a common language. He explains why precision in the language used is vital to the credibility of responsible investment in the context of client expectations and robustness of investment products.

We conclude that clarity around the nomenclature on ESG issues and their materiality and enhanced disclosure will facilitate better informed dialogue about costs and benefits of ESG investment integration and stewardship including potential

---

[28] See the related SEC filing by the proponent of the resolution, https://www.sec.gov/Archives/edgar/data/1364742/000121465922005689/b422225px14a6g.htm.

trade-offs between investment returns and real-world outcomes. It will also allow different types of investors to choose the outcomes they (or their beneficiaries or end investors) desire within the applicable legal framework and other constraints. The goal needs to be clarity and disclosure along the investment chain.

v. The Way Forward

In sum, the expectations gap regarding the industry's conduct is not merely a contest between financially-focused, materiality framing and broader social framing with internalisation of non-financial goals. The former is rooted in legal traditions that reflect the legitimate roles and limitations of private sector 'financialisation', while there is elasticity in the industry's appreciation for financial and double materiality which can crucially be supported by clearer policy leadership.

Nevertheless, to date key regulations, such as the UK Stewardship Code, the EU's Shareholders Rights Directive in 2017 and the EU Sustainable Finance Disclosure Regulation remain firmly market-based, as discussed in section II. In particular, as Birkmose argues in her chapter, the regulative steer towards environmental and social objectives in the key pieces of EU regulation is limited and leaves the private law and fiduciary duty framework largely intact. Chiu explains how the 2020 version of the Stewardship Code breaks new ground by articulating purpose-based steers for the investment management industry in the form of public interest objectives to be internalised in fund management activities. While recent ESG regulation does address wider environmental and social issues, it primarily provides more and better disclosure about ESG investment integration and stewardship. This should help asset owners in choosing asset managers and enhance competition on ESG capability.

None of the contributors to this book advocated for an intervention that would challenge the private law based and fiduciary framing of key relationships in the investment chain between asset owners and asset managers. Market-based regulation appears to be without a real alternative in our financial system. However, as Chiu argues in her chapter, the purpose-based approach used by the Financial Reporting Council (FRC) in the latest version of its Stewardship Code may be a blueprint for future regulation.

Such purpose-guided regulation could be complemented by fine-tuning of the current system addressing market failures, for example the lack of pricing of externalities, such as carbon emissions. Regulators could also look at the transparency, the bargaining process around and key provisions of fund management mandates to enhance the alignment of interests between asset owners and managers.

Model mandates should be clear about what type of ESG issues a fund seeks to address and what the cost/benefit and investment return implications are for the asset owner (and beneficiaries or end investors) in the short, medium and long term. This way, asset owners and their investors can assess the alignment of interests between them and the asset managers they are contracting with for fund management services.

Moreover, as highlighted in Birkmose's and Hirt's chapters, considering recent EU regulation and the latest version of the UK Stewardship Code, which arguably develop already existing duties, there is a question whether the fiduciary duties of key participants in the investment chain, specifically regarding indirect and long-term investment benefits of addressing ESG issues, should be clarified.

Finally, Birkmose, Hirt and Van der Elst highlight in their chapters the importance of focusing on the interests of clients and the ultimate beneficiaries or end investors. This should inform and guide future policies and regulation. The new UK Stewardship Code provides an example of what this could look like.

Having said all this, the contributions of both academic and practitioner highlight that while the investment industry can play an important role in addressing wider environmental and social issues, there seems a real danger that its influence and impact is overestimated and necessary policy and regulatory interventions remain indispensable.

B. The Impact of Regulation and Policy on Materiality and Incentives for Investment Management

It is arguable that regulatory law and policy have been emerging attempts to change or steer the default incentive-driven investment management paradigm discussed above. It will be argued below in Section IV that such regulatory policy and law are based on a mixture of market failure and public interest rationales, with public interest rationales featuring more prominently in relation to sustainable finance reforms in the EU. Although the UK's proposed Green Taxonomy[29] resembles EU approaches in sustainable finance regulation, a strong market-based governance ethos is still detected[30] and, in time, we may be better able to appraise the differences between the EU and UK regimes.

The first 'policy steer' in relation to institutional investors' investment management conduct is found in the UK Stewardship Code 2010, which is followed by the EU Shareholder Rights Directive 2017. As Birkmose's chapter argues, this 'steer' is relatively nuanced and does not represent the working of the 'visible hand' of mandatory policy. This policy steer relates to long-termism, and nudges[31] relevant institutions to be more accountable for their long-term horizons and investment management goals. The nature of the policy steer in the EU Directive, which is disclosure-based for asset owners and managers, in a 'comply or explain' approach, is arguably ultimately market-based, as the application of the provision would cohere with market structures and market discipline is the expected modus of 'enforcement'. Birkmose's chapter argues that: (a) only the relevant institutions are covered, ie institutions such as pension funds and their asset managers that have a long-term horizon anyway; and (b) the disclosures made by asset owners are intended to be scrutinised by

---

[29] HM Government, 'Greening Finance: A Roadmap to Sustainable Investing' (October 2021), https://assets.publishing.service.gov.uk/government/uploads/system/uploads/attachment_data/file/1031805/CCS0821102722-006_Green_Finance_Paper_2021_v6_Web_Accessible.pdf.

[30] See ibid 7 on relying on disclosures and the market to effect discipline as a primary stage of reforms; see also 11, 18–19.

[31] MB Madsen, 'Behavioural Economics in European Corporate Governance – Much Ado about Nudging?' (2021) 32 *European Business Law Review* 295.

beneficiaries, although it can be queried to what extent beneficiaries act upon these, given collective action problems and passivity.

In examining the concept and evolution of 'stewardship' for institutions as introduced in the UK, Chiu's and Johnston's chapters also highlight the relative weakness of any 'public interest' element. Johnston argues that the Code is a culmination of policy approval for a form of shareholder activism that has arisen in the 1980s and 1990s relating to the needs for 'value protection' for investors, such as observed in US-style pension fund activism by the California Public Employees' Retirement System (CalPERs). Chiu also argues that market-based governance pervades the earlier UK Stewardship Codes before the overhaul in 2020, and analyses the critiques against the Codes and their implementation. It can be argued that the advent of 'stewardship' provides a certain form of framing for the investment management industry in the sense-making of its conduct and making its conduct more accountable, but such framing does not intervene in the primarily incentive-driven materiality-based investment management conduct which prevails. Section III explains why investment management conduct is incentive-driven, but in this manner, we should also not mistake the policy steer in 'stewardship' as introducing something different from reinforcing market-based governance.

The chapters in Part II of this volume flesh out best practices in stewardship, such as Hirt's chapter on systematic stewardship, which arguably achieve sounder monitoring and accountability within the investment chain, particularly between asset owners and managers. This is an important achievement, as weaknesses on the part of asset owners have been observed, in terms of how mandates are to be structured, how performance is to be scrutinised, and how expenses can be mitigated, in the UK's Asset Management Market Study.[32] Yet in the UK, mandatory regulation is only resorted to to address practices that are seen as subject to persistent market failures, such as the lack of mitigation of fund expenses, therefore affecting beneficiaries' ultimate return.[33] One of us argues elsewhere,[34] that regulatory intervention into the conduct of investment management or in relation to how investment chain relationships are framed, is still relatively sparing and patchwork in nature.

The more pronounced recent regulatory steer relates to sustainable finance reforms, principally the EU's leading reforms as the UK and US are only beginning to consider the role of regulation in sustainable finance policy.[35] In particular, Harper Ho's chapter highlights the challenges and difficulties for regulating sustainable or climate risk disclosures under the overriding framework of material concerns for fiduciary-based investment management.

---

[32] FCA, *Asset Management Market Study: Final Report* (June 2017), https://www.fca.org.uk/publication/market-studies/ms15-2-3.pdf. Rule changes: FCA, *Asset Management Market Study Remedies and Changes to the Handbook – Feedback and final rules to CP17/18* (April 2018), FCA, *Asset Management Market Study – Further Remedies* (February 2019).

[33] Such as the obligation for fund entity to scrutinise the 'value for money' for beneficiaries and its disclosure: FCA Handbook COLL 4.5.7, 6.6.20–22; 8.3.5A, 8.5.16–19.

[34] IH-Y Chiu, 'Charting the Indefatigable Rise of Public Regulation of the Investment Management Industry' in IH-Y Chiu and IG MacNeil (eds), *Research Handbook on Global Capital Markets* (Edward Elgar, forthcoming).

[35] SEC, 'SEC Proposes Rules to Enhance and Standardize Climate-Related Disclosures for Investors' (21 March 2022), https://www.sec.gov/news/press-release/2022-46. For the UK, see n 29 above.

Malecki's chapter provides an overview of the hub-and-spoke approach in EU sustainable finance reforms, building out from the crucial EU Taxonomy Regulation 2020. The Taxonomy provides scientifically-established outcomes-based criteria for labelling environmentally sustainable activities, so that financing these activities can then be labelled as 'sustainable' for the purposes of marketing, performance evaluation and monitoring by the investment market broadly. Further, sustainability must include 'doing no harm' to a range of environmental, social and governance matters, so that 'sustainability' labels do not legitimate harms that are traded off for certain sustainable payoffs. The Taxonomy Regulation would be the central plank that is implemented in financial regulation relating to investment inter-mediaries, funds, green bonds, financial benchmarks etc.

Birkmose's and Chiu's chapters argue that the EU's sustainable finance reforms take on a more authoritative character but it can still be queried to what extent this body of reforms 'steer' the investment management industry and in what manner. As Chiu's chapter argues, the baseline expectation that all investment intermediar-ies 'integrate' material sustainability matters in investment management and disclose how they do so as a matter of public reporting and pre-contractual disclosure, can potentially shift the needle. Sustainability matters are no longer optional for the quar-ter of the industry that markets 'responsible', 'ESG' or 'sustainable' products. On the other hand, the integration of 'material' sustainability concerns is not different from what is expected of considerations for financial materiality.

Further, the labelling and marketing of 'sustainable' financial products are optional market opportunities for investment intermediaries. There is no compulsion to turn all currently self-regulatory 'responsible' or 'ESG' products into 'sustaina-ble' financial products in the EU. Although EU regulation[36] provides that products labelled as 'responsible' or 'ESG' need to be properly described and marketed in relation to the outcomes they aim to achieve and how these are measured, such a regulatory measure does not prescribe what 'responsible' or 'ESG' means, therefore still leaving it to industry self-regulation, and to potentially weak market discipline on the part of investors.[37] Indeed Hickey's chapter points out poignantly the failures of self-regulation in such forms of incentive-based labelling.

Ultimately it may be argued that the EU's sustainable finance label, which is the 'gold standard' tied to scientifically-established Taxonomy definitions, is a market-building measure seeking to stimulate the demand side to ask for quality and standardised sustainably labelled investment products, so as to motivate the supply side to comply and offer such products, gradually weeding out self-regulatory labels that are not underpinned by regulatory compliance. Is such a measure only market-based governance in nature, or has it achieved a balance between an authoritative steer and allowing market-based governance to work in optimal ways? The effective-ness of the EU sustainable finance reforms are unlikely to be appraised until after several years for us to take stock of the market products that are offered and their credibility.

---

[36] EU Sustainable Disclosure Regulation 2019/2088, Art 8.
[37] 'Greenwashing Biggest Challenge of ESG Investing, Say Institutions' (6 July 2021), https://www.corpo-ratesecretary.com/articles/esg/32633/greenwashing-biggest-challenge-esg-investing-say-institutions.

IV. THE MAPPING OF DIFFERENT POLICY INSTRUMENTS
ON INVESTMENT MANAGEMENT PRACTICE

This section discusses another key theme that recurs throughout the chapters in the volume: the impact of different types of legal and policy instruments that affect the practice of investment management, therefore having an impact upon the resolution or otherwise of the expectations gaps discussed.

The mapping of these instruments can be a complex exercise as the industry is regulated by a number of legislative and regulatory instruments, pertaining to pensions, investment management conduct and investment funds, and also subject to laws such as company law that is more 'private' and enabling in nature in relation to how shareholders' rights are framed and exercised. Further, there are soft law instruments such as the Stewardship Code in the UK and other iterations in other capital markets. At an even more self-regulatory level, there may be industry associations' policies or codes, such as the ICGN's Global Governance[38] or Stewardship Principles,[39] and Net Zero Alliance Asset Owners' common principles. Major asset managers also have their own policies such as the BlackRock ESG Integration Statement.[40] In the responsible, ESG or sustainable investing paradigm, there are also a plethora of industry codes such as the UN Principles for Responsible Investment,[41] or Shareaction's policy positions[42] or campaigns, as well as asset owner or manager groups' policies such as those of the Net Zero Alliance mentioned above. Asset owners such as the Brunel Pension Fund discussed in Ward's chapter have their own responsible investment policies, and so does the renowned Norges Bank which is famous for its ethical investment policies. Many asset managers would also have their own policies, which can act as a form of 'branding' as they seek to bid for mandates. Asset managers with an outsized influence, an example of which is BlackRock mentioned above, are also likely to have their own policies. Further, contractual governance between asset owners and asset managers is envisaged, such as in the development of the ICGN's Model Mandate discussed in Dallas' and Hodge's chapter. In sum, what are the roles of instruments positioned at these different regulatory, legal and soft law levels and how do they affect investment management practice?

First, we turn to 'soft law' instruments, including the Stewardship Code. The soft law instruments reflect the space for mandate setting, contractual governance and monitoring and best practice principles that are not fully addressed at the legal or regulatory level. Law, especially in financial regulation, hesitates to engage in regulation of conduct that can best be determined between equal and sufficiently sophisticated parties, as private bargaining can be more efficient than a one-size-fits-all solution imposed by law. Private remedies would also be more appropriate ex post. In this manner we seek to take stock of the achievements and limitations of a broad

---

[38] See https://www.icgn.org/icgn-global-governance-principles.

[39] See https://www.icgn.org/sites/default/files/2021-06/ICGN%20Global%20Stewardship%20Principles%202020_1.pdf.

[40] See https://www.blackrock.com/corporate/literature/publication/blk-esg-investment-statement-web.pdf.

[41] See https://www.unpri.org/about-us/what-are-the-principles-for-responsible-investment.

[42] See https://shareaction.org/policy-hub.

range of 'soft law' for the investment management industry. We then discuss the precise roles for hard and regulatory law, the rationales that motivate the introduction of such instruments, such as market failures and more recently, market steering, in the EU's sustainable finance reforms. Hard law and regulatory instruments, however, produce certain effects on investment management conduct, which are also discussed critically in our volume.

A. Market-based Developments and Soft Law

The investment industry has enthusiastically embraced ESG associations and initiatives since the launch of the Principles for Responsible Investment in 2006, which now have more than 4,500 signatories.[43] More recent initiatives, such as the various net-zero focused projects of asset owners and managers, banks and insurers, and Climate Action 100+, the global carbon engagement coalition (bringing together more than 700 investors with more than $68 trillion in assets[44]), have been joined or are supported by most major institutional investors.

Similarly, soft law, such as the UK's Stewardship Code, have been welcomed and supported by the investment management industry. However, this enthusiasm for industry initiatives and soft law broadly defined could be driven by a desire to avoid hard law and/or purely commercial considerations rather than a genuine commitment towards ESG investment integration and stewardship. Let us try to assess what the practical impact has been of some of the soft law and ESG initiatives.

Having been introduced in 2010, the UK Stewardship Code provides a great case study for the assessment of the practical impact of soft law with a regulatory underpinning in a market such as the UK and beyond.

i. The UK Stewardship Code

Looking at whether stewardship will drive long-termism and sustainability amongst investee companies, Johnston concludes in his chapter that there is little evidence that the UK Stewardship Code has been effective in changing the approach and focus of investors in steering companies they invest in. He believes that short-termism of institutional investors prevails and identified the investment chain as the underlying structural problem. On this basis, Johnston concludes that regulatory intervention becomes more likely.

In his chapter, Hirt describes the experience from a practitioner's perspective. He suggests that the practice of stewardship has improved over the last decade, pointing to the fact that many large asset owners and managers now employ stewardship professionals and produce a considerable amount of reporting. However, he questions whether more activity and reporting have translated into effectiveness in practice in the form of stewardship-related outcomes, including the prevention of

---

[43] See https://www.unpri.org/signatories/signatory-resources/quarterly-signatory-update.
[44] See https://www.climateaction100.org/.

corporate governance failures and significant changes in the activities and behaviours of companies, including on key ESG issues.

The general sentiment about the status quo of stewardship practice in the UK was summarised in an unusually damning assessment of the impact of the original UK Stewardship Code published within a wider independent review of the FRC in December 2018.[45] John Kingman, who led the review, described it as 'a major and well-intentioned intervention' but 'not effective in practice'[46] and concluded, 'If the Code remains simply a driver of boilerplate reporting, serious consideration should be given to its abolition'.[47]

This critical assessment of the 2010 version of the UK Stewardship Code reflects the views of both academics[48] and practitioners. However, as Birkmose, Chiu and Hirt explain in their chapters, the 2020 version of the UK Stewardship Code breaks new ground and differs from the 2010 version in steering the activities of the investment industry towards wider environmental and social objectives and requiring more outcomes-focused reporting from signatories in the change to 'apply-and-explain' from a 'comply-or-explain' approach.

While this purpose-led direction is still a firmly market-based approach, Chiu argues in her chapter that the revised Code should be appreciated against the wider context of governance concerns regarding the power and conduct of the investment management more broadly. She shows that the new Code is increasingly clearer on the purpose of investment management, articulates public interest objectives and suggests how they should be internalised within investment management mandates. Chiu highlights that the Stewardship Code 2020 only provides general guidance as to the contractual governance within the investment chain towards public interest objectives. However, she concludes that the Code's public purpose steer for the investment management industry could prove to be the starting point for a type of governance that could define investment management regulation in the future.

It is clearly too early to assess conclusively the practical impact of the 2020 version of the UK Stewardship Code. However, the FRC's review of the first reporting under the new Code[49] confirms significant improvements in application by signatories. Hirt's chapter comes to a similar conclusion, highlighting that the revised Code has led to considerable improvements in stewardship reporting which reflect better implementation and practice by asset managers investing in relevant resources. The formal signatory application process required by the Stewardship Code 2020 has accelerated such investments, as unsuccessful applications seemed to have triggered a wave of recruitment across the investment management industry. More resource and focus are likely to continue to enhance the stewardship activities.

---

[45] Independent Review of the Financial Reporting Council (December 2018) (Kingman Review), https://assets.publishing.service.gov.uk/government/uploads/system/uploads/attachment_data/file/767387/frc-independent-review-final-report.pdf.

[46] ibid, 8.

[47] ibid, 46.

[48] For some academic studies, see Chapter 2 in this volume by Chiu.

[49] FRC, 'Effective Stewardship Reporting – Examples from 2021 and Expectations for 2022' (November 2021), https://www.frc.org.uk/getattachment/42122e31-bc04-47ca-ad8c-23157e56c9a5/FRC-Effective-Stewardship-Reporting-Review_November-2021.pdf.

However, as Hirt shows in his chapter, the reporting of engagement outcomes and crucially the evidence of stewardship investment integration remains largely anecdotal rather than being based on systematic practice. There is still a long way to go in evidencing the effectiveness and impact of stewardship activities across the sector. And, not surprisingly, despite the enhanced reporting, there is no hard evidence to date that the Stewardship Code 2020 has had an impact regarding wider environmental and social objectives and other systemic risks.

Stewardship codes in other markets seem to have had even less impact in practice.[50] This is not surprising, as most of them lack any regulatory underpinning and thus at least some teeth.

In conclusion, Stewardship Codes seem helpful in spreading best practice across the investment industry, enhancing transparency for asset owners and creating commercial incentives for more activity and reporting, which are required for signatory status in some markets. While best practice will necessarily differ between asset managers of different sizes and investment styles, the measurement of engagement outcomes remains largely qualitative rather than being based on a systematic approach and measurement. This should not be a surprise, as Stewardship Codes do not fundamentally change the incentives of asset managers and in isolation they do not provide transparency and, critically, alignment of interests across the investment chain, which would be required to make more progress on systemic issues. As Hirt explained in his chapter, more could be done within the industry, for example by clarifying what ESG objectives are being pursued and highlighting related benefits (both in terms of returns and real world outcomes) and costs, as well as potential trade-offs, but ultimately regulation might be required to tackle the underlying challenges.

ii. EU Shareholder Rights Directive 2017

The 2010 version of the UK Stewardship Code significantly influenced the drafting of the EU's 2017 revision of the Shareholder Rights Directive (SRD II). However, as Birkmose describes in her chapter, in some regards SRD II developed and added to the principles in the original UK Code, not least regarding the inclusion of ESG issues in engagement policies of institutional investors. It also embedded the 'comply or explain' requirement for institutional investors in law and established a link between stewardship and investment strategies.

Perhaps not surprisingly given the experience in the UK with the 2010 version of the Stewardship Code, as Johnston highlights in his chapter, it is unclear whether SRD II has had much impact on ESG investment integration and the stewardship activities of institutional investors. Birkmose highlights in her chapter that although SRD II contains a normative element regarding engagement, it should be viewed as a disclosure framework. Though it does require some reporting on activities of institutional investors, this is at a much higher level and lacks the breadth and depth that is expected under the UK's Stewardship Code 2020, including on outcomes. It is thus questionable whether the additional reporting is of help to asset owners.

---

[50] D Katelouzou and D Puchniak, *Global Shareholder Stewardship* (Cambridge University Press, 2022).

For this reason, the practical impact of the new UK Code over the next few years, as evidenced in tangible outcomes to which institutional investors contributed, will most likely provide a better indication of whether soft law can contribute towards enhanced sustainability of investee companies and progress towards wider environmental and social objectives.

iii. Model Mandates

As Dallas and Hodge describe in their chapter, the aim of the ICGN's Model Mandate Initiative,[51] launched in 2012, was to help asset owners to express what they expected of the asset managers that they engaged in terms of investment stewardship, and to reflect those expectations in investment contracts and mandates.

The original Model Mandate made an important contribution to the debate by identifying some of the key challenges in the investment chain and offering potential solutions to them. It was followed by similar initiatives from other organisations. However, there is no evidence that it has had a significant practical impact regarding key terms between asset owners and managers in investment mandates since it was launched. While the underlying challenges regarding issues such as performance measurement and time horizons and related to these commercial incentives are well understood and increasingly discussed, little progress seems to have been made across the investment industry.

But there are some notable exceptions, for example, the Brunel Pension Partnership which is one of eight UK Local Government Pension Scheme pools and brings together more than £35 billion of investments of ten like-minded pension funds. As Ward describes in her chapter on embedding accountability for portfolio decarbonisation and resilience in the relationship between asset owners and asset managers, Brunel has succeeded in introducing enhanced requirements in its investment management agreements (IMAs) for segregated mandates. They include the requirement to adhere to its climate policy and provide climate data and regular stewardship reporting. Even in pooled investment vehicles, Brunel seeks to agree side letters that set out enhanced expectations of asset managers.

Moreover, as Ward explains in her chapter, recognising the rapid development of Brunel's approach to climate change and the related risk that requirements in an IMA become obsolete, the organisation also developed the Brunel Asset Management Accord,[52] which sets out principles-based expectations of asset managers in the implementation of mandates. The Accord is not intended to create legal obligations, but to capture the spirit of the relationship and the partnership approach that Brunel is seeking to establish.

However, at least in the UK context, Brunel appears to be a special case amongst asset owners, due to its nature and clients, significant size and sophistication and ultimately bargaining power. It is not surprising, therefore, that the Financial Conduct Authority highlighted investment mandates between asset owners and managers

---

[51] International Corporate Governance Network, *ICGN Model Mandate Initiative: Model Contract Language between Asset Owners and Their Fund Managers* (2012).
[52] *Brunel Asset Management Accord* (Brunel Pension Partnership, 2018).

that are not fully aligned with the investment and stewardship objectives of asset owners and their beneficiaries as a barrier to effective stewardship in its 2019 feedback statement following consultation together with the FRC on the revision of the Stewardship Code.[53] It also set out some actions it proposed to pursue working with the Investment Association to address this issue.[54]

As Dallas and Hodge describe in their chapter, one of the primary purposes of the new Model Mandate, launched in June 2022, is to provide a common understanding of how asset owners and managers should engage, both when agreeing the terms of the mandate and when reporting on how it has been implemented. However, it seems questionable whether without any regulatory support or underpinning the new Model Mandate will have a greater practical impact than its predecessor, specifically in the alignment of interests between asset owners and managers.

iv. Industry Associations and Initiatives

The PRI has made a significant contribution to the investment industry in mainstreaming ESG investment integration and stewardship activities. It has also developed into the leading hub for sharing best practice which has particularly helped institutional investors with limited internal resources or in markets which historically have focused less on ESG. Finally, the significant, annual signatory reporting requirements and related scores have introduced some internal rigour and external transparency and accountability for institutional investors. However, perhaps not surprisingly given its voluntary nature and the broad scope of its initiatives and actions, it is impossible to assess its impact on ESG investment integration and stewardship practice.

While it is early days for some of the recent net-zero initiatives, the chapter by Cojoianu et al looking at the climate voting records of Net-Zero Asset Owner Alliance members suggests that meaningful actions by institutional investors and real-world outcomes have not yet materialised. And while the global Climate Action 100+ initiative can point to some encouraging developments at the companies it engages with, including the setting of a net-zero target for 2050 or sooner, in many cases, medium-term 1.5°C aligned emission targets and net-zero aligned capex strategies are still lacking.[55]

In summary, industry associations and initiatives can play a significant role in sharing best practice, agreeing on common expectations of investee companies and approaches and bringing together resources for engagement. However, there seems a danger that membership becomes a tick-box exercise which is desirable for marketing purposes and in some cases necessary to win mandates from asset owners rather than a genuine commitment to ESG investment integration and stewardship on the part of the institutional investor.

---

[53] FCA, 'Building a Regulatory Framework for Effective Stewardship – Feedback Statement – FS 19/7' (October 2019) 29–31, https://www.fca.org.uk/publication/feedback/fs19-7.pdf.

[54] ibid 32.

[55] Climate Action 100+, 'Net Zero Company Benchmark' (March 2022), https://www.climateaction100. org/news/climate-action-100-net-zero-company-benchmark-shows-an-increase-in-company-net-zero-commitments-but-much-more-urgent-action-is-needed-to-align-with-a-1-5c-future/.

v. Potential Solutions to the Fundamental Challenges

The commercial incentives of asset managers regarding ESG investment integration and stewardship activities are not optimally aligned with the long-term interests of asset owners and their beneficiaries. Unsurprisingly, soft law and bottom-up governance initiatives do not address this fundamental issue and can be seen more as industry supporting in nature. They work within the industry's capacity and limitations as a form of market-based governance, and can be seen not to 'make significant differences' especially where social expectations or perceptions are concerned.

In this light, it is queried whether 'harder forms' of regulatory governance are needed for market failures that have to be addressed by regulation and hard law to support existing and future soft law, such as Stewardship Codes. Clearer definitions and more transparency of asset managers about their ESG objectives, including related benefits and costs, as well as potential trade-offs, are needed along the investment chain.

Regulatory interventions could also involve the fine-tuning of the current system addressing market failures, for example the lack of pricing of externalities, such as carbon emissions. Moreover, fiduciary duties of key participants in the investment chain, specifically regarding indirect and long-term investment benefits of addressing ESG issues could be clarified.

And finally, regulators could also look at the transparency, the bargaining process around and key provisions of fund management mandates to enhance the alignment of interests between asset owners and their beneficiaries and asset managers. As Chiu argued, the new UK Stewardship Code's public purpose steer for the investment management industry could prove to be the starting point for a type of governance that could define investment management regulation and mandates in the future.

B. Looking Forward to the Roles of Hard Law or Regulatory Policy

In light of the limitations of soft law or bottom-up best practices discussed above, is hard law or regulation an appropriate instrument for governing investment management conduct? The law governing investment fund management has been largely private law in character, flanked by aspects of public regulation that are mapped onto regulatory objectives such as consumer protection. In the US, the fiduciary law of investment management characterises the main body of governing law, ensuring that those who entrust funds to investment managers are protected by duties of loyalty, care and diligence.[56] The predominance of this private law framework has, also discussed in Harper Ho's and Bertsch's chapters, crucially shaped the practice of investment management regarding ESG issues, resisting public interest influence upon core private law. In the UK, the private law tradition of fiduciary proscriptive duties,

---

[56] AR Laby, 'The Fiduciary Structure of Investment Management Regulation' in WA Birdthistle and J Morley (eds), *Research Handbook on the Regulation of Mutual Funds* (Edward Elgar, 2018) Ch 4.

the duty of care and diligence, as well as contractual duties frame the investor-fund relationship.[57]

The advent of regulation in the US, EU and UK arguably provide for similar themes in relation to market failures. One important rationale for hard law is the presence of market failures that impede optimal working of markets, such as to facilitate the allocation of investment resources to opportunities that are most optimal, or market failures that relate to inadequate internalisation of cost of activities, therefore producing externalities for society. It is arguable that such forms of hard law are ultimately market-based in nature, and although they entail compliance conduct and produce compliance cost, they reinforce market workings and are ultimately 'absorbed' by industry. For example, the SEC's regulation of mutual funds[58] focuses on consumer protection objectives via transparency regarding fund objectives, policies and the regular valuation of funds in order to facilitate exit.[59] Further, investment advisers are registered and subject to customer protection regulation such as anti-fraud.[60] The introduction of increased regulatory governance for investment fund intermediaries in the UK is attributed to EU harmonised regulation, but it also caters for similar market failure themes as such mandatory disclosure to mitigate information asymmetry at pre-contractual stages and periodic transparency to protect investors in relation to funds' stated objectives and facilitating rights to exit.[61]

Regulatory regimes do not generally deal with investment management design, as competitive market forces shape fund managers' strategies and innovations. Further, the institutional relationships in the investment chain are generally subject to contractual governance and there is little regulatory incursion in this area. However there is a general trend of expanding public regulatory law in the investment management industry. A key area of discussion in this volume is the quasi-regulation of institutional shareholder stewardship or corporate engagement discussed in Johnston's, Chiu's and Birkmose's chapters. Institutional investors' engagement activities with their companies, which are essentially an aspect of equity owning investment management,[62] have been articulated as important policy imperatives, situated between hard and soft law. The Stewardship Code is soft law. While the EU Shareholders' Rights Directive 2017 adopts the expectation of institutional shareholder engagement, it allows investment intermediaries to comply or explain. At the very least, disclosure is mandatory but conduct is ultimately to be determined by relevant investment intermediaries.

The relevant chapters in this volume do not disagree that the quasi-hard laws regarding stewardship and institutional engagement are market-based in character, and ultimately not out of sync with industry practices, and furthermore have

---

[57] L van Setten, *The Law of Institutional Investment Management* (Oxford University Press, 2009).

[58] Investment Company Act of 1940 (US).

[59] J Morley, 'The Separation of Funds and Managers: A Theory of Investment Fund Structure and Regulation' (2013–14) 123 *Yale Law Journal* 1228.

[60] Investment Advisers Act of 1940 (US).

[61] In relation to the Prospectus Directive 2003, recast as the Prospectus Regulation 2017/1129; UCITs Directive 2009/65/EU, Art 68 ff.

[62] Discussed in R M Barker and IH-Y Chiu, *Investment Management and Corporate Governance* (Edward Elgar, 2017).

been absorbed by the industry. Moreover, hard law can produce undesirable effects, besides not completely addressing the weaknesses perceived in soft law. Compliance obligations do produce an impact on investment management practice, and Parry's chapter critiques the application of such intermediate hard law as having strait-jacketing effects on investment management conduct, an inevitable consequence of compliance. Mandatory disclosure obligations are periodic in nature and require yearly accountability. In this way, compliance with stewardship or institutional engagement disclosure entails regulatory cost in preparing for such disclosure. Further, Parry's chapter raises questions as to how a yearly disclosure requirement could shed light on effective stewardship that may take a longer period to culti-vate and bear fruit. Such stewardship involves research on the part of investment intermediaries into issuers, before strategising as to how such engagement is to be conducted. Looking at Hirt's chapter on systematic stewardship, it is also queried as to whether time horizons for effective stewardship to be carried out, and then to be evaluated for its outcomes, may exceed regular reporting periods. In this manner, it can be queried whether there is optimal synergy between hard legal instruments that entail compliance conduct and the substantive effects desired to be produced, such as double materiality.

However, the trend towards more marked regulatory incursion into investment management practices or the interrelationships within the investment chain can be discerned of late.

First, prudential regulatory interventions have ramped up. This is in light of systemically important banks being brought under more regulatory control to address the faultlines that led to the global financial crisis 2007–2009.[63] Although the partial intermediation funding model for investment funds and asset managers means that the types of systemic risks banks are susceptible to do not play out in the same way, policy-makers are concerned for the effects of liquidity runs on funds,[64] as well as the use of leverage.[65] Hence, more regulatory governance for investment intermediaries in the prudential aspects followed in the EU.[66] Further, regulatory governance is introduced for products whose failure may produce significant and perhaps 'systemic' effects, such as market runs and significant asset price movements. These underlie heightened regulatory prescription for money market funds,[67] increasingly reflecting the integration of macro objectives into regulatory governance. The rise in regula-tory governance for liquidity management for mutual funds more generally in the EU is a response to issues such as the H2O fund suspensions and the collapse of the Woodford funds in the UK.[68]

---

[63] Systemically important banks are identified for enhanced capital regulatory and resolution treatment: Basel Committee, 'Global Systemically Important Banks: Updated Assessment Methodology and the Higher Loss Absorbency Requirement' (2013, updated 2020), https://www.bis.org/publ/bcbs255.htm.

[64] P Hildebrand, 'Systemic Risk and Financial Regulation: Where Do We Stand?' in OJ Blanchard et al (eds), *The State of Macroeconomic Policy* (MIT Press, 2016) Ch 7; C Lopez, 'The Asset Management Industry, Systemic Risk, and Macroprudential Policy' (2017) 45 *Journal of Financial Transformation* 121, https://papers.ssrn.com/sol3/papers.cfm?abstract_id=2953076.

[65] L Enriques and G Hertig, 'Post-crisis Regulation of Asset Management' (2018) *Réalités Industrielles* 88.

[66] Investment Firms Regulation 2019/2033.

[67] Money Market Funds Regulation 2017/1131.

[68] 'FCA Issues Warning to Fund Managers after Woodford Scandal' (23 January 2020), https://citywire.co.uk/funds-insider/news/fca-issues-warning-to-fund-managers-after-woodford-scandal/a1316137.

Next, conduct regulatory intervention has also been steadily introduced. The UK's retail distribution reforms overhauled investment advisers' upstream relationships so they do not compromise the objectivity of advice given to customers. The EU MiFID was also recast in 2014 to strengthen investor protection affected by investment chain relationships. The MiFID 2014 prevents independent investment advisers from being paid by product providers' commissions.[69] Most spectacularly, the MiFID disrupted the industry practice of bundling research charges into trading commissions.[70] This practice allowed brokers' analysts to be paid out of trading revenues although their output may not be directly consumed by investors. Such charges now have to be accounted for and approved by customers, if not absorbed in-house.[71] Public policy interventions are not shy of disrupting interrelationships between investment intermediaries based on financial incentives.

The UK commissioned an Asset Management Market Study from 2016 in order to consider market failures in the agency problems within the investment chain, as well as the state of competition in the market. The study found weaknesses in asset owners' scrutiny of asset managers' performance and charges, and this would have adverse ultimate impact for retail investors saving in pooled funds such as pension and mutual funds.[72] Reforms specific to the UK were introduced to compel asset owners to assess 'value for money'[73] in their delegation to asset managers and other service providers, as well as to engage with performance monitoring of asset managers based on more clearly articulated performance metrics and benchmarks,[74] and objectives regarding environmental social and governance performance.[75] These monitoring duties therefore reflect regulatory incursion into a space hitherto left to private contractual governance between asset owners and managers.

This landscape of indefatigable regulatory intervention arguably reflects the intervention based on public interest concerns, such as systemic stability, as well as losses of large-scale investor confidence should opaque or unchecked conduct on the part of investment managers affect financial goals of social and public importance. Although such regulation is framed by public interest, yet it is still possible to argue that these are responses to unaddressed externalities and market failures, such as gaps where investment management conduct is unchecked or where systemic risks are not accounted for by individual firms. In this light, the recent sustainable finance reforms, which the EU leads, may be contextualised with an aura of greater authoritativeness than their market-based nature suggests. Birkmose's chapter points out that the public interest punctuating these reforms is more pronounced than under the Shareholders' Rights Directive, and the compliance obligations for investment

---

[69] Art 24(7).
[70] Commission Delegated Directive (EU) 2017/593.
[71] Subject to some carveouts, eg FCA, *Changes to UK MIFID's Conduct and Organisational Requirements* (2021), https://www.fca.org.uk/publication/policy/ps21-20.pdf that exempts research for smaller listed companies with a market capitalisation of £200m and below from the 'bundling prohibition'.
[72] FCA, *Asset Management Market Study Final Report* (2017), https://www.fca.org.uk/publication/market-studies/ms15-2-3.pdf.
[73] FCA Handbook COLL 4.5.7, 6.6.20–22; 8.3.5A, 8.5.16–19.
[74] FCA Handbook COLL 4.2.5; 4.5.12–15.
[75] Sustainability Disclosures Regulation 2019/2088; Taxonomy Regulation 2020/852.

intermediaries' new sustainability disclosures may not merely be 'absorbed' in market practice.[76] The context of new mandatory obligations for the corporate sector,[77] which are the subject of equity investments, also loom large in the space for imagining the future of mandatory regulation in sustainable finance. Hence, it remains a highly dynamic phenomenon as to how far regulatory governance for the investment management industry would stretch and produce significant impact for changing the conduct of investment management. In this manner, regulatory governance in incremental steps may indeed bridge the expectations gaps discussed in section III in relation to how 'legitimate' conduct is framed and perceived and therefore what ought to result from it.

V. CONCLUDING REMARKS ON THE THREE ROLE PERCEPTIONS FOR THE INVESTMENT MANAGEMENT INDUSTRY AND WHERE NEXT FOR THE EXPECTATIONS GAP

The investment management industry's practices in stewardship, and increasingly, the integration of ESG or sustainability concerns, are shaped by the intersection of incentives and policy/legal steering. Incentives range from the desire to protect financial performance and portfolios from material non-financial problems to the seizing of new opportunities and market shares for assets under management as social appetites and demands shift. Policy and legal steering are crucially nested within an institutional framework of regulatory capitalism,[78] that is: the role of regulation is chiefly to address market failures and to 'steer' market actors and participants accordingly, not to 'row', in terms of imposing directions for economic actions. That said, in times of extreme exigencies, such as the imposition of economic sanctions against Russia for its aggression against Ukraine, the almost 'martial' financial law of economic sanctions would forcibly compel market actors to comply, such as to divest[79] or to write off assets.[80] These instances are ad hoc and generally in the overriding public interest. In this manner, we conceive of the investment management industry in liberal democracies as subject largely to regulatory policy that ultimately works with efficient markets.

---

[76] Large firms need to prepare an adverse impact statement, which has generated a lot of anxiety regarding compliance: see https://www.dechert.com/knowledge/onpoint/2020/10/survey---eu-sustainable-finance-disclosure-regulation--sfdr----a.html.

[77] The proposed Corporate Due Diligence Directive, note 18 and Sustainability Disclosure Act, https://ec.europa.eu/info/publications/210421-sustainable-finance-communication_en#csrd.

[78] D Levi-Faur, 'The Global Diffusion of Regulatory Capitalism' (2005) 598 *The Annals of the American Academy of Political and Social Science* 12.

[79] 'European Investors Keep Shedding Russian Assets Amid Additional Sanctions' (28 February 2022), https://www.ipe.com/news/european-investors-keep-shedding-russian-assets-amid-additional-sanctions/10058319.article; 'Abrdn, DWS, Nordea and Storebrand Divest from Russian Assets' (1 March 2022), https://citywire.com/new-model-adviser/news/abrdn-dws-nordea-and-storebrand-divest-from-russian-assets/a2381148.

[80] 'Russia-focused Funds with More Than €4bn in Assets Freeze Redemptions' (*Financial Times*, 2 March 2022), https://www.ft.com/content/471a38c2-9bf5-4f1b-9bcd-82463b9323ab; 'BP to Offload Stake in Rosneft Amid Ukraine Conflict' (*BBC News*, 28 February 2022), https://www.bbc.co.uk/news/business-60548382.

We argue that there are possibly three not mutually exclusive role perceptions of the investment management industry that the industry, policy-makers, stakeholders and society must ultimately work together to support, reinforce or legitimise. The investment management industry ultimately performs a financial intermediation role. Financial intermediaries can shape economic activities and therefore the effects that entail from these, whether on the environment, climate or society, but the actors in economic activities remain mainly businesses and corporations. In this way, the roles played by the investment management industry should be conceptualised as follows: the resource-based thesis in terms of leveraging upon the resources, capacity and influence of the industry upon its corporate investees/debtors; the 'gatekeeper' thesis in terms of being in a position to prevent harmful externalities from occurring from corporate strategies and activities; and the 'agent for change' thesis that encapsulates broader social and policy expectations in actively bringing about change in corporate and economic conduct. These role perceptions, which have ultimately given rise to the expectations gaps observed and discussed in this volume, need to be debated widely in order to feed into both top-down policy measures as well as bottom-up soft law/industry-based measures that frame the investment management industry's purposes and roles.

First, on the 'resource-based' thesis, regulation theorists have argued for a long time that in complex problems involving many actors and avenues of problem-solving, a 'de-centred'[81] view of governance can be taken, ie 'de-centring' from exclusive reliance on state-based or regulator action, and considering a broader framework of governance actors, capacity, resources and influence, in order to grapple with the problem. The role of the investment management industry in relation to corporate behaviour and activities can be seen in this light, that the industry wields a financial lever for incentivising corporate behaviour, and is one of the governance actors that can be deployed to shape corporate behaviour. For example, as Hickey's chapter mentions, if the investment industry refuses to buy the corporate debt of certain companies due to environmental or sustainable concerns, that would exact a powerful financial lever in terms of companies' access to finance and cost of debt. Policy-makers have, however, relied much more strongly on equity investors, as the policy admonition towards active engagement, framed as 'stewardship' in many jurisdictions, is meant to leverage upon the investment management industry's role as shareholders, not just financiers, therefore using the 'corporate governance' lever.[82] The 'corporate governance' lever is seen as directly relevant to corporate behaviour, as accountability has to be made to shareholders by the Board and shareholders can also directly participate in proposals for strategic changes, by tabling resolutions at general meetings or voting on resolutions that have to be decided at general meetings. The struggles

---

[81] J Black, 'Critical Reflections on Regulation' (2002) 27 *Australian Journal of Legal Philosophy* 1.

[82] Envisaged in Kay (n 2 above). Also see D Katelouzou, 'Shareholder Stewardship: A Case of (Re)Embedding the Institutional Investors and the Corporation?' in B Sjåfjell and CM Bruner (eds), *The Cambridge Handbook of Corporate Law, Corporate Governance and Sustainability* (Cambridge University Press, 2019) ch 41 but critically, LE Talbot, 'Polanyi's Embeddedness and Shareholder Stewardship: A Contextual Analysis of Current Anglo-American Perspectives on Corporate Governance' (2011) 62 *Northern Ireland Legal Quarterly* 451.

with motivating the 'corporate governance' lever have been well-discussed, and this connects to our discussion and mapping above of the debate regarding incentives and purposes of investment management, extensively canvassed in the academic and practitioner chapters in this volume.

Next, on the 'gatekeeper' thesis, this arguably flows from the resource-based thesis regarding the role of the investment management industry but centring upon its equity financing and shareholder roles. This is akin to Lord Myners' accusation against institutional investors for having been 'asleep' prior to the global financial crisis, while invested in a number of major banks in the UK that have almost failed.[83] The 'gatekeeper' thesis is also the underlying perception of European policy-makers in encouraging active engagement in the Shareholders' Rights Directive in 2017, as Birkmose has discussed in her chapter in this volume.[84] The 'gatekeeper' thesis puts into sharper conflict the debate regarding investment managers' incentives and the expectations put on their roles as 'capable' shareholders who could safeguard the prevention of harm to the company and other stakeholders as a whole.[85] As Birkmose argues in this volume, one way to reconcile the conflict is to see investment managers with longer-term horizons – such as pension funds and insurance companies – as being more aligned with the 'gatekeeper shareholder' role, as their incentives for the long-term performance of companies should be the same as the company's need to continue to be viable and perform over the long term. The 'gatekeeper' role may be less aligned with short-term investors and hence the comply-or-explain regime introduced in the Directive is the right one. However, much as policy-makers and academic commentators are able to theorise this 'gatekeeper' capacity, practitioner chapters shed light on the limitations of investors' actions. For example, Gjessing's chapter on the Norwegian sovereign wealth fund, Norges Bank, crucially reminds us of potential limitations on the part of sovereign wealth asset owners and their managers in relation to the need for political neutrality and maintaining a stance of economic primacy in their actions. Parry's chapter also highlights the limitations of shareholders in relation to the wisdom and business judgement of corporate strategies.

Thirdly, the 'agent for change' thesis arguably more explicitly connects the role of investment management to policy-makers' and social expectations in terms of transcending incentives and playing a part to advance 'other' goals, such as net-zero goals, the achievement of global temperatures not rising above 1.5°C,[86] or even certain sustainable development goals.[87] This paradigm is discussed in Chiu's and Malecki's chapters regarding the intrusion of regulatory policy and how this challenges or reshapes the incentives of the investment management industry. In this regard theorisation or discussions in law and policy go further than practitioners perceive to be

---

[83] 'Myners Lashes out at Landlord Institutional Shareholders' (*Financial Times*, 21 April 2009). Also 'Institutional Institutional Shareholders Admit Oversight Failure on Banks' (*The Daily Telegraph*, 27 January 2009).

[84] D Ahern, 'The Mythical Value of Voice and Stewardship in the EU Directive on Long-term Shareholder Engagement: Rights Do Not an Engaged Shareholder Make' (2018) 20 *Cambridge Yearbook of European Legal Studies* 88.

[85] Kay (n 2 above).

[86] Campaigned for by such as the UN Global Compact, see https://unglobalcompact.org/take-action/events/climate-action-summit-2019/business-ambition.

[87] See https://sdgs.un.org/goals.

optimal or achievable in mainstream investment. Bertsch's, Parry's and Hickey's chapters all provide perspectives of practitioners who see incoming challenges but also see the industry being left on its own to reconcile the needs to meet private contractual mandates and obligations. However, Ward's chapter provides an insight into what asset owners are doing for self-implementation, in terms of deriving mutual guidance and wisdom from groups such as the Net-Zero Asset Owner Alliance, as well as coming up with recruitment, monitoring and mandate templates for asset managers. In particular, even in the context of a pooled mandate, asset owners can pull their weight in relation to climate change objectives by using a soft Accord to 'loosely' hold asset managers to account. There is a need to interrogate any expectations in relation to the 'agent for change' perspective in terms of the different roles played by different entities in the investment chain. Further the desirability of relying on the investment management industry's 'agency for change' or influence should also be queried. In Mahoney's view, such reliance can hazardously exonerate policy-makers from making more difficult policy choices such as in mandatory conduct regulation or tax laws.[88] However, there is also the question of how much further the industry can stretch and transform itself in the face of such expectations.

Nevertheless, it can be argued that we should perhaps not have undue expectations of the investment management industry. Although the EU Taxonomy Regulation has taken pioneering steps to define sustainability and put a backstop to greenwashing, it forms part of market-building premises in policy, such as in relation to sustainable finance product marketing, standardisation of labels, benchmark designs etc. The European 'Green Bonds' and 'sustainable finance' standards are 'opt-in' rather than mandatory approaches. Hence, regulators are providing enabling policies to build up for better information signalling and pricing in financial markets, in order for financial participants to make their decisions in a free market consistent with the liberal democratic ethos. Overall this policy package reflects the European policy-makers' reliance on financial sector participants, but in relation to that which they have been professionally mandated and trained to do. It is increasingly clear that this policy package is not to be exclusive of, for example, the EU's agenda in influencing changes in corporate behaviour and activities. It is observed that the EU is embarking on: (a) making listed and large private companies disclose non-financially important information that affects environmental and sustainable matters as such;[89] and (b) introducing an overarching regulatory duty for threshold listed and private corporations to carry out due diligence in relation to their group entities and supply chains in relation to human rights and environmental impact.[90]

---

[88] PG Mahoney and JD Mahoney, 'The New Separation of Ownership and Control: Institutional Investors and ESG' (2021) *Columbia Business Law Review* 840.

[89] European Commission, Proposal for a Directive of the European Parliament and of the Council amending Directive 2013/34/EU, Directive 2004/109/EC, Directive 2006/43/EC and Regulation (EU) No 537/2014, as regards corporate sustainability reporting, https://eur-lex.europa.eu/legal-content/EN/TXT/?uri=CELEX:52021PC0189.

[90] European Commission, Proposal for a Directive of the European Parliament and of the Council on Corporate Sustainability Due Diligence and amending Directive (EU) 2019/1937 (23 February 2022), https://ec.europa.eu/info/sites/default/files/1_1_183885_prop_dir_susta_en.pdf.

We are of the view that the three role perceptions will persist and interact with each other, with respect to contesting expectations framed around the investment management industry's role in contest and debate, for some time to come. The industry cannot shrug off its increasing global profiles and the expectations placed on it, but it is also important for discourses to take place in order to subject the expectations gaps to questioning and reframing. This volume hopes to advance such discourse by bringing together senior investment management industry representatives' reflections alongside the perspectives of academic theorists who are conversant in 'law and policy'. We believe the discussions here are of use to:

(a) policy-makers in terms of regulatory design, on how best to leverage upon market-based regulation and recognition of limitations and the need for a variety of policy measures to achieve broader sustainable goals;
(b) academics in relation to bringing together the interrelated disciplines of financial law and regulation, corporate law and governance, other public policy and in interrogating objectives, purposes of legal, regulatory and soft law instruments and their efficacy;
(c) policy-makers in the US in particular in relation to resolving the issues of financial materiality of sustainable and ESG issues and their positions in the face of international convergence or divergence. This issue also pertains to the siloed preferences for law and policy, versus the more fluid approaches that integrate legal disciplines and policy in Europe;
(d) practitioners in terms of reflecting upon the expectations gaps and their reasonableness or otherwise and shaping up strategies in relation to the industry's customer and socially-facing relations;
(e) society and stakeholders in relation to the achievements and limitations of experts, whether in the public or private sector, and for the purposes of contributing to the discourse generally in terms of the relationship between finance, society and collective interest.

Part I

The Conception, Policy and Expectations of Investment Management Stewardship and Sustainable Finance

1

From Universal Owners to Hedge Funds and Indexers: Will Stewardship Drive Long-Termism and Sustainability?

I. INTRODUCTION

POLICY-MAKERS IN THE UK have, since the early 1970s at least, sought to encourage institutional investors (IIs) to engage with investee companies. This policy has remained remarkably consistent, considering the shifting challenges confronting both corporate governance and wider society, as well as the significant changes in the structure of institutional investment over the last 50 years. If anything, the demands made of shareholders have only increased, with the UK's post-global financial crisis Stewardship Code variously expecting large shareholders to: steer companies towards 'long-term returns to shareholders';[1] 'promote the long term success of companies in such a way that the ultimate providers of capital also prosper';[2] and, most recently, 'create long-term value for clients and beneficiaries leading to sustainable benefits for the economy, the environment and society'.[3]

In this chapter, shareholder engagement refers to dialogue between shareholders and investee companies, backed by voting and collective action where necessary. The Cadbury Report highlighted that shareholders can make their views known to Boards 'by communicating with them direct and through their attendance at general meetings'.[4] Shareholder engagement was often referred to as 'activism' before 2008, highlighting that shareholders were pressing for changes intended to enhance shareholder value.[5] After the 2008 global financial crisis, it was rebranded

---

[1] Financial Reporting Council (FRC), *Stewardship Code 2010* (July 2010) Preface.
[2] FRC, *Stewardship Code 2012* (September 2012) 1.
[3] FRC, *The UK Stewardship Code 2020* (December 2019) (SC 2020) 4.
[4] Sir Adrian Cadbury, *Report of the Committee on the Financial Aspects of Corporate Governance* (Gee, 1992) para 6.5.
[5] See eg P Myners, *Institutional Investment in the United Kingdom: A Review* (2001) paras 5.73–5.89; Institutional Shareholders' Committee, *Statement of Principles* (2002).

as stewardship, highlighting the 'duty' of institutional investors as a counterpart to their 'significant rights of ownership', which entailed adopting 'a long as well as a short-term horizon'.[6] As such, they were expected to exercise influence through monitoring, meeting with Board members, drawing up intervention strategies and adopting voting policies.[7] Under the influence of the Stewardship Code (and latterly the EU's revised Shareholder Rights Directive), institutional investors are expected to disclose publicly their stewardship and voting policies, and periodically report on their implementation. Stewardship was clearly intended to mark a qualitative change in approach, away from earlier short-term oriented shareholder activism towards an approach that benefits shareholders over the long term and leads to more sustainable economic activity.

As the implications of climate change become clearer, and as it becomes evident that sustainability must be embedded across all areas of policy and regulation, the mainstream belief that it is appropriate to rely shareholder empowerment as the primary means of bringing corporate governance into alignment with sustainability and long-termism is being called into question like never before. Shareholder stewardship as a policy initiative is in the last chance saloon, and if shareholders fail to use their powers to push large businesses to take account of sustainability considerations, then it seems likely that, before long, there will be – as Charkham warned in 1989 – 'political activity to make boards once again more accountable'.[8] There are already signs of this in the EU, which, having mainstreamed stewardship as part of its 2017 revisions to the Shareholder Rights Directive (SRD II),[9] committed, in its Sustainable Finance Action Plan, to giving serious consideration to using directors' duties to reinforce a corporate obligation to conduct human rights and environmental due diligence. Most recently, the European Commission has published proposals for directives mandating corporate sustainability due diligence and corporate sustainability reporting.[10] This suggests that, if stewardship fails to achieve the goals set for it, then more far-reaching regulation of Boards and senior management is likely in the future.

This chapter sets out to evaluate whether existing efforts to encourage IIs to engage with companies are likely to achieve the goal of steering companies towards

---

[6] D Walker, *A Review of Corporate Governance in UK Banks and Other Financial Industry Entities, Final Recommendations* (26 November 2009) para 5.7. The Walker Review largely eschews discussion of activism in favour of stewardship. In particular, para 5.27 distinguishes stewardship in the form of 'dialogue and longer-term engagement between investors and boards' from 'short-term pressure' involving 'analyst and activist investor argument for short-term initiative'.

[7] ibid at 5.14.

[8] J Charkham, 'Corporate Governance and the Market for Companies: Aspects of the Shareholders' Role' *Bank of England Discussion Paper No 44* (November 1989) 9.

[9] Directive (EU) 2017/828 of the European Parliament and of the Council of 17 May 2017 amending Directive 2007/36/EC as regards the encouragement of long-term shareholder engagement, OJ L 132, 20 May 2017 (SRD II).

[10] European Commission, 'Action Plan: Financing Sustainable Growth' (COM(2018) 97 final, Brussels, 8 March 2018), Action 10, which commits to carry out analytical and consultation work on requiring companies to develop and disclose corporate sustainability strategies and possible clarification of directors' duties; for the recent proposals see European Commission, 'Proposal for a Directive on Corporate Sustainability Reporting' (COM(2021) 189 final, 21.4.2021) and 'Proposal for a Directive on Corporate Sustainability Due Diligence', (COM(2022) 71 final, 23.2.2022).

long-termism and sustainability. Section II briefly traces the attempts to encourage shareholder engagement, from the Bank of England's efforts in the early 1970s through to the 2008 global financial crisis, and sets them against academic debates at the time, from Useem's 'investor capitalism' to Hawley and Williams' 'universal owners'. Section III examines stewardship as the major corporate governance policy response to the global financial crisis, leading to the UK Stewardship Code and influencing the EU's SRD II. These two sections of this chapter highlight the remarkable consistency of this policy prescription despite far-reaching changes in the world of institutional investment and different aspirations for what engagement was supposed to achieve. Section IV examines the rapid expansion of activist hedge funds, with academic commentary casting them alternately as 'governance arbitrageurs' or 'predatory value extractors'. Section V then focuses on the implications of the explosive growth, post-2008, of passive investors that track indexes of various kinds, focusing on their 'issue-specific' engagement and asking whether this is likely to drive long-termism and sustainability. In the short conclusion, we highlight that if – as seems likely – the activities of these types of institutional investor fail to steer companies towards a more long-term and sustainable approach on the part of companies, then more company-side regulatory intervention (at least in the EU if not in the UK) will occur, beginning with mandatory sustainability due diligence.

II. THE LONG-STANDING POLICY OF ENCOURAGING INSTITUTIONAL INVESTOR ENGAGEMENT

From the early 1970s, the Bank of England sought to encourage IIs to collaborate in order to 'improve efficiency in industrial and commercial companies where this is judged necessary',[11] an initiative which ultimately led to the establishment of the Institutional Shareholders' Committee (ISC).[12] At the end of the 1970s, as institutional share ownership approached 50 per cent of listed UK equities,[13] the Wilson Report concluded that IIs 'generally do have the capacity to exercise the responsibilities of ownership, especially those of fostering efficient management

---

[11] Bank of England, *Annual Report 1972* 25–26. Whilst its involvement in matters of corporate governance looks surprising today, the Bank of England staged wide-ranging interventions in industrial policy and finance from the 1970s onwards, with one David Walker heading up the Industrial Finance Division from 1980, working on numerous restructurings of failing companies, coordinating refinancing operations by consortia of banks, pushing for management improvements, consulting with shareholders and appointing non-executive directors: see H James, *Making a Modern Central Bank: The Bank of England 1979–2003* (Cambridge University Press, 2020) Ch 9. With the Bank largely working on companies in financial difficulty, it makes sense that they tried to harness institutional investors to improve the management of companies that were not (yet) in financial difficulty. The Bank also played a key role in encouraging companies to appoint non-executive directors and in the establishment of the Cadbury committee, and as we will see below, its former employee and later executive director, David Walker, also wrote the report that led to the Stewardship Code.

[12] 'Institutional Shareholders Committee' (June 1973) *Bank of England Quarterly Bulletin* 148.

[13] P Davies, 'Institutional Investors: A UK View' (1991) 57 *Brooklyn Law Review* 130 at 131; by 1981 institutions owned 54% of UK shares, and pension funds owned 30% of British listed shares by 1984: see Lord Wedderburn, 'Trust, Corporation and the Worker' (1985) 23(2) *Osgoode Hall Law Journal* 203 at 219.

and encouraging development'.[14] It clearly viewed II engagement with companies as crucial, emphasising that those investors 'should be prepared to take a long-term view'.[15] However, whilst it was aware that the ISC was not particularly active, the Report concluded that the ISC 'was adequate for any collective action that may be needed' and that there was no need to strengthen it.[16]

In fact, the activity of the ISC subsequently declined to the point where it was 'virtually inactive'.[17] In the late 1980s, Jonathan Charkham, an adviser to the Bank of England and later a member of the Cadbury Committee, put the issue of II engagement forcefully back onto the Bank's agenda. He argued that shareholders had to take a more active approach and hold Boards accountable, this time in order to justify shareholder supremacy and head off the danger of regulatory intervention.[18] Again, shareholders were expected, in the event of corporate decline, to 'use their influence and, in the last resort, their powers under the Companies Acts in relation to the composition of the Board to cause remedial action to be taken, rather than simply wash their hands of the whole matter by selling their shares and walking away'.[19] Yet, as the Myners Review highlighted in 2001,[20] the slew of soft law initiatives that followed, from industry-led initiatives such as the ISC to Bank of England-sponsored initiatives such as the Cadbury Report, had failed to reorient institutional investors towards a long-term approach.

How can this ongoing passivity on the part of IIs be explained? As early as 1989, Charkham highlighted one of the main obstacles to institutional investors playing this role: the performance of fund managers was assessed over short time horizons, potentially encouraging a 'trading' approach which runs contrary to the 'longer term view which is concerned with the underlying quality of a business and its management'.[21]

---

[14] *Committee to Review the Functioning of Financial Institutions* (Cmnd 7937, 1980) (the Wilson Report) para 898.

[15] ibid, para 902. The Report alluded to the necessary reliance of institutions on the work of financial analysts, and that they may be 'more cautious than company managements and less imaginative about long-term investment opportunities', although it was not 'immediately obvious' whether this caution would be beneficial or harmful.

[16] ibid, para 925.

[17] See ISC, 'The Institutional Shareholders' Committee' (24 June 1991), available from the Cadbury archive: http://cadbury.cjbs.archios.info/_media/files/CAD-01221.pdf.

[18] Charkham (n 8 above) 8–9.

[19] ibid 4.

[20] In 2001, Myners expressed particular concern about 'the value lost to institutional investors through 'the reluctance of fund managers to actively engage with companies in which they have holdings, even where they have strong reservations about strategy, personnel or other potential causes of corporate under-performance': Myners (n 5 above) para 79. Myners acknowledged 'considerable movement in recent years' but levels of activism were 'not always sufficient' and 'concerns about the management and strategy of major companies can persist among analysts and fund managers for long periods of time before action is taken': ibid paras 5.73–5.74. Indeed, Myners' threat of regulatory intervention along the lines of the US Department of Labor triggered fresh activity on the part of the ISC. In addition to avoiding confrontation and conflicts of interest, the reasons for the lack of activism and engagement included the same one noted repeatedly over the years: 'current manager selection and performance measurement processes can mean that there is little incentive to adopt activist strategies, which do not deliver the quick results which a perceived focus on quarterly figures tends to demand': ibid para 5.83.

[21] Charkham (n 8 above) 12. A similar point was made by David Walker in 1985 when he drew attention to short-termism in capital markets, as well as increased turnover of institutional shareholdings and 'the increased attention to performance on the part of portfolio managers, which, since it is measured only on a short-term basis, means that they are unavoidably driven to concentrate on the short term rather than

As the asset management industry developed from the late 1950s through the 1960s and 1970s,[22] pension funds increasingly rewarded 'the more successful with a greater share of the portfolio management'.[23] Reviewing the role of IIs, the Wilson Report of 1980 did not disaggregate the investment chain, but identified a 'lack of industrial, as distinct from financial, expertise' on the part of IIs, so that regular contact with investee companies was 'exceptional'.[24] It also noted that, whilst IIs had formed Investment Protection Committees, they could decline to take part, preserving 'their freedom to deal'.[25] Trading would be key to outperforming peers and increasing assets under management. Indeed, pre-2008 empirical research highlighted that trading was the dominant approach adopted by asset managers.[26] As we will see in the next section, problems arising from the investment chain were highlighted once again in the Kay Review of 2012, and remain a major obstacle to the stewardship agenda achieving its goals.

Much greater academic attention was paid to II engagement in the US than the UK, and expectations and evaluations shifted over time. The reconcentration of the 'ownership' side of corporate governance in the hands of IIs was variously expected to lead to 'pension fund socialism',[27] 'pension fund capitalism'[28] or 'investor capitalism'.[29] In 1976, Drucker was concerned that pension funds would not

---

long haul'. One of Walker's proposed solutions to the problem of 'shorter horizons militating against long-term investment decisions' was the provision of better information about innovation and encouragement of dialogue between executives and IIs, another theme to which corporate governance has returned repeatedly over the years: D Walker, 'Capital Markets and Industry' (1985) Q4 *Bank of England Quarterly Bulletin* 570, 571–72.

[22] For historical background on the development of the asset management industry, see L Hannah, *Inventing Retirement: The Development of Occupational Pensions in Britain* (Cambridge University Press, 1986) 65–78.

[23] ibid 76.

[24] Wilson Report (n 14 above) 900.

[25] ibid 911.

[26] J Hendry et al, 'Owners or Traders? Conceptualizations of Institutional Investors and their Relationship with Corporate Managers' (2006) 59 *Human Relations* 1101.

[27] P Drucker, *The Unseen Revolution: How Pension Fund Socialism Came to America* (Harper & Row, 1976), referring to workers coming to own the means of production through their pension funds. At the same time, Drucker was one of the first writers to recognise the flaws in the existing model of institutional investment. For example, at 71: 'Pension funds cannot beat the market – they are the market … But because the ability of the asset managers to attract pension fund business heavily depends on their promise to perform such miracles, they tend to concentrate on short-term results: the next ninety days or, perhaps, the next swing in the stock market. Yet, by definition, pensions are long-term. Pension fund management therefore requires long-term strategies for true performance. It is an axiom proven countless times that a series of short-term tactics, no matter how brilliant, will never add up to a successful long-term strategy'; see also P Drucker, 'Pension Fund "Socialism"' (1976) (Winter) *National Affairs* 3, arguing that the growth of pension funds meant that workers were going to own the means of production.

[28] G Clark, 'Pension Fund Capitalism: A Causal Analysis' (1998) 80(3) *Geografiska Annaler: Series B, Human Geography* 139, noting that 'The concentration of financial assets in pension funds coupled with the fact that trustees and their investment advisers have considerable autonomy from plan beneficiaries is analogous to the separation of ownership from control characteristic of modern corporations'. Robert Clark refers to 'the third stage of capitalism' which 'split ownership into capital supplying and investment', describing this separation as 'one of the most striking institutional developments in our century': see RC Clark, 'The Four Stages of Capitalism: Reflections on Investment Management Treatises' (1981) 94 *Harvard Law Review* 561, 564.

[29] M Useem, *Investor Capitalism* (Basic Books, 1996).

hold management accountable because they would sell their stock where they were unhappy with the company.[30] As the takeover wave of the 1980s receded, however, and the number of formal resolutions on governance matters, as well as informal contact between investors and managers, increased during the 1990s, Michael Useem referred to the emergence of a kind of joint decision-making in relation to many key corporate decisions.[31] Since this was the 1990s, 'Consistent executive reference to "shareholder value" [was] de rigueur',[32] with investors pressing for performance, for strategic change and company restructuring, for changes to the governance system, for information and mutual influence, and insisting that strategy and organisation should be more responsive to investor concerns.[33] At this point, shareholder activism had become a reality, in the US at least, where the threat of a proxy contest created pressure for management to be responsive to shareholder demands for change. In contrast, institutional investors in the UK remained passive, happy to take the 'lazy way out' of waiting for a hostile takeover to come along rather than 'use voice as an instrument for improving poor management'.[34] At the same time, the rise of shareholder influence observed in the US was quite different from the current notion of stewardship, which expects structured dialogue between mainsteam investors and Boards oriented towards the long term. For example, there is no hint in Useem's work that 'investor capitalism' was concerned with anything more than increasing shareholder value and influence.

During this period, Pound influentially argued that a political model of corporate governance had superseded takeovers as a means of protecting shareholder interests and solving the 'oversight problem'.[35] Pound used the term 'political model' to refer to

> an approach in which active investors seek to change corporate policy by developing voting support from dispersed shareholders, rather than by simply purchasing voting power or control. I call it 'political' because this form of corporate governance bears a strong resemblance to the model of governance that we typically associate with the public sector. Within a political model of corporate governance, insurgents use public processes to educate voters and to propose alternatives to the policies of incumbents. This process, and the debate it engenders, promotes an informed, participatory, and substantive approach to oversight of management.[36]

Behind the emergence of the political model was the concentration of institutional ownership, which was 'sufficient to create a wholly different set of market incentives, one that promotes the "political" approach to governance'.[37] As institutional

---

[30] Drucker (n 27 above) 82–83.
[31] Useem (n 29 above) 25–28.
[32] ibid 253.
[33] ibid 274–75.
[34] J Charkham, 'Corporate Governance and the Market for Control of Companies', *Bank of England Panel Paper No 25* (March 1989) 11–12.
[35] J Pound, 'The Rise of the Political Model of Corporate Governance and Corporate Control' (1993) 68 *New York University Law Review* 1003, 1013.
[36] ibid 1007.
[37] ibid 1042; see also Useem (n 29 above) 31.

investors responded to those incentives, they engaged in activism, opting for both informal negotiation and formal voting, with formal proxy voting challenges just the most visible part of the resurgent political model.[38] Pound emphasised that the political model was a more continuous, lower cost, less disruptive and more creative method of corporate oversight than the system of takeovers that it superseded. For example, shareholder activism could result in the divestment of a division rather than a wholesale change of control. There are echoes here of what Charkham was demanding in the UK in the late 1980s and, like Charkham, Pound was focused on shareholder activism as a means to managerial accountability and shareholder value.

After Useem and Pound, a gradual but clear drift beyond a pure shareholder value conception of shareholder activism can be identified, starting with the seminal analysis of Hawley and Williams. They identified an emergent shift to 'fiduciary capitalism', in which well diversified institutions were becoming 'universal owners' more akin to stakeholders because their holdings represent the entire economy. They expected that, as universal owners, institutions would recognise that actions taken at one company can impact on the entire corporate sector and from there to global public goods. Hence this type of investor arguably had a breadth of concern that aligns with the public interest; for example, 'universal owners may have (and indeed they should have) interests in form activities that minimize negative externalities (eg environmental damage) by taking account of them to a greater degree and reducing social, third-party costs for the portfolio as a whole'.[39] Similarly, universal owners should support companies producing positive externalities by investing in education and training, even if they are unable directly to internalise all the benefits, because it will make the economy more productive. Ultimately they claimed, these investors were increasingly being 'forced to consider issues that can be seen as quasi-public policy in nature'. Even if fiduciary duty requires investors to exclude 'purely' social issues, this distinction becomes fluid because they should focus on 'issues that affect the *economic* return on a portfolio investment'.[40] At this point a concern about social and environmental externalities becomes relevant because these costs impact on the portfolio via their impact on the real economy.

Like Useem, Hawley and Williams recognised that, in the US at least, institutional investors appeared to be moving away from rational apathy. In large part, this was because exit was increasingly blocked, leaving voice as the only solution.[41] They expected that professional shareholders would increasingly monitor their investee companies and communicate with management.[42] But unlike Useem, who assumed that the aim was simply direct increases in shareholder value, and highlighted that low levels of staffing at indexed funds left little scope 'for sustained attention to any company',[43] Hawley and Williams expected that IIs would increasingly take account

---

[38] ibid 1012.
[39] J Hawley and A Williams, *The Rise of Fiduciary Capitalism* (Pennsylvania University Press, 2000) 4.
[40] ibid 29.
[41] ibid 125.
[42] ibid 124.
[43] Useem (n 29 above) 61.

of wider social considerations as a means of discharging their fiduciary duty to their beneficiaries. In this regard, their work marks the beginning of the (rhetorical) shift from activism to stewardship. Their study highlighted that, although CalPERS' proxy voting guidelines were still dominated by corporate governance issues aimed at 'enhancing shareholder value', they also mentioned a number of 'social issues', in relation to which information disclosure was demanded.[44] Whilst this tendency was clearly still in its infancy, it arguably highlighted an emerging 'awareness that the actions of individual companies can have spillover effects that impact the owner's entire portfolio'.[45] With the benefit of hindsight, Hawley and Williams' expectations were not met, and their argument was perhaps the highpoint of academic belief in institutional investors having incentives to steer companies towards a long-term, sustainable approach, at least until the emergence of recent Panglossian litera- ture (evaluated in section V below) claiming once more that index funds will drive sustainability. Certainly, their analysis highlighted increasing levels of indexation, giving the asset owner an interest in the index as a whole,[46] and foreshadowed more recent commentary about the incentives of index funds to focus on non-diversifiable, 'systematic' risk.[47]

Overall, then, shareholder activism before 2008 was patchy, and was primar- ily focused on increasing short-term shareholder value, with some IIs beginning to pay attention to what we now know as environmental, social and governance (ESG) issues. In the US, activism served as a substitute for the market for corporate control as takeovers became much harder to carry out from the end of the 1980s. In the UK, policymakers reversed this logic, hoping that IIs would engage more frequently with companies so that there would be fewer takeovers, allowing the end beneficiaries of pension funds to share in the long-term returns that accrue to shareholders in well-run companies. However, there was little evidence of this happening, and as we will see next, shareholder pressure for returns played its part in the run up to the 2008 crisis.

III. THE POST-GLOBAL FINANCIAL CRISIS STEWARDSHIP AGENDA

Given the apparent failure of efforts to encourage engagement, in the UK at least, the 2008 global financial crisis provided a golden opportunity for policymakers

---

[44] Hawley and Williams (n 39 above) 32–40. CalPERS (the California Public Employees' Retirement System) was (and still is) the largest US retirement fund. From 1987, it was a trailblazer among pension funds, taking an activist approach to corporate governance issues. It began by opposing poison pills and staggered Boards that protected against takeovers, then in the 1990s began pushing for improvements among its portfolio companies with poor financial performance: see CalPERS, *Global Governance Principles*, March 2015. Useem noted (at 65) that 'for some investors, the stress on company performance came to displace any concern with governance and related executive practices'. Whilst CalPERS now publicly professes a belief that ESG issues can affect financial performance (*Global Governance Principles* 6), its most recent proxy voting guidelines do not go much further than the 1998 Guidelines discussed by Hawley and Williams, being largely confined to supporting resolutions seeking information disclosure across environmental and social matters: see *CalPERS Proxy Voting Guidelines* (April 2021) 10–12.

[45] Hawley and Williams (n 39 above) 171.

[46] ibid 7.

[47] See further section V below.

to change tack. After all, institutional investors had been identified as one of the drivers of the crisis, chasing returns and pushing for financial institutions to take more – not less – risk in the period leading up to the financial meltdown.[48] Yet, the 2009 review of corporate governance in UK banks, carried out by Sir David Walker, referred to Institutional Investors' 'at least acquiescence in and some degree of encouragement to high leverage'. Walker noted that major fund managers were 'slow to act', and whilst he concluded that they 'could not have prevented the crisis', he also thought the Board-level shortcomings 'would have been tackled more effectively had there been more vigorous scrutiny and engagement by major investors acting as owners'.[49] Walker ultimately recycled Charkham's position from two decades earlier by concluding that, in order to obtain 'at least implicit social legitimacy', 'the larger fund manager' had to be attentive 'to the performance of investee companies over a long as well as a short-term horizon'.[50] In converting the ISC's 2009 Code on the Responsibilities of Institutional Shareholders into a Stewardship Code, and encouraging pension funds, insurance companies and the asset managers they hire to comply and disclose an engagement policy or explain their non-compliance, the assumption was that this would call forth the right kind of shareholder engagement from the 'naturally longer-term holders'.[51]

As will be clear from the history set out above, the 2010 introduction and 2012 revision of the Stewardship Code represented a continuation of business as usual, and it is unsurprising that little changed. Echoing Charkham and Walker in the 1980s, the 2012 Kay Review noted the 'short performance horizon' of asset managers,[52] concluding that 'short-termism is a problem in UK equity markets', caused by 'the decline of trust and the misalignment of incentives throughout the equity investment chain'.[53] Research carried out by the Department of Business, Innovation and Skills in 2014 once again highlighted problems in the investment chain, especially a failure to communicate expectations between asset owners and asset managers, leading asset managers to 'over focus on the benchmark and a short-term mindset' because of misunderstandings about time horizons, as well as a lack of clarity as to who is responsible for stewardship.[54] This communication failure is further compounded by the infinite complexity of the investment chain, with huge variety in the extent to

---

[48] J de Larosière, *Report of the High-Level Group on Financial Supervision in the EU* (25 February 2009) 10; Walker referred to 'widespread acquiescence by institutional investors and the market in the gearing up of the balance sheets of banks (as also of many other companies) as a means of boosting returns on equity': Walker Review (n 6 above) para 5.10.

[49] Walker Review (n 6 above) paras 5.10–5.11.

[50] ibid para 5.8.

[51] Walker emphasised 'the need for those who are naturally longer-term holders to be ready to engage proactively where they have areas of concern', both to address Board shortcomings and to offset the short timeframe of shareholders such as 'hedge funds with significant stakes': Walker Review (n 6 above) para 5.11.

[52] J Kay, *The Kay Review of UK Equity Markets and Long-Term Decision Making* (July 2012) para 5.18.

[53] ibid 10.

[54] Department for Business, Innovation & Skills, 'Metrics and models used to assess company and investment performance', *BIS Research Paper No 190* (October 2014). This apparent misunderstanding about the relevance of past performance and short time horizons was identified in the Myners Review of 2001 (n 5 above) paras 5.30 and 5.69, but apparently remains unresolved.

which asset owners rely on asset managers, as well as secrecy around mandates,[55] making it impossible for the Stewardship Code to state clearly whether asset owners or asset managers have primary responsibility for engagement.[56] Stewardship, then, remains at best a hope and an aspiration, making highly questionable the prominent and continued reliance on IIs and private incentives to drive UK companies towards a long-term approach.

Given the UK's sustained failure to nurture significant II engagement with investee companies, it is perhaps surprising that the UK's approach acted as such a powerful influence on the EU's SRD II of 2017. In rolling out obligations analogous to those contained in the UK's Stewardship Code, SRD II added three innovations: engagement policies had to cover ESG matters; the 'comply or explain' obligation on pension funds, insurance companies and asset managers was embedded in law; and these investors were required to report annually and publicly on the implementation of their engagement policy, including disclosure of voting behaviour and how specific votes were cast.[57] With SRD II fully implemented in the UK before Brexit,[58] the 2020 revision to the Stewardship Code (SC 2020) became a best practice document once again, encouraging IIs to identify and respond to market-wide and systemic risks, and to integrate 'material environmental, social and governance issues, and climate change'.[59]

Hence, the response to a financial crisis that was driven at least in part by shareholder pressure for short-term returns, was more shareholder empowerment. That this step was rather illogical was not lost on Bratton and Wachter, who asked:

> Was the crash of financial stocks the result of a system that gave managers too much power, or did it follow from managers catering to stockholders as they expressed their views through stock prices?[60]

They argued that banks came under considerable pressure, as a result of a lagging stock price, to abandon their strict risk management practices as the housing bubble expanded. The way the banks behaved in the lead-up to the crash was shaped by the incentives given to executives, with their decisions validated by shareholder approval as expressed in the share price:

> The financial sector undertook high-risk/high-return strategies to enhance return on equity and raise stock prices. The executives who danced to the rhythm were compensated

---

[55] For further discussion of the different (dysfunctional) behaviours that can arise out of the structure of the investment chain, and an argument about the legitimate scope of shareholder engagement, see A Johnston et al, 'Governing Institutional Investor Engagement: from Activism to Stewardship to Custodianship?' (2021) *Journal of Corporate Law Studies* https://doi.org/10.1080/14735970.2021.1965338.

[56] The BIS research paper (n 54 above) noted at 28 that asset owners share the responsibility 'through the mandates they give to fund managers and the monitoring of these', which 'can influence behaviour that leads to improved stewardship by fund managers'.

[57] SRD II (n 9 above). For further discussion, see Birkmose, Ch 3 below.

[58] See COBS 2.2B.5R and 2.2B.6R (for asset managers); SYSC 3.4.4R and 3.4.5R (for life insurance companies); The Occupational Pension Schemes (Investment) Regulations 2005, SI 2005/3378, reg 2(3)(c) and The Occupational and Personal Pension Schemes (Disclosure of Information) Regulations 2013, SI 2013/2734, Sch 3 (as amended) (for pension schemes).

[59] SC 2020 (n 3 above) Principles 4 and 7.

[60] W Bratton and M Wachter, 'The Case against Shareholder Empowerment' (2010) 158 *University of Pennsylvania Law Review* 653 at 718.

with stock options and restricted stock in addition to cash bonuses, and so had incentives roughly in alignment with those of their shareholders ... Shareholder power was a part of the problem and is not a part of the solution.[61]

This brief history highlights that the corporate governance prescription has remained broadly the same since the 1970s, despite repeated reports concluding that the structure of the investment chain was a key driver of short-termism and despite an enormous financial crisis. Despite decades of failure, there was a clear unwillingness to move beyond soft law and long-standing assumptions that simply empowering shareholders would resolve whatever corporate governance issue was considered most pressing at the time. However, whilst corporate governance policy remained largely unchanged in the aftermath of the global financial crisis, monetary policy did not, and this triggered enormous upheaval in the market for institutional investment, further undermining the assumption that empowered institutional investors would drive more long-term and sustainable behaviour on the part of companies.

IV. THE RISE OF HEDGE FUND ACTIVISM

Hawley and Williams did not anticipate (and nor could they have) that the global financial crisis of 2008 would call forth more than a decade of zero interest rates and extraordinary central bank monetary policies (in the form of quantitative easing), forcing institutional investors into a quest for yield in order to meet current liabilities. As Millon makes clear, IIs were forced, in the new era after 2008, to adopt increasingly short-term strategies in order to meet current liabilities fixed on the basis of a now impossible 8 per cent annual return.[62] Indeed, the shift to structurally low interest rates ought to call into question the assumption that most IIs, burdened by liabilities taken on in an earlier, higher interest rate era, remain capable of acting as long-term providers of patient capital.

Likewise, Duruigbo asked whether long-term investors still existed, noting that:

Some people that invest for the long-term may be properly characterized as 'short-term investors with long-term interests'... such investors may prefer a series of short-term investments that yield higher returns cumulatively than single investments that are held for longer

---

[61] ibid 723. At the same time, in the UK, it apparently made sense further to empower shareholders by giving them a binding say on forward-looking executive pay policy: see Enterprise and Regulatory Reform Act 2013, s 79(4).

[62] In his examination of the drivers of shareholder short-termism, Millon notes the 'substantial current obligations' of pension funds, which creates a 'need for large amounts of cash on a monthly basis'. In order to meet those obligations, pension funds 'have historically assumed an annual rate of return of 8%, give or take a half point depending on the plan. This is still largely true in the wake of the 2008 financial crisis, although some plans are considering reducing their assumed rate of return by a point or so'. This pressure for returns is amplified by the enormous deficits being run by many funds. With that level of return being impossible in the current climate, funds have to 'focus on short-term stock price performance' by trading, moving into riskier 'alternative investments' such as hedge funds or cutting costs through greater reliance on indexing strategies. See D Millon, 'Shareholder Social Responsibility' (2013) 36 *Seattle University Law Review* 911 at 930–33.

periods of time but generate lower returns. If that is the case, focusing on the long-term investor's interest clearly misses the point.[63]

In a pre-global financial crisis contribution, Kahan and Rock recognised that hedge funds fall into just this category, holding out exactly the prospect of a series of short-term investments that yield higher returns cumulatively. Kahan and Rock highlighted that hedge funds push for significant changes at target companies, changes which are identified before shareholdings are purchased rather than as a response to underperformance. They also identified a potential divergence of interests between hedge funds and other shareholders, as hedge funds seek short-term payoffs at the expense of long-term profitability.[64] Noting that hedge funds require support from independent directors and other shareholders in challenging management, Kahan and Rock suggested that companies should head off the threat of short-term oriented interventions by 'maintaining regular and close contact with major institutional investors'.[65]

However, with interest rates effectively at zero from the global financial crisis until very recently, hedge funds increasingly came to be viewed as a solution by 'long-term' investors facing ever more expensive liabilities. As institutional investors shifted into 'alternative investments', this increasingly (ought to have) called into question the reliance of policymakers on shareholder engagement as a means to an end of companies adopting more long-term and sustainable strategies. Following the financial crisis, hedge fund activism increased, with Coffee and Palia referring to an 'almost hyperbolic' spike in 2015.[66] Capital flowed into hedge funds, enabling shareholder activism in the US which further reduced barriers to shareholder influence, as resolutions sought removal of classified Boards and poison pills.[67] In the UK, hedge fund activism was less obvious, partly because the UK Corporate Governance Code and the Takeover Code had long ensured that managers had less insulation from shareholder influence than their counterparts in the US. However, as pension funds and insurance companies sold off their listed UK company shareholdings following the financial crisis, 'other financial institutions', including hedge funds (with investments from those very same pension funds and insurance companies), took up some of those shares.[68] As of 2021, hedge funds and other activist investors were taking advantage of COVID- and Brexit-related uncertainty in the UK.[69]

---

[63] E Duruigbo, 'Tackling Shareholder Short-Termism and Managerial Myopia' (2012) 100(3) *Kentucky Law Journal* 531 at 580.

[64] M Kahan and E Rock. 'Hedge Funds in Corporate Governance and Corporate Control' (2007) 155 *University of Pennsylvania Law Review* 1021 at 1083–84; for further analysis of the implications of diverging shareholder interests, see I Anabtawi, 'Some Skepticism About Increasing Shareholder Power' (2006) 53 *UCLA Law Review* 561.

[65] Kahan and Rock (n 64 above) 1088–1090.

[66] J Coffee and D Palia, 'The Wolf at the Door: The Impact of Hedge Fund Activism on Corporate Governance' (2016) 41 *Journal of Corporation Law* 545, 548. There were no signs of this abating by 2020: see L Fortado, 'Companies Faced More Activist Investors Than Ever in 2019' (*Financial Times*, 15 January 2020).

[67] S Bainbridge, 'Preserving Director Primacy by Managing Shareholder Interventions' in J Hill and R Thomas (eds), *Research Handbook on Shareholder Power* (Edward Elgar, 2015).

[68] Office for National Statistics, 'Ownership of UK Quoted Shares: 2018', https://www.ons.gov.uk/economy/investmentspensionsandtrusts/bulletins/ownershipofukquotedshares/2018.

[69] P Hollinger et al, 'Activists Eye Targets in Weak and Vulnerable Corporate UK' (*Financial Times*, 7 January 2021). They were joined in this by private equity firms: see K Wiggins et al, 'Private Equity and the Raid on Corporate Britain' (*Financial Times*, 12 July 2021).

In the debate about whether hedge funds have a harmful or beneficial effect on companies, on the end beneficiaries of other institutional investors, such as pension funds, and on wider society, Coffee and Palia contrasted two 'polar characterisations': that of hedge funds as natural leaders of shareholders, and that of hedge funds as short-term 'predators, intent on a quick raid to boost the stock price and then exit before long-term costs are felt'.[70]

Gilson and Gordon's hedge fund-friendly model of 'fiduciary capitalism' sees hedge funds acting as 'governance arbitrageurs' who 'identify strategic and governance shortfalls with significant valuation consequences' and present a value proposition, which involves changes to the investee company's strategy or structure, to the other, 'rationally reticent', institutional shareholders.[71] Hedge funds cannot bring about change on their own, and rely on support from more passive institutions, which are trying to produce superior relative performance in order to gain competitive advantage, and do not have the incentive to engage in active monitoring of investee companies. Nor do they have the expertise to do this: as Gilson and Gordon put it, 'institutions can be expected to be skilled at managing portfolios, not at developing more profitable alternatives to a portfolio company's business strategy, creating better governance structures for the firm, or mastering the skills of governance activism'.[72] Hence Gilson and Gordon present hedge funds as a solution to possible agency problems in the investment chain, setting up intervention proposals that institutional investors can vote on.

In contrast, the critique of hedge fund-led activism is that it demands increased distributions to shareholders in the form of dividends and share buybacks. In their account of predatory value extraction, Lazonick and Shin highlight that activist shareholders, including hedge funds, will seek to influence distribution policies, either working 'harmoniously in looting the corporation' with 'senior executives who have already been incentivized to act as value-extracting insiders',[73] or seeking support from other institutional investors, who also have co-invested in the sense of making an investment into the hedge fund that is pressing for change to the distribution policy.[74] Regardless of who they work with, Lazonick and Shin emphasise that:

> the goal of the hedge fund activist is … *not* to improve a target company's operations or its financial stability. Nor is it to contribute expertise to formulating an innovative investment strategy … Hedge fund activists have neither the abilities nor the incentives to engage in the allocation of corporate resources to innovative strategies, which require massive financial commitments in pursuit of inherently uncertain outcomes combined with an intimate understanding of the company's productive capabilities and competitive possibilities … Their goal is to extract value that was created in the past, not to engage in the innovative strategies that may create value in the future.[75]

---

[70] Coffee and Palia (n 66 above) 549.

[71] R Gilson and J Gordon, 'The Agency Costs of Agency Capitalism: Activist Investors and the Revaluation of Governance Rights' (2013) 113(4) *Columbia Law Review* 863, 896.

[72] ibid 895.

[73] This point reminds us that we should not view the drive for stewardship in isolation from the UK and EU rules giving shareholders a binding 'say on pay'.

[74] W Lazonick and J-S Shin, *Predatory Value Extraction* (Oxford University Press, 2020) 137.

[75] ibid 137–38.

Whether increasing the level of payout requires leverage, which in turn increases the riskiness of the firm, or simply involves disgorging cash flow to shareholders rather than investing it in the business, it is likely to entail future cuts to expenditure, whether on R&D and capital assets or on employment, wages and other employee benefits.[76] For example, Coffee and Palia note that 'most studies find that research and development expenditures decline significantly in the wake of hedge fund pressure' and that 'one needs to look beyond the targeted firms and consider the general deterrent impact of hedge fund activism on R&D expenditures across the broader landscape. For every firm targeted, several more are likely to reduce R&D expenditures in order to avoid becoming a target'.[77] Moreover, they say, this may undermine the positive externalities of research, so that 'even if reducing investment in R&D makes sense for an individual company (because it increases its profitability), this reduction in investment likely involves a social cost (as fewer new drugs and products are introduced)'.[78] In this sense, among others, hedge fund activism runs counter to policymakers' expectations that shareholder stewardship would lead to companies taking more long-term, sustainable decisions.

In his 2017 intervention, Strine emphasised the pervasiveness of the disconnect between the short time horizons of hedge funds, asset managers and other actors in the investment chain and the much longer time horizons of end beneficiaries. As he put it:

> If it is the case that these money managers are acting for their own short-term motives and if most hedge funds themselves have no incentive to think long term, that illustrates that we are relying on the law of unintended consequences to drive important elements of decision making in a context critical to human investors' wellbeing.[79]

Strine's contribution highlights the assumption on the part of the authors of the Stewardship Codes that simply encouraging shareholders to engage with companies (and leaving the investment chain unregulated) will necessarily inculcate a longer-term approach on the part of corporate management, 'creat[ing] long-term value for clients and beneficiaries leading to sustainable benefits for the economy, the environment and society'.[80] Yet, as Strine puts it, there is simply no reason to assume that 'this debate among those with short-term perspectives' will produce 'optimal policy for human investors with far longer time horizons'.[81] Whilst payouts in the form of dividends and share buybacks are presumably very welcome to the institutional

---

[76] Lazonick and Shin add to this list 'avoidance of corporate taxes, price gouging of customers, sale of corporate assets, and acquisition of other cash-rich companies': ibid 138.

[77] Coffee and Palia (n 66 above) 576.

[78] ibid 576–77.

[79] L Strine, 'Who Bleeds When the Wolves Bite?: A Flesh-and-Blood Perspective on Hedge Fund Activism and Our Strange Corporate Governance System' (2017) 126 *Yale Law Journal* 1870 at 1907. Along similar lines, Silver emphasises that where companies attempt to boost their share price 'by paying out large dividends or buying back its shares, this would be in the interest of the asset manager, but not in the interest of the ultimate beneficiaries who would want the company to be prospering when they retire': N Silver, *Finance, Society and Sustainability: How to Make the Financial System Work for the Economy, People and Planet* (Palgrave Macmillan, 2017) 118.

[80] SC 2020 (n 3 above) 4.

[81] Strine (n 79 above) 1873–74.

investors and rich individuals who invest in hedge funds, this does leave the 'stuck-in investor' having to figure out where to reinvest the dividends and buyback proceeds, which ultimately 'have to be invested back into the very companies paying them out'.[82] Ultimately, with central banks continuing to flood economies with liquidity through quantitative easing and buying up government bonds, the primary problem facing institutional investors, and by implication their end beneficiaries, has recently been not a shortage of liquid assets, but a shortage of places to put their money where it can generate a return.

Moreover, there is a real question about the legitimacy of hedge fund interventions into areas currently reserved for managerial prerogative. As Anabtawi and Stout put it, there is 'a new genre of public company shareholder that is aggressive, wealthy, and eager to play a role in setting corporate policy'.[83] Not only do these shareholders not face liability where they engage in self-interested behaviour and other forms of rent-seeking, there are also serious questions as to their competence to dictate matters of strategy to incumbent management. Indeed, the 2020 iteration of the UK Stewardship Code invites institutional investors to intervene in a range of issues, including diversity, remuneration and workforce interests, environmental and social issues and compliance with covenants and contracts, which in law fall within the scope of the managerial prerogative, and in relation to which there is no reason to believe the investors have any expertise, yet for which IIs are very unlikely to bear any legal responsibility.[84] Lazonick and Shin point out that advocates of agency theory, such as Bebchuk, 'do not explain how public shareholders, who merely buy and sell shares on the stock market, could and would make contributions to "long-term value" if they could exercise more power over management'.[85] Strine adds that even those who are optimistic about hedge fund interventions recognise that they tend to focus on matters of corporate finance. For example, Brav admits that:

> many of the hedge funds in our sample are not experts in the specific business of their target firms. Focusing on issues that are generalizable to other potential target firms helps hedge funds lower the marginal cost of launching activism at a new company.[86]

Those who support hedge fund activism claim that forcing payouts through activism helps to resolve 'the agency problem of free cash flows, such as relatively low

---

[82] ibid 1939. Silver estimates that the pension fund industry invests less than 4% of its funds in the real economy (that is, new investment), whilst the rest is spent on buying existing assets on secondary markets. As he emphasises, payouts that boost the share price serve the interests of asset managers, but do not serve the interests of long-term end beneficiaries who want investee companies to make long-term investments in productivity: Silver (n 79 above) 113.

[83] I Anabtawi and L Stout, 'Fiduciary Duties for Activist Investors' (2008) 60 *Stanford Law Review* 1255, 1279.

[84] For further discussion of the legitimate scope of intervention, see Johnston et al (n 55 above) 35–37.

[85] Lazonick and Shin (n 74 above) 160.

[86] Strine (n 79 above) 1940; A Brav et al, 'Hedge Fund Activism, Corporate Governance, and Firm Performance (2008) *Journal of Finance* 1729, 1754–55. The recent successful proxy fight, which resulted in Engine No 1, a provider of index funds, having three nominees appointed to the Board of Exxon Mobil on the back of a very small shareholding, has been called a game changer, although more sceptical commentators such as Sharfman highlight the absence of concrete transition proposals from the insurgent, as well as the huge marketing boost it obtained: see BS Sharfman, 'The Illusion of Success: A Critique of Engine No 1's Proxy Fight at ExxonMobil' *George Mason Law & Economics Research Paper No 21-20*.

dividend yield and diversifying investments ... that might not be in the best interest of shareholders'.[87] For them, these 'investment-limiting' interventions move companies towards an optimal level of long-term investment, correcting for the tendency of management to build empires and 'pursue projects without the discipline generated by having to raise outside financing'.[88] However, increasing payouts to shareholders through share buybacks and dividends is not only a corporate finance issue; it also constrains the range of options open both to management teams facing hedge funds acting as 'governance arbitrageurs', and to other management teams that experience the 'governance externalities' of these activities, and feel obliged to increase payouts to shareholders in order to avoid attracting attention from hedge funds.

Ultimately, this debate comes down to a question of whether capital should be allocated by corporate management under the oversight of the general meeting (as company law expects) or by institutional investors following distributions from companies (as shareholder primacy advocates increasingly claim).[89] Besides a lack of clarity as to who is actually supposed to be taking decisions on behalf of the company, and a concern about whether the distributions are primarily used to further bid up the price of existing assets, there are significant doubts about whether hedge fund activism is compatible with the goals of stewardship, that is, long-term and sustainable decision-making producing benefits for shareholders and wider society. Whilst some might say that this does not matter, because shareholder engagement is simply about resolving the 'agency problem', this is not what policymakers are claiming. After the 2008 global financial crisis, they sought legitimacy for their continued reliance on shareholder engagement by referencing wider social benefits that went beyond shareholder value. As such, it is submitted, whether or not engagement drives long-term and sustainable decision-making is fundamental to any assessment of the success or failure of the stewardship agenda. Ultimately, as I have argued elsewhere, the legitimate scope of shareholder engagement needs to be more clearly delineated than it is at present if it is to achieve these goals.[90]

V. THE RISE OF PASSIVE OR INDEX INVESTORS

A. Background to the Rise of Indexers

Alongside the growth of hedge funds discussed in the previous section, the other critical development since 2008 has been the massive growth in indexed funds (or 'indexers') as retail and institutional investors alike have switched from active to

---

[87] Brav et al (n 86 above) 1755.

[88] L Bebchuk et al, 'The Long-Term Effects of Hedge Fund Activism' (2015) 115(5) *Columbia Law Review* 1085, 1135–36.

[89] Indeed, Lazonick and Shin (n 74 above, 162) express some doubt as to whether, 'after a quarter century of embracing MSV ideology, incumbent directors and executives of US business corporations have the incentives, or even the abilities, to make resource-allocation decisions consonant with "the long-term success of the business enterprises" over which they exercise strategic control'.

[90] Johnston et al (n 55 above) part five.

passive management,[91] driven by lower fees and by the ongoing failure of many higher cost, actively managed funds to outperform the market benchmark.[92] This section explores the implications of this shift, asking whether it is likely to drive long-termism and sustainability.

A passive or index fund is a pool of assets, normally set up as a separate legal entity by a sponsoring company within the same corporate group, with administrative, advisory, engagement and stewardship services delegated to other companies within that corporate group. They may take the form of exchange traded funds (ETFs), the shares of which can be bought and sold on a stock exchange, or a mutual fund, which can be bought and sold based on a daily valuation.[93] These types of funds commit to tracking a particular index, whether a mainstream index such as FTSE100 or a more bespoke index, for example focusing on ESG-screened companies, created for them by an index provider. These funds are therefore 'locked in' to their shareholdings, which must mirror the index on a weighted basis, and are unable simply to sell shares in response to events within investee companies. When the various funds managed under a single corporate group are considered together, that group is normally among the largest shareholders on the register of every listed companies, giving it considerable influence over whether resolutions are approved, and greater weight with Boards than the highly fragmented institutional investors of the past. At the same time, they attract investors by charging low fees, so clearly face constraints on their capacity to process firm-specific information and engage with investee companies. This combination of factors means that the engagement behaviour of indexers will be absolutely crucial in determining whether stewardship achieves its goals of long-termism and sustainability.

The sector is dominated by a handful of large corporate groups, with BlackRock and Vanguard the largest, whilst State Street, LGIM and others are smaller but still very large. These corporate groups offer a whole suite of passive funds to their investors, as well as a variety of active funds. For example, Vanguard primarily offers passive funds to its investors, whilst two thirds of BlackRock's assets are in passive funds. The majority of BlackRock's customers are institutional investors,[94] whilst

---

[91] In the EU, passive equity funds grew from 15% of investment fund assets in 2007 to 30% in 2017; in the US passive funds controlled 43% of total equity fund assets in 2018; and in the UK, passive funds account for about one-third of total assets managed by members of the investment association: see K James et al, 'Does the Growth of Passive Investing Affect Equity Market Performance?: A Literature Review' *FCA Research Note* (February 2019) 6.

[92] V Sushko and G Turner, 'The Implications of Passive Investing for Securities Markets' (2018) *BIS Quarterly Review* 113, 117.

[93] Secondary market trading means that ETFs are more frequently traded than mutual funds, especially in times of market turmoil: see ibid 123–26. Mutual funds may also be active funds, buying and selling shares in an effort to outperform other active funds as well as passive funds in order to increase assets under management. Anabtawi points out that the combination of investor liquidity in mutual funds, 'coupled with widespread availability of information on fund performance, has led to pressure on mutual fund managers to maximize short-term returns at the expense of any longer-term focus in order to attract and retain investors': Anabtawi, (n 64 above) 579–80.

[94] BlackRock, Inc's SEC Form 10-K filing of February 2022 discloses that, as of. December 2021, $5,694,080m out of total $10.01 trn of AUM were institutional, the remainder divided between retail (£1,048,709m) and ETFs ($3,267,354m).

Vanguard is more focused on retail investors.[95] Other groups, such as Fidelity, are more focused on actively managed funds.[96] The higher costs of active funds will normally be reflected in higher fees, although Fidelity, for example, offered fee-free passive funds in order to attract new investors and new assets, highlighting the potential for cross-subsidisation between funds.[97]

Unlike the funds, which are locked into holdings, the fund's investors have liquidity and can sell their shares or units at any time and receive the net asset value. One result of this is that competition to attract new investors and retain existing ones is fierce. The normal business model of these groups is to maximise revenue across the whole range of funds, with revenue coming from the fees they charge their investors as well as from other activities such as securities lending.[98] The fees which come into the group will increase as assets under management increase, so groups compete to increase investment and reduce costs in order to increase returns to their own shareholders. Vanguard is an important exception to this as its mutual funds are the shareholders of the company which provides asset management services to them at cost.[99]

The rise of passive funds over the last decade has given rise to much debate about their contribution to stewardship, both about whether they will engage in activism and about the orientation of their contribution (especially whether it will be focused on individual companies or the index as a whole). This section sets out to evaluate whether – and if so, how – indexed funds are likely to make a significant contribution to the stewardship goals of long-termism and sustainability.

B. What Kind of Stewardship Activities Are Indexers Expected to Conduct?

Sceptics and optimists alike recognise that indexers have little or no incentive to improve performance of individual companies in their portfolio.[100] Among sceptics, Lund argues that indexers lack firm-specific information acquired through the process of trading, and may also lack governance expertise (although she accepts that there may be some information sharing within big investors).[101] As such, they may either fail to engage with management or intervene to demand low cost, one-size-fits-all

---

[95] As of June 2022, Vanguard managed £7.5trn of assets on behalf of more than 30m investors across 411 funds: see https://corporate.vanguard.com/content/corporatesite/us/en/corp/who-we-are/sets-us-apart/facts-and-figures.html. Vanguard's origins lie in providing services to retail investors, and this is where its focus remains: see A Massa, 'Vanguard Makes Rare Retreat as Price War It Started Takes a Toll' (*Bloomberg*, 7 December 2020), https://www.bloomberg.com/news/articles/2020-12-07/vanguard-makes-rare-retreat-as-price-war-it-started-takes-a-toll.

[96] J Fisch et al, 'The New Titans of Wall Street: A Theoretical Framework for Passive Investors' (2019) 168 *University of Pennsylvania Law Review* 17, 28–29.

[97] Fisch et al (n 96 above) 24.

[98] ibid.

[99] For a history of Vanguard see J Bogle, *Stay the Course: The Story of Vanguard and the Index Revolution* (Wiley, 2019).

[100] Sushko and Turner (n 92 above), for example, note at 119 that 'passive portfolio managers have scant interest in the idiosyncratic attributes of individual securities in an index'.

[101] D Lund, 'The Case against Passive Shareholder Voting' (2018) 43 *Journal of Corporation Law* 493, 495.

measures, normally following the recommendations of proxy advisers.[102] Lund highlights the 'lock-step consistency of voting across funds', with very few funds not following standard, proxy-adviser given guidelines.[103] Moreover, she claims that indexers are less likely than active institutional investors to act as a 'keel' to hedge fund activism, which, she says, evaluate proposals and block them where they are not in the interests of their long-term shareholders.[104] Lund is concerned about convergence on a particular model of corporate governance (which increases Board independence, removes takeover defences and eliminates dual class structures) that pays little heed to firm-specific circumstances. Indeed, there is some evidence that, for example, innovative activity increases as non-index fund ownership increases, and that companies with a higher proportion of passive shareholders invest less and pay out more.[105]

Bebchuk and Hirst's main concern is that indexers defer excessively to managers.[106] Whilst they publicly claim to be maximising the long-term value of their portfolios, index fund managers have incentives which give rise to agency costs: the private interest of the fund manager in fees prevails over the investor interest in stewardship.[107] Moreover, they have private incentives to be excessively deferential, including business ties and fear of a potential regulatory backlash if they intervene in matters conventionally reserved to management.[108] They lament that indexers do not intervene in ways that link pay to performance, eliminate takeover defences and monitor and if necessary remove CEOs for underperformance.[109] Competition for assets does not solve this problem because passive funds which commit more resources to stewardship will have a higher cost base than other passive funds tracking the same index, which will free ride on their efforts.[110] Likewise, if they do succeed in bringing about improvements in portfolio companies, this will benefit those actively managed funds that are overweight those companies.[111]

Perhaps because they were written in a US context, and are therefore grounded in an agency approach, these accounts pay less attention to stewardship activities aimed at ESG matters, which are treated as extraneous to the core task of producing shareholder value. Bebchuk and Hirst view indexer claims in this regard merely as an effort to distract attention away from their growing power and the agency costs they impose on their investors,[112] whilst Lund appears to view claims to ESG activism

---

[102] ibid 495 and 516.

[103] ibid 517.

[104] ibid 520.

[105] See sources cited in James et al (n 91 above) 9–10.

[106] L Bebchuk and S Hirst, 'Index Funds and the Future of Corporate Governance: Theory, Evidence, and Policy' (2019) 119 *Columbia Law Review* 2029.

[107] ibid 2048–55.

[108] ibid 2060–70.

[109] ibid 2068.

[110] ibid 2057.

[111] ibid 2059.

[112] Bebchuk and Hirst (n 106 above) note at 2073 that some investors might choose indexers on the basis of their non-financial preferences for stewardship quality, giving indexers 'an incentive to emphasize their commitment to stewardship in their public communications. This might also lead index fund managers to take positions on subjects that they expect to appeal to such investors, such as gender diversity on boards and climate change disclosure'.

as advertising aimed at attracting additional assets by appearing to meet investor preferences.[113]

More optimistic accounts similarly focus on engagement to improve corporate governance, such as supporting 'higher quality financial reporting' or 'better-functioning audit committees',[114] but again, perhaps reflecting their US origins, pay little or no attention to issues like long-termism and sustainability. Fisch et al emphasise the highly competitive nature of the market for passive investment creates incentives to improve the governance of investee companies.[115] Passive funds are competing with an enormous array of other investment alternatives, and need to attract investors, increasing assets under management, and deter outflows, allowing the corporate group to achieve its goal of maximising revenue. The key question is how much scope these considerations leave for stewardship activities. Fisch et al argue that passive funds have an incentive to focus their efforts on improving corporate governance across their portfolio as a whole, rather than on firm-specific improvements. Where 'a passive investor can identify governance "best practices" that are likely to reduce the risk of underperformance with little firm-specific information', that approach 'can be deployed across a broad range of portfolio companies'.[116] Combined with their scale, passive investors have 'a comparative advantage in using voting and engagement to address issues such as corporate governance'. While their holdings generate significant fees and hence resources for engagement, the cost of engagement is likely to be low, 'especially if a fund sponsor supports a particular governance reform across its entire portfolio', and given that 'passive investors are likely to be pivotal voters', this will allow them to exercise informal influence in many cases.[117]

Kahan and Rock agree that passive funds have very strong incentives to increase 'corporate value' through informed engagement and voting.[118] The primary incentive is direct: higher share prices lead to higher returns to portfolios which brings in more assets under management which produces higher fees. Since indexers hold large numbers of shares, they have a good incentive to cast informed votes, knowing that they are likely to influence investee companies. The costs of becoming informed will be met out of the additional fees that flow from higher portfolio value. Moreover, with very large shareholdings and with customers who hold for long periods of time, these higher fees will be received over a long period of time.[119] However, like Fisch et al, they recognise that passive investors who hold shares in multiple companies are likely to focus on 'issue-specific' rather than 'company-specific information', because a focus on the former will allow them to enjoy 'economies of scope', as they will

---

[113] Lund (n 101 above) 525.
[114] Fisch et al (n 96 above) 37.
[115] ibid 30–32.
[116] ibid 37.
[117] ibid 38–40.
[118] M Kahan and E Rock, 'Index Funds and Corporate Governance: Let Shareholders be Shareholders' (2020) 100 *BU L Rev* 1771, 1779. The fund is an entity to which management is provided by an external adviser, normally identified with the fund family, and which hires portfolio managers. The investment adviser will normally make all voting decisions, even in active funds, and this function is normally centralised in an in-house stewardship or proxy voting group.
[119] ibid 1787–88.

already have considered particular issues in relation to other portfolio companies. This, they say, 'may explain why some investment advisers have developed detailed voting guidelines on many recurring issues',[120] and their lack of company-specific focus is confirmed by evidence on voting which 'suggests that it is often governed by published policies that apply equally to all companies'.[121]

The literature highlights three main areas in which passive funds might engage with investee companies: system-level issues, specific externalities and, as we have just seen, corporate governance.

i. System-level Issues

In arguments echoing Hawley and Williams two decades earlier, Condon claims that passive funds are no longer 'rationally reticent'; instead, they put forward proposals with the aim of improving returns across the whole portfolio by addressing systemic risk (in the climate context, this includes transition, physical and liability risks) that the investor cannot avoid through diversification. Climate risk 'is substantially generated by the publicly traded companies within institutional investors' own portfolios', and so is a systemic risk over which investors 'can uniquely exercise control'.[122] Gordon, too, argues that index funds ought to focus not on firm-level engagement but on actions that seek to 'mitigate systematic risk, which most notably would include climate change risk, financial stability risk, and social stability risk'.[123]

However, whilst indexers might support firm-specific activism on climate matters (led by others), and might also take part in collective action to push for appropriate regulation, most of their activities in this area involve pushing companies to disclose information, including compliance with private standards such as those produced by the Sustainability Accounting Standards Board and Taskforce on Climate-Related Financial Disclosures (TCFD).[124] So the big indexers are very publicly putting pressure on companies to comply with TCFD,[125] and putting

---

[120] ibid 1800–1801.

[121] ibid 1797.

[122] M Condon, 'Externalities and the Common Owner' (2020) *Washington Law Review* 1 at 18.

[123] J Gordon, 'Systematic Stewardship' *ECGI Law Working Paper No 566/2021*. In modern portfolio theory, systematic risk is risk that cannot be diversified away, contrasted with firm-level, idiosyncratic risk, which can.

[124] For an overview of TCFD, see A Johnston, 'Climate-Related Financial Disclosures: What Next for Environmental Sustainability?' *University of Oslo Faculty of Law Research Paper No 2018-02*, https://papers.ssrn.com/sol3/papers.cfm?abstract_id=3122259.

[125] The largest indexers, along with many other institutional investors, have expressed their support for the TCFD Recommendations: see https://www.fsb-tcfd.org/supporters/. For example, BlackRock asked companies to report under TCFD and SASB in January 2020, and notes that 'it seeks to understand how a company's strategy, operations and long-term performance would be affected by the transition to a low-carbon economy'. It adds that 'all investors need a clearer picture of how companies are managing sustainability-related risks and opportunities'. In 2020, it flagged up 244 companies as making insufficient progress on climate risk, whether in terms of their business models or disclosures, voting against 53 (22%) of them and putting the remaining 191 on watch: BlackRock, *Our Approach to Sustainability: BlackRock Investment Stewardship* (July 2020) 4, 7 and 17. In November 2020, the Investment Association, which represents investment managers with £8.5 trillion AUM, reaffirmed its position that FTSE-listed companies should report in line with TCFD, committed to engaging with them to improve the quality of their disclosures, and called on the government to amend company law to require all large UK incorporated

pressure on governments to require companies to carry out environmental and human rights due diligence.[126] What explains this strategy of focusing on information production and disclosure?

Condon advances a number of possibilities, all of which would benefit a passive investor with a portfolio focus: it might encourage governments to regulate when they see company projections; it might enable firm-specific targeting by climate activists; it may lead to 'regulation by revelation' (elimination of undesirable practices by disclosure alone); or 'disclosure may lead to a decline in the value of fossil fuel industry stock, which in turn will limit present capital expenditures on the exploration and development of reserves'.[127] Others, such as Gordon, argue that sustainability disclosures 'lead to better capital market pricing of the risks in question, which is both informative and disciplinary, and deepens the fund's ability to evaluate systematic risk associated with a particular company's activities'.[128]

However, sustainability disclosure regimes such as TCFD are at a comparatively early stage in their development, and, to the extent that it is being disclosed, scenario analysis is a long way from being comparable and capable of being used to price shares.[129] Moreover, whilst actively managed funds within the same corporate group might be able to make use of and profit from the information, it is unclear why passive funds would want to contribute to assisting third party active shareholders to

---

companies, whether public or private, to report in line with TCFD: see The Investment Association, 'Investment Association Position on Climate Change' (11 November 2020) 6–7. The UK Treasury has published a 'roadmap' towards mandatory TCFD-aligned disclosures, which would apply to companies as well as asset managers, life insurers and pension schemes: see HM Treasury, 'A Roadmap towards mandatory climate-related disclosures' (November 2020). In December 2020, the FCA announced that the UK Listed Rules (9.8) would require premium listed companies to include a statement in their annual financial report setting out whether and where they have made TCFD-compliant disclosures, and if they have not, explaining why and setting out a time frame for doing so. These rules will apply to accounting periods beginning on or after 1 January 2021, so the first annual financial reports including disclosures should appear in Spring 2022: see FCA, 'Proposals to enhance climate-related disclosures by listed issuers and clarification of existing disclosure obligations' *Policy Statement PS20/17* (December 2020).

[126] See eg Investor Alliance for Human Rights, 'The Investor Case for Mandatory Human Rights Due Diligence', https://investorsforhumanrights.org/sites/default/files/attachments/2020-04/The%20 Investor%20Case%20for%20mHRDD%20-%20FINAL_3.pdf, signed by 105 institutional investors with US$5 trillion of AUM calling on 'all governments to develop, implement, and enforce mandatory human rights due diligence requirements for companies headquartered or operating within their own jurisdictions or, where appropriate, to further strengthen these regulatory regimes where they already exist'.

[127] Condon (n 122 above) 39.

[128] Gordon (n 123 above) 9.

[129] In *The Green Swan*, 'the development of forward-looking approaches grounded in scenario-based analyses' is described as an 'epistemological break' within the financial community, as it is increasingly recognised that backward-looking risk assessment models cannot address future systemic risk of climate change, not least because 'physical and transition risks … interact with complex, far-reaching, nonlinear, chain reaction effects'. It recognises the limits of scenario analysis arising out of 'the deep uncertainties involved' (hence the notion of Green Swan or 'climate black swan') so that 'no single model or scenario can provide a full picture of the potential macroeconomic, sectoral and firm-level impacts caused by climate change'. See Bank for International Settlements, *The Green Swan* (January 2020) 1, 3 and 10. *The Green Swan's* pessimistic conclusion about scenario analysis is that 'although the generalised use of forward looking, scenario-based methodologies can help financial and economic agents to better grapple with the long-term risks posed by climate change, they will not suffice to "break the tragedy of the horizon" and induce a significant shift in capital allocation towards low-carbon activities'. Whilst they might be useful for firms to explore their underlying vulnerabilities, they can become operational only in the context of a system-wide transition: ibid 23–24.

contribute to the public good of more accurate share prices and engagement aimed at greater sustainability. One possibility is that passive funds desire to avoid the disorderly transition which would occur if climate risks were suddenly priced in (this was one of the goals of the drafters of TCFD), leading to gyrations in asset prices and outflows that significantly reduce fee income. Yet it is also far from clear that active funds will actually make use of this information in their share trading and activism, as hedge funds continue to prioritise short-term shareholder value as discussed above, whilst active funds are being squeezed by indexers, potentially leaving a significant stewardship gap in relation to sustainability.

This leaves one last explanation for passive investor activism in relation to sustainability disclosures: it brings these issues more forcefully to the attention of the regulatory authorities, and so acts as a complement to collective demands for regulators to implement legally enforceable due diligence regimes or TCFD compliance obligations. This makes sense from three perspectives. First, passive investors are exposed to high levels of climate-related risk which 'remain unhedgeable as long as system-wide transformations are not undertaken'.[130] Hence, passive investors need to put pressure on governments to change the whole system in order to ensure the long-term viability of their investment model. Secondly, this type of action might enhance their reputation with certain types of investors, especially millennials who are viewed as a key future market,[131] and create a 'halo effect' by engaging on ESG matters.[132] Thirdly, and more cynically, activism in relation to disclosure standards is akin to the CSR activities of companies, creating the impression that these investors are fulfilling their social responsibilities, potentially heading off the threat of regulatory action to limit their power[133] as debate increases about the deleterious effects of common ownership on competition.[134]

ii. Specific Externalities

Another parallel to Hawley and Williams' universal owner approach can be found in Enriques and Romano's argument that portfolio value maximising indexers might press for emissions reductions, making their efforts as visible as possible in order to improve the group's reputation, potentially attracting investors and assets.[135] Condon goes further, arguing that indexers tracking an entire market rather than just one industry should rationally act to internalise intra-portfolio negative externalities, provided that its share of the costs to the externality-creating firms is lower than the benefits that accrue to its entire portfolio from the elimination of the externality.[136]

---

[130] *The Green Swan* (n 129 above) 4.

[131] M Barzuza et al, 'Shareholder Value(s): Index Fund ESG Activism and the New Millennial Corporate Governance' (2020) 93 *Southern California Law Review* 1243.

[132] P Jahnke, 'Ownership Concentration and Institutional Investors' Governance through Voice and Exit' (2019) 21(3) *Business and Politics* 327, 341.

[133] Bebchuk and Hirst (n 106 above) 2073.

[134] For a recent overview of the anticompetitive effects of common ownership, see M Schmalz, 'Recent Studies on Common Ownership, Firm Behavior, and Market Outcomes' (2021) 66(1) *Antitrust Bulletin* 12.

[135] L Enriques and A Romano, 'Rewiring Corporate Law for an Interconnected World' *ECGI Law Working Paper No 572/2021* 23–25.

[136] Condon (n 122 above) 6.

In other words, indexers should engage with companies with the aim of protecting and enhancing the value of the portfolio in the long term by forcing companies to reduce carbon emissions. In support of her argument, she cites recent examples of climate change activism, with asset managers acting collectively, for example, to outline expectations that portfolio companies should not lobby against carbon regulation[137] and to use private persuasion to induce major oil companies to set targets to reduce total emissions impact and to link executive pay to these targets.[138]

Such activism is no doubt welcome, but is there potential for indexers to go further on externalities? After all, reducing externalities is a major way in which companies can become more sustainable, and so contributes to the goals of the stewardship agenda. Enriques and Romano are doubtful, noting that, despite very wide diversification, 'institutional investors only have stakes in one subset of the economy. Thus, they do not internalize the losses imposed on non-portfolio companies, final consumers, and others'.[139] Even this may be expecting too much of indexers: will cost-constrained parent groups spend money trying to identify and distinguish which externalities should be discouraged, because they impact on portfolio valuations, and which fall on consumers and citizens, who likely would never have been savers in the first place? Even at the more enlightened end of indexing, where companies are encouraged to mitigate certain impacts, there is no obvious focus on intra-portfolio externalities as opposed to negative externalities more generally.[140] Condon highlights that passive investors do not have sufficiently large stewardship and engagement teams realistically to be able to track and quantify intra-portfolio externalities, so it makes more sense to focus on issue-specific engagement that can be scaled up.[141] This means that, headline issues like oil firms' carbon emissions aside, firm-specific externalities are likely to remain the preserve of active investors, corporate social responsibility initiatives, or, where regulation is lacking, be left where they fall.

iii. Corporate Governance

In their public communications, the large indexers emphasise that they 'advocate for robust corporate governance and the sound and sustainable business practices core to long-term value creation for our clients'[142] or 'speak with thousands of executives and board members each year to understand how they intend to deliver enduring value to investors'.[143] So how does this commitment to 'long-term' or 'enduring' value creation translate into engagements on corporate governance matters?

---

[137] ibid 7.

[138] ibid 20–21.

[139] Enriques and Romano (n 135 above) 27. Condon (n 122 above) also notes (at 68) that the incentive to internalise is limited to costs that affect portfolio value, and does not extend to costs that affect others.

[140] For example, in its April 2022 'Global Corporate Governance and Responsible Investment Principles' at 31, Legal & General Investment Management (LGIM) calls for investee companies to carry out a 'dynamic risk-mapping exercise' in relation to environmental and social risks, and then disclose policy statements which commit to managing and mitigating 'risks [that] have been identified for the business'. That holistic approach should cover 'business operations that either can be considered exposed to environmental and social-related risks, and/or that may produce negative externalities'.

[141] Condon (n 122 above) 69.

[142] BlackRock, *Investment Stewardship Annual Report* (September 2020) 2.

[143] Vanguard, *Investment Stewardship 2020 Annual Report* 1.

Numerically, BlackRock's ESG engagements are dominated by 'governance' engagements,[144] and if we look at its proxy guidelines for Europe, we find a large investor committed to most, if not all, of the conventional shareholder value mechanisms commonly associated with short-termism and social and environmental externalities. Only a brief flavour can be given here. It begins by noting that the 'majority of our equity investments are made through indexed strategies, so our clients are going to be invested as long as the companies are in the index'.[145] As for takeovers, which will normally lead to companies being removed from the index, BlackRock is clear that it does not support anti-takeover defences,[146] but does not otherwise mention its approach to takeovers. On remuneration, BlackRock supports linking it to 'strategy and long-term value creation', assessed over a three- to five-year horizon, but is hardly encouraging of ESG-linked incentives. It notes that, if they are used, ESG-type criteria should be linked to material issues, and be quantifiable, transparent and auditable. Moreover, companies should offer an explanation if financial issues make up less than 60 per cent of performance measures.[147] Finally, BlackRock 'usually approves' share repurchases on the basis that they are 'generally supportive of the share price'.

Vanguard's European proxy voting policies are not dissimilar. Its policy on mergers and acquisitions is more detailed, with funds voting on a case-by-case basis, albeit that financial and market considerations weigh very highly.[148] On remuneration, alignment of pay with performance is 'mainly assessed through analysis of three-year total shareholder return', whilst structurally pay 'should be aligned with the company's long-term strategy and should support pay-for-performance alignment'.[149] Long-term performance is assessed 'ideally for a period of three years or more',[150] with relative performance in terms of Total Shareholder Return (TSR) strongly emphasised.[151] Finally, on share repurchases, Vanguard states that funds will typically vote to authorise share repurchases.[152]

C. The Implications of the Rise of Indexers for Long-Termism and Sustainability

Overall, then, as we saw in section V.B.i and iii, these indexers very visibly press for sustainability-related disclosures, but when it comes to engaging with companies on

---

[144] BlackRock reports 1,230 environmental engagements, 870 social engagements and 2,835 governance engagements in 2020: see BlackRock, *Our Approach* at 8.

[145] BlackRock, *Proxy voting guidelines for European, Middle Eastern, and African securities*, effective as of January 2021, 3.

[146] ibid 9.

[147] ibid 11–15.

[148] Vanguard, 'Summary of the proxy voting policy for UK and European portfolio companies', effective 1 December 2020, 11: 'The strategic, operational and financial benefits (and drawbacks) of the transaction are evaluated based on a number of criteria, including … Board and management oversight of the deal process; Valuation; Prospects for long-term enterprise value under a standalone/alternate scenario; Market reaction; The surviving entity's governance profile; Fairness opinions from independent financial advisers; Effect on stakeholders, if relevant to long-term value'.

[149] ibid 14.

[150] ibid.

[151] ibid.

[152] ibid 22.

matters of governance, their approach tends very strongly towards shareholder value. Where takeovers are proposed, it seems likely that BlackRock, which lacks company-specific information, will simply accept any bid that offers a significant premium over market price, even if the effect is to remove companies from the index. This may deliver a short-term gain for BlackRock's 'long-term' indexed investors, but, as Strine highlights, the money still has to go somewhere.[153] In the case of an index fund, it will simply be reallocated across the recomposed index, regardless of whether the change of composition of the index presents a better or worse prospect for the long-term investors. Vanguard's position is slightly more nuanced, but beyond a reference to taking account of 'effect on stakeholders, if relevant to long-term value', there is no evidence of considering wider social costs or other externalities which might impact on the portfolio over the longer term. On remuneration, BlackRock hardly looks like an investor committed to incentivising management to pursue long-term social and environmental sustainability. Its focus on a 3–5 year time horizon is a purely conventional shareholder value approach and is also likely to undermine the quality of its much-trumpeted support for TCFD disclosures: incentivising executives in investee companies to keep the share price high during that time period makes it less likely that they will disclose scenarios that will lead to significant (negative) share repricing to reflect physical and transition risks. Likewise, there is no real pressure from BlackRock for companies to link executive pay to issues identified in their sustainability strategies, whilst Vanguard does not encourage aligning pay with anything other than relative TSR.[154]

We might wonder whether the priority given to shareholder value governance by these two institutions can be explained by reference to their American origin. UK and Ireland-based LGIM is committed to 'inclusive capitalism' and promises that its index funds will benefit from 'meaningful dialogue with corporate boards and executives on matters that impact long-term financial returns'.[155] In 2021, it managed £1.3 trillion of assets on behalf of individuals and institutions, of which around £430bn was indexed. Like Vanguard and BlackRock, its 'statement of principles' places emphasis on gender and racial diversity on the Board, and it demands TCFD and other sustainability disclosures from investee companies.[156] However, it goes further than its US counterparts in a number of respects. First, and this may be driven by the recent evolution of the UK Corporate Governance Code, it encourages investee companies to 'embrace the value of their workforce' and establish an 'appropriate structure' for employee voice. Going further, it encourages all companies to pay employees a living wage; to ask their suppliers to do the same; and to make annual disclosures about how employees are treated and whether all are offered the opportunity to elect to work at least 15 hours per week. Second, it encourages companies 'that are exposed to high levels of ... ESG risks [to] include relevant and clearly measurable targets that focus management on mitigating these risks' in the annual incentive part of their remuneration arrangements. Third, it encourages dynamic risk-mapping of sustainability risks and opportunities as mentioned above.[157] At the same time, large swathes of

[153] Strine (n 79 above).
[154] ibid 15.
[155] See https://www.lgim.com/uk/ad/capabilities/index-funds/#esg-integration.
[156] See LGIM (n 140 above) 34.
[157] ibid 5, 14, 20–21 and 31.

its policy remain straightforward demands for shareholder value – long-term incentive plans should have a minimum three-year assessment period making up at least 50 per cent of executive pay, with 'at least one measure that is linked to shareholder returns' alongside Board-determined KPIs that 'reflect the company's ESG risks as well as target opportunities';[158] share buybacks are viewed as 'a flexible way to return cash to shareholders';[159] M&A proposals will be supported where they 'create value for investors over the long term';[160] and it is opposed to poison pills that 'protect the company from market pressures, which is not in investors' best interests'.[161] LGIM, then, tempers its pursuit of shareholder value with some stakeholder and sustainability demands, bringing it more into line with the European discourse around corporate governance and sustainability. At the same time, whilst its demands are welcome, it is difficult to see them leading to wholesale transformation in the way large companies are governed.

VI. CONCLUSION

As we saw in section I above, the policy of relying on institutional investors to solve the corporate governance problem of the day has been remarkably consistent, as has the failure of the policy to reorient corporate governance. The focus is now on institutional investors to steer companies towards prioritising long-termism and sustainability. Whilst there was a period of optimistic commentary about their potential contribution, as we saw in section II, along with a gradual ramping up of pressure and legal obligations with the post-global financial crisis introduction of the Stewardship Code and SRD II, as seen in section III, there is little evidence that these measures have been effective in steering companies towards more long-termism and sustainability. The pressure for short-term returns, identified in section IV, has led to rapid expansion of flows into hedge funds and greater activism aimed at short-term shareholder value. Meanwhile, the exponential growth of indexers described in section V is unlikely to contribute to this goal either, as they push for sustainability disclosures that they cannot act on, but otherwise largely support conventional shareholder value, itself a key driver of unsustainability.

The polarisation of institutional investment between activist funds that push for higher payouts and passive funds that compete on cost and engage in an issue-specific way across their portfolio seems likely to continue. The result is likely to be indexers trying to ensure that sufficient sustainability-related information is available so that active investors can incorporate it into the share price. Yet this is likely to fall on deaf ears as hedge funds focus on helping their clients meet their short-term financial obligations.

Both the Financial Conduct Authority (FCA) and the Financial Reporting Council (FRC) appear to have a good understanding of the implications of the rise of indexers. An FCA research note recognises that, although it has not been conclusively

---

[158] ibid 22.
[159] ibid 28.
[160] ibid.
[161] ibid 29.

proven either way, the massive growth of passive investment may reduce the amount of informed trading, which in turn may affect market quality, especially as regards pricing. Likewise, it recognises that 'the growth of passive investing may shift shareholder monitoring towards routine engagement and away from deep engagement'.[162] That certainly appears to be borne out by our brief exploration in the final section of the proxy voting policies of BlackRock and Vanguard, which are highly generic. The FCA cites evidence that the routine engagement that characterises indexers may lead to increases in firm value, something which is unsurprising, as all the proxy voting policies are straight out of the shareholder value playbook. However, there is much more doubt about whether this 'routine engagement', combined with encouragement to comply with disclosure regimes such as TCFD, will steer companies towards long-termism and sustainability, which are the stated goals of the SC 2020. In a joint paper, the FRC and FCA note that there is value in both routine engagement and the 'idiosyncratic issuer-specific' focus of actively managed funds, but note that 'the balance of engagement strategies observed may influence overall market quality'.[163] There is no reference in this discussion paper to whether the balance of engagement strategies might impact on the goals of the Stewardship Code, something for which the FRC is responsible.

It is clear that SC 2020 strives to accommodate indexers and their issue-specific engagements by expecting signatories to 'identify and respond to market-wide and systemic risks to promote a well-functioning financial system'.[164] This is a long way from the original conception of stewardship, as evident in the Walker Report and SC 2010 and 2012, which focused on the role of IIs in ensuring the quality of the leadership team and giving 'broad endorsement of the company's principal strategies and objectives'.[165] The SC 2020 also expects signatories to 'systematically integrate stewardship and investment, including material environmental, social and governance issues, and climate change'.[166] Here again, the expansion beyond the original corporate governance focus of Walker and the early iterations of the Stewardship Code is clear, as is the influence of SRD II. However, early evidence is that signatories tend simply to 'list collaborative initiatives to which they are signed up', whilst 'many reports fell short of meeting the requirements of the Code' in relation to the integration of sustainability or responsible across 'the organisation as a whole'.[167]

In many ways, the disappointing effect of SC 2020 only serves to highlight the limits of soft law, even where the 'comply or explain' obligation is embedded in law, as it has been since SRD II. As climate change becomes an ever more pressing issue, and as institutional investors continue to fail to play their part in steering companies in

---

[162] James et al (n 91 above) 9.

[163] FRC and FCA, 'Building a Regulatory Framework for Effective Stewardship' DP 19/1 (January 2019) para 5.21.

[164] SC 2020 (n 3 above) Principle 4.

[165] See Walker Review (n 6 above) para 5.30.

[166] SC 2020 (n 3 above) Principle 7. For further discussion of SC 2020, see Chapter 2 below, by Chiu.

[167] See FRC, 'The UK Stewardship Code: Review of Early Reporting' (September 2020) 21 and 28.

that direction, regulatory intervention becomes more likely, as Charkham recognised so clearly in the 1980s. The continued failure of stewardship is likely to see greater attention being paid to other, company side reforms (at least in the EU, even if not in post-Brexit UK). As noted in the introduction, this process is already under way, with the recent publication of proposals for EU directives mandating corporate sustainability due diligence and corporate sustainability reporting,[168] two instruments that have significant potential complementarities.[169]

---

[168] See n 10 above.

[169] For recommendations as to how due diligence could usefully be linked to the development and implementation of a sustainability strategy, see A Johnston et al, 'Corporate Governance for Sustainability' (January 2020) https://papers.ssrn.com/sol3/papers.cfm?abstract_id=3502101.

2

The Evolution of 'Engagement' as a Norm in Investment Stewardship in the UK and the Impact of Sustainability Demands

IRIS H-Y CHIU*

I. INTRODUCTION

S INCE THE DEVELOPMENT of the UK Stewardship Code in 2010 as a result of both private sector and public sector coordination,[1] the practice of institutional shareholder engagement has become 'normified' for investment management conduct, in the UK and globally. Commentators show that such 'normification' is not limited to the UK, as bodies with transnational reach such as the International Corporate Governance Network (ICGN) and European Fund and Asset Management Association (EFAMA) have also spurred the global 'normification' of shareholder engagement as 'stewardship', and have influenced the adoption by many jurisdictions of Stewardship Codes.[2]

However, over the last decade, a plethora of critique has been levied at institutions[3] in relation to how the expectations of stewardship have been met (or otherwise). Such critiques range from theoretical discussions of the nature of engagement (or lack of incentives to so engage),[4] to empirical research findings showing that

* Professor of Corporate Law and Financial Regulation, University College London. The support of the UCL Centre for Ethics and Law is gratefully acknowledged. I thank Hans-Christoph Hirt for very insightful comments and feedback on an earlier draft. All errors and omissions are mine.

[1] The Code was adapted from the Institutional Shareholder Committee's statement on the responsibilities of institutional shareholders, see IH-Y Chiu, 'Turning Institutional Investors into "Stewards" – Exploring the Meaning and Objectives in "Stewardship"' (2013) 66 *Current Legal Problems* 443.

[2] D Katelouzou and M Siems, 'The Global Diffusion of Stewardship Codes' (2020), https://papers.ssrn.com/sol3/papers.cfm?abstract_id=3616798.

[3] Pension and mutual funds, their asset managers, excluding alternative funds such as hedge or private equity funds which employ different strategies.

[4] RJ Gilson and JN Gordon, 'The Agency Costs of Agency Capitalism Activist Investors and the Revaluation of Governance Rights' (2013) 113 *Columbia Law Review* 863 on institutions' reticent corporate governance roles, contrasting with shareholder activists; also L Bebchuk and S Hirst, 'Index Funds and the Future of Corporate Governance: Theory, Policy and Evidence' (2019) 119 *Columbia Law Review* 2029 on the lack of incentives to engage by index funds.

engagement is 'feeble',[5] symbolic,[6] or makes little difference to corporate behaviour[7] or performance.[8] The UK Kingman Review,[9] which was commissioned to examine the role of the Financial Reporting Council (FRC),[10] also levied critique at the Stewardship Code, viz:

> A fundamental shift in approach is needed to ensure that the revised Stewardship Code more clearly differentiates excellence in stewardship. It should focus on outcomes and effectiveness, not on policy statements. If this cannot be achieved, and the Code remains simply a driver of boilerplate reporting, serious consideration should be given to its abolition.[11]

The FRC has issued a majorly revised Stewardship Code in 2020.[12] The Stewardship Code 2020 seems to be a product of tacit acknowledgment that the earlier 'normification' of shareholder engagement needs to be refined. As the Stewardship Code 2020 has taken a markedly different approach from previous iterations, the investment management community may not be entirely certain what signals are being sent to them regarding the expectations of 'stewardship'. This chapter argues that the earlier 'normification' of 'shareholder engagement' reflects a relatively narrow understanding of stewardship.[13] This seems to be giving way to an acceptance of a variety of investment management practices that can also deliver good stewardship. In this manner, regulators and policy-makers seem to be moving away from their earlier fixation upon the 'normification' of shareholder engagement.

The UK Stewardship Code 2020 may be regarded as returning to a point of re-setting 'normification'. This move has nevertheless been criticised as a 'weakening' of the Stewardship Code.[14] This chapter, however, takes a different perspective.

---

[5] J Fichtner and EM Heemskerk, 'The New Permanent Universal Owners: Index Funds, Patient Capital, and the Distinction Between Feeble and Forceful Stewardship' (2020) 49 *Economy and Society* 493.

[6] ibid; for ESG engagement see J Li and D Wu, 'Do Corporate Social Responsibility Engagements Lead to Real Environmental, Social, and Governance Impact?' (2021) 66 *Management Science* 2564.

[7] Li and Wu (n 6 above).

[8] MR Denes et al, 'Thirty Years of Shareholder Activism: A Survey of Empirical Research' (2015), https://papers.ssrn.com/sol3/papers.cfm?abstract_id=2608085. Specific studies on ESG engagement that matter for financial performance in terms of risk reduction or supporting improved performance, see AGF Hoepner et al, 'ESG Shareholder Engagement and Downside Risk' *ECGI Working Paper* (2020), https://papers.ssrn.com/sol3/papers.cfm?abstract_id=2874252; T Barkó et al, 'Shareholder Engagement on Environmental, Social, and Governance Performance' (2017), https://research.tilburguniversity.edu/en/publications/shareholder-engagement-on-environmental-social-and-governance-per; E Dimson et al, 'Active Ownership' (2015) 28 *Review of Financial Studies* 3225.

[9] Sir John Kingman, *Independent Review of the Financial Reporting Council* (December 2018), https://assets.publishing.service.gov.uk/government/uploads/system/uploads/attachment_data/file/767387/frc-independent-review-final-report.pdf.

[10] Audit and financial reporting watchdog in the UK, oversight body for the UK Corporate Governance Code for listed companies and UK Stewardship Code for institutional shareholders.

[11] Kingman Review (n 9 above) 10.

[12] https://www.frc.org.uk/getattachment/5aae591d-d9d3-4cf4-814a-d14e156a1d87/Stewardship-Code_Dec-19-Final-Corrected.pdf.

[13] RM Barker and IH-Y Chiu, *Corporate Governance and Investment Management: The New Financial Economy* (Edward Elgar, 2017) Ch 3 arguing that fixation on engagement may be misplaced, as investment management practices can be optimal in a variety of models.

[14] BV Reddy, 'The Emperor's New Code? Time to Re-Evaluate the Nature of Stewardship Engagement under the UK's Stewardship Code' (2021), https://ssrn.com/abstract=3773156.

The Stewardship Code 2020 kickstarts discourse for a richer slate of eventual 'normification' in investment management practices, from its starting point as soft law. Further, we see the Stewardship Code 2020 as encompassing a range of private, contractual interests as well as social interests and regulatory objectives.

Finally, 'normification' in investment management is far from being relaxed, although the new Stewardship Code takes a more flexible and expansive view of investment management practices as 'stewardship'. This is because the Code is increasingly clearer on the purpose of investment management, articulating public interest objectives to be internalised within investment management mandates. The articulation of public interest objectives in investment management has also been significantly ramped up in the area of sustainable finance, hence this area of reform in the EU and UK may provide a significant impetus for the increasing framing of investment management within public interest terms.

Section II discusses the initial development of institutional shareholder engagement as a norm in investment management stewardship. The section discusses the context and explores the unreconciled and sometimes contesting narratives that underlie the expectations of shareholder engagement by institutions. The nature of such narratives has arguably given rise to vagueness and dissatisfaction regarding the characterisation and conceptualisation of engagement behaviour.

Section III explores the Stewardship Code 2020 as a platform to 'reset' the 'normification' of investment management behaviour. The Code should be appreciated against the broader context of governance concerns surrounding the conduct of investment management more broadly. These include: (a) market failure findings with regard to relations within the investment chain, in the Financial Conduct Authority (FCA)'s Asset Management Market Study;[15] and (b) policy-makers' expectations of the allocative roles of investment managers and funds in relation to economy and market-building, particularly in long-term,[16] sustainable[17] and developmental finance.[18] The section argues that the Stewardship Code 2020 articulates certain

---

[15] FCA, *Asset Management Market Study: Final Report* (June 2017), https://www.fca.org.uk/publication/market-studies/ms15-2-3.pdf. Rule changes: FCA, *Asset Management Market Study Remedies and Changes to the Handbook – Feedback and Final Rules to CP17/18* (April 2018), FCA, *Asset Management Market Study – Further Remedies* (February 2019).

[16] EU Shareholders' Rights Directive 2017/828, Arts 3h and 3i, and Preambles 3, 14 and 15, implemented in the UK for all investment fund entities and managers, FCA Handbook COBS 2.2B.5–9, and The Occupational Pension Schemes (Investment and Disclosure) (Amendment) Regulations 2019, SI 2019/982, for occupational pension schemes.

[17] Led by the EU Sustainability Disclosure Regulation 2019/2088 and EU Taxonomy Regulation 2020/852, see section IV. In the UK, the *Green Finance Strategy* (2019), https://assets.publishing.service.gov.uk/government/uploads/system/uploads/attachment_data/file/820284/190716_BEIS_Green_Finance_Strategy_Accessible_Final.pdf envisages that besides public sector action in mobilising finance, along with the actions of central banks, private sector actors in finance play a part in allocational steering towards green finance, for example by mobilising green exchange-traded funds (at 11). The UK may look at industry standards for certifying green investment management rather than relying on regulatory fiat (at 27).

[18] See EU's and UK's commitment to the UN Social Development Goals (see https://sdgs.un.org/goals), one strategy of which is to mobilise private sector finance to achieve SDGs: EU Commitment to UN SDGs: 'Sustainable Development: EU sets out its priorities', https://ec.europa.eu/commission/presscorner/detail/en/IP_16_3883. UK commitment to the UN SDGs: 'Implementing the Sustainable Development Goals' (July 2019), https://www.gov.uk/government/publications/implementing-the-sustainable-development-goals/implementing-the-sustainable-development-goals--2. On the role of private finance for UN SDGs alongside public-led finance, see C Tan, 'Creative Cocktails or Toxic Brews? Blended Finance and the Regulatory

wider and socially-facing expectations in relation to investment purpose, although it provides only general guidance as to the contractual governance within the investment chain towards these purposes. Although the Code is soft law, it provides a meta-level governance as a starting point to signal policy 'steer'.

Section IV then turns to the governance initiatives for sustainable finance and how these further shape new 'normification' in investment management steward-ship. The EU has introduced new Regulations for sustainable finance,[19] and the UK has embarked on its own version of regulation for the same subject.[20] We examine whether there is a clear purpose-based pivot in investment management regulation and what this achieves in relation to 'normification' for investment management, or shareholder engagement. Section V concludes.

II. THE 'NORMIFICATION' OF INSTITUTIONAL SHAREHOLDER ENGAGEMENT AND THE NARRATIVES THAT LED TO ITS RE-SETTING

In the wake of the global financial crisis 2007–2009 which also saw the near-failure of two large listed banks in the UK, the Royal Bank of Scotland and Halifax Bank of Scotland, institutional shareholders were accused of having been 'asleep'[21] – being too uncritical of risky business practices in their investee banks and neglecting to monitor Board risk management. Although institutional shareholder apathy was not regarded as the key cause of the UK banking crisis,[22] the Walker Review[23] on corporate governance in banks and financial institutions took the view that such institutional shareholder apathy provided a tolerant context for misjudgements of risk made at the Board level of the failed UK banks. The UK banking and global financial crisis provided an opportunity for reflections upon corporate and investment culture, and the role of institutional investors in foster-ing general economic and social well-being. Against this context, 'stewardship' was articulated and developed to characterise, in particular, the role of institu-tional investment. The FRC reframed the Institutional Shareholders' Committees' Principles of Responsibilities in 2010[24] in order to introduce a Stewardship Code

---

Framework for Sustainable Development' in C Gammage and T Novitz (eds), *Sustainable Trade, Investment and Finance: Toward Responsible and Coherent Regulatory Frameworks* (Edward Elgar, 2019) Ch 13; J Griffiths, 'Financing the Sustainable Development Goals (SDGs)' (2018) 61 *Development* 62.

[19] See n 17 above.

[20] J Fitzgerald, 'ESG disclosure rules for advisers shelved amid Brexit doubts' (20 November 2020), https://citywire.co.uk/new-model-adviser/news/esg-disclosure-rules-for-advisers-shelved-amid-brexit-doubts/a1427945; FCA, *Enhancing Climate-Related Disclosures by Asset Managers, Life Insurers and FCA-Regulated Pension Providers* (December 2021), https://www.fca.org.uk/publication/policy/ps21-24.pdf.

[21] 'FSA Chief Lambasts Uncritical Investors' (*Financial Times*, 11 March 2009).

[22] J Mukwiri and M Siems, "The Financial Crisis: A Reason to Improve Shareholder Protection in the EU?" Leeds Law School Conference (6 December 2012).

[23] D Walker, *A Review of Corporate Governance in Banks and Financial Institutions* (November 2009), https://webarchive.nationalarchives.gov.uk/ukgwa/+/www.hm-treasury.gov.uk/d/walker_review_261109.pdf.

[24] FRC, *Revisions to the UK Stewardship Code Consultation Document* (April 2012) 1, https://www.frc.org.uk/getattachment/69188de6-3dcf-46ab-afd9-050886ef0c5d/-;.aspx.

for institutional shareholders on a comply-or-explain basis. The first Stewardship Code contained seven principles which revolved around institutions having policies and implementing engagement with their investee companies, including voting, informal engagement, escalation of engagement and collective engagement. They also needed to disclose how they managed conflicts of interest in carrying out their engagement roles.[25]

The 'normification' of shareholder engagement by institutions is arguably a result of crystallising 'blame' upon the state of institutional shareholder behaviour which had already been subject to criticism prior to the events of the global financial crisis. It has been observed[26] that institutional shareholder holding periods have declined over the years. This is largely due to trading having become a focus for asset management, as trading gains are more easily exploited and quicker to achieve than investing for longer term capital growth.[27] Although dispersed ownership structures quite naturally entail shareholder apathy, as has been pointed out decades ago in Berle and Means' original work,[28] it was not until the 1970s, with the rise of law and economics scholarship in corporate governance, that the lack of shareholder monitoring in dispersed ownership companies was articulated as a distinct *problem*, in particular, reinforcing the agency problem of the unmonitored corporate management.[29] In the 1990s, Useem's[30] and Hawley and Williams'[31] theses of universal owners and fiduciary capitalism reignited hope in pension funds and pooled entities that invest on behalf of the saving public that they would monitor corporations on behalf of the broad public interest. This vision, however, did not quite come to pass as empirical evidence[32] continued to reflect shareholder apathy, low voting turnout and institutions' focus on trading on financial instrument markets to generate returns. Actively managed funds may tend towards exit and trading, a phenomenon which

---

[25] Chiu (n 1 above).

[26] AG Haldane, 'Control Rights (and Wrongs)' (speech, Wincott Annual Memorial Lecture, London, 24 October 2011), https://www.bankofengland.co.uk/-/media/boe/files/speech/2011/control-rights-and-wrongs-speech-by-andrew-haldane.pdf, 12.

[27] K Ho, 'Corporate Nostalgia? Managerial Capitalism from a Contemporary Perspective' in G Urban (ed), *Corporations and Citizenship* (University of Pennsylvania Press, 2014).

[28] The separation of ownership from control was described by Berle and Means as the 'atomisation of property'. They observed that as shareholding in a corporation became diffuse, fragmentation into smaller holdings occurred as corporations grew. Shareholders became passive, leaving decision-making into the hands of managers. Berle and Means questioned the appropriateness of the quasi-proprietary fabrication of ownership in light of separation of ownership from control: AA Berle and GC Means, *The Modern Corporation and Private Property* (1932, Transaction Publishers, 1999 edn) 66.

[29] MC Jensen and WH Meckling, 'Theory of the Firm: Managerial Behavior, Agency Costs and Ownership Structure' (1976) 3 *Journal of Financial Economics* 305.

[30] M Useem, *Investor Capitalism: How Money Managers are Rewriting the Rules of Corporate America* (Basic Books, 1999).

[31] JP Hawley and AT Williams, *The Rise of Fiduciary Capitalism: How Institutional Investors Can Make Corporate America More Democratic* (University of Pennsylvania Press, 2000).

[32] For early evidence see R Stratling, 'General Meetings: A Dispensable Tool for Corporate Governance of Listed Companies?' (2003) 11 *Corporate Governance* 74. However, shareholder voting levels around the world have improved after the global financial crisis: P Iliev et al, 'Shareholder Voting and Corporate Governance around the World' (2012), http://www.bris.ac.uk/efm/media/conference-papers/corporate-finance/shareholder-voting.pdf.

has been termed investor 'short-termism',[33] while passively managed funds have little incentive to behave as engaged shareholders in any particular company. Corporate executives have also tended to bend towards market short-termism, bringing about corporate short-termism[34] as their remuneration packages are usually tied to stock performance.[35] Developments in corporate short-termism include the rise of frequent share buybacks,[36] and shifts in investment in long-term research and development to short-term goals with quicker payoffs.[37]

The confluence of a long-running observation of sub-optimal institutional share-holder behaviour and the global financial crisis 2007–2009 brought about policy reform targeted at such behaviour, although some commentators argue that share-holder behaviour was neither key to the problems with excessive risk-taking by banks[38] prior to the financial crisis, nor was increased shareholder engagement necessarily salutary for the specific issue of corporate risk-taking.[39] The Kay Review of 2012[40] in the UK nevertheless articulated that one of the needs of economic recovery post-crisis would be institutional shareholder engagement with their investee companies for the purposes of securing a long-term well-performing corporate economy.

The Review concluded that institutions were undertaking short-termist invest-ment strategies that would ultimately affect the long-term well-being of the corporate sector to serve social and economic good.[41] In this manner, the Kay Review framed market and corporate short-termism as malaises pitted against the optimal goal of long-termism, and recommended that changes in institutional ownership behaviour would be key to reversing the unhealthy trend. The Review in particular recommended that institutional shareholders should be more engaged as monitors of their investee companies for long-term economic well-being which is in the public interest, and such

---

[33] Corporate Values Strategy Group, *Overcoming Short-termism: A Call for a More Responsible Approach to Investment and Business Management* (Aspen Institute Business and Society Programs, 2009), http://www.aspeninstitute.org/publications/overcoming-short-termism-call-more-responsible-approach-investment-business-management.

[34] C Helms et al, 'Corporate Short-Termism: Causes and Remedies' (2012) 23 *International and Comparative Company Law Review* 45; E Duruigbo, 'Tackling Shareholder Short-Termism and Managerial Myopia' (2011–12) 100 *Kentucky Law Journal* 531. However, Roe disagrees that corporations suffer from systemic short-termism: M Roe, 'Stock Market Short-Termism's Impact' (2020), https://papers.ssrn.com/sol3/papers.cfm?abstract_id=3171090.

[35] Helms et al (n 34 above).

[36] J-M Gaspar et al, 'Can Buybacks be a Product of Shorter Shareholder Horizons?' (2005), https://papers.ssrn.com/sol3/papers.cfm?abstract_id=649482; JM Fried, 'Open Market Repurchases: Signaling or Managerial Opportunism?' (2001) 2 *Theoretical Inquiries in the Law* 865; 'Informed Trading and False Signaling with Open Market Repurchases' (2005) 93 *California Law Review* 1323.

[37] MT Moore and E Walker-Arnott, 'A Fresh Look at Stock Market Short-termism' (2014) 41 *Journal of Law and Society* 416.

[38] E Avgouleas and J Cullen, 'Market Discipline and EU Corporate Governance Reform in the Banking Sector: Merits, Fallacies, and Cognitive Boundaries' (2014) 41 *Journal of Law and Society* 28.

[39] L Bebchuk and H Spamann, 'Regulating Bankers' Pay' (2010) 98 *Georgetown Law Journal* 247; PO Mülbert, 'Corporate Governance of Banks after the Financial Crisis – Theory, Evidence, Reforms', *ECGI Law Working Paper* (2010), https://papers.ssrn.com/sol3/papers.cfm?abstract_id=1448118, arguing that shareholders were incentivised to support banks in higher levels of risk-taking as payoffs would be enjoyed by them but risks are borne by banks' creditors, including depositors.

[40] J Kay, *The Kay Review of UK Equity Markets and Long-term Decision Making*' (Final Report, July 2012), https://assets.publishing.service.gov.uk/government/uploads/system/uploads/attachment_data/file/253454/bis-12-917-kay-review-of-equity-markets-final-report.pdf.

[41] ibid, para 5.16ff.

engagement should be of a type that is specific and involves strategic and governance matters at companies. The Review suggested that such behaviour could be incentivised, in terms of lowering the barriers and cost to collective engagement,[42] as well as potentially legalised, in terms of reviewing the fiduciary law that governs investment management.[43] Finally, institutions should emulate Warren Buffett's investment ethos of more concentrated holdings in smaller numbers of companies in order to monitor and engage effectively.[44] Hence, the 'issuer-specific' form of shareholder engagement[45] became endorsed. This form of shareholder engagement envisages that institutional shareholders should 'go alongside' in order to monitor corporate management, raise critical questions and exert a benign influence. Issuer-specific engagement has arguably become the optimal norm in institutional shareholder behaviour, as reinforced in the Stewardship Code 2012. This development will, however, shortly be discussed as not necessarily being compatible with investment management strategies in the market, contributing to what this chapter calls 'contesting narratives' in relation to the expectations of shareholder engagement.

These developments in the UK did not go unnoticed in the EU, where policymakers were also convinced that institutional shareholders needed to change their behaviour to support the long-term recovery and well-being of the corporate economy in the EU after the global financial crisis.[46] Shareholder engagement came close to being mandated in the Shareholders' Rights Directive 2017.[47] The Directive introduced increased shareholder powers in order to reinforce and support their monitoring role, such as in relation to executive remuneration policies and related-party transactions.[48] In particular, institutional shareholders – ie both asset owners and managers – need to institute an engagement policy and provide explanation if they choose not to do so.[49] The implementation of the engagement policy relates to long-termism and includes non-financial concerns such as environmental, social and governance issues relating to investee companies.

There is chequered practice on the ground in relation to issuer-specific engagement. The implementation of the Stewardship Code in the UK and shareholder engagement generally under the EU Directive were criticised in many quarters. In the next section, the key critiques are surveyed. We argue that these critiques are based on unresolved contests of narratives surrounding the norm of shareholder engagement. Shareholder engagement is essentially a means to a purpose or for certain outcomes, not an end in itself. The lack of clarity surrounding what shareholder engagement 'is for' has entailed debates on many sides as to what shareholder engagement 'ought to be for'. The lack of resolution of such debates has left all sides disappointed with the state

---

[42] ibid, paras 7.2–7.7, p 51.
[43] ibid, Recommendation 9, p 13; paras 9.1–9.25.
[44] ibid, para 7.28, p 55.
[45] Reddy (n 14 above).
[46] D Ahern, 'The Mythical Value of Voice and Stewardship in the EU Directive on Long-term Shareholder Engagement: Rights Do Not an Engaged Shareholder Make' (2018) 20 *Cambridge Yearbook of European Legal Studies* 88, commenting on the Commission's Action Plan leading to the Directive.
[47] Directive (EU) 2017/828.
[48] ibid, Arts 9a, 9b and 9c.
[49] ibid, Art 3g.

of implementation of shareholder engagement. Hence, regulators and policy-makers need to step back from the fixation upon issuer-specific engagement and engage with the normative debates regarding expectations of the investment management industry. The following unpacks the contesting narratives and expectations surrounding shareholder engagement to explain why disappointment has been felt on many sides leading to the resetting of the Stewardship Code 2020.

A. Contesting Narratives for the Norm of Issuer-specific Shareholder Engagement

The policy discourse surrounding the encouragement towards 'long-termist' investment management behaviour seems to underlie the first iterations of the UK Stewardship Code. Critique against investor and corporate short-termism underpinned the call to shareholder engagement. In this manner, shareholder engagement is arguably synonymous with holding for the long term, and exercising voice instead of exit. Yet, this call to optimal investment management conduct using 'voice' is an oversimplification, as it cannot be assumed that investment management mandates are homogenous. Even the Kay Review acknowledges that investment managers carry out a range of mandates and states that '[n]ot all investors have long holding periods in mind: nor, necessarily, should they. An activist investor who seeks changes in strategy or management may anticipate that the effects of those actions on the share price will be felt in a short period and plan an early sale'.[50] Although the Kay Review is of the view that a majority of traders rather than long-term investors present in UK equity markets would have a marked adverse effect upon corporations in the long-run, the variety of investment management mandates existing as private arrangements cannot be completely disavowed.

Indeed Pacces,[51] in his critique of the European Shareholders' Rights Directive that favours shareholder engagement for long-termist objectives, argues that whether 'long-termism' is optimal or efficient for a company or otherwise is not susceptible of a standard answer. The question is whether what companies decide to forgo in terms of long-term thinking is wrongly priced and undervalued in markets. However, in light of literature in behavioural economics that highlight the tendency in markets towards under-pricing, and hence mis-pricing, of long-term benefits,[52] can it not be argued that the legislative endorsement of 'long-termism' as a preferred purpose for investment management serves to make a correction for market failure? This market failure also entails social consequences as many ordinary savers and pensioners depend on the long-term financial health of the corporate economy to meet their needs. Nevertheless, it can be counter-argued that mandating long-termism by regulatory fiat is over-inclusive, as this treads upon the freedom for investment management

---

[50] Kay Review (n 40 above) para 5.4, p 37.
[51] AM Pacces, 'Shareholder Activism in the CMU' in D Busch et al (eds), *Capital Markets Union in Europe* (Oxford University Press, 2019) Ch 23.
[52] D Marginson and L McAulay, 'Exploring the Debate on Short-Termism: A Theoretical and Empirical Analysis' (2008) 29 *Strategic Management* 273.

mandates as private arrangements. As both the UK Stewardship Code and the EU Shareholders' Rights Directive provide a comply-or-explain framework for institutions regarding policies on shareholder engagement, it can be argued that even the 'long-termism' purpose is not hardened in law. In this manner, the policy encouragement towards issuer-specific engagement should be clarified as based on compatibility with institutions' investment time horizons.

However, it may be argued that policy-makers, though not explicit, have been implicitly encouraging long-termism as being compatible with wider social good. Hence, the expectations of stewardship reflect a contest between the perception of investment management as a private mandate fulfilled for contractual purposes, and the perception that it should perform as a 'force for public or social interest' in bringing about a healthy and well-performing corporate economy in the long-term.[53]

Although Katelouzou[54] characterises the 'normification' of shareholder stewardship or engagement as a Polanyian moment, where institutions' shareholder roles are not atomistically carried out for merely private purposes but cognisant of a broader social agenda of gatekeeping the health and optimal conduct of the corporate economy, Talbot[55] is more pessimistic. She argues that shareholder stewardship or engagement is borne out of private incentives and this 'financialised' lever, in the absence of clearer embedding of societal expectations and norms into investment management conduct, would only be used for the self-interest of the investment management industry. The contest of private-public narratives underlying the preference for long-termism and the purpose of shareholder engagement is arguably unresolved.

Further, there are indications that policy-makers also see shareholder engagement as a channel to address issues of corporate behaviour and implications for wider society, ie the EU Directive's reference to non-financial considerations[56] such as environmental, social and governance (ESG) concerns, which connect shareholder engagement to a form of gatekeeping towards broader social good or mitigation of social harm.[57] Although the engagement provisions in the Directive are 'comply-or-explain' in nature, the expectations surrounding issuer-specific shareholder engagement[58] raise questions regarding reconciliation between the private law of the fiduciary nature of investment management and the more socially-facing role that institutions are expected to assume. Case law in the UK has clearly supported investment managers discharging their legal duties based on conduct focused

---

[53] Ahern (n 46 above); also see FCA, *Building a Regulatory Framework for Effective Stewardship* (October 2019), https://www.fca.org.uk/publication/feedback/fs19-7.pdf, paras 4.13–4.15.

[54] D Katelouzou, 'Shareholder Stewardship: A Case of (Re)Embedding the Institutional Investors and the Corporation?' in B Sjåfjell and CM Bruner (eds), *The Cambridge Handbook of Corporate Law, Corporate Governance and Sustainability* (Cambridge University Press, 2019) Ch 41.

[55] LE Talbot, 'Polanyi's Embeddedness and Shareholder Stewardship: A Contextual Analysis of Current Anglo-American Perspectives on Corporate Governance' (2011) 62 *Northern Ireland Legal Quarterly* 451.

[56] Shareholders' Rights Directive 2017, Art 3g.

[57] HS Birkmose, 'From Shareholder Rights to Shareholder Duties – A Transformation of EU Corporate Governance in a Sustainable Direction' (2018) 5 *InterEULawEast: Journal of International and European Law, Economics and Market Integrations* 69.

[58] IH-Y Chiu and D Katelouzou, 'From Shareholder Stewardship to Shareholder Duties: Is the Time Ripe?' in H Søndergard Birkmose (ed), *Shareholder Duties* (Wolters Kluwer International, 2016) Ch 7.

on generating financial returns.[59] However, the United Nations Environmental Programme's report[60] has clarified that modern fiduciary duty in investment management should encompass consideration of ESG issues where material or where mandated. The scope of financial materiality may, however, be expanding as dynamic entanglement is observed between non-financial considerations with financial performance, and there is increasing scope too for investment mandates to pivot more explicitly towards non-financial objectives.[61] In sum, underlying contesting narratives framing the roles and purposes of shareholder engagement make it highly challenging for institutions to satisfy their critics in relation to their implementation of stewardship. We turn to specific and well-articulated criticisms against institutions and show how these are deeply steeped in the contesting narratives.

B. The Criticism against Institutions for Formalistic/Symbolic Engagement

Institutions' shareholder 'stewardship' roles have often been criticised to be formalistic and symbolic,[62] lacking real substance in terms of 'outcomes', as mentioned in the Kingman Review. However, in the context of the unresolved contesting narratives as to what 'stewardship' is for, can institutions rightly be criticised for performing a 'form' of stewardship, which is largely manifested in terms of having policies[63] for engagement and voting?

Institutions who signed up to the earlier Stewardship Codes were asked to make disclosure of their policies for stewardship. Hence, having a policy is treated as a proxy for the performance of stewardship. The FRC's evaluation of institutions' compliance with the Code was based on the text of their stewardship policies only, but this inevitably left a sense of vacuum as to discerning what institutions have actually *achieved*. Further, stewardship policies could be written in a boilerplate and meaningless manner. This prompted the FRC to introduce a 'tiering regime'[64] in 2016, so that institutions are ranked in relation to their disclosure quality. The tiering reform at least pushed institutions towards more meaningful articulation of their policies.

What has attracted criticism to institutions' stewardship practices is this sense of vacuum in terms of connecting policy to outcomes, or the lack of demonstration of the difference policies have made. Stewardship achievements can only be meaningfully evaluated against expected purposes and outcomes. Empirical research shows

---

[59] *Cowan v Scargill* [1985] 1 Ch 270; *Harries and Others v The Church Commissioners for England and Another* [1992] WLR 1241.

[60] Freshfields Bruckhaus Deringer, 'A Legal Framework for the Integration of Environmental, Social and Governance Issues into Institutional Investment' (Report for the UNEP Finance Initiative, 2005), https://www.unepfi.org/fileadmin/documents/freshfields_legal_resp_20051123.pdf; UNEPFI, *Fiduciary Duty in the 21st Century* (2019), https://www.unepfi.org/wordpress/wp-content/uploads/2019/10/Fiduciary-duty-21st-century-final-report.pdf.

[61] UNEPFI, Generation Foundation and PRI, *A Legal Framework for Impact* (2021), https://www.freshfields.com/en-gb/our-thinking/campaigns/a-legal-framework-for-impact/.

[62] A Reisberg, 'The UK Stewardship Code: On the Road to Nowhere?' (2015) 15 *Journal of Corporate Law Studies* 217.

[63] Pacces (n 51 above).

[64] FRC, 'Tiering of Signatories to the Stewardship Code' (2016), https://www.frc.org.uk/news/november-2016/tiering-of-signatories-to-the-stewardship-code.

that institutional stewardship activities have mixed impact on companies' operating performance.[65] But is this the yardstick against which we ought to measure stewardship efficacy? Empirical research has also shown that institutional stewardship activities bring about a reduction in audit cost for companies,[66] suggesting that auditors perceive benefits in terms of institutional monitoring and efficacy. However, is the achievement of 'substitute' gatekeeping between external audit and shareholder monitoring the yardstick for evaluating what stewardship or engagement achieves?

Davies pointed out that the UK's Stewardship Code is more procedural than substantive in nature,[67] as *what* is written in the policies for engagement and voting, and how these are implemented, are up to institutions to determine. Unless the law is unambiguous about what engagement or stewardship should seek to achieve, especially in measurable terms, institutions must default to a stewardship purpose that is consistent with their objectives defined by: (a) the legal framing of investment management conduct; and (b) the contractual framing of their investment management mandates. In this manner, it can be argued that the Code's as well as the Directive's provision for institutions *having* policies, but not prescribing further, would mean that there is no other top-down purpose for stewardship that changes the objectives for investment management conduct.

We also need to query why policy-makers and regulators strongly encourage issuer-specific shareholder engagement as an optimal manner of investment management conduct.[68] Whether shareholder engagement is optimal for carrying out institutions' investment mandates would surely have to be evaluated on a case-by-case basis taking into account the nature and purpose of the mandate and agreed strategies of investment.[69] This is also linked to the critique made against 'untailored' forms of stewardship[70] as opposed to issuer-specific engagement, as there seems to be an assumption made by policy-makers and commentators that the latter is superior.[71]

The fiduciary framing of investment management conduct provides for its legal parameters, chiefly in relation to duties focused on securing financial returns for beneficiaries, in a manner that is loyal and with diligence and care.[72] The fiduciary

---

[65] C Lu et al, 'The UK Stewardship Code and Investee Earnings Quality' (2018) 31 *Accounting Research Journal* 388 but see Dimson et al (n 8 above).

[66] J Routledge, 'Institutional Investors, Stewardship Code Disclosures and Audit Fees' (2020) 29 *Asian Review of Accounting* 61.

[67] P Davies, 'The UK Stewardship Code 2020: From Saving the Company to Saving the Planet?' (2020), https://ssrn.com/abstract=3553493.

[68] Variety of investment management objectives and strategies is discussed in T McNulty and D Nordberg, 'Ownership, Activism and Engagement: Institutional Investors as Active Owners' (2016) 24 *Corporate Governance* 346; JC Coates IV, 'Thirty Years of Evolution in the Roles of Institutional Investors in Corporate Governance' in JG Hill and RS Thomas (eds), *Research Handbook on Shareholder Power* (Edward Elgar, 2015) Ch 4.

[69] ibid.

[70] Discussed shortly below.

[71] Eg J Fichtner and EM Heemskerk, 'The New Permanent Universal Owners: Index Funds, Patient Capital, and the Distinction Between Feeble and Forceful Stewardship' (2020) 49 *Economy and Society* 493.

[72] B Richardson, 'Governing Fiduciary Finance' in T Hebb et al (eds), *The Routledge Handbook of Responsible Investment* (Routledge, 2015) Ch 50; Chiu (n 1 above). Empirical research on institutions reflects dominant adherence to financial primacy: A Tilba and A Reisberg, 'Fiduciary Duty under the Microscope: Stewardship and the Spectrum of Pension Fund Engagement' (2019) 82 *Modern Law Review* 456.

framing in the US is more expansive than in the UK[73] and commentators argue that investment objectives can be subject to more organic development.[74] Nevertheless, the upshot is that investment purpose or objectives are privately determined. Although US law provides much clearer articulation of the connection between institutions' corporate governance roles and their fiduciary governance, as pension fund institutions are required to vote the shares they hold in portfolio companies,[75] this regulatory fiat deals with a mandatory *means* of investment management and not its ends. It would also be clear that voting as a prescribed means says nothing about *how to vote*, as that would be in the freedom of institutions to designate. In the eyes of the regulator, adhering to these means reflects meaningful management of the portfolio and of diligence. The regulatory mandate to vote can be seen as supportive of institutions' investment management conduct and their accountability to their beneficiaries. Such an underlying narrative is one that focuses on stewardship as serving the private purposes of the investment management mandate.

For the UK and EU, it is questioned to what extent an alternative purpose for engagement implicitly lurks in its underlying narrative. As argued above, the purpose of 'long-termism' is part of a comply-or-explain regime in the Directive, and not all institutions are managing funds according to a long investment horizon. The objectification of 'long-termism' can therefore only mean the long-term well-being and performance of investee companies. In the UK and EU, the underlying narrative arguably frames institutions into a gatekeeping role to safeguard the long-term well-being of the corporate sector as a social good. This is a much more public interest-oriented objective external to and not derived from the private paradigm of fiduciary investment management. Such an objective can only transform investment management conduct if it is legalised unambiguously, therefore allowing the clear framing of engagement as a norm that is part of institutions' corporate governance roles, as *owed to portfolio companies*.[76] Such a development is not discerned in UK or EU company law developments. It is, however, arguable that both the UK and EU have now taken steps now to address the clearer articulation of investment management objectives, therefore shaping the regulatory governance of institutions' conduct of investment management according to more public interest expectations. These are canvassed in sections III and IV below.

---

[73] The US notion of fiduciary investment management is an umbrella concept comprising both loyalty and care (see T Frankel, *Fiduciary Law* (Oxford University Press, 2011) 169 ff) while the UK sees fiduciary duty in its proscriptive sense, ie loyalty only. The duty of care is separately regarded and now largely governed by regulation, in terms of suitability for portfolio management, Art 25, Markets in Financial Instruments Directive 2014/65/EU, and precise duties regarding diversification and delegation by pension funds: Trustee Act 2000, ss 1–6; Pensions Act 2005, s 36.

[74] JP Hawley et al, 'Reclaiming Pension Fund Fiduciary Duty Fundamentals' in T Hebb et al (eds), *Routledge Handbook of Responsible Investment* (Routledge, 2015) Ch 49; AR Laby, 'The Fiduciary Structure of Investment Management Regulation' in WA Birdthistle and J Morley (eds), *Research Handbook on the Regulation of Mutual Funds* (Edward Elgar, 2018) Ch 4.

[75] Employee Retirement Income Security Act of 1974, 29 US Code Article 18, Sections 1101–1114.

[76] IH-Y Chiu and D Katelouzou, 'Making a Case for Regulating Institutional Shareholders' Corporate Governance Roles' (2018) *Journal of Business Law* 67.

C. Criticism against Institutions in Relation to Lack of Issuer-specific Stewardship

An oft-raised critique against the manner of shareholder stewardship or engagement is that some institutions do not engage in issuer-specific monitoring and hence
do not fulfil intelligent gatekeeping roles for each of their portfolio companies.[77]
These institutions in particular offer passive investment management strategies
based on curating portfolios that match an established index. Passive investment
managers tend to show interest, particularly in voting, in 'across the board' issues
such as best practice in corporate governance or ESG issues for portfolio companies
without much discrimination.[78] This is regarded as sub-optimal compared to issuer-
specific engagement such as conducted by activist hedge funds,[79] as well as certain
socially responsible themed funds. The latter have the mandate to engage with ESG
issues, such as by filing shareholder proposals or engaging in informal dialogue with
companies.[80]

However, why should passive investment strategies such as exclusion or untailored
stewardship be regarded as sub-optimal *from the point of view* of fiduciary investment management? Or divestment in the case of actively managed funds?

Despite Bebchuk and Hirst's[81] pessimistic account of passive investment managers' disengagement from their corporate governance roles, there is evidence to the
usefulness of passive investment managers' techniques.[82] This should be considered
carefully by policy-makers as the shift of assets under management from active to
passive is marked,[83] and the 'Big Three', BlackRock, Vanguard and State Street,
would come to assume importance in corporate governance discussions. In particular, commentators argue that passive investment funds vote intelligently in face of
hedge fund activism, showing that they provide a moderating gatekeeping influence
even if they do not initiate actions.[84] It is also to be noted that active managers who
stock-pick are not likelier to adopt issuer-specific shareholder engagement as part of
their optimal investment management strategy.[85]

---

[77] Bebchuk and Hirst (n 4 above); JE Fisch et al, 'The New Titans of Wall Street: A Theoretical Framework
for Passive Investors' (2019) 168 *University of Pennsylvania Law Review* 17.

[78] S Gomstian, 'Voting Engagement by Large Institutional Shareholders' (2020) 45 *Journal of Corporation
Law* 659.

[79] Pacces (n 51 above); Reddy (n 14 above).

[80] L King and E Gish, 'Marketizing Social Change: Social Shareholder Activism and Responsible
Investing' (2015) 58 *Sociological Perspectives* 711; N Semenova and LH Hassel, 'Private Engagement by
Nordic Institutional Investors on Environmental, Social, and Governance Risks in Global Companies'
(2019) 27 *Corporate Governance* 144; N Uysal et al, 'Shareholder Communication and Issue Salience:
Corporate Responses to 'Social' Shareholder Activism' (2018) 46 *Journal of Applied Communication
Research* 179; E Eding and B Scholtens, 'Corporate Social Responsibility and Shareholder Proposals'
(2017) 24 *Corporate Social Responsibility and Environmental Management* 648. These papers document
shareholder social activism/engagement (SSE) through filing shareholder proposals, voting and informal
discourse.

[81] Above n 4.

[82] M Kahan and EB Rock, 'Index Funds and Corporate Governance: Let Shareholders Be Shareholders'
(2020) 100 *Boston University Law Review* 1771; A Hamdani and S Hannes, 'The Future of Shareholder
Activism' (2019) 99 *Boston University Law Review* 971.

[83] K Anadu et al, 'The Shift from Active to Passive Investing: Potential Risks to Financial Stability?'
Federal Reserve Bank of Boston Working Paper (2018), https://ssrn.com/abstract=3321604.

[84] Kahan and Rock (n 82 above); Hamdani and Hannes (n 82 above).

[85] Kahan and Rock (n 82 above).

A number of commentators find that passive investment managers exert considerable influence in relation to *issue-specific matters*, not necessarily *issuer-specific
concerns*. These matters relate generally to corporate governance practices, shareholder power and rights and increasingly, ESG issues.[86] Such influence is usually
exercised by voting,[87] which on the one hand may be regarded as visible and low
cost, but on the other hand is still a definitive exercise of shareholder power. The
Big Three are also not susceptible to merely voting according to proxy advisers'
recommendations.[88] In this sense, Gordon[89] has forcefully argued that passive investment managers can be positioned as optimal gatekeepers for portfolio systematic risk,
relating to issues that affect the corporate economy as a whole, such as ESG issues,
rather than idiosyncratic risk associated with individual portfolio companies. This is
a form of beta stewardship[90] where issues-specific engagement can result in improvement in performance across a range of portfolio companies, delivering not only on the
fiduciary responsibility for beneficiaries but also common good for the sector and for
society. In this manner, the corporate governance roles of passive investment managers can be looked at differently in terms of what they achieve within their investment
management strategies and mandates, and not be judged by a narrow yardstick
focused on the expression of issuer-specific engagement.

Further, divestment actions by actively-managed funds would seem contrary to
issuer-specific engagement aimed at changing corporate behaviour. However, actions
directed at certain types of portfolio companies, such as those engaged in traditional
energy activities like fossil fuels, is often expected and perceived as supporting the
public interest, and actually called upon by the public.[91] Although divestment is not in
the vein of issuer-specific engagement seeking to change corporate behaviour, it may
achieve beneficiaries' objectives as well as resonate with public interest. Given that
much of the socially responsible investment universe adopts exclusion strategies,[92]
why should exclusion or exit be regarded as less important than issuer-specific
engagement?

It is arguable that the preference for issuer-specific engagement being *the norm*
for shareholder engagement must be based on an underlying narrative that seeks to
enhance institutions' corporate governance roles in the belief that their monitoring

---

[86] Gomstian (n 78 above); V Harper Ho, 'From Public Policy to Materiality: Non-Financial Reporting,
Shareholder Engagement, and Rule 14a-8's Ordinary Business Exception' (2019) 76 *Washington and Lee
Law Review* 1231.

[87] ibid.

[88] Gomstian (n 78 above) and Bebchuk and Hirst (n 4 above) differ on this observation.

[89] JN Gordon, 'Systematic Stewardship', *ECGI Working Paper 2020*, https://ecgi.global/sites/default/
files/gordon_systematic_stewardship_draft_1.0._101820.pdf.

[90] Eg see https://theshareholdercommons.com/beta-stewardship/.

[91] GJ Cundill et al, 'Non-financial Shareholder Activism: A Process Model for Influencing Corporate
Environmental and Social Performance' (2018) 20 *International Journal of Management Reviews* 606.
Public appetite for divestment perceived as in line with social expectations: Friends of the Earth, 'Divestment
and Climate', https://friendsoftheearth.uk/climate-change/divestment; 'Cambridge University to divest
from fossil fuels by 2030' (*The Guardian*, 1 October 2020), https://www.theguardian.com/education/2020/
oct/01/cambridge-university-divest-fossil-fuels-2030-climate#:~:text=Cambridge%20University%20
is%20to%20divest,by%20students%2C%20academics%20and%20politicians, as a result of a five-year
long campaign by students, staff and politicians.

[92] Eurosif, 'SRI Study 2018', https://www.eurosif.org/wp-content/uploads/2021/10/European-SRI-2018-
Study.pdf.

benefits portfolio companies in the long-term.[93] Such a preference cannot be based on a narrative that is focused only on the investment management dimension, ie premised on institutions performing optimally for their ultimate savers. The narrative supporting institutions' private roles to deliver for their savers would accommodate greater freedom in designing the various means in investment management conduct for meeting beneficiaries' objectives,[94] and would unlikely be fixated upon issuer-specific engagement. In this manner, the encouragement towards issuer-specific engagement is arguably beyond the fiduciary and contractual framing of institutions' obligations.

D. Criticism against Institutions in Relation to Incentive-based Limitations to Stewardship

Next, institutions may be criticised for ineffective engagement or stewardship because they lack incentives to do so, not because their investment strategies are carefully considered and incompatible with issuer-specific engagement. A number of commentators[95] argue that institutions' incentives to engage in stewardship is determined by private factors within the chain of investment management relationships, such as how pension consultants influence pension funds as asset owners, and how such influence plays out in the delegation to asset managers, and other service providers in the investment chain.[96] Hence, institutional shareholders are incentivised to behave as 'agency capitalists'[97] rather than Hawley & Williams' 'fiduciary capitalists'.[98] In particular, short-term (such as quarterly) evaluations of asset managers by asset owners,[99] intense competition in the asset management market,[100] and chain intermediaries who tend to maximise their own interests by rent extraction,[101] are all phenomena that affect investment management behaviour. The non-assumption of effective shareholder engagement can thus be perceived to be a market failure. In this manner, it can be argued that the reason for institutions falling short of issuer-specific shareholder engagement is not due to the ambiguities and inappropriateness surrounding such normification, but rather, due to institutions' structural weaknesses.

In order to overcome institutions' lack of incentives to engage in shareholder stewardship, the Kay Review has opined that facilitating collective engagement, so that

---

[93] J Kay, *Other People's Money* (Profile Books, 2015) Ch 7.
[94] McNulty and Nordberg (n 68 above); Coates (n 68 above).
[95] See below.
[96] MR Ivanova, 'Institutional Investors as Stewards of the Corporation: Exploring the Challenges to the Monitoring Hypothesis' (2017) 26 *Business Ethics: A European Review* 175.
[97] RJ Gilson and JN Gordon, 'The Agency Costs of Agency Capitalism: Activist Investors and the Revaluation of Governance Rights' (2013), https://papers.ssrn.com/sol3/papers.cfm?abstract_id=2206391.
[98] Hawley and Williams (n 31 above).
[99] SCY Wong, 'Is Institutional Investor Stewardship Still Elusive?' (2015) *Butterworths Journal of Banking and Financial Law* 508.
[100] D Del Guercio and P A Tkac, 'Star Power: The Effect of Morningstar Ratings on Mutual Fund Flow' (2007), https://papers.ssrn.com/sol3/papers.cfm?abstract_id=286157.
[101] *Kay Review* (n 40 above) paras 3.9, 3.10, 4.10, 4.12; BIS, 'Exploring the Intermediated Shareholding Model' (January 2016), https://www.gov.uk/government/uploads/system/uploads/attachment_data/file/489357/bis-16-20-intermediated-shareholding-model.pdf; K Judge, 'Intermediary Influence' (2015) 82 *University of Chicago Law Review* 573.

the cost of stewardship can be reduced and shared, would be important.[102] This has empirically been observed to be beneficial for institutions in a few jurisdictions who would otherwise be put off engagement due to perceived cost.[103] However, the UK Investors' Forum does not seem to be well-used. It records only 40 engagements with listed company boards to date.[104]

In another work,[105] I critically questioned whether perceived structural weaknesses, such as investor short-termism and disincentives for long-term shareholder engagement, are due to other legitimate drivers and rationale, such as the regulatory framework for investment funds. The regulatory framework for investment funds revolves around regular and periodic reporting of performance, in order to mitigate the perceived principal-agent problems inherent in the design of pooled and collective investing. Hence pension funds, albeit being long-term in horizon, are subject to regular reporting,[106] and defined benefit funds subject to yearly actuarial review.[107] Mutual funds that are open-ended are regulated to protect investors by way of strong redemption rights,[108] hence regular valuation[109] and reporting[110] are required to support these regulatory objectives.

Regular accountability and reporting entail certain consequences. The insistence of regulatory frameworks on regular evaluation and accountability exacerbates the short-termist preferences in investment management because such evaluation and accountability, pursuant to the need of being standardised and objective, is necessarily based on market price, therefore reinforcing a narrow-minded attention to marketised values.[111] Regular reporting also forces funds to regularly evaluate their performance, and funds may be under pressure to boost such performance from one reporting interval to the next. For open-ended investment schemes, past performance may also be crucial to attracting new inflows.

The regulatory regime for regular reporting has played no small part in encouraging funds and their asset managers to pursue short-termist investment performance.[112]

---

[102] *Kay Review* (n 40 above) paras 7.2–7.7, pp 50–51.

[103] Semenova and Hassel (n 80 above) in relation to Nordic institutions' collective engagement; C Yamahaki, 'Responsible Investment and the Institutional Works of Investor Associations' (2019) 9 *Journal of Sustainable Finance & Investment* 162 on collective shareholder engagement for socially responsible causes; C Doidge et al, 'Collective Action and Governance Activism' (2019) *Review of Finance* 893 on collective engagement by Canadian institutions.

[104] See https://www.investorforum.org.uk/activities/collective-engagement/case-studies/; also Davies (n 67 above). I am thankful to Hans-Christoph Hirt for suggesting that the relative under-utilisation of the Investors' Forum may reflect the high levels of agreement needed for collective engagement, usually in cases where spectacular problems have occurred.

[105] Barker and Chiu (n 13 above) Ch 2.

[106] Pensions Act 2004, s 244.

[107] ibid, s 224.

[108] Right to request redemption for UCITs investors: UCITs Directive 2009/65/EU, Art 84; FCA Handbook COLL 6.2.

[109] FCA Handbook COLL 6.3.

[110] FCA Handbook, COLL 4.5 for annual and half-yearly reporting.

[111] M Maher and T Andersson, 'Corporate Governance: Effects on Firm Performance and Economic Growth' OECD *Working Paper* 1999.

[112] Empirical research on investment short-termism: BJ Bushee, 'Do Institutional Investors Prefer Near-Term Earnings Over Long-Run Value?' (2001) 18 *Contemporary Accounting Research* 207; A Manconi et al, 'The Role of Institutional Investors in Propagating the Crisis of 2007–2008' (2012) 104 *Journal of Financial Economics* 491. Opposite view: JL Callen and X Fang, 'Institutional Investor Stability

Guyatt[113] argues that investor myopia is entrenched as it is seen as a defensible practice in light of regulatory requirements. Funds and asset managers may be reluctant to move away from the norm unless incentivised by mandates that build in longer-term incentives and evaluations.[114]

Institutions may be disincentivised from issuer-specific shareholder engagement because of competing legal imperatives that pull in different directions. The matter may not be simply framed as a market failure on institutions' part. It can be argued that resolving the 'normification' of issuer-specific shareholder engagement requires a wider institutional apparatus, addressing the competing regulatory demands placed on institutional investors and the contest between the private and public expectations of what shareholder engagement is for.

Fixation upon issuer-specific engagement has resulted in an unproductive cycle of criticisms against institutions that are narrowly focused. It is, however, arguable that policy-makers are finally 'out of the woods' as steps have been taken to articulate more clearly the desired purposes of investment management in law and soft law. These developments would enrich the private investment management dimension by adding public interest impetus for governing investment managers. In this light a more comprehensive rubric of policy measures is being developed, away from the singular fixation on issuer-specific shareholder engagement.

The UK Stewardship Code 2020, adopting an apply-and-explain modus for voluntary signatories, contains goal-based articulations in relation to long-termism, market-wide stability and ESG objectives. The next section proceeds to discuss the Code, in order to analyse the beginnings of purpose-based articulation for investment management conduct, as well as to offer suggestions as to how institutions should respond to the initiative.

III. STEWARDSHIP CODE 2020

The UK Stewardship Code was revised in 2020 from its 2012 version, in light of the Kingman Review's critique[115] against the lack of demonstration of 'outcomes' by signatories adopting the Code. The Stewardship Code 2012[116] contained seven principles which all revolved around issuer-specific shareholder engagement and forms of engagement that were encouraged, ie having an engagement policy (Principle 1),

---

and Crash Risk: Monitoring Versus Short-Termism?' (2013) 37 *Journal of Banking and Finance* 3047; MJ Roe, 'Corporate Short-Termism – In the Boardroom and in the Courtroom' (2013) 68 *Business Lawyer* 977.

[113] D Guyatt, 'Meeting Objectives and Resisting Conventions: A Focus on Institutional Investors and Long-Term Responsible Investing' (2005) 5 *Corporate Governance: The International Journal of Business in Society* 139.

[114] See work by the FCLT Global, *Institutional Investment Mandates: Anchors for Long-term Performance* (2017), https://www.fcltglobal.org/wp-content/uploads/institutional-investment-mandates-anchors-for-long-term-performance.pdf.

[115] Kingman Review (n 9 above) 10.

[116] IH-Y Chiu, 'Institutional Shareholders as Stewards: Towards a New Conception of Corporate Governance?' (2012) 6 *Brooklyn Journal of Financial, Corporate and Commercial Law* 387; Chiu (n 1 above).

informal dialogue with portfolio companies (Principle 3), escalation of engagement (Principle 4), collective engagement (Principle 5), and voting (Principle 6). Principles 2 and 7 dealt, respectively, with institutions having a conflict of interest management policy and accountability to their beneficiaries.

The 2012 Code was for voluntary adoption and signatories needed to 'comply or explain'. Where signatories deviated from any of the Principles, an explanation for such decision had to be provided. Many asset managers signed up to the Code, as being a signatory could be attractive to asset owners looking to delegate portfolio management. However, over the years, the FRC found that signatories made boiler-plate disclosures of policies and explanations,[117] and the 'stewardship' label could be eroded in terms of quality for market confidence. In 2016, the FRC introduced a tiering regime in order to rank the quality of signatories' disclosure.[118] Nevertheless, the quality signals sent by the FRC were entirely based on what signatories *said* about their stewardship activities. These were not further mapped against what they *did*, as stewardship reporting was not required to be assured. Hence both the FCA and the market could not tell for certain what has been *achieved* in terms of improvement or transformation of corporate behaviour.

The 2020 Stewardship Code is an attempt to address the limitations of the previous Code by introducing a set of 12 new principles for asset owners and managers, and a set of six new principles for service providers. The Code also adopts a new 'apply and explain' regime for signatories. An 'apply and explain' regime may transcend the limitations of disclosure under a 'comply or explain' regime.[119] In the latter regime, 'explain' is regarded as the antithesis to 'comply'. Hence, institutions who regard themselves as broadly 'compliant' would likely say little, as the narrative in 'explain' is treated as an alternative mode of action. 'Comply or explain' based disclosure requirements therefore do not encourage knowledge-building about what institutions *do* as a whole. In contrast, 'apply and explain' is premised on the basis that application of the Code's principles is mandatory for signatories, and 'explain' is meant to flesh out how the application takes place. 'Explain' is therefore no longer optional or is regarded as 'fringe' action, but is expected and purposed towards knowledge-building of what institutions do. In this manner, the FRC's adoption of 'apply and explain' is a direct response to the Kingman Review's critique that outcomes of stewardship remained shrouded in mystery.

The FRC, in its first survey[120] of asset owner and manager signatories' reports under the 'apply and explain' approach, finds encouraging signs of disclosure by signatories who understand that the 'explain' approach requires them to shed light on what they do. The survey also extracts good explanatory practices as examples to encourage other signatories.

---

[117] FRC (n 64 above).
[118] ibid.
[119] P Natesan, 'The Evolution and Significance of the "Apply and Explain" Regime in King IV' (2020) 11 *Journal of Global Responsibility* 135.
[120] FRC, *The UK Stewardship Code Review of Early Reporting* (September 2020), https://www.frc.org.uk/getattachment/975354b4-6056-43e7-aa1f-c76693e1c686/The-UK-Stewardship-Cod-Review-of-Early-Reporting.pdf.

This chapter argues that there are four key aspects to transformative behaviour for institutions provided in the Code. These aspects reflect the trend of increased governance endeavour on the part of policy-makers vis-à-vis institutions' investment management conduct, usually thought to be a discretionary universe subject to private contractual design and governed only by the private law of investment management. Even if the Code is regarded as soft law and not in the same manner as legislative rules, the Code signals an emerging governance initiative. This initiative should also be understood against a broader context of developments in increased *regulatory* governance of investment management conduct introduced in the EU and UK. These regulatory initiatives have resulted from the FCA's Asset Management Market Study[121] and the recent developments in the EU's and UK's sustainable finance reforms.[122]

The four key aspects are:

(a)   articulation of wider public interest purposes of stewardship (Principles 1, 2, 4, 6 and 7) in the Code;
(b)   moving away from exclusively normifying shareholder engagement as equivalent to stewardship but adopting a wider understanding of investment management conduct and strategies in achieving the purposes in (a) (Principles 2, 3, 5 and 12);
(c)   continuing support for shareholder engagement but requiring disclosure of what such engagement seeks to achieve and its efficacy (Principles 9, 10, 11, 12, also 5 more broadly); and
(d)   cognisance and reporting of investment chain monitoring and activities, possibly for knowledge-building in relation to agency problems (Principle 8, Principles 1–6 for service providers).

(a)   Articulation of Wider Public Interest Purposes of Stewardship

The Code now articulates a number of purpose-based goals for stewardship more clearly than under the previous Code. This goes some extent towards addressing the previous critiques levied against stewardship. Stewardship processes or activities can now be evaluated against particular goals, which have been debatable and implicit surrounding the previous Codes. The move to articulating purposes and goals for investment management may be regarded as a radical 'governance' measure. The regulation of investment management has primarily been focused on the intermediary-client relationship, in order to mitigate principal-agent problems,[123] in the regimes in the US[124] and UK/EU.[125] Regulation is focused on the pre-sale context,

---

[121] See n 15 above.

[122] See section IV below.

[123] A M Pacces, 'Financial Intermediation in the Securities Markets Law and Economics of the Conduct of Business Regulation' (2000) 20 *International Rev of Law and Economics* 479.

[124] D DeMott, 'Fiduciary Contours: Perspectives on Mutual Funds and Private Funds' in Birdthistle and Morley (n 74 above) Ch 3.

[125] Private law of fiduciary and contractual management: L van Setten, *The Law of Institutional Investment Management* (Oxford University Press 2009) paras 1.21, 3.15–3.69, 4.92; UCITs Directive 2009/65/EU and Markets in Financial Instruments Directive 2014/65/EU (MiFID 2014).

in terms of advice[126] and product disclosure[127] but the universe of post-sale investment management conduct and outcomes is largely left to the working of private
market forces[128] subject to certain investor protection rights which relate more to exit
than voice.[129] In this manner, articulating what investment management is for can be
regarded as radical and potentially transformative.

The Code's purpose-based articulations complement recent regulatory reforms.
In the FCA's recent reforms for pension funds, whether defined benefit or contribution schemes, funds need to set out investment objectives with their asset managers.[130]
This may be regarded partly as a response to principal-agent problems, as expert
asset managers and pension consultants can be seen to wield significant influence over
less expert pension scheme trustees and governance boards.[131] However, the regulatory mandate to specify and clarify purpose also engages with social accountability
more widely for the benefit of beneficiaries, and allows regulators and policy-makers
to scrutinise how funds conceive of their purposes and what these are. This is especially relevant in light of policy-makers' interest in mobilising the private sector,
particularly private assets under management, towards purposes that are aligned with
public interest, such as sustainability goals,[132] and social development, for example
in impact investing.[133]

Principle 1 now defines stewardship as delivering long-term value for clients and
beneficiaries and also sustainable benefits for the economy, society and environment. This is inherited from the previous Code that articulates long-termism as a
preferred goal, but being nested in a 'comply or explain' regime, it is arguable that
long-termism could be regarded as a strong but not binding steer. With the 'apply and
explain' regime, the goal of long-termism is not optional. But as asset owners and
managers can elect to be signatories, those who do not identify with long-termism

---

[126] MiFID 2014, Art 25, on the suitability of advice, UK FCA Handbook COBS 9 and 9A. See P Giudici, 'Independent Financial Advice' in D Busch and G Ferrarini (eds), *Regulation of the EU Financial Markets: MiFID II and MiFIR* (Oxford University Press, 2017) Ch 6.

[127] Pre-sale disclosure of prospectuses and short-form key information sheets for mutual funds, UCITs Directive Arts 68, 69 and Commission Regulation 583/2010.

[128] The universe of investment management strategies, like active, passive, hybrid forms, alternative strat-
egies etc. Specific EU funds are regulated for portfolio composition, prudential and investor protection, ie long-term investment funds, venture capital funds or social entrepreneurship funds marketed across the Single Market, Regulation (EU) No 346/2013; Regulation (EU) 2015/760; Regulation (EU) No 345/2013.

[129] J Morley, 'The Separation of Funds and Managers: A Theory of Investment Fund Structure and Regulation' (2013–14) 123 *Yale Law Journal* 1228.

[130] The Statement of Investment Principles for Occupational Pensions, s 2, The Occupational Pension Schemes (Investment) Regulations 2005, also the FCA's Policy Statement for other non trust-based occupational schemes, FCA, *Independent Governance Committees: Extension of Remit* (September 2019) Ch 2, https://www.fca.org.uk/publication/policy/ps19-30.pdf.

[131] FCA, *Final Report* (n 15 above) para 4.23.

[132] N Dorn, 'Capital Cohabitation: EU Capital Markets Union as Public and Private Co-regulation' (2019) 11 *Capital Markets Law Journal* 84 on the EU's endeavour to marry private finance with public interest goals.

[133] A Pekmezovic, 'The New Framework for Financing the 2030 Agenda for Sustainable Development and the SDGs' in J Walker et al (eds), *Sustainable Development Goals: Harnessing Business to Achieve the SDGs through Finance, Technology, and Law Reform* (John Wiley & Sons, 2019) Ch 5; M Blessing and T Naratil, 'The Contribution of the International Private Sector to a More Sustainable Future' in Walker et al (ibid) Ch 6; D Wood et al, 'Institutional Impact Investing: Practice and Policy' (2013) 3 *Journal of Sustainable Finance & Investment* 75.

as such could choose not to be signatories. Mainstream institutions, especially with pension and mutual fund portfolios, may be faced with demand-side pressure to opt in, which means subscribing to the investment purpose of long-termism.

In an 'apply and explain' regime, mainstream institutions opting into the Code would have to explain how they manage investments for long-term value creation, as opposed to short-term performance. In this sense, it is queried whether active management strategies would be reshaped by the long-termism goal and perhaps their churning tendencies may be moderated. The long-termism purpose articulated here is arguably inherently biased against trading strategies, but these are neither necessarily inefficient or mispriced. Securities mispricing is due to behavioural sub-optimalities,[134] information inefficiencies and structural conditions of markets that promote these. For example, allowing high frequency traders' servers to be co-located with stock exchange servers[135] brings about a structural advantage for traders in exploiting a short window of information inefficiency. Trading itself is merely an information signal to the market that allows price to be adjusted. At the macro level, one needs to ask whether it is trading frequencies and efficiencies that have contributed more to price bubbles[136] or whether other drivers such as central bank liquidity tools are more significant for such phenomena.[137] It remains uncertain if investment intermediaries explaining their long-termist strategies need to show moderation of trading behaviour, or otherwise. Nevertheless, the opportunity to 'explain' can afford investment intermediaries the space to account for broader structural factors affecting trading behaviour. Signatory reporting is, however, not assured and continues to be susceptible of self-selectivity, so it remains highly uncertain how stewardship reports would shed precise light on investment managers' interpretation of 'long-termism' and the proxy indicators for adhering to this goal.

Principle 1 can also be regarded as encouraging investment value creation to be holistic and aligned with sustainable benefits for the economy and society, and the environment as well. The outward-facing purposes for investment management are not only found in this Principle but continue through Principles 4 and 7, where these purposes are more clearly defined. Principle 4 relates to institutions' roles in promoting a well-functioning financial system and not contributing to market-wide systemic risk. Principle 7 relates to integrating material ESG issues and climate change targets.

---

[134] R Shiller, *Irrational Exuberance*, 3rd edn (Princeton University Press, 2016) Chs 7–9.

[135] M Aitken et al, 'Trade Size, High Frequency Trading, and Co-Location around the World' (2014), https://citeseerx.ist.psu.edu/viewdoc/download?doi=10.1.1.1026.159&rep=rep1&type=pdf; A Frino et al, 'The Impact of Co-Location of Securities Exchanges' and Traders' Computer Servers on Market Liquidity' (2014) 34 *Journal of Futures Markets* 20.

[136] There is some evidence: J Chen et al, 'Forecasting Crashes: Trading Volume, Past Returns and Conditional Skewness in Stock Prices' NBER *Working Paper* (2000), https://www.nber.org/system/files/working_papers/w7687/w7687.pdf, but only amongst other explanations; O Blanchard and M Watson, 'Bubbles, Rational Expectations and Financial Markets' NBER *Working Paper* (1982), https://www.researchgate.net/publication/5184534_Bubbles_Rational_Expectations_and_Financial_Markets; C Noussair et al, 'Price Bubbles in Laboratory Asset Markets with Constant Fundamental Values' (2001) 4 *Experimental Economics* 87.

[137] JH Huston and RW Spencer, 'Quantitative Easing and Asset Bubbles' (2018) 25 *Applied Economics Letters* 369.

Systemic risk in the financial system is defined in relation to the preservation of the functioning of the financial system in a manner that does not result in domino-type failures of connected institutions or disruption to key services that may be unsubstitutable.[138] Does Principle 4 mean that institutions should identify and manage these risks, ensuring that they do not contribute to these? In this manner, institutions should institute systems that mitigate trading disruptions for clients and markets,[139] or counterparty risk.[140] There is an existing regulatory requirement to mitigate the possibility of systemic risk creation by investment intermediaries engaged in high frequency algorithmic trading.[141] This MiFID requirement ensures that where algorithmic high frequency traders become key suppliers of market liquidity in particular financial instruments, they continue to carry out that role under all market conditions and do not unexpectedly withdraw market liquidity which may destabilise market prices. Is the application of Principle 4 envisaged more widely to all investment intermediaries to be aware of and mitigate systemic risks?

The FRC seems to take a widely inclusive interpretation to Principle 4. It has raised an example of good practice in its survey, focusing on thematic risk in the corporate economy,[142] ie issue-specific or systematic risk, which is addressed by Principles 9–11 as discussed below. This is further clarified in the FRC's later report on how it has assessed stewardship reporting against the 2020 Code.[143] Market-wide or systemic risks include not only macro-economic risks but also environmental, social, governance and other risks that could have market-wide impact. Arguably this can be a tall order and institutions can nevertheless be selective about their perceptions of what matter. However, given that Principle 7 deals with ESG risks, it is questioned whether a narrower interpretation of Principle 4 is apt – for example to focus on institutions' risks in trading strategies, leverage employment if any, settlement risk, market abuse risk etc.

Principle 7 relates to investment management conduct that integrates material ESG matters and climate change. It is arguable that such integration is not only demonstrated by shareholder engagement which is more specifically dealt with in Principles 9–11, but also encompasses the whole investment management process including asset allocation decisions. In this manner, Principle 7 takes in both ESG engagement consistent with the Shareholders' Rights Directive provisions as well as strategic decisions regarding allocation. One point that may be made is that Principle 7 refers to material ESG matters, and therefore does not break new ground in terms of institutions' perception of the needs for fiduciary investment management. The call to integrate 'material ESG' does not compel institutions to demand

---

[138] M Dijkman, 'A Framework for Assessing Systemic Risk' (2010) *World Bank Policy Research Working Paper*, http://elibrary.worldbank.org/content/workingpaper/10.1596/1813–9450-5282; F Allen et al, 'Financial Connections and Systemic Risk' *NBER Working Paper* (2010), https://www.nber.org/papers/w16177; M Beville, 'Financial Pollution: Systemic Risk and Market Stability' (2010) 36 *Florida State University Law Review* 245.

[139] Such as limit or stop-loss orders offered by brokerages to protect investors from unexpected financial losses, https://www.hl.co.uk/shares/share-dealing/limits.

[140] Mitigating defaults where leverage is used, eg by collateral management.

[141] MiFID 2014, Art 17.

[142] FRC, *The UK Stewardship Code Review of Early Reporting* (2020) 21.

[143] FRC, *Effective Stewardship Reporting* (November 2021).

ESG performance beyond that connected to financial value creation (albeit in the long term). However, it is arguable that the EU sustainable finance regulations, discussed in Section IV, demand more of institutions in their investment management conduct.

Finally, Principle 6 articulates the need for signatories to take into account the needs of clients and beneficiaries as a whole, and make appropriate communication with them as to how stewardship meets their needs. This Principle is an extension from the previous Code, which requires accountability to beneficiaries on stewardship activities. However the Principle is different as it goes beyond *ex post* accountability, to require that asset managers take *ex ante* steps to ascertain the wishes of asset owners and beneficiaries and to consider how these may be translated into investment management conduct. We regard it as a purpose-based articulation for investment management conduct to be carried out with the consciousness of investment managers' representative capacity. In this manner, institutions need to explain how this representative capacity is implemented. The FRC has signalled generally weak reporting by signatories, as signatories are not comprehensive or consistent in terms of reporting their investor base or what is communicated to investors. However, the FRC's expectations also seem minimal, as it focuses on reporting on the client base as the mainstay of Principle 6.[144]

Arguably, Principle 6 goes further than the legal framing of rights within the investment chain. Beneficiaries are usually unable to exercise their economic interest rights due to the no-look through rule that accords the legal registered holder of shares,[145] usually a custodian, with corporate governance rights. It is possible for asset owners to instruct and steer asset managers, who should ensure that such communications are conveyed to the custodian, to exercise corporate governance rights. However structural impediments and incentive weaknesses exist in the investment chain.[146] Criticism has been made of the dilutive effects of the investment chain upon institutions' engagement with their corporate governance rights, prompting research into potential reform to English law on intermediated securities.[147] If beneficiaries were empowered to feed their voice into the corporate governance processes, the corporate economy could be more effectively subject to social voice and pressure.[148] In this manner, Principle 6 could deal more overtly with mitigation of principal-agent problems in the investment chain, incorporating a stronger social basis for investment

---

[144] ibid, 27.

[145] E Micheler, 'Intermediated Securities from the Perspective of Investors: Problems, Quick Fixes and Long-term Solutions' in L Gullifer and J Payne (eds), *Intermediation and Beyond* (Hart Publishing, 2019) Ch 12; Law Commission, *Intermediated Securities: Who Owns Your Shares? A Scoping Paper* (November 2020), https://s3-eu-west-2.amazonaws.com/lawcom-prod-storage-11jsxou24uy7q/uploads/2020/11/Law-Commission-Intermediated-Securities-Scoping-Paper-1.pdf; paras 2.18–2.34 on challenges for asset owners in pooled funds to instruct their wishes. For benefits of the intermediated shareholder system, see ibid para 2.91.

[146] E McGaughey, 'Does Corporate Governance Exclude the Ultimate Investor?' (2016) 16(1) *Journal of Corporate Law Studies* 221. See Law Commission (n 145 above) paras 1.33, 3.17–3.54, 3.58.

[147] Law Commission (n 145 above). The Law Commission does not recommend structurally changing intermediated structures to facilitate direct beneficiary voting: para 1.30. Commentators arguing for legal facilitation of beneficiaries to vote: C van der Elst and A LaFarre, 'Blockchain and Smart Contracting for the Shareholder Community' (2019) 20 *European Business Organisations and Law Review* 111.

[148] Law Commission (n 145 above) paras 3.6, 3.7; 3.83–3.90.

management conduct, and potentially having a radical impact on the principal-agent problems affecting voiceless beneficiaries in particular. In this manner, the FRC should require institutions to report more clearly on how they ascertain beneficiaries' and asset owners' wishes and perceptions, in order to map out a balanced representative strategy.

(b) Moving Away from Exclusively Normifying Shareholder Engagement as Equivalent to Stewardship but Adopting a Wider Understanding of Investment Management Conduct and Strategies in Achieving the Purposes in (a)

The Code may be interpreted as moving away from exclusively 'normifying' issuer-specific shareholder engagement. Engagement activities are now articulated in Principles 9–11, while the rest of the Code adopts a wider understanding of stewardship conduct. Principle 2, which requires institutions to ensure that their governance, resources and incentives support stewardship, can broadly be interpreted to mean that institutions should disclose how their strategies meet beneficiary needs and how such strategies are resourced and capabilised within institutions' governance and incentive structures.

In this manner, asset owners can discuss asset allocation[149] and outsourcing strategies as meeting stewardship demands, and asset managers can discuss their choice of strategies and how these meet asset owners' and beneficiaries' needs. A wider range of investment management conduct and strategies can therefore be acceptable forms of 'stewardship' beyond the hitherto 'normification' of issuer-specific shareholder engagement.[150] Indeed the FRC's survey even highlights institutions' disclosures of their own governance initiatives, such as improving diversity in their own outfits, as being connected with stewardship. This acceptance of a wide range of 'stewardship' activities is reinforced in Principle 12 which requires signatories to exercise their rights and responsibilities effectively. These rights and responsibilities are recognised as different across different asset classes, including fixed income, equities and possibly other asset classes.

Following this new broad perception of what constitutes stewardship, Principle 5 requires institutions to regularly review their policies, assure their processes and assess the effectiveness of their activities. This is buttressed by the more specific Principle 3 that deals with effective management of conflicts of interest in order not to compromise beneficiaries' interests (inherited from the previous Code). The breadth of Principle 5 is not presumptive as to what manners of conduct count as stewardship, as long as adequate explanation is made of them in Principle 2. The FRC noted in its survey that signatories tended to discuss engagement process reviews. This is possibly a path dependent response carried over from adherence to the previous Code. Signatories have yet to improve on satisfactory reporting against internal governance, structures and reviews,[151] and it may take time for signatories to realise the import

---

[149] This seems to be a highlight in FRC: *Effective Stewardship Reporting* (November 2021) pp 27–29.
[150] Davies (n 67 above).
[151] FRC, *Effective Stewardship Reporting* (November 2021) pp 43–45.

of the broader approach in order to report a wider range of review, assurance and evaluation measures for a broader spectrum of investment strategies and conduct accommodated under Principle 2.

(c) Continuing Support for Shareholder Engagement but Requiring Disclosure of what Such Engagement Seeks to achieve and its Efficacy

Principles 9, 10 and 11 arguably inherit the previous Code's provisions on the forms of shareholder engagement regarded as desirable practice. It may be argued that in light of the discussion in (b), Principle 9 has adopted a wider conception of engagement that need not be issuer-specific. Principle 9 envisages institutions may be issues-focused rather than issuer-specific, and that engagement can be delegated. This is also reflected in Principle 11, which deals with escalation of engagement activities. Principle 10 also accommodates this wider conception of engagement by articulating that collaborative engagement, where necessary, could be issuer-specific or could be thematic in nature.

In this manner, it is arguable that Principles 9–11 would likely negate many previous critiques focused on non issuer-specific engagement. However, what has changed with Principles 9–11 from the previous Code is that disclosure is now required not only of policies, but of implementation, processes and outcomes achieved. The FRC further clarifies that engagement is different from monitoring and both sets of activities and their outcomes should be reported.[152] Effective reporting in this area can contribute to knowledge-building as to whether and to what extent shareholder engagement should itself be normified.

(d) Cognisance and Reporting of Investment Chain Monitoring and Activities, Possibly for Knowledge-building in Relation to Agency Problems

Agency problems exist between the different links in the investment chain. It has been posited that conflicts of interest exist between asset managers and their investors. The former may maintain business relationships with portfolio companies, and this could affect asset managers' exercise of corporate governance rights.[153] Hence the previous Code and the 2020 Code require the effective management of conflicts of interest.[154] This remains a weak area of 'explanation' for institutions as noted in the FRC's survey.[155] Agency problems in investment management conduct can be seen as market failures, and the FCA has intervened into market failures in order to mitigate these problems.[156]

---

[152] ibid, p 58.
[153] Bebchuk and Hirst (n 4 above); earlier evidence: JS Taub, 'Able but Not Willing: The Failure of Mutual Fund Advisers to Advocate for Shareholders' Rights' (2009) 34 *Journal of Corporation Law* 102.
[154] Stewardship Code 2020, Principle 3.
[155] FRC, *The UK Stewardship Code Review of Early Reporting* (2020) p 17.
[156] FCA 2017 (n 15 above) paras 1.10–1.16, 6.8.

The introduction of precise regulatory duties to correct market failures and agency problems is the backdrop to the soft law in the Code. Provisions in the Stewardship Code 2020 now address more generally the monitoring of service providers (Principle 8) and how service providers should ensure that they effectively support their clients' stewardship (Principles 1, 2, 5 and 6 for service providers). Disclosure can be treated as part of knowledge-building as to the extent of agency problems that may exist in the investment chain. Asset owners and managers should also scrutinise how service providers manage conflicts of interest (Principle 3) in order not to compromise their support of effective stewardship by institutions.

It is noted that although a key service provider, the proxy adviser industry, came under the spotlight for regulatory consideration in light of the potential power they wield in influencing institutions in their corporate governance roles,[157] it was ultimately agreed in the EU/UK that they should be subject to self-regulation.[158] The Shareholders' Rights Directive 2017 introduced mandatory disclosure obligations for proxy advisers in order to secure market and public scrutiny of their roles and influence,[159] but arguably the standards of conduct remain self-regulatory.[160]

The FRC's survey surprisingly did not include service providers, and its later Report in 2021 also does not raise examples of service provider reporting. This seems to indicate that focus is placed much more on asset owners and managers. Further, it may be perceived that the Asset Management Market Study has yielded comprehensive findings, so regulatory responses are targeted at precise agency problems and market failures.

It is arguable that the UK Stewardship Code 2020, despite being soft law, has made significant strides in articulating purpose for stewardship and clarifying a broader range of investment management strategies and activities that can be scrutinised for stewardship purposes. Being a measure in soft law and relying on a meta-governance framework, the Code guides investment firms towards internalisation of its purpose-based articulations, but implementation is a private matter for contractual mandates. This remains necessary as investment allocation is a market-based matter and not under the command of regulatory fiat. Bilateral monitoring by contracting parties would be the 'supervisory' framework and it remains uncertain if the performance of signatories would be carefully scrutinised by regulators. The FRC relies on unassured reporting[161] by signatories and it is uncertain to what extent the FRC would be able to tell if signatories 'walk the talk'. The FRC's surveys, if regularly carried out, may send signals of moral suasion for best practice.

---

[157] MC Schouten, 'Do Institutional Investors Follow Proxy Advice Blindly?' (2012), https://papers.ssrn.com/sol3/papers.cfm?abstract_id=1978343; SJ Choi et al, 'The Power of Proxy Advisors: Myth or Reality?' (2010) 59 *Emory Law Journal* 869.

[158] ESMA, *Final Report on The Proxy Advisor Industry* (19 February 2013); ESMA, *Report: Follow-up on the Development of the Best Practice Principles for Providers of Shareholder Voting Research and Analysis* (2015).

[159] Shareholders' Rights Directive 2017, Art 3j.

[160] UK Proxy Advisors (Shareholders' Rights Directive) Regulations 2019, SI 2019/926. Although the FCA is empowered to enforce against non-disclosure, the exact standards of conduct are for industry best practice.

[161] Reddy (n 14 above).

However, it may also be argued that soft law can often be experimental and transitory,[162] providing further information and empirical bases for governance and regulatory development. A new regulator, the Accounting and Governance Reporting Authority,[163] is to replace the FRC and poised to be a fully-fledged regulatory body with significant enforcement powers. Hence, a new 'supervisory' approach may come about for monitoring Code signatories. Further, the FRC has been coordinating with the investment firm regulator in the UK, the FCA, and it cannot be ruled out that regulatory governance may be introduced to address issues of public interest if market discipline continues to leave gaps. The coordination between the FRC and FCA[164] in relation to investment management regulation and the implementation of the Stewardship Code 2020 may signal trends towards regulatory governance' of investment management conduct where it matters- not only to resolve agency problems but also to serve public interest goals. The next Section turns to examine if firmer legalisation has been achieved by sustainable finance regulations and its purpose-based articulation for investment management entities to heed sustainability.

IV. THE IMPLICATIONS OF THE SUSTAINABLE FINANCE REFORMS IN THE EU AND UK

The push for sustainable finance regulatory reforms in the EU and UK has been pronounced in recent years. Former Bank of England Governor Mark Carney played a significant role as chair of the Financial Stability Board during his term to highlight the importance of counting climate risk in financial institutions' assets.[165] With the launch of the Financial Stability Board's Taskforce for Climate-related Financial Disclosures in 2017,[166] and the adoption of the UN Sustainable Development Goals in 2015,[167] policy-makers in the EU and UK have begun to address regulatory risk management by financial institutions of climate and sustainability risks, as well as the role of private finance in addressing sustainability goals and objectives. The EU has commissioned a sustainable finance strategy[168] since 2018 in order to inquire into the mobilisation of private sector finance for sustainable goals and purposes, as the investment sector wields significant influence, with global assets under management estimated to be at US$145 trillion by 2025.[169] Besides policy-makers' initiatives,

---

[162] G-P Calliess and M Renner, 'From Soft Law to Hard Code: The Juridification of Global Governance' (2009) 22 *Ratio Juris* 260.

[163] BEIS, *Restoring Trust in Audit and Corporate Governance* (March 2021) Ch 10.

[164] Work coordinated between the FRC and FCA, *Building a Regulatory Framework for Effective Stewardship* (Discussion Paper January 2019), https://www.fca.org.uk/publication/discussion/dp19-01. pdf and *Feedback Statement* (October 2019), https://www.fca.org.uk/publications/feedback-statements/ fs19-7-building-regulatory-framework-effective-stewardship.

[165] M Carney, 'TCFD: Strengthening the Foundations of Sustainable Finance' (8 October 2019), https://www.bankofengland.co.uk/-/media/boe/files/speech/2019/tcfd-strengthening-the-foundations-of-sustainable-finance-speech-by-mark-carney.pdf?la=en&hash=DAF.

[166] See https://assets.bbhub.io/company/sites/60/2020/10/FINAL-2017-TCFD-Report-11052018.pdf.

[167] See EU's and UK's commitments to the UN SDGs, n 18 above.

[168] HLEG, *Financing a Sustainable European Economy* (2018), https://ec.europa.eu/info/sites/info/ files/180131-sustainable-finance-final-report_en.pdf.

[169] PwC, *Asset & Wealth Management Revolution: Embracing Exponential Change* (2017), https://www. pwc.com/ng/en/press-room/global-assets-under-management-set-to-rise.html.

market appetite and industry initiatives have also blossomed. The United Nations Environment Programme Finance Initiative has, for example, led the way in facilitating legal clarity and discourse in order to encourage the private sector to engage in sustainable investments.[170]

Sustainable finance reforms can introduce gradual regulatory 'normification' for the conduct of investment management, arguably aligned with public interest concerns in sustainability. However, such regulatory 'normification' cannot go too far in micro-managing how investment management is conducted, and the accountability of investment managers continues to be framed within a private framework of legal duties and obligations. We observe a mix of mandatory and market-based governance being developed in the EU and UK.

A. EU Sustainable Finance Reforms

The EU Sustainable Disclosure Regulation 2019 now compels all financial market participants who engage in portfolio or fund management (whether as mainstream pension or collective investment schemes, or alternative investments funds)[171] to integrate sustainability risks in their investment decision-making.[172] This also includes financial services providers who provide investment-based products as part of an insurance product. Such 'integration' relates to both conventional and sustainable portfolios or funds.

Further, if funds wish to market sustainably-labelled financial products,[173] they have to ascertain and report on sustainable achievements as meeting doubly material criteria. This means that sustainably-labelled funds should achieve sustainable performance as such, apart from such achievement being related to financial performance. The EU has begun to provide outcomes standards for environmentally sustainable financial products[174] and this will in time extend to socially sustainable products.[175] The sustainable label for investment products is an attempt to mobilise a market for investment products that exceed conventional 'socially responsible investing' or 'ESG-based' investing, which relate non-financial criteria primarily to their materiality for financial performance.[176] The latter market has grown due to investors' pro-social preferences, on the parts of many institutions and individuals,[177]

---

[170] UNEPFI, PRI and the Generation Foundation, *A Legal Framework for Impact* (2021), https://www.unepfi.org/legal-framework-for-impact/.

[171] Sustainability Disclosures Regulation 2019, Art 2.

[172] ibid, Art 3.

[173] ibid, Arts 8–11.

[174] Taxonomy Regulation 2020, Arts 9–17.

[175] The forthcoming Social Taxonomy envisaged by the Commission, https://ec.europa.eu/info/sites/default/files/business_economy_euro/banking_and_finance/documents/finance-events-210226-presentation-social-taxonomy_en.pdf.

[176] IG MacNeil and I-M Esser, 'From a Financial to Entity Model of ESG' (2022) 23 *European Business Organisations Law Review* 9.

[177] G Apostolakis et al, 'Predicting Pension Beneficiaries' Behaviour When Offered a Socially Responsible and Impact Investment Portfolio' (2018) 8 *Journal of Sustainable Finance & Investment* 213; A Wins and B Zwergel, 'Comparing Those Who Do, Might and Will Not Invest in Sustainable Funds: A Survey Among German Retail Fund Investors' (2016) 9 *Business Research* 51; L Delsen and A Lehr, 'Value Matters or

but is often criticised as offering opaque and uncertain quality in terms of sustainable achievement.[178]

Under the Sustainability Disclosure Regulation 2019, investment fund intermediaries are under a universal obligation to make mandatory disclosure of how they 'integrate sustainability risks'. 'Sustainability risk' is defined as 'environmental, social or governance event or condition that, if it occurs, could cause an actual or a potential material negative impact on the value of the investment'.[179] Such a definition adopts a 'single materiality' approach of treating sustainability risk as salient only if it materially affects investment performance. At a baseline, this is not novel and consistent with the interpretation of fiduciary duty in private investment management.[180] It may even be argued that this baseline duty pertains only to disclosure and does not change the nature of the financially-focused duty of fiduciary investment management. Policy-makers in the EU have responded by clarifying that the baseline duty is not merely a duty of disclosure but also a duty to integrate sustainability risks as such in the governance and risk management of investment intermediaries.[181] In this way, the achievement in this legalisation is that all mainstream investment intermediaries are at least bound to consider material sustainability issues in their investment management, this is not limited to funds that opt to be labelled as Socially Responsible Investment (SRI) or ESG. On the other hand, it may be argued that the baseline duty is not terribly potent, as enforcement is likely to come from market discipline, relying on the mandatory disclosure by investment intermediaries. It is also challenging for regulators to undertake clear enforcement actions regarding how firms integrate sustainability risks into their governance and risk management processes. This aspect is meta-regulatory in nature[182] and allows firms a certain scope of open-endedness for implementation within its systems, processes and culture. Reinforcing regulatory measures have been introduced in investment management regulation so as to compel investment firms to integrate sustainability risks in terms of their organisational governance, risk management, management of conflicts of interest, product governance and design, as well as in relation to suitability obligations owed to investors

---

Values Matter? An Analysis of Heterogeneity in Preferences for Sustainable Investments' (2019) 9 *Journal of Sustainable Finance & Investment* 240.

[178] 'Unregulated "greenwashing"? ESG investing is under the microscope as the money rolls in' (*CNBC News*, 14 October 2020), https://www.cnbc.com/2020/10/14/esg-investing-meaning-is-under-the-microscope-as-the-money-rolls-in.html.

[179] Art 2(22).

[180] Freshfields Bruckhaus Deringer (n 60 above), UNEPFI 2019 (n 60 above); B Richardson, 'From Fiduciary Duties to Fiduciary Relationships for Socially Responsible Investing: Responding to the Will of Beneficiaries' (2011) 1 *Journal of Sustainable Finance and Investment* 5.

[181] Commission Delegated Regulation to amend the Alternative Investment Fund Managers Directive, https://ec.europa.eu/finance/docs/level-2-measures/aifmd-delegated-act-2021–2615_en.pdf (21 April 2021); Commission Delegated Directive to amend the UCITs Directive, https://ec.europa.eu/finance/docs/level-2-measures/ucits-directive-delegated-act-2021–2617_en.pdf (21 April 2021); Commission Delegated Directive to amend the Markets in Financial Instruments Directive, https://ec.europa.eu/finance/docs/level-2-measures/mifid-2-delegated-act-2021–2612_en.pdf (21 April 2021).

[182] C Parker, *The Open Corporation* (Cambridge University Press, 2000). Critics discuss the opaque and unsupervised nature of meta-regulation: J Black, 'Paradoxes and Failures: "New Governance" Techniques and the Financial Crisis' (2012) 75 *Modern Law Review* 1037.

where investment advice is provided.[183] These regulatory specifications provide steer for firm implementation and therefore reduce the risk that meta-regulatory measures may be cosmetically applied.

Next, investment intermediaries of a certain scale, defined as having 500 employees or more, or being a parent company of such an undertaking,[184] are mandated to account for principal adverse sustainability impacts (applying from 30 June 2021). This applies whether or not such intermediaries engage with sustainably-labelled products. They must account for any adverse impact of their investment decision-making processes on sustainability objectives, how adverse impacts are discovered and what due diligence policies are deployed.[185] Smaller entities are able to declare that they do not consider adverse sustainability impacts in their investment decision-making process but must clearly explain why and whether this practice cuts across all their products.[186] This means that smaller entities are subject to the broad duty to integrate sustainability risks, but not specifically to measurement of adverse sustainability impact. In this manner, larger investment intermediaries are imposed with an obligation that is more socially-facing in nature, ie to account for sustainability cost *as such*. The type and nature of principal adverse impact that will be disclosed is based on double materiality ie these are measured not only in terms of their impact upon investment performance but for their impact upon sustainability performance.[187] Further, by 30 December 2022, financial services providers mandated to integrate and disclose sustainability risks in relation to adverse impacts must also make that transparency available at the level of each financial product.[188] These disclosures are also regarded as pre-contractual in nature, therefore attracting market and legal discipline from investors.[189]

The need to integrate and account for adverse sustainability impact compels large investment fund intermediaries to internalise such impact as part of their investment management purpose. This means that for all investment intermediaries, counting sustainability cost in their investment footprint is no longer an option, which would have been mostly pursued by 'socially responsible' funds.[190] However, the counting of sustainability cost would only change behaviour if asset owners and beneficiaries care about adverse sustainability impact, producing a market response to discourage such harms and therefore influencing allocational steer. There is increasing evidence that asset owners such as pension funds[191] and pro-social individuals value the avoidance of adverse sustainable impact in their investment allocations.[192] However, this is not

---

[183] See n 181 above.
[184] Regulation 2019/2088, Art 4(3), (4).
[185] ibid Art 4(1)(a).
[186] ibid Art 4(1)(b).
[187] European Securities and Markets Authority's draft technical standards, 23 April 2020, https://www.esma.europa.eu/press-news/esma-news/esas-consult-environmental-social-and-governance-disclosure-rules.
[188] Sustainability Disclosure Regulation 2019, Art 7.
[189] ibid Art 6.
[190] Such as strategies excluding investments that perpetuate harm to sustainability goals.
[191] See n 170 above.
[192] M Ammann et al, 'The Impact of the Morningstar Sustainability Rating on Mutual Fund Flows' (2018), https://ssrn.com/abstract=3068724.

necessarily the case with many conventional institutions[193] and investment beneficiaries have highly heterogenous preferences.[194]

Although we perceive large investment intermediaries to come under more radical obligations that may shape the market's perceptions and preferences for double materiality, many smaller investment intermediaries can elect to be principally 'private-facing' and potentially 'exempt', subject to their explanation, from a scope of socially-facing accountability imposed on larger firms. There is a large sector of investment firms that are medium sized and employ under 500 employees. In this manner, there could still be a sizeable market focusing only on single materiality. Nevertheless, it may be argued that the reforms recognise the potential systemic impact of large investment firms' stewardship actions, and that it is not disproportionate to require their greater demonstration of social accountability in investment management.

Next, the Sustainable Disclosure Regulation clarifies that sustainably-labelled finance goes beyond 'harm-based analysis' and the starting point for sustainably-labelled financial products is based on a higher departure point, ie the achievement of positive sustainability outcomes. Indeed 'sustainable investment' is defined as 'investment products [that] should positively achieve specified sustainable outcomes and at least do 'no significant harm' to environmental and social objectives as a whole'.[195] The definition of sustainably-labelled relates to:

> an economic activity that contributes to an environmental objective, … [such as], by key resource efficiency indicators on the use of energy, renewable energy, raw materials, water and land, on the production of waste, and greenhouse gas emissions, or on its impact on biodiversity and the circular economy, or an investment in an economic activity that contributes to a social objective, … [such as] tackling inequality or that fosters social cohesion, social integration and labour relations, or an investment in human capital or economically or socially disadvantaged communities, provided that such investments do not significantly harm any of those objectives and that the investee companies follow good governance practices, in particular with respect to sound management structures, employee relations, remuneration of staff and tax compliance.

Investment intermediaries who provide explicitly sustainably-labelled products must explain how the environmental or social characteristics promoted by each product meet its characterisation, whether in active or passive management. In an actively managed product, disclosure is to be made of the strategies designed to meet the relevant characteristics, including how the intermediary defines the sustainability objective and measures its attainment or otherwise.[196] The European Securities and

---

[193] MJ Jansson and A Biel, 'Investment Institutions' Beliefs About and Attitudes toward Socially Responsible Investment (SRI): A Comparison Between SRI and Non-SRI Management' (2014) 22 *Sustainable Development* 33; F Ielasi and M Rossolini, 'Responsible or Thematic? The True Nature of Sustainability-Themed Mutual Funds' (2019) 11 *Sustainability Journal* 3304.

[194] G Apostolakis et al, 'Pension Beneficiaries' and Fund Managers' Perceptions of Responsible Investment: A Focus Group Study' (2016) 16 *Corporate Governance* 1; prosocial individual investors remain a minority: C Christiansen et al, 'Who are the Socially Responsible Mutual Fund Investors?' (2019), https://papers.ssrn.com/sol3/papers.cfm?abstract_id=3128432.

[195] Sustainability Disclosure Regulation 2019, Art 2(17).

[196] ibid, Arts 8, 10.

Markets Authority (ESMA) will prescribe a template[197] for such disclosure so that it attains certain standards and comparability.

In relation to passively managed products, investment intermediaries must disclose if the environmental or social characterisation is derived by benchmarking against indices for sustainable finance.[198] It is not sufficient to refer to a designated index to be satisfied of a product's environmental or social characteristics. They must disclose how the index is aligned or consistent with those characteristics and how alignment with it differs from a broad market index.[199] Although investment intermediaries are in substance relying on an index provider's diligence and evaluation, there needs to be some level of intelligent engagement with indexers' methodologies[200] in order to demonstrate why the index has been selected and the difference to sustainable performance made by adhering to the index.

The Regulation provides new standards for the design and offering of sustainable financial products. Although the Taxonomy Regulation does not outlaw 'lower' labels such as 'ESG' or 'socially responsible' products,[201] the regulatory governance of the 'sustainable' label is intended to set standards as well as galvanise market choice. These are regulatory steers for the market building of investment products that would meet the purposes of double materiality. However, the effectiveness of such regulatory policy depends on the alignment between market choice and regulatory steering. If sustainably-labelled products are more costly due to the more demanding compliance obligations, this could affect market choice and the demand side may be incentivised to settle for 'lower' labels.

In sum, can it be argued that sustainability has been legalised as a new purposed-based norm for investment management conduct in the EU? The EU Regulation's framing seems non-optional and can be understood to have introduced a regulative modification to the understanding of fiduciary investment management in private law. However, the regulatory provisions work with meta-regulatory firm implementation (where 'integrating sustainability risks' are concerned), market-based discipline for the disclosure dimensions and uncertainty in relation to market appetite for the orientation of investment products. It is arguable that despite the mandatory nature of new obligations for investment intermediaries to integrate sustainability risks, and for larger fund intermediaries to report on specific matters of adverse sustainability impact, the substantive nature of such obligations is that of a nudge,[202] as the purpose is ultimately to provide information and framing to guide asset owners' and beneficiaries' choices. Whether such market-based regulation ultimately changes allocative steer and influences behaviour at the level of the corporate economy, can only be observed in time.[203]

---

[197] See n 187 above.
[198] Sustainability Disclosure Regulation 2019, Arts 8, 9.
[199] ibid, Art 9(1)(b).
[200] RJ Bianchi and ME Drew, 'Sustainable Stock Indices and Long-Term Portfolio Decisions' (2012) 2 *Journal of Sustainable Finance & Investment* 303 on the differences between Indices.
[201] Taxonomy Regulation 2020, Art 7.
[202] R Thaler and C Sunstein, *Nudge: Improving Decisions About Health, Wealth and Happiness* (Penguin, 2009).
[203] 'Fifty Shades of Green: How Prevalent is ESG Window Dressing?' (Citywire), https://citywire.co.uk/wealth-manager/news/investor-faith-risks-drowning-in-a-rising-tide-of-greenwash/a1363868.

However, it can be argued that with prescriptive templates for disclosure of adverse sustainability risks imposed on larger intermediaries, sustainability risks would be evaluated as a matter of double materiality, not merely single materiality. In this manner, some of the largest and most well-known investment intermediaries would be compelled to engage with granular items of sustainability cost that would appeal to the public interest, in order to adhere to mandatory disclosure. In turn, these investment intermediaries may weigh in more pronouncedly against their portfolio companies, or in an issue-specific manner across the board, in order to demand information of a nature that meets double materiality needs. The Taxonomy Regulation contains amendments to the EU Non-financial Reporting Directive 2013 in order to further support the mandatory disclosure of environmental, social, human rights and anti-corruption matters by listed corporations.[204] Reforms are also afoot to revamp the EU Non-financial Disclosure provisions into comprehensive disclosure obligations for corporations so that they can provide standardised and comprehensive disclosures on sustainability matters.[205] The ESMA welcomes and is collaborating with bodies such as the International Financial Reporting Standards body to develop meaningful metrics of sustainability performance.[206] The legalisation carried out in the EU reforms is poised to being about a new landscape of transparency that galvanises public alongside market pressure. It may be too early to dismiss these reforms as merely market-based regulation that would be subservient to market behaviour.[207]

B. UK's Sustainable Finance Reforms

Although the UK made early indications[208] that it did not necessarily wish to adopt the EU's sustainable finance regulations for the investment sector,[209] some alignment is being proposed[210] perhaps in view of the advantages of regulatory equivalencies and reducing complex costs of compliance for the asset management sector.

---

[204] Taxonomy Regulation 2020, Art 8, supplementing the Non-financial Reporting Directive 2013/34/EU.

[205] Ongoing reform, European Commission, *Communication from the Commission to the European Parliament, the Council, the European Economic and Social Committee and the Committee of the Regions: EU Taxonomy, Corporate Sustainability Reporting, Sustainability Preferences and Fiduciary Duties: Directing finance towards the European Green Deal* (21 April 2021), https://ec.europa.eu/finance/docs/law/210421-sustainable-finance-communication_en.pdf; European Commission, Proposal for a Directive of the European Parliament and of the Council amending Directive 2013/34/EU, Directive 2004/109/EC, Directive 2006/43/EC and Regulation (EU) No 537/2014, as regards corporate sustainability reporting (April 2021), https://eur-lex.europa.eu/legal-content/EN/TXT/?uri=CELEX:52021PC0189.

[206] 'ESMA Supports IFRS Foundation's Efforts on International Standardisation in Sustainability Reporting' (16 December 2020), https://www.esma.europa.eu/press-news/esma-news/esma-supports-ifrs-foundation%E2%80%99s-efforts-international-standardisation-in.

[207] F Möslein and KE Sørensen, 'The Commission's Action Plan for Financing Sustainable Growth and its Corporate Governance Implications' *Nordic & European Company Law Working Paper No 18-17* (2018), https://ssrn.com/abstract=3251731.

[208] See n 20 above.

[209] Finalised on 31 December 2020.

[210] FCA, 'Sustainability Disclosure Requirements (SDR) and Investment Labels' (November 2021), https://www.fca.org.uk/publication/discussion/dp21-4.pdf.

In December 2021, the UK FCA finalised a baseline duty for all investment asset management entities, including life insurers, to make mandatory reporting based on the Task-Force on Climate-related Financial Disclosures (TCFD).[211] This is also seen as a reasonable introduction of a mandatory duty, as the TCFD is already imposed on all listed entities on the London Stock Exchange.[212] Mandatory TCFD reporting is to be made by investment managers at an 'entity-level' and at a 'product or portfolio-level'. In relation to 'entity-level' reporting, investment managers subject to this duty would need to disclose how they as a whole manage climate risks according to the four components of TCFD reporting, ie how their business strategy and governance take into account of climate risk, how their risk management policies and framework take into account of climate risk, how firms employ scenario analysis to map and evaluate climate risks, and what metrics and targets are used for measuring financial risks and opportunities from climate risks (guided by examples provided in the TCFD framework). It is envisaged that when the International Sustainability Standards Board issues its reporting standards, these, incorporating the TCFD's input, would be mandated for entity-level reporting.[213]

Product disclosure would however be focused on scope 1, 2 and 3 greenhouse gas emissions and carbon footprint and emissions, including the metrics adopted for their measurement. These disclosures are envisaged to be backed up by entity level and product level disclosures in accordance with the TCFD and International Sustainability Standards Board (ISSB) bases discussed above.[214]

Nevertheless, the UK's approach would be clearly focused on single materiality. The UK's regulatory approach is arguably different from the EU as its adoption of the TCFD and in due course, ISSB standards would likely be focused on single materiality, therefore more clearly refraining from importing public interest goals as such into regulating investment management. The TCFD focuses on the financial risks from climate-related risks and opportunities, and is therefore complementary to mainstream financial institutions' focus on financial performance. The ISSB's work, developing from the IFRS' familiarity with material financial information, may also have the same bent. This could be narrower than the EU's embrace of double materiality for large investment firms' mandatory reporting of adverse sustainability impact which is to be evaluated in non-financial as well as financial terms; as well as for sustainably-labelled products.

In the absence of an indication that the EU is willing to endorse the ISSB's standards in due course, its approach of adopting a mixed public and private approach to developing and governing metrics for sustainability indicators[215] may provide

---

[211] FCA (n 20 above).

[212] FCA, *Proposals to Enhance Climate-Related Disclosures by Listed Issuers and Clarification of Existing Disclosure Obligations: Policy Statement* (21 December 2020), https://www.fca.org.uk/publications/policy-statements/ps20-17-proposals-enhance-climate-related-disclosures-listed-issuers-and-clarification-existing; and FCA, *Enhancing Climate-Related Disclosures by Standard Listed Companies* (December 2021), https://www.fca.org.uk/publication/policy/ps21-23.pdf.

[213] ibid.

[214] FCA (n 210 above).

[215] IH-Y Chiu, 'The EU Sustainable Finance Agenda: Developing Governance for Double Materiality in Sustainability Metrics' (2022) 23 *European Business Organization Law Review* 87.

longer-lasting influence of public interest infusion into metrics development, which has hitherto been dominated by the private sector.[216] This furthers a broader agenda of steering sustainable finance reforms according to public interest and preventing disengagement of the sustainable finance market from public interest goals. In contrast, by mandating investment institutions to focus on single materiality, UK policy-makers need to ask whether incentive-based calculations and internalisation of climate risk are always aligned with public interest goals and to what extent these goals are really served. For example, a focus on single materiality may lead investment institutions to price solar energy investments favourably, but these are not uncontroversial in relation to community rights, such as in relation to farming and food security.[217] Would such holistic 'social risks' be priced into investment allocations and valuations, and what would the social impact be of a narrow approach? However, it may be argued that regulators could overstretch their mandates by extending into public interest goals that are not primarily related to financial regulatory goals such as investor protection.[218]

It may nevertheless be argued that the EU's reforms do not achieve markedly different effects from the UK, as its introduction of a mandatory duty to 'integrate sustainability risks' for all investment management entities is also based on single materiality. The connection with public interest goals and double materiality are imposed on a small set of large investment management entities only.

Further, it may be argued that the UK's focus on single materiality in reporting by asset managers does not necessarily indicate that the public interest in sustainable outcomes is not reflected. Similar to the EU, the UK is adopting a Taxonomy, especially for environmentally beneficial outcomes.[219] Both the EU's Taxonomy for environmentally-sustainable financial products and the UK's Green Taxonomy provide standards for investment objectives and performance that can shore up investor confidence, as well as double materiality baselines for the public interest goals sought to be concurrently achieved. This therefore more robustly appeals to pro-social investors looking to be able to verify double materiality outcomes.

The coupling of public interest goals with sustainable finance regulation in the EU and UK provides an interesting hybrid approach to nudging financial allocation as well as governing investment management conduct. In this manner, the Stewardship Code 2020 reinforces such objective-based governance of investment management.

---

[216] Such as by bodies for social reporting and accounting like the GRI and SASB, and by indices and ratings providers for sustainable or 'ESG' related investment products.

[217] For example, 'Campaigners Fight Plans for One of the World's Biggest Solar Farms on Suffolk-Cambridgeshire Border' (*ITV News*, 4 December 2020), https://www.itv.com/news/anglia/2020-12-04/campaigners-fight-plans-for-one-of-the-worlds-biggest-solar-farms-on-suffolk-cambridgeshire-border.

[218] DA Katz and LA McIntosh, 'SEC Regulation of ESG Disclosures' (Harvard Law School Forum on Corporate Governance, 28 May 2021), https://corpgov.law.harvard.edu/2021/05/28/sec-regulation-of-esg-disclosures/; PG Mahoney and JD Mahoney, 'The New Separation of Ownership and Control: Institutional Investors and ESG' (2021) *Columbia Business Law Review* 840, https://papers.ssrn.com/sol3/papers.cfm?abstract_id=3809914.

[219] HM Government, 'Greening Finance: A Roadmap to Sustainable Investing' (October 2021) Ch 2, https://assets.publishing.service.gov.uk/government/uploads/system/uploads/attachment_data/file/1026224/CCS0821102722-006_Green_Finance_Paper_2021_v5_Bookmarked_48PP.pdf.

In consolidating with the purpose-based steers in the UK Stewardship Code 2020, code signatories can no longer ignore the wider context for investment fund allocation and management, and meta-level policy scrutiny. Although the framework seems to comprise of soft law, meta-level governance and market-based discipline, the visibility of policy steer is still remarkable, and strikes a balance between leaving to contractual implementation and painting the boundaries of public interest. Such designs of modern governance are not in the vein of central planning or allocation, but do not subscribe to a laissez-faire attitude either.[220] The UNEPFI reports of 2019 and 2021 have also done much to pave the way for the integration of a traditionally private law-based paradigm with modern concerns of a broader nature.[221]

Modern investment management contributes to and is part and parcel of global capital allocation. Policy-makers are increasingly scrutinising the purposes to which such capital is put. It may be argued that as many countries struggle with economic recovery in the wake of the COVID-19 pandemic, the needs for financial allocation at a macro level would more than ever become questions of public interest, in addition to the long-running issues of climate change, environmental sustainability and social development that have been on policy-makers' agendas for a long time. The governance of investment fund management is transcending the paradigm revolving around the micro needs of private entrustment and allocation, moving towards the macro needs of global capital allocation.

V. CONCLUSION

From the introduction of shareholder engagement as a 'norm' for stewardship, the regulatory governance of investment management conduct has been ramping up, not to mention areas not covered in this chapter such as policy-makers' scrutiny for systemic risks.[222] As investment funds and asset managers assume control of increasing global assets under management and enjoy significant allocative power, public interest in the exercise of such power increases correspondingly. It is inevitable that societal and public expectations would be augmented and the governance needs for the industry would rise. This chapter argues that the UK Stewardship Code 2020 is a 'graduation' from an earlier experimental period which focused on the narrower and process-based 'norm' of shareholder engagement. The Code has broken new ground by articulating purpose-based steers for investment management, providing the starting point for a type of governance that may come to define the regulation of investment management in the future. Indeed, sustainable finance reforms such as in the EU and UK may provide the crucial kickstart to introducing non-optional

---

[220] I Goldin, *Rescue: From Global Crisis to Better World* (Sceptre, 2021) 95, where the author admonishes going beyond stale central planning and capitalist divides in political economy and modernising the hybrid roles of public and private sector.

[221] See https://www.unepfi.org/investment/fiduciary-duty/.

[222] Financial Stability Board, 'Policy Recommendations to Address Structural Vulnerabilities from Asset Management Activities' (January 2017), https://www.fsb.org/wp-content/uploads/FSB-Polic y-Recommendations-on-Asset-Management-Structural-Vulnerabilities.pdf.

integration of sustainability risks and goals into mainstream investment management in due course. Purpose-based governance, albeit in its soft law beginnings, is arguably a new trajectory for calibrating the relationship between private investment management and regulation, reflecting the public interest and expectations for the future of the industry.

3

Institutional Investors and Sustainable Finance – Developing the Shareholder Engagement Framework in Light of the Emerging Sustainable Finance Regime in the EU

HANNE S BIRKMOSE

I. INTRODUCTION

T HE ADOPTION IN 2017 of the amended Shareholder Rights Directive[1] (hereinafter the SRD II) was the culmination of almost a decade of intense European focus on the role of shareholders and in particular the role of the institutional investor in corporate governance, following the financial crisis. Five years later, after Member States had gone through the process of implementing the Directive into national law, another policy agenda came to the fore, that of sustainable finance.

However, this is not a new agenda. In particular, since the adoption in 2015 of the UN's 2030 agenda and its sustainable development goals,[2] as well as the Paris climate agreement,[3] the EU Commission has been increasingly focused on the green agenda. Over the years, the European sustainable finance agenda has become ever more ambitious, and the overall political objectives are now starting to materialise with regard to European companies, the financial sector and investors. Thus, institutional investors must divide their attention between a somewhat established engagement agenda and an emerging, sustainable finance agenda.

These two agendas should not be viewed as two separate agendas. Rather they are interlaced in different ways, and this chapter aims to develop the shareholder

---

[1] Council Directive 2017/828/EU of 17 May 2007 amending Directive 2007/36/EC, as regards the encouragement of long-term shareholder engagement [2017] OJ L 132/1.

[2] See https://sustainabledevelopment.un.org/topics/sustainabledevelopmentgoals.

[3] See https://unfccc.int/process-and-meetings/the-paris-agreement/the-paris-agreement.

engagement framework established by the SRD II, in light of the emerging sustainable finance regime in the EU.

The amended SRD II imposes duties on institutional investors and asset managers in relation to their engagement with investee companies.[4] Hence, they must disclose information on their engagement policy, as well as information on their actual engagement with investee companies. According to Article 3g of the SRD II, the policy must describe how institutional investors and asset managers 'monitor investee companies on relevant matters, including strategy, financial and non-financial performance and risk, capital structure, social and environmental impact and corporate governance ...' Although Article 3g is applied according to the comply-or-explain principle, it articulates a normative direction in which institutional investors and asset managers are expected to include ESG considerations in their engagement with investee companies. However, the Directive does not provide any guidance on the nature of such considerations and leaves this to the discretion of institutional investors. As such, the amended SRD II and the engagement by institutional investors are important elements of the overall corporate governance framework, which serve to ensure long-term value creation in investee companies. However, as an additional requirement of the SRD II, institutional shareholders must disclose information on their equity investment strategy, *cf* Article 3h. This requirement links to their role as financial intermediaries, whereby they invest in their capacity as investors on behalf of the beneficiaries. Interestingly, the SRD II is silent in relation to the content of said strategy, and Article 3h does not include any reference to ESG matters. However, although Article 3g contains a normative element, the SRD II should be viewed as a disclosure framework. Therefore, to fully understand the investment management component of the institutional investors' practice,[5] it is necessary to consider specific sector regulation, such as the Solvency II Directive, the IORP Directive, the AIFM Directive, the UCITS Directive and the MiFID II Directive, which for a long period of time have regulated the investment element of financial institutions' practices.[6] Investment is also the focus of the sustainable finance agenda and institutional investors and asset managers are targeted in different ways by this emerging agenda. First, their role as

---

[4] The definition of an institutional investor has a rather limited scope in the amended SRD II, as it entails undertaking activities of life assurance and of reinsurance, as well as institutions for occupational retirement. See also MB Madsen, 'Articles 1 and 2: Scope and Definitions' in HS Birkmose and K Sergakis, *The Shareholder Rights Directive II. A Commentary* (Edward Elgar, 2021) 2.35–2.42.

[5] For the discussion of the 'investment management' side of institutional investment practices, see IH-Y Chiu, 'Turning Institutional Investors into "Stewards": Exploring the Meaning and Objectives of "Stewardship"' (2013) *Current Legal Problems* 3 ff.

[6] Council Directive 2009/138/EC of 25 November on the taking up and pursuit of the business of Insurance and Reinsurance [2009] OJ L 335/1 (Solvency II), Council Directive (EU) 2016/2341 of 14 December 2016 on the activities and supervision of institutions for occupational retirement provisions (IORPs) [2016] OJ L 354/37; Council Directive 2011/61/EU of 8 June 2011 on Alternative Investment Fund Managers and amending Directives 2003/41/EC and 2009/65/EC and Regulations (EC) No 1060/2009 and (EU) No 1095/2010 [2011] OJ L 174/1 (AIFMD); Council Directive 2009/65/EC of 13 June 2009 on the coordination of laws, regulations and administrative provisions relating to undertakings for collective investment in transferable securities (UCITS) as regards depositary functions, remuneration policies and sanctions [2009] OJ L 302/2 and Council Directive 2014/65/EU of 15 May 2014 on markets in financial instruments and amending Directive 2002/92/EC and Directive 2011/61/EU [2014] OJ L 173/349 (MiFID).

financial intermediaries is stressed, which means that they must disclose information in relation to sustainability considerations to end investors, according to the
Sustainable Finance Disclosure Regulation (hereinafter the SFDR).[7] However, they
are also investors, and it is stressed that in this capacity they must carefully consider
the way in which they integrate sustainability considerations into their investment
decisions and how sustainability risks may affect their investments. In summary,
both agendas impose new duties on institutional investors and asset managers, but
they also develop already existing duties, particularly in relation to the investment
management element of institutional investors' practice. However, it is less clear if
and how the development of the investment management element affects the institutional investors' and asset managers' engagement with investee companies.

Therefore, the aim of this chapter is to discuss institutional shareholder engagement under SRD II and the new EU sustainable finance regime. The chapter will
start out by exploring the duties that are imposed on the institutional investors and
assets managers by the SRD II. In particular, the relationship between Article 3g and
Article 3h will be explored, first, in order to establish the scope of the duties outlined
by the two provisions, and secondly, to discuss whether there is any interconnectedness
between the two. Next, the chapter will move on to discuss the emerging sustainable
finance agenda. In particular, the focus of the discussion will be whether – and if so
how – this agenda may affect and perhaps channel institutional investors' and assets
managers' engagement duties in a direction which takes cognisance of sustainability
to a much greater extent.

II. INSTITUTIONAL ENGAGEMENT UNDER SRD II

Following the financial crisis in 2008–2009, the European Commission initiated a
debate on how to secure better corporate governance and more accountability within
European listed companies, in particular. The most significant outcome of this
process was the amendment of the 2007 Shareholder Rights Directive. This Directive
was adopted in order to secure and harmonise fundamental shareholder rights across
Member States and aimed to pave the way for increased shareholder engagement.
However, the financial crisis showed that there was a continued lack of monitoring and control by shareholders and, in particular, the institutional investors were
accused of failing their obligations as long-term owners of companies.[8] Consequently,
the amendment of the SRD II in 2017 maintained the focus on increasing shareholder engagement but, with clear inspiration from the 2010 UK Stewardship Code,[9]
the European Commission took a different approach to the engagement challenge.
Rather than solely paving the way for engagement by strengthening shareholder

---

[7] Council Regulation (EU) 2019/2088 of 27 November 2019 on sustainability-related disclosures in the
financial services sector [2019] OL J L 317/1.
[8] The European Commission, 'Green Paper. Corporate Governance in Financial Institutions and
Remuneration Policies' (COM(2010) 284).
[9] FRC, *The UK Stewardship Code* (July 2010).

rights, the European Commission mandated that institutional investors and asset managers disclose information regarding their engagement with investee companies. This includes disclosure of an engagement policy, the implementation of said policy and how votes have been cast in the general meeting of investee companies. Moreover, the SRD II linked the engagement of the institutional investors and asset managers with their investment strategy. Although the European Commission upheld the focus on shareholder engagement, the shift from shareholder rights to institutional investor disclosure duties also indicate a shift in the market failure thesis that drives the development. The post-crisis narrative seems to rely on a market failure thesis where a sub-optimal level of shareholder engagement is detrimental to the long-term viability and performance of companies.[10] The role of shareholders in the European corporate governance framework is repeatedly emphasised. However, it is not a clear traditional corporate governance perspective that drives the promotion of shareholder engagement though, as it is also argued by the European Commission that institutional investors' beneficiaries will benefit from more efficient engagement with investee companies.[11] The appearance of a beneficiary perspective in a corporate governance framework may be surprising, and the different interests that were driving the development of the SRD II is therefore further discussed below in section II.C.iii.

A. The SRD II's Engagement Duties

Regarding the engagement policy, Article 3g, paragraph (1)(a) of the SRD II states that:

> [i]nstitutional investors and asset managers shall develop and publicly disclose an engagement policy that describes how they integrate shareholder engagement in their investment strategy. The policy shall describe how they monitor investee companies on relevant matters, including strategy, financial and non-financial performance and risk, capital structure, social and environmental impact and corporate governance, conduct dialogues with investee companies, exercise voting rights and other rights attached to shares, cooperate with other shareholders, communicate with relevant stakeholders of the investee companies and manage actual and potential conflicts of interests in relation to their engagement.

Even though shareholder engagement was a key priority for the European Commission in the making of the SRD II, the Directive does not provide a clear definition of the concept.[12] However, as shown in the aforementioned wording, a definition seems to be integrated into the provision. Thus, the first paragraph defines the various elements of shareholder engagement, which the institutional investors and asset managers are

---

[10] ibid 3.5; The European Commission, 'Green Paper. The EU Corporate Governance Framework' (Communication) COM (2011) 164, 2.1; The European Commission, 'Action Plan: European Company Law and Corporate Governance – A Modern Legal Framework for More Engaged Shareholders and Sustainable Companies' (Communication) COM (2012) 740 final, 3 and the SRD II (n 1 above) Recitals 2 and 15.

[11] COM (2012) 740 final (n 10 above) 2.4 and the SRD II (n 1 above) Recital 14.

[12] See also, HS Birkmose, 'Article 3g: Engagement Policy' in Birkmose and Sergakis (n 4 above) 151–52.

expected to cover in their engagement policy. This is consistent with the definition put forward in the 2011 Green Paper. Here it was said that:

> [s]hareholder engagement is generally understood as actively monitoring companies, engaging in a dialogue with the company's board, and using shareholder rights, including voting and cooperation with other shareholders, if need be to improve the governance of the investee company in the interests of long-term value creation.[13]

Article 3g does not incorporate a duty to engage. Rather, the SRD II is a disclosure framework that is based on the comply-or-explain principle, which is why an institutional investor or an asset manager can choose not to comply with one or more of the provisions and instead disclose a clear and reasoned explanation as to why this approach has been chosen.

At the core of the provision is the monitoring of investee companies, as monitoring precedes the other engagement activities. The European Commission has repeatedly stressed the importance of effective monitoring of the board of directors by the shareholders, and how it is essential to the European corporate governance model that they hold the board of directors accountable on issues that promote the company's value creation.[14] According to Article 3g, some of these issues – such as establishing the strategy of the company, defining the company's risk profile or capital structure, or ensuring the financial performance of the company – relate to the traditional core duties of the board of directors. Other duties, which institutional investors and asset managers must monitor, have been shaped and refined in recent times. This includes the boards' corporate governance duties, as well as duties in relation to the company's non-financial performance. Boards of directors' corporate governance duties may encompass a number of different issues,[15] however, in relation to the individual company, compliance can be assessed against the corporate governance statement, which the board of listed companies has to include in their management report.[16] Non-financial performance is also a concept, which may be ambivalent. However, since 2018, large undertakings have had to include a non-financial statement in their management report, to provide an understanding of the company's development, performance, position and impact of its activity, relating to, among other things, environmental, social and employee matters, respect for human rights and issues regarding anti-corruption and bribery.[17] Both reporting obligations

---

[13] COM (2011) 164 (n 10 above).

[14] COM(2010) 284 (n 8 above) 5 and in particular ibid 3.

[15] Most recently, the European Commission has planned a directive on sustainable corporate governance to clarify corporate boards' duties in relation to sustainability and companies' long-term interest. However, the proposal is yet to be adopted. See also The European Commission, 'Action Plan: Financing Sustainable Growth' (Communication), Action 10. COM(2018) 97 final and European Parliament Resolution of 17 December 2020 on sustainable corporate governance (2020/2137(INI)) (2021/C 445/12).

[16] Art 20, Council Directive 2013/34/EU of 26 June 2013 on the annual financial statements, consolidated financial statements and related reports of certain types of undertakings, amending Directive 2006/43/EC of the European Parliament and of the Council, and repealing the Council Directives 78/660/EEC and 83/349/EEC [2013] OJ L 182/19.

[17] Council Directive 2014/95/EU of 22 October 2014 amending Directive 2013/34/EU as regards disclosure of non-financial and diversity information by certain large undertakings and groups, introducing Article 19a to Dir 2013/34/EU.

are subject to the comply-or-explain principle.[18] For institutional investors and asset managers, the reporting duties make up a natural point of reference when assessing the performance of investee companies. Arguably, the duty to monitor investee companies in terms of their social and environmental impact may be rather more difficult to pin down. I have previously argued that this duty should most likely be considered in relation to the aforementioned duty to monitor non-financial performance, as it will be difficult for institutional investors and asset managers to monitor companies' social and environmental impact beyond the information provided in the already established reporting requirements.[19] In general, institutional investors and asset managers depend on available data to be able to monitor financial, as well as non-financial, performance; company reporting, therefore, makes up an essential source of information. Considering how heavily the monitoring task depends on financial and non-financial information provided by investee companies,[20] it is not surprising that the European Commission has adopted a proposal for a directive regarding corporate sustainability reporting (CSRD),[21] which amends – among other things – non-financial reporting requirements. When adopted, the CSRD will provide a stronger basis for the assessment of investee companies' performance as regards sustainability and for engagement in respect of non-financial performance. The strengthening of companies' disclosure duties in this area also aims to allow for stakeholders to take part in the emerging transformation, which is initiated with the sustainable agenda in the EU. Here investors play an important role as they can use their financial leverage and governance rights to press for a transformation that will not only benefit their own investment but will also be for the good of society. Therefore, it may be argued that the CSRD emphasises that monitoring has another dimension than the dominant corporate governance dimension.

B. The Scope of the SRD II's Engagement Duties

Based on the wording of Article 3g, the provision has a clear focus on institutional investors and asset managers but not shareholders in general. This focus should be understood in relation to the role of institutional investors and asset managers, as financial investment intermediaries in the financial markets.[22]

In the documents leading to the adoption of the SRD II, the European Commission repeatedly referred to the European corporate governance framework and the role

---

[18] Council Directive 2013/34/EU of 26 June 2013 on the annual financial statements, consolidated financial statements and related reports of certain types of undertakings, amending Directive 2006/43/EC of the European Parliament and of the Council and repealing Council Directives 78/660/EEC and 83/349/EEC, Articles 19a and 20.

[19] Birkmose (n 12 above) 153.

[20] The 2018 Action Plan (n 15 above) section 4.1.

[21] Proposal for a Directive of The European Parliament and of the Council amending Directive 2013/34/EU, Directive 2004/109/EC, Directive 2006/43/EC and Regulation (EU) No 537/2014, as regards corporate sustainability reporting, section 1. COM(2021) 189 final.

[22] See also IH-Y Chiu 'Building a Single Market for Sustainable Finance in the EU – Mixed Implications and the Missing Link of Digitalisation' (2022) 18(5) *European Company and Financial Law Review* 181.

of shareholder engagement. For instance, it was stated in the 2012 Action Plan that '[s]hareholders have a crucial role to play in promoting better governance of companies'[23] and '[e]ffective, sustainable shareholder engagement is one of the cornerstones of listed companies' corporate governance model'.[24] This focus was upheld despite the shortcomings of the corporate governance framework, including shareholder passivity, which emerged during the financial crisis.[25] However, such shortcomings were not surprising, as free riding and collective action problems, among others, characterise shareholder engagement efforts in general.[26] Still, large shareholders have been highlighted in corporate governance theory as a means of overcoming these shortcomings.[27] While the adoption of the Shareholder Rights Directive in 2007 aimed to strengthen and increase shareholder engagement in general,[28] there has been a shift in the SRD II from a general focus on the role of shareholders in corporate governance to a focus on institutional investors and asset managers.[29] Therefore, even though the European Commission refers to *shareholder* engagement, the SRD II's initiatives target, in particular, the institutional investors and asset managers.[30] This shift cannot be explained by the size of institutional investors and asset managers alone, although part of the explanation may be found here. Institutional investors and asset managers have played an increasingly important role in international capital markets, as they hold an increasing proportion of the shares traded on capital markets around the world. These large blocks of shares create an important potential source of influence. However, although they may be considered large shareholders with respect to their importance in financial markets in general, this may not be the case when their investment in individual companies is considered. Therefore, to understand why the European Commission did not focus on large investors, in general, to remedy shareholder passivity, one aspect of the investment element, in particular, needs to be considered.

Institution investors and asset managers are a heterogeneous mass with very different characteristics.[31] However, in the context of SRD II there is a strong link

---

[23] COM (2012) 740 final (n 10 above) 3.

[24] ibid 9. Repeated in the SRD II, Recital 14.

[25] See, among others, the Green Paper COM(2010) 284 (n 8 above) 8. Even though this green paper focused on financial institutions, many of the conclusions also apply to non-financial companies.

[26] See, among others, HS Birkmose, 'European Challenges for Institutional Investor Engagement – Is Mandatory Disclosure the Way Forward' (2014) *European Company and Financial Law Review* 226 and 243 ff.

[27] See, among others, A Shleifer and RW Vishny, 'Large Shareholders and Corporate Control' (1986) 94 *Journal of Political Economy* 461.

[28] Council Directive 2007/36/EC of 11 July 2007 on the exercise of certain rights of shareholders in listed companies [2007] OJ L 184/17.

[29] See, among others HS Birkmose, 'Duties Imposed on Specific Shareholders Only, and Enforcement Implications' in HS Birkmose and K Sergakis (eds), *Enforcing Shareholders' Duties* (Edward Elgar, 2019) 48 ff.

[30] The 2012 Action Plan (n 10 above) 13; The European Commission: 'Consultation and hearing on future priorities for the action plan on modernising company law and enhancing corporate governance in the European Union' (20 December 2005) 7 ff; Commission Staff Working Document: Annex to the Proposal for a Directive on the exercise of voting rights (SEC(2006) 181); and COM (2011) 164 (n 10 above) 11.

[31] See, among others, MB Madsen, 'A New Approach to Shareholder Heterogeneity' in HS Birkmose (ed), *Shareholder Duties* (Kluwer Law International, 2017) § 5.03.

between supposed long-term investors and the SRD II engagement duties, and the European Commission has emphasised the importance of long-term investors on several occasions. Although, the European Commission has recognised that engagement by short-term investors can have a positive effect on investee companies' value creation,[32] shareholder engagement is said to be 'generally understood as an activity which improves long-term returns to shareholders'. Therefore, the European Commission believes 'that it is primarily long-term investors who have an interest in engagement'.[33]

The long-term perspective is closely related to the obligations that many institutional investors owe to their beneficiaries, including pension funds, life insurance companies, state pension reserve funds and sovereign wealth funds.[34] However, the SRD II's definition of institutional investors in Article 2, paragraph 1(e),[35] does not include all long-term investors and only encompasses certain undertakings carrying out activities of life assurance and of reinsurance, and certain institutions for occupational retirement provision. The activities of these institutional investors are characterised by being regulated by harmonised EU frameworks that aim to support credible capital markets and at the same time protect the beneficiaries' interests. However, in order to ensure the interests of the beneficiaries, the long-term focus that defines the relationship between institutional investors and beneficiaries should also characterise the relationship between institutional investors and asset managers[36] and explains why the SRD II obligations are extended down the investment chain to asset managers.[37]

Thus, because institutional investors and asset managers are expected to be long-term investors, due to the nature of the obligations they owe to their beneficiaries, they are the focus of SRD II's engagement objective and not large shareholders in general. Therefore, it is clear that even though SRD II's engagement agenda is part of the European corporate governance framework, the scope of the engagement disclosure duties is framed by the investment side of institutional investment practice.

C. Integration of Shareholder Engagement and Investment Strategy

The link between engagement – the governance side – and the investment side also manifests itself more explicitly in the SRD II than through the scope. According to

---

[32] As an example, a reference was made to engagement by 'activist' hedge funds, which can be beneficial despite their typical short-term nature, because such activism can act as a catalyst for a change in governance and raise awareness among other shareholders.

[33] COM(2011) 164 final (n 10 above), Sec. 2.1. See also the SRD II (n 1 above) Recital 15.

[34] However, the Commission does recognise that engagement by short-term investors may have a positive effect on companies' value creation, as it may 'act as a catalyst for a change in governance and raise awareness among other shareholders': COM(2011) 164 (n 10 above) 11.

[35] See also Madsen (n 4 above) 2.35–2.42.

[36] See also HS Birkmose, 'Article 3h': Investment Strategy of Institutional Investors and Arrangements with Asset Managers' in Birkmose and Sergakis (n 4 above) 7.21–7.45 and S Gomtsian, 'Article 3i: Transparency of Asset Managers' in Birkmose and Sergakis (n 4 above), in particular 8.19.

[37] Asset managers are defined for the purpose of SRD II in Art 2, para 2(e). See further Madsen (n 4 above) 2.43–2.47.

Article 3g, paragraph 1(a), it is not sufficient that institutional investors and asset managers publicly disclose an engagement policy that describes how they engage with investee companies as discussed above; the engagement policy must also describe 'how they integrate shareholder engagement in their investment strategy'.

Arguably, this requirement is an additional dimension to the traditional financial dimensions that make up an investment strategy, but it demonstrates clearly that shareholder engagement is expected to be part and parcel of investment management by institutions.[38] Due to the long-term obligations of the targeted institutional investors, it is an implicit presumption that the integration of shareholder engagement in the investment strategy will improve the long-term value of the investments. However, paragraph 1(a) does not set out any guidelines as to how engagement should be integrated, leaving it to the individual institutional investor or asset manager to describe how integration is to be achieved. Some guidance may be found in the UK 2020 Stewardship Code, Principle 7, though. Here it is stated that '[s]ignatories systematically integrate stewardship and investment, including material environmental, social and governance issues, and climate change, to fulfil their responsibilities'. As mentioned above, the SRD II was clearly inspired by the 2010 Stewardship Code. Although the Code has developed significantly since then and comparison should be made with care, it is still relevant to look to the UK for inspiration. It should also be noted that paragraph 1 is applied on the basis of the comply-or-explain principle, for which reason shareholder engagement may be left out in the investment strategy, if the institutional investors or asset managers publicly provide a clear and reasoned explanation as to why they have chosen not to comply with one or more of those requirements.

The link discussed also stresses that to fully understand the engagement agenda set out in Article 3g, it is necessary to look more closely at the investment side and the significance of the investment strategy. Although some guidance may be found in the SRD II, as Articles 3h and 3i set out disclosure provisions regarding the investment strategy of institutional investors and arrangements with asset managers, the link to the investment side seems to have gone unnoticed in the debate on shareholder engagement, following the adoption of the Directive. However, it is clear that shareholder engagement in the context of SRD II has a corporate governance function (Article 3g), as well as an investment management function (Article 3h). The latter concerns the relationship between the institutional investor that makes investment decisions on behalf of individual beneficiaries, whereas the former concerns the relationship between the institutional investor and the investee companies in which equity is held. Moreover, the investment management function also includes institutional investors' arrangements with asset managers (Article 3i).[39] Together, these provisions seek to align the interests of institutional investors' beneficiaries, the asset managers and the investee companies,[40] thereby stressing the role of institutional investors as financial intermediaries. Consequently Articles 3h and 3i require closer examination.

---

[38] See Chiu (n 5 above) 3 for a discussion of investment management in relation to stewardship.
[39] See Gomtsian (n 36 above) Ch 8 for a detailed analysis of this article.
[40] SRD II (n 1 above) Recital 19.

i. The SRD II's Investment Strategy Disclosure Duties

Article 3h, paragraph 1 of the SRD II states that:

> Member States shall ensure that institutional investors publicly disclose how the main elements of their equity investment strategy are consistent with the profile and duration of their liabilities, in particular long-term liabilities, and how they contribute to the medium to long-term performance of their assets.

As can be seen from the wording, the provision only applies to institutional investors. The equivalent disclosure obligations of asset managers are found Article 3i.

Even though many institutional investors invest in balanced portfolios, only the elements of the equity investment strategy are covered by the disclosure requirements of paragraph 1. This is also the case where the balanced portfolio requires the overall investment strategy to embrace a wider range of assets than just equity investments. Neither the SRD II nor the proceeding documents give a reason for the narrow application, but a natural explanation may the close link to the governance side, as it is focused on holdings in listed companies. However, the 2020 UK Stewardship Code shows that a narrow application is not a given, as it is being applied across all asset classes. Still, the Code contains more detailed reporting expectations for listed equity assets than for other asset classes.[41]

Interestingly, the SRD II does not define 'investment strategy'. Neither do any of the preceding documents. However, it is clear from reading Article 3h that it implies an understanding which differs from a narrow focus on an active or passive investment strategy.[42] The investment strategy called for in paragraph 1 must guide actual investment decisions, and consequently, the investment strategy has to be made operative. In this respect, institutional investors' objectives and risk tolerance, as well as their need for capital are important. Consequently, the main elements of the equity investment strategy may include a number of different aspects. These include not only questions relating to active or passive investment and direct or indirect investment, but also risks associated with investments, ESG considerations, geographical allocation, allocation based on different sectors or industries, currency or the weight of different types of securities in the portfolio.[43] Moreover, the investment strategy must reflect the portfolio diversification requirements, to which the institutional investors must adhere.[44] Therefore, for many institutional investors ESG considerations will

---

[41] See The UK Stewardship Code 2020, https://www.frc.org.uk/getattachment/5aae591d-d9d3-4cf 4-814a-d14e156a1d87/Stewardship-Code_Final2.pdf.

[42] See among others Chiu (n 5 above) 7, S Gomtsian, 'Shareholder Engagement by Large Institutional Investors' (2020) 45(3) *Journal of Corporation Law* 66–67; and J Fisch, 'The Uncertain Stewardship Potential of Index Funds', section III, https://papers.ssrn.com/sol3/papers.cfm?abstract_id=3525355 for details on active vs passive investing.

[43] Regarding IORPs, the IORP Directive, Art 30 requires that an IORP prepares a written statement of investment policy principles, which must be made public and which includes inter alia how the investment policy takes environmental, social and governance factors into account. Although these principles are not mentioned in the SRD II or in any of the preparatory documents, it must be assumed that these, to some extent, overlap the investment strategy. In the context of Art 3h, the latter is more narrow, as it only covers equity investments.

[44] See among others RM Barker and IH-Y Chiu, *Corporate Governance and Investment Management. The Promises and Limitations of the new Financial Economy* (Edward Elgar, 2017) 94 ff.

be a natural part of the investment strategy, although this is not stressed in any way by Article 3h.[45]

However, the investment strategy as such is not the aim of Article 3h. Rather, it is a disclosure provision, which requires that:

> Member States shall ensure that institutional investors publicly disclose how the main elements of their equity investment strategy are consistent with the profile and duration of their liabilities, in particular long-term liabilities, and how they contribute to the medium to long-term performance of their assets.[46]

As mentioned above, there is a clear link between the institutional investors covered by the SRD II's disclosure provisions and their long-term investment focus. These institutional investors per se have long-term liabilities, but Article 3h stresses that they must not only demonstrate their equity investment strategy's consistency with their long-term liabilities by disclosing the main elements of their equity investment strategy, but must also disclose how the main elements of their equity investment strategy contribute to the medium to long-term performance of their assets. If an institutional investor engages with an asset manager, then the institutional investor must still comply with Article 3h, paragraph 1, however, the institutional investor must also disclose information on the arrangement with the asset manager, to ensure that the consistency of the investment strategy with the institutional investor's long-term liabilities are extended to the asset manager.[47] Consequently, the asset managers must:

> disclose, on an annual basis, to the institutional investor with which they have entered into the arrangements referred to in Article 3h how their investment strategy and implementation thereof complies with that arrangement and contributes to the medium to long-term performance of the assets of the institutional investor or of the fund.[48]

Thus, the long-term obligations which the institutional investors owe to the beneficiaries also define the disclosure duties of the asset managers.

Hence, the core aim of Article 3h is to ensure that institutional investors are transparent with regard to the main elements of their investment strategy, so as to enable the beneficiaries to evaluate their practices. Moreover, this transparency must be extended to asset managers whenever institutional investors make use of their services, as part of their investment management. Thus, institutional investors must not only disclose information relating to their own equity investment strategy but also regarding their arrangements with asset managers, in order to demonstrate how the delegation of investment decisions may affect their obligations towards the beneficiaries. Thus, Articles 3h and 3i seem to build on the assumption that greater

---

[45] Moreover, the specific focus in Art 3h on institutional investors' medium to long-term liabilities indicates that sustainability can play a role in relation to the development of the investment strategy, as sustainability is often linked with a long-term perspective. Thus, it is stated in the 2018 Action Plan (n 13 above) section 1.3, that sustainability and long-termism go hand in hand.

[46] This is contrary to Art 3g, according to which institutional investors must disclose in full how they integrate shareholder engagement in their investment strategy.

[47] See also Birkmose (n 36 above) 7.21–7.45.

[48] See also Gomtsian (n 36 above) Ch 8.

transparency in relation to investment practices may ultimately promote better investment decisions and strengthen the accountability of institutional investors to their
beneficiaries, as it will allow them to optimise their investment decisions.[49] However,
this dependence on the beneficiaries may prove to be overrated, as it is arguable
whether they can and will rely on the disclosed information to invest and hold the
institutional investors to account for their investment strategy[50] (see section II.C.iii
below).

At the same time, Article 3h does not impose any duties on institutional investors
in relation to their investment management or their investment strategy. Rather, it
refers to existing duties. As discussed above, the SRD II clearly builds on the assumption that the specific institutional investors covered by the Directive apply long-term
investment models, because they have long-term obligations to their beneficiaries,
due to the nature of their commitments. Therefore, in order to fully understand the
link between investment management and shareholder engagement, it is necessary
to look beyond the SRD II and include other regulatory frameworks that address
the institutional investors' and asset managers' business model and obligations to
their beneficiaries. The Solvency II Directive and the IORP Directive are particularly
relevant for this purpose, as the definition of institutional investors found in SRD II
Article 1, paragraph 2 links to these regulatory frameworks.[51]

ii. The Investment Management Side Unfolded

The so-called 'prudent person' principle is key to understanding the fundamental
duties, which institutional investors owe to their beneficiaries. The prudent person
principle is a financial standard that aims to ensure that institutional investors have
assets of sufficient quality to cover their overall financial requirements at all times, and
that investments are made in the best interests of their beneficiaries.[52] Thus, according
to the Solvency II Directive,[53] Article 132, Member States must assure 'that insurance
and reinsurance undertakings invest all their assets in accordance with the prudent
person principle'. As far as the Institutions for Occupational Retirement Provisions
(IORPs) are concerned, the IORP Directive,[54] Article 19, states that Member States
must require IORPs to invest in accordance with the 'prudent person' principle, which
among other aspects states that 'the assets shall be invested in the best long-term interests of members and beneficiaries as a whole'. Interestingly, the long-term perspective
is an explicit focus of the IORP Directive,[55] while it seems to be an only implicit

---

[49] Recital 16 and also ibid, paras 24–25.

[50] See F Möslein and KE Sørensen, 'The Commission's Action Plan for Financing Sustainable Growth
and Its Corporate Governance Implications' (2018) 15(6) *European Company Law* 227 for similar reflections as regards the 2018 Action Plan.

[51] Directive 2009/138 (n 6 above) and Directive 2016/2341 (n 6 above). See also the discussion in Madsen
(n 4 above).

[52] See also, Directive 2016/2341 (n 6 above), Recital 71 and R Galer, OECD, '"Prudent Person Rule"
Standard for the Investment of Pension Fund Assets' (2002) https://www.oecd.org/finance/private-
pensions/2763540.pdf for an older account.

[53] Directive 2009/138 (n 6 above).

[54] Directive 2016/2341 (n 6 above).

[55] Recital 45 also states that 'IORPs are very long-term investors'.

focus of the Solvency II Directive. Therefore, even though the European Commission clearly takes the view that insurance and reinsurance undertakings also rely on a long-term business model, their duties in that respect may be more opaque. Thus, while the prudent person principle establishes an overarching guiding principle for the institutional investors' investment practices, it does not set any specific requirements regarding the individual investments.[56] Rather, both Directives establish that Member States cannot require the institutional investors to invest in any particular categories of assets but leaves it to them to apply an investment strategy which they consider to be in the best interests of the beneficiaries.[57] Both directives also have provisions that are more specific in relation to the institutional investors' investments, and which also aim to secure the interests of the beneficiaries, such as portfolio diversification requirements.[58] Therefore, even though institutional investors have considerable freedom to decide on an investment strategy, they have to invest within the framework of the specific provisions on investment and the prudent person principle, aiming to support the long-term interests of their beneficiaries.

Under common law, understanding the prudent person principle is integrated with fiduciary duties that characterise the relationship between the institutional investor and the individual beneficiary.[59] Here, the governance of pension funds is traditionally based on trust law,[60] while other insurance schemes fall outside trust-based relations.[61] In this case, the duties of the institutional investors are defined by contract or legislation and are comparable with those found in civil law jurisdictions, where there is no equivalent to the common law trust.[62] Still, the idea of a 'fiduciary' – a trusted person who must uphold the interests of the beneficiary or final owner of the funds – may also be found in civil law legislation. Therefore, even though the genesis of institutional investors' fiduciary duties varies, it can be argued that, in general, the understanding of the prudent person principle in the Solvency II and IORP Directives rests on the notion of institutional investors owing fiduciary duties to their beneficiaries.

Moreover, the fiduciary relationship between the institutional investors and the beneficiaries also has a spill over effect on the relationship between the institutional

---

[56] However, both directives clarify the understanding of the prudent person principle, *cf* Art 132, respectively, Art 19. In respect of the IORP Directive it includes a reference to ESG factors, as Art 19, para 1(b) states that 'within the prudent person rule, Member States shall allow IORPs to take into account the potential long-term impact of investment decisions on environmental, social, and governance factors'. Thus, it does not include a duty to address ESG considerations, it merely establishes that fund managers are not precluded from considering the impact of their investments on ESG factors.

[57] Directive 2009/138 (n 6 above) Art 133; and Directive 2016/2341 (n 6 above) Art 19, para. 4.

[58] See also Barker and Chiu (n 44 above) 94 ff.

[59] See, among others, D Guyatt 'Challenging Conventional Wisdom: The Role of Investment Tools, Investment Beliefs and Industry Conventions in Changing our Interpretation of Fiduciary Duty' in JP Hawley et al (eds), *Cambridge Handbook of Institutional Investment and Fiduciary Duty* (Cambridge University Press, 2014) 322 ff. See also EU High-level Expert Group (HLEG) on Sustainable Finance, *Financing a Sustainable European Economy*, section 3, Interim Report (July 2017).

[60] See, among others, C Molinari, 'The Future of Fiduciary Obligation for Institutional Investors' in Hawley et al (n 59 above) 161.

[61] ibid 164 ff.

[62] See, among others, JP Hawley et al, 'Introduction' in Hawley et al (n 59 above) 1 ff.

investors and the asset managers,[63] and institutional investors must monitor the asset managers to ensure that their investment and engagement activities also support long-term value creation in the interests of the ultimate beneficiaries.

Although the reference to the prudent person principle does not really clarify how the overall obligations to beneficiaries should relate to specific duties concerning institutional investors' investment management, beyond that found in the Solvency II Directive and the IORP Directive, it still needs to be considered whether the duty to act in the best interests of the beneficiaries, may have implications for the engagement of institutional investors with investee companies. Since Recital 19 of the SRD II makes it clear that Articles 3g–3i seek to align the interests of institutional investors' beneficiaries, the asset managers and the investee companies, one can argue that the fiduciary duties, found in the Solvency II and IORP Directives, must carry over to the SRD II's disclosure duties. Therefore, the fiduciary duties that characterise the investment side also influence the duties of institutional investors in relation to their engagement with investee companies, due to the link established by the SRD II. Hence, when institutional investors manage the funds with which they have been entrusted, they must act prudently and uphold the (long-term) interests of their beneficiaries. This role as a financial intermediary includes engagement with investee companies, as successful management of the investments may have a positive effect on the financial performance of the institutional investors. However, this argument does not go as far as to say that institutional investors must engage. Rather, they must consider whether engaging is in the best interests of the beneficiaries.

iii. To Whom Must the Institutional Investors and Asset Managers Disclose Engagement and Investment Information?

Finally, in order to understand the relationship between engagement and investment management, it may also be relevant to consider the question to whom must the institutional investors and asset managers disclose engagement and investment information? As stated above, Articles 3g–3i seek to align the interests of institutional investors' beneficiaries, asset managers and investee companies,[64] and the link between the governance dimension and the investment management dimension, which was explored above, seems to suggest that the interests of the beneficiaries are critical in understanding the disclosure duties. Both dimensions are also reflected in the preamble to the SRD II, Recital 16, which states that:

> [i]nstitutional investors and asset managers are often not transparent about their investment strategies, their engagement policy and the implementation thereof. Public disclosure of such information could have a positive impact on investor awareness, enable ultimate

---

[63] However, the extent to which asset managers owe fiduciary duties is not clear. See, among others, Molinari, in Hawley et al (n 59 above) 163. See also *The Kay Review of UK Equity Markets and Long-Term Decision Making* (2012), https://assets.publishing.service.gov.uk/government/uploads/system/uploads/attachment_data/file/253454/bis-12-917-kay-review-of-equity-markets-final-report.pdf and J Winter, 'Shareholder Engagement and Stewardship. The Realities and Illusions of Institutional Share Ownership' (2011) 6 https://papers.ssrn.com/sol3/papers.cfm?abstract_id=1867564.

[64] SRD II, Recital 19.

beneficiaries such as future pensioners optimise investment decisions, facilitate the dialogue between companies and their shareholders, encourage shareholder engagement and strengthen their accountability to stakeholders and to civil society.

According to this recital, the beneficiaries seem to be only one of several recipients of the disclosed information, and the clear focus of the investment management side, which was stressed above, is absent. Thus, one could read the recital in such a way that the SRD II extends the institutional investors' and asset managers' accountability to include a number of different stakeholders. However, this is not necessarily the case. To answer the question asked at the beginning of this section, separating the two dimensions might be helpful.

Starting with the governance dimension, shareholder engagement is stressed as an important aspect of the European Corporate Governance Framework, as previously discussed. Therefore, one would expect that the corporate governance dimension of the SRD II's engagement regime would prevail. However, although Recital 16 does mention that increased transparency could encourage shareholder engagement and facilitate the dialogue between companies and their shareholders, this creates several problems when it comes to accountability. Even if it was assumed that disclosure is aimed at the investee companies, it cannot be expected that the latter will hold the shareholders (the institutional investors) accountable, if the shareholders do not engage.[65] Therefore, it is also relevant to include the investment management dimension in this respect. Recital 16 also mentions that disclosure could enable ultimate beneficiaries, such as future pensioners, to optimise investment decisions. While the institutional investors' beneficiaries in many cases do not have the right to hold the institutional investor accountable from an internal corporate governance perspective, they may still be able to sanction institutional investors by deselecting a life insurance undertaking or IORP, when choosing to take out a life insurance or pension policy. Moreover, the policy holder is sometimes able to transfer a policy from one undertaker or IORP to another. Finally, Recital 16 also mentions accountability to stakeholders and to civil society. While the disclosed information may be of value to other stakeholders, as well as to society in general, they may have very few or no tools available to hold the institutional investors and asset managers to account for their fulfilment of duties, set forward in Articles 3g–3h.[66] Moreover, such wider accountability is neither captured by the governance side nor by the investment management side, and although there may be a wider social dimension in the practices of institutional investors,[67] it is unclear if and how this is reflected in the SRD II. The national financial authorities (NFA), who are given a strong role in securing the public interest in the sound functioning of listed markets and the well-being of financial institutions, could also be regarded as relevant public sector stakeholders. However, they are not given a particularly strong role in the SRD II. Although Member States have to ensure some enforcement of the provisions of the

---

[65] See also Birkmose (n 29 above) 58.

[66] ibid.

[67] See IH-Y Chiu, 'Institutional Shareholders as Stewards: Towards a New Conception of Corporate Governance' (2011–2012) 6 *Brooklyn Journal of Corporate, Financial and Commercial Law* 396 ff in relation to the UK Stewardship, which partly inspired the SRD II.

SRD II (see Article 14b) it is not required that the NFAs are entrusted with specific powers or duties in that regard.[68] Moreover, it may also be questionable whether legal enforcement by NFAs will ensure stronger accountability towards society, if that is an explicit aim of the Directive.[69]

Although the focus of the disclosure duties in Articles 3g and 3h is somewhat ambivalent, because of Recital 16, the interests of beneficiaries also seem to guide the duties of the institutional investors in SRD II. This conclusion partly rests on the intermediary role which institutional investors play in the financial markets and the fiduciary duties they owe to the beneficiaries, but also partly on SRD II, Article 3g, which requires that shareholder engagement is integrated in the investment strategy. Thus, engagement must also be seen as a means of fulfilling the fiduciary duties which institutional investors owe the beneficiaries. This is an interesting – and somewhat surprising – finding as company law and the corporate governance framework traditionally deals with the relationship between shareholders and the investee companies, whereas the underlying interests of the shareholders are irrelevant.

Thus, the consequence of such an understanding is that developments in relation to the investment side may also have a derived effect on the engagement of institutional investors. Therefore, the development of the European sustainable finance agenda is also of great interest in relation to the shareholder engagement agenda.

III. THE EUROPEAN SUSTAINABLE FINANCE AGENDA

The European Commission's sustainable finance agenda has become increasingly ambitious, as it has developed over the last few years. Following the adoption in 2015 of both the UN's 2030 agenda and sustainable development goals,[70] as well as the Paris climate agreement,[71] the Commission issued several policy documents outlining the European agenda for a sustainable European future.[72] A priority in these documents is the focusing of the EU's economy on a greener and more sustainable future. The investments needed for this transformation are huge and in order to secure sufficient finance the Commission ascribes a key role to private sector and financial market participants.[73]

---

[68] See A Bartolacelli et al, 'Article 14a and 14b: Enforcement of SRD II Provisions' in Birkmose and Sergakis (n 4 above) 322–24.

[69] See K Sergakis, 'Legal vs Social Enforcement of Shareholder Duties' in Birkmose and Sergakis (n 29 above) 143–47.

[70] See n 2 above.

[71] See n 3 above.

[72] The European Commission, 'Next steps for a sustainable European future. European action for sustainability' (Communication) COM(2016) 739 final. The European Commission, 'The European Green Deal' (Communication) COM(2019) 640 final. See also https://ec.europa.eu/info/strategy/priorities-2019–2024/european-green-deal_en.

[73] 'Financial Market Participants' are defined in Regulation 2019/2088, Art 2(1). This covers various kinds of institutional investors and assets managers. In relation to the discussions regarding the SFDR, this term will be used, whereas the wider discussions in this section focusing on the duties of institutional investors and asset managers will continue to use these terms.

A. The Road to Sustainable Finance in the EU

To support the green transformation and direct financial and capital flows to green investments, the Commission adopted an Action Plan, 'Financing Sustainable Growth' in 2018 (hereinafter the 2018 Action Plan).[74] Thus, one of the key objectives of the 2018 Action Plan is to reorient capital flows towards sustainable investments, in order to achieve sustainable and inclusive growth.[75] The other two key objectives are to manage financial risks stemming from, among other things, climate change and social issues, and to foster transparency and long-termism in financial and economic activity. The key objectives are materialised in ten actions, some of which were planned to be tabled as legislative initiatives. The most important in respect of this chapter are the establishment of an EU classification system for sustainable activities (action 1); the clarification of institutional investors' and asset managers' duties in relation to sustainability considerations (action 7) and the strengthening of companies' sustainability disclosure (action 9), as these have direct implications for the SRD II's disclosure duties.[76] The initiatives of the 2018 Action Plan were scheduled for Q2 2018 until Q2 2019; it was therefore a very ambitious workplan, timewise.[77] While the European Commission's ambitions have not been met regarding all of the initiatives that were set out, several important milestones have been achieved. This includes the Regulation on the Establishment of a Framework to facilitate Sustainable Investment (hereinafter, the Taxonomy Regulation)[78] and the SFDR.[79] Additionally, a number of Delegated Regulations have been adopted, which link to the two said regulations.[80] At the same time, the European Commission has indicated that it is necessary to accelerate the transition,[81] and in April 2020 it presented a new strategy for sustainable financing.[82] After a public consultation, a summary of the responses submitted by stakeholders were published in February 2021.[83]

The sustainable finance plans have been accompanied by investment plans, which establish the level of investments needed to secure the policy goals going forward.

---

[74] The 2018 Action Plan (n 15 above). The action plan builds on the work of the expert group, which the European Commission set up in 2016 and which published its final report on 31 January 2018. See https://ec.europa.eu/info/sites/default/files/180131-sustainable-finance-final-report_en.pdf.

[75] The 2018 Action Plan (n 15 above) 2. See Möslein and Sørensen (n 50 above) 221–31 for a discussion on the 2018 Action Plan.

[76] This link is explored below in section V.

[77] The 2018 Action Plan (n 15 above) Annex III.

[78] Council Regulation (EU) 2020/852 of 18 June 2020 on the establishment of a framework to facilitate sustainable investment, and amending Regulation.

[79] Regulation 2019/2088 (n 7 above).

[80] Some of the delegated acts are discussed below in section IV. A Delegated Regulation on disclosures related to the environmentally sustainable economic activities of undertakings was adopted by the European Commission on 6 July 2021. C(2021) 4987 final. The same is the case with a Delegated Regulation to Regulation (EU) 2020/852 on criteria for climate change mitigation or adaptation. This was adopted by the European Commission on 21 April 2021. C(2021) 2800 final.

[81] See among others, the European Commission, 'Sustainable Europe Investment Plan, European Green Deal Investment Plan' (Communication) COM(2020) 21 final, 4.1.

[82] See https://ec.europa.eu/info/sites/default/files/business_economy_euro/banking_and_finance/documents/2020-sustainable-finance-strategy-consultation-document_en.pdf.

[83] See https://ec.europa.eu/info/sites/default/files/business_economy_euro/banking_and_finance/documents/2020-sustainable-finance-strategy-summary-of-responses_en.pdf.

The European Commission presented an investment plan in January 2020 as part of the so-called green pact,[84] which set out to mobilise at least €1 trillion of sustainable investments over the course of 10 years. The European Commission has estimated that achieving the current 2030 climate and energy targets alone will require €350 billion of additional annual investment.[85] The European Commission assumes in the investment plan that not only will the Member States increase their investments in the green transition, but that private companies and households will provide the bulk of sustainable investments in the coming decade. In that respect the institutional investors and asset managers will play a huge role as financial intermediaries.[86] This argument is also essential for the understanding of institutional investors' engagement duties, as discussed above. The connection made here also supports the fact that it is relevant to consider how the European sustainable finance agenda interacts with institutional investors' and asset managers' duties in relation to engagement with investee companies. The discussion opens with a brief presentation of the Taxonomy Regulation[87] and the SFDR,[88] as they make up the nucleus of the current regulatory framework.[89]

B. The Green Taxonomy and Sustainability Disclosure

Action 1 of the 2018 Action Plan was the establishment of an EU classification system for sustainable activities. This aim was key to reorienting capital flows towards a more sustainable economy, as it set out to create a harmonised understanding of the meaning of 'sustainable'. Thus, such a classification was one of the first initiatives the Commission tabled, and in 2020 the Taxonomy Regulation was adopted.[90] The uniform criteria established here can be regarded as a governance ordering for setting the priorities of sustainability, which express strong public interest notions, and which aim to steer how finance is allocated. In the recital, it is stated that harmonisation will make it easier for European companies to raise funding across borders for their environmentally sustainable activities, as their economic activities may be compared against uniform criteria, to be selected as underlying assets for environmentally sustainable investments. Furthermore, disclosure by the European companies of their environmentally sustainable activities will allow financial market

---

[84] COM(2020) 21 final (n 81 above); and COM(2019) 640 final (n 72 above).

[85] See among others, n 82 above. This is a significant increase from the €180 billion which the European Commission assumed necessary just a couple of years ago. COM(2018) 97 final (n 15 above) 2 and The European Commission, 'Proposal for a regulation of the European Parliament and of a framework to facilitate sustainable investment' COM(2018) 353 final, 1.

[86] ibid COM(2018) 353 final, 1 and COM(2020) 21 final (n 81 above).

[87] Regulation 2020/852 (n 78 above).

[88] Regulation 2019/2088 (n 7 above).

[89] If the two regulations are compared, one should be aware that their scope is not identical. The definition of financial market participants in the SFDR, Article 2(1) is wider than the definition of institutional investors and asset managers in SRD II, Article 2(e) and (f). See Madsen (n 4 above) regarding the latter. Consequently, institutional investors and asset managers covered by the SRD II are also covered by the SFDR in their capacity as financial market participants.

[90] Regulation 2020/852 (n 78 above).

participants to make financial products available, which pursue environmentally sustainable objectives, an effective way of channelling private investments into sustainable activities. Moreover, trust in the green financial market is essential in the financial transition, and if the market and investors cannot trust in the given information, there is a risk that they will be misled by greenwashing.[91] Therefore, it is important that a classification of products that claim to be sustainable build on the taxonomy. This will ultimately benefit end investors, as they will be able to find and compare environmentally sustainable products, helping them make more informed investment decisions.[92] A sustainability taxonomy may also support different investment strategies and reward companies that prioritise sustainable activities and potentially lower their capital costs and reputational risk.[93] It should be noted that activities are classified according to the taxonomy, and not companies, products or assets. Moreover, the taxonomy only establishes a framework for environmentally sustainable investments, while a similar framework for socially sustainable investment is yet to come.[94]

To be classified as an environmentally sustainable activity, an activity must fulfil the criteria set out in the Taxonomy Regulation, Article 3, ie the activity must contribute substantially to one of the six objectives set out in Article 9, in accordance with Articles 10–16.[95] The objectives are: climate change mitigation; climate change adaptation; the sustainable use and protection of water and marine resources; the transition to a circular economy; pollution prevention and control; and the protection and restoration of biodiversity and ecosystems. Moreover, an activity that contributes to one of these six objectives must not at the same time significantly harm any of the other environmental objectives set out in Article 9 (the 'do no harm' principle). Finally, economic activities only qualify as environmentally sustainable when they are carried out in alignment with the OECD Guidelines for Multinational Enterprises and UN Guiding Principles on Business and Human Rights, including the declaration on Fundamental Principles and Rights at Work of the International Labour Organization (ILO), the eight fundamental conventions of the ILO and the International Bill of Human Rights.[96]

Besides the qualification of activities as environmentally sustainable, disclosure of information on activities that are classified as environmentally sustainable is key to ensuring that investments are channelled from the financial sector, in particular, to companies that are either involved in or are becoming involved in more sustainable activities. Therefore, the Taxonomy Regulation, Article 8, includes an obligation for

---

[91] 'Greenwashing' is defined in the Taxonomy Regulation as the practice of gaining an unfair competitive advantage by marketing a financial product as environmentally friendly, when, in fact, basic environmental standards have not been met: Regulation 2020/852 (n 78 above) Recital 11.

[92] ibid Recitals 11–13.

[93] See EU Technical Expert Group on Sustainable Finance, https://ec.europa.eu/info/sites/default/files/business_economy_euro/events/documents/finance-events-190624-presentation-taxonomy_en.pdf.

[94] See Regulation 2020/852 (n 79 above) Recital 6. See also the European Commission, 'Strategy for Financing the Transition to a Sustainable Economy (Communication) COM(2021) 390 final, 11 and Action 2(d).

[95] Furthermore, the European Commission must establish technical screening criteria in accordance with Arts 10–15.

[96] See Regulation 2019/2088 (n 7 above) Art 18.

companies and other undertakings, which are obliged to publish non-financial information pursuant to Article 19a or Article 29a of Directive 2013/34/EU, to include in that statement information relating to the extent to which their activities are associated with economic activities that are deemed to be environmentally sustainable.[97] It allows investors and suppliers of financial products that build on the taxonomy to make informed investment decisions. However, the supply of financial products which build on the taxonomy will not only allocate funds to environmentally sustainable activities, but will also benefit end investors, as they will be able to find and compare environmentally sustainable products, helping them make better-informed investment decisions.[98] Therefore, the taxonomy is not only important in securing an environmentally sustainable economic system, it is also the starting point for understanding the sustainability implications of financial products that are marketed by financial market participants as sustainable. Disclosure with a view to end investors on the integration of sustainability risks, on the consideration of adverse sustainability impacts, on sustainable investment objectives, or on the promotion of environmental or social characteristics, in investment decision-making and in advisory processes are, therefore, also key objectives in the transition of sustainable finance.[99] Thus, these particular objectives are the main focus of the SFDR,[100] which was adopted in 2019, seven months prior to the adoption of the Taxonomy Regulation.[101]

If end investors are to be able to make an informed choice when investing, disclosure is essential. This includes information on the financial products that are produced and marketed as being sustainable. In this respect, the Taxonomy Regulation is fundamental, as it harmonises the understanding of what is sustainable, and the taxonomy links the disclosure duties of the SFDR to the taxonomy.[102] Moreover, it is also important that information on sustainability-related issues relating to investment decisions is disclosed to end investors. This includes whether the principal adverse impacts of investment decisions on sustainability factors are considered, as well as the way in which risks stemming from environmental and social considerations are integrated in investment decisions and managed. Therefore, the SFDR also goes beyond the taxonomy framework, in order to ensure that end investors receive sufficient information on sustainability-related issues, so as to make informed investment decisions. In other words, the SFDR's disclosure duties relate to financial products, as well as to financial market participants[103] and financial advisers.[104]

---

[97] Article 8 is supplemented by Delegated Regulation C(2021) 4987 final (n 80 above). Moreover, the European Commission has adopted a proposal for a directive regarding corporate sustainability reporting, which amends, among other things, the non-financial reporting requirements (n 21 above).

[98] Regulation 2020/852 (n 78 above) Recitals 11–13.

[99] Regulation 2019/2088 (n 7 above) Recital 5.

[100] ibid.

[101] Due to the timing, the adoption of the Taxonomy Regulation included a few amendments to the SFDR, *cf* Art 25.

[102] Regulation 2020/852 (n 78 above), Arts 5 and 6.

[103] As defined in Regulation 2019/2088 (n 7 above) Art 2, 1. The term 'financial market participants' includes among others insurance undertakings which make available an insurance-based investment product (IBIP), investment firms which provide portfolio management, institutions for occupational retirement provision (IORP), Alternative Investment Fund Managers (AIFM) and management companies for collective investment in transferable securities (UCITS management company).

[104] As defined in Regulation 2019/2088 (n 7 above) Arts 2, 11.

First, all financial market participants and financial advisers must publish information on their websites regarding their policies and the integration of sustainability risks in their investment decision-making process and their investment or insurance advice.[105] This requirement applies to all financial market participants and financial advisers, whether or not they actively integrate sustainability risks into their business models. Sustainability risks refer to a potential environmental, social or governance event or condition, which could cause an actual material negative impact on the value of the investment and hence the end investors.[106] The financial market participants must present the policy in their pre-contractual disclosures and describe the manner in which sustainability risks are integrated into their investment decisions. They should also clarify the results of the assessment of the likely impact of sustainability risks on the returns of the financial products that they make available.[107] A similar requirement applies in relation to the financial advisers. If, however, financial market participants or financial advisers regard sustainability risks not to be relevant, the descriptions must include a clear and concise explanation of the reasons. In this way, sustainability risk is treated like any other risk that might impact the financial value of an investment and, for this reason, the financial market participant's or financial adviser's risk management system must be aligned with the policy. It also means that financial market participants or financial advisers cannot disregard sustainability risks, which must be monitored and managed according to the risk management policy in the same way as other financial risks.

All financial market participants and financial advisers must also include in their remuneration policies information relating to the way in which those policies are consistent with the integration of sustainability risks, and they must publish this information on their websites.[108]

If financial market participants consider the principal adverse impacts of investment decisions on sustainability factors, or financial advisers consider the principal adverse impacts on sustainability factors in their investment advice or insurance advice,[109] these financial market participants or financial advisers must disclose additional information. In that case financial market participants or financial advisers must make a statement on due diligence policies with respect to those adverse impacts, taking due account of their size, the nature and scale of their activities and the types of financial products they make available or on which they advise.[110] This will show how they identify and manage such adverse impacts, whether material or likely to be material, as part of their due diligence processes. However, these provisions also apply on a comply-or-explain basis. If financial market participants and financial advisers do not consider the adverse impacts of investment decisions on sustainability factors, they must provide clear reasons for not doing so, including, where relevant, information as to whether and when they intend to consider such adverse impacts.[111]

---

[105] ibid Art 3.

[106] ibid Art 2(1)(22).

[107] ibid Art 6(1) and (2).

[108] ibid Art 5(1).

[109] Sustainability factors refer to environmental, social and employee matters, respect for human rights, anti-corruption and anti-bribery matters, *cf* ibid Art 2(1)(24).

[110] ibid Arts 4(1)(a) and 4(2).

[111] ibid Art 4(1)(b). This option is not available for large financial market participants or financial market participants, which are parent undertakings: *cf* Art 4(3) and (4).

The described disclosure requirements relate to the *entity* that offers financial products or provides investment advice. However, the entities must also disclose information on adverse sustainability impacts at financial *product* level. Thus, pre-contractual disclosure must also include information on whether, and, if so, how a financial product considers the principal adverse impacts on sustainability factors, if the financial market participant considers such principal adverse impacts.[112]

Disclosure at product level ties closely to the Taxonomy Regulation, as the products may be based on investments in economic activities that qualify as environmentally sustainable within the taxonomy. In that case, the disclosure requirements are more wide-reaching. The requirements differ depending upon whether the financial product promotes, among other characteristics, environmental or social characteristics, or a combination of those characteristics (Article 8-product),[113] or whether the financial product has sustainable investment as its objective (Article 9-product). If a product is characterised as an Article 8-product, then the disclosed information must include details on how those characteristics are met.[114] If, on the other hand, a product is characterised as an Article 9-product, then the information must include an explanation as to how the objective is to be attained.[115] If in the latter case an index has been designated as a reference benchmark, then the information must include an explanation as to why and how the designated index, aligned with that objective, differs from a broad market index. For both types of products, the SFDR states, that the ESAs shall develop draft regulatory technical standards to specify the details of the presentation and the content of the information to be disclosed.[116] As Article 8 and 9 are essential in understanding the disclosure duties of the financial market participant, it is to be expected that both provisions have been criticised, due to the uncertainties they hold. In a letter, dated 7 January 2021 to the European Commission, the ESAs stressed that it is unclear how the scope of Articles 8 and 9 is to be interpreted.[117] In July 2021, the Commission replied to the letter in the form of a Q & A.[118] Here some clarification was provided, as it was said that on the one hand, integration per se of sustainability risks, is not sufficient for Article 8 to apply. More has to be done in relation to the promotion of the defined characteristics. This includes direct or indirect claims, information, reporting, disclosure, impressions or general ambitions that the investments pursued, consider environmental or social characteristics in terms of investment policies, goals, targets or objectives. Such promotion may appear in pre-contractual and periodic documents or marketing communications, advertisements, product categorisation, description of investment strategies or asset allocation,

---

[112] ibid Art 7(1)(a). If the financial market participant does not consider the adverse impacts of investment decisions on sustainability factors, the financial market participant must instead include for each financial product a statement in the pre-contractual disclosure that this is the case and the reasons for this: *cf* Art 7(2).

[113] It is an additional requirement that the companies in which the investments are made follow good governance practices.

[114] Disclosure on Article 8 products must also comply with the Taxonomy Regulation, Art 6.

[115] Disclosure on Article 8 products must also comply with the Taxonomy Regulation, Art 5.

[116] Regulation 2019/2088 (n 7 above), Arts 8(3) and 9(5).

[117] See https://www.esma.europa.eu/document/letter-eu-commission-priority-issues-relating-sfdr-application.

[118] See https://www.esma.europa.eu/sites/default/files/library/sfdr_ec_qa_1313978.pdf.

information on the adherence to sustainability-related financial product standards and labels and use of product names or designations. Moreover, where a financial product complies with certain environmental, social or sustainability requirements or restrictions laid down by law, including international conventions or voluntary codes, and these characteristics are 'promoted' in the investment policy, the financial product is subject to Article 8. This includes subscription to the UNPRI, the SASB or other sustainability frameworks or standards.[119] The examples given are non-exhaustive and extremely broad.[120] Article 8-products are, on the other hand, demarcated by Article 9 where sustainable investment is the objective of the investment. In the Q & A, it is stated that although Article 9 financial products must primarily consist of sustainable investments,[121] they may also include investments for certain specific purposes, such as for hedging and liquidity purposes, once these are in line with the sustainable investment objective. The difference between sustainable investments that comply with the definition in Article 2(17) and investments that are in line with the sustainable investment objective is, however, unclear. For a product to qualify as an Article 9-product, the Danish FSA states that each individual investment must comply with Article 2(17), which appears to make the European Commission's distinction redundant. Finally, it is stated in the Q & A that should a product have an environmental objective but not meet the principle of 'do no significant harm',[122] as set out in Article 2(17) of the SFDR, it qualifies as an Article 8-product.[123]

The SFDR adds to the disclosure duties for financial market participants, including institutional investors and asset managers covered by the SRD II, which ultimately aim to safeguard the interests of the end investors, namely the beneficiaries. Such information is closely related to the institutional investors' fiduciary duties; it is for this reason that the SFDR also aids in the understanding of institutional investors' fiduciary duties, in particular, with regard to the relationship between sustainability issues and institutional investors' investment management practices. The need for clarification of the institutional investors' and asset managers' duties in relation to sustainability was discussed in the 2018 Action Plan (action 7). While the SFDR might add to the clarification, it arguably leaves certain questions unanswered.

IV. SUSTAINABLE FINANCE AND THE INTERESTS OF THE END INVESTOR

As discussed in section II.C.ii above, institutional investors' and asset managers' obligations to their beneficiaries and clients are partly defined by their fiduciary duties, which require them to act in the best interests of the beneficiaries and clients. However, the content of the fiduciary duty is not well-defined, in particular, in relation

---

[119] See also Maples Group, Newsletter 29 July 2021 https://maples.com/en/knowledge-centre/2021/7/european-commission-replies-on-sfdr-priority-issues.

[120] ibid.

[121] Sustainable investments are defined in Regulation 2019/2088 (n 7 above) Art 2(17).

[122] Regulation 2020/852 (n 78 above) Art 25, inserts Art 2a in the SFDR in relation to the 'do no significant harm' principle.

[123] See n 118 above, 7.

to sustainability-related issues. The 2018 Action Plan, Action 7 is built on similar observations.[124] Here, as an introduction, it is stated in section 3.2 that 'current EU rules on the duty of institutional investors and asset managers to consider sustainability factors and risks in the investment decision process are neither sufficiently clear nor consistent across sectors'.[125]

Current EU rules include, inter alia, the MiFID II,[126] and sector regulation is established by the UCITS Directive, the FAIF Directive, the IORP Directive and the Solvency II Directive.[127] Even though these directives also aim to ensure the end investors' or beneficiaries' interests and consider the risks in the investment process, in general, they do not address sustainability-related issues. The only exception is the IORP Directive, which mentions ESG considerations in relation to investment decisions.[128] However, the starting point here is that funds are not precluded from considering the impact of their investments on ESG factors, but there is no obligation to include ESG considerations. If such considerations are included, this will trigger several duties, including disclosure duties.[129]

On this basis, to standardise and streamline the duties of financial market participants and financial advisers in relation to sustainability, assistance by ESMA and EIOPA was requested to provide technical advice to supplement the initial package of proposals and to assist the European Commission in implementing potential amendments to or introducing delegated acts under the existing directives. Subsequently, in April 2019, the ESMA and EIOPA published their recommendations.[130] Next, the European Commission published draft proposals for amendments in six different fields for consultation[131] and in 2020 the European Commission published proposals for amendments of the delegated legislative acts relating to MiFID II, UCITS FAIF and Solvency II. The amended legislative acts were adopted in April 2021 and formulated on existing duties.[132] Thus, while the overall contours of the sustainability

---

[124] See also HLEG (n 59 above) section 3.
[125] COM(2018) 97 final (n 15 above). See also Regulation 2019/2088 (n 7 above) Recitals 5, 8–10.
[126] Directive 2014/65 (n 6 above).
[127] Directive 2009/65 (n 6 above); Directive 2011/61 (n 6 above); Directive 2016/2341 (n 6 above) and Directive 2009/138 (n 6 above) respectively. See in addition Regulation 2019/2088 (n 7 above) Recital 4.
[128] Directive 2016/2341 (n 6 above), Art 19, para 1(b); see also above section II.C.ii.
[129] cf in particular Arts 25 and 28.
[130] EIOPA's Technical Advice on the integration of sustainability risks and factors in the delegated acts under Solvency II and IDD, 30 April 2019, EIOPA-BoS-19/172, https://www.eiopa.europa.eu/document-library/advice/technical-advice-integration-of-sustainability-risks-and-factors-solvency-ii_en; ESMA's technical advice to the European Commission on integrating sustainability risks and factors in MiFID II, 30 April 2019, ESMA35-43-1737 https://www.esma.europa.eu/sites/default/files/library/esma35-43-1737_final_report_on_integrating_sustainability_risks_and_factors_in_the_mifid_ii.pdf and ESMA's technical advice to the European Commission on integrating sustainability risks and factors in the UCITS Directive and AIFMD, 30 April 2019, ESMA34-45-688 https://www.esma.europa.eu/sites/default/files/library/esma34-45-688_final_report_on_integrating_sustainability_risks_and_factors_in_the_ucits_directive_and_the_aifmd.pdf.
[131] For an overview, see Clifford Chance, June Newsletter 2020 https://www.cliffordchance.com/content/dam/cliffordchance/briefings/2020/06/sustainable-finance-european-commission-consults-on-how-insurers-and-asset-managers-integrate-sustainability-into-their-operations.pdf.
[132] Commission Delegated Regulation (EU) 2021/1253 of 21 April 2021 amending Delegated Regulation (EU) 2017/565 as regards the integration of sustainability factors, risks and preferences into certain organisational requirements and operating conditions for investment firms; Commission Delegated Directive (EU) 2021/1269 of 21 April 2021 amending Delegated Directive (EU) 2017/593 as regards the integration

duties are found in the SFDR, it is the amendments to the sector regulation that are important, so as to understand how the fiduciary duties are clarified for different institutional investors and asset managers.

In relation to MiFID II, it is inter alia a consequence of the amended Delegated Regulation[133] that investment firms, providing financial advice and portfolio management, must carry out a mandatory assessment of the sustainability preferences of their clients or potential clients.[134] These sustainability preferences shall be considered in the selection process of the financial instruments that are recommended to clients. Additionally, the management of sustainability risks must be an integrated element of the investment companies' organisational set-up; it must be an integrated component of the risk management system and the client's sustainability preferences must also be regarded when handling conflicts of interest.[135] Moreover, in relation to MiFID, the investment firms must take sustainability factors and sustainability related objectives into account in the product oversight and governance process.[136] In relation to UCITS, according to the amendment of the Delegated Directive, the management company, respectively the investment company, must integrate sustainability risk in the management of each of the UCITS funds. Moreover, management companies, when identifying the types of conflicts of interest that may damage the interests of a UCITS, must include conflicts of interest that may arise as a result of the integration of sustainability risks in their processes, systems and internal controls.[137] Finally, the management company must ensure that it has the necessary resources and expertise to be able to fulfil the Delegated Directive's requirements. Similar requirements are found in the amendment of the Delegated Regulation concerning AIFs.[138] Finally, as for insurance undertakings and insurance intermediaries manufacturing insurance products, they must consider sustainability factors in the product approval process of each insurance product, and in product governance in general. Moreover, insurance intermediaries and insurance undertakings that provide advice on insurance-based investment products should also ask questions to

---

of sustainability factors into the product governance obligations; Commission Delegated Regulation (EU) 2021/1255 of 21 April 2021 amending Delegated Regulation (EU) No 231/2013 as regards the sustainability risks and sustainability factors to be taken into account by AIFM; Commission Delegated Directive (EU) 2021/1270 of 21 April 2021 amending Directive 2010/43/EU as regards the sustainability risks and sustainability factors to be taken into account for UCITS; Commission Delegated Regulation (EU) 2021/1257 of 21 April 2021 amending Delegated Regulations (EU) 2017/2358 and (EU) 2017/2359 as regards the integration of sustainability factors, risks and preferences into the product oversight and governance requirements for insurance undertakings and insurance distributors and into the rules on conduct of business and investment advice for insurance-based investment products; Commission Delegated Regulation (EU) 2021/1256 of 21 April 2021 amending Delegated Regulation (EU) 2015/35 as regards the integration of sustainability risks in the governance of insurance and reinsurance undertakings (Solvency II). Some apply from 1 August 2022, while others apply from 2 August 2022.

[133] ibid Delegated Regulation 2021/1253/EU, Art 1(6).

[134] ibid. Sustainability preferences are included in the new Art 2, point (7).

[135] ibid Art 1(2)–(4).

[136] Delegated Directive 2021/1269 (n 132 above).

[137] Delegated Directive 2021/1270 (n 132 above). For an overview of the amendments, see Eversheds Sutherland, 'More ESG from the EU: updates to the UCITS and AIFMD Regimes' https://www.eversheds-sutherland.com/global/en/what/articles/index.page?ArticleID=en/Financial_services/EU-ESG_UCITS-AIFMD-updates_091020.

[138] Delegated Regulation 2021/1255 (n 132 above).

identify a customer's individual sustainability preferences, in order to include such preferences in the suitability statement that must be provided to the customer.[139]

Hence, there is a straight line between the disclosure duties, which originate in the SFDR, and the procedures and systems, which the sector regulation obliges financial market participants to establish, and which aim to ensure that sustainability considerations become an integrated element of the financial market participants' practices. For many institutional investors and asset managers, sustainability considerations are already an established element of their business model, but the amended requirements aim to ensure that procedures are followed in a more systematic and uniform way across the different sectors.

On this basis, it is noteworthy that the SFDR does not make reference to the prudent person principle,[140] which is an explicit component of the obligation that institutional investors, covered by the SRD II, owe to their beneficiaries. In particular, since 2016, it has been stated in the IORP Directive, Article 19(1)(b) that 'within the prudent person rule, Member States shall allow IORPs to take into account the potential long-term impact of investment decisions on environmental, social, and governance factors'.[141] Initially, the proposal for the Disclosure Regulation did include a provision in Article 10, according to which the European Commission was conferred the authority to adopt delegated acts, which should allow for a clarification of the prudent person principle mentioned in the IORP Directive.[142] It was stated that it was necessary to ensure consideration of environmental, social and governance risks, the integration of ESG factors in internal decision and risk management processes and to ensure means to equally safeguard consumer protection and a level playing field between IORPs and other financial market participants.[143] However, the proposed Article 10 was not part of the final text of the adopted SFDR and the relationship between the prudent person principle and ESG considerations is not mentioned directly in the SFDR's provisions. Thus, for IORPs, the duties in relation to sustainability are found in the IORP Directive and the general duties of SFDR. This includes the policy aims found in the preamble, inter alia Recital 12, which affirm that the SFDR 'maintains the requirements for financial market participants and financial advisers to act in the best interest of end investors, including but not limited to, the requirement of conducting adequate due diligence prior to making investments', provided for in sector regulation. Moreover, in Recital 12 it was highlighted that for the purpose of fulfilling their duties in relation to the SFDR, financial market participants and financial advisers:

> should integrate in their processes, including in their due diligence processes, and should assess on a continuous basis not only all relevant financial risks but also including all

---

[139] Delegated Regulation 2021/1257 (n 132 above); and Delegated Regulation 2021/1256 (n 132 above).

[140] Directive 2016/2341 (n 6 above) Art 19(1)(b), and Directive 2009/138, Art 132, require the encompassed institutional investors to invest according to the prudent person principle, see above section II.C.ii.

[141] Directive 2016/2341 (n 6 above) Art 19(1)(b) states that 'within the prudent person rule, Member States shall allow IORPs to take into account the potential long-term impact of investment decisions on environmental, social, and governance factors'.

[142] Proposal for a Regulation of the European Parliament and of the Council on disclosures relating to sustainable investments and sustainability risks and amending Directive (EU) 2016/2341, COM(2018) 354 final.

[143] ibid sections 2 and 5.

relevant sustainability risks that might have a relevant material negative impact on the financial return of an investment or advice.

However, clarification of the IORPs' sustainability duties is still an issue and the European Commission's Strategy for Financing the Transition to a Sustainable Economy includes an Action 4, according to which the Commission will 'ask EIOPA to assess the need to review the fiduciary duties of pension funds and investors to reflect sustainability impacts as part of investment decision making processes, including stewardship and engagement activities by 2022'.[144] Moreover, Solvency II mentions the prudent person principle. Here, the amendment of the Delegated Regulation inserts Article 275a, which refers to Article 132, and according to which the sustainability risk must be integrated in the prudent person principle.[145] This includes taking account of the potential long-term impact of the investment strategy and decisions on sustainability factors and, where relevant, that strategy and those decisions on sustainability factors reflecting the sustainability preferences of its customers, which are taken into account in the product approval process.

Arguably, understanding of the financial market participants' fiduciary duties has been clarified with the SFDR and later with the adoption of the delegated acts. The underlying duties of loyalty and prudence have to some extent been standardised across the different market participants in relation to inter alia inclusion of sustainability risks, sustainability considerations in investment decision-making, inclusion of clients' sustainability preferences, disclosure and handling of conflicts of interest. However, uncertainty relating to the financial market participants' overall obligation to act in the end investors' financial interests in the best possible way, still exist. Although some duties apply to all financial market participants and advisers, inter alia SFDR, Articles 3 and 5, others depend upon whether the financial market participants and advisers consider the principal adverse impacts of investment decisions on sustainability factors/consider such principal adverse impacts in their advice; others depend upon whether the financial products offered, either promote, among other characteristics, environmental or social characteristics or have sustainable investment as their objective. Thus, the sustainable finance agenda aims to facilitate a transition towards a more sustainable and resilient economy. This is an ambition and there is no legal requirement to invest sustainably. Therefore, investors are not obliged to invest in assets that fall within the taxonomy, but investment decisions continue to be based on an assessment of the individual investment's potential.[146] Consequently, there may be situations in which the fiduciary duty hinders sustainable investments, because of the duty to act in the best (financial) interests of the beneficiaries. For instance, in Denmark,[147] the traditional

---

[144] The European Commission 'Strategy for Financing the Transition to a Sustainable Economy' (Communication) 14, COM(2021) 390 final.

[145] Delegated Regulation 2021/1256 (n 132 above).

[146] See also Pensions Europe, *Position Paper on Legislative Package on Sustainable Finance* (28 November 2018) 5, https://www.pensionseurope.eu/system/files/Sustainable%20Finance%20Package%20position%20paper.pdf.

[147] See also HS Birkmose, 'Skærpede forventninger til de institutionelle investorers rolle i corporate governance. Perspektiver og udfordringer' (2020) 2/3 *Nordisk Tidsskrift for Selskabsret* 112 ff and A Horvathova et al, 'Occupational Pension Funds (IORPs) & Sustainability: What Does the Prudent Person Principle Say' (2017) 28 *Nordic Journal of Commercial Law* 44–45.

understanding of the prudent person principle has been that investments which do not aim for the greatest possible return or the managers of which know with great certainty that the largest possible return is unlikely, are against regulations, as stipulated in particular, in the Financial Business Act § 158.[148] These trade-offs may also have short-term versus long-term implications that result in sub-optimal investment decisions in relation to the sustainable finance agenda.

Despite the lack of clarity that still exists in relation to institutional investors' and asset managers' fiduciary duties, the investment management side of institutional investors' and asset managers' practice has been subject to fundamental changes, because of the EU sustainable finance agenda. The adoption of the Taxonomy Regulation and, in particular, the SFDR, has clarified institutional investors' and asset managers' duties in relation to sustainability. Sustainability has become part of their core duties, as sustainability considerations are now defined by specific legal duties. Still, the question of whether this development on the investment management side affects the duties which were imposed on institutional investors by the SRD II and the engagement agenda, is largely left unanswered.

V. SUSTAINABLE FINANCE AND THE CONNECTION WITH SRD II

In the 2021 Strategy for Financing the Transition to a Sustainable Economy,[149] the Commission states that it will explore how the Shareholder Rights Directive II may better reflect EU sustainability goals and align with global best practices in stewardship guidelines. It suggests that more needs to be done to link the investment management side and the governance side. Still, some progress may have been made with the sustainable finance agenda.

As a starting point, there is no doubt that the duties relating to Article 3h (*cf* section IV above), are affected by the sustainability agenda. This link was stressed by the European Commission in the proposal for the SFDR, where it was stated that the existing disclosure requirements in SRD II entail a lack of transparency regarding the way in which institutional investors, asset managers and financial advisers consider sustainability risks in their investment decision making or advisory processes. As a result, their clients do not receive the complete set of information that they need to inform their investment decisions or recommendations.[150] Arguably, one would expect this to be a reference to Article 3h, which only requires institutional investors to disclose the main elements of their equity investment strategy; undoubtedly the SFDR will supplement Article 3h with details on the investment strategy in relation to sustainability considerations. Interestingly, however, in the proposal for the SFDR, this lack of transparency is linked to institutional investors' engagement duties, which presumably is a reference to Article 3g. Arguably, the connection made here could stress the link between the investment management side and the

---

[148] Consolidating Act no 174 of 31 January 2017, https://www.dfsa.dk/Rules-and-Practice/Acts.
[149] COM(2021) 390 final (n 94 above).
[150] COM(2018) 354 final (n 142 above).

governance side and it could also support the argument that the SRD II mainly aims to support the end investors' investment decisions.

The duty in SFDR Article 4, for financial market participants to disclose on their website whether they consider the principal adverse impacts (PAI) of its investment decisions on sustainability factors, also brings the investment side and the governance side together.[151] Financial market participants must disclose whether or not they consider sustainability factors, as defined in Article 2(24), before making investment decisions. If they do, they must disclose a statement on due diligence processes, including information about their procedures for considering the principal adverse impacts. However, the due diligence processes must also include information on whether the financial market participants monitor and mitigate relevant impacts. Specifically, according to the SFDR, Article 4, paragraph 2(c), financial market participants must include a brief summary of their engagement policy in accordance with Article 3g of the SRD II, where applicable, given they consider the principal adverse impacts of investment decisions on sustainability factors in the information they publish on their website. The added value of this requirement seems somewhat unclear, as institutional investors must disclose their engagement policy in full on their website or publish a clear and reasoned explanation as to why they have chosen not to comply (*cf* the SRD II, Article 3g, paragraph 2). Thus, it is unclear how adding a requirement to publish a brief summary of the same policy contributes to informing end investors. Some guidance may be found in the SFDR, Recital 18, which states that the information on procedures for considering the principal adverse impacts might describe how financial market participants discharge their sustainability-related stewardship responsibilities or other shareholder engagements. Therefore, it may be agued that the summary must be designed to support end investors' understanding of how the specific engagement practices enable the institutional investors to consider the principal adverse impacts of their investment decisions.

Moreover, the link made in the SFDR between investment and engagement also supports the argument that to fulfil the overarching aim of securing sustainable finance, it is not enough that sustainability considerations become an integrated part of investment decisions and that institutional investors and asset managers are transparent regarding this. Institutional investors and asset managers must also disclose information on their engagement with investee companies for end investors to assess and compare sustainability considerations in relation to investment decisions and sustainability considerations with regard to engagement. Only then can end investors make fully informed investment decisions. Moreover, one may also argue that a natural element of institutional investors' fiduciary duty is to ensure that sustainability considerations are an integrated component of engagement with investee companies, in particular, if institutional investors consider the principal adverse impacts of investment decisions on sustainability factors or offer financial products within the taxonomy.[152] Still, it is probably too far-reaching to conclude that engagement

---

[151] The provision applies under a proportionality principle and is also subject to the comply-or-explain-principle.
[152] COM(2021) 390 final (n 94 above) 15.

by the institutional investors is required for them to fulfil their sustainability disclosure duties, even in relation to Article 8 and 9 products. Rather, it can be argued that in particular in relation to these investments, institutional investors must consider whether engagement is necessary to become satisfied that the investments meet the taxonomy characteristics established by the SFDR. It may also be argued that there is a preference for engagement, as engagement gives insights on a continuous basis, which otherwise may be hard to obtain. It may also be argued that in general, the sustainable finance agenda will have a much larger impact on the institutional investors' focus on ESG and sustainability issues than the SDR II has. This is particularly the case in relation to the investment management side, where Article 3h leaves it to institutional investors to decide on the substance of the investment strategy, but it may also be the case in relation to the governance side, as the reference in Article 3g to ESG and non-financial performance is unclear. Moreover, it may also be important that the development of the institutional investors' sustainability duties takes place in a context where it belongs, rather than in a corporate governance context, where the relationship between institutional investors and their beneficiaries does not belong – at least not in a traditional perspective. Still, the focus on sustainability leaves a role for the SRD II to play as a general corporate governance mechanism. Moreover, the sustainable finance agenda does not success in bridging the gap between the investment management side and the governance side, which is caused by the uncertainty that remains in relation to institutional investors' fiduciary duties. This calls for further research.

VI. CONCLUDING REMARKS

Institutional investors and asset managers have been placed at centre stage in the European sustainable finance agenda. In their capacity as financial intermediaries, they are able to channel funds towards sustainable investments and support the EU's grand policy ambitions of an environmentally and socially sustainable economic system. The taxonomy regulation and, in particular, the SFDR, impose duties on institutional investors and asset managers in relation to the integration of sustainability risks, the consideration of adverse sustainability impacts, the promotion of environmental or social characteristics and sustainable investment. Consequently, financial market participants and financial advisers must make pre-contractual and ongoing disclosures to end investors, when acting on behalf of those end investors.

The intermediary role of institutional investors and asset managers is evident in the sustainable finance agenda, but much less so in the engagement agenda expressed by the SRD II. Nevertheless, this chapter has argued that the governance side of institutional investors' practice, represented by Article 3g of SRD II, must be viewed as an integrated element of the institutional investors' and asset managers' investment management side, represented by Article 3h of SRD II. However, to fully understand the investment management side, sector regulation must be consulted. The SFDR brings about substantial change to the relevant directives, first, in the form of a systematic and harmonised approach to sustainability duties across different sectors, and secondly in the development of institutional investors' fiduciary duties.

Although it has become clear that sustainability and fiduciary duties are not opposites, the relationship between the two has not been fully clarified.

Thus, the chapter concludes that such uncertainty may have implications for the sustainable finance agenda, as well as for the engagement agenda, and that uncertainty on the investment management side may have spill-over effects on the governance side, due to the link between Articles 3g and 3h. Therefore, the European Commission's intention to explore how the SRD II may better reflect sustainability seems timely and relevant, to ensure the required development of institutional investors' and asset managers' engagement within their fiduciary duties.

4

Sustainable Investment and Asset Management: From Resistance to Retooling

VIRGINIA HARPER HO

I. INTRODUCTION

ROUND THE WORLD, market demand is rising for investment products and practices that take 'environmental, social, and governance' (ESG) factors into account, challenging asset managers and capital markets in new ways. These trends are also motivated by government and private sector commitments to promote a sustainable finance transition so that markets can more accurately price ESG risks, and so that capital can be redirected from less sustainable uses and toward sustainable development goals.[1] Some of these efforts go beyond attention to the economic impacts of ESG risk on companies and investors and seek to harness shareholder power to drive corporate behaviour in ways that will reduce environmental impacts and other externalities. All of these factors are fueling growing demand for better standardisation of how ESG and sustainability concepts are defined across investment chains and for ESG integration across asset classes and across markets. There are also growing expectations that large investors will play a greater monitoring role in corporate governance around climate risk and other ESG concerns.

In this transition, asset managers have a key role to play. They are intermediaries with fiduciary obligations to investors, and many of their clients are themselves fiduciaries. They are also competitors in the market for financial products and services, as well as shareholders of the public and private companies that drive economies around the world. Many are actively engaged in shaping the future of finance and financial regulation in industry working groups and other fora. This volume is itself a testament to the fact that the importance of ESG considerations to asset managers and their clients has increased rapidly over the past decade.

---

[1] See eg Commission, 'Action Plan: Financing Sustainable Growth' (Communication) COM (2018) 97 final. On regulatory goals and standards of relevance to asset managers, see IOSCO, 'Recommendations on Sustainability-Related Practices, Policies, Procedures and Disclosure in Asset Management' FR08/21 (November 2021).

This chapter begins by outlining why sustainability issues are increasingly relevant to mainstream asset owners and asset managers. It then explores the evolving regulatory landscape for sustainable investment in the US, focusing on the degree to which it supports or facilitates ESG integration into investment management and the exercise of shareholder governance rights. As this discussion shows, the sustainable finance landscape in the US is still defined largely by private standard setters and service providers and by the financial sector itself. This market-driven path parts course from the more regulatory approach that the EU, the UK, and many other capital markets featured in this volume are taking.

In fact, as this chapter explores, some aspects of the US regulatory framework constrain the expansion of ESG integration in investment analysis, fund management, and shareholder activism, amplifying the economic disincentives to activism for many investors and fund managers. These limits can be traced to regulatory concerns about 'mission creep' and scepticism about the financial materiality of ESG and climate risk to investors.[2] However, the Biden administration has included the financial sector in its climate change response,[3] and as investors' expectations change and sustainable finance regulation moves forward elsewhere, the regulatory context of sustainable finance in the US is also shifting from resistance to a modest 'retooling'. These developments may more strongly support asset manager and institutional investors' ability to take account of ESG in investment, proxy voting, and engagement decisions. At the same time, asset managers still face key challenges in implementing ESG-sensitive investment and engagement strategies in a manner that aligns with their fiduciary duties.

II. THE MAINSTREAMING OF SUSTAINABLE INVESTMENT

In the US, ESG-oriented investment strategies have entered the mainstream, and ESG-themed investment products have proliferated in recent years.[4] In fact, by some measures, nearly half of all institutional investors in the US and an even higher percentage of financial analysts currently include ESG factors in investment decision-making.[5] Market demand for 'sustainable' investment products and services has also

---

[2] Regulatory resistance by the US Securities and Exchange Commission (SEC) has defined a number of past ESG-related rulemaking and policy initiatives: C Williams and D Nagy, 'ESG and Climate Change Blind Spots: Turning the Corner on SEC Disclosure' (2021) 99 *Texas Law Review* 1453.

[3] Executive Order on Climate-Related Financial Risk (20 May 2021), https://www.whitehouse.gov/briefing-room/presidential-actions/2021/05/20/executive-order-on-climate-related-financial-risk/ (calling for a 'comprehensive, Government-wide strategy' on the 'measurement, assessment, mitigation, and disclosure of climate-related financial risk to [the federal government]' and an assessment of the capital investment required to limit global temperature rise to 1.5°C, achieve net-zero greenhouse gas emissions by 2050, and reach climate adaptation goals); 'Fact Sheet: Biden Administration Roadmap to Build an Economy Resilient to Climate Change Impacts' (15 October 2021), https://www.whitehouse.gov/briefing-room/statements-releases/2021/10/15/fact-sheet-biden-administration-roadmap-to-build-an-economy-resilient-to-climate-change-impacts/.

[4] See eg J Hale, 'Sustainable Funds Landscape – Highlights and Observations' (*Morningstar*, 18 February 2022), https://www.morningstar.com/articles/1080300/sustainable-funds-landscape-highlights-and-observations.

[5] 'Callan Survey Finds Nearly 50% of Respondents Incorporate ESG, Highest Level Ever', https://www.callan.com/blog-archive/2021-esg-survey/ (reporting results of a 2021 survey of 114 institutional investors).

been fuelled by the exponential growth of 'sustainable, responsible, and impact' (SRI) funds whose investment objectives respond to investors' diverse ethical or social preferences.[6] All of these trends are being pushed forward from many directions, reflecting a diversity of approaches to ESG investment.

A. 'Values' Investing and Shareholder Expectations

The growing number of SRI or 'values' investors includes those who prioritise a social, ethical, sustainability or impact objective, as well as those with a dual focus that incorporates ESG factors while prioritising financial return. Major index funds are also responding to a generational shift that is driving demand for ESG investment options from millennial employees and other investors, raising expectations that even passively managed funds will use their power to bring about change in corporate practice.[7] According to the Certified Financial Analysts' (CFA) Institute, the leading industry organisation for financial analysts, '73 percent of institutional investors and 67 percent of retail investors would be willing to give up some [financial] return' in order to meet their values goals.[8] The COVID-19 pandemic has also brought to light previously overlooked areas of workforce-related risk and other 'human capital management' considerations that are attracting greater investor attention to these ESG dimensions.[9]

At the same time, sustainable investments adopt a range of different investment strategies that are no longer limited to negative screening of undesirable sectors. Instead, they include positive screening or 'best-in-class' strategies that identify companies in each sector that outperform peers on identified ESG measures within a fully diversified portfolio, as well as ESG integration, voting and stewardship, and thematic strategies.[10] Demand for climate- and sustainability-oriented investment products is expected to drive further demand for better ESG metrics, investment benchmarks, and sustainability reporting standards.

Asset managers are also under scrutiny from their own shareholders and clients to take sustainability issues seriously in their investment and voting policies, and

---

According to another survey of 2,800 practitioner members of the Certified Financial Analysts (CFA) Institute in 2020, over 70% report that they consider environmental factors in investing; 65% reported considering social factors: CFA Institute, 'Future of Sustainability in Investment Management' (2021), https://www.cfainstitute.org/-/media/documents/survey/future-of-sustainability.ashx 13.

[6] As of 2020, SRI investments accounted for US$ 17 trillion or over one-third of all assets under management in the United States, representing a four-fold increase since 2015: US SIF, 'Report on US Sustainable and Impact Investing Trends' (2020), https://www.ussif.org/trends.

[7] M Barzuza et al, 'Shareholder Value(s): Index Fund ESG Activism and the New Millennial Corporate Governance' (2020) 93 *Southern California Law Review* 1243.

[8] CFA Institute (n 5 above) 4.

[9] M Souders, 'Survey Analysis: ESG Investing Pre- and Post-Pandemic' (2020) 4–6, https://www.issgovernance.com/file/publications/ISS-ESG-Investing-Survey-Analysis.pdf (reporting results of a broad survey of asset managers based primarily in North America and Europe).

[10] CFA Institute (n 5 above) 4 (reporting that a majority of survey respondents use positive screening or ESG integration, with 48% using ESG exclusionary screening).

in their engagement with companies.[11] In fact, BlackRock and Vanguard began to revisit their voting practices of consistently voting with management on ESG resolutions only after they came under pressure from key clients and when SRI activist funds that were among their own shareholders filed shareholder proposals calling on them to do so.[12] Asset managers' public visibility, changing client expectations, and grassroots activism by investment managers' own shareholders are raising the bar for how asset managers approach ESG issues.

B. ESG and Systematic Risk

For mainstream investors and asset managers, the primary justifications for incorporating ESG factors into investment analysis have to do with their potential impact on portfolio-level risk-adjusted returns and specifically on the relationship between ESG factors and risk. A sizeable body of academic work has found nonnegative relationships between ESG factors and systematic risk and some evidence of the financial materiality of different ESG factors to portfolio risk-adjusted returns, although the magnitude of the observed effects vary.[13] These findings are also less consistent for studies focusing on the portfolio level than on firm-level financial performance.[14] However, studies have also found that ESG factors have a moderating 'insurance-like' effect on portfolio risk.[15] Interpreting the empirical evidence in the aggregate

---

[11] According to a 2020 survey by Institutional Shareholder Services, over 50% of asset managers surveyed indicated that their main driver for undertaking ESG investing was client or beneficiary demand: Souders (n 9 above) 11.

[12] See eg Attracta Mooney, 'BlackRock's Environmental Voting Record Attacked' (*Financial Times*, 26 November 2016) (reporting on demands by Walden Asset Management and others); R Kerber and T McLaughlin, 'Biggest US Index Funds Oppose Most Climate Proposals in Shareholder Votes' (*Reuters*, 8 October 2019). See also Attracta Mooney, 'BlackRock Vows to Back More Shareholder Votes on Climate Change' (*Financial Times*, 9 December 2020) (noting BlackRock's revision of its policies after pressure around its voting record).

[13] See U Atz et al, 'Does Sustainability Generate Better Financial Performance? Review, Meta-analysis, and Propositions' (2022) *Journal of Sustainable Finance & Investment* (surveying 24 meta-studies and over 1,000 peer-reviewed studies since 2015). This study finds evidence of a 'robust and positive association between sustainability and financial performance at the firm level' and that ESG integration has positive risk-mitigating effects at the portfolio level: ibid. However, the authors did not identify significant differences in the performance of ESG-oriented and traditional portfolios, findings which they attribute to inadequate investor access to ESG data and the fact that many of the studies on portfolio effects conflate different investment strategies: ibid 4–5, 17–19. See also S Gillan et al, 'Firms and Social Responsibility: A Review of ESG and CSR Research in Corporate Finance' (2021) 66 *Journal of Corporate Finance* 929 (reviewing studies on ESG and corporate responsibility with respect to various firm characteristics and performance measures).

[14] Atz et al (n 13 above) 4–5, 17–19. See also J-C Plagge and D Grim, 'Have Investors Paid a Performance Price? Examining the Behavior of ESG Equity Funds' (2020) 46 *Journal of Portfolio Management* 123 (testing equity fund performance for the 2004–2018 period); G Freide et al, 'ESG and Financial Performance: Aggregated Evidence From More Than 2000 Empirical Studies' (2015) 5 *Journal of Sustainable Finance & Investment* 210, 220–21, 225–26 (aggregating the results of nearly 2,200 individual studies and concluding that the majority find positive correlations between corporate financial and ESG performance but that portfolio-level studies identify more mixed results).

[15] Atz et al (n 13 above) 20–22 (finding support for this effect across a broad dataset of studies since 2015). See also P Bolton and M Kacperczyk, 'Do Investors Care about Carbon Risk?' (2021) 142 *Journal of Financial Economics* 487 (finding a risk premium related to carbon emissions risk); R Albuquerque et al,

is complicated by the fact that some studies include SRI investments, which may sacrifice risk-adjusted returns, depending on their strategy.

The growing literature on common ownership also observes that highly diversified investors are essentially exposed to systematic risk across the entire market portfolio, which includes environmental and social risks that affect all firms or an entire sector.[16] Costs that one firm externalises through poor ESG practices may therefore fall on other portfolio companies, and some ESG risks may have an aggregate effect on portfolio risk-adjusted returns even if the associated effects for each portfolio firm are small. Evidence that firms have often failed to adequately monitor or report these risks has raised concerns that sectoral or even economy-wide 'climate blindness' or 'ESG myopia' may be amplifying investors' ESG risk exposure, and has motivated several of the largest asset managers to indicate in their voting and engagement policies that they will advocate for better corporate reporting of these risks.[17]

C. Chasing Alpha

Although the empirical evidence does not show a consistent relationship between ESG factors and portfolio outperformance, ESG information asymmetries may also create unique opportunities for some investment managers to undertake more comprehensive ESG analysis in order to outperform the market.[18] Climate change in particular is creating new business and investment opportunities as different sectors move forward in a post-carbon transition.[19] And while some empirical studies find evidence that certain ESG and climate risks are priced in the market,[20] the limitations

'Resiliency of Environmental and Social Stocks: An Analysis of the Exogenous COVID-19 Market Crash' (2020) 9(3) *Review of Corporate Finance Studies* 593. The implications of these findings for investors are nuanced, since lower volatility is typically associated with lower investment returns.

[16] M Condon, 'Externalities and the Common Owner' (2020) 95 *Washington University Law Review* 1; J Coffee Jr, 'The Future of Disclosure: ESG, Common Ownership, and Systematic Risk' (2021) *Columbia Business Law Review* 602; J Gordon, 'Systematic Stewardship' (2022) *Journal of Corporation Law* (forthcoming).

[17] The 2017 report of the Financial Stability Board's Task Force on Climate-Related Financial Disclosure (TCFD) raised concerns about the low awareness among financial institutions of the *financial* effects of climate change and the lack of data to help them better evaluate it: TCFD, 'Final Report: Recommendations of the Task Force on Climate-related Financial Disclosures' (2017) 1–22, https://www.fsb.org/wp-content/uploads/P290617-5.pdf; see also M Condon 'Market Myopia's Climate Bubble' (2022) *Utah Law Review* 63.

[18] See nn 13–16 above and sources cited therein.

[19] Early estimates for the world's largest companies were that climate-related business opportunities would reach around US$2 trillion, produced at estimated costs to exploit them of approximately US$300 billion: CDP, 'World's Biggest Companies Face $1 trillion in Climate Change Risks' (4 June 2019), https://www.cdp.net/en/articles/media/worlds-biggest-companies-face-1-trillion-in-climate-change-risks. The same report estimated climate-related risks to separately impose about US$1 trillion in costs on these leading companies: ibid.

[20] Studies indicating that markets are beginning to price climate risk include: Bolton and Kacperczyk (n 15 above) (finding a risk premium related to carbon emissions risk); S Giglio et al, 'Climate Finance' (2021) 13 *Annual Review of Financial Economics* 15 (surveying the literature on climate risk and physical and financial assets); R Balvers et al, 'Temperature Shocks and the Cost of Equity Capital: Implications for Climate Change Perception' (2017) 77 *Journal of Banking and Finance* 18 (finding that temperature shocks increase the cost of equity capital).

of the underlying data suggest continued market mispricing that some investors may be able to exploit.[21] At the same time, empirical studies of the link between corporate governance and investor returns in earlier periods suggest that opportunities to generate *alpha* through ESG arbitrage are likely to decline as markets are able to more accurately price these factors over time and as underlying corporate practice among investee companies becomes more homogeneous.[22]

D. Systemic Risk Effects

The systemic risk associated with climate change is also driving more institutional investors and asset managers to incorporate ESG factors into investment analysis, voting policies, and direct engagement with portfolio firms. Financial regulators have emphasised the materiality of climate risk to financial institutions and have identified a range of associated physical and transition risks that are expected to affect different sectors and asset classes differently but that cannot be mitigated through diversification. Studies by the G20 Financial Stability Board's Task Force on Climate-Related Financial Disclosure (TCFD), as well as the US Commodity Futures Trading Commission (CFTC) and the Financial Stability Oversight Council (FSOC) explain further that financial institutions and markets may experience significant and unpredictable effects if major climate risk events materialise or if companies across the economy fail to effectively manage a post-carbon transition.[23] Regulators outside the US have already responded to the threat of climate change by requiring asset managers to measure and disclose their own climate-related risks and to ensure that the companies they invest in do the same.

Identifying, disclosing, and mitigating climate-related financial risk is therefore a top priority for the entire financial sector and one that requires new capacities to measure climate risk across investment chains. At the same time, data limitations continue to impede assessment of the nature, scale, and correlation of these risks.[24]

---

[21] Commodity Futures Trading Commission (CFTC) 'Managing Climate Risk in the US Financial System' (2020) 59–60, 79, https://www.cftc.gov/ (emphasising the lack of climate risk data and raising concerns about mispricing).

[22] Lucian Bebchuk and colleagues have tested the link between the corporate governance index developed by Gompers and others and have found that above-market returns for companies with better corporate governance disappeared over time: L Bebchuk et al, 'Learning and the Disappearing Association Between Governance and Returns' (2013) 108(2) *Journal of Financial Economics* 323 (attributing this result in part to market participants' improved ability to identify and understand good governance indicators).

[23] TCFD (n 17 above); CFTC (n 21 above) 88–92; FSOC (US), 'Report on Climate-related Financial Risk' (October 2021), https://home.treasury.gov/system/files/261/FSOC-Climate-Report.pdf; International Organization of Securities Commissions (IOSCO), 'Mitigating Systemic Risk: A Role for Securities Regulators' (2011) 19–20, https://www.iosco.org/research/pdf/publications/Discussion%20Paper%20on%20Systemic%20Risk.pdf.

[24] Financial Stability Board, 'The Availability of Data with Which to Monitor and Assess Climate-related Risks to Financial Stability' (2021) 4 and table 1, 8, 34, https://www.fsb.org/2021/07/the-availability-of-data-with-which-to-monitor-and-assess-climate-related-risks-to-financial-stability/ (identifying data gaps); Condon (n 17 above) 78–104 (identifying lack of asset-level data, reliance on outdated risk assessment models, and climate-blind risk management practices as barriers to accurate climate risk assessments at the firm level).

It is also unclear at present how sustainability risks should be allocated across the investment chain and who should ultimately bear the financial risk and oversight responsibility with respect to complex financial products whose value and risk profile are impacted by climate change and other ESG risk factors.

III. THE EVOLVING ESG REGULATORY LANDSCAPE IN THE UNITED STATES

As the previous discussion shows, asset managers and their clients have diverse reasons to consider sustainability or ESG factors when setting and implementing investment policies, and when deciding to exercise voting rights or engage directly with portfolio companies. These decisions are of course informed by relevant regulatory requirements and are subject to the exercise of fiduciary duties. In this regard, in contrast to many other jurisdictions, the key question for institutional investors and asset managers in the US is generally not whether they are *required* to undertake ESG investment or engagement strategies but whether they are *permitted* to do so. A related question, explored later in this chapter, is how fiduciaries should exercise such discretion consistent with their fiduciary duties.

The following discussion focuses on the primary authorities governing the fiduciary duties of asset managers and their clients in the US – the Investment Advisers Act of 1940 (the '40 Act), which is interpreted and enforced by the Securities and Exchange Commission (SEC),[25] and the Employee Retirement and Income Security Act of 1974 (ERISA), which governs private pension plans and is interpreted and enforced in part by the Department of Labor (DOL).[26] The Investment Company Act of 1940 (the ICA), which governs mutual funds, also imposes requirements regarding proxy voting, disclosure, and fiduciary duty.[27]

Other institutional investors such as insurance companies and public pension funds are subject to different federal and state regulatory regimes, and this heterogeneity may also affect how willing they are to take on a 'stewardship' role or to engage in activism around ESG issues.[28] For example, state law governs state pension

---

[25] Investment Advisers Act of 1940, 15 USC 80b ff (the '40 Act). The '40 Act does not apply to banks, bank holding companies, or broker-dealers, which are separately regulated, nor does it apply to smaller advisers and advisers to hedge funds, venture capital funds, and other private funds, which are regulated under state law: SEC (US), 'Regulation of Investment Advisers by the US Securities and Exchange Commission' (2013) 4–5, 8–9, 14–17, 22–23, https://www.sec.gov/about/offices/oia/oia_investman/rplaze-042012.pdf (SEC 2013 Investment Adviser Regulation Report). Non-US advisers are not generally exempt from registration under the '40 Act: ibid 7–8, 12–13 (discussing exemptions for certain foreign private advisers). This chapter also does not address circumstances under which foreign investors or asset managers may be subject to US regulation.

[26] Employee Retirement Income Security Act of 1974 (ERISA) Pub L No 93-406, 88 Stat 829 (codified as amended at 29 USC ss 1001–1461 and in scattered sections of 5, 18, and 26 USC).

[27] 15 USC 80a-1 ff.

[28] A discussion of these rules is beyond the scope of this chapter. According to a recent study by Dasgupta and others, equity ownership in the US is concentrated among institutional investors, namely 'mutual funds (20.8%), exchange traded funds (ETFs) (6.6%), public pension funds (5.3%), and private pension funds (5.4%)': A Dasgupta et al, 'Institutional Investors and Corporate Governance' (2021) 12(4) *Foundations and Trends in Finance* 276. Foreign institutional investors hold an additional 16.4%, and insurance companies, hedge funds, and financial institutions' proprietary funds make up the remainder: ibid 4 and table 1.

funds and may impose obligations on investment advisers that differ from the federal requirements enforced by the SEC.[29] In addition, the voting and information rights of shareholders, and their right to sue for breach of corporate director and officer fiduciary duties, are determined for US companies under the corporate law of their state of incorporation, while the federal securities laws govern proxy voting and information disclosure requirements for public companies, including publicly traded financial institutions.[30] Federal law also governs reporting requirements for blockholders and corporate insiders, discussed below, that may also affect shareholder activism around governance or sustainability concerns. Other relevant sources include the many voluntary standards, codes, and principles endorsed by asset managers and financial institutions that relate to the exercise of shareholder rights or that commit them to greater transparency around ESG investment.

A. Asset Manager Fiduciary Duties

A basic starting point for understanding the scope of investment managers' responsibilities with respect to ESG matters is the fiduciary duties financial intermediaries owe to their clients.[31] The fiduciary duties institutional investors owe to fund beneficiaries are also equally important, as these inform investment policies, the oversight that institutional investors must exercise when delegating authority to asset managers, and the extent to which they may take account of ESG factors within the scope of their fiduciary role.

i. Investment Advisers Act of 1940 and the Investment Company Act of 1940

Asset managers' fiduciary duties and many of the rules governing their reporting obligations are governed by the '40 Act, although the ICA also requires mutual funds and other registered investment companies to provide complete and accurate information to investors.[32] The '40 Act does not contain any specific provisions regarding fiduciary duties, but both the common law and the SEC's regulatory guidance have interpreted it as establishing fiduciary duties of care and loyalty of investment

---

[29] SEC (US), 'Commission Interpretation Regarding Standard of Conduct for Investment Advisers' 84 Fed Reg 33669 (12 July 2019) (regarding the standard of conduct for investment advisers under the Investment Advisers Act of 1940, 15 USC 80b and following) (SEC 2019 Standard of Conduct Guidance).

[30] For non-corporate entities, other bodies of law apply under state law and as a matter of contract. For example, the fiduciary duties and voting rights for funds organised as partnerships are subject to the terms of the partnership agreement.

[31] For example, investor fiduciary duties may necessitate consideration of systemic risk. See ICGN, 'ICGN Guidance on Investor Fiduciary Duties' (2018), https://www.icgn.org/policy/icgn-guidance.

[32] The ICA imposes additional reporting and fiduciary obligations on investment advisers with respect to compensation paid by a mutual fund: section 36(b), 15 USC s 80a-35(b). US state law also imposes general fiduciary duties on investment advisers, including as a matter of trust law and the law of agency: A Laby, 'Fiduciary Principles in Investment Advice' in E Criddle et al (eds), *The Oxford Handbook of Fiduciary Law* (Oxford University Press, 2019) 152–54.

advisers toward their clients.[33] These duties extend to all investment activities and are enforced under the general anti-fraud prohibitions of section 206 of the '40 Act, which forbid fraud, self-dealing, deception and manipulation.[34] In addition, compliance rules under the '40 Act and the ICA require registered investment advisers and certain funds, respectively, to implement compliance procedures and policies to ensure that portfolio management is consistent with the information provided to investors, clients, and regulators about investment objectives and portfolio management processes.[35]

The duty of loyalty requires that 'an adviser not subordinate its clients' interests to its own' and that advisers disclose any conflicts of interests to the client.[36] This duty may be of relevance if an adviser and a client have differing preferences with respect to investment time horizons or the objectives of particular ESG-oriented investments.

Fiduciary duties also require investment advisers who have been given authority to vote client proxies to do so in the client's best interest.[37] Part of the duty of loyalty includes an obligation of investment advisers to implement voting policies with regard to their exercise of proxy voting authority and to describe these voting policies and procedures to clients.[38] Investment advisers must also provide 'full and fair' disclosure of any 'material facts' and conflicts of interest', and must make available to clients upon request records of how proxies were voted.[39]

The duty of care requires investment advisers to provide only 'suitable' investment advice in the best interest of the client based on the client's objectives and to have a 'reasonable' basis for their recommendations.[40] The SEC has emphasised that in order to do so, advisers must make a reasonable inquiry into the client's situation, experience, and objectives.[41] Some commentators have argued further that investment advisers should also be subject to a positive duty to consider funds' ESG performance if those considerations are important to the ultimate beneficial owners of an institutional client, but no such requirements exist at present unless the institutional client

---

[33] SEC 2019 Standard of Conduct Guidance (n 29 above) 33669 (citing case law under section 206 of the '40 Act). Given space limitations, this chapter does not address the separate standard of conduct that broker-dealers owe to retail clients. See generally SEC (US), 'Regulation Best Interest: The Broker-Dealer Standard of Conduct' 84 Fed Reg 33318 (12 July 2019).

[34] SEC 2013 Investment Adviser Regulation Report (n 25 above) 22–23 (citations omitted).

[35] SEC, 'Enhanced Disclosures by Certain Investment Advisers and Investment Companies About Environmental, Social, and Governance Investment Practices' Rel No 33-11068 (25 May 2022) 165–68 (discussing current rules).

[36] SEC 2019 Standard of Conduct Guidance (n 29 above) 33675 and 33675–78 (discussing the scope of the duty of loyalty).

[37] SEC 2013 Investment Adviser Regulation Report (n 25 above); SEC (US), 'Proxy Voting by Investment Advisers' 68 Fed Reg 6585 (7 February 2003). The duty of care also requires investment advisers to 'seek best execution of a client's transactions' and to 'provide advice and monitoring over the course of the relationship': SEC 2019 Standard of Conduct Guidance (n 29 above) 33672, 33674–75.

[38] SEC Proxy Voting by Investment Advisers Release (n 37 above) (citing Rule 206(4)–6(a) of the '40 Act); SEC (US), 'Supplement to Commission Guidance Regarding Proxy Voting Responsibilities of Investment Advisers' Release No IA-5347 (22 July 2020) 6 (citing 17 CFR 275.206(4)–6(c) with regard to automated voting).

[39] SEC 2019 Standard of Conduct Guidance (n 29 above) 33675–76.

[40] ibid 33673–74; SEC 2013 Investment Adviser Regulation Report (n 25 above) 24.

[41] ibid 33673; SEC 2013 Investment Adviser Regulation Report (n 25 above) 24–25.

so directs.[42] Incorporating beneficial owner preferences also requires pension funds and other institutional investors to develop processes to identify what beneficial owners' preferences are.[43]

The ICA also imposes disclosure and voting obligations on mutual funds that are an important starting point in understanding the governance or 'stewardship' obligations of these funds and their advisers. Under the ICA, a mutual funds' registration statement must accurately describe all 'matters of fundamental [investment] policy,' which includes any ESG factors or strategies of the fund, and the fund will be bound to comply with those terms.[44] In 2003, the SEC also introduced requirements under the ICA that mutual funds and other registered investment companies must vote proxies for the securities held by the fund and must disclose to their shareholders the policies and procedures that govern proxy voting, as well as a record of how those securities have been voted.[45] These disclosures apply to any policies and procedures of a fund's investment adviser or third party, such as a proxy advisory firm, that the fund relies on in deciding how to vote its proxies.[46] As the SEC has emphasised, investment advisers who act on behalf of mutual funds are also subject to the same fiduciary obligation to vote proxies related to portfolio securities held by the fund.[47] In such cases, the investment adviser 'is a fiduciary that owes the fund a duty of 'utmost good faith, and full and fair disclosure'' and must exercise its proxy voting responsibilities in a manner consistent with the best interests of the fund and its shareholders'.[48]

In sum, the SEC's 2019 guidance on investment adviser fiduciary duties does not specifically address the extent to which investment adviser fiduciary duties may take account of ESG factors or any other particular matters affecting investment risk or return or the implementation of a client's objectives, all of which are matters left to the discretion of the fiduciary. However, the 2019 guidance emphasises that investment advisers remain bound by the scope and terms of client instructions, which requires consideration of the client's delegation of authority and its expectations with regard to systemic risk concerns, investment time horizons, and the exercise of voting rights with respect to ESG matters.[49] The costs associated with investment advice may also be relevant in determining what is in the client's best interest.[50]

---

[42] See eg L Palladino and R Alexander, 'Responsible Asset Managers: New Fiduciary Rules for the Asset Management Industry' (June 2021), https://rooseveltinstitute.org/wp-content/uploads/2021/07/RI_ResponsibleAssetManagers_IssueBrief_202106.pdf.

[43] Various approaches for engaging fund beneficiaries are being used by some investors. UN Princ Resp Investment, 'Understanding and Aligning with Beneficiaries' Sustainability Preferences' (2021), https://www.unpri.org/download?ac=13321. See also C Griffin, 'We Three Kings: Disintermediating Voting at the Index Fund Giants' (2020) 79 *Maryland Law Review* 954 (suggesting mechanisms for beneficial owner voting).

[44] M Schanzenbach and R Sitkoff, 'Reconciling Fiduciary Duty and Social Conscience: The Law and Economics of ESG Investing by a Trustee' (2020) 74 *Stanford Law Review* 381, 385 and n 8 (citations omitted) (citing examples from past SEC enforcement actions against an SRI fund).

[45] SEC (US), 'Disclosure of Proxy Voting Policies and Proxy Voting Records by Registered Management Investment Companies' Release No 33-8188 (31 January 2003).

[46] ibid.

[47] ibid.

[48] ibid.

[49] SEC 2019 Standard of Conduct Guidance (n 29 above) 33672–73 (noting that for institutional investors, the adviser must understand the client's investment mandate).

[50] ibid 17.

In general, then, investment advisers must consider ESG factors if ESG considerations are part of the client's objectives and if doing so is in the client's best interest, while taking into account the costs associated with providing such advice.

ii. The Employee Retirement Income Security Act

Private pension fund trustees who manage corporate employee benefit plans are subject to the Employee Retirement and Income Security Act (ERISA).[51] Depending on the scope of the discretionary authority delegated by the client, fund managers may also themselves be deemed ERISA fiduciaries.[52] ERISA is therefore another important source of authority governing the ability of institutional investors and asset managers to consider ESG factors in making investment, voting, and engagement decisions. ERISA will also inform the investment options that pension funds provide to plan beneficiaries. Non-regulatory interpretive guidance on ERISA from the US DOL is also influential with respect to public pension funds and other trustee relationships that are not directly subject to ERISA.[53]

As Max Schanzenbach and Robert Sitkoff explain in their seminal article on this question, ESG-integrated investment is permitted under ERISA (and under trust law) so long as '(1) the trustee reasonably concludes that the ESG investment program will benefit the beneficiary directly by improving risk-adjusted return; and (2) the trustee's exclusive motive for adopting the ESG investment program is to obtain this direct benefit'.[54] Under ERISA, a distinction must therefore be made between the inclusion of ESG factors on economic and non-economic grounds. This view has generally been supported in guidance issued by the DOL since 2015, including in its 2021 proposed guidance;[55] however, the DOL's position has shifted to some extent over successive administrations, creating uncertainty for plan fiduciaries.

ERISA fiduciaries are subject to duties of prudence and loyalty with regard to the choice of investments and the exercise of proxy voting and other shareholder rights.[56] These duties generally require plan fiduciaries to diversify plan investments,[57] and to 'act solely in the interest of the plan's participants and beneficiaries and for the exclusive purpose of providing benefits' to them while covering the reasonable expenses of plan administration.[58] Because the US Supreme Court has held that the 'sole interest' rule applies to the 'financial benefits' of plan beneficiaries, considering

---

[51] Employee Retirement Income Security Act of 1974 (ERISA), Pub L No 93-406, 88 Stat 829.

[52] ERISA fiduciaries may delegate management authority under section 402(c)(3) of ERISA. 29 USC 1102(c)(3).

[53] On the regulation of public pension funds and the influence of ERISA, as well as distinctions, see P Rose, 'Public Wealth Maximization: A New Framework for Fiduciary Duties in Public Funds' (2018) *University of Illinois Law Review* 891, 899–911.

[54] Schanzenbach and Sitkoff (n 44 above) 386–87. Trust law is the foundation of ERISA fiduciary principles, particularly in view of the trust structure it mandates for private pension plans: ibid.

[55] DOL (US), 'Proposed Rule on Prudence and Loyalty in Selecting Plan Investments and Exercising Shareholder Rights' 86 Fed Reg 57272, 57272 (14 October 2021) (2021 Proposed Rules).

[56] ibid 57272 and nn 1–2 (citing sections 403 and 404 of ERISA, 29 USC 1103, 1104).

[57] 29 USC 1104.

[58] 29 USC 1103(c) and 1104(a).

non-financial goals in an ERISA plan with respect to asset allocation, proxy voting, or the choice of investment options for beneficiaries, could breach the trustee's duty of loyalty.[59] ERISA fiduciaries also have an obligation to monitor an investment manager's exercise of proxy voting rights if discretionary authority has been retained by the fiduciary.[60] It is important to note, however, that these obligations only apply to ERISA fiduciaries, and do not prevent other investors or funds from pursuing investments that may sacrifice returns or increase risk in order to achieve particular non-financial objectives.

The DOL's guidance has also recognised that some investments may provide 'collateral benefits' to plan beneficiaries beyond investment return, such as the pursuit of social or sustainability goals.[61] The DOL has therefore generally permitted plan fiduciaries to take these factors into account as 'tie-breakers' among investments that equally advance the plan's economic objectives.[62] The DOL has also recognised that ESG factors may themselves be financially material to investment risk and return and are therefore appropriate economic considerations in their own right for ERISA fiduciaries.[63] However, it has cautioned that not all ESG-oriented investments are necessarily prudent investments[64] and has interpreted the duties of prudence and loyalty to prohibit ERISA fiduciaries from sacrificing investment returns or taking on greater investment risks in pursuit of non-economic 'collateral benefits'.[65] Because of the inconsistency and low reliability of ESG corporate data, ensuring that ESG integration does not fall afoul of these fundamental duties presents challenges.[66]

More difficult is the question of whether ERISA fiduciaries may expend plan resources to research the ESG implications of proxy voting or to engage in more direct ESG-related activism. As some commentators have noted, changing corporate practice would be consider a 'collateral benefit' under ERISA if it is not intended to improve investment risk-adjusted returns.[67] In addition, ERISA fiduciaries are allowed to vote proxies or take other action to influence corporate management only if the costs are reasonable with respect to the anticipated economic benefits; in fact, the DOL has emphasised that an ERISA fiduciary is obligated *not* to vote if it determines that the research and other costs of doing so outweigh the expected economic benefits

---

[59] Schanzenbach and Sitkoff (n 44 above) 403–405 and n 110 (citing *Fifth Third Bancorp v Dudenhoeffer* 134 S Ct 2459, 2468 (2014) for its interpretation of 29 USC s 110(a)(1)(A)(i)–(ii)).

[60] DOL 2021 Proposed Rules (n 55 above) 57274.

[61] ibid 57278.

[62] ibid. Some commentators have criticised this approach as creating a false assumption that equivalent investments can in fact be identified, yet with different ESG profiles: Schanzenbach and Sitkoff (n 44 above) 408–11 (arguing that the tie-breaking concept is '"irreconcilable" with the "sole interest" or "exclusive benefit" rule').

[63] DOL 2021 Proposed Rules (n 55 above) 57275–76. DOL, 'Field Assistance Bulletin 2018-01' (23 April 2018), superseded by 85 Fed Reg 72846 and 85 Fed Reg 81658 (2018 Field Assistance Bulletin).

[64] DOL 2018 Field Assistance Bulletin ibid.

[65] DOL 2021 Proposed Rules (n 55 above) 57273.

[66] The limitations of ESG data and ratings are discussed further below. See nn 82, 153–154 and accompanying text.

[67] Schanzenbach and Sitkoff (n 44 above) 398.

of voting.[68] Moreover, the DOL's 2021 proposed rules reaffirm its position that plan fiduciaries may not undertake engagement or adopt voting or investment policies to advance the plan fiduciaries' 'personal public policy preferences at the expense of participants' economic interests'.[69]

The proposed rules attempt to clarify that ERISA fiduciaries may consider financially material ESG factors, including climate-related risk, in investment analysis and in the exercise of voting rights on behalf of plan beneficiaries, consistent with plan fiduciaries' duty of loyalty.[70] They also state that consideration of portfolio risk-adjusted return and the benefits of investment-related decisions may in fact *require* an assessment of the economic effects of climate change and other ESG factors.[71] This proposal was prompted in part by earlier amendments issued during the Trump administration that, in the view of many ERISA fiduciaries, had chilled their ability to take even financially material ESG factors into account.[72] Those rules had required the choice of investments and other investment actions to be based solely on 'pecuniary factors' and had therefore cast doubt on the ability of plan fiduciaries to consider ESG factors in their exercise of voting rights.[73] At the time of this writing, the DOL has also sought public comment on regulatory actions the agency could take under ERISA to protect plan beneficiaries from climate-related financial risk.[74]

iii. State Law

Although federal regulations do not mandate that asset managers or institutional investors take account of ESG factors in investment decisions, and indeed may constrain their ability to do so, there have been efforts at the state level to encourage ESG-oriented investing by public pension funds. Most notably, the state of Illinois requires its pension funds and other state agencies to publish and implement sustainable investment policies for all public funds that they control and to take account of sustainable investment factors to the extent consistent with relevant fiduciary duties.[75]

---

[68] DOL 2021 Proposed Rules (n 55 above) 57274–75 (citing its 1994 and 2008 interpretive guidance). DOL Interpretive Bulletin 2008-02, 73 Fed Reg 61731 (17 October 2008), replacing 59 Fed Reg 38860 (29 July 1994). The DOL's 2021 proposed rules would also eliminate any requirement to maintain records of proxy voting activities, out of concern that such rules would discourage or burden proxy voting: DOL 2021 Proposed Rules (n 55 above) 57281–82.

[69] ibid 57275.

[70] ibid 57272–76. The DOL is seeking guidance on whether climate risk should be considered presumptively material to investment risk and return: ibid 57290.

[71] ibid 57276–78. The proposed rules also reaffirm that integrating ESG factors into investment decisions as a 'tie-breaking' collateral benefit is permitted even if it is not material with respect to financial risk or return: ibid 57278–81.

[72] ibid 57281.

[73] ibid. They also were understood to prevent the selection of ESG-oriented funds as a default option for plan beneficiaries, since the rules prevented default selections from including funds whose investment objectives or strategies reflected non-economic goals. See DOL, 'Financial Factors in Selecting Plan Investments' 85 Fed Reg 72846 (13 November 2020), DOL 'Fiduciary Duties Regarding Proxy Voting and Shareholder Rights' 85 Fed Reg 81658 (16 December 2020).

[74] DOL, 'Request for Information on Possible Agency Actions to Protect Life Savings and Pensions from Threats of Climate-Related Financial Risk' 87 Fed Reg 8289 (14 February 2022).

[75] The Illinois Sustainable Investing Act, ILCS 238 (2020) https://www.ilga.gov/legislation/ilcs/fulltext.asp?DocName=004000050K1-113.17.

Other states have introduced legislation to encourage ESG integration or require divestment of fossil fuels for public investment funds.[76] State pension funds in California and New York that are not subject to similar rules have nonetheless adopted investment mandates that incorporate ESG criteria and have been leaders in stewardship and engagement around ESG issues.[77] These funds have also announced a goal to achieve carbon neutrality or 'net zero' greenhouse gas emissions by 2040.[78] In addition, insurers in six states are already required by regulators to provide various climate risk disclosures on a report-or-explain basis.[79]

B. Regulation of ESG Investment Products

The exponential growth in demand for sustainable investments has attracted regulatory attention in recent years because of the potential for ESG 'greenwashing' due to the lack of clear definitions and standards for ESG investment funds or products.[80] ESG ratings or indices that investors or fund managers may reference to assess the ESG performance of a company or a portfolio have also been found to be of uncertain reliability.[81] At the same time, some ESG funds use higher fee structures and may in some cases offer lower risk-adjusted returns, depending on their non-financial or social goals and the ESG integration approach they adopt.[82]

The need to establish clear indicators for green finance targets has led the EU and over 20 other jurisdictions to adopt or develop green 'taxonomies' that may

[76] See 'Navigating State Regulation of ESG Investments by Investment Managers: A Rapidly Evolving and Contradictory Landscape' *Ropes & Gray Client Alert* (30 June 2021), https://www.ropesgray.com/en/newsroom/alerts/2021/June/Navigating-State-Regulation-of-ESG-Investments-by-Investment-Managers-A-Rapidly-Evolving.

[77] See CalPERS, 'Sustainable Investments Program', https://www.calpers.ca.gov/page/investments/sustainable-investments-program; New York State Comptroller, 'Sustainable Investments and Climate Solutions Program', https://www.osc.state.ny.us/common-retirement-fund/sustainable-investments-and-climate-solutions-program.

[78] New York State Comptroller, 'New York State Pension Fund Sets 2040 Net Zero Carbon Emissions Target' Press Release (9 December 2020), https://www.osc.state.ny.us/press/releases/2020/12/new-york-state-pension-fund-sets-2040-net-zero-carbon-emissions-target; R Tuttle, 'California's Public Pensions are Major Fossil Fuel Investors' (*Bloomberg*, 8 December 2021) (criticising California's two largest public pension funds for endorsing 'voice' rather than 'exit' strategies to reach net-zero goals).

[79] The required disclosures are made under a survey administered by the National Association of Insurance Commissioners: NAIC, 'Proposed Redesigned NAIC Climate Risk Disclosure Survey' (11 March 2022), https://content.naic.org/sites/default/files/call_materials/2022ProposedClimateRiskSurvey.pdf.

[80] IOSCO Asset Management Recommendations (n 1 above) 11–14, 28–35.

[81] F Berg et al, 'Aggregate Confusion: The Divergence of ESG Ratings' (2022) *Review of Finance*, https://papers.ssrn.com/sol3/papers.cfm?abstract_id=3438533; A Rzeźnik et al, 'Investor Reliance on ESG Ratings and Stock Price Performance' *SAFE Working Paper No 310* (2022), https://papers.ssrn.com/sol3/papers.cfm?abstract_id=3801703; F Berg et al, 'Is History Repeating Itself? The (Un)Predictable Past of ESG Ratings' *ECGI Working Paper 708/2020*, https://ssrn.com/abstract=3722087.

[82] See DOL 2021 Proposed Rules (n 55 above) 57290–91 (citing studies on this issue); AMAC, 'Recommendations for ESG' 4–6 (7 July 2021), https://www.sec.gov/files/amac-recommendations-esg-subcommittee-070721.pdf (discussing divergent conclusions on ESG materiality). See also R Moore, 'Morningstar Finds ESG Funds Are More Expensive than Conventional Funds' (26 October 2021), https://www.planadviser.com/morningstar-finds-esg-funds-expensive-conventional-funds/.

improve standardisation in how 'green' or 'sustainable' investments are defined and the transparency of green investment characteristics.[83] These taxonomies form a basis for the reporting requirements for investment managers that are also being introduced in these jurisdictions.[84] Voluntary standards have also been developed for this purpose, including the widely referenced Green Bond Principles and other guidelines adopted by the International Capital Market Association (ICMA). There are also efforts underway transnationally to harmonise green taxonomies to promote fair pricing and transparency across global capital markets.[85]

Since 2020, the SEC has identified ESG investing and climate risk as examination priorities for registered investment advisers due to these investor protection concerns, and in 2021 it created a Climate and ESG Task Force to assess investment advisers' and funds' disclosure and compliance with their stated ESG strategies.[86] The SEC has also published guidance to retail investors to help them better understand the range of ESG funds and investment strategies.[87] The focus of the ESG Task Force to date has been on the extent to which ESG investments and proxy voting processes are consistent with the information funds provide to their clients and shareholders in marketing materials and ESG disclosures, and on the adequacy of internal controls and compliance programmes that implement ESG investment and proxy voting policies and ensure adherence to any ESG frameworks a fund claims to follow, as well as clients' ESG directives.[88] Although asset managers' exercise of voting rights on behalf of their clients is ultimately subject to the scope of the responsibilities that fund clients delegate to them by contract, the SEC's findings suggest that some funds are not in fact voting in accordance with their own investment policies and in accordance with client direction.[89]

In 2022, the SEC therefore proposed for the first time reporting obligations for investment advisers and funds with respect to ESG investment practices, objectives, and products in order to address these ESG greenwashing and investor protection concerns.[90] Under the proposal, funds that engage in ESG investing will be obligated to describe how they do so and what ESG factors they consider. More extensive

[83] IPSF, 'Common Ground Taxonomy – Climate Change Mitigation Instruction Report' 35–43 (November 2021), https://ec.europa.eu/info/sites/default/files/business_economy_euro/banking_and_finance/documents/211104-ipsf-common-ground-taxonomy-instruction-report-2021_en.pdf.

[84] One of the most prominent is the EU green taxonomy: Council Regulation (EC) 2019/2088 on Sustainability-related Disclosures in the Financial Services Sector [2019] OJ L317 2(24); Council Regulation (EC) 2020/852 on the Establishment of a Framework to Facilitate Sustainable Investment [2020] OJ L198. A social taxonomy is under development: EU Platform on Sustainable Finance, 'Final Report on Social Taxonomy' (February 2022).

[85] IPSF (n 83 above).

[86] 'SEC Announces Enforcement Task Force Focused on Climate and ESG Issues' (4 March 2021), https://www.sec.gov/news/press-release/2021-42; US SEC Division of Examinations, '2021 Examination Priorities' (2021) 28, https://www.sec.gov/files/2021-exam-priorities.pdf; https://www.sec.gov/about/offices/ocie/national-examination-program-priorities-2020.pdf 15.

[87] SEC (US), 'Environmental, Social and Governance (ESG) Funds – Investor Bulletin' (26 February 2021), https://www.investor.gov/introduction-investing/general-resources/news-alerts/alerts-bulletins/investor-bulletins-1.

[88] US SEC Division of Examinations, 'Review of ESG Investing Risk Alert' (9 April 2021) https://www.sec.gov/exams/announcement/risk-alert-esg.

[89] ibid 4 (reporting findings from fund investigations).

[90] SEC Enhanced ESG Disclosures (n 35 above).

information about ESG strategies, metrics, impact targets and performance, and in some cases, portfolio greenhouse gas emissions would be required depending on how extensively a fund integrates ESG factors into its investment strategies and whether its goals include specific ESG impacts.[91] In 2022, the SEC also proposed amending the rules that prohibit funds from using names that may mislead investors about the funds' investments and risks.[92] If adopted, the amended naming rules would prohibit a fund that does not consider ESG factors as more significant than non-ESG factors from using 'ESG' or similar terms in its name.[93]

Pending these reforms, the CFA Institute, a non-profit association, has developed Global ESG Disclosure Standards for Investment Products in order to reduce greenwashing and 'facilitate fair representation and full disclosure of an investment product's consideration of ESG issues in [terms of] its objectives, investment process, or stewardship activities'.[94] The CFA Institute's standards reference and seek to align with the EU's Sustainable Financial Disclosure Regulation (SFDR),[95] but they are limited to product-specific disclosure and so do not speak to asset managers' disclosures to clients, shareholders, or regulators about their own incorporation of ESG factors in investment and voting decisions or other firm-level disclosure policies.

The SEC's Asset Management Advisory Committee (AMAC) has noted that one of the challenges for developing new standards or guidance for investment manager disclosure is that corporate issuer disclosure of material ESG matters is still inadequate 'to support performance measurement and validation of ESG related features' for investment products, particularly since many ESG products have a longer-term time horizon and may be directed to goals beyond financial risk and return.[96] As discussed below, the SEC is also considering how to align its reporting requirements for corporate issuers with the international standards that are being developed by the International Sustainability Standards Board (ISSB). These rules may offer some grounding for ESG investment products and services and for investment manager's own disclosure to current and prospective clients.

C. Investor Stewardship

In 2010, the concept of 'investor stewardship' was introduced formally by the UK in its voluntary guidelines for institutional investors in order to encourage greater

---

[91] ibid.

[92] SEC, 'Investment Company Names' Rel No 33-11067 (25 May 2022). Under the Names Rule of the Investment Company Act of 1940, 15 USC s 35(d) and related rules, Rule 35d-1, 17 CFR 270.35d-1, funds must invest at least 80% of their assets in accordance with the type of investment suggested by its name.

[93] ibid.

[94] CFA Institute, 'Global ESG Disclosure Standards for Investment Products' (2021) v–vi, https://www.cfainstitute.org/-/media/documents/ESG-standards/Global-ESG-Disclosure-Standards-for-Investment-Products.pdf. These standards are 'global' in the sense that they are intended to apply across all investment vehicles, asset classes, ESG approaches, and investment strategies: ibid vii.

[95] CFA Institute, 'Global ESG Disclosure Standards for Investment Products: Sustainable Finance Disclosure Regulation (SFDR) Cross-Reference' (November 2021), https://www.cfainstitute.org/-/media/documents/ESG-standards/Global-ESG-Disclosure-Standard-for-Investment-Products---SFDR-Cross-Reference.pdf.

[96] AMAC (n 81 above) 6.

transparency around how investors exercise their shareholder governance rights and engage with portfolio companies.[97] The concept has come to be understood to include both the exercise of shareholder voting rights and more direct forms of activism, as well as related disclosure obligations for the benefit of clients and fund beneficiaries. The 2020 amendment of the UK stewardship code extended its scope to encouraging investor monitoring of corporate ESG performance.[98]

In recent years, a growing number of jurisdictions, including the EU and Japan, have followed the UK's lead and have introduced stewardship guidelines or regulatory mandates for asset managers and their clients that encourage or require them to incorporate sustainability factors into investment policies, fund management, and voting and engagement practices. Investor stewardship guidelines also encourage investors to collaborate on engagement efforts, and to provide more expansive disclosure about their compliance with stewardship policies to their clients and to regulators.[99] Many of these initiatives are intended to improve transparency requirements around voting and investment policies.

Thus far, the only regulatory guidance and formal rules on investor stewardship in the US are those discussed above that generally govern fund managers' disclosure obligations and exercise of proxy voting rights. Common forms of ESG activism in the US are direct engagement by asset managers and other large investors with investee companies, proxy voting on ESG proposals, and the adoption of voting guidelines that signal support for certain ESG practices, such as board diversity or corporate climate change policies. The regulatory space for these kinds of activism, and for collaborative engagements by investors, is subject to some of the same constraints as other forms of governance-related activism, discussed below, although the SEC has taken a more expansive approach toward shareholder proposals that may further encourage their use with respect to climate change risk and other ESG concerns. The ESG disclosures for investment advisers and investment companies proposed by the SEC at the time of this writing would not affect these rules, but would require certain ESG funds to disclose information about their engagement activities other than proxy voting.[100] The following discussion introduces the mechanisms for investor stewardship in the US context.

i. The Debate over Shareholder Activism and the Question of Corporate Externalities

Regulatory interest in encouraging sustainable investment, ESG integration, and shareholder monitoring of corporate environmental and social externalities has renewed long-standing debates around the question of which investors, if any, have

---

[97] The UK stewardship code was updated in 2019: FRC, 'The UK Stewardship Code 2020' (2019) https://www.frc.org.uk/getattachment/5aae591d-d9d3-4cf4-814a-d14e156a1d87/Stewardship-Code_Final2.pdf.

[98] P Davies, 'The UK Stewardship Code 2010–2020: From Saving the Company to Saving the Planet?' in D Katelouzou and D Puchniak (eds), *Global Shareholder Stewardship: Complexities, Challenges and Possibilities* (Cambridge University Press, 2022) 6–7.

[99] Katelouzou and Puchniak, ibid. With regard to collaborative engagement, see UK Stewardship Code (n 97 above) s 10 ('Collaboration').

[100] SEC Enhanced ESG Disclosures (n 35 above).

adequate incentives to take an active role in corporate governance, and if so, to what effect.[101] The literature has shown that passive investors, such as index funds, and most institutional investors and asset managers have little economic incentive to bear the costs of proxy voting and other governance rights (absent regulatory mandates), much less to actively monitor portfolio firms.[102] Hedge funds, in contrast, have economic incentives that are more aligned with activism and are not constrained by the regulatory barriers, discussed below, that prevent even the largest investors from engaging in the more aggressive forms of activism like proxy contests that hedge funds are able to undertake.[103] Institutional investors who may be unwilling to engage in activism on their own have also proven willing to support activist campaigns initiated by hedge funds.[104]

The ability and willingness of asset managers to push for greater ESG transparency and related corporate governance reforms at investee companies is subject to the same constraints that apply to shareholder activism generally, and it, too, has been catalysed by investors that, like hedge funds, have unique incentives to engage in activism – SRI funds, individual activists, and to a lesser extent, pension funds.[105] While pension funds are subject to greater constraints, many SRI funds have sustainability impact goals that give them incentives to engage in activism even when it involves significant costs. For many SRI investors, changing corporate behaviour is also an important goal of investment strategy, and they are more likely to adopt investment criteria that consider the ESG impacts of the company's operations on external stakeholders in addition to the financial materiality of sustainability factors to the company itself. One of the most visible examples of activism spearheaded by an SRI fund was the successful effort in 2021 by impact hedge fund Engine No 1 to seat dissident directors on the board of Exxon Mobil. It did so at a cost of about $ 12.5 million, ultimately with the support of the 'Big Three' – BlackRock, State Street, and Vanguard.[106] SRI funds are also likely to continue actively monitoring how

---

[101] See eg L Bebchuk, 'The Case for Increasing Shareholder Power' (2005) 118 *Harvard Law Review* 833; *cf* L Stout, 'The Mythical Benefits of Shareholder Control' (2007) 93 *Virginia Law Review* 789. See also J Hill and R Thomas (eds), *Research Handbook on Shareholder Power* (Edward Elgar, 2015).

[102] See eg D Lund, 'The Case against Passive Shareholder Voting' (2018) 43 *Journal of Corporation Law* 101; R Gilson and J Gordon, 'The Agency Costs of Agency Capitalism: Activist Investors and the Revaluation of Governance Rights' (2013) 113 *Columbia Law Review* 863. See also Y Yadav, 'Too-Big-to-Fail Shareholders' (2018) 103 *Minnesota Law Review* 587; L Bebchuk and S Hirst, 'Index Funds and the Future of Corporate Governance: Theory, Evidence, and Policy' (2019) 119 *Columbia Law Review* 2029; JD Morley, 'Too Big to Be Activist' (2019) 92 *Southern California Law Review* 1407.

[103] V Harper Ho, 'Risk-Related Activism: The Business Case for Monitoring Nonfinancial Risk' (2016) 41 *Journal of Corporation Law* 647; *cf* Gilson and Gordon (n 102 above); A Brav et al, 'Hedge Fund Activism, Corporate Governance, and Firm Performance' (2008) 63 *Journal of Finance* 1729.

[104] Gilson and Gordon (n 102 above) 897–98.

[105] Public pension funds face cost constraints, but some have led highly visible campaigns on ESG issues through shareholder proposals, direct engagement, and at times, litigation. Individual investors have also historically been regular proponents of both governance and environmental and social shareholder proposals: K Kastiel and Y Nili, 'The Giant Shadow of Corporate Gadflies' (2021) 94 *Southern California Law Review* 469.

[106] M Phillips, 'Exxon Mobil Defeated by Activist Investor Engine No. 1' (*NY Times*, 9 June 2021), https://www.nytimes.com/2021/06/09/business/exxon-mobil-engine-no1-activist.html; S Herbst-Bayliss, 'Little Engine No 1 Beat Exxon with Just $12.5 mln' (*Nasdaq*, 29 June 2021), https://www.nasdaq.com/articles/little-engine-no.-1-beat-exxon-with-just-%2412.5-mln-sources-2021-06-29.

these major asset managers implement their own policies and whether their voting records around corporate climate impacts and other ESG practices align with those policy guidelines. As with other aspects of ESG, the impact of shareholder monitoring and engagement around ESG performance varies by jurisdiction and issue, but research to date suggests that it can bring about identifiable changes in corporate sustainability practice and focus.[107]

However, economic rationales for sustainable investment are not likely to be strong enough to motivate mainstream investors to engage in oversight with respect to corporate externalities unless ESG portfolio risk effects and climate risk impacts are taken seriously. This is especially so if externalising environmental and social costs remains profitable for investee firms. This is often the case if corporate harms present no real legal liability, if the associated financial risk to the firm itself is not seen to be material to investors, or if the risks are difficult to measure. Investor activism around ESG matters also implicates potential tensions between shareholders' economic goals and the more stakeholder-oriented nature of many ESG concerns, as well as the differing goals of short-term and long-term investors and the potential tensions between competing ESG factors.

ii. Basic Approaches and Comparative Divergence

Internationally, the EU has adopted perhaps the most comprehensive framework to encourage investor stewardship and sustainable asset management, although ESG regulation of asset management is rapidly expanding in other jurisdictions as well.[108] The EU framework includes a 2017 amendment to its Shareholder Rights Directive, which requires greater transparency on a comply-or-explain basis about the voting and engagement policies and activities of institutional investors and asset managers, as well as greater disclosure regarding conflicts of interest, the use of proxy advisors and related matters.[109] In addition, the EU SFDR, which took effect in 2021, modifies the existing rules governing fund managers and investment advisers to require them to provide sustainability disclosures, including reporting on the negative externalities of investment advice and investment products.[110] To comply with the SFDR, ESG considerations must be incorporated into funds' investment and advisory functions, risk management and internal operational controls.[111] These measures also require US asset managers, including US hedge funds, to provide SFDR-compliant

---

[107] W-G Ringe, 'Investor-led Sustainability in Corporate Governance' *ECGI working paper 6* (November 2021) 16, https://ecgi.global/content/working-papers (citing anecdotal examples of specific impacts); A Dyck et al, 'Do Institutional Investors Drive Corporate Social Responsibility? International Evidence' (2019) 131 *Journal of Financial Economics* 639.

[108] On international developments, see IOSCO Asset Management Recommendations (n 1 above) 36–52.

[109] Council Directive 2017/828 of 20 May 2017 amending Directive 2007/36/EC as Regards the Encouragement of Long-Term Shareholder Engagement [2017] OJ L132/1, https://eur-lex.europa.eu/legal-content/EN/TXT/?uri=CELEX:32017L0828.

[110] Regulation (EU) 2019/2088 of 27 November 2019 on Sustainability-related Disclosures in the Financial Services Sector [2019] OJ L317/1, https://eur-lex.europa.eu/legal-content/EN/TXT/?uri=CELEX:32019R2088.

[111] On related measures adopted in the EU, see ESMA, 'Investment Services and Asset Management', https://www.esma.europa.eu/policy-activities/sustainable-finance/investment-services-and-asset-management.

disclosures on a firm-wide basis rather than only with respect to investment products marketed in the EU.[112] Asset managers and asset owners in the UK are also subject to climate-related risk disclosure rules that require reporting on how these risks are incorporated into investment management, and to climate risk disclosure rules for financial products.[113]

Prior to 2022, no specific affirmative obligations applied to asset managers or institutional investors in this regard, although some aspects of disclosure that other jurisdictions include in investor stewardship codes or mandates is already required under existing US law. These include, for instance, the obligation of asset managers and their institutional clients to disclose information about their investment and voting policies and in the case of mutual funds, their voting records. And as discussed above, investment managers are also obligated to engage in appropriate operational risk management and to comply with the contractual investment responsibilities and parameters that their clients have delegated to them, including those concerning investment strategy or voting and engagement practices.[114] The further reporting requirements that investor stewardship regimes now generally impose with respect to engagement activities or ESG-specific policies were not, however, required as a matter of US law, and opponents of sustainable finance reforms in the US have argued that the SEC and other regulators do not have the authority to adopt rules to encourage better ESG governance or disclosure practices by issuers or regulated financial institutions.[115]

The SEC's proposed disclosure rules for investment advisers and funds would not mandate shareholder activism or investor stewardship. However, if adopted, they would require funds to disclose how they use proxy voting to influence portfolio companies.[116] A fund for whom proxy voting is a significant means of implementing its ESG strategy would also need to disclose in its annual report the percentage of voting matters during the reporting period for which it voted in furtherance of such matters.[117] Under the proposed rules, funds whose ESG strategy depends significantly on engagement with issuers other than through proxy voting, would instead disclose any key performance indicators of their engagement.[118] Such funds would also have to disclose the total number of ESG engagement meetings and the number or percentage of issuers with whom such meetings were held during the reporting period.[119]

---

[112] J Ainger and F Schwartzkopff, 'Hedge Funds Hit by "Onerous" ESG Rule Turn to Lawyers for Help' (*Bloomberg*, 22 December 2021) (discussing the challenges of compliance with the SFDR's 'Principal Adverse Impact rule').

[113] FCA, 'Enhancing Climate-Related Disclosures by Asset Managers, Life Insurers and FCA-Regulated Pension Providers' *Policy Statement PS21/24* (December 2021), https://www.fca.org.uk/publication/policy/ps21-24.pdf (introducing final rules).

[114] The SEC has also proposed risk management and reporting rules for investment advisers and funds with respect to cybersecurity incidents occurring at advisers and funds, which build on existing regulatory compliance obligations under the '40 Act and the ICA: SEC (US), 'Proposed Rule on Cybersecurity Risk Management for Investment Advisers, Registered Investment Companies, and Business Development Companies' 87 Fed Reg 13524 (9 March 2022).

[115] V Harper Ho, 'Modernizing ESG Disclosure' (2022) *Illinois Law Review* 277, 304–306.

[116] SEC Enhanced ESG Disclosures (n 35 above) 60–65.

[117] ibid 77–78.

[118] ibid 80–83.

[119] ibid.

In addition, funds that seek to achieve specific ESG impacts would need to identify the intended impacts, key performance indicators they use over disclosed timeframes, and the relationship between those impacts and financial returns.[120] If adopted, these reporting requirements would bring greater clarity and standardisation to funds' ESG goals and potentially portfolio firms' ESG performance, although they are not designed to encourage or expand investor stewardship as many stewardship codes are designed to do.

iii. Shareholder Proposals

Although the US has no investor stewardship code and shareholders have no legal obligation to engage with portfolio companies around ESG issues, there have been some modest expansions under the Biden administration of investors' ability to do so through the use of shareholder proposals. Shareholder proposals have long been an important lever for shareholder engagement and have raised the visibility of many ESG issues. Under Rule 14a-8 of the Securities Exchange Act of 1933, shareholder proposals are advisory even if they earn majority shareholder support, but they are nonetheless a powerful tool of shareholder activism for investors seeking better ESG information or for those who want to push corporate boards to give greater attention to corporate environmental and social impacts.

With the exception of public pension funds and labour union funds, institutional investors and asset managers are rarely the proponents of shareholder proposals and do not often initiate activist campaigns, but their support has been critical to the growing number of ESG proposals that achieve majority voting approval or are ultimately withdrawn after successful engagement with corporate management.[121] All of the largest asset managers and proxy advisory firms have adopted voting guidelines that call on companies to pay attention to ESG risks and signal support for ESG shareholder proposals.[122] Importantly, the federal rule governing shareholder

---

[120] ibid 56–58.

[121] Ringe (n 107 above) 18–29 (discussing the role of coalitions in supporting ESG shareholder proposals). Examples of leading investor coalitions around ESG concerns include the Climate Action 100+ and signatories to the United Nations' Principles for Responsible Investment (UNPRI). See Climate Action 100+, 'About Climate Action 100+', https://www.climateaction100.org/about; UNPRI, 'The PRI Collaboration Platform', https://collaborate.unpri.org/; Institutional Shareholder Services (ISS), '2021 United States Environmental & Social Issues Proxy Season Review' (2021), https://insights.issgovernance.com/posts/2021-united-states-environmental-social-issues-proxy-season-review/ (reporting that ESG proposals at listed companies in the US received a record level of majority support in 2021). Individual activists are frequent proponents: Kastiel and Nili (n 105 above).

[122] BlackRock, 'Investment Stewardship: Global Principles (2022)' (2022), https://www.blackrock.com/corporate/literature/fact-sheet/blk-responsible-investment-engprinciples-global.pdf; BlackRock, 'Investment Stewardship: Proxy Voting Guidelines for US Securities', https://www.blackrock.com/corporate/literature/fact-sheet/blk-responsible-investment-guidelines-us.pdf; C Taraporevala, 'CEO's Letter on SSGA 2021 Proxy Voting Agenda' (*State Street Global Advisors*, 11 January 2021) https://www.ssga.com/us/en/institutional/ic/insights/ceo-letter-2021-proxy-voting-agenda (endorsing the TCFD framework and requiring portfolio companies to use the SASB framework); 'Fidelity Proxy Voting Guidelines' (February 2022), https://www.fidelity.com/bin-public/060_www_fidelity_com/documents/Full-Proxy-Voting-Guidelines-for-Fidelity-Funds-Advised-by-FMRCo-and-SelectCo.pdf; ISS, 'United States Proxy Voting Guidelines Benchmark Policy Recommendations (2022)', https://www.issgovernance.com/file/policy/latest/americas/US-Voting-Guidelines.pdf; Glass Lewis, '2022 Policy Guidelines – Environmental, Social & Governance (ESG) Initiatives', https://www.glasslewis.com/wp-content/uploads/2021/11/ESG-Initiatives-Voting-Guidelines-GL-2022.pdf.

proposals is not limited to matters that are material to the company financially. Indeed, it was specifically designed to give shareholders a voice on public policy concerns regardless of their financial significance.[123]

Concerned about the costs to companies of responding to proposals put forth by small investors or those that attracted low levels of support, the SEC under the Trump administration adopted tighter eligibility rules for shareholder proposals under Rule 14a-8.[124] Those rules remain in force. However, the SEC has now liberalised its guidance on proposals that implicate the 'ordinary business' of the company.[125] Because sustainability and risk-related proposals often fall within this category, these measures make such proposals more likely to be submitted to a shareholder vote. The SEC also plans to further clarify the circumstances under which companies may keep a proposal from going to a shareholder vote because it is duplicative, has been 'substantially implemented', or because the company considers it to be a resubmission of a prior failed proposal.[126] The purpose of these amendments is to 'enhance the ability of shareholders to express diverse objectives' and to facilitate shareholder voting on matters that companies were previously able to block from going to a vote.[127] Taken together, these changes could allow shareholders to engage companies more successfully on climate-related risk and other ESG issues and to bring these matters to a vote through the shareholder proposal process.

iv. Regulatory and Practical Disincentives to Investor Stewardship

Although large asset managers have shown their willingness to throw their weight behind more ESG proposals over time, regulatory barriers, as well as economic and practical disincentives, still prevent many asset managers and institutional investors from engaging in more confrontational forms of activism, such as proxy contests, or indeed from actively engaging with portfolio companies at all.[128] As explained above, the cost-benefit analysis for shareholder activism does not always add up for index funds and other passive investors. In addition, for the largest fund families, the chance that activism by one fund may conflict with the interests of other funds or clients increases as the number of clients and the diversity of other managed funds increases.[129] Similar practical constraints have limited investors' interest in undertaking

---

[123] V Harper Ho, 'From Public Policy to Materiality: Non-Financial Reporting, Shareholder Engagement & the Rule 14a-8 Ordinary Business Exception' (2019) 76 *Washington and Lee Law Review* 1231, 1244, 1248–49.

[124] 'Procedural Requirements and Resubmission Thresholds under Exchange Act Rule 14a-8' 85 Fed Reg 70240 (4 November 2020).

[125] Staff Legal Bulletin No 14L (3 November 2021), https://www.sec.gov/corpfin/staff-legal-bulletin-14l-shareholder-proposals (rescinding prior guidance with respect to Rule 14a-8's 'ordinary business' exception).

[126] SEC (US), 'Substantial Implementation, Duplication, and Resubmission of Shareholder Proposals Under Exchange Act Rule 14a-8' Release Number 34-95267 (13 July 2022).

[127] ibid at 7, 16.

[128] See nn 102–104 and accompanying text.

[129] Morley (n 102 above) 1449.

issuer-specific monitoring and engagement in the UK, where shareholders' role in corporate governance is even stronger than in the US.[130]

One of the greatest challenges to ESG activism for US asset managers is that many of the basic compliance obligations imposed by federal regulation create barriers to collaborative engagement and impede the more direct forms of activism, such as nominating dissident directors or engaging in proxy contests. Ironically, these barriers are higher for the largest asset managers that may be expected to gain the most from addressing portfolio-wide systematic risk concerns, and that should also have the greatest capacity to engage companies around ESG issues.[131] And indeed, the largest asset managers have generally not sought to influence corporate sustainability practice in this way.

As John Morley and others have explained, the federal ownership reporting requirements under section 13(d), as well as other rules that take an aggregate view of managed fund holdings, create legal barriers for large fund managers that discourage them from engaging in activism via any of their managed funds. The section 13(d) reporting requirements for investors who cross a 5 per cent ownership threshold with the intent to exercise control (a term that includes many more typical activist strategies) apply on an aggregate basis to 'the entire investment management complex.'[132] For managers with many clients, this threshold can be met even if each client's holdings are much smaller.[133] More critically, activism at a company that is held by one fund would require an investment management firm like Fidelity or State Street to comply with section 13(d) reporting obligations with respect to the target company's stock across all of its funds, not just the activist fund, and would disqualify it from filing the less onerous blockholder reporting under section 13(g) that applies if the blockholder does not intend to exercise control.[134] Section 13(d) also requires investment managers to make frequent, costly updating of any changes in their holdings of the company's stock of greater than 1 per cent, which is determined on an aggregate basis and therefore would likely be regularly met if the fund manager has a large number of funds holding the target company's stock. As Morley points out, section 13(d) reporting also requires disclosure of the 60-day trading history in the target company's stock, which could create immense obligations for managers of

---

[130] See eg B Reddy, 'The Emperor's New Code? Time to Re-Evaluate the Nature of Stewardship Engagement under the UK's Stewardship Code' (2021) 84(4) *Modern Law Review* 842; I Chiu, 'Reviving Shareholder Stewardship: Critically Examining the Impact of Corporate Transparency Reforms in the UK' (2014) 38 *Delaware Journal of Corporate Law* 983.

[131] Morley (n 102 above) 1422.

[132] Morley (n 102 above) 1429. At the time of this writing, the SEC has proposed amendments to these reporting requirements that shorten the filing deadlines: SEC (US), 'Modernization of Beneficial Ownership Reporting' 87 Fed Reg 13846 (10 March 2022).

[133] Morley (n 102 above) 1423–25 (noting that 'as a manager and its clients get bigger' (and thus potentially more influential), the '5 percent threshold becomes easier and easier to cross' in addition to the effects of group aggregation rules under Section 13(d)(3). At present, each of the top four asset management firms – BlackRock, State Street, Vanguard and Fidelity – already hold more than 5% of thousands of publicly traded companies: Morley (n 102 above) 1425 and fnn 49–51, citing J Fitchner et al, 'Hidden Power of the Big Three? Passive Index Funds, Re-Concentration of Corporate Ownership, and New Financial Risk' (2017) 19 *Business & Politics* 298, 312.

[134] Morley (n 102 above) 1427–30.

large number of issuers and clients, in addition to revealing publicly information about the manager's trading practices.[135] Activism by any single managed fund can also bring an investment adviser within the scope of the short-swing insider trading prohibitions of section 16 of the Exchange Act.[136] Uncertainty surrounding the bounds of these rules has also discouraged cooperative or collaborative engagement with portfolio companies, even though shareholders are only be deemed a 'group' under Section 13(d) if they agree to act in concert or together for the purpose of 'acquiring, holding, voting, or selling shares.[137] While space constraints prevent a more complete discussion, these regulatory limits help explain why the largest asset managers have limited their stewardship activities to policy and voting statements and occasional support for activist campaigns led by others.[138]

v. Voluntary Regimes and Self-Regulation

In the absence of more robust investor stewardship guidance or affirmative ESG engagement mandates for asset managers and institutional investors, voluntary standards of best practice have emerged that many US asset managers endorse or reference. In addition to private standards for ESG investment products, the most prominent private initiative for investment stewardship is the 'Framework for US Stewardship and Governance,' a set of six stewardship principles developed by the Investor Stewardship Group, an organisation of institutional investors and asset managers.[139] The framework has been endorsed by over 75 leading asset managers, including all of the Big Three, and represents around US$ 35 trillion in assets under management.[140] The ISG is a forum that supports and encourages members' own engagement initiatives but it is not designed to coordinate or facilitate collective engagement by its members.[141]

In addition to the ISG, the largest US asset managers, as well as many in the SRI space, are also signatories of the United Nations' Principles for Responsible Investment (UNPRI), which urges signatories to actively engage with portfolio firms around ESG risks and impacts.[142] The International Corporate Governance Network

---

[135] ibid.

[136] ibid 1430–34.

[137] 15 USC s 78m(d)(3) (2015); Rule 13d-5(b)(1), 17 CFR s 240.13d-5(b)(1) (2019). See eg *CSX Corpn v Children's Investment Fund Management (UK) LLP*, 654 F3d 276, 283–84 (2nd Cir 2015); *Dreiling v America Online*, 578 F3d 995, 1002 (9th Cir 2009); *Roth v Jennings*, 489 F3d 499, 507–508 (2nd Cir 2007).

[138] Other limits include the shareholding thresholds and procedural rules governing proxy access, the rules governing proxy solicitations, and the costs of proxy contests. See Dasgupta et al (n 28 above) 19–21, 53–66 (surveying these rules and the empirical literature on their use). See also Yadav (n 102 above) (discussing investor passivity with respect to monitoring of banks).

[139] ISG, 'Stewardship Principles', https://isgframework.org/stewardship-principles/. See also 'About the Investor Stewardship Group and the Framework for US Stewardship and Governance', https://isgframework.org/.

[140] ISG, 'Signatories', https://isgframework.org/signatories-and-endorsers/; email from ISG Chair to author (25 March 2022).

[141] Email from ISG Chair to author (25 March 2022).

[142] 'About the PRI', https://www.unpri.org/pri/about-the-pri. The G20/OECD Principles of Corporate Governance are another source of investor stewardship guidance. They provide that '[i]nstitutional investors acting in a fiduciary capacity should disclose their corporate governance and voting policies with respect to their investments, including the procedures that they have in place for deciding on the use of their voting rights': OECD Principles of Corporate Governance (2015) 30.

(ICGN), an association of global institutional investors, has also introduced a suite of principles and guidelines to establish best practices for the exercise of shareholder rights, the role of institutional investors in the corporate governance of investee companies,[143] and the exercise of institutional investor fiduciary duties with respect to the selection, retention, and oversight of asset managers.[144]

US asset managers also participate in voluntary initiatives to encourage greater corporate attention to ESG issues. One prominent example is the 'Net Zero Asset Managers Initiative' organised during the 2021 UN Conference of the Parties (COP26), which commits signatories to report on the percentage of their assets that will be managed in line with net-zero greenhouse gas emission goals by 2050 or sooner.[145] The initiative has over 220 signatories, and US asset manager signatories pledged over $200 billion under the initiative as an initial AUM net zero target.[146]

D. ESG Data and the Fiduciary Challenge of ESG Integration

To no small extent, the 'elephant in the room' for ESG integration stewardship has to do with the limits of corporate ESG information. Reliable, consistent ESG information is essential to asset managers' ability to satisfy their fiduciary duties and their reporting obligations to their own shareholders and clients. It is also essential if they are to monitor the ESG performance of portfolio companies and assess its impact. At present, however, uncertainty about the scope of ESG, the lack of consensus about which ESG factors are material to particular firms, and the use of ESG ratings that are inconsistent and lack transparency has made ESG integration challenging for investors.

The urgent need for reliable, investment-grade data, particularly for climate-related risk, has led many US asset managers to endorse and apply internationally recognised standards to their own reporting and to encourage portfolio firms to do the same. One of the most prominent is the TCFD framework for climate-related financial risk disclosure, which was developed with a focus on asset owners and asset managers.[147] The TCFD framework includes sector-specific guidance for the asset management industry that encourages disclosure and reporting against recommended quantitative indicators, such as weighted average carbon intensity, for each product or investment strategy.[148] The industry-specific standards developed by the Value Reporting Foundation/Sustainability Accounting Standards Board (SASB) are based on the materiality standards that apply under the US federal securities laws

---

[143] These include the ICGN Global Stewardship Principles and related Model Disclosure Templates: 'ICGN Global Stewardship Principles', https://www.icgn.org/policy/stewardship.

[144] ICGN, 'ICGN Guidance on Investor Fiduciary Duties' (2018), https://www.icgn.org/policy/icgn-guidance.

[145] 'Net Zero Asset Managers' Initiative', https://www.netzeroassetmanagers.org/.

[146] 'Net Zero Asset Managers' Initiative Progress Report' (2021), https://www.netzeroassetmanagers.org/media/2021/12/NZAM-Progress-Report.pdf. These levels have been criticised as too limited: A Marsh, '"Net Zero" Asset Managers Fall Short of Targets Set by Scientists' (*Bloomberg*, 11 November 2021).

[147] TCFD (n 17 above).

[148] TCFD (n 17 above) 33–35, 38–44.

and have also been widely adopted; these include sector-specific materiality stand-ards for asset management and custody activities.[149] The largest US asset managers have also encouraged investee companies to use the TCFD guidelines and the relevant SASB industry-specific indicators as the basis of internal materiality assessments, in selecting key performance indicators (KPIs), in managing ESG risks, and in preparing disclosures for investors.[150]

The SEC's 2022 proposed mandatory corporate reporting requirements for climate-related financial risk would be an important foundation for standardised climate disclosure, and the SEC plans to strengthen public company reporting on other ESG matters, such as human capital management and diversity.[151] The SEC's climate disclosure proposal draws on the core elements of the TCFD framework and the Greenhouse Gas Protocol.[152] It also appears intended to align with the interna-tional reporting standards being developed by the ISSB, which build on these same established frameworks.[153] Both the SEC and ISSB proposals would require manda-tory GHG emissions reporting, which is one of the key indicators of corporate climate impacts. However, unlike the EU approach, neither the SEC nor the ISSB's draft standards endorse a 'double materiality' standard that would require reporting on companies' own environmental and social impacts.[154] Therefore, with the signifi-cant exception of emissions disclosure, which may be required regardless of whether it presents a material financial risk to a reporting company, ESG reporting rules in the US are likely to apply only to financially material climate or ESG risks.

These efforts to standardise mandatory reporting frameworks are noteworthy and should help address some of the current limitations of ESG data and the ratings

---

[149] SASB, 'Asset Management & Custody Activities Standards' https://www.sasb.org/standards/download/?lang=en-us.

[150] BlackRock, State Street, and Vanguard have each taken steps to encourage implementation of the TCFD framework and the SASB standards. See Sullivan & Cromwell LLP 'The Rise of Standardized ESG Disclosure Frameworks in the United States' (8 June 2020), https://www.sullcrom.com/files/upload/SC-Publication-Rise-Standardized-ESG-Disclosure-Frameworks.pdf (discussing these initiatives and guidelines). For their specific voting and engagement guidelines, see sources referenced above (n 122 above).

[151] SEC (US), 'Proposed Rule on the Enhancement and Standardization of Climate-Related Disclosures for Investors' 87 Fed Reg 21334 (11 April 2022) (Proposed Climate Disclosure Rule). See 'SEC Announces Regulatory Agenda' *Press Release* (11 June 2021) https://www.sec.gov/news/press-release/2021-99. The SEC's early guidance on climate-related financial risk disclosure in 2010 identifies information that is already subject to disclosure under the current reporting regime: SEC (US) 'Commission Guidance Regarding Disclosure Related to Climate Change' 75 Fed Reg 6,290 (8 February 2010).

[152] SEC (US), Proposed Climate Disclosure Rule (n 149 above); IFRS, 'Exposure Draft IFRS S1 General Requirements for Disclosure of Sustainability-related Financial Information' (31 March 2022), https://www.ifrs.org/content/dam/ifrs/project/general-sustainability-related-disclosures/exposure-draft-ifrs-s1-general-requirements-for-disclosure-of-sustainability-related-financial-information.pdf; IFRS, 'Exposure Draft IFRS S2 Climate-related Disclosures' (31 March 2022), https://www.ifrs.org/content/dam/ifrs/project/climate-related-disclosures/issb-exposure-draft-2022-2-climate-related-disclosures.pdf.

[153] IFRS Foundation, 'ISSB Delivers Proposals That Create Comprehensive Global Baseline of Sustainability Disclosures' (31 March 2022), https://www.ifrs.org/news-and-events/news/2022/03/issb-delivers-proposals-that-create-comprehensive-global-baseline-of-sustainability-disclosures/.

[154] The EU Corporate Sustainability Reporting Directive (CSRD), which takes effect in 2023, extends reporting obligations beyond those that are material to investors to include information that is material from the standpoint of external stakeholders, such as environmental, social, climate, and human rights impacts: Commission, 'Proposal for a Directive of the European Parliament and of the Council as Regards Corporate Sustainability Reporting' COM (2021) 189 final.

that rely on them. At present, however, uncertainty about which measures should be used and to what ends create very real difficulties for investment managers and their clients, whose fiduciary duties require them to serve the financial interests of their clients and fund beneficiaries.[155] These challenges lead many asset managers to expend their own resources to identify basic ESG information at added cost, which also has fiduciary implications.[156] Even for investors and funds that are permitted to sacrifice investment returns in order to invest only in ESG leaders or to more actively push companies to reduce externalities, the choices of which ESG issues to prioritise and how to do so in a principled and transparent way are complex in light of the wide range of ESG factors and measures, the long-term nature of many ESG risks, the potential tradeoffs among different ESG factors, and these underlying data limitations. These practical questions are now more pressing as regulator and investor demand for greater transparency around ESG investment strategies and products has increased.

IV. NAVIGATING THE SUSTAINABLE FINANCE TRANSITION

In sum, there are rising investor and regulator expectations globally that financial institutions will begin to more actively monitor emerging ESG risks across their portfolios and improve transparency around ESG products and services. In many respects, the approach of US regulators to these issues has been to defer to private standard setters, leading industry players, and investors themselves to decide whether ESG factors should be integrated into investment analysis and voting policies, and if so, to what extent. As this chapter has explored, some aspects of the US regulatory framework also limit they types of ESG activism or stewardship in which asset managers and their clients can engage.

Relying on private initiatives to standardise ESG investment practice and reporting, or to create clear definitions for new investment products, has allowed flexibility but has also created costly fragmentation and slowed the development of a level playing field for all investors. In contrast to other jurisdictions, the US federal government's climate finance plans also do not as yet commit to a broader sustainable finance transition, and so the SEC and other federal agencies may continue to look to the asset management industry itself to promote greater harmonisation of ESG standards, definitions, and reporting requirements.

In this context, more fundamental regulatory reforms may be hampered by continued lack of consensus on the business case for ESG integration and engagement, the need for a sustainable finance transition, and whether regulatory frameworks should adhere to or move away from traditional economic understandings of materiality.

---

[155] John Coffee has argued, however, that to the extent that asset managers assess the costs and benefits of ESG investing and engagement decisions at the portfolio level, they are more likely to be able to justify ESG integration as complying with even the strict 'sole interest' fiduciary obligation of ERISA: Coffee (n 16 above) 636–41.

[156] See n 81 and accompanying text.

Given the influence of US financial regulation and its capital markets, its narrower, more incremental approach may also dampen momentum behind more fundamental changes that are being introduced elsewhere.

Nonetheless, some of the changes in the US regulatory landscape discussed in this chapter suggest a modest retooling of the environment for sustainable investment that may improve investors' ability to incorporate ESG information into investment decisions and indirectly encourage greater corporate accountability around sustainability impacts. These include, for example, the DOL's proposed guidance for ERISA fiduciaries and the SEC's proposed disclosure reforms for public companies and for investment advisers. The SEC's enforcement focus on the internal policies and compliance processes of ESG funds and its proposal to amend the 'Names Rule' may also stimulate further efforts to standardise ESG indicators for investment products.

In the face of changing client needs and shifting compliance demands, asset managers must continue to anticipate the next phases of the sustainable finance transition. Despite the limitations discussed in this chapter, asset managers can focus their engagement and advocacy on the need for better ESG data and can support greater harmonisation of ESG definitions, reporting standards, and disclosure obligations, whether for investment products, issuers, or for the industry itself. As ESG information and investment strategies mature, they can also develop and follow emerging best practices for ESG risk assessment across asset classes, and can adopt clear and consistent disclosure for ESG products, investment policies, and voting practices. Working to better align their public support for sustainability with engagement and voting practices will also help demonstrate to clients and portfolio companies their commitment to sustainable business practice. If they do so, asset managers may not only be able to navigate the sustainable finance transition but may continue to shape its course as well.

5

The EU Taxonomy: A Key Step for Sustainable Finance

CATHERINE MALECKI*

I. GENERAL INTRODUCTION

THE OBJECTIVE OF a climate-neutral European continent by 2050 was set by the EU some 20 years ago. To achieve this 'low-carbon' continent, the sustainable finance sector can mobilise both public and private capital. One of the objectives set for 2030 is to reduce greenhouse gas emissions by 40 per cent. However, the EU Green Deal is well underway. The most recent steps already taken are: the Taxonomy (EU) Regulation 2020/852 of the European Parliament and Council on establishing a framework to foster sustainable investment and amending Regulation (EU)[1] of 18 June 2020 and the Sustainable Disclosure Regulation (EU) 2019/2088 of 27 November 2019.[2] The aim is to build a climate-resilient Europe. A draft European climate 'Bill' is also being drawn up. The EU is 'institutionally equipped' to carry out this task, based on Article 11 TFEU, Article 115 TFEU and Article 191 TFEU (health, environment, protection of natural resources, combating climate change). A European signal exists, embodied by EU Climate Action and the European Commission which are part of this movement,[3] and the EU Green Paper of 18 February 2015 on 'Building a Capital Markets Union', whose aims specifically include 'increasing and diversifying the sources of finance provided by investors in the EU and elsewhere in the world'.[4] The European Parliament and Council Resolution of 29 May 2018 on Sustainable Finance (2018/2007(INI))[5] sets out a general roadmap

---

* Professor of Private Law, Rennes 2 University, LiRIS EA 7481, Campus Villejean, Place du Recteur Henri Le Moal CS 24307, 35043 Rennes cedex, France, Institut universitaire de France (IUF).
[1] OJEU, 22 June 2020, L 198/14.
[2] OJEU, 9 December 2019, L 317/1, https://eur-lex.europa.eu/legal-content/EN/TXT/?uri=celex%3A32 019R2088.
[3] cf the Green Paper on 'Building a Capital Markets Union: Measures Relating to Company Law', COM (2015) 63 final, p 17, http://ec.europa.eu/finance/consultations/2015/capital-markets-union/docs/green-paper_fr.pdfsp; B Lecourt, *Livre vert "Construire l'Union des marchés de capitaux": mesures ayant trait au droit des sociétés* 2015, p. 338.
[4] Green Paper (n 3 above) 6.
[5] See https://www.europarl.europa.eu/doceo/document/TA-8-2018-0215_FR.html.

for sustainable finance, with many references to French legislation. This resolution is essential because it lays the foundations for sustainable finance with a global perspective. The main aspects of this roadmap concern the following points:

> Financial markets can and must play a key role in supporting the transition to a sustainable economy in the EU which extends beyond climate transition and environmental issues and also concerns social and governance issues; whereas there is an urgent need to address related market failures.[6]

Cooperation between the public and private sectors to accelerate the environmental transition is reflected in the promotion of 'sustainable public investment within the framework of an EU Observatory on Sustainable Finance'[7] and 'publicly issued green bonds'. Integration of sustainable finance criteria in all legislation related to the financial sector lies in the creation of a pan-European framework to oblige investors to 'prevent, mitigate and account for ESG factors after a transitional period' based on the French Corporate Duty of Vigilance Law.[8] This new regulatory obligation is arguably an extension of the 'prudent person' principle,[9] and puts on legislative footing best investment management practices such as embodied in the soft law of the United Nations Principles of Responsible Investment. Other EU initiatives uphold the 'green oath' of 'do not harm', which is stated in the major communication entitled 'The European Green Deal' of 11 December 2019,[10] which lays a solid foundation for the measures. This paragraph heading speaks for itself: '2.2.1. Pursuing green finance and investment and ensuring a just transition'. Achieving the ambitions set out in the European Green Deal will require significant investment. The Commission has estimated that achieving the current 2030 climate and energy targets will require €260 billion of additional annual investment – about 1.5 per cent of 2018 GDP. This investment flow will need to be sustained over time. The magnitude of the investment challenge requires the mobilisation of both the public and private sectors. The COVID-19 crisis has arguably also exacerbated the need for funding to combat social inequalities.

As the Commission's Action Plan emphasises the need for more ESG-friendly legislation and financial regulation, including with regard to climate change, this implies strengthening the role of the European Supervisory Authorities (ESAs), which have been invited to participate in these measures. The Commission thus

---

[6] Resolution 2018/2007(INI) recital A.

[7] Resolution 2018/2007(INI) §5.

[8] 'Loi n°2037/3099 relative au devoir de vigilance des sociétés mères et entreprises donneuses d'ordre, 27 March 2017, JORF n°0074, 28 March 2017; C Malecki, 'Devoir de vigilance des sociétés mères et entreprises donneuses d'ordre: est-ce bien raisonnable?' (2017) mai 2017, n° 116j8*BJS* 298; T Sachs, 'La loi sur le devoir de vigilance des sociétés mères et donneuses d'ordre: les ingrédients d'une corégulation' (2017) 6 *Revue de droit du travail* 380. This law must be analysed with regard to the Commission's Proposal on CSDD (Corporate Sustainability Due Diligence) published on 23 February 2022, https://eur-lex.europa.eu/legal-content/EN/TXT/HTML/?uri=CELEX:52022PC0071&from=EN.

[9] Resolution 2018/2007(INI) §10.

[10] Communication from the Commission to the European Parliament, the European Council, the Council, the European Economic and Social Committee and the Committee of the Regions: The European Green Deal (COM/2019/640 final), https://eur-lex.europa.eu/legal-content/FR/TXT/HTML/?uri=CELEX:52019DC0640&from=EN.

states that these agencies 'should play an important role in assessing and reporting the risks to financial stability posed by sustainability factors'. The High Level Expert Group (HLEG) was created in the wake of the Paris Climate Agreement.[11] It proposed potential topics to be covered by the Commission's Sustainable Finance Action Plan.

The EU roadmap makes important contributions in two areas that are, in practice, inseparable realities and part of the strategy for 2030. Taxonomy and ESG disclosure – two cornerstones of sustainable finance – are closely linked. It will be necessary to calculate the alignment of investments on the Taxonomy and prepare the information to be disclosed in relation to investment products.

II. TAXONOMY: A CLASSIFICATION TOOL FOR ENVIRONMENTALLY SUSTAINABLE ACTIVITIES, OR THE NOVELTY OF AN OPERATIONAL DEFINITION[12]

A form of urgency, associated with the climate emergency, underlies the introduction of the Climate Bill and the future role of the European Securities and Markets Authority (ESMA). In France, the Autorité des marchés financiers (AMF) created a Climate and Sustainable Finance Commission on 2 July 2019,[13] and its latest report in July 2020, entitled 'Progress made and elements to be completed: the regulator's perspective' on sustainable finance[14] is very revealing, emphasising the need for completion of regulatory frameworks at EU level to facilitate sustainable finance on a credible footing.

This is arguably now found in EU Regulation 2020/852 of the European Parliament and Council of 18 June 2020 on establishing a framework to foster sustainable investment and amending Regulation (EU) 2019/2088[15] of 18 June 2020, which introduces a Taxonomy for environmental sustainability, designed as a tool to enable investors to comply with future European regulations on sustainable finance.[16]

The taxonomy is a classification tool that should enable the identification of what are considered to be 'sustainable' economic activities, in the context of the need to reorient financial flows in order to meet European requirements on tackling climate change and reducing carbon emissions by 2050. 'Sustainable finance will be essential to mobilising the financing vital to the attainment of a climate-neutral Europe by 2050', declared Valdis Dombrovskis, Executive Vice-President of the European Commission and responsible for the European Commission's Sustainable Finance Programme.

---

[11] High-Level Expert Group on Sustainable Finance (E03485), http://ec.europa.eu/transparency/regexpert/index.cfm?do=groupDetail.groupDetail&groupID=3485&NewSearch=1&NewSearch=1&Lang=EN.

[12] C Malecki, 'The EU Taxonomy Regulation: Giving a Good Name to Sustainable Investment' (2021) 26(4) *Environmental Liability* 149; CN Wang et al, 'Addressing the missing linkage in sustainable finance: the "SDG Finance Taxonomy"' (2022) 12(2) *Journal of Sustainable Finance & Investment* 630.

[13] See https://www.amf-france.org/fr/lamf/notre-organisation/la-commission-climat-et-finance-durable.

[14] See https://www.amf-france.org/sites/default/files/2020-07/finance-durable_juillet2020_final.pdf.

[15] OJEU, 22 June 2020, L 198/14.

[16] See https://ec.europa.eu/commission/presscorner/detail/fr/ip_20_335.

A. How the Taxonomy Works: Defining What Makes an Activity Economically and Environmentally Sustainable – A Classification Tool

The Taxonomy Regulation introduces a classification system or 'taxonomy' to iden-tify the extent to which an economic activity is environmentally sustainable, based on standard criteria. This European Taxonomy will be used to determine the degree of sustainability of investments in companies operating in each of these areas. This very general text required long and painstaking work, and yet was produced at unprec-edented speed. It is a regulation tool for a low carbon EU – a low-carbon continent based on the Matryoshka principle.

The Taxonomy is a classification tool that provides all financial market partic-ipants with a common understanding of what is to be considered a 'green' or 'sustainable' activity. It deals in detail with 70 economic activities based on the Technical Expert Group's (TEG) report. The TEG report of 18 June 2019 follows in the wake of the first proposal for a regulation that will create a framework to facilitate sustainable investment.[17] This report specifies the key areas of 'sustainable' activities listed by the proposed regulation. It was recommended that a framework of activities per sector be created.[18] The NACE classification[19] is useful even if it is not perfect in this regard because it provides a classification of industrial activi-ties already used by certain financial institutions, and it can be used with the Global Industrial Classification System (GICS). All of the TEG's activities make a welcome contribution as they provide excellent input that helps us develop our final standards on climate change mitigation and adaptation. Developed by more than 200 technical experts after 20 months of work, the Taxonomy finally establishes the framework and the environmental targets to be aimed at.

The Taxonomy is ultimately aimed at '… an effective way of channelling private investments into sustainable activities'. 'To that end, sustainable finance needs to become mainstream and consideration needs to be given to the sustainability impact of financial products and services'.[20]

i. Harmonising the Concept of Sustainability: First Steps

This harmonisation of the concept of sustainability is part of the vast programme of standardising quality-labelling criteria, financial products and improving clarity for market players. This classification is a world first: it aims to create a common language for investors. The aim is to enable comparability of sustainable financial instruments. The Taxonomy must be analysed in accordance with the definition of a sustainable investment proposed by the EU Regulation of 27 November 2019. Under the 2019 Sustainable Disclosure Regulation, sustainable investment is defined as:

> investment in an economic activity that contributes to an environmental objective, as measured, for example, by key resource efficiency indicators on the use of energy, renewable

---

[17] See https://ec.europa.eu/info/law/better-regulation/initiatives/com-2018-353_en.
[18] ibid 23 ff.
[19] Statistical Classification of Economic Activities in the European Community.
[20] EU Regulation 2019/2088, Recital 10.

energy, raw materials, water and land, on the production of waste, and greenhouse gas emissions, or on its impact on biodiversity and the circular economy, or an investment in an economic activity that contributes to a social objective, in particular an investment that contributes to tackling inequality or that fosters social cohesion, social integration and labour relations, or an investment in human capital or economically or socially disadvantaged communities, provided that such investments do not significantly harm any of those objectives and that the investee companies follow good governance practices, in particular with respect to sound management structures, employee relations, remuneration of staff and tax compliance.[21]

The environmental outcomes specified in the Sustainable Disclosure Regulation are fleshed out and standardised by the Taxonomy in terms of what indicators and aspects of achievement have to be made, in order to secure a harmonised sense of credibility. The Taxonomy, however, does not yet deal with social outcomes or the harmonisation of sound management or governance matters that the Sustainability Disclosure Regulation deals with. These may be regarded as future steps ahead in the EU's legislative pipeline.

ii. How the Taxonomy Works

The Taxonomy defines a list of economic activities as well as performance thresholds ('Technical Screening Criteria') that measure the contribution of these activities to six environmental objectives. It consists of seven macro-sectors and 72 sub-activities, which are named after the NACE code.

The seven macro-sectors are: agriculture and forestry; manufacturing; electricity, gas, steam and air conditioning supply; water, waste and sewerage remediation; transport; buildings; information and communication technologies. This taxonomy meets the need for a definition that is useful for the future, combining scientifically-consulted input with the need for financial certainty, viz the concept of 'environmentally sustainable' economic activity.

Article 3 of the EU Taxonomy Regulation proposes a list of 'criteria for the environmental sustainability of economic activities'. An economic activity is 'environmentally sustainable' if it complies with all of the following cumulative criteria:

(1) it contributes substantially to one or more of the environmental objectives set out in Article 5 in accordance with Articles 6 to 11a;
(2) it does not significantly harm any of the environmental objectives set out in Article 5 in accordance with Article 12; (the 'DNSH': see below);
(3) it is carried out in compliance with the minimum safeguards set out in Article 13;
(4) it complies with technical screening criteria specified by the Commission in accordance with Articles 6(2) 7(2), 8(2), 9(2), 10(2) and 11(2).

These technical screening criteria rules will be specified in delegated regulations.[22] The TEG Report proposes flexible tools to implement this taxonomy, for example

---

[21] Art 2(17).
[22] One proposal of a Delegated Act was adopted on 21 April 2021, see below.

in relation to the European Green Bonds Standards which are being introduced by the EU.[23] The aim is to allow any 'organisation' to specify the proportion of its activities that contribute substantially to the environmental objectives.

Six environmental objectives are specified in Article 5 of the Taxonomy Regulation as follows:

- climate change mitigation;
- climate change adaptation;
- sustainable use and protection of water and marine resources;
- the transition to a circular economy, and waste prevention and recycling;
- pollution prevention and control;
- the protection of healthy ecosystems.

The environmental objectives form the basis for investment product labelling as well as disclosure under the 2019 Sustainability Disclosure Regulation if investment firms offer products labelled in this manner. Article 4 of the Regulation provides that:

> Financial market participants offering financial products or corporate bonds shall disclose the relevant information allowing them to establish whether the products they offer qualify as environmentally sustainable investments or as investments having similar characteristics, shall disclose information on how and to what extent the criteria for environmentally sustainable economic activities set out in Article 3 are used to determine the environmental sustainability of the investment.

The Taxonomy Regulation also standardises how each objective is to be evaluated as being met, which is discussed in the following sections.

a. Substantial Contribution to Climate Change Mitigation (Article 6)

In particular, this entails the 'stabilization of greenhouse gas concentrations in the atmosphere at a level which prevents dangerous anthropogenic interference with the climate system by avoiding or reducing greenhouse gas emissions or enhancing greenhouse gas removals through …' certain specified means. The details in Article 6 reflect the intensity of scientific input in order to underpin the credibility of investments labelled as achieving sustainable outcomes.

b. Substantial Contribution to Climate Change Adaptation (Article 7)

This definition is broader and more flexible, as techniques in this area depend on general scientific and technological developments. Activities pursuant to this objective must contribute 'substantially to climate change adaptation' if they reduce the 'negative effects of the current and expected future climate' or 'prevent' 'an increase or

---

[23] European Commission, Proposal for a Regulation of the European Parliament and of the Council on European green bonds, COM/2021/391 final, 6 July 2021, https://eur-lex.europa.eu/legal-content/EN/TXT/?uri=CELEX:52021PC0391.

shifting of negative effects of climate change'. This will involve either 'preventing or reducing the location- and context-specific negative effects of climate change, which shall be assessed and prioritised using available climate projections, on the economic activity', or 'preventing or reducing the negative effects that climate change may pose to the natural and built environment within which the economic activity takes place, which shall be assessed and prioritised using available climate projections'.

c. Substantial Contribution to the Sustainable Use and Protection of Water and Marine Resources (Article 8)

This objective concerns the marine environment: the challenges of sustainable water management, especially drinking water and marine resources, water in quality and quantity. It includes a very detailed section on the 'good status of waters, including freshwater, transitional inland surface waters, estuaries and coastal waters', and also on the 'good ecological status of marine waters'. The protection of human health is specified. It should also be remembered that access to drinking water is a fundamental human right. There are two aspects: on the one hand, 'protecting the aquatic environment … from the adverse effects of urban and industrial wastewater discharges' and, on the other, 'protecting human health from the adverse effects of any contamination of drinking water'.

d. Substantial Contribution to the Circular Economy, Waste Prevention and Recycling (Article 9)

This objective concerns an essential aspect of sustainable development which is already becoming widespread under the impetus of the French Law on Energy Transition and green Growth.[24] The main aim is to increase the 'durability, reparability, upgradability or reusability of products' by insisting on the recyclability of products. However, these aspects will once again depend on the constant evolution of technologies and inventions in this field. Pollution and waste production are targeted.

e. Substantial Contribution to Pollution Prevention and Control (Article 10)

This objective sets out the methods (currently identified) used to provide a high level of environmental protection against pollution.

f. Substantial Contribution to Protection of Biodiversity and Healthy Ecosystems (Article 11)

This objective concerns the protection, conservation and enhancement of biodiversity and ecosystem services.

One pertinent question regarding the establishment of the Taxonomy system is how the attainment of these objectives is to be verified or assured, and whether a public

---

[24] Called LTECV (loi sur la transition énergétique et la croissance verte) 17 August 2015.

body would ultimately be responsible for upholding compliance with the Taxonomy standards. While no sanctions for non-compliance with the Taxonomy are envisaged at present, an external body will most probably be tasked with performing compliance checks in the future. This is likely to be ESMA at European level. This supervision will be very relevant to the promotion of pan-European fund offerings. However, it is also envisaged that private sector verification and assurance services may arise, such as those in relation to green bonds.[25] Indeed, according to the annual indicator of sustainable funds published by Novethic, a French Rating Agency, the volume of sustainable fund assets under management in France almost doubled in 2019 (+ 89 per cent), and this increase was combined with excellent financial performance.

B. The New Concept of the 'Do No Significant Harm' Principle

The Taxonomy Regulation also incorporates the new version of the 'do no harm' principle, the DNSH.[26] The notion of avoiding doing significant harm to environmental objectives is a new one. This emblematic notion is defined in Article 17, where the outcomes achieved run counter to the objectives intended to be attained in the six aspects discussed above. This definition fleshes out and complements the 2019 Sustainable Disclosure Regulation which generally requires investment products labelled as sustainable to be consistent with the DNSH.

The DNSH is defined in relation to each of the six objectives above, specifying what it means to be counterproductive to the attainment of each of the sustainability objectives. For example, in relation to the sustainability objective to climate change mitigation under Article 6 discussed above, significant harm would be done if an activity leads to significant greenhouse gas emissions. Or for example in relation to the sustainable objective promoting a circular economy under Article 13, significant harm is defined as:

'... activity lead[ing] to significant inefficiencies in the use of materials or in the direct or indirect use of natural resources such as non-renewable energy sources, raw materials, water and land at one or more stages of the life cycle of products, including in terms of durability, reparability, upgradability, reusability or recyclability of products; or

'... activity lead[ing] to a significant increase in the generation, incineration or disposal of waste, with the exception of the incineration of non-recyclable hazardous waste; or

'the long-term disposal of waste [that] may cause significant and long-term harm to the environment'.

The DNSH arguably provides clear indicators of when significant harm is found and when sustainable objectives are compromised, hence performing a control against greenwashing or the lack of credibility of the Taxonomy or labels of investment products based on the Taxonomy. Although it seems clear that the DNSH is defined in relation to counterproductive achievements, it is arguably less clear in relation

---

[25] Such as the Climate Bonds Initiative.
[26] Also called the 'do no significant harm' principle.

to the degree of severity for significant harm, and it is questioned to what extent shortfalls from sustainable objects would be tolerated before they breach the DNSH.

Moreover, the DNSH is used in the Recovery and Resilience Facility (RRF), which is the key instrument at the heart of NextGenerationEU to help the UE emerge stronger and more resilient from the COVID crisis.[27] Regarding nuclear energy, for example, the Commission published a huge technical assessment with respect to the DNSH principle.[28]

III. APPLICATION OF THE TAXONOMY TO SUSTAINABLE FINANCE

As soon as the Taxonomy Regulations come into force, financial market participants will be obliged to disclose precise information concerning any of their investment products that are qualified as 'sustainable'. These are mainstream investment products including fund products and investment-linked insurance products. For other types of offerings not labelled as sustainable, financial markets participants nevertheless must disclose if there are certain characteristics that the product should attain and how such attainment is to be evaluated.[29] For the products covered by the regulation, financial market participants will be required to indicate:

- the environmental objectives to which the investments contribute;
- the proportion of the underlying investments that are aligned with the Taxonomy, expressed as a percentage of the investment, fund or portfolio. This proportion must be calculated separately for each of the environmental objectives for which performance criteria have been defined.

For example, an asset-management company will need to be able to provide the total percentage of alignment of the underlying activities in its portfolio with the Taxonomy. Investment intermediaries would have to grapple with accessing corporate information as well as making sense of it in order to evaluate their portfolios' Taxonomy-alignment. Investment intermediaries should identify which activities carried out by the company could be eligible, and for which environmental objective. For each potentially eligible activity, investment intermediaries should check whether the company or issuer meets the relevant selection criteria (eg electricity generation $<100g\ CO_2/kWh$). Investment intermediaries should verify that the DNHP for other environmental objectives is not breached. They should also carry out a due diligence review to avoid any violation of minimum social guarantees. On the availability of data, it may be easier to retrieve data from large companies which will themselves be obliged to disclose information relating to the Taxonomy under the Non-Financial

---

[27] See Commission Notice, 'Technical guidance on the application of "do no significant harm" under the Recovery and Resilience Facility Regulation', Brussels, 12.2.2021, C(2021) 1054 final.

[28] JRC report, 'Technical assessment of nuclear energy with repect to the "do no significant harm" criteria of Regulation (EU) 2020/852 ("Taxonomy Regulation")', Ares(2021)1988129–19/03/2021 (387 pages).

[29] EU Sustainability Disclosure Regulation 2019/2088/EU, Art 8. This is further discussed in detail in Birkmose, see Ch 3 above.

Reporting Directive (NFRD). However non-financial reporting is highly unstandard-ised at the moment and the nature of the data may also prove to be challenging for investment intermediaries attempting to process them. In this respect an EU initia-tive is underway for standardisation of corporate sustainability data, including both environmental and social aspects, amending the 2014 NFRD.[30] Corporate disclosure is dicussed in more detail below.

The Taxonomy can also be applied to the voluntary label of the 'European Green Bond' (EuGB) proposed by the Commission. This regime is for issuers to opt in, not a mandatory framework for all green bond issues, so those aligned with CBI or ICMA principles remain legally marketable in the EU. Under this regime, issuers may choose to adopt the standard of an EuGB. The EuGB standards are supported by the Taxonomy in that the green bonds must relate to one of the Taxonomy objectives. This means that the green bonds should not only fund activities pertain-ing to the objectives and consistent with the DNHP, but that the performance of those activities funded by the bonds would also ultimately be measured according to the Taxonomy standards. The EuGB may be an attractive label for investors, as the bonds are underpinned by regulatory mechanisms that could not be offered in market-based governance, such as regulatory supervision and oversight of third party verifiers and assurers and standardised regulatory standards for certification and disclosure.

Next, and fundamentally, the Taxonomy would shape corporate disclosure of sustainable activities, profiles and performance. Corporate disclosure is the building block for investors to assess their equity and debt-based portfolios in mainstream investment.

An activity may be Taxonomy-aligned for three reasons:

(1) it is already a low-carbon activity (Own performance);
(2) it contributes to the transition to a net-zero-emission economy by 2050 ('Transi-tional activity'); or
(3) it enables other activities to reduce their CO_2 emissions ('Enabling activity').

In terms of the the breakdown between 'transition' and 'enabling' activities, enabling activities are economic activities that, by the provision of their products or services, enable a substantial contribution to be made in other activities, for example, an economic activity that manufactures a component that improves the environmental performance of another activity. Although the activities mentioned above concern the environmental aspects – in particular, climate change – there are more gener-ally applicable disclosures for corporations that proxy their attainment of social or environmental objectives. The Commission proposes that in order to capture the full spectrum of companies' dedication and performance in social and environmental aspects, each company whose field of activity is included in the scope of application

---

[30] See Corporate Sustainability Reporting Directive as proposed by the European Commission, https://www.europarl.europa.eu/legislative-train/theme-a-european-green-deal/file-review-of-the-non-financial-reporting-directive.

of the Sustainable Disclosure and Taxonomy regulations will be required to calculate the percentage sustainable alignment of its turnover, capital expenditures (Capex) or operating expenditures (Opex). For example, a renewable energy company may not necessarily have a 100 per cent alignment percentage. Its activity would therefore be considered not totally 'green'. Further, for example, a manufacturing plant which does not comply with the criteria for substantial contribution to climate change mitigation but is being renovated to improve its resilience against climate change could count expenditure linked to that renovation but not the turnover linked to its activity as a manufacturer, even after the plant has been made climate-resilient'.[31]

In time the sustainability disclosure by corporations, both public and private, are envisaged to be captured under the new Corporate Sustainability Reporting Directive amending the 2014 NFRD. This initiative would support the investment curation and allocation that is intended to be Taxonomy-aligned.

IV. THE FUTURE OF THE TAXONOMY REGULATION: FOCUS ON TWO KEY AREAS

The Taxonomy Regulation is arguably an evolving text, a necessarily flexible tool due to the rapid and constant evolution of knowledge in this field. The Commission's first task is to define a framework in order to establish uniform criteria to determine when an economic activity can be considered environmentally sustainable. Then, as this is an evolving process, the Commission will identify activities that can be considered sustainable in light of the technical advice received from a platform of experts. The objectives of any future taxonomy are unchanged: the attainment of the EU's environmental objectives (reduction of greenhouse gas emissions, transition to a circular economy and resource use). The green sectors (environmental restoration, waste management, energy efficiency, investment in renewable energy) are expected to have immediate impacts and enable the reduction of pollution (air, water, soil) in the longer term.

A. Technological Developments and Future Improvements

Although the Taxonomy is an exceptional advance, it is still insufficient and needs to be improved. It is regrettable that the social dimension is omitted and is still under development. On this point, the TEG has envisaged several complementary developments to improve the solution: adding social objectives to the environmental objectives and determining performance thresholds for 'brown' activities. As it will

---

[31] See p 5 of the draft of the EU Taxonomy Delegated Act, https://ec.europa.eu/finance/docs/level-2-measures/taxonomy-regulation-delegated-act-2021–2800_en.pdf and for example 'Thus any undertaking whose activities are not covered by the taxonomy EN 6 EN could count and disclose as taxonomy-aligned relevant expenditures in, for example, the purchase and installation of solar panels, energy efficient heating systems or energy efficient windows from manufacturers that comply with taxonomy criteria for these activities'.

be incorporated into the disclosure requirements of the NFRD, the European standard on 'Green Bonds', and the future 'European Eco-label', the EU is also aiming to
use the Taxonomy as an eligibility criterion for this European Eco-label. While the
threshold has not yet been determined, it is reasonable to imagine this label being
awarded as soon as 20 per cent of a fund's underlying activities are aligned with the
Taxonomy.

The Platform on Sustainable Finance[32] is also a permanent expert group of the
Commission that has been established under Article 20 of the Taxonomy Regulation.
Although it favours the financing of green activities, it cannot be considered a
complete response to the climate emergency, which requires the reduction of carbon
emissions within existing energy systems. For the time being, the Taxonomy only
concerns firms and management companies under the jurisdiction of the EU. Certain
activities could have been taken into account, such as maritime and air transport, fishing, and above all, fossil fuels (coal, oil) and the software sector as facilitators of the
climate transition. Further, it remains as open question as to how the criteria for each
of the objectives may be made more comprehensive with innovation in new activities.
At the same time, it remains important to be vigilant as to new ways in which significant harm may be done beyond the stipulated criteria for the DNHP, particularly
throughout the entire product life cycle and supply chain.

B. Emphasis on a 'Minimum' of Social Rules

The strong environmental dimension of this text is immediately apparent, but the
future development of social aspects, especially in accordance with Article 8 (access
to water in general), is clearly implied. But what about the notion of social objectives
and social rules? These rules will hopefully be specified in future delegated regulations. Well-being and health for example, are referred to in the recent communication
from the Commission of 24 February 2021 'Forging a climate-resilient Europe – the
new EU Strategy on Adaptation to Climate Change'.

The Taxonomy sets mandatory requirements on disclosure with the aim of providing transparency on environmental performance. Large financial and non-financial
companies that fall under the scope of the Non-Financial Reporting Directive will
have to disclose to what extent the activities that they carry out meet the criteria
defined in the Taxonomy.

This text should be considered as just one component of a larger scheme (applying the Matryoshka principle throughout Europe): a set of texts that aims to create
a general framework for sustainable finance (duty of disclosure, securities regulation, sustainability reporting, benchmarks and indices, EuGB principles, supervision
of national regulatory authorities and ESMA's role, the roles of non-financial rating

---

[32]See https://ec.europa.eu/info/business-economy-euro/banking-and-finance/sustainable-finance/overview-
sustainable-finance/platform-sustainable-finance_en.

agencies, etc). There are still points to be improved, such as the difficulty of forming a general understanding, but the parties have managed to put the parts together like a technical jigsaw puzzle on an unprecedented scale. Rarely has so much work by the AMF, ESMA, and the Commission led to the publication of texts such as regulations within such a short time frame.

C. Implementation of the Taxonomy

The ultimate aim of European taxonomisation of environmental and social objectives is to cover all the sustainability objectives, ie both environmental and social in terms of 'finance climat' (climate-oriented finance) or 'finance résiliente' (resilient finance). In all these areas, given the speed of technological developments, the Commission plans to adopt delegated acts in order to supplement the above-mentioned articles with a view to establishing 'technical examination criteria' to determine whether a particular economic activity makes a 'substantial contribution' in relation to each article. Indeed, the Taxonomy empowers the Commission to adopt delegated and implementing acts to specify how competent authorities and market participants shall comply with the obligations laid down in the directive. One complication is the many levels of delegated legislation and ESMA's Guidelines that would follow, therefore representing a complex framework for corporations and the financial industry to comply with.

The EU Taxonomy Delegated Act, the first Delegated Act, also called the Climate Delegated Act[33] politically adopted by the College of Commissioners on 21 April 2021, defines the technical screening criteria for economic activities that can make a substantial contribution to climate change mitigation and climate change adaptation, and determines whether those economic activities cause significant harm to any of the other relevant environmental objectives. One of the main questions is about nuclear energy. Is nuclear power included or excluded from the EU taxonomy? There is already a technical report on the 'do no significant harm' aspects of nuclear energy.[34] At this stage, the Taxonomy Regulation neither includes nor excludes natural gas.[35] This Delegated Act which is applicable from 1 January 2022 foresees that the Commission will review the screening criteria for both bioenergy and forestry based on upcoming Commission policies and taking into account legislation. It has been decided to delay the inclusion of the agricultural sector until the next Delegated Act.

Two other Delegated Acts have been adopted by the Commission: (i) the Disclosures Delegated Act, which specifies the content and presentation of information to be disclosed by undertakings subject to Article 19a or 29a of Directive 2013/34/EU

---

[33] Commission Delegated Regulation (EU) 2021/2139 of 4 June 2021, OJUE, 9.12.2021, L 442/1.
[34] See https://ec.europa.eu/info/sites/default/files/business_economy_euro/banking_and_finance/documents/210329-jrc-report-nuclear-energy-assessment_en.pdf.
[35] See https://ec.europa.eu/commission/presscorner/detail/en/qanda_21_1805.

(Accounting Directive) concerning environmentally sustainable economic activities, and specifying the methodology to comply with that disclosure obligation;[36] and (ii) the Complementary Climate Delegated Act adopted on 9 March 2022, which includes under strict conditions specific nuclear and gas energy activities in the list of economic activities covered by the Taxonomy.[37] This act will apply as of January 2023.

A careful alignment had to be found between the requirements of the Taxonomy Regulation, notably the 'do no significant harm' requirements, and the requirements of existing law, such as the Water Framework Directive.

D. Entry into Force and Remaining Questions

The entry into force of the European Taxonomy regulation is envisaged in two phases. The first disclosures concerning activities contributing to the first two environmental objectives will have to be carried out from 2022 by undertakings, asset management companies and insurance undertakings. The Disclosure Delegated Act also specifies the content, methodology and presentation of information to be disclosed by large financial and non-financial undertakings. The timeline for the application of reporting requirements is provided in Article 10 of the Disclosures Delegated Act.

Then, from 2023, these companies will be required to disclose information relating to the six environmental objectives. For financial market participants, information concerning compliance with the Taxonomy should be provided as part of the existing pre-contractual and periodic requirements, and on websites. The pre-contractual reports must include the environmental objectives of the fund, the percentage of alignment with the Taxonomy (eg 20 per cent of the fund invested in companies whose turnover is at least 50 per cent aligned with the Taxonomy), and how the Taxonomy will be used to achieve these objectives. The periodic reports must include descriptions of how the strategies have been implemented as well as the one-off calculations of percentage alignment with the Taxonomy.

E. Taxonomy as a Key Element for Other EU Regulations/Initiatives

i. *The Disclosure Regulation in the Financial Services Sector*

Although EU Regulation 2019/2088 on sustainability-related disclosures in the financial services sector has established duties for public and pre-contractual disclosures by all investment intermediaries on their management of sustainability risks and the characteristics and accountability regarding sustainably-labelled investment products,

---

[36] Commission Delegated Regulation (EU) 2021/2178 of 6 July 2021, OJUE 10.12.2021, L 443/9.
[37] Commission Delegated Regulation (EU) 2022/1214 of 9 March 2022, OJUE, 15.7.2022, L 188/1.

it is queried how these disclosures may expand or be changed with new developments such as in relation to the social aspects of the Taxonomy. Further, it should be considered whether the EU should standardise investment products characterised as 'ESG' or responsible with the sustainable label, or whether the sustainable label should still be for voluntary adoption, signalling certain quality standards.

ii. *Sustainable Corporate Governance?*

The European Parliament Resolution of 17 December 2020 on sustainable corporate governance (2020/2137(INI))[38] insists on the Taxonomy being in the centre of the regulations on sustainable finance and on sustainable corporate finance. Indeed, it is useful to mention §6 of this Resolution:

> Notes that the Taxonomy Regulation establishes a series of environmental objectives, namely on climate change, the use and protection of water and marine resources, the transition to a circular economy, pollution prevention and control, and on biodiversity and ecosystems; considers that the concept of environmental matters in the NFRD should be interpreted in line with the Taxonomy Regulation and include all forms of pollution.

Non-financial corporate disclosure is at the centre of sustainable corporate governance, as such disclosure provides the necessary basis for shareholders' exercise of power, such as engagement referred to in the Shareholders' Rights Directive 2017,[39] as well as the necessary background and context for corporate Boards to consider their strategic and stakeholder orientations. A revised NFDR[40] adopted by the Commission on 21 April 2021, called the Corporate Sustainability Reporting Directive (CSRD) is the much-anticipated way forward. This proposal is an important step not only by extending the scope to all large companies and all companies listed on EU regulated markets (removing the employee threshold but excluding listed micro-entreprises) but also by introducing more detailed sustainability requirements, in particular a requirement to report according to mandatory EU sustainability standards developped by the European Financial Reporting Advisory Group. The European Single Access Point will require companies to digitally 'tag' the reporting information – a 'one-stop shop' which would be very useful for investors.

There is no doubt that the non-financial information is quite complex but this will supplement the basic financial or quantitative information that corporations are now required to disclose under the Taxonomy Regulation, ie Article 8, which provides for the disclosure of the proportion of corporations' turnover, Capex and Opex, associated with activities included in the taxonomy.

iii. *Other Initiatives*

Although regulatory harmonisation for investment entities' basic duties, as well as the marketing of sustainable finance, is important in the EU for building a credible

---

[38] European Parliament Report, Text tabled A9-0240/2020.
[39] See Birkmose, Ch 3 above.
[40] See https://eur-lex.europa.eu/legal-content/EN/TXT/HTML/?uri=CELEX:52021PC0189&from=EN.

sustainable finance market, there remain certain developments that would be necessary to complement regulatory governance.

A European sustainable observatory would be useful as a post-regulatory monitoring mechanism. The future creation of a 'European Sustainable Finance Observatory' by the European Environment Agency, in cooperation with the ESAs will be responsible for monitoring, reporting and publishing information on sustainable investment bu EU funds and institutions (European Fund for Stretegic Investments (EFSI), European Investment Bank (EIB), European Central Bank (ECB)).

Further, Article 20 of the Taxonomy Regulation aims at the creation of a sustainable finance platform. This platform can play an advisory role. This platform satisfies the wishes of the HLEG, in particular. It will be chaired by the Commission and composed of members drawn from the European Investment Agency, the ESAs, the EIB and the European Investment Fund, experts representing private-sector stakeholders, and experts recognised for their knowledge or proven experience. The EU Platform on Sustainable Finance, created on 18 June 2020, whose membership list[41] was published on 26 October 2020, will play a role together with the International Platform on Sustainable Finance. This platform has a varied mission and will be essential for the future of sustainable finance (analysing the impact of technical review criteria, tendering advice, providing analytical support, and reporting to the Commission, particularly on the 'channelling of capital flows into sustainable investments').

V. CONCLUSION

Step by step the European Green Deal is bringing about a new growth strategy. The EU Taxonomy Regulation, which is very technical and innovative regarding the 'Do no significant harm' principle is at the centre of many other regulations, such as Sustainable Disclosure Regulation for financial intermediaries, the future CSRD, the Resolution on Sustainable Corporate Governance and the EU Green Bonds Regulation to name but a few.[42] Non-financial information which should be meaningful, comprehensive, comparable, assurable and electronically accessible would be the most important tool for shareholders, stakeholders and boards members. The Taxonomy Regulation provides an objective basis for non-financial information and representations to be made, and actual financial allocations to be deployed, as well as corporate activities and performance to be evaluated, upon a harmonised footing. It is not doubted that EuGBs and Social Bonds are on the rise in terms of investment interest. The current climate emergency and even the COVID-19 crisis could boost mainstream interest in resilient finance. As Christine Lagarde, President of the ECB,

---

[41] See https://ec.europa.eu/info/sites/info/files/business_economy_euro/banking_and_finance/documents/eu-platform-on-sustainable-finance-members_en.pdf.

[42] For example, the new rules for EU regional, cohesion and social funds for the period 2021–2027 will also need to respect the DNSH principle within the meaning of Art 17 of the Taxonomy Regulation, but without requiring the use of the delegated acts and related technical screening criteria.

explained in a speech in 2020, climate change constitutes a major challenge for this century. 'The transition to a carbon-neutral economy provides opportunities, not just risks'.[43] Sustainable finance is poised to deliver not only public interest outcomes but also new opportunities, and the EU has again pinned its hopes on legal harmonisation to achieve these outcomes.

[43] Speech by Christine Lagarde, President of the European Central Bank, at the COP 26 Private Finance Agenda, London 27 February 2020; see also 'Towards a Green Capital Markets Union for Europe' at the European Commission's high-level conference on the proposal for a Corporate Sustainable Reporting Directive, 6 May 2021 Frankfurt am Main, https://www.ecb.europa.eu/press/key/date/2021/html/ecb. sp210506~4ec98730ee.en.html.

6

Direct Mandatory Corporate Social Responsibility Legislation: Lessons from China and Indonesia

LI-WEN LIN* AND IRIS H-Y CHIU

I. INTRODUCTION

THIS CHAPTER DISCUSSES a legislative development adopted by some emerging economies as they contend with the need to change corporate behaviour so as to meet social and political goals and objectives. These goals may be aligned with what investors increasingly value as goals with regard to environmental, governance and social effects. However the legislative approach reflects policy-makers' preference not merely to rely on capital markets channels to incentivise changes in corporate behaviour, but to implement industrial and social policy. This approach may particularly meet emerging economies' needs for a stronger economic steer while addressing social issues, where political institutions may be more powerful and developed than market or private sector institutions.[1] This chapter discusses such an institutional approach to shaping corporate behaviour, in contrast to investor-led, market-based approaches which have been predominantly accepted in the Western developed jurisdictions of the US, UK and EU discussed elsewhere in this volume.

Corporate social responsibility (CSR) is typically understood as a voluntary undertaking by corporations rather than a legal obligation imposed by the government. Yet, this understanding is no longer true. In recent years, a growing number of countries around the world have adopted a wide variety of innovative legislation with the purpose of improving corporate social and environmental performance.

---

*Portions of the chapter are adapted from my previous work, Li-Wen Lin, 'Mandatory Corporate Social Responsibility Legislation around the World: Emergent Varieties and National Experiences' (2021) 23 *University of Pennsylvania Journal of Business Law* 429.

[1] S Parnell and S Oldfield (eds), *The Routledge Handbook on Cities of the Global South* (Routledge, 2014) Ch 16, which deals with China's strong government steering policies in urbanisation for example.

The most common type of CSR legislation is mandatory reporting,[2] in which companies are required to disclose extensive information about their social and environmental plans, actions or performance. While disclosure is mandatory, the law does not require any substantive social or environmental performance. The effectiveness of this disclosure-based legislation relies on market and societal participants such as consumers, investors and non-governmental organisations (NGOs) to utilise disclosed information and pressure companies to change behaviour. More recently, not only companies but also financial investors have been subject to disclosure regulation. For instance, EU Sustainable Finance Disclosure Regulation (SFDR), which came into force on 10 March 2021, requires certain asset managers and financial advisers to disclose whether and how environmental, social and governance (ESG) factors are integrated into their risk assessments, investment decisions or advice.[3] Firms not adopting ESG factors are required to publish their reasons for not doing so, which often is referred to as the 'comply-or-explain' model.

Mandatory CSR disclosure is *indirect* regulation. It does not directly impose any legal obligations on companies, asset managers or financial advisers to achieve any substantive social or environmental goals. Instead, it relies on a chain of market reactions to ultimately trigger any behaviour change of companies. With CSR information available, consumers are expected to choose to patronise socially or environmentally friendly products and boycott unfriendly ones. Further, the most significant market actors would be investors. Investors can study such disclosures and determine if they wish to allocate capital to particular companies, and by their market discipline also signal the importance of particular ESG criteria, or may avoid or divest from companies that do not meet certain ESG criteria or are 'irresponsible'. The disclosure-based legislation expects market reaction to drive companies toward accountability. For example, reforms in the EU such as the Non-Financial Reporting Directive[4] in 2014 mandate certain non-financial disclosures such as environmental, human rights and anti-corruption etc disclosures so that investors can determine the market importance of these matters. This is now reinforced by sustainable finance reforms such as the SFDR imposed directly on many institutional investors. Such legislation follows an *indirect* approach, yet with a longer chain of market reactions. It is hoped that retail investors would channel their money to asset managers and financial advisers who consider ESG factors, and in turn such financial agents have stronger leverage to influence corporate behaviour.

---

[2] According to a recent report by KPMG International, Global Reporting Initiative (GRI), United Nations Environmental Programme (UNEP), and the Centre for Corporate Governance in Africa, at least 64 countries in the world have introduced almost 400 sustainability reporting instruments and more than two thirds of the instruments are mandatory regulations: Global Reporting Initiative, 'Carrots and Sticks: Global Trends in Sustainability Reporting Regulation and Policy', 10, 12 (2016), https://www.carrotsandsticks.net.

[3] Regulation (EU) 2019/2088 of the European Parliament and of the Council of 27 November 2019 on Sustainability-Related Disclosures in the Financial Services Sector, https://eur-lex.europa.eu/legal-content/EN/TXT/?uri=celex%3A32019R2088.

[4] EU Non-financial Reporting Directive 2014/95/EU.

Despite its worldwide popularity, mandatory disclosure has been controversial in its effectiveness in improving substantive corporate behaviour.[5] An obvious yet rarely asked question in the debate about this indirect disclosure-based regulation is: if the ultimate goal is to hold companies accountable, why not just directly impose an encompassing CSR duty on companies? Recently, this direct approach has been adopted in a few countries, among which China and Indonesia are the earliest pioneers. Since more than a decade ago, their corporate statutes respectively have expressly required companies to undertake 'corporate social responsibility'. Important to note is that their corporate statutes impose a general CSR duty on *companies*, rather than merely part of directors' fiduciary duties as often discussed in scholarship.[6] This chapter reviews the legal experience of China and Indonesia. It shows that politics – and, importantly, the inherent vagueness of CSR itself – explain the implementation (or lack thereof) in legal practice. The lack of specificity of the general CSR duty significantly weakens the compulsory nature of the law. The law does not set any substantive requirements about any specific behaviour but leaves the implementation entirely in the hands of corporations.

A general CSR duty imposed on companies is a form of *direct* but *unspecific* CSR regulation. The law has limited enforceability and largely only serves an expressive function. The explicit legal recognition of CSR may send signals about appropriate corporate behaviour and reform business norms that exclusively focus on profits. But it requires *direct* and *specific* regulation to make CSR truly mandatory and enforceable. The law should have precise behaviour requirements and rigorous enforcement. To the extent that specific corporate performance is required, it probably entails specific legal requirements under specialised laws, such as topic-focused, industry-specific, geography-targeted and behaviour-specified regulations. A general CSR duty, if in place, should not and would not able to act as substitutes for regulatory modes that require specific and substantive performance, though the CSR law may have a complementary role to play through promoting responsible business norms.

---

[5] See generally O Ben-Shahar and CE Schneider, 'The Failure of Mandated Disclosure' (2011) 159 *University of Pennsylvania Law Review* 647 (noting that a series of required conditions for mandated disclosures to succeed are rarely met, leading to dubious indirect benefits and various costs). For a review of empirical evidence on mandatory disclosure, see D Hess, 'The Transparency Trap: Non-Financial Disclosure and the Responsibility of Business to Respect Human Rights' (2019) 56 *American Business Law Journal* 5 (finding that CSR disclosure legislation often increases information quantity but without much improvement in quality).

[6] See B Sheehy and D Feaver, 'Anglo-American Directors' Legal Duties and CSR: Prohibited, Permitted or Prescribed?' (2012) 37 *Dalhousie Law Journal* 345, 386–92 (comparing whether directors have a CSR duty in Australia, Canada, the UK and the US). For instance, the UK Companies Act 2006 requires directors to consider the interests of employees, consumers, suppliers, the environment, and the community when pursuing the interests of shareholders: Companies Act 2006, s 172; see also VE Harper Ho, 'Enlightened Shareholder Value: Corporate Governance Beyond the Shareholder-Stakeholder Divide' (2010) 36 *Journal of Corporation Law* 59, 78–79, 92 (explaining how s 172 mandates greater corporate social responsibility); and AR Keay and H Zhang, 'An Analysis of Enlightened Shareholder Value in Light of Ex Post Opportunism and Incomplete Law' (2011) 8 *European Company and Financial Law Review* 445, 446–48 (evaluating whether s 172 is too vague a requirement to effectively ensure that directors consider the interests of all stakeholders).

II. ARTICLE 5 OF CHINESE COMPANY ACT 2006

In 2006, China made a comprehensive revision to its corporate statute. A salient feature of this revision was a new provision explicitly requiring companies to undertake CSR. Article 5 provides that '[i]n the course of doing business, a company shall comply with laws and administrative regulations, conform to social morality and business ethics, act in good faith, subject itself to the government and the public supervision, and undertake social responsibility'.[7] The official legislative documents provide little clue about why legislators decided to adopt the CSR provision. Nevertheless, some government officials and legal scholars who were involved in the legislation compiled and published the opinions considered in the law-making process, which may shed some light on the legislative history.[8] According to the sources, legislators of various provinces advocated explicit recognition of CSR in corporate law.[9] For instance, Shanghai delegates at the National People's Congress proposed that CSR should be included as one of the legislative purposes of company law and 'companies shall protect and improve the interests of other stakeholders in addition to shareholders'.[10]

Although the CSR provision was passed into law with strong legislative support, its practical application since enactment has been controversial among legal scholars and practitioners. The statutory language of Article 5 appears mandatory, yet Chinese law scholars have different interpretations about the nature of the CSR provision. Some scholars view the CSR provision as purely ethical and legally unenforceable, as the corporate statute does not define CSR or provide any remedies in case of non-compliance.[11] In contrast, some scholars see Article 5 as compulsory in nature.[12] They argue that the CSR provision is a fundamental principle of corporate law and should be applied to interpretations of all provisions throughout the statute.[13] Moreover, they maintain that the corporate statute has implemented the broad CSR principle through some specific requirements such as employee participation in corporate governance. Other scholars argue that the CSR provision is both a moral obligation and a legal obligation.[14]

Despite the lack of consensus among Chinese legal scholars on the nature of the CSR provision, it is generally accepted that the CSR law probably has little use in

---

[7] Company Law of the People's Republic of China (promulgated by Standing Committee, National People's Congress, 27 October 2005, effective 1 January 2006), Art 5, Westlaw China.

[8] K Cao et al, *A Research Report on the Amendments to Company Law* (2005) (in Chinese). The Chinese government did not disclose official documents concerning the legislative history. The editors of this report compiled the opinions considered in the legislative process. The leading editor was the head of the State Council's Legislative Affairs Office, responsible for drafting laws and regulations. Other editors were also affiliated with the Office; and some are prominent law professors in China.

[9] ibid, 21, 141.

[10] ibid.

[11] See eg X Chen, 'Rational Consideration on the Legal Rule of Corporate Social Responsibility: A Comment on Article 5 of Chinese Company Law' in B Wang (eds), *China Commercial Law Annual 2009* (2009) (in Chinese) 50–53.

[12] J Liu, *Institutional Innovation of New Company Law: Legislative and Judicial Controversies* (2006) (in Chinese) 555.

[13] ibid.

[14] See eg J Lou, 'The Literal Interpretation and Implementation Path of Article Five Paragraph One of Chinese Company Law' (2008) 20 *Peking University Law Journal* 36, 36–37 (in Chinese).

legal practice. Indeed, Chinese courts seldom apply the law in a way that has any real legal consequences as a matter of company law. Nevertheless, it is not useless in judicial decisions. As I have shown elsewhere, Chinese courts have expressly referred to Article 5 in around a hundred cases.[15] These cases are seldom litigation in relation to corporate law, but private law litigation regarding contractual and tort liability or breaches of regulatory duties resulting in private harm. Nevertheless the CSR provision has on occasion been used to pierce the corporate veil so that shareholders became personally liable for harm caused by the company, although the reasoning for invoking the CSR provision and its legal connection to piercing the corporate veil has not been clearly articulated. The most common application of the CSR provision relates to legal compliance. Chinese courts used the CSR provision as an additional legal ground to require companies to comply with contracts or other legal rules or to shoulder liability or compensatory responsibility. For example, in one case where the defendant corporation refused to make any social security payments for a long-term employee, the court stated that '[t]imely and sufficient payment of social security charges for employees is the corporation's legal obligation as well as a representation of corporate social responsibility'.[16]

In some cases, the courts used the CSR provision to exhort companies to go beyond legal compliance. For instance, a company that managed a dam for fishing and recreation purposes breached a water supply agreement with the local farming community. At the end of its ruling, the court emphasised CSR under Article 5 and 'remind[ed] the [defendant] corporation to try its best to balance the relationship between profitability and social responsibility while legally operating its business, thereby increasing its long-term competitiveness'.[17]

More importantly, in a few cases, the courts applied the CSR provision to determine the outcome of judicial dissolution under corporate law.[18] Chinese courts denied judicial dissolution sought by shareholders if such dissolution would potentially cause mass protests by employees or consumers.[19] The courts interpreted CSR to include a responsibility to maintain 'social stability'.[20] This interpretation of CSR is closely connected with China's political institutions. The Chinese government (ultimately the Chinese Communist Party) suppresses any social unrest that would possibly threaten its rule. The Chinese courts subject to the Party's control draw on the legal term of CSR to advance and legitimise the Party's political interests.[21]

---

[15] L-W Lin, 'Mandatory Corporate Social Responsibility? Legislative Innovation and Judicial Application in China' (2020) 68 *American Journal of Comparative Law* 576.

[16] See Shamen Shi Bisite Shizhuang Youxian Gongsi Yu Shamen Shi Shehui Baoxian Guanli Zhongxin Xingzheng Panjueshu An [*Xiamen Bisite Fashion Co Ltd v Xiamen Municipal Social Security Management Center*, An Administrative Judgement] (Fujian Province Xiamen City Simin District People's Court, 1 December 2014) (China Law Info).

[17] See Beijing Dadi Yujia Shengtai Luyou Kaifa Youxian Gongsi Deng Yu Beijing Shi Huairou Qu Changshaoying Manzu Xiang Dadi Cun Cunmin Weiyuanhui Hetong Jiufen Shangsu An [*Beijing Dadi Yujia Ecological Travel Development Co Ltd v Beijing Huairo District Shaoyingmenzu Village Committee*, An Appeal of Contract Dispute] (Beijing City Third Intermediate People's Court, 13 December 2016) (China Law Info).

[18] Lin (n 15 above).

[19] ibid.

[20] ibid 28.

[21] ibid.

Chinese courts have used the CSR provision to require legal compliance or to encourage something beyond legal compliance; yet, they have never used the CSR provision to impose any additional legal obligations on corporations. As a standard of conduct, the CSR provision permits corporations to pursue goals other than profits but it does not require any additional legal responsibilities. Meanwhile, as a judicial review standard illustrated in the cases of judicial dissolution sought by shareholders, the CSR provision gives an additional legal ground based on which the court may justify its decision in favour of the interests of society (or government). From a legal perspective, the importance of the CSR provision under the Chinese corporate statute is more for a court ruling standard than a corporate behaviour standard.[22] It seems that Chinese judges have some social consciousness and legal capacity to meaningfully apply the vague CSR law. Chinese courts have been quite competent in dealing with cases that require the exercise of equity and discretion, such as cases involving fiduciary duties, piercing the corporate veil and oppression actions.[23] These related practical experiences provide the courts with complementary skills to apply the vague CSR law.

To date, the effect of the general CSR duty has been largely extra-judicial, non-adjudicative and expressive. China's corporate statute does not provide non-shareholders with any rights to enforce the CSR duty against the corporation or directors. Even in relation to shareholders, it is uncertain if shareholders can rely on this provision in shareholder litigation, such as for breaches of fiduciary duties, as the legal connection between the CSR provision, which is the company's responsibility, is not clearly made with directors' fiduciary duties.

The compulsory nature of the CSR duty can arguably be significantly weakened if enforcement is not generally found as a matter of corporate law. However, it may be argued that the CSR provision is a form of social policy that transcends the corporate law framework, and is unique to China as the notion of company law as 'private law' is not necessarily dominant in China,[24] since there are strong public interest elements framing company law as a form of public regulatory law. In particular, commentators anchor Chinese company law, in particular the CSR provision, upon the 'harmonious society' political agenda.[25] As Zhao[26] argues, this agenda conceives of company law and the development of the private corporate sector in China as being part of broader economic development plans. However, as private sector-led economic development

---

[22] A standard of conduct specifies how an actor should conduct a given activity or play a given role, while a standard of review is the rule with which the court determines whether to impose liability or grant relief. See MA Eisenberg, 'The Divergence of Standards of Conduct and Standards of Review in Corporate Law' (1993) 62 *Fordham Law Review* 437 (discussing the importance of recognising the differences between standards of conduct and standards of review as they may sometimes differ, especially in corporate law).

[23] See G Xu, 'Directors' Duties in China' (2013) 14 *European Business Organization Law Review* 57; DC Clarke and NC Howson, 'Pathway to Minority Shareholder Protection: Derivative Actions in the People's Republic of China' in D Puchniak et al (eds). *The Derivative Action in Asia: A Comparative and Functional Approach* (Cambridge University Press, 2012) 243–95; NC Howson, 'Fiduciary Principles in Chinese Law' in EJ Criddle et al, *The Oxford Handbook of Fiduciary Law* (Oxford University Press, 2019) 603.

[24] CX-C Weng, 'Inside or Outside the Corporate Law Box? Shareholder Primacy and Corporate Social Responsibility in China' (2017) 18 *European Business Organisations Law Review* 155.

[25] J Zhao, 'The Harmonious Society, Corporate Social Responsibility and Legal Responses to Ethical Norms in Chinese Company Law' (2012) 12 *Journal of Corporate Law Studies* 163.

[26] ibid; J Zhao, 'Promoting More Socially Responsible Corporations through a Corporate Law Regulatory Framework' (2017) 37 *Legal Studies* 103.

can bring about social externalities, such as the scandal involving the Sanlu infant milk powder contamination,[27] as well as environmental degradation, social discontent where companies treat their employees or stakeholders poorly, and wealth inequalities, the 'harmonious society' agenda is meant to ameliorate unchecked private sector incentives in order to bind everyone to a social contract respecting social stability and common civic expectations. In this manner, company law legislation functions as a public regulatory instrument as well, setting out the state's expectations for corporate behaviour, internally amongst its constituents, as well as externally-facing aspects. Hence, one can accept that broader enforcement outside of corporate law in relation to the CSR provision is justified upon this unique social contract, and both the state and private litigants (not litigating in corporate law as such) are stakeholders that call for articulations of corporations' responsibility to society generally in the appropriate case. Can one therefore regard this wider 'socialised' form of enforcement as being more imperative for shaping corporate behaviour and hence more effective than the constraints faced by Western jurisdictions which treat company law as private law, and rely on shareholders and market channels to translate discipline?

While judicial application of the CSR provision is generally limited, there are regulatory measures with a view to implementing the CSR provision within the frameworks of corporate legislation.[28] Mandatory sustainability reporting is a good example, and in this manner, it seems that shareholders – who are the main recipients of such reporting – are regarded as potential sources of discipline for companies in relation to ESG or sustainability matters. For instance, in an explicit attempt to further Article 5 of China's corporate statute, the Shanghai Stock Exchange has required certain types of listed companies to issue annual CSR reports since 2008.[29] Recently, Chinese regulators have further mandated all listed companies by the end of 2021 to disclose key environmental information in their annual reports.[30] In 2016, the Chinese government published the Guidelines for Establishing the Green Financial System, which sets comprehensive policies for sustainable lending, insurance and investing.[31] Over the years, China now has become the world's second largest issuer of climate-aligned

[27] 'True Horror of Sanlu Milk Scandal Revealed', https://www.dairyindustries.com/news/838/true-horror-of-sanlu-milk-scandal-revealed/#:~:text=The%20scandal%20surrounding%20China's%20toxic,can%20also%20cause%20kidney%20failure.

[28] Lin (n 15 above) at 10–12.

[29] Three types of companies are subject to this disclosure requirement, including: companies in the Shanghai Stock Exchange Corporate Governance Index, companies that list shares overseas, and companies in the financial sector. According to information released by the Shanghai Stock Exchange, 290 listed companies published CSR reports for the fiscal year of 2008. Of these 290 companies, 258 companies issued CSR reports due to the regulatory requirement while only 32 companies did so voluntarily. For a detailed discussion about the Chinese stock exchanges' CSR disclosure rules and the implementation effects, see L-W Lin, 'Corporate Social and Environmental Disclosure in Emerging Securities Markets' (2009) 35 *North Carolina Journal of International Law* 1, 18–22.

[30] China Securities Regulatory Commission, 'Notice of the China Securities Regulatory Commission on Promulgating the Standards Concerning the Contents and Formats of Information Disclosure by Companies Offering Securities to the Public No 2 – Contents and Formats of Annual Reports' (6 June 2021), http://lawinfochina.com/display.aspx?id=36782&lib=law&EncodingName=big5.

[31] People's Bank of China et al, 'Guidelines for Establishing the Green Financial System' [guanyu goujian luse jinrong tixi de zhidao yijian] (31 August 2016) http://www.scio.gov.cn/32344/32345/35889/36819/xgzc36825/Document/1555340/1555348.htm. For more research about green finance, see V Harper Ho, 'Sustainable Finance & China's Green Credit Reforms: A Test Case for Bank Monitoring of Environmental Risk' (2018) 51 *Cornell International Law Journal* 609.

bonds since its first corporate green bond was issued in 2015.[32] As of June 2020, there were 47 ESG mutual funds and ETFs operating in China and managing assets worth US$7.3 billion.[33] There is empirical evidence showing that shareholders 'care' about sustainability reporting, and adverse reporting does result in negative stock price reactions on China's main stock exchanges.[34] However it remains uncertain in what sense shareholders really engage with companies' ESG matters, and whether shareholders matter in that regard, given the preceding discussion on the mandatory CSR provision and its main enforcement dimensions.

There is little sense of shareholder engagement or activism in China. In part, one queries whether this is because of the adverse perception of activism or campaigns for causes being 'socially disruptive'. Zhao[35] documents an episode where, during the eruption of the Sanlu infant milk powder scandal, an activist demanding compensation for infant victims was imprisoned for causing 'social disruption' although he was championing what many would objectively regard as a just cause. Indeed the most pronounced enforcement against the company came in the form of criminal prosecutions and sentences, reflecting the preference for public law and regulation for dealing with corporate irresponsibility as a form of anti-social conduct.

That said, reforms to Chinese law in relation to the institution of private securities litigation[36] as a remedial outlet for investors with respect to securities misrepresentations may reflect a gradual move towards enrolling shareholders into the discipline landscape for corporations via litigation. But it may be said that even if shareholders' private rights are augmented, the broader context of 'harmonious society' looms large in relation to the interpretation of such rights. Further, it is unlikely that shareholders, or market-based channels are regarded as a key means of signalling discipline for corporations. The distrust of economic primacy by the state ensures that economic developments are firmly embedded within social policy.

Can it be argued that international developments converging upon the endorsement of shareholder stewardship[37] would also influence Chinese developments in relation to their conception of shareholders' roles? For example, Ping An, one of the largest insurers and asset owners in China has recently become a signatory to the PRI and to the Climate Action 100+ network.[38] Although the embrace of ESG investing is

---

[32] *See* Climate Bonds Initiative and China Central Depository & Clearing Company (CCDC), 'China Green Bond Market 2017', https://www.climatebonds.net/files/files/China_Annual_Report_2017_EN_Final_14_02_2018.pdf.

[33] Cerulli Associates, 'Sustainable Investing Evolves in China' (21 December 2020), https://www.cerulli.com/news/sustainable-investing-evolves-in-china.

[34] H Huang et al, 'Chinese Shareholders' Reaction to the Disclosure of Environmental Violations: A CSR Perspective' (2017) 2 *International Journal of Corporate Social Responsibility* 12.

[35] Zhao (n 25 above).

[36] Reform in the Chinese Securities Law allowing a representative action to be taken by the China Securities Investor Services as authorised by investors. The successful litigation against Kangmei Pharmaceutical was discussed in Clyde & Co, 'Chinese Court delivers decision on first securities class action: Implications for the D&O market' (3 December 2021), https://www.clydeco.com/en/insights/2021/12/chinese-court-on-first-securities-class-action.

[37] Eg see D Katelouzou and M Siems, 'The Global Diffusion of Stewardship Codes' (2020), https://papers.ssrn.com/sol3/papers.cfm?abstract_id=3616798.

[38] See 'China Awakens to the Power of Responsible Investing', https://group.pingan.com/media/news/News-2020/China-awakens-to-the-power-of-responsible-investing.html.

very much aligned with Chinese social and economic policy, it seems that ESG invest-ing is based on data analytics and stock selection, allocation rather than engagement actions.

To date, it remains unclear to what extent Article 5 in the corporate statute has improved the ESG performance of Chinese companies. Existing empirical studies seem to suggest that Chinese companies have made some gradual improvement in ESG performance, yet they still lag far behind their global peers.[39] Absent consensus on how to measure CSR performance, any performance evaluation may be contro-versial. Still, the bottom line appears to be that the Chinese government's various measures including the CSR provision in the corporate statute have raised CSR aware-ness among companies. In this regard, the CSR principle stated in the company law may serve an expressive function to 'reconstruct existing norms and to change the social meaning of action through a legal expression or statement about appropri-ate behavior'.[40] Overall, except for a few judicial cases, the general CSR duty under Article 5 *alone* as a corporate behavioural standard, is largely de facto voluntary, despite the mandatory tone of the statute.

While Article 5 in the corporate statute itself has not generated significant legal impact and may be uncertain in its impact towards positive ESG performance for Chinese companies, Chinese companies have recently observed its political impor-tance in response to the Chinese Communist Party's 'common prosperity' campaign. In October 2020, the Chinese Communist Party declared 'common prosperity' as a national goal and called for help from business enterprises and entrepreneurs to resolve wealth inequality.[41] Large Chinese companies are pledging their political allegiance through charitable donations in the name of 'CSR' and 'common prosperity'. For example, Alibaba has announced to pledge 100 billion yuan (approximately US$15.7 billion) to help small businesses, local development, etc; Tencent has declared that it will donate 50 billion yuan (US$7.8 billion) to assist rural development.[42]

In this regard it is arguable that specific campaigns led by the state or by local governments that mobilise corporations to 'do something' may be more effective in achieving particular outcomes in the non-financial aspects. Empirical evidence[43] shows that the Chinese 'poverty alleviation' campaign, for example, mobilised many

---

[39] F Pan, 'Revisiting ESG In China: Has Company Performance Improved?' (30 May 2018), https://www.sustainalytics.com/esg-research/resource/investors-esg-blog/revisiting-esg-in-china-has-company-performance-improved (reviewing the historical ESG scores of Chinese companies).

[40] See CR Sustein, 'On the Expressive Function of Law' (1996) 144 *University of Pennsylvania Law Review* 2031.

[41] Xinhua, 'Xi Focus: Xi Leads Efforts To Draw China's New Development Blueprint' (31 October 2020), http://www.xinhuanet.com/english/2020-10/31/c_139480851.htm; Bloomberg, 'Billionaire Donations Soar in China Push for "Common Prosperity"' (26 August 2021), https://www.bnnbloomberg.ca/billionaire-donations-soar-in-china-push-for-common-prosperity-1.1644292 (reporting that on 17 August 2021, the government stated that 'should reasonably adjust excessive incomes and encourage high-income people and companies to give back more to society').

[42] A Kharpal, 'China's Tech Giants Pour Billions Into Xi's Vision Of 'Common Prosperity' (*CNBC*, 3 September 2021), https://www.cnbc.com/2021/09/03/chinas-tech-giants-pour-billions-into-xis-goal-of-common-prosperity.html.

[43] Y Chang et al, 'Government Initiated Corporate Social Responsibility Activities: Evidence from a Poverty Alleviation Campaign in China' (2021) 173 *Journal of Business Ethics* 661.

state-owned enterprises and local companies pressured by local governments to engage in significant philanthropy to fund particular social projects with clear social outcomes, such as lifting certain numbers of individuals or families out of poverty to become fully participatory and capabilised citizens. In this regard the general and foundational nature of the CSR provision may itself justify more specific state-led campaigns and actions even if it remains an uncertain basis for corporate implementation or judicial enforcement. However, we note critically that while CSR seems to gain huge traction along with this 'common prosperity' campaign, it seems to be focused on an outdated aspect of CSR, namely corporate philanthropy, rather than sustainable management in daily business operations. It is thus questioned whether the sustainability or responsibility footprint of companies is measured in terms of actions such as philanthropy that may be external or peripheral to its activities, while 'emitting companies may carry on their emissions'. The ad hoc judicial enforcement of the CSR provision outside of corporate law also does not help in terms of 'integrating' sustainability or responsibility within core business decision-making or operations. Nevertheless, the generality of this provision continues to provide possibilities in terms of its application to constrain or shape corporate behaviour, notwithstanding the lack of legal certainty as to what these channels of influences may be. One thing, however, is clear, and that is the state's range of actions in terms of public campaigns, regulation or other forms of political pressure would continue to play a significant part in shaping corporate behaviour that is judged holistically for both economic and social impact.

III. ARTICLE 74 OF INDONESIAN LIMITED LIABILITY COMPANY ACT

The history of mandatory CSR legislation in Indonesia began with the regulation of state-owned enterprises (SOEs). After independence from Dutch colonial control in 1945, the Indonesian government nationalised Dutch businesses as a way to gain economic sovereignty.[44] Since then, SOEs have played an important role for economic development purposes. Since 1999, every Indonesian SOE has been required by law to allocate four per cent of their profit to partnerships with small and medium enterprises and environmental management programmes.[45] Indonesian SOEs often implement the law through charitable donations and philanthropic activities.[46] Such mandatory CSR programmes, however, have been rife with corruption due to lack of regulatory implementation details, external auditing and enforcement.[47]

---

[44] See RR Sinaga, 'The Indonesian Government's Role in the Development of Corporate Social Responsibility in Indonesia' (November 2017) (PhD thesis, Griffith University) 103 (discussing the Decree and rules adopted), https://research-repository.griffith.edu.au/handle/10072/370832.

[45] The Ministry of SOEs of Indonesia issued a Minister Decree No Kep-216/M-PBUMN/1999, the Law No 19 of Year 2003 concerning SOEs, and the SOE Ministry Regulation No Per-05/MBU/2007 concerning SOE's partnership with small enterprises and environmental management programme.

[46] See B Sheehy and C Damayanti, 'Sustainability and Legislated Corporate Social Responsibility in Indonesia' in B Sjåfjell and CM Bruner (eds), *Cambridge Handbook of Corporate Law, Corporate Governance and Sustainability* (Cambridge University Press, 2019) Ch 34, 475–89.

[47] ibid.

Unlike the state-owned sector, the private sector's CSR movement originated from outside Indonesia. The global anti-sweatshop movement in the 1990s pushed multinational companies and their suppliers to improve labour conditions in Indonesia. As a result, it raised local awareness of CSR and led to the emergence of indigenous CSR NGOs.[48]

In 1995, Indonesia adopted its first indigenous corporate statute, the Limited Liability Company Act. At that time, the legislators took shareholder wealth maximisation as the purpose of the corporation and dropped any consideration of wider social purposes suggested in the earlier drafts.[49] In 2005, the government made a comprehensive amendment to its 1995 corporate statute. With shareholder primacy as the accepted principle, the intended purpose of the 2005 revision was to promote trade, investment and economic growth. Unsurprisingly, the original draft submitted to the parliament did not mention CSR at all. The parliamentary committee responsible for preparing the final draft held a series of public hearings with key stakeholders. Representatives of Business Watch Indonesia (BWI), a prominent CSR-focused NGO in Indonesia, attended one of the hearings and argued for the inclusion of CSR in the statute.[50] After this hearing, BWI funded a trip to the Netherlands for three parliamentary members to investigate CSR issues.[51] A subsequent parliamentary committee meeting was held in June 2006, which occurred two weeks after the massive mud flow pollution caused by a mining corporation owned by Aburizal Bakrie (then Coordinating Minister for People's Welfare and a key leader of the Golkar Party, a conservative party).[52] In the meeting, various political factions, including the Golkar's opponents, supported mandatory CSR in the law, partly intending to embarrass Bakrie and his party and partly intending to direct CSR money to the indigenous Indonesian businesses in their own electoral districts.[53]

After the agreement on the inclusion of mandatory CSR into the new corporate law, the parliamentary committee's deliberation focused on how much companies should spend on CSR programmes. The proposed amount ranged between three to five per cent of a company's net profit. Several business associations were strongly opposed to mandatory CSR. They demanded that the parliament abandon the mandatory approach and opt for a voluntary approach. Consistent with the business sector's wishes, the Golkar representatives on the parliamentary committee submitted a proposal to replace mandatory CSR with a voluntary CSR statement in the law. However, the committee rejected this proposal. The Golkar representatives then proposed that mandatory CSR should be limited to natural resources companies. The

---

[48] See M Kemp, 'Corporate Social Responsibility in Indonesia, Quixotic Dream or Confident Expectation', United Nations Research Institute for Social Development, Technology, Business and Society Programme, *Paper No 6*, 11–13, (December 2001), https://perma.cc/FUG3-XKSF (discussing how the anti-sweatshop movement originating outside Indonesia impacted CSR in Indonesia).

[49] P Mahy, 'The Evolution of Company Law in Indonesia: An Exploration of Legal Innovation and Stagnation' (2013) 61 *American Journal of Comparative Law* 377, 412.

[50] A Rosser and D Edwin, 'The Politics of Corporate Social Responsibility in Indonesia' (2010) 23 *The Pacific Review* 1, 11–12.

[51] ibid.

[52] ibid, at 12.

[53] ibid, at 12–13.

committee partially accepted the proposal; it agreed that the law would be applied to natural resources companies and companies that have activities connected with natural resources.[54]

As a result, Article 74 of Limited Liability Company Act, passed in July 2007, provides that:

(1)   a limited liability company that carries out business activities in natural resources sectors or in connection with natural resources is obliged to implement corporate social and environmental responsibility;
(2)   the social and environmental responsibility undertaken by the corporation shall be budgeted and calculated as expenses of the company and its implementation must be undertaken by considering appropriateness and reasonableness;
(3)   failure to implement the CSR obligation will incur sanctions in accordance with further regulations.[55]

Although the business sector failed to stop the law at the legislature, it continued its battle against the mandatory CSR law by resorting to the constitutional court. Indonesia's Chamber of Commerce and Industry, along with certain other associations and companies, jointly filed a judicial review of Article 74 with the constitutional court. They argued that the law violated the principle of legal certainty because the CSR mandate would contradict the voluntary nature of CSR and essentially amount to double taxation. The court reasoned that the meaning of CSR must be in line with the culture of each country and therefore that the voluntary nature of CSR is not universally true.[56] Moreover, the court took the position that CSR as a legal obligation, as opposed to a voluntary initiative, provides more legal certainty, not less.[57] The court also made a distinction between taxation and CSR spending. According to the court, tax levies are used for national development, while CSR funds are used for communities and the restoration of the environment where the company is located. The court also explained that there is no double taxation because the costs incurred for CSR are calculated as the company's costs and its implementation ability.[58] As a result, the court upheld the CSR law.

The legal battle did not end there. The business sector then effectively delayed and weakened the law at the regulatory implementation stage.[59] The implementation regulation was belatedly released in 2012, five years after the CSR legislation.[60] The regulation holds the Board of directors responsible for the practical details of CSR implementation, including the preparation of annual CSR operations plans and budget plans. However, the regulation adds little substance to implementation.

---

[54] ibid (detailing the legislative history leading up to the law).
[55] For an English-translated version of the Law of the Republic of Indonesia No 40 of 2007 Concerning Limited Liability Company, see http://dlplawoffices.com/pdf/limitedliabilitycompanies.pdf.
[56] Indonesian Constitutional Court Decision No 53/PUU-VI/2008, https://mkri.id/index.php?page=download.Putusan&id=283.
[57] ibid.
[58] ibid.
[59] See Rosser and Edwin (n 38 above) 8–11, 16–17 (describing the political dynamics that shaped the introduction of mandatory legal requirements for corporate social responsibility in Indonesia).
[60] Government Regulation, 2012 (Regulation No 47/2012) (Indon).

The regulation vaguely explains the meaning of 'appropriateness and reasonableness' as being 'the financial capacity of the company having regard to the risks that give rise to the social and environmental responsibilities that must be borne by the company, subject to the obligations of the company as set out in the legislation governing the company's business operations'.[61] Article 7 of the regulation provides that if a company fails to fulfil its CSR obligations, it will be sanctioned as prescribed by laws and regulations in effect. However, the regulation itself imposes no sanctions. In fact, Article 3 of the regulation provides that 'CSR shall be mandatory for companies that carry on business in the natural resources sector or related fields, where such CSR obligations are imposed by a specific sectoral statute'. The regulation echoes the constitutional court's view that 'CSR has been implicitly regulated by other laws and regulations such as Forestry Law, Environmental Law, Water Resources Law and the Law on Gas and Oil', and administrative sanctions imposed under such laws serve as an important way to punish companies failing to perform the CSR obligation under the corporate statute.[62] As a result, the CSR obligation under Article 74 of the Limited Liability Company Act turns out to be no more than a legal obligation to comply with existing laws and regulations.

The battle in Indonesia for the mandatory legislation for CSR highlights an interesting contrast to the Chinese case study. Unlike in China where the policy has been clearly centralised, top-down and articulated in order to bind everyone to a social contract, the Indonesian policy has been fraught by contesting interests and represents a sort of political compromise. This inevitably affects the manner in which it has been implemented and its effectiveness in bringing about change in corporate behaviour.

The Indonesian case study must also be understood against the backdrop of its hybrid capitalism, whereby the private sector controls much wealth-creation in the country, alongside state-owned enterprises.[63] In this manner, the acceptance of shareholder primacy and the needs of corporations to generate returns for their financiers is more similar to capitalist jurisdictions in the West. Hence, Indonesia's CSR law may be seen to be a way for the state to attempt to ameliorate social externalities that can be imposed by private sector activity, that are inadequately accounted for by regulation or taxation. The contests during the passage of the legislation also showed the difficulties in framing regulation that would reach into and shape corporate behaviour, since the compromise was reached in terms of providing for CSR budgets as a way of ameliorating the potential environmental and sustainability damage that can be inflicted by Indonesia's vast resources sector where many of its powerful private sector companies are found.

It may be argued that while controlling shareholders of private sector companies may have little incentive to demonstrate ESG or CSR performance, states as controlling

---

[61] ibid.

[62] Indonesian Constitutional Court, Decision No 53/PUU-VI/2008 (Indon). See also L Andrini, 'Mandatory Corporate Social Responsibility in Indonesia' (2016) 28 *Mimbar Hukum* 512, 519 (discussing the various forms of sanctions for when companies fail to meet their CSR obligations).

[63] K Kim, 'Indonesia's Restrained State Capitalism: Development and Policy Challenges' (2021) 51 *Journal of Contemporary Asia* 419.

shareholders of state-owned enterprises ought to lead by example. However, the OECD[64] reports that state-owned enterprises have become huge opportunities for cronyism and corruption, and the state's ideal position as ESG champion in its share-holder capacity may be under-realised. While structural issues in the economy remain in the country, it is uncertain whether minority or foreign investors can do much by way of engagement or stewardship. That said, Indonesia is not immune to the desire to attract foreign and diverse investment into its growing economy and is looking at strengthening sustainability reporting by corporations to better assist investors. From 2020, all listed companies are required to publish sustainability reports, according to Indonesia Financial Services Authority (Otoritas Jasa Keuangan – OJK).[65] The rule provides guidance for sustainability reporting, including a list of content that issuers should consider disclosing. Financial services providers must also submit a Sustainable Finance Action Plan, which describes their plan for implementing sustainable finance.

IV. ASSESSMENT OF THE EFFICACY OF A GENERAL, ALL-ENCOMPASSING CSR DUTY FOR COMPANIES

On its face, a general CSR duty directly imposed on companies seems a powerful way to force companies to act socially and in an environmentally responsible manner in business operation. It appears to be an encompassing legal obligation. This may apparently be a stronger measure of compulsion for responsible corporate behaviour than relying on market actors' incentives, usually investors', channelled through financial decisions. Further, these issues being broadly social and non-financial, should arguably not be disciplined merely through a financialised lens.[66] Yet, there are various drawbacks. One is that the all-encompassing nature is not specific as to the nature of activities and operations that need implementation and can be cosmetically applied by companies until they are challenged. Further, it is uncertain who has standing to challenge and enforce, in both the case studies of China and Indonesia. Hence in practice, the general CSR duty as adopted in China and Indonesia arguably remains largely voluntary in reality.

Why is the apparently ambitious law legally powerless in practice and seems to contribute little to shaping corporate behaviour? One might argue that China, Indonesia and many developing countries alike do not have strong legal institutions to enforce a general CSR duty. One might further argue that the CSR duty could be effectively enforced and truly mandatory if adopted in developed countries that have

---

[64] The OECD is quoted in article 'Asia Media Tycoon Takes on Reform of Indonesia's State-owned Enterprises amid the Covid-19 Pandemic' (20 July 2020), https://www.riskadvisory.com/news/asia-media-tycoon-takes-on-reform-of-indonesias-state-owned-enterprises-amid-the-covid-19-pandemic/.

[65] Indonesia Financial Services Authority (Otoritas Jasa Keuangan) (2017), 'Implementation of Sustainability Finance for Financial Services Institutions, Issuers and Public Companies', International Finance Corporation, https://www.ifc.org/wps/wcm/connect/bab66a7c-9dc2-412f-81f6-f83f94d79660/Indonesia+OJK+Sustainable+Finance+Regulation_English.pdf?MOD=AJPERES&CVID=lVXU.Oy.

[66] P Ireland, 'Financialization and Corporate Governance' (2008), https://papers.ssrn.com/sol3/papers.cfm?abstract_id=2068478.

mature legal institutions. There might be some truth in such an argument. However, the challenge of enforcing a general CSR duty runs much deeper than the apparent gap in the quality of legal institutions between developed and developing countries.

When enacting a law that requires companies to undertake CSR, legislators would face a challenging question: how to define CSR? At the enforcement stage, how would regulators or judges understand CSR? The general CSR duty in China and Indonesia simply requires companies to undertake 'CSR' without defining what CSR is. Given that scholars and international organisations such as the United Nations and the EU have provided many CSR definitions ready to use, why did the legislators decide to leave it blank? It might be possible that the legislators did not have genuine intention to implement the law. Further, it is uncertain whether emerging economies would readily adopt international standards on ESG or CSR bearing in mind compatibility with political agendas, coherence with social fabric and the tendency for international organisations' standards to be regarded as Western-centric.[67] Meanwhile, great vagueness seems necessary. Chinese and Indonesian courts suggest a context-dependent approach to CSR, where the meaning of CSR depends on the organisational, cultural, and national contexts. A context-dependent approach makes sense from a business management perspective because it considers the different needs of business organisations. As CSR is sensitive to business contexts, the best people to determine appropriate CSR measures would be corporate managers rather than legislators, regulators or judges, who lack business expertise. Lawmakers could declare a CSR duty in law but companies could decide what CSR means at the implementation stage. As a result, the compulsory nature of the general CSR duty would be significantly adapted.

A general CSR duty appears a comprehensive obligation. It requires companies to properly handle a wide range of social, environmental, human rights issues, etc. The goal appears ambitious – wishing to hold corporations accountable for all kinds of behaviour through one statutory instrument. This ambition comes at a price: vague statutory language which hinders implementation and enforcement. The business reality – that there is no one-size-fits-all CSR strategy – necessitates some vagueness to accommodate the diverse needs of corporations. This suggests a great limitation on the residual lawmaking and enforcement functions undertaken by regulators and courts. It would be unlikely for regulators to proactively stipulate CSR standards suitable for each company and it would be often inappropriate for judges to substitute their own opinions for CSR policies made by corporate managers. Even if possible, the interpretation and specification of a very vague CSR law would place high demands on legal infrastructure, which is particularly challenging for developing countries. As a result, in practice corporations would have great discretion in interpreting and implementing the law.

---

[67] Eg see J Mende, 'Are Human Rights Western – And Why Does It Matter? A Perspective from International Political Theory' (2021) 17 *Journal of International Political Theory* 38; on the challenges for shareholder advocacy and activism on the basis of contested 'universal' notions, see A Dhir, 'Shareholder Engagement in the Embedded Business Corporation: Investment Activism, Human Rights and TWAIL Discourse' *Osgoode CLPE Research Paper No 12/2009* (2008), https://papers.ssrn.com/sol3/papers.cfm?abstract_id=1416198.

When writing a general CSR duty into law, legislators need to consider who has the right to enforce the duty. A law without any enforcement mechanism is unlikely to be mandatory in effect. If the CSR duty is enacted under corporate law, as the case in China and Indonesia, the enforcement right presumably rests with shareholders. However, compared to shareholders, non-shareholder stakeholders such as employees and local communities might be more interested in bringing CSR issues before court. Yet, neither China nor Indonesia provide non-shareholders with the right to enforce the CSR duty. In fact, China and Indonesia are not outliers in this regard. Comparative evidence from developed countries consistently shows that shareholders rarely address non-shareholders' interests through derivative action and non-shareholder stakeholders rarely have access to enforcement under corporate statutes. For instance, while the UK Companies Act 2006, section 172 requires directors to consider various stakeholders' interests when pursuing the benefits for shareholders, there exists only one UK court decision where shareholders sought to address non-shareholder stakeholders' interests as outlined in that section.[68] In that case, the court refrained from forcing the Board to consider stakeholders' interests because the decision-making power ultimately remained with the Board of directors. Similarly, the Supreme Court of Canada expressly allows (perhaps even requires) directors to consider non-shareholders' interests when discharging their fiduciary duties; nevertheless, judicial cases remain focused on shareholder interests.[69] Tellingly, prevailing statutes of benefit corporations around the world, which are supposed to protect various stakeholders through corporate governance, often explicitly preclude non-shareholder stakeholders enforcing directors' fiduciary duties.[70]

If the purpose of a general CSR duty is to hold the corporation accountable to various stakeholders, why do legislators hesitate to give non-shareholders the right to enforce the CSR duty? One possible concern could be frivolous litigation. Nevertheless, this concern may be mitigated by setting procedural standards. Shareholders are often required by law to satisfy some procedure requirements in order to launch a derivative action. Similarly, non-shareholders could be asked to follow certain procedural steps and prove good faith in order to launch a suit to enforce the CSR duty.

Given that legal design faces no technical problem in giving non-shareholder stakeholders the right to enforce a general CSR duty, politics may be a more plausible reason that prevents such legal arrangement from happening. As illustrated in the case of Indonesia, the CSR law experienced a difficult legal journey. The law faced strong opposition from the business sector, which is unsurprising as the law explicitly targets corporations, especially large oil corporations with lobbying prowess. The law was significantly watered downed after the legal battles. The implementation regulations in Indonesia were long delayed and, when finally promulgated, were too vague to provide any meaningful guidance for implementation. In China, there was no

---

[68] G Tsagas, 'Section 172 of the Companies Act 2006: Desperate Times Call for Soft Law Measures' in N Boerger and C Villiers (eds), *Shaping the Corporate Landscape: Towards Corporate Reform and Enterprise Diversity* (Bloomsbury Publishing, 2018) 137–38.

[69] L-W Lin, 'The 'Good Corporate Citizen' Beyond BCE' (2021) 58 *Alberta Law Review* 551.

[70] E Winston, 'Benefit Corporations and The Separation of Benefit and Control' (2018) 39 *Cardozo Law Review* 1783.

evidence to suggest that corporate lobbying weakened the CSR legislation. However, the judicial practice there suggests that the government is motivated more by political interest in 'social stability' than by the pursuit of social/environmental justice. The government has great discretion in deciding how CSR may be enforced on a case-by-case basis. When the government turns its focus on wealth inequality issues and calls for corporate charities, Chinese companies answer the political call. It relies on government agencies to invoke the CSR law, rather than empowering non-shareholder stakeholders to press for enforcement.

Politicians may find it attractive to write a general CSR duty into law. CSR looks appealing to the public and generates favourable political publicity. Politicians may use it as an easy way to signal their commitments to social and environmental justice. They may be more concerned with political signalling value than actual implementation of the law, especially when lack of legal enforcement is a taken-for-granted systemic problem, particularly in developing countries where the vast body of law already suffers from poor enforcement.

V. CONCLUSION

Legislation that imposes a broad CSR duty on corporations appears a promising way to force companies to operate in a socially and environmentally responsible way. Such legislation also appears to transcend the limitations of market-based discipline and investors' influence. Yet, such legislation is likely to be a hollow promise. A broad CSR duty is inevitably vague, leaving companies with great discretion to decide how to implement the law. At best, such legislation serves an expressive function – raising awareness and hopefully giving rise to a pro-CSR business norm. However, it has the potential to justify *direct* and *specific* regulation to make CSR truly mandatory and enforceable. The legal infrastructure of CSR lies in specialised laws that set precise behaviour standards and clear enforcement mechanisms, rather than in a vague and seemingly encompassing CSR duty. Even then, in emerging economies, specific campaigns and regulations are a conflation of politics, social demand and law, therefore rendering such measures legally uncertain in terms of interpretation and scope of application. Further, broad mandatory CSR provisions may seem lacking in credibility if the legal regime lacks clear standards and rigorous enforcement in important areas such as labour and environmental regulation, which remain works in progress in the jurisdictions studied above. A general CSR duty, if adopted, should not and could not act as a substitute for regulatory modes that mandate specific and substantive behaviour, though the CSR law may play a complementary role in forming responsible business norms. This not only provides a clearer pathway for behavioural change, but also helps to support the development of consistent and predictable expectations on the parts of market actors and stakeholders, so that in time they too may be able to develop and mature as constructive agents of change.

7

The Voting Behaviour of Institutional Investors and Retail Shareholders and the Interests of Beneficiaries

CHRISTOPH VAN DER ELST

I. INTRODUCTION

I AM A small retail investor, and I invest in different ways, both directly and indirectly. First, I directly invest in a limited number of companies, and I admit that my portfolio is not optimally diversified for lowering risks in accordance with finance theory. The latter theory is nice to know but the level of my savings does not allow for the appropriate application of the theory. My banker fully understands my position and is very friendly, referring to a number of the bank's investment funds 'providing in a diversified portfolio for any amount you want to invest, Mr Van der Elst'. So, and secondly, I yielded and for regions I had hardly heard of in my younger years, accessed some inaccessible markets with my participation in one of the bank's undertakings for the collective investment in transferable securities (UCIT). Thirdly, the Dutch legal framework results in my mandatory membership of a pension fund, in my case the Dutch ABP, one of the largest pension funds in the world which, at the moment of writing,[1] governs €486 billion of assets.[2]

I care about my investments and do my best to keep track of the investees (and their behaviour). This includes acting as an engaged retail shareholder and voting the shares directly and looking after the behaviour of the UCIT and the pension fund. For my holdings of shares in investees, the EU has facilitated my participation in the general meetings of shareholders (AGMs) significantly over recent decades.[3]

---

[1] June 2022.
[2] APB, *bezittingen*, https://www.abp.nl/over-abp/financiele-situatie/actuele-financiele-situatie/.
[3] Especially Directive 2007/36/EC of the European Parliament and of the Council of 11 July 2007 on the exercise of certain rights of shareholders in listed companies [2007] OJ L184/17 and Directive (EU) 2017/828 of the European Parliament and of the Council of 17 May 2017 amending Directive 2007/36/EC as regards the encouragement of long-term shareholder engagement [2017] OJ L132/1.

When I started investing, I travelled, usually in the month of May, several times to the headquarters of the investees in Brussels, attending the meeting in person. It was the only feasible way of signalling my support or displeasure with the current company's performance and practices. Several times I got stuck in traffic jams when entering the city and arrived at the meeting's venue when the small number of other shareholders were already sipping glasses of bubbly, making my young age even more conspicuous. In those days, I appreciated the French voting by mail system: my two French investees sent all documents related to their AGMs via the postal service, including a stamped envelope for sending back my 'yes/no' votes, which encouraged my remote participation.[4]

For my indirect investments through the UCIT and the pension fund, acting as an engaged beneficiary is more complex. Neither fund provides their beneficiaries with any direct say in the investees of the fund. The pension fund is structured as a trust.[5] The articles of association of the pension fund define in every detail who can become a member of the (supervisory) Board of directors. The Board of directors elects the members of the (supervisory) Board based on binding proposals of different organisations of employers and employees and the pensioners of the fund. The Board members of the pensioners are proposed by the representatives of the pensioners in the accountability body. The latter body has, among many other powers, an advisory role in the determination of the fund's strategic investment policy. Considering its important role, reaching out to the membership can be an option for steering the engagement policy and behaviour of the pension fund. However, the accountability body is composed of representatives of the employers, working beneficiaries and retired beneficiaries. Several employers' and employees' organisations present a list of candidates for the accountability body. As a beneficiary it is possible to present yourself as a candidate if more than 500 beneficiaries of your class support your candidacy. This is a too cumbersome procedure for signalling my pension fund of the necessity of its active ownership, especially in industries like oil and gas for increased investing in the transition towards other energy sources.

Similarly, my plea for active ownership as a beneficiary of the UCIT is even more theoretical. An asset manager governs the fund(s) and 'makes its voice heard at shareholder meetings and engages with companies'.[6] The asset manager requests a dialogue with the investees in case of a lack of transparency, poor performance in sustainable

---

[4] See R La Porta et al, 'Law and Finance' (1998) 106 *Journal of Political Economy* 1113; R La Porta et al, 'Legal Determinants of External Finance' (1997) 52 *Journal of Finance* 1131. However, these studies are also heavily criticised (see for example S Cools, 'The Real Difference in Corporate Law between the United States and Continental Europe: Distribution of Powers' (2005) 30 *Delaware Journal of Corporate Law* 697).

[5] Information on the organisation of the pension fund can be found at https://www.abp.nl/over-abp/onze-organisatie/.

[6] See the report of the Asset Manager, https://multimediafiles.kbcgroup.eu/ng/feed/AM/funds/AF/Proxy_Voting_Codex/Proxy_Voting_and_Engagement_Activity_Report_EN.pdf.

business criteria and measures that threaten the creation of shareholder value. The engagement of the asset manager recently focused on three specific themes: (1) anti-bribery and corruption policies, especially of investees operating in a controversial regime (identified by the asset manager's parent company); (2) improving governance by sending the proxy voting policy (to the investees of the major Belgian index); and (3) companies producing cement in a non-sustainable way. It also makes use of the ISS voting services. How it worked in practice was less clear, and if I needed to know how it affected its voting behaviour, I had to plough through hundreds of pages of voting results. There is no doubt that the fund and the asset manager offer significantly more transparency[7] than they did a decade ago and I am very pleased with the shift towards activism and sustainability. Yet, there remains a feeling of unease with the level of alignment of my beneficial interests with the engagement practices of the asset manager.

With my investment in an UCIT and participation in a pension fund, I became part of a long investment 'chain of finance' with a set of intermediaries between me and the companies.[8] Together with millions of other 'savers', including governments, companies, other (institutional) investors, I allocate part of my financial resources to asset owners like pension funds, insurance companies, mutual funds, etc. The latter owners either internally make use of asset managers that govern the resources and invest the money, or – which is frequently the case – make use of an asset management company that pools the resources of these asset owners and redirects these resources towards different types of investments in shares, bonds and other assets. These companies, which reside at the buy side, make use of sell-side intermediaries, brokers and dealers working for investment banks, providing the services of executing of orders for shares and other financial instruments as well as research reports. These orders go via the market of stock exchanges and other trading platforms. Figure 1 provides a simplified overview of the investment chain. One important consequence of these investment chains is the opaqueness of the allocation and the use of the rights attached to the financial instruments, like the voting right of the shares. When one or more intermediaries is involved in the investment chain, these rights remain with an intermediary, which can be the investment management firm or the asset owner, while a direct investor can vote the shares of the investees.[9]

---

[7] See for example the information document in n 6.

[8] D-L Arjaliès et al, *Chains of Finance* (Oxford University Press, 2017).

[9] In previous times this was often not the case when investing in companies overseas. Investing in overseas companies makes use of another intermediated chain, which hindered investors from become 'recognised' as the shareholder: see C Van der Elst and A Lafarre, 'Blockchain and Smart Contracting for the Shareholder Community' (2019) 20(1) *European Business Organization Law Review* 111; Association of Member Nominated Trustees, *Bringing Shareholder Voting into the 21st Century* (6 November 2020), and A Lafarre and C Van der Elst, 'Shareholder Voice in Complex Intermediated Proxy Systems: Blockchain Technology as a Solution?' (2021) 4(1) *The Stanford Journal of Blockchain Law and Policy* 29.

Figure 1 The Investment Chain

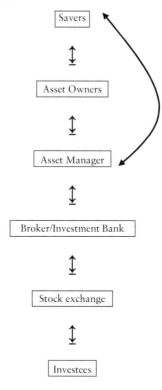

The investment chain raises the question how well aligned the behaviour of the intermediaries is vis-à-vis the 'savers' interests. For example, do these different types of intermediaries vote and engage in accordance with the interests of the ultimate beneficiaries? Pension funds and mutual funds, with their thousands – and even millions – of beneficiaries[10] cannot always be expected to consider all interests of all different beneficiaries. Using different mechanisms, like offering a proxy voting choice of votes,[11] surveys, focus groups, interviews and member AGMs are all helpful in bridging the gap between the intermediaries' behaviour and the beneficiaries' interests.[12]

---

[10] The pension fund ABP, of which I am a beneficiary, serves the interests of close to three million other beneficiaries.

[11] See Recommendation 20 of the Report of the Taskforce on Pension Scheme Voting Implementation: Recommendations to Government, Regulators and Industry (20 September 2021), https://www.gov.uk/ government/publications/taskforce-on-pension-scheme-voting-implementation-recommendations- to-government-regulators-and-industry/the-report-of-the-taskforce-on-pension-scheme-voting- implementation-recommendations-to-government-regulators-and-industry.

[12] These mechanisms are considered among the best practices of involvement of the beneficiaries of Step 2 of the Principles for Responsible Investment: United Nations Global Compact, 'Understanding and Aligning

To the best of my knowledge, research on this alignment of behaviour and interests is scarce. Therefor, in this chapter I study the voice, exit and loyalty of the three different types of shareholders – retail shareholders, pension funds and mutual funds/asset managers – of the Italian company Telecom Italy between 2012 and 2021. This company publishes the voting records of all the participating shareholders, allowing for an analysis at the individual level of shareholders' voting behaviour. I combine this analysis, the new evidence, and the results, with the findings of the limited number of studies that address the beneficiaries' expected engagements of institutional investors and the effective engagement of these investors. The major finding is that the alignment between beneficiaries and funds is imperfect. The chapter opens the debate on how arrangements between the different interested parties can be further addressed.

This chapter is structured as follows. In section II, I introduce Telecom Italia. Section III gives the methodological background. Section IV provides the results of the analysis of the entry, voting terms and exit of retail shareholders, pension funds, mutual funds and asset managers, and other shareholders. In section V we address the findings of the voting behaviour of these different shareholder classes related to a specific ESG-issue, the governance issue of the remuneration policy, in the corporate governance literature also known as say-on-pay. Section VI presents the findings of other research that studies the preferences of beneficiaries of pension funds and other institutional investors and the latter's engagement behaviour. Section VII discusses the main findings and concludes.

II. THE TURBULENT LIFE OF TELECOM ITALIA

Telecom Italia is a formerly stated-owned telecommunications company that was established in 1994 with the merger of several Italian telecommunications companies. Soon after its formation it was privatised and turned into a large multimedia group. The company was highly leveraged and confronted with other significant difficulties, Telecom Italia's stock price slid from more than €2 in 1995 to less than €0.60 in early 1997.[13] Controlling ownership blocks in Telecom Italia have changed several times since the second half of the 1990s. In 1999 Olivetti, another Italian telecommunications company with a pyramidal ownership structure, 'de facto' controlled by Roberto Colaninno, launched a successful hostile takeover bid for Telecom Italia, acquiring 56 per cent of the shares. However, only two years later, Pirelli & Co acquired a controlling voting block in one of the pyramidal companies, Bell, via an intermediary vehicle Olimpia. Pirelli is, via a chain of other intermediaries, controlled

---

with Beneficiaries' Sustainability Preferences' (21 April 2021), https://www.unpri.org/strategy-policy-and-strategic-asset-allocation/understanding-and-aligning-with-beneficiaries-sustainability-preferences/7497. article. See also section VII below.

[13] Stock prices of MarketWatch.com (more than likely, the stock price is converted from the former currency, the Italian Lira).

by Marco Tronchetti Provera. The acquisition of this voting block did not cross the mandatory bid threshold, and no public offer was launched.[14] These operations did not prevent Telecom Italia experiencing further increasing debt levels and in 2007, after several failed negotiations with other telecom operators like AT&T, Telco, a consortium with the Spanish telecommunications company Telefónica, acquired the holding company controlling Telecom Italy. Telefónica controlled 46 per cent of Telco. In 2014 Telefónica announced its intention to fully take over Telco. However, the Brazilian competition authorities opposed the transaction as both Telefónica and Telecom Italia were the largest telecommunication companies in Brazil and the acquisition of Telco would distort competition. A third important Brazilian tele-communications player is GVT, a subsidiary of the French company Vivendi. The latter received offers from both Telefónica and Telecom Italia.[15] In a number of transactions that followed these bids, Vivendi acquired approximately 8 per cent of Telecom Italia and purchased in different transactions close to 12 per cent of Telecom Italia's shares on the market, creating a strong relationship of more than 20 per cent in Telecom Italia in early 2016.[16] Ever since, Vivendi has been the largest shareholder of Telecom Italia, owning close to 24 per cent of the shares. In between, Vivendi and Telecom Italia were confronted with a concentration investigation by the European Commission, as Vivendi de facto controlled Telecom Italia when most of the Board members were elected from the slate of Vivendi. Simultaneously, Vivendi holds a significant minority stake of 29 per cent in the digital broadcasting operator Mediaset SpA, an activity that Telecom Italia also exploits. The investiga-tion resulted in the European Commission's conditional decision that the acquisition of the 'de facto control' of Telecom Italia was not incompatible with the internal market.[17]

In the meantime, two other major shareholders appeared in the shareholder base: first, the activist fund Elliott and later the Italian Cassa Depositi e Prestiti. Two years after Vivendi acquired its stake in Telecom Italia, the activist built this stake in Telecom Italia in 2018 and complained that the strategy and governance of Telecom Italia was weak due to 'Vivendi's poor stewardship with its broken promises, track record and prolonged and pervasive value destruction'.[18] The specific Italian

---

[14] For a short overview of these developments see J Grant et al, 'Financial Tunnelling and the Mandatory Bid Rule' (2009) 10 *European Business Organization Law Review* 240.

[15] Vivendi, 'GVT: Telecom Italia Offer and New Telefonica Offer' (28 August 2014), https://www.vivendi.com/wp-content/uploads/2014/08/20140828_Two_new_offers_for_GVT.pdf.

[16] Vivendi, 'Vivendi Holds 19.9% of Telecom Italia' (6 October 2015), https://www.vivendi.com/wp-content/uploads/2015/10/20151006_Vivendi_PR_Vivendi_holds_19_9_pc_of_Telecom_Italia.pdf.

[17] European Commission, 'Case M.8465 – Vivendi/Telecom Italia, Commission decision pursuant to Article 6(1)(b) and 6(2) of Council Regulation No 139/20041 and Article 57 of the Agreement on the European Economic Area' (30 May 2017), https://ec.europa.eu/competition/mergers/cases/decisions/m8465_568_3.pdf.

[18] Businesswire, 'Elliott Statement on Telecom Italia' (11 March 2019), https://www.businesswire.com/news/home/20190311005218/en/Elliott-Statement-on-Telecom-Italia.

Board election process with slate voting resulted in the election of eight (a majority number in the Board) representatives of Elliott's candidates, all of whom were considered independent directors. In 2020, Elliott sold its stake in Telecom Italia, leaving Vivendi and Cassa Depositi e Prestiti as the only two major shareholders. Table 1 provides an overview of the development of the ownership structure of Telecom Italia between 2011 and 2021.

Table 1 Evolution of the Large Shareholders of Telecom Italia

	2011	2012	2013	2014	2015	2016	2017	2018	2019	2020	Jun–21
Telco	22.40%	22.39%	22.39%	22.39%	22.30%						
Vivendi						24.68%	23.94%	23.94%	23.94%	23.94%	23.75%
Elliott								8.85%	9.55%	6.98%	
Findim	4.99%	4.99%	4.99%	5.00%							
Brandes Investment Partners LP	4.02%										
Blackrock	2.89%	2.89%		4.81%	4.79%		3.10%				
AllianceBernstein LP	2.07%	2.06%									
BNP Paribas	2.53%										
Cassa Depositi e Prestiti								4.78%	9.89%	9.89%	9.81%
Canada Pension Plan Inv. Board									3.24%	3.24%	3.19%
JP Morgan						2.14%					
Bank of China					2.07%	2.07%					
Novator Capital Ltd.											2.96%
Norges Bank											1.05%
Banca d'Italia											1.00%

Source: Telecom Italia, annual reports, and minutes of the AGMs.

The instability at both shareholder level and Board level correlates with a modest performance record. The company suffered significant losses and even experienced a negative operational income. As a result, the company had to abolish any dividend payments (Table 2). The stock price fluctuated significantly between a low of less than €0.4 in 2020 during the pandemic and a high of €1.18 in 2015, around the time that Vivendi stepped in as major shareholder. Consequently, while many companies in this industry experienced a difficult decade, as is shown in the development of the STOXX Telecom index, Telecom Italia underperformed on the stock market relative to its peers as the index is higher in 2021 than in 2011, whilst the stock price of Telecom Italia dropped by almost 50 per cent between 2011 and 2021.

Table 2 Evolution of Telecom Italia's Performance

	2011	2012	2013	2014	2015	2016	2017	2018	2019	2020	Jun-21
EBIT (€ mio.)	−1190	−1709	2718	4529	2963	3722	3291	561	3175	2104	501
Net earnings (€ mio.)	−4676	−1277	−238	1960	657	1966	1287	−1038	1242	7352	−137
Dividend	0.043	0.02	0	0	0	0	0	0	0.01	0.01	
Share price (€, year end)	0.83	0.70	0.69	0.88	1.18	0.84	0.72	0.48	0.56	0.38	0.42
Share price evolution		−15.7%	−1.4%	27.8%	33.2%	−28.8%	−13.9%	−33.0%	15.0%	−32.0%	11.0%
STOXX Telecom	252	225	298	320	347	292	282	245	245	206	287
STOXX Tel. evolution		−11%	32%	7%	8%	−16%	−3%	−13%	0%	−16%	39%

Source: Telecom Italia, annual reports and semi-annual report, STOXX.

In November 2021 the financial press reported that Telecom Italia received a take-over offer from KKR.[19] KKR would offer the shareholders a significant premium compared to the current stock price but many long(er) term investors, like Vivendi, would still suffer major losses as the shares were traded at prices more than twice the announced bid price when Vivendi stepped in. KKR's move resulted in the resignation of the CEO, who was already in troubled waters with the largest shareholder. Stability at the top of Telecom Italia is a major concern, as the recent resignation means that a new CEO must now be found – the fifth since 2015. Telecom Italia turned down the non-binding bid of KKR in April 2022 as KKR did not confirm the bid terms.[20] Overall, the eventful life of the Italian telecom operator makes it an interesting case study for my research.

III. METHODOLOGY

A. Identification and Classification of Shareholders

In this study, I analyse the entry, voting and exit behaviour of the shareholders. The Italian minutes of the meeting of Telecom Italia provide a detailed overview of the partici-pating shareholders in its AGMs, their voting blocks and how they voiced their votes.

---

[19] See E Polina et al, 'KKR Makes $12 Billion Approach to Take Telecom Italia Private' (21 November 2021), https://www.reuters.com/markets/deals/telecom-italia-board-meet-sunday-kkrs-takeover-proposal-sources-2021-11-21/.
[20] See E Polina, 'Telecom Italia Draws Line under KKR Bid Approach' (7 April 2022), https://www.reuters.com/business/media-telecom/telecom-italia-rejects-kkr-request-due-diligence-2022-04-07/.

This information allows for a detailed analysis of the investment behaviour of the different shareholders and in particular their voting behaviour. In the classification of the seminal work of Hirschman, this chapter identifies whether the shareholders vote or not (voice), whether the shareholders (presumably) exited the company (exit) or whether the shareholder remained loyal (loyalty).[21]

I collected all minutes of AGMs between 2012 and 2021, a 10-year time frame, and classified every shareholder according to pre-defined shareholder classes (and sizes). The following shareholder classes are used: (foreign) banks; (foreign) foundations; (foreign) non-financial companies; (foreign) governments; (foreign) other entities; foreign churches; foreign universities; insurance companies; pension funds; mutual funds and asset managers; and retail shareholders. Some of these classes could not further be divided according to nationality or seat of incorporation, as this information was not disclosed in the AGM minutes. For this study, I am interested in the shareholder voting engagement behaviour of three classes of shareholders, namely the retail shareholders, the pension funds, and the mutual funds/asset managers. All other shareholders are regrouped together.

Combined with the identification of the type of the participating shareholder based on its name disclosed in the minutes, I harmonised the different names that Telecom Italia used in its minutes for the same shareholder over the years. Indeed, Telecom Italia used different abbreviations – like pension fund often being abbreviated as 'PF' or investment as 'inv' – in one year but not in another year. The shareholder 'Municipal Employees' Annuity and Benefit Fund of Chicago' serves as an illustration of the different presentation modes. This shareholder was present and participated in all AGMs of Telecom Italia from 2012 to 2021. As is shown in Table 3, this shareholder is presented in five different ways in the minutes of these ten AGMs.

Table 3 Identification of the Municipal Employees' Annuity and Benefit Fund of Chicago in the Minutes of Telecom Italia

AGM 2012	MUNICIPAL EMP ANNUITY E BEN FD CHICA
2013	MUNICIPAL EMP ANNUITY E BEN FD CHICA
2014	MUNICIPAL EMP ANNUITY E BEN FD CHICAGO
2015	MUNICIPAL EMPLOYEES' ANNUITY AND BENEFIT FUND OF CHICAGO
2016	MUNICIPAL EMPLOYEES' ANNUITY AND BENEFIT FUND OF CHICAGO
2017	MUNICIPAL EMPLOYEES' ANNUITY AND BENEFIT FUND OF CHICAGO
2018	MUNICIPAL EMPLOYEES ANNUITY & BENEFIT FUND CHICAGO
2019	MUNICIPAL EMPLOYEES' ANNUITY AND BENEFIT FUND OF CHICAGO
2020	MUNICIPAL EMPLOYEES' ANNUITY AND BENEFIT FUND OF CHICAGO
2021	MUNICIPAL EMPLOYEES' ANNUITY AND BENEFIT FUND OF CHICAGO

Source: Telecom Italia, minutes of the AGMs.

---

[21] A Hirschman, *Exit, Voice, and Loyalty: Responses to Decline in Firms, Organizations, and States* (Harvard University Press, 1970).

Where there were doubts whether it was the same or a different shareholder that appeared in these AGMs, the differences in the name were maintained and consequently the shareholders are reported as two different shareholders. As an example, I refer to the shareholder 'Florida Retirement System' and the shareholder 'Florida Retirement System Trust Fund'. As a result, I can report a slightly higher number of different shareholders over the years than the number that effectively participated.

It was found that several shareholders appear several times in the participants' list in the minutes of the AGM for a particular year. During the 2018 AGM the Peoples' Bank of China voted with four different stakes in the meeting. The way the shareholder voted the different share blocks was also recorded differently for several agenda items. As no further information was available, I considered, for the purposes of studying the evolution of the participation, this shareholder as just one shareholder for counting the total numbers of participating shareholders in the AGM, but I continued to study separately all the different voting blocks of that shareholder.

B. Measuring Entry, Loyalty and Exit of Shareholders

Next, for each AGM I studied which shareholders of each class that participated in the general meeting at year t also participated in the meeting at $t+1$. This measures both the mechanisms of voice (being present in the meeting $t+1$) and exit (not present in the meeting $t+1$) as well as, over the years, the loyalty of shareholders. Similarly, I also measured the voting stakes with which the shareholder participated in both t and $t+1$. This second approach gives further insights into whether the voicing shareholders became more or less 'loyal', to the extent that their investment behaviour in combination with their voting behaviour is a good proxy for measuring the loyalty of shareholders. Whether the shareholder types developed their behaviour over the years differently is also empirically tested. Therefore, I make use of the survival analysis technique of the Kaplan-Meier estimator and curves. This is a nonparametric technique for measuring survival time probabilities.[22] In this type of analysis, censored observations are also considered. Censored observations are observations where is known that the time of an event – which in this study is a shareholder that is no longer participating in the AGM – exceeds the duration of the period of observation of the study. In this study, I have the voting behaviour over the years of all individual shareholders. Some shareholders only stepped in and voted their Telecom Italia shares after 2012, the first year for which I collected all the shareholders voting at the AGM, while others were already shareholders before 2012. Of the latter, there is no information on the exact time the shareholder started its voting engagement.

---

[22] For this kind of empirical analysis see for example D Hosmer and S Lemeshow, *Applied Survival Analysis* (John Wiley & Sons, 1999).

Both types of shareholders are included in a Kaplan-Meier analysis measuring the probability of showing voting engagement past a certain time *t*. Next, many shareholders had not (yet) exited the company in 2021. Of these shareholders, I do not have the total number of years of (future) voting engagement. The Kaplan-Meier survival analysis also considers these observations for estimating the survival time. I estimate if the survival time probability of exiting the company is different for the different classes of shareholders, including the shareholders that only after 2012 voted their shares and comprising the shareholders that were engaged in the company after the AGM of 2021. More precisely if retail shareholders show different exit and voting behaviour than the pension funds and the mutual funds and asset managers, it is an indication that the engagement behaviour of these shareholders is different and signals that the beneficiaries of these funds would prefer another engagement behaviour.

Next, I also study whether the different types of shareholders respond differently on one of the recurring environmental, social and governance (ESG) AGM agenda items, the policy of the executive remuneration of directors. Since 2011, the shareholders of listed Italian companies have been provided with a right to approve the first section of the remuneration report of the Board of directors.[23] That part of the report provides the remuneration policy of the company, as well as the process of the adoption and implementation of this policy. Italian legislative decree No 259 of 30 December 2010 provides that, in a mandatory shareholder vote of an advisory nature, companies must provide the shareholders with the right to vote on this part of the report, but the voting result is only advisory. The Revised Shareholders' Right Directive 2018/828 of May 2017 required an update to the Italian system of reporting and voting of remuneration into a binding and an advisory vote. The company's remuneration policy, including the procedures used to adopt and implement this policy, must contribute to the corporate strategy, the pursuit of long-term interests and the company's sustainability. It must also explain how it makes this contribution. This policy, the first part of an Italian remuneration report, must be voted in a binding resolution at least every three years. The second part of the remuneration report, which comprises information on the remuneration packages, must be voted yearly but the result of the vote is not binding. Telecom Italia provided the shareholders a yearly vote of the first part of the remuneration report, including the remuneration policy from 2012 onwards as well as in 2020 and 2021 when the voting results were binding. In these final two years, the shareholders also voted, in a non-binding manner, for the second part of the remuneration report, containing details of the remuneration packages. In this analysis, I study the results of the votes for the first part of the remuneration report related to the remuneration policy from 2012 to 2021. Empirically an assessment is carried out on whether the number of shareholders belonging to the different shareholder classes, as well as the total number of voting rights they

---

[23] M Solinas, 'Directors' Remuneration in Italy' in C Van der Elst (ed), *Executive Directors' Remuneration in Comparative Corporate Perspective* (Wolters Kluwer, 2015).

voted in the AGM, is significantly different: a non-parametric chi-square test of independence determines the associations in voting between the different shareholder classes. It measures whether these types voted differently for the remuneration policy between 2012 and 2021.

IV. LOYALTY, VOICE AND EXIT OF RETAIL SHAREHOLDERS, PENSION FUNDS AND MUTUAL FUNDS

A. Attendance at the AGM of Telecom Italia and Other large Italian Companies

Telecom Italia is known as one of the Italian companies with the largest number of participating shareholders. Consob's Report on the corporate governance of Italian listed companies states that the maximum number of participating number of shareholders at any AGM fluctuated between 3,886 and 5,501 shareholders in 2012 to 2020.[24] My findings show that the AGM with the largest number of participating shareholders is thus, for several reporting years, the AGM of Telecom Italia. This large number of participating shareholders is only a tiny fraction of all shareholders of Telecom Italia. The minutes of the meetings also contain, for five years between 2015 and 2021, and divided into six different size classes, the distribution of voting stakes of all shareholders.[25] Until 2020 the shareholder base of the company comprised approximately 500,000 shareholders; this remained stable between 2015 and 2020. In 2021 the base dropped drastically, by approximately 40 per cent, to less than 300,000 shareholders.[26] Over 98 per cent of all the shareholders hold less than 100,000 shares, a voting block of less than 0.001 per cent of all issued voting shares. The other size classes of shareholders each count for less than 1 per cent of the number of shareholders but hold the bulk of all issued shares, the largest shareholder class – each holding more than 0.07 per cent of the shares – together controlling more than 50 per cent of all issued shares and votes. Overall, approximately 1 per cent of the total number of shareholders engage in voting at the AGM. In 2021, due to the large drop in the shareholder base, the number of participating shareholders passed 1.5 per cent of all the shareholders of Telecom Italia. This very low figure is largely due to the absence of the smallest class of shareholders. Less than 0.7 per cent of those shareholders voted their shares at the 2017 AGM of Telecom Italia. In 2021,

---

[24] Consob, *Report on Corporate Governance of Italian Listed Companies 2020* (Rome 2021), https://www.consob.it/documents/46180/46181/rcg2020.pdf/023c1d9b-ac8b-49a8-b650-3a4ca2aca53a.

[25] The size classes are: 1–100,000 shares; 100,001–500,000; 500,001–1,000,000; 1,000,001–5,000,000; 5,000,001–10,000,000; and more than 10,000,000 shares. As the total number of issued voting shares of Telecom Italia increased between 2015 from 13.4 billion shares to 15.3 billion shares in 2021, these ownership classes go from 0.0007% (100,000 shares) to 0.07% (10,000,000 shares).

[26] There is no explanation in the minutes of what caused this significant decrease in the number of shareholders in 2021. It could be that the 2015–2020 numbers include the holders of the saving shares of Telecom Italy, and the 2021 number excludes this class of shareholders.

their relative participation more than doubled to 1.3 per cent of the total number of that shareholder class.

In all other shareholder classes, a significant number of the shareholders vote their shares. In the group next to the smallest shareholders, with an individual voting stake of 0.003 to 0.007 per cent, 10–15 per cent of all the shareholders vote their shares. For the three largest groups, with individual voting stakes of 0.007 to 0.03 per cent, of 0.03 to 0.075 per cent and more, active engagement with the company – measured as voting at the AGM – is to be considered normal. In some of these groups and for some of the years more than two thirds of all these shareholders participated in the voting. Only in 2020, when the pandemic hit Italy very hard around the date of the AGM of Telecom Italia, was the participating rate lower than 20 per cent.

While Telecom Italia has an adequate participation rate, the average representation of voting shares in the AGM is significantly lower than in other large Italian companies, as can be seen from Figure 2. The participation in the AGM of Telecom Italia – measured as the total number of enrolled shares with voting rights – increased from 44 per cent in 2013 to 67 per cent in 2019. Thereafter, the participation levels dropped again, to 59 per cent in 2021. Both this significant increase, and the absolute percentage of the increase, and the relapse differ significantly from other large Italian companies, which experienced stable participation levels of represented voting shares of 70–74 per cent between 2012 and 2020.

Figure 2 Evolution of the Representation of Voting Shares in AGMs of Telecom Italia and the 100 Largest Italian Companies

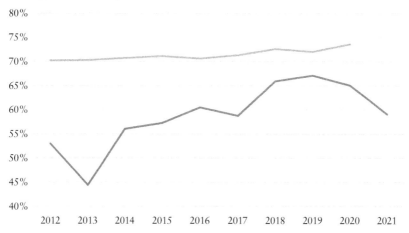

——— Average participation AGM 100 largest ——— Participating shares Telecom Italia

Source: Minutes of the meeting of Telecom Italia and Consob.

B. Participation Behaviour of Different Shareholder Classes

Table 4 summarises the total number of observations of participating shareholders in all AGMs of Telecom Italia from 2012 to 2021 as well as the number of different shareholders per class. Over a period of 10 years, 42,390 shareholders participated in the AGMs of Telecom Italia. In total 14,803 different shareholders attended at least one meeting and their median voting block was 9,176 shares. The latter median is significantly affected by an overwhelming majority of participating retail shareholders. More than two-thirds of all observations, close to 60 per cent of the shareholders, are individual retail shareholders that participated in one or more of the meetings. Retail shareholders have very small voting blocks of 4,760 shares (median block), less than 1 per cent of the median voting block of for example pension funds, holding each meeting a median of more than 0.5 million shares. Participating retail shareholders attended almost three AGMs before exiting the company.[27] The second largest class of shareholders is 'other institutional investors', predominantly foreign mutual funds and asset managers. Almost 24 per cent of the shareholders that participated in one of the AGMs of Telecom Italia belong to this class, and one out of three shareholders is an institutional investor of this kind. The significant larger number of shareholders belonging to this group compared to the total number of observations (Table 4) is due to the shorter voting engagement term of this type of shareholder. These shareholders exit after just two years (two AGMs), whereas retail shareholders voted their Telecom Italia shares for more than three years. This confirms other research that found relatively shorter investment horizons of mutual funds.[28] The median voting block of this kind of institutional investors is approximately 361,000 shares. A significantly smaller group of institutional investors are the pension funds: 733 different pension funds participated 2,183 times in one of the AGMs of Telecom Italia. Pension funds individually hold the largest median voting block and are also keen to engage with the company during a longer term than the other institutional investors. The average pension fund participated in three AGMs before 'going dark'.[29]

---

[27] We will provide more specific details of retail shareholders' behaviour in section IV. Some shareholders exited and returned to a later general meeting several times during the decade of investigation.

[28] M Cremers and A Pareek, 'Patient Capital Outperformance: The Investment Skill of High Active Share Managers who Trade Infrequently' (2016) 122 *Journal of Financial Economics* 288 (finding for mutual funds an average 'duration' of stock of 1.36 years); J Harford et al, 'Do Long-term Investors Improve Corporate Decision Making' (2018) 50 *Journal of Corporate Finance* 424 (considering as long-term investors, institutional investors that have a portfolio turnover of 35% or less).

[29] A shareholder that no longer votes the shares has not necessarily exited the company. However, many shareholders, and especially institutional investors, have a fiduciary or even mandatory duty to vote the shares: K Schmolcke, 'Institutional Investors' Mandatory Voting Disclosure: The Proposal of the European Commission against the Background of the US Experience' (2006) 15 *European Business Organization Law Review* 767. Therefore, when those types of shareholders disappear from the list of participating shareholders in the AGM, it is likely that they have exited the company as a shareholder. Shareholders can also 'disappear' from the attendance list when they start, as asset owners, outsourcing the management (and voting) of their portfolio to an asset manager. The records do not provide this information and both asset managers and asset owners are presented in the attendees' lists.

Table 4 Participating Shareholder Types and their Average Loyalty Term and Median Voting Block

	Observations	Shareholders	Average term	Median voting block
Individuals	28,875	8,795	3.28	4,760
Pension funds	2,183	733	2.98	562,222
Mutual fund/asset managers	10,146	4,866	2.09	361,073
Other types of shareholders	1,186	409	2.90	271,264
Total	42,390	14,803	2.86	9,176

Source: Own research based on the minutes of the AGMs of Telecom Italia.

The other shareholders include a wide variety of different types: foreign investors include several (American) churches and universities, local communities in the UK and the US, some foundations and a significant number of banking institutions and insurance companies and some, predominantly Italian, other non-financial companies. These classes of shareholder participate on average in 2.9 AGMs but the subtypes differ significantly in their loyalty behaviour. Foreign non-financial companies participated in less than two AGMs on average, whereas some Italian foundations were very loyal and attended on average 4.7 meetings. However, the number of participating shareholders of this subclass is very limited. The largest shareholders of all participating shareholders are also part of this group: the Spanish Telefónica group held its major voting share in Telecom Italy via its Italian subsidiary Telco. In 2015 it sold its stake to the French group Vivendi, which is part of the foreign other shareholders. The median voting block of these types of shareholders of 271,264 shares hides huge differences of voting blocks, ranging from one share of GSC Proxitalia SPA in the 2018 AGM to more than three billion shares of Telco in the AGMs of 2012 to 2015.

These observations result in a first conclusion. Voting retail shareholders show more loyalty than the mutual funds and pension funds of which some of the retail shareholders are also beneficiaries.[30] The retail shareholders vote, on average, in more than three AGMs of Telecom Italia; mutual funds and asset managers barely exceed voting in two AGMs.

C. Long-Term Voting Behaviour of the Different Classes of Shareholders

These first observations are further explored in another way. I measured the number of shareholders as well as their voting blocks that reappeared yearly in the AGM of Telecom Italia or entered the company. Figures 3A and 3B show the loyalty of

---

[30] While the pension funds hold and vote their shares during a longer period than mutual funds and asset management, an *anova* analysis show that the differences of voting shares between the latter shareholder types and retail shareholders is significant at the 1% level.

shareholders (attending the meeting at year *t*+1 after attending the meeting at year *t*) (Figure 3A) or entering the company at year *t*+1 as a voting shareholder (Figure 3B).

Figure 3A Relative Number of Participating Shareholders at the AGM at *t*+1 Compared to the AGM at *t*

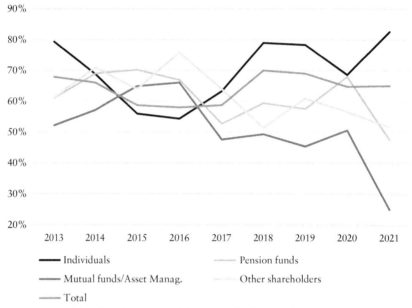

Source: Own research based on the minutes of the AGMs of Telecom Italia.

Figure 3B Relative Number of Voting New Shareholders Compared to Voting Shareholders at *t*

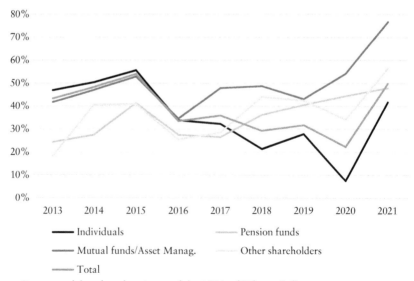

Source: Own research based on the minutes of the AGMs of Telecom Italia.

These figures show a more complex picture of the loyalty, exit and voice of shareholders than Table 4 illustrates. Every year between 58 and 70 per cent of all shareholders attending a meeting at year t had already attended the meeting at year t-1. Retail shareholders show a relative high level of loyalty in the early and more recent years. Starting in 2013, with a loyalty rate of almost 80 per cent of the retail shareholders participating in a follow up AGM at year t, this loyalty significantly decreases in the first years of the analysis to an absolute low of only 54 per cent of the retail shareholders participating in the 2015 AGM and attending the meeting in 2016. No other shareholder type shows this low level of loyalty in the years 2015 and 2016. After 2016, there is a steep increase in the loyalty to a record high of almost 83 per cent of the retail shareholders that participated in the meeting in 2020 showing up in the meeting of 2021. Since 2018 no other shareholder type showed similar levels of loyalty. At the opposite end of the spectrum, one can find the mutual funds and asset managers. At the start of the analysed period, those investors increased their level of loyalty from 52 per cent in 2013 to 66 per cent in 2016. However, after 2016 this level of loyalty was decreasing significantly to levels of less than 50 per cent participating in the meeting of the following year and to an all time low in 2021. That year less than 25 per cent of the mutual funds and asset managers who voted at the 2020 AGM participated in the meeting of 2021. The other shareholder types hold the middle between the loyal retail shareholders and 'disloyal' mutual funds. Note that a mirror image of Figure 3A would show the number of exiting shareholders.

Every year, new shareholders enter the company and start with an engagement policy, including voting at AGMs. Figure 3B shows the relative inflow of shareholders. The nominator of every relative observation is the number of participating shareholders of a class that attended the meeting at time t but did not participate in the AGM of year t-1; the denominator is the total number of that type of shareholders that participated in year t. Overall, the number of 'new' shareholders that are voting grows the first years from 43 to 54 per cent of all attending shareholders, decreasing afterwards to an all-time low of 22 per cent in 2020. The COVID-19 pandemic seems to have lowered interest in becoming an active shareholder. The 'entrance behaviour' seems to be different for some groups of shareholders at the start of our research period. The first group were the individuals and mutual funds and asset managers that experience similar number of entries varying in the first half of the period from 34 to 55 per cent but diverging afterwards sharply. While the retail shareholders experienced a significant drop in the number of newly entering shareholders to 7 per cent in 2020 and returning to a high level of 41 per cent in 2021, the entry of new mutual funds and asset managers increased gradually after 2015 to more than 75 per cent of all participating mutual funds and asset managers in 2021. The number of new pension funds and other shareholders differs from the other two groups and show similar patterns of 20 to 50 per cent of the total number of voting shareholders of that class over the whole research period.

Figures 3A and 3B measure the number of loyal, exiting and new entering shareholders. They provide a more balanced view of the loyalty of shareholders than Table 4. However, loyal shareholders in each group can, from one AGM to the next, also show their loyalty in another way: they can increase or decrease their voting block.

Further, shareholders that enter the company and start voting in the AGM acquired relatively large blocks of shares compared to the current loyal shareholders. In Figure 4A, Figure 4B and Figure 4C, I address the changing numbers of voted shares of the different voting classes. Figure 4A measures the relative size of the summed voting blocks of the shareholders in the different classes of shareholders that already voted in the previous AGM of Telecom Italia. For example, the results of the retail shareholders for 2014 show that the total voting block of loyal retail shareholders that had already voted in the 2013 AGM of Telecom Italia was 87 per cent, indicating that the 69 per cent loyal retail shareholders (Figure 3A) increased their voting blocks between 2013 and 2014.

Overall, only in the first year of our study, the loyal shareholders maintained their relative position in the company: the loyal shareholders voted 98.5 per cent of the shares voted at the 2012 AGM also at the 2013 AGM. As only 68 per cent of the share-holders were loyal (see Figure 3A), loyal shareholders increased their voting stake in the company between 2012 and 2013. Except for the pension funds that only voted 84 per cent of the shares voted in 2012 in the AGM of 2013, all other classes of share-holders had loyal shareholders voting similar number of shares in the meeting of 2013 compared to the meeting of 2012. Afterwards the yearly changes in the relative voting blocks of the different classes of loyal shareholders were significant. The development of the overall relative number of loyal voted shares differs significantly from year to year with an absolute high in 2013 of 98.5 per cent and an absolute low of 35 per cent in 2019. Similarly, loyalty of retail shareholders, measured as the summed voting stakes of the shareholders also voting at the previous AGM, diverged from 52 per cent in 2020 to more than 101 per cent in 2021, meaning that the 82 per cent loyal retail shareholders in 2021 increased their voting block in Telecom Italy by more than 20 per cent. In 2020 the 68 per cent remaining loyal retail shareholders decreased their voting block by almost 25 per cent. The cut down was even higher in 2018: 79 per cent of the retail shareholders remained loyal but their combined voting stake diminished by 30 per cent compared to the summed voting stake of 2017.

Mutual funds and asset managers followed a significantly different path to that of the retail shareholders. From 2013 onwards the summed voting block of the loyal funds and managers diminished yearly to an absolute low of only 20 per cent in 2021, hence the 25 per cent loyal funds and managers that also voted their shares in 2020 did not exit like the large majority of their colleagues but they did lower their interests. These results are in sharp contradiction with 2013. The 52 per cent loyal funds and managers voted in 2013 more than the total number of shares that all funds and managers voted in 2012. When comparing the development of the total loyal voting blocks of retail shareholders and that of the mutual funds and asset managers the differences are striking. A similar observation can be made for the pension funds. Some years, like 2014, 2017 and 2020 the loyal pension funds increase their voting stakes significantly and to levels higher than the total voting block of all loyal pension funds voted in the previous AGM, whilst in other years, like in 2018, even the loyal pension funds decreased their voting block. Further, at six AGMs the pension funds participated with the relatively largest voting blocks, which had voted at the previous AGM, compared to those of the other sharehold-ers. It includes the three years that the loyal pension funds increased their voting blocks to levels that exceeded the voting block of all pension funds voting in the previous AGM. This results in a strongly diverging pattern of loyalty between retail shareholders and pension funds.

Note that the largest yearly changes in voting blocks can be found in the class of other shareholders. This is due to the entry or exit of some of Telecom Italia's blockholders. In 2015, the subsidiary of the Spanish Telefónica, Telco, sold its stake of more than 22 per cent. As a result, only 3 per cent of the shares of other shareholders voted in 2015, were also voted at the AGM in 2016. Later, Vivendi stepped in and acquired a voting block of approximately 21 per cent. This French group later increased its stake to 24 per cent and shifted shares in its group, resulting in 2018 again in a large fluctuation in the number of 'loyal' voted shares.

Figure 4A Voting Block of the Loyal Shareholders at the AGM at $t+1$ Compared to t

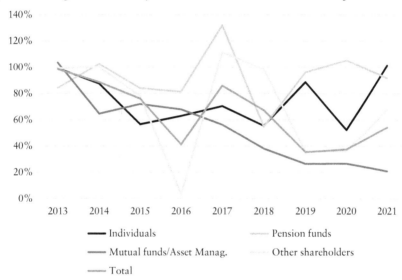

Source: Own research based on the minutes of the AGMs of Telecom Italia.

Differently from the development of the number of loyal shareholders in Figure 3A which includes information on the relative number of exiting shareholders, namely the difference between 100 per cent and the number of loyal shareholders, Figure 4B does not include information on the size of the voting blocks of the exiting shareholders. As the loyal shareholders can increase their voting blocks from one year to another – a good example of which is the pension funds in 2017 – we present in Figure 4B the relative size of the voting blocks of exiting shareholders, divided into the defined shareholder classes. The size of the voting blocks of the exiting retail shareholders fluctuates from 16 per cent in 2014 to 55 per cent in 2020, a strongly different development than that of the exiting pension funds and mutual funds and asset managers. The first type of shareholders, the pension funds, show a relative stable turnover of shares: between 9 and 26 per cent of the shares held by pension funds that voted, exit the company every year. Mutual fund and asset managers exited in large volumes at the starting years of our analysis and show an even stronger exiting behaviour towards the end, with more than 83 per cent of the shares belonging to these share-holders in 2020 which were no longer voted in 2021.

Figure 4B Voting Block of the Exiting Shareholders at the AGM at *t*+1 compared to the AGM at *t*

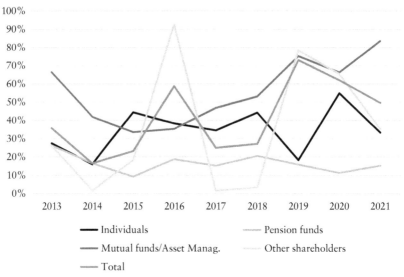

Source: Own research based on the minutes of the AGMs of Telecom Italia.

The combination of both developments described in the previous paragraphs resulted in similar patterns of newly entering shareholders over the years. While pension funds step in and acquire voting blocks similar to the size of the exiting voting blocks, hold-ing shares of 10 to 20 per cent of the total voting block of pension funds, there were more new mutual funds and asset managers towards the end of our research period. From 2018 onwards the total voting block of the newly entered mutual funds and asset managers is significantly larger than that of the mutual funds and asset manag-ers that stepped in in a previous year. The yearly differences of entering and exiting shares held by retail shareholders and other shareholders show another pattern. Both types of shareholders experienced the relative highest and the lowest entry of new voting blocks. In 2014 more than 70 per cent of the voting block of retail shareholders belonged to retail shareholders that were not yet voting in 2013. In 2020 this number was at an all-time low of only 5 per cent, probably due to the pandemic. In 2016 with more than 96 per cent and 2019 with 70 per cent the new voting blocks of other share-holders peaked, in 2013 with less than 1 per cent and 2015 and 2017 with less than 4 per cent the new voting blocks of other shareholders were negligible compared to the voting blocks of other shareholders that earlier started their engaging behaviour. In short, these results show another different behaviour of retail shareholders on the one side and the pension funds and mutual funds on the other side. Along with a different term of voting the shares, the entry and exit behaviour is different between these types of shareholders.

Figure 4C Voting Blocks of New Shareholders Compared to Loyal Shareholders at *t*

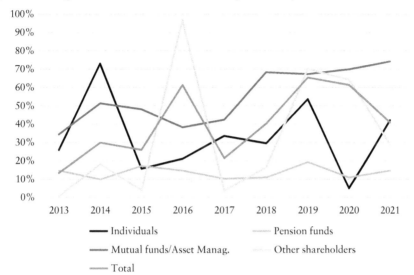

Source: Own research based on the minutes of the AGMs of Telecom Italia.

D. Empirical Assessment of the Long Term Voting Behaviour of Different Shareholder Classes

The previous section addressed the yearly changes of the voting practices of different shareholder classes. In this section I study the long-term voting behaviour of the different shareholder classes. First, I provide an overview of the distribution of the different voting terms of the different shareholder classes in Figure 5. In Table 5 it was shown that the average number of years of voting the shares is highest for retail shareholders and lowest for mutual funds and asset managers. Figure 5 provides more details of the long-term voting behaviour of the different classes of shareholders. Slightly more than 40 per cent of the pension funds, the retail shareholders and other shareholders only vote their voting block once at an AGM of Telecom Italia. This number is significantly higher for mutual funds and asset managers. Almost 58 per cent of this class of shareholders vote only once. Engaging periods of two to five years are more equally distributed, although retail shareholders leave the company as voting shareholders less frequently than the other types of shareholders: 14 per cent of retail shareholders leave after two years, 8 per cent after three years and 5 per cent after five years. None of the other shareholder types have similar low levels of exiting. The numbers for pension funds are 20 per cent, 14 per cent and 7 per cent, those for mutual funds and asset managers, 18 per cent, 9 per cent and 6 per cent. The significantly lower relative numbers for the shorter voting terms of retail shareholders of up to five years, result in a much higher number of retail shareholders with voting terms of more than five years; 23 per cent of all retail shareholder vote in more than five AGMs of Telecom Italia. These retail shareholders are relatively equally distributed between the different classes of years of voting, with even in the longest voting terms of 8 to 10 years, every year close to 4 per cent of all retail shareholders belong to this group. The difference between this and the mutual funds and asset managers is striking. Only 6 per cent of all funds and managers participate in the AGMs of Telecom Italy more than five times. The other shareholders and pension funds 'perform' better with 11 and 13 per cent of all other shareholders and funds that voted, which is still significantly lower than the retail shareholders.

Figure 5 Number of Years of Voting Engagement per Shareholder Class

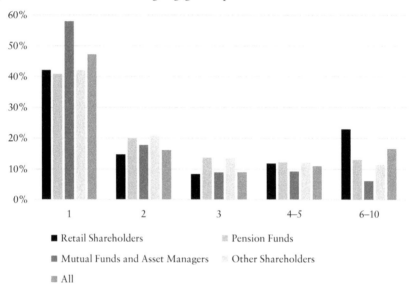

Source: Own research based on the minutes of the AGMs of Telecom Italia.

These differences are confirmed in the Kaplan-Meier survival analysis. The results are presented in Figure 6. This figure shows the relative number of 'surviving' shareholders in the different classes. As the previous assessments of the differences in voting behaviour between, especially, retail shareholders, and pension funds and mutual funds and asset managers illustrated, the Kaplan-Meier survival analysis reveals significantly different long-term voting behaviour between the different classes of shareholders. The estimated survival times are only 2.4 years for the mutual funds and the asset managers, 3.0 and 3.1 years for the pension funds and the other shareholders, while the Kaplan-Meier analysis predicts a participation period of 4.1 years for the retail shareholders. It results in an expected period of 3.5 years for all shareholders.[31] When looking at the lower and upper bound 95 per cent intervals, it reveals that only the periods of pension funds and other shareholders overlap. The three additional tests[32]

---

[31] These results are higher than my findings in Table 3 because this empirical method does take into account censored data, like engaged shareholders that will be present in AGMs of Telecom Italia to come.

[32] The Log Rank (Mantel-Cox), the Breslow and the Tarone-Ware tests. The Breslow test the early years of voting behaviour (fast exit), the Log Rank test the last years of voting behaviour (many years of voting), the Tarone-Ware tests the intermediate years: https://www.real-statistics.com/survival-analysis/kaplan-meier-procedure/kaplan-meier-comparison-tests/.

addressing in which part of the survival analysis, the first years (early exit) the middle years or the later years (long voting terms) the differences tend to be significant, show that for all survival periods the differences remain significant. Even after the first year, but also at the medium and long term, shareholder classes demonstrate significantly different voting behaviour.

Figure 6 Kaplan Meier Survival Function of the Long-Term Voting Engagement of Different Shareholder Classes

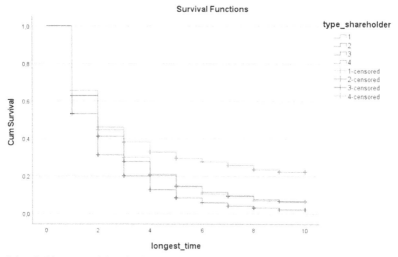

Type of shareholder: 1: retail shareholders; 2: pension funds; 3: mutual funds and asset management and 4: other shareholders.

Source: Own research based on the minutes of the AGMs of Telecom Italia.

V. SAY ON PAY VOTING BEHAVIOUR OF SHAREHOLDER CLASSES

In the previous section I showed that the voting behaviour of the different shareholder classes varies significantly. In relative numbers, more retail shareholders participate in a larger number of AGMs than the other classes of shareholders, especially mutual funds and asset managers. In this section I analyse whether similar differences exist in the voting behaviour of a specific governance issue, the approval of the remuneration policy, presented in the first part of the remuneration report.

The say-on-pay voting item often receives significant opposition.[33] I used these say-on-pay voting outcomes for studying whether the different shareholder classes experienced the proposed remuneration policy as adequate. Table 5 shows the voting results of the agenda item 'remuneration policy' of Telecom Italia for the period 2012–2021. The numbers show that this voting item is regularly heavily

---

[33] Y Ertimur et al, 'Shareholder Votes and Proxy Advisors: Evidence from Say on Pay' (2013) 51 *Journal of Accounting Research* 951; C Van der Elst and A Lafarre, 'Shareholder Voice on Executive Pay: A Decade of Dutch Say on Pay' (2017) 18 *European Business Organization Law Review* 51.

contested at the AGMs of Telecom Italia. From 2012 to 2019 shareholders holding more than 30 per cent of all the participating votes, voted against the remuneration policy or had their votes withheld. The remuneration policy was even rejected in 2019. In 2020 and 2021 a supermajority of all the shareholders voted for the remuneration policy.

Table 5 Voting Results of the Remuneration Policy of Telecom Italia

	2012	2013	2014	2015	2016	2017	2018	2019	2020	2021
Vote for	67.77%	67.91%	84.82%	66.05%	61.58%	56.05%	66.99%	43.76%	94.98%	94.03%
vote against	21.56%	31.92%	5.09%	33.63%	37.93%	43.49%	25.15%	20.40%	3.85%	4.51%
vote withheld/ not voted	10.67%	0.17%	10.09%	0.31%	0.50%	0.46%	7.86%	35.84%	1.17%	1.46%
Total	100%	100%	100%	100%	100%	100%	100%	100%	100%	100%

Source: Minutes of the AGMs of Telecom Italia.

Figure 7 reports how the shareholders voted for the remuneration policy. The figure presents the evolution of the relative number of shareholders of each class voting for the remuneration policy. The difference between these relative numbers and 100 per cent marks the number of shareholders voting against the proposed policy or abstained from voting. The total results show that a large majority of the participating shareholder were against the remuneration policy of Telecom Italia in the period of 2012 to 2019. The number of shareholders voting against the policy increased over the years from 75 per cent of all shareholders in 2012 to 96.5 per cent of all participating shareholders in 2018. Nevertheless, the voting power of the other 3.5 per cent of the shareholders was sufficient to approve the remuneration policy in 2018. It was not until 2019, with 93 per cent of the shareholders voting against the remuneration policy that their voting power was sufficient to reject the policy; 35 per cent of the votes abstained. The class of the retail shareholders significantly influenced these totals as this class overtakes all other classes in the absolute number of participating shareholders.

Pension funds, mutual funds and asset managers and other shareholder voted almost identically during the whole research period. Over the years these classes of shareholders tend to vote more and more against the remuneration policy, reaching an absolute low of only 10 per cent of all pension funds, mutual funds and asset managers and other shareholders voting for the remuneration policy. The only exception was 2014, when 85 per cent (mutual funds and asset managers) to 93 per cent (pension funds) of these shareholders approved the policy. From 2019 onwards the number of shareholders supporting the remuneration policy steeply increased to levels of 70–80 per cent of these shareholder classes approving the presented voting policy.

Retail shareholders voted completely differently. From 2012 to 2019, each year less than 2.6 per cent of the number of attending retail shareholders approved the remuneration policy. From 2012 to 2016 and in 2019 more than 99 per cent of the participating retail shareholders voted against the remuneration policy. In 2020 and 2021 the sentiment of the retail shareholder shifted completely. In those two years the retail shareholders supported, close to unanimously, the remuneration policy of Telecom Italia. More than 99.5 per cent of retail shareholders voted yes for the remuneration policy.

Given the previous findings, it does not come as a surprise that a chi-square test of independence examining the relationship between the class of shareholders and the voting behaviour was significant. The retail shareholders were more likely than the other shareholder classes to vote against the remuneration policy between 2012 and 2019 and more likely to vote for the remuneration policy in the years 2020 and 2021. Further study is needed to assess whether the different types of shareholders use the voting item of the remuneration policy to signal their discontent with this policy or use it (also) to warn of other areas of corporate displeasure.[34]

Figure 7 Evolution of how Shareholders Voted for the Remuneration Policy

Source: Own research based on the minutes of the AGMs of Telecom Italia.

Figure 8 presents the relative number of votes 'for' the remuneration policy of the different shareholder classes. This second method of presenting the voting for the remuneration policy, confirms the different voting behaviour of retail shareholders versus the other types of shareholders except for 2020 and 2021. Until 2019 retail shareholders holding less than 12 per cent of all the votes of the retail shareholders

---

[34] For example, in 2016 the stock price of Telecom Italia dropped by almost 30%, significantly more than the referential Telecom STOXX index (Table 2). Nevertheless, the remuneration report showed that the CEO achieved 123% of the criteria of the short-term bonus in 2016, resulting in a bonus of more than €1.7m. At the same time the ownership base of the company significantly changed. These developments and results could trigger the different voting behaviour of the different kinds of shareholders.

participating in the AGM approved the remuneration policy. In 2016 the number of votes was close to 0. However, except for 2016, more of the larger retail shareholders were supportive for the remuneration report. With approval voting rates diverging from 1.1 per cent in 2015 to 12 per cent in 2017, the number of votes was at least four times as high as the total number of retail shareholders voting for the remuneration policy between 2012 and 2019. As almost all retail shareholders approved the remuneration policy in 2020 and 2021 – this difference according to the size of the voting block of the retail shareholders disappeared.

The other classes of shareholders show a more mixed picture in their voting behaviour for the remuneration policy. The most divergent from retail shareholders' voting behaviour can be noticed in the class of the other shareholders. These shareholders always approved the remuneration policy with a supermajority of the votes ranging from 75 per cent in 2012 to 99.9 per cent in 2020. Only in 2019 did several shareholders of this class, holding most of the votes of this class of shareholders, vote against the remuneration policy, resulting in the rejection of the policy. Also in this class, the comparison between the number of shareholders voting for the policy and the number of votes voting for the policy is striking. From 2012 to 2018 the wedge between these numbers and these votes increased from 50 per cent to 900 per cent. In 2018 only 9.7 per cent of the other shareholders approved the remuneration policy, but their voting power resulted in an approval rate of more than 83 per cent of the votes of this class of shareholders and a 66 per cent overall approval of the remuneration policy.

The pension funds and the mutual funds and asset managers voted similarly in several years, but also between these classes of shareholders, significant differences can be noticed in Figure 8. Like retail shareholders, pension funds voted with a majority of the votes against the remuneration policy for five years between 2012 and 2018. Also, the pension funds voted 94 per cent of the votes against the remuneration policy in 2018. Remarkably, in 2019 when the remuneration policy was voted down, close to 80 per cent of the pension fund votes voted for this policy. While retail shareholders overwhelmingly approved the remuneration policy in 2020 and 2021, pension funds were more critical. In both years, 12 per cent of the votes of the pension fund opposed this agenda item. The same holds for the mutual funds and asset managers: 12 to 17 per cent of the votes held by the participating mutual funds and their managers voted against the remuneration policy. During the period 2012–2018, the mutual funds tend one year to vote more in a similar way to the retail shareholders, whereas another year the voting result of this class resembles that of the pension funds. In 2018, 57 per cent of the votes were supportive of the remuneration report, whilst only 2 per cent of the votes of the retail shareholders and 6 per cent of the pension funds approved the remuneration policy. In 2017 12 per cent of the votes of the retail shareholders approved the report whereas 18 per cent of the votes of the mutual funds voted yes, while 44 per cent of the votes of the pension funds gave this voting item a yes.

The chi-square test of independence examining the relationship of the voting results of the different classes of shareholders was also significant, even in 2020 when the difference in approval rates of the votes of the different shareholder classes was only 12 per cent. Again, the retail shareholders were more likely than the other shareholder classes to vote against the remuneration policy between 2012 and 2019 and more likely to vote for the remuneration policy in the years 2020 and 2021.

Figure 8 Evolution of the Number of Votes 'for' the Remuneration Policy of the Different Shareholder Classes

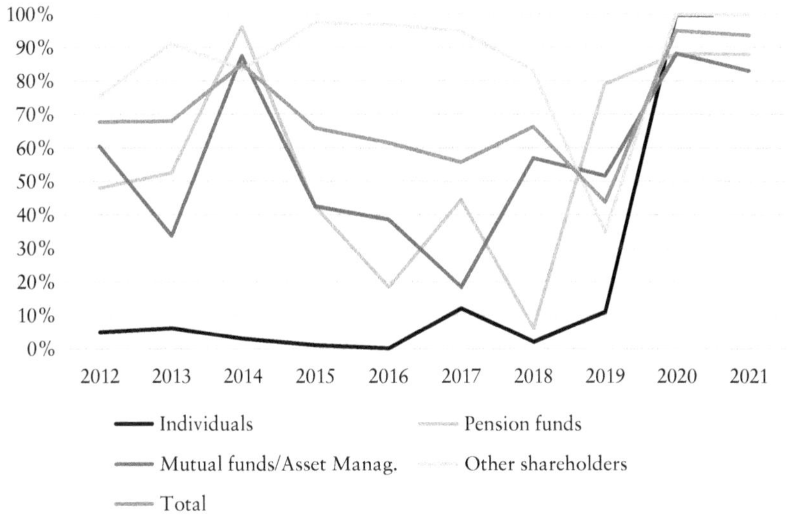

Source: Own research based on the minutes of the AGMs of Telecom Italia.

VI. PREFERENCES OF RETAIL SHAREHOLDERS AND BENEFIARIES OF FUNDS AND FUNDS' BEHAVIOUR

The long-term voting behaviour of shareholder classes differs. Retail shareholders are more loyal to the company but voice their concerns more often than pension and mutual funds. However, retail investors in companies are not identical to investors in mutual funds and beneficiaries of pension funds. The previous findings prove only partially, at best, that the beneficiaries of pension funds and mutual funds would respond differently to the investees of these funds than the funds currently do. Whereas my approach vis-à-vis companies is likely to be identical whether I am a direct investor or a beneficiary of a pension fund and a mutual fund, only in the former can I effectively vote. However, my way of engagement should not be like that of the other direct or indirect retail shareholders or beneficiaries. Therefore, I also investigated whether other research provides evidence that beneficiaries support another engagement policy than the one that the (mutual or pension) fund is applying.

Bauer, Ruof and Smeets show in their survey research that the beneficiaries of a Dutch pension fund overwhelmingly support an increased engagement of the fund in its investees.[35] Importantly, the majority of the participants are in favour of an increased support of the pension fund for the United Nations Social Development Goals (SDG), independent of return expectations. Even if the participants expect a negative financial effect of more sustainable behaviour of the pension funds, almost

---

[35] R Bauer et al, 'Get Real! Individuals Prefer More Sustainable Investments' (2021) 34 *The Review of Financial Studies* 3976.

twice as many beneficiaries favour the more sustainable option. Related to my research, it signals that the current behaviour of a pension fund is more than likely not well aligned with the expectations of the beneficiaries, particularly regarding its engagement in companies for more sustainable development. The study confirms the research of Riedl and Smeets for mutual fund investors.[36] These scholars invited a large number of investors of a large Dutch fund manager offering a range of investment funds to participate in a survey and experiments with monetary incentives. Investors in mutual funds that favour socially responsible investments (seem to) accept lower financial returns. Like the study by Bauer, Ruof and Smeets, the research was carried out with (at least predominantly) Dutch investors. Both studies provide convincing arguments that the international investor community would show similar results.[37]

In another, experimental, study of the behaviour of retail investors of Siemroth and Hornuf, the experiment shows that investors are willing to give up some of their investment returns if the environmental impact is sufficiently large.[38] It was found that a specific impact – in the experiment, reducing greenhouse gas emissions – is preferred over a general environmental impact, in the experiment of a donation to Greenpeace. The study found that a significant number (25 per cent) of the investors never want to substitute a higher financial return for any kind of impact. A large majority of 60 per cent considers giving up a higher return for a substantial large impact. Siemroth and Hornuf show that investors prefer an environmental impact over a social impact. I studied a core governance issue which makes a comparison with the results of Siemroth and Hornuf challenging. However, the approval of the remuneration policy can be considered as a high-impact proposal, which a company must duly consider, especially when experiencing significant opposition, and certainly after it became a binding vote.

Brav, Cain and Zytnick similarly show that retail shareholders, like other investors, are driven by financial arguments.[39] They found that retail shareholders make their decision to vote depending on the cost of the participation and the benefits of success. However, the scholars also confirmed that there are benefits from voting that financial fluctuation cannot easily explain. Non-financial motives steer the voting turnout. Unrelated to my study, the findings of Brav et al. confirm the results of Schmidt who, in a survey among 425,000 German retail investors of a German blue-chip company, found that well-informed retail investors use their corporate voting rights more frequently.[40] Brav et al also show that retail shareholders support less ESG-proposals than institutional investors do. However, the authors identified a significant degree of

---

[36] A Riedl and P Smeets, 'Why Do Investors Hold Socially Responsible Mutual Funds' (2017) 72 *Journal of Finance* 2505.

[37] Some other studies are more critical towards the (non-financial) interests of beneficiaries, see D Katelouzou and E Micheler, 'The Market for Stewardship and the Role of the Government' in D Katelouzou and DW Puchniak (eds), *Global Shareholder Stewardship: Complexities, Challenges and Possibilities* (Cambridge University Press, 2022).

[38] C Siemroth and L Hornuf, 'Do Retail Investors Value Environmental Impact? A Lab-in-the-Field Experiment with Crowdfunders' *CESIFO Working Papers* 9197 (July 2021).

[39] A Brav et al, 'Retail Shareholder Participation in the Proxy Process: Monitoring, Engagement, and Voting' *Journal of Financial Economics* (forthcoming).

[40] A Schmidt, 'Determinants of Corporate Voting – Evidence from a Large Survey of German Retail Investors' (2017) 18 *Schmalenbach Business Review* 71.

heterogeneity in voting for environmental and social proposals of retail shareholders. Smaller retail shareholders more often support the environmental and social proposals, and even more than institutions do. I also found many thousands of very small retail shareholders that faithfully vote their small stake, which did not have any effect on the voting outcome. Even when year after year more than 99 per cent of all the retail shareholders voted against the remuneration policy, it was only when some major shareholders abstained from voting that the remuneration policy of Telecom Italia was not approved in 2019. This confirms that some shareholders derive other than financial benefits from voting. Second, most of the retail shareholders that voted against the remuneration policy were the shareholders that had smaller stakes. The approval rates of the retail shareholders were up to ten times higher when their voting block was measured compared to the number of voters, signalling that the larger retail shareholders voted with management. The latter findings are aligned with the findings in Brav et al's study. Third, as the remuneration policy is a governance issue, it confirms the findings of Brav, Cain and Zytnick for environmental and social policy issues.

Zytnick evaluates the relationship between mutual fund ideology and the ideology of the beneficiaries of the mutual funds.[41] His research shows that mutual funds that focus on ESG especially attract beneficiaries that are keen to have their preferences reflected in the policies of the fund. Conversely, the research of Curtis, Fisch and Robertson indicates that the ESG-funds deliver more ESG exposure.[42] However, outside the ESG-funds this relationship of preferences and policies does not hold, Zytnick's study argues. Funds that support responsible investing do not attract beneficiaries that align with this ideology. Zytnick's research concludes: 'mutual fund voting features a diversity of opinion not captured by the simple binary of ESG and non-ESG, and most variation in voting across mutual funds is not reflected in the investors in the funds'. These findings of Zytnick support my research of all mutual funds and asset managers as one class, as it was unfortunately not possible to break down the mutual funds and asset managers into different subclasses of funds.

While more research is certainly necessary, these studies confirm that voting practices differ between different classes of shareholders as well as within the classes of shareholders. Further, there is reasonable evidence that the participants in different types of funds do not see their voting preferences fully reflected in the voting practices of the fund. It is more than likely that many investors in mutual funds and beneficiaries of pension funds would vote similarly to current retail shareholders.

VII. DISCUSSION AND CONCLUSIONS

In my study of the AGMs of Telecom Italia, I found that long-term voting practices of retail shareholders differ from those of other kinds of shareholder classes. Between

---

[41] J Zytnick, 'Do Mutual Funds Represent Individual Investors?' (24 April 2021) *NYU & Econ Research Paper No 21-04* (24 April 2021), https://ssrn.com/abstract=3803690.

[42] Q Curtis et al, 'Do ESG Mutual Funds Deliver on Their Promises' (2021) 120(3) *Michigan Law Review* 393, https://papers.ssrn.com/sol3/papers.cfm?abstract_id=3839785.

58 per cent and 70 per cent of the shareholders that voted at an AGM had also voted at the previous AGM. It is often the class of the retail shareholders that show the largest continuous voting engagement, but sometimes pension funds or other shareholders show more commitment. For several years most of the mutual funds and asset managers have made use of 'exit'. Less than 25 per cent of those shareholders who participated in 2020 also voted in the AGM 2021. When measured by the size of the voting blocks, the yearly divergences of voting engagements between the different shareholder classes were even larger. In some years almost all votes in some of the shareholder classes came from newly entered shareholders, while in other years the loyal shareholders of a particular class further increased their voting blocks. Overall, my empirical analysis shows significant differences in long-term voting engagement of the different shareholder classes and especially between the retail shareholders and the mutual funds and the asset managers. Second, voting practices of a governance-related voting item diverges between retail shareholders and other classes of shareholders, especially pension funds and mutual fund and asset management. Almost all retail shareholders disapproved for many years the remuneration policy of Telecom Italia, which was supported by most of the shareholders belonging to the other shareholder class and, to a lower extent, the pension funds and the mutual funds and asset management. For many years, over 90 per cent of all participating shareholders voted no, but due to the large voting blocks of the class of the other shareholders, the voting result of the remuneration policy was broadly supportive of the Board of directors. Only when some of the largest shareholders voted against this agenda item – or abstained in 2019 – did the voting results require the Board of directors to act.

As the pension funds, mutual funds and asset managers should consider the interests of beneficiaries or investors of the fund and act accordingly, the voting practices of these institutional investors often seem to be badly aligned with the expectations and wishes of these fund investors and beneficiaries. This is certainly the case if investors in these funds behave in the same way as the retail shareholders who directly invest in portfolio companies.

Griffin recently noted that funds are not aware of the best interest of the beneficiaries. Only by blind luck could these funds, which make no serious attempts to discern investors' preferences, be accurately reflecting investors' interests with their voting behaviours.[43] Currently, I tend to agree with this statement. Recently, my pension fund decided to step out of companies in the oil and gas industry. The appropriateness of excluding less sustainable industries is a heavily debated issue in the Netherlands, certainly after this year's shareholder proposal at the AGM of Shell receiving over 30 per cent support. The resolution requested the company 'to set and publish targets that are consistent with the goal of the Paris Climate Agreement'.[44] According to the financial press the beneficiaries of the pension fund and the affiliated employers

---

[43] C Griffin, 'Environmental & Social Voting at Index Funds' (2020) 44 *Delaware Journal of Corporate Law* 169.

[44] Royal Dutch Shell plc, *Notice of Annual General Meeting Tuesday May 18* (2021) 6.

exerted significant pressure for exiting investments in coal, gas, and oil.[45] It could be the case that there were beneficiaries making a plea for this strategic investment change.[46] However, certainly not all beneficiaries (including me) exerted pressure. I am against such an exit as I still believe that my pension fund can put (far more) pressure on changing the behaviour of the investees towards sustainability than I can. Bauer even argued that such a change in policy is not effective. ABP should stimulate this industry to invest in innovation.[47] Bebchuk and Hirst also found, for the largest investment funds – the Big Three: BlackRock, Vanguard and State Street – that the funds are more deferential to the managers of the investees than is optimal, and invest less in stewardship than beneficiaries would prefer.[48] Therefore it comes as no surprise to find that a number of scholars asked some years ago for an adequate regulatory framework matching the beneficiaries' expectations and investment management practices.[49]

My findings, as well as the results of many other studies, raise the question how the alignment can be established between the preferences of the beneficiaries of the funds and the voting practices of these funds. Currently, the institutional investors' voting behaviour raises concerns about the legitimacy of the outcomes.[50] Further, mutual funds are more likely to exit the company if the voting result is inconsistent with how the fund voted.[51] As the fund's voting behaviour does not necessarily match with its beneficiaries' preferences, exit can also be contrary to the beneficiaries' expectations. However, most beneficiaries are unaware, especially ex ante, of the voting practices of the fund. Fortunately, several solutions are rapidly gaining ground.

First, over recent years, the stewardship of asset owners and asset managers has progressed.[52] Since the first stewardship codes were issued in 2010, it is expected that these types of shareholders will engage with companies for long-term sustainable value creation. Many of the codes consider the promotion of the long-term interest

---

[45] M Wolzak and J Groot, 'Pensioenbelegger ABP verkoopt olie- en gasbedrijven: Noodzakelijke koerswijziging' (27 October 2021) *Financieele Dagblad* 2.

[46] In one newspaper they were identified as a 'small pushy action group' (een klein drammerig actiegroepje).

[47] Reddit, 'Hoogleraar over besluit ABP tot stoppen beleggen fossiele industrie' (26 October 2021), https://www.reddit.com/r/DutchFIRE/comments/qgwo2r/hoogleraar_over_besluit_abp_tot_stoppen_beleggen/.

[48] L Bebchuk and S Hirst, 'The Power of the Big Three, and Why it Matters' *Working Paper* (21 February 2021), http://www.law.harvard.edu/faculty/bebchuk/The_Power_of_the_Big_Three_and_Why_It_Matters.pdf. It should not come as a surprise as the incentives of managers of funds are towards not monitoring: H Spamann, 'Indirect Investor Protection: The Investment Ecosystem and Its Legal Underpinnings' *NUY Working Paper No 594/2021* (23 August 2021), https://www.law.nyu.edu/sites/default/files/Spamann%20Indirect%20Investor%20Protection_v3.0.pdf.

[49] R Barker and I Chiu, *Corporate Governance and Investment Management* (Edward Elgar, 2017) 187.

[50] J Fisch, 'Mutual Fund Stewardship and the Empty Voting Problem' *ECGI Working Paper No 612/2021* (October 2021), https://papers.ssrn.com/sol3/papers.cfm?abstract_id=3939112.

[51] SZ Li et al, 'When Shareholders Disagree: Trading after Shareholder Meetings' (2022) 35(4) *The Review of Financial Studies* 1813.

[52] D Katelouzou and D Puchniak, *Global Shareholder Stewardship* (Cambridge University Press, 2022). Currently there exist more than 20 stewardship codes (for an overview see https://www.icgn.org/global-stewardship-codes-network).

of the clients and beneficiaries of these investors as part of this value creation.[53] It includes reaching out to their beneficiaries with information on 'how investee companies will be monitored; [...] the policy on voting and the use made of, if any, proxy voting or other voting advisory service, including information on how they are used'.[54] The policy informs the beneficiaries of the engagement behaviour of the asset owners/asset manager and aligns both interests as the beneficiaries can redirect their savings to those owners/managers whose engagement policies they support. However, it should be noted that the latter redirection of resources is not open to all beneficiaries.[55] The stewardship practices are supported in the Shareholder Rights Directive, in which institutional investors and asset managers are requested to provide an engagement policy and its implementation, including 'a general description of the voting behaviour, an explanation of the most significant votes [...] how they have cast votes in the general meetings of companies in which they hold shares'.[56]

Bolton et al disclosed the voting preferences of institutional investors on a left-right dimensional scale, with those investors who support a more social and environmentally friendly behaviour from investees appearing on the left side, and 'money-conscious' investors on the right side.[57] This offers beneficiaries of the funds the opportunity to find the fund that represents their engagement interests in the best way. However, the classification is based on the former voting behaviour of the fund and cannot guarantee that the future voting policy remains unchanged. It is also of limited use for beneficiaries of many pension funds, who do not have any freedom in selecting their pension fund. Emphasising stewardship engagement, therefore, continues to play an important role.[58]

Third, more mature stewardship codes, like the UK Stewardship Code 2020, endorse a more developed relationship between asset owners and asset managers. According to principle 6 of the UK Code, these parties must take into account the needs of the beneficiaries. As one of the most important activities for complying with principle 6, these managers and owners could investigate beneficiaries' and clients' views.[59] Beneficiaries of funds can also be provided with the right to communicate their voting preferences to the fund managers and help the latter in preparing their voting decision.

A more advanced technique is extending the proxy voting choice. The asset manager provides clients with a choice on how the holdings are voted. From 2022,

---

[53] D Katelouzou, 'Shareholder Stewardship: A Case of (Re)Embedding Institutional Investors and the Corporation?' in B Sjåfjell and CM Bruner (eds), *Cambridge Handbook of Corporate Law, Corporate Governance and Sustainability* (Cambridge University Press, 2019) 585.

[54] Guidance of Principle 1 of the 2010 edition of the UK Stewardship Code: FRC, *UK Stewardship Code* 5.

[55] Working at a Dutch university automatically results in my participation in the Dutch pension fund APB.

[56] Art 3g(1) of Directive (EU) 2017/828 of the European Parliament and of the Council of 17 May 2017 amending Directive 2007/36/EC as regards the encouragement of long-term shareholder engagement [2017] OJ L132/1.

[57] P Bolton et al, 'Investor Ideology' (2020) 137 *Journal of Financial Economics* 320.

[58] I Chiu, 'Governing the Purpose of Investment Management: How the "Stewardship" Norm is being (Re)Developed in the UK and EU' *ECGI Working Paper No 602/2021* (August 2021), https://papers.ssrn.com/sol3/papers.cfm?abstract_id=3908561.

[59] FRC, *The UK Stewardship Code 2020*, 13.

BlackRock offers several of its institutional clients the opportunity to vote the proxies in accordance with the policy of the client insofar it is consistent with the fiduciary standards that apply to the fund.[60] In the 'context' of Principle 12 of the UK Stewardship Code 2020, this means that the fund managers 'should disclose their policy on allowing clients to direct voting in segregated and pooled accounts'.[61] Experience with the organisation of AGMs of investees suggests that the administrative and organisational workload should not be underestimated; the time between disclosure of the investees' agenda and the AGM is short.[62] A major advantage for pension and investment funds compared to listed companies is that the identification of the beneficiaries is easier than that of the shareholders of listed companies. New technologies like blockchain can be helpful.[63] Platforms for shareholder communication have already been launched[64] and these organised systems can be superior to online tools like Reddit,[65] and there is no reason why it could not be an appropriate tool for beneficiaries of funds.[66] Some service providers are already offering savers and beneficiaries tools to engage with the asset owners.[67]

---

[60] M McCombe et al, 'Expanding Proxy Voting Choice' (19 October 2021), https://corpgov.law.harvard. edu/2021/10/19/expanding-proxy-voting-choice/#7b.

[61] FRC, *The UK Stewardship Code 2020*, 21.

[62] See for an assessment of this and other barriers, Association of Member Nominated Trustees, 'Bringing Shareholder Voting into the 21st Century' (6 November 2020), https://amnt.org/report-2020/.

[63] A Lafarre and C Van der Elst, 'Shareholder Voice in Complex Intermediated Proxy Systems: Blockchain Technology as a Solution?' (2021) 4 *The Stanford Journal of Blockchain Law and Policy* 29; C Van der Elst and ALafarre, 'Blockchain and Smart Contracting for the Shareholder Community' (2019) 20 *European Business Organization Law Review* 111.

[64] See Say at https://www.saytechnologies.com/investor.

[65] G Ricci and CM Sautter, 'Corporate Governance Gaming: The Power of Retail Investors' (2021) 22 *Nevada Law Journal* 51, https://papers.ssrn.com/sol3/papers.cfm?abstract_id=3815088.

[66] J Fisch, 'Mutual Fund Stewardship and the Empty Voting Problem' (2021) 16(1) *Brooklyn Journal of Corporate, Financial & Commercial Law* 71, https://papers.ssrn.com/sol3/papers. cfm?abstract_id=3939112.

[67] See for example Tumelo at www.tumelo.com.

8

Common Ownership and Corporate Social Responsibility: Evidence from the BlackRock-BGI Merger

KENNETH KHOO*

'COMMON OWNERSHIP' IS a phenomenon where shareholders hold substantial stakes in firms that impose externalities on each other. The 'common ownership' hypothesis suggests that these shareholders may internalise some of these externalities amongst their portfolio firms. While most of the empirical research in the area has focused on whether common ownership can induce anti-competitive outcomes, the question of whether common ownership can influence portfolio-wide externalities – such as the Environmental, Social and Governance (ESG) externalities associated with the portfolio firms of common owners – has not been examined. In this chapter, I exploit a merger between two large institutional investors – BlackRock and Barclays Global Investors – as an exogenous shock to evaluate the effect of common ownership on environmental and social (E&S) scores. I find no evidence that the resulting increase in common ownership had a positive influence on E&S performance amongst the investors' portfolio firms. Similarly, I find no evidence that the increase in common ownership had any significant impact on greenhouse gas emission levels. On the contrary, I find significant evidence that the merger induced lower E&S scores for these firms, as well as evidence that the negative relationship is stronger for environmental scores relative to social scores. I find that the increase in common ownership induced by the merger was attributable to an increase in overlapping ownership despite a concurrent decrease in investor concentration, possibly exacerbating collective action problems associated with shareholder monitoring. My results suggest that institutional investors are unlikely to become 'climate stewards' in pushing companies to reduce their carbon footprint, even if they are assumed to maximise the value of their entire portfolios.

* The author would like to thank Iris Chiu, Wan Wai Yee, Ernest Lim, Umakanth Varottil, Hans Tjio, Martin Schmalz, Ivan Png, Suren Gomtsian, Alessandro Romano, Anne Lafarre and an anonymous referee for helpful comments, as well as Matthew Backus, Christopher Conlon and Michael Sinkinson for kindly sharing some of their data.

I. INTRODUCTION

'Common ownership' arises where shareholders hold substantial stakes in firms that impose externalities on each other.[1] This phenomenon fundamentally challenges the assumption in neoclassical economics that firms take actions that maximise their own profits.[2] While a firm's decision-making power is ordinarily vested in its managers and Board of directors, most shareholders retain control over the appointment and dismissal of the firm's managers and its Board.[3] Furthermore, firm managers are obligated by corporate law to take into account the interests of its shareholders when exercising decisions on behalf of the firm. Accordingly, if the interests of a firm's shareholders includes the profits of other firms, one might not expect the firm to solely maximise its own profits, but to also take these profits into account when making decisions. This hypothesis reflects the idea that shareholders may internalise some or all of the externalities amongst their portfolio firms, and is often referred to as the 'common ownership hypothesis'.[4] The common ownership hypothesis is particularly salient in terms of its potential for anti-competitive effects, as a common owner clearly has the prima facie incentive to internalise the pecuniary externalities between its portfolio firms competing in similar industries, resulting in higher industry profits and portfolio returns.[5]

In 2018, Azar et al published a seminal article providing some empirical support for the common ownership hypothesis. Azar et al found that an increase in common ownership was associated with ticket price increases in the US airline industry. Importantly, the authors also put forth evidence that within-flight-route changes in common ownership concentration were strongly correlated with within-flight-route changes in airline ticket prices. This sparked a heated debate as to whether their findings were generalisable to more industries,[6] and as an ancillary matter, whether the anti-competitive effects of common ownership were sufficiently severe to warrant regulatory intervention.[7] Some scholars argued that the methodologies employed by Azar et al were flawed,[8] while others failed to find a significant effect of common

---

[1] In this context, an 'externality' is a cost or benefit resulting from a firm's actions which affects other firms.

[2] M Friedman, *Essays in Positive Economics* (University of Chicago Press, 1953).

[3] R Kraakman et al, *The Anatomy of Corporate Law: A Comparative and Functional Approach* (Oxford University Press, 2017).

[4] M Backus et al, 'Common Ownership in America: 1980–2017' (2021) 13(3) *American Economic Journal: Microeconomics* 273.

[5] J Rotemberg, 'Financial Transaction Costs and Industrial Performance' (Massachussets Institute of Technology, 1984).

[6] A Koch et al, 'Common Ownership and Competition in Product Markets' (2021) 139(1) *Journal of Financial Economics* 109.

[7] E Elhauge, 'How Horizontal Shareholding Harms Our Economy – and Why Antitrust Law Can Fix It' (2020) 10 *Harvard Business Law Review* 207; EA Posner et al, 'A Proposal to Limit the Anti-Competitive Power of Institutional Investors' (2017) 81 *Antitrust Law Journal* 1–2; C Scott Hemphill and M Kahan, 'The Strategies of Anticompetitive Common Ownership' (2019) 129 *Yale Law Journal* 1392.

[8] P Kennedy et al, 'The Competitive Effects of Common Ownership: Economic Foundations and Empirical Evidence' (2017), https://papers.ssrn.com/sol3/papers.cfm?abstract_id = 3008331; PJ Dennis et al, 'Common Ownership Does Not Have Anti-Competitive Effects in the Airline Industry' (forthcoming) *Journal of Finance*.

ownership on firm conduct in other industries (eg the ready-to-eat cereal industry in Backus et al[9]).

On the theoretical front, there is also a considerable divergence in views as to whether common owners have both the incentives and abilities to influence the behaviour of their portfolio firms. This divergence should be seen in the context of how common ownership has dramatically risen over time, especially over the past two decades or so. Backus et al illustrate how the 'profit weight' of an average firm in the S&P 500 – a measure which indicates the degree of importance that a given firm places on the profits of other firms – has risen from about 0.2 in 1980 to almost 0.7 in 2017.[10] Much of the rise in common ownership is associated with the accompanying rise in institutional investing. Institutional investors hold almost 70–80 per cent of public company stock today,[11] and three firms alone (Vanguard, BlackRock and State Street) own about 40 per cent of the S&P 500.[12] In European markets, institutional investing is also on the rise. Today, BlackRock is already the largest shareholder of a third of the largest companies in the UK and German public-exchange markets.[13]

Opponents of the common ownership hypothesis have focused on the nature of common owners as institutional investors, arguing that these investors are driven by incentives distinct from those of high-networth-individuals. Morley, for instance, has pointed out that the economic agents acting on behalf of common owners are systemically disincentivised from interfering with product market decision-making in portfolio firms due to the potential risk of breaching the fiduciary duties owed to their client funds.[14] Similarly, Bebchuk and Hirst have argued that index funds incur large information costs when intervening in the management decisions of their portfolio firms.[15] On the other hand, scholars like Rock and Rubinfeld have noted that institutional investors have both the incentives and abilities to induce coordination through subtle means, such as through regular (non-binding) engagement with firm managers.[16] Ultimately, the extent to which common owners internalise these pecuniary externalities between their portfolio costs may boil down to the transaction costs they face in doing so.[17]

Putting these contemporary debates aside, earlier economic literature has acknowledged that absent transaction costs, common owners will have the incentives to internalise *any* form of externality across their portfolio firms.[18] This subtle point is crucial, as most scholars writing on common ownership have focused on

---

[9] M Backus et al, 'Common Ownership and Competition in the Ready-to-Eat Cereal Industry' *NBER Working Paper 28350* (January 2021).

[10] Backus et al (n 4 above).

[11] J Fichtner et al, 'Hidden Power of the Big Three? Passive Index Funds, Re-Concentration of Corporate Ownership, and New Financial Risk' (2017) 19(2) *Business and Politics* 298.

[12] J Azar et al, 'Anticompetitive Effects of Common Ownership' (2018) 73(4) *The Journal of Finance* 1513.

[13] J Weche and A Wambach 'The Fall and Rise of Market Power in Europe' *ZEW Discussion Paper 18-003* (2018).

[14] JD Morley, 'Too Big to Be Activist' (2019) 92 *Southern California Law Review* 1407.

[15] L Bebchuk and S Hirst, 'Index Funds and the Future of Corporate Governance: Theory, Evidence, and Policy' (2019) 119(8) *Columbia Law Review* 2029.

[16] EB Rock and DL Rubinfeld, 'Antitrust for Institutional Investors' (2018) 82 *Antitrust Law Journal* 221.

[17] K Khoo, 'Transaction Costs in Common Ownership' (2022) available at SSRN 4067883.

[18] R Gordon, 'Do Publicly Traded Corporations Act in the Public Interest?' (2003) 3.1 *Advances in Economic Analysis & Policy* 1013.

the internalisation of *pecuniary* externalities between portfolio firms. As a pecuniary externality is the effect that a given firm's *competitive behaviour* (eg pricing) has on another firm's profits, it is a particular *type* of externality that harms consumers through higher product market prices when internalised.[19] Nevertheless, if common owners have the ability to internalise other externalities that have little or no effect on other third parties, such an internalisation of externalities may be socially desirable. For instance, the internalisation of horizontal innovation spillovers,[20] disclosures,[21] vertical spillovers,[22] and governance[23] externalities may improve social welfare by incentivising investments which would otherwise be under-provided due to free-riding problems. In terms of innovation externalities, a common owner could raise the overall level of investments in research and development across its portfolio firms by taking into account the positive impact of a portfolio firm's innovation on the profits of its other portfolio firms. In the absence of the common owner, each (independent) firm would free-ride on the innovations of rival firms to the extent permitted by intellectual property law.

In recent work, some scholars have suggested that common owners may have the potential to take collective action to curb the negative E&S externalities caused by portfolio firms. Condon, for instance, argues that diversified investors should be rationally motivated to internalise intra-portfolio negative externalities with a view to maximising portfolio returns – especially in relation to externalities related to climate change and greenhouse gas emissions.[24] In a similar vein, Coffee and Gordon note that large common owners (who are also institutional investors) may resist attempts by large public companies to impose environmental externalities on other firms.[25] Like Condon, both scholars argue that large common owners who 'own most of the market' are primarily concerned with systemic risk over firm-specific risk. According to these scholars, common owners would be highly incentivised to internalise ESG externalities that tend to disproportionately increase systemic risk over firm-specific risk. Indeed, given the far-reaching and catastrophic consequences of climate change in the long run, many environmental externalities are now commonly seen

---

[19] More precisely, pecuniary externalities benefit firms and harm consumers when they are internalised. Competitive behaviour by a given firm imposes a negative externality on other firms (since a reduction in prices by firm *a* reduces competitor firm *b*'s profits), while imposing a positive externality on consumers (since a reduction in prices by firm *a* increases the utility of consumers). See J Tirole, *The Theory of Industrial Organization* (MIT Press, 1989).

[20] M Anton et al, 'Innovation: The Bright Side of Common Ownership?' (2021), https://papers.ssrn.com/sol3/papers.cfm?abstract_id = 3099578; ÁL López and X Vives, 'Overlapping Ownership, R&D Spillovers, and Antitrust Policy' (2019) 127(5) *Journal of Political Economy* 2394.

[21] J Park et al, 'Disclosure Incentives When Competing Firms Have Common Ownership' (2019) 67(2–3) *Journal of Accounting and Economics* 387.

[22] A Romano, 'Horizontal Shareholding and Network Theory' (2021) 38 *Yale Journal on Regulation* 363.

[23] A Edmans et al, 'Governance under Common Ownership' (2019) 32(7) *The Review of Financial Studies* 2673; JJ He et al, 'Internalizing Governance Externalities: The Role of Institutional Cross-Ownership' (2019) 134(2) *Journal of Financial Economics* 400; S Ramalingegowda et al, 'Common Institutional Ownership and Earnings Management' (2021) 38(1) *Contemporary Accounting Research* 208.

[24] M Condon, 'Externalities and the Common Owner' (2020) 95 *Washington Law Review* 1.

[25] JC Coffee Jr, 'The Future of Disclosure: ESG, Common Ownership, and Systemic Risk' *European Corporate Governance Institute – Law Working Paper* 541/2020 (2021) 602; JN Gordon, 'Systematic Stewardship' (forthcoming) *Journal of Corporation Law*.

as externalities which impose systemic risk.[26] These hypotheses go beyond prevailing narratives where common owners are seen to focus on internalising externalities *within industries*.[27] Instead, the focus here is on the internalisation of *porfolio-wide* externalities with a view to maximising portfolio profits.[28]

In this chapter, I attempt to examine the validity of the hypothesis that common ownership may influence portfolio-wide externalities, such as E&S externalities. To exogenously identify changes in common ownership, I exploit a merger between two large institutional investors – BlackRock and Barclays Global Investors – as an exogenous shock to evaluate the effect of common ownership on the E&S performance of portfolio firms. Drawing on data provided by an ESG rating agency, Refinitiv, I find no evidence that the resulting increase in common ownership had a positive influence on E&S performance amongst the investors' portfolio firms. On the contrary, I find substantial evidence that the merger induced lower E&S scores for these firms. I find that the negative relationship between common ownership and E&S performance is primarily driven by the negative relationship between common ownership and environmental scores, as opposed to the relationship between common ownership and social scores which is far less robust. To target externalities (other than pecuniary externalities) that have the greatest potential to influence portfolio value, I also draw on granular greenhouse gas emissions data used as a component to determine environmental scores. Contrary to much of the existing literature, I find no evidence that an exogenous increase in common ownership had an impact in reducing greenhouse gas emissions.[29]

To investigate the plausible causal mechanisms behind these results, I consider two key components of the increase in common ownership induced by the merger. As Backus et al have illustrated, a given increase in common ownership may be attributable to an *increase in overlapping ownership* (a measure of investor portfolio similarities) or an increase in *relative investor concentration* (a measure of the costs associated with exercising control rights over multiple firms).[30] I find that the increase in common ownership induced by the BlackRock-BGI merger was largely attributable to an increase in overlapping ownership as opposed to an increase in relative investor concentration – a hallmark of increasing diversification. If corporate social responsibility (CSR) is associated with a fixed governance cost, an increase in the level of overlapping ownership without a corresponding increase in investor concentration (eg if there were a decrease in investor concentration) could possibly exacerbate collective action problems associated with shareholder monitoring, *reducing* the optimal level of investor engagement with portfolio firms.[31] Indeed, I find evidence that

---

[26] N Stern, *Why Are We Waiting?: The Logic, Urgency, and Promise of Tackling Climate Change* (Mit Press, 2015); B Choudhury, 'Climate Change as Systemic Risk' (2021) 18 *Berkeley Business Law Journal* 52.

[27] S Bindal and J Nordlund, 'When Does Common Ownership Matter?' (2022), https://papers.ssrn.com/sol3/papers.cfm?abstract_id = 4009316; K Lewellen and M Lowry, 'Does Common Ownership Really Increase Firm Coordination?' (2021) 141(1) *Journal of Financial Economics* 322; Koch et al (n 6 above).

[28] Tallarita terms the maximisation of portfolio value a view of 'portfolio primacy' as opposed to 'shareholder primacy' where the values of individual portfolio firms are maximised: R Tallarita, 'The Limits of Portfolio Primacy' (forthcoming) 76 *Vanderbilt Law Review*.

[29] J Azar et al, 'The Big Three and Corporate Carbon Emissions around the World' (2021) 142(2) *Journal of Financial Economics* 674.

[30] Backus et al (n 4 above).

[31] AR Admati et al, 'Large Shareholder Activism, Risk Sharing, and Financial Market Equilibrium' (1994) 102(6) *Journal of Political Economy* 1097.

the BlackRock-BGI merger induced a decrease in investor concentration amongst its portfolio firms.

These results are consistent with recent empirical work suggesting the rational passivity of institutional investors,[32] as well as other work suggesting that institutional investors are unlikely to become 'climate stewards' in pushing companies to reduce their carbon footprint.[33] More importantly, while I do not rule out the potential for the growing ESG movement to change firm behaviour, this chapter provides evidence that meaningful E&S reform does *not* occur through the mechanism of portfolio primacy. Rather, positive changes in E&S policies are likely to be led through other mechanisms which are consistent with shareholder primacy, such as the creation of norms induced by the ESG movement[34] or the adoption of 'E&S conscious' shareholder preferences.[35] As Tallarita argues, policymakers should not rely on portfolio primacy as an effective substitute for climate regulation.[36]

This chapter is organised as follows. In section II, I discuss some of the associated literature relevant to my identification strategy and my outcome variables of interest. In section III, I provide a detailed derivation of the measure of common ownership I use in this chapter, the data sources used for it, and some summary statistics on the variables of interest. Notably, the skewed nature of the dependent variables I examine merits the use of an estimation methodology distinct from much of the existing literature – that of the Poisson generalised linear model (GLM).[37] In section IV, I implement some baseline GLM Poisson panel regressions before describing the identification strategies I use to evaluate the impact of common ownership on E&S performance. Furthermore, I present results on how the identification strategy of choice influences common ownership and investor concentration. In section V, I present my findings on the relationship between common ownership and E&S performance, harnessing the identification strategy detailed in section III. I also present my findings on the relationship between common ownership and greenhouse gas emissions. Finally, in section VI, I provide some theoretical justifications for my results, before making some concluding remarks.

II. LITERATURE REVIEW

Having motivated my empirical study in section I, I turn to the related literature concerning: (1) challenges in identifying common ownership; and (2) ESG outcomes. I will discuss the former before turning to the latter.

---

[32] M Antón et al, 'Common Ownership, Competition, and Top Management Incentives' *CEPR Discussion Paper No DP12674* (2018).

[33] Tallarita (n 28 above); D Heath et al, 'Does Socially Responsible Investing Change Firm Behavior?' *European Corporate Governance Institute – Finance Working Paper No 762/2021* (2021).

[34] D Katelouzou and DW Puchniak, *Global Shareholder Stewardship* (Cambridge University Press, 2022).

[35] O Hart and L Zingales, 'Companies Should Maximize Shareholder Welfare Not Market Value' (2017) 2 *Journal of Law, Finance, and Accounting* 247.

[36] Tallarita (n 28 above).

[37] J Cohn et al, 'Count (and Count-Like) Data in Finance' (2022), https://papers.ssrn.com/sol3/papers.cfm?abstract_id = 3800339.

Despite the large volume of empirical research on common ownership in recent years, identifying a truly exogenous change in common ownership continues to pose challenges for researchers. This obstacle stems from the fact that the ownership of firms is influenced by many factors that are *in turn* affected by ownership.[38] For instance, information of firm *a*'s profitability may induce existing or potential investors to increase their ownership stakes of firm *a* in liquid capital markets, in turn affecting the profitability of firm *a*. Due to the potential for such bilateral causality between ownership and observable firm outcomes, any statistical inference from a statistical model that links ownership data to firm outcomes could suffer from problems associated with endogeneity, detracting from the persuasiveness of the inferences made.[39]

A secondary challenge associated with the common ownership hypothesis (*cf* mere 'ownership' like in Dyck et al[40]) is the fact that common ownership is a *relational* concept. In other words, common ownership is a measure of the *extent to which* firm *f* takes firm *g*'s profits into account when making decisions at the firm-level. The construction of a measure of common ownership has attracted considerable controversy. Azar et al, for instance, harness the modified Herfindahl-Hirschman Index (MHHI) created by Bresnahan and Salop to measure the competitive effects of common ownership across industries.[41] As the MHHI depends on the market shares of the firms involved, it is useful for measures of common ownership within industries, but not measures of common ownership across industries. More recently, however, economists have constructed more generalisable measures of common ownership that can be used across industries.[42] I will turn to the usage of these measures in section III.A of this chapter.

Turning back to the issue of endogeneity, scholars have attempted to address this problem through several means. The crux lies in the identification of an exogenous change in common ownership unrelated to the outcome variable in question. For instance, a researcher may be interested in understanding the relationship between common ownership and profitability, product market prices, or innovation measures. Three broad classes of events have been harnessed in the literature to identify changes in common ownership (ostensibly) unrelated to these variables of interest. The first of these classes is that of index entries, where a given firm enters into an index for the first time.[43] Index entry is likely to change common ownership as index funds are

---

[38] Koch et al (n 6 above).

[39] In econometrics, a model's 'endogeneity' broadly refers to situations in which an explanatory variable in the model is correlated with its error term. This violates exogeneity assumptions required in most statistical models, such as Ordinary Least Squares. See B Hermalin and M Weisbach, *The Handbook of the Economics of Corporate Governance*, Vol 1 (Elsevier, 2017) and WH Greene, *Econometric Analysis* (Pearson Education India, 2003).

[40] A Dyck et al, 'Do Institutional Investors Drive Corporate Social Responsibility? International Evidence' (2019) 131(3) *Journal of Financial Economics* 693.

[41] Azar et al (n 12 above); TF Bresnahan and SC Salop, 'Quantifying the Competitive Effects of Production Joint Ventures' (1986) 4(2) *International Journal of Industrial Organization* 155; DP O'Brien and SC Salop, 'Competitive Effects of Partial Ownership: Financial Interest and Corporate Control' (1999) 67 *Antitrust Law Journal* 559.

[42] Lewellen and Lowry (n 27 above); Backus et al (n 4 above).

[43] PN Afego, 'Effects of Changes in Stock Index Compositions: A Literature Survey' (2017) 52 *International Review of Financial Analysis* 228.

(at least in the short run) compelled to purchase shares of the index entrant in the index which they are tracking, and also to sell shares of the firms leaving the relevant index.[44] Boller and Scott-Morton exploit index entries in the S&P 500 to estimate the effect of common ownership on future expected profits.[45] They find that the stock returns of the index entrant's product market rivals are positively associated with increases in common ownership, consistent with a hypothesis that common owner-ship raises profits. In a different context, Lewellen and Lowry examine index entries in the S&P 500 to estimate changes to the nature of ownership changes after a firm enters an index.[46]

The second of these classes is that of the annual reconstitution of Russell indices, where the top 1,000 to 3,000 US equities are rebalanced to reflect accurate representa-tion of the largest firms in the US stock market.[47] Like index entries, resultant changes in the Russell indices should lead to changes in common ownership, as mutual funds (and other capital market participants) which are constructed to track these indices are compelled to re-balance their portfolios in light of the updated indices.

Finally, the third of these classes is the merger of institutional investors. As institutional investors tend to be large common owners, the merger of institutional investors is also likely to change common ownership, as the post-merger institutional investor tends to preserve most of its holdings previously owned by its pre-merger institutions.[48] Thus, it is unsurprising that a large number of papers in the literature have relied on the mergers of institutional investors as a source of exogenous varia-tion in common ownership.[49]

While some concerns are associated with all of these identification strategies, index entries and Russell reconstitutions pose particular challenges for common ownership research. In relation to index entries, Robertson[50] documents how a substantial fraction of 'passive' index funds track indices that they or their affili-ates create, confounding the ostensibly 'exogenous' relationship between variables of interest (eg profitability) and common ownership.[51] Insofar as Russell reconstitutions

---

[44] AF Gygax and I Otchere, 'Index Composition Changes and the Cost of Incumbency' (2010) 34(10) *Journal of Banking & Finance* 2500; S-S Chen and Y-H Lin, 'The Competitive Effects of S&P 500 Index Revisions' (2018) 45(7–8) *Journal of Business Finance & Accounting* 997.

[45] L Boller and F Scott Morton, 'Testing the Theory of Common Stock Ownership' *NBER Working Paper* 27515 (2020).

[46] Lewellen and Lowry (n 27 above).

[47] Y-C Chang et al, 'Regression Discontinuity and the Price Effects of Stock Market Indexing' (2015) 28(1) *The Review of Financial Studies* 212; IR Appel et al, 'Passive Investors, Not Passive Owners' (2016) 121(1) *Journal of Financial Economics* 111; Lewellen and Lowry (n 27 above).

[48] JJ He and J Huang, 'Product Market Competition in a World of Cross-Ownership: Evidence from Institutional Blockholdings' (2017) 30(8) *The Review of Financial Studies* 2674.

[49] Azar et al (n 12 above); Anton et al (n 20 above); Bindal and Nordlund (n 27 above); He and Huang (n 48 above); He et al (n 23 above); O Kini et al, 'Common Institutional Ownership and Product Market Threats' (2021), https://www.semanticscholar.org/paper/Common-Institutional-Ownership-and-Product-Market-Kini-Lee/731a79d5051363e7d7a8b53ab3bef74f58bfcbd8; Koch et al (n 6 above).

[50] AZ Robertson, 'Passive in Name Only: Delegated Management and Index Investing' (2019) 36 *Yale Journal on Regulation* 795.

[51] Lewellen and Lowry also argue that the use of index entries as an identification strategy also creates a distinct problem where associated changes in monitoring incentives (due to the fact that index entries are associated with significant declines in ownership by large (5% or more) blockholders) may affect firm policies independently of any changes in common ownership. However, as I will illustrate in section IV.B.i, this problem is unavoidable where the measure of common ownership is inextricably tied with the cost of

are concerned, Lewellen and Lowry[52] show that there is little evidence that common ownership increases with Russell re-constitutions, consistent with Schmidt and Fahlenbrach's[53] findings that Russell indices re-constitutions did not significantly affect index funds or 13F-bound institutions – both of which have contributed to the massive rise in common ownership over the years.[54] Thus, following Azar et al, I rely on the BlackRock-BGI merger in 2009 as an exogenous source of variation in common ownership to identify potential changes in ESG scores.[55] As I will detail in section IV.B.i, the choice of this instrument is motivated by the substantial change in common ownership induced by the merger relative to a set of institutional investor mergers (eg in Bindal and Nordlund[56]) which often induces a much smaller change. Furthermore, exploiting a single merger avoids the complications associated with identification strategies with multiple time periods (as would be the case with a set of institutional investor mergers) where a two-way fixed effects model is no longer robust to the heterogeneity of treatment effects.[57]

The second strand of literature relevant to my study is the literature concerned with ESG outcomes. Much of the literature focusing on ESG outcomes has used proxy scores created by ESG rating agencies like Thomson Reuters (now Refinitiv), Sustainalytics, BoardEx, ISS, MSCI and Compustat. These vendors construct firm-level environmental and social (E&S) performance measures using observable metrics like CO_2 emissions, renewable energy use, human rights violations, and employment quality, amongst others.[58] Reliance on these ESG scores has exploded in recent years, with one in three US dollars invested now managed pursuant to ESG principles.[59] Although researchers have begun to raise questions concerning the reliability and quality of these scores in recent years,[60] Amel-Zadeh and Serafeim show that almost 82 per cent of investment professionals continue to use ESG scores in the investment process.[61] Furthermore, fund flows react strongly to the ESG ratings of mutual funds which are constructed in accordance with the ESG ratings of their portfolio firms.[62]

Two papers are closely related to my work. The first of the two is Dyck et al.[63] Using Thomson Reuters' ASSET4 (now Refinitiv) ESG database, Dyck et al show

---

exercising control. Indeed, I show that the merger of institutional investors *also* induces a similar change in monitoring incentives: Lewellen and Lowry (n 27 above).

[52] Lewellen and Lowry (n 27 above).

[53] C Schmidt and R Fahlenbrach, 'Do Exogenous Changes in Passive Institutional Ownership Affect Corporate Governance and Firm Value?' (2017) 124(2) *Journal of Financial Economics* 285.

[54] Backus et al (n 4 above).

[55] Azar et al (n 12 above).

[56] Bindal and Nordlund (n 27 above).

[57] A Goodman-Bacon, 'Difference-in-differences with Variation in Treatment Timing' (2021) 225(2) *Journal of Econometrics* 254; B Callaway and PHC Sant'Anna, 'Difference-in-differences with Multiple Time Periods' (2021) 225(2) *Journal of Econometrics* 200.

[58] Artikel Refinitiv, 'Environmental, Social and Governance (ESG) Scores from Refinitiv' (2020) *ESG Scores Methodology* 18.

[59] See https://www.ussif.org/blog_home.asp?display = 155.

[60] F Berg et al, 'Rewriting History II: The (Un) Predictable Past of ESG Ratings' *ECGI Finance Working Paper No 708/2020* (2020).

[61] A Amel-Zadeh and G Serafeim, 'Why and How Investors Use ESG Information: Evidence from a Global Survey' (2018) 74(3) *Financial Analysts Journal* 87.

[62] SM Hartzmark and AB Sussman, 'Do Investors Value Sustainability? A Natural Experiment Examining Ranking and Fund Flows' (2019) 74(6) *The Journal of Finance* 2789.

[63] Dyck et al (n 40 above).

evidence that institutional ownership is positively associated with E&S performance.[64] However, Dyck et al also find that when the same estimates are reported for firms domiciled in the US, the effect of institutional ownership is positive but not always significant. Furthermore, Dyck et al find that US institutional investors have no impact on the environmental performance of US portfolio firms, consistent with their lack of impact on environmental performance when these investors invest abroad. The authors also exploit a quasi-experiment provided by the Deep Water Horizon oil spill, finding that firms with greater institutional ownership at the time of the shock were more reactive in improving environmental performance in the years following this shock.

As distinguished from Dyck et al, this chapter examines the relationship between common ownership and E&S performance. In contrast to Dyck et al, I find no evidence that an exogenous change in common ownership had a positive influence on E&S performance. Indeed, I find robust evidence that the change in common ownership induced lower environmental scores for treated firms. While common ownership may be correlated with institutional ownership, the two are distinct concepts and should not be conflated with each other. In particular, measures of institutional ownership do not incorporate information as to the extent to which ownership is *overlapping* and the *relative* costs of exercising control rights over multiple firms.[65] Thus, institutional ownership per se fails to provide an accurate measure of the extent to which a common owner is incentivised to internalise externalities across its portfolio firms.[66]

Separately, Berg et al note that Refinitiv has made both substantive and methodological changes in how it evaluates the ESG performance of firms under study since Dyck et al's paper.[67] At the time of writing this chapter, Refinitiv Support has also officially announced these changes.[68] To address the changes associated with Refinitiv's percentile scoring methodology, I harness a different methodology from Dyck et al – the Poisson GLM – to estimate the relationship between common ownership and my outcome variables of interest. As I will explain in section IV.A below, the Poisson GLM is far more robust to the bounded and skewed distributions of the E&S scores I examine in my study.

The second of the two papers is Azar et al.[69] Azar et al examine the role of the 'Big Three' institutional investors (ie BlackRock, Vanguard and State Street) on the reduction of corporate carbon emissions around the world. Drawing on a dataset of CO_2 emissions provided by Trucost, Azar et al find a strong and robust negative

---

[64] Dyck et al. draw on a large dataset of both US and non-US institutional investors and portfolio firms. In contrast, my study only examines US institutional investors and portfolio firms: Dyck et al (n 40 above).

[65] Backus et al (n 4 above).

[66] Note that institutional ownership does capture the costs of exercising control rights over a single firm.

[67] Berg et al (n 60 above).

[68] According to Refinitiv Support in April 2022: 'Prior to Q2 2017, the scoring methodology was based on a Z-score. To better optimise and meet the changing needs for relevant and material ESG data across more markets, the methodology changed to use a Percentile scoring methodology. In doing so, some data types became inactive and data collection stopped for some measures beginning in 2014 w/ additional stoppage for several measures from 2017 onward. These include the Economic Pillar Score, and content has suggested to not rely on this measure as it contains stale data.'

[69] Azar et al (n 29 above).

association between Big Three ownership and subsequent carbon emissions among MSCI index constituents. Azar et al also find that the Big Three focus their engagement efforts on large firms with high CO_2 emissions in which these investors hold a significant stake. While I also examine granular data on greenhouse gas emissions in this chapter (including CO_2 emissions), I also assess the relationship between the more general phenomenon of common ownership and greenhouse gas emissions.[70] As distinct from Azar et al, I draw on granular emissions data provided by Refinitiv, include portfolio firms outside of the MSCI index constituents, and adopt a different methodology (the Poisson GLM) to evaluate the aforementioned relationship. Unlike Azar et al, I find no evidence that an exogenous increase in common ownership had any significant impact on greenhouse gas emission levels.

III. PROFIT WEIGHTS, DATA SOURCES, AND SUMMARY STATISTICS

A. Profit Weights

As explained in section II above, common ownership is a *relational* concept – it measures the *extent to which* firm f takes firm g's profits into account when making decisions at the firm-level. A firm under common ownership departs from own-firm profit maximisation due to the influence of its shareholders who also own other firms, who are known as 'common owners'. To formally define the profits of a common owner, consider the case where a shareholder s is assumed to have cash flow rights corresponding to β_{fs} of firm f's profits π_f, where β_{fs} is equal to the fraction of firm f that it owns.[71] Here, an investor is a common owner if $\beta_{fs} > 0$ for multiple firms. The profits of a common owner, v_s, is thus defined by the sum of the profits from its portfolio investments weighted by its cash flow rights:

$$v_s = \sum_{\forall g} \beta_{gs} \pi_g \qquad (1)$$

Absent transaction costs, the common owner s will seek to induce its portfolio firms to make decisions which would maximise its own portfolio profits, v_s.[72] However, as common owners will have different portfolios, they will disagree on the optimal strategy which the firm should pursue (ie common owner s would prefer firm g to pursue a strategy that maximises v_s as opposed to v_k if $v_s \neq v_k$). To provide a tractable notion of how firms would resolve such disagreements, Backus et al assume that firm managers will place a Pareto weight γ_{fs} on the portfolio profits of investor s and maximise the Pareto-weighted sum of their investors' profits.[73] In other words, a firm is assumed

---

[70] Backus et al note that the rise in common ownership incentives predates the 'rise of the Big Three', with the average 'profit weight' rising from 0.2 to 0.5 from 1980 to 1999: Backus et al (n 4 above).

[71] O'Brien and Salop (n 41 above); Backus et al (n 4 above).

[72] Khoo (n 17 above).

[73] Backus et al (n 4 above).

to maximise a weighted sum of its shareholders' profits, with Pareto weights that correspond to the control rights of its shareholders.

Letting Q_f denote the objective function of firm f (with s investors holding investments in firms f and g and where $g \neq f$) under these assumptions:

$$
\begin{aligned}
Q_f &= \sum_{\forall s} \gamma_{fs} \upsilon_s \\
&= \sum_{\forall s} \gamma_{fs} \left(\sum_{\forall g} \beta_{gs} \pi_g \right) \\
&= \sum_{\forall s} \gamma_{fs} \beta_{fs} \pi_f + \left(\sum_{\forall s} \gamma_{fs} \sum_{\forall g \neq f} \beta_{gs} \pi_g \right)
\end{aligned}
\tag{2}
$$

where $\upsilon_s = \sum_{\forall g} \beta_{gs} \pi_g$ as per equation (1). Dividing Q_f by $\sum_{\forall s} \gamma_{fs} \beta_{fs}$, we have a normalised objective function $Q_{fnorm} = \dfrac{Q_f}{\sum_{\forall s} \gamma_{fs} \beta_{fs}}$ defined by:

$$
\begin{aligned}
Q_{fnorm} &= \pi_f + \sum_{\forall g \neq f} \frac{\sum_{\forall s} \gamma_{fs} \beta_{gs}}{\sum_{\forall s} \gamma_{fs} \beta_{fs}} \pi_g \\
&= \pi_f + \sum_{\forall g \neq f} \kappa_{fg}(\gamma_f, \beta) \pi_g
\end{aligned}
\tag{3}
$$

where $\dfrac{\sum_{\forall s} \gamma_{fs} \beta_{gs}}{\sum_{\forall s} \gamma_{fs} \beta_{fs}}$ represents the *implied profit weight* $\kappa_{fg}(\gamma_f, \beta)$ arising from common ownership. The profit weight $\kappa_{fg}(\gamma_f, \beta)$ can be interpreted as the value of firm g's profits relative to firm f in firm f's maximisation problem. Importantly, the derivation of $\kappa_{fg}(\gamma_f, \beta)$ is very general and is not contingent on firm g being firm f's industry rival. Rather, the presence of firm g's profits in firm f's objective function is driven by the firm managers' incentives to maximise the profits of its common owners as per equations (1) and (2).

As Backus et al note, the notation in equation (3) is also able to nest a range of behavioural models.[74] Where $\kappa_{fg}(\gamma_f, \beta) = 0 \; \forall g \neq f$, for instance, own-firm profit maximisation results – firm f does not take firm g's profits into account. In the context of mergers and acquisitions, a large body of literature in industrial organisation assumes unified control of the merged entity's actions, where both $\kappa_{fg}(\gamma_f, \beta)$ and $\kappa_{gf}(\gamma_g, \beta)$ change from 0 to 1.[75] Finally, γ_{fs} represents the *control weight* of investor s in firm f. Intuitively, firm managers will accord a higher weight to investors with more control over the firm. Absent an obvious alternative, I follow the rest of the literature[76] in

---

[74] ibid.

[75] Bresnahan and Salop (n 41 above); A Nevo, 'Measuring Market Power in the Ready-to-eat Cereal Industry' (2001) 69(2) *Econometrica* 307.

[76] O'Brien and Salop (n 41 above); Azar et al (n 12 above); Backus et al (n 4 above).

assuming that $\gamma_{fs} = \beta_{fs}$, a model of *proportional control* which corresponds to the 'one share, one vote' rule in most corporations.[77]

Given the further assumption that $\gamma_{fs} = \beta_{fs}$, the profit weight $\kappa_{fg}(\beta)$ ($\forall f \neq g$) may be represented as:

$$\kappa_{fg}(\beta) = \frac{\sum_{\forall s} \beta_{fs}\beta_{gs}}{\sum_{\forall s} \beta_{fs}\beta_{fs}}$$

$$= \frac{\sum_{\forall s} \beta_{fs}\beta_{gs}}{\sum_{\forall s}\left[\beta_{fs}\right]^2} \tag{4}$$

The expression $\kappa_{fg}(\beta)$ remains a *pairwise* relation between firms f and g. To obtain a *firm-level* measure of $\kappa_f(\beta)$ that represents the average weight which firm f places on other firms' profits, I follow Bindal and Nordlund and Backus et al in aggregating the profit weights across all firms g ($\forall g \neq f$) for each firm f.[78] Accordingly, $\kappa_f(\beta)$ may be represented as:

$$\kappa_f^{mc}(\beta) = \sum_{\forall g \neq f} w_g \frac{\sum_{\forall s} \beta_{fs}\beta_{gs}}{\sum_{\forall s}\left[\beta_{fs}\right]^2} \tag{5}$$

where w_g is a weight $\frac{mc_g}{\sum_{\forall g \neq f} mc_g}$ corresponding to firm g's market capitalisation mc_g.[79]

$\kappa_f^{mc}(\beta)$ reflects a market capitalisation weighted average of firm f's profit weights. Alternatively, $\kappa_f(\beta)$ may be represented as:

$$\kappa_f^n(\beta) = \frac{1}{G} \sum_{\forall g \neq f} \frac{\sum_{\forall s} \beta_{fs}\beta_{gs}}{\sum_{\forall s}\left[\beta_{fs}\right]^2} \tag{6}$$

where G is the total number of firms related to firm f through its common owners. Thus, $\kappa_f^n(\beta)$ reflects an equal weight average of firm f's profit weights. As Backus et al note, weighing the observations by either market capitalisation or revenue does not qualitatively change the results.[80] As such, I focus on the equal weight average to identify portfolio-wide externalities in sections IV and V.[81]

---

[77] Kraakman et al (n 3 above).

[78] Bindal and Nordlund (n 27 above); Backus et al (n 4 above).

[79] A similar methodology may be used to calculate a revenue weighted average of firm f's profit weights.

[80] Backus et al (n 4 above).

[81] The use of $\kappa_f^{mc}(\beta)$ also introduces measurement problems related to data availability, as not all of the firms g will have corresponding market capitalisation data at a given time t.

B. Data Sources

I collect and process data from four different sources. First, data on common ownership was procured from Backus et al, who share public data on all 13F filings from 1980 to 2017.[82] While data on common ownership is also available from the Refinitiv's (formerly Thomson Reuters) S34 dataset used by many researchers, Backus et al note that there are still significant discrepancies in this database. In their dataset, Backus et al parsed all 13F filings (available on SEC's EDGAR repository) from 1980 to 2017, extracting the reporting dates and Central Index Keys. Coupled with CRSP data on market capitalisation and monthly prices, Backus et al were able to compute the implied profit weights arising from common ownership weights (defined in section III.A) from 1980 to 2017. Second, data on portfolio firm financial characteristics was procured from the Compustat/CRSP Merged Database. This data includes information on, inter alia, the firms' total assets, market to book ratio, leverage, and profitability.

Third, data on ESG metrics and granular emissions data was acquired from Refinitiv's ESG database. Formerly known as the 'Thomson Reuter's ASSET4' database, Refinitiv's ESG database provides data on a company's relative ESG performance, commitment, and effectiveness across several categories (in emissions, environmental product innovation, human rights, etc.) based on publicly-reported data such as company annual reports, company websites, stock exchange filings, CSR reports, and news sources.[83] Refinitiv's ESG database also contains data on some components which feed into the construction of these scores – including but not limited to data on greenhouse gas emissions. Finally, data on the BlackRock-BGI merger was obtained from BlackRock's Schedule 14C proxy statement associated the aforementioned merger.[84]

C. Summary Statistics

i. Ownership Variables

Table 1 provides some summary statistics on the processed dataset. The full sample consists of 6,582,283 observations, with 7,267 common owners and 3,134 portfolio firms[85] across 256 industries from 2002 to 2017. There are 15,320 unique firm-year pairs, 1,908,672 unique common owner-firm pairs, and 6,582,283 unique common owner-firm-year triplets. My processed dataset is limited to firms with complete ESG data under Refinitiv's ESG database. As Refinitiv's ESG database only commences from 2002 (with no data available prior to 2002), all portfolio firms which did not meet these requirements were dropped from the sample.

---

[82] Backus et al (n 4 above).
[83] Artikel Refinitiv (n 58 above).
[84] See https://www.sec.gov/Archives/edgar/data/1364742/000134100410000059/def14c.htm.
[85] I use 'firms' synonymously with 'securities' in this chapter.

Table 1 Summary Statistics of Ownership Variables

	Mean	1Q	Median	3Q	N	Max	Min	Range	SD
13F Common Owners	N.A.	N.A.	N.A.	N.A.	6,582,283	7,267	1	N.A.	N.A.
Portfolio Firms	N.A.	N.A.	N.A.	N.A.	6,582,283	3,134	1	N.A.	N.A.
Years	N.A.	N.A.	N.A.	N.A.	6,582,283	16	1	N.A.	N.A.
Industries	N.A.	N.A.	N.A.	N.A.	6,582,283	356	1	N.A.	N.A.
Firm-Year Pairs	N.A.	N.A.	N.A.	N.A.	6,582,283	15,320	1	N.A.	N.A.
CO-Firm Pairs	N.A.	N.A.	N.A.	N.A.	6,582,283	1,908,672	1	N.A.	N.A.
CO-Firm-Year Pairs	N.A.	N.A.	N.A.	N.A.	6,582,283	6,582,283	1	N.A.	N.A.
Profit Weights (Equal Weights)	0.3081	0.2069	0.2923	0.3898	6,582,283	1.9829	0.0009	1.9820	0.1457
Profit Weights (Weighted by Mkt Cap)	0.4713	0.3206	0.4382	0.5954	6,582,283	3.4589	0.0003	3.4586	0.2178
Investor HHI (for each Firm)	0.0101	0.0078	0.0099	0.0122	6,580,649	0.0432	0.0000	0.0432	0.0033
% of Firm Collectively Owned by Inst Investors	0.6284	0.5486	0.6400	0.7261	6,580,649	2.0461	0.0001	2.0460	0.1401
% of Firm Owned by Individual CO	0.0015	0.0000	0.0001	0.0007	6,582,283	0.0553	0.0000	0.0553	0.0048

Note: "1Q" refers to the 25th percentile value of the variable's distribution, "3Q" refers to the 75th percentile value of the variable's distribution, and SD refers to the variable's standard deviation. Mean, Quartile, Range and SD Statistics are not reported for identifier variables. Ownership variables are rounded off to 4 decimal points.

Table 1 also provides summary statistics on ownership variables. As detailed in section III.A, we can obtain a firm-level measure of common ownership by aggregating the profit weights across all firms g ($\forall g \neq f$) for each firm f. Accordingly, Table 1 presents summary statistics for $\kappa_f^n(\beta)$ and $\kappa_f^{mc}(\beta)$. The mean value of $\kappa_f^n(\beta)$ is about 0.31, implying that the average firm values the profits of other firms (on average) under common ownership 0.3 times as much as it values its own profits. The maximum value of $\kappa_f^n(\beta)$ is about 1.98. As Backus et al have noted, this implies that the firm would value the profits of other firms *more* than it would value its own profits. Such a firm would have an incentive to *divert* profits to other firms, a phenomenon known as 'tunnelling'.[86] Indeed, Matvos and Ostrovsky show that in the context of mergers and acquisitions, institutional investors vote to approve mergers that seem to reduce the share value of acquiring firms when these losses are offset by gains to their holdings in the target firms.[87]

Finally, Table 1 provides summary statistics on *firm-specific* ownership variables. These variables are distinguished from common ownership variables like $\kappa_f^n(\beta)$ and $\kappa_f^{mc}(\beta)$ as they do not measure the extent to which ownership is overlapping across firms.[88] The first variable, *Investor HHI*, is defined for firm f as the sum of the squared ownership

---

[86] Backus et al (n 4 above).
[87] G Matvos and M Ostrovsky, 'Cross-ownership, Returns, and Voting in Mergers' (2008) 89(3) *Journal of Financial Economics* 391.
[88] O'Brien and Salop (n 41 above); Backus et al (n 4 above).

measure β_{fs} within firm f, $\sum_{s=1}^{S}\beta_{fs}^{2}$. Investor HHI is a measure of the concentration of institutional investorship within a firm, and provides an indirect proxy for the costs of collective action in shareholder monitoring. A higher Investor HHI is associated with less diffuse ownership – thereby ameliorating the collective action problems associated with shareholder monitoring of firm managers.[89] The second variable, the Percentage of a Firm Collectively Owned by Institutional Owners (*Total Institutional Ownership*), represents the sum of the ownership measure β_{fs} within a given firm f, $\sum_{s=1}^{S}\beta_{fs}$. The Percentage of Firm Collectively Owned by Institutional Owners illustrates the dominance of institutional investors in public capital markets, with 62.8 per cent of the average firm owned. This percentage is inversely correlated with the retail share $1-\sum_{s=1}^{S}\beta_{fs}$, where retail investors are assumed to be diffuse and have little to no control rights over the firm. Finally, a third variable, the Percentage of a Firm Owned by an Individual Common Owner, represents the plain ownership measure β_{fs}. On average, each common owner only owns 0.15 per cent of a given portfolio firm. Given the large percentage of institutional ownership, the latter two variables suggest the large diversification of ownership amongst institutional investors in my sample.

Figure 1 provides an illustration of common ownership profits over time. The figure depicts both $\kappa_{f}^{n}(\beta)$ and $\kappa_{f}^{mc}(\beta)$ over time from 2002 to 2017. Regardless of the measure used, Figure 1 shows that common ownership has been increasing over time. For instance, $\kappa_{f}^{n}(\beta)$ has risen from about 0.18 to about 0.32 over the course of 16 years. As Backus et al have noted, much of this rise in common ownership incentives is 'driven not by [a] concentration in asset management, but rather a broader increase in diversification of investor portfolios'.[90] Figure 2 provides a graphical illustration of this increase in diversification over time. Panel A of Figure 2 plots the institutional ownership for a given time t averaged across the total number of common owners S_t and observations, $\frac{1}{F \cdot S_t}\sum_{fs=1}^{F \cdot S_t}\left[\frac{1}{S_t}\sum_{s=1}^{S_t}\beta_{fs}\right]$, against time.[91] In contrast, Panel B of Figure 2 plots the institutional ownership for a given time t averaged across the total number of firms F and observations, $\frac{1}{F \cdot S_t}\sum_{fs=1}^{F \cdot S_t}\left[\frac{1}{F}\sum_{f=1}^{F}\beta_{fs}\right]$, against time. The ownership time series in Panel A has an increasing trend, indicating that the *average institutional ownership in each firm* has risen over time from about 0.22 per cent in 2002 to about 0.25 per cent in 2017. On the other hand, the ownership time series in Panel B has a decreasing trend, indicating that the *average institutional ownership per common owner* has declined over time from about 0.27 per cent in 2002 to about 0.18 per cent in 2007. While these time trends might seem ostensibly contradictary, they are reconciliable once we take into account the phenomenon of increasing diversification over time. While average institutional ownership in each firm has indeed increased, institutional investors invest in many more portfolio firms over time, driving down the average institutional ownership per common owner (since each firm has more common owners in subsequent years).

---

[89] ibid.

[90] Backus et al (n 4 above).

[91] Note that S_t, the total number of common owners across all firms, differs from S, the total number of common owners within a firm. Note that the normalisation $\frac{1}{F \cdot S_t}\sum_{fs=1}^{F \cdot S_t}[\cdot]$ is used as $\frac{1}{F}\sum_{f=1}^{F}\left[\frac{1}{S_t}\sum_{s=1}^{S_t}\beta_{fs}\right]=\frac{1}{S_t}\sum_{s=1}^{S_t}\left[\frac{1}{F}\sum_{f=1}^{F}\beta_{fs}\right]$.

Figure 1 Profit Weights over Time

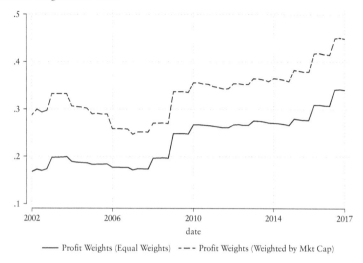

— Profit Weights (Equal Weights) - - - Profit Weights (Weighted by Mkt Cap)

Panel C of Figure 2 shows the ownership time series for the *total institutional owner-ship* in each firm averaged across the total number of firms, $\frac{1}{F}\Sigma_{f=1}^{F}\left[\Sigma_{s=1}^{S_1}\beta_{fs}\right]$ for a given time t. Total institutional ownership increases over time from about 0.50 in 2002 to about 0.65 in 2014, before falling to 0.57 in 2017. Panel D of Figure 2 shows the ownership time series for the *Investor HHI* in each firm, defined as $\frac{1}{F}\Sigma_{f=1}^{F}\left[\Sigma_{s=1}^{S_1}\beta_{fs}^2\right]$ for a given time t. Similarly, Investor HHI increases over time from about 0.008 in 2002 to about 0.011 in 2014, before falling to 0.009 in 2019.

Figure 2 Ownership Variables over Time

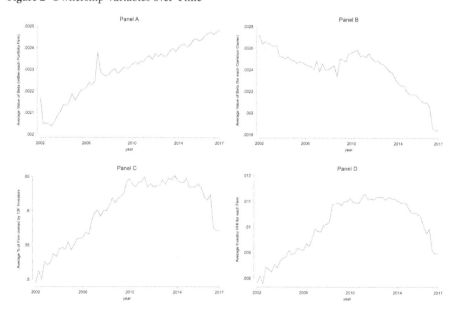

ii. E&S Scores and Granular Emissions

Table 2 provides summary statistics on the E&S scores of the portfolio firms under study. As per Dyck et al, the E&S score reflects a broad measure of the environmental and social performance of these firms.[92] E&S scores are, in turn, based on sub-categories of scores.[93] Refinitiv assigns 'category weights' to these categories and sub-categories of scores. The category weights reflect the relative importance which Refinitiv places on the various categories which represent a firm's overall score as a whole. For instance, a firm's E&S score is a weighted average of its environmental score (with a category weight of 0.587) and its social score (with a category weight of 0.413). In turn, a firm's environmental score is based on a weighted average of three sub-categories of scores, namely a 'resource use' score (reflecting a company's capacity to reduce the use of materials, energy or water, and attempts at improving the carbon footprint of its supply chain management), an 'emissions' reduction score (measuring a company's commitment towards reducing environmental emissions in its operational processes), and an 'innovation' score (reflecting a company's capacity to reduce the environmental costs for its customers by creating new environmental technologies or products).[94] The social score is also based on a weighted average of four sub-categories of scores, namely a 'workforce' score (reflecting a company's effectiveness in providing job satisfaction, a healthy workplace, and maintaining diversity and development opportunities for its workforce), a 'human rights' score (reflecting a company's effectiveness in respecting human rights conventions), a 'community score' (reflecting a company's commitment to public health and business ethics), and finally a 'product responsibility' score (reflecting a company's capacity to produce goods and services that protect their customers' health, safety, and privacy).[95]

Unlike the former ASSET4 database, all of the new Refinitiv E&S scores (whether categorical or sub-categorical) are bounded between 0 and 1. Sub-category scores are comprised of *components* that are generated pursuant to a combination of boolean and percentile-based calculations.[96] Insofar as the boolean-based calculations are concerned, Refinitiv considers 'yes/no/null' responses to a checklist of questions. For instance, Refinitiv considers whether a given firm has a water efficiency policy. It assigns a value of 1 if the firm does indeed have such a policy, and assigns a value of 0 if the firm does not or if it reports only partial information on that policy. A default value of 0 is assigned if no relevant data is found. These binary (0/1) scores are then converted to a percentile based score where the component score for a given firm is:

component score

$$= \frac{\text{no. of firms with a worse value} + \frac{\text{no. of firms with the same value included in the component}}{2}}{\text{no. of firms with a value}}$$

(7)

---

[92] Dyck et al (n 40 above).

[93] Refinitiv terms these categories 'pillars' and 'sub-pillars'.

[94] As per Refinitiv, the resource use score is assigned a category weight of 0.35, the emissions score is assigned a category weight of 0.35, and the innovation score a category weight of 0.29: Artikel Refinitiv (n 58 above).

[95] As per Refinitiv, the workforce score is assigned a category weight of 0.43, the human rights score is assigned a category weight of 0.17, the community score a category weight of 0.28, and the product responsibility score a category weight of 0.13: Artikel Refinitiv (n 58 above).

[96] Artikel Refinitiv (n 58 above).

Table 2 Summary Statistics of E&S Scores and Granular Emissions Variables

	Mean	1Q	Median	3Q	N	Max	Min	Range	SD
Envrn and Social Score	0.4080	0.1743	0.3736	0.6260	6,582,283	0.9650	0.0000	0.9650	0.2514
Envrn and Social (Compensated) Score	0.2992	0.1230	0.2325	0.4562	6,582,283	0.9650	0.0000	0.9650	0.2192
Environmental Score	0.3319	0.0078	0.2917	0.5843	6,582,283	0.9744	0.0000	0.9744	0.2941
Resource Use Score	0.3880	0.0000	0.3448	0.7355	6,582,283	0.9983	0.0000	0.9983	0.3588
Emissions Score	0.3755	0.0000	0.3288	0.6964	6,582,283	0.9975	0.0000	0.9975	0.3489
Innovation Score	0.2229	0.0000	0.0000	0.4449	6,582,283	0.9937	0.0000	0.9937	0.3034
Social Score	0.5162	0.3385	0.5069	0.6891	6,582,283	0.9957	0.0000	0.9957	0.2215
Workforce Score	0.5280	0.3026	0.5324	0.7558	6,582,283	0.9993	0.0000	0.9993	0.2704
Human Rights Score	0.2312	0.0000	0.0000	0.5000	6,582,283	0.9929	0.0000	0.9929	0.3234
Community Score	0.6959	0.5422	0.7375	0.8955	6,582,283	0.9988	0.0000	0.9988	0.2343
Product Resp Score	0.4235	0.1750	0.3763	0.7010	6,582,283	0.9974	0.0000	0.9974	0.3088
CO_2 Emissions (Total)	7,338,497	187,609	884,976	4,399,127	2,983,058	166,000,000	0	166,000,000	20,340,808
CO_2 Emissions (Direct)	5,902,577	31,329	229,384	2,078,600	2,559,315	156,300,000	0	156,300,000	18,609,055
CO_2 Emissions (Indirect)	1,205,742	105,261	385,140	1,167,992	2,488,949	32,299,000	0	32,299,000	2,312,951
NOx Emissions	26,929	243	3,157	24,857	820,772	317,314	0	317,314	48,811
SOx Emissions	53,531	37	1,655	20,306	771,566	18,600,000	0	18,600,000	582,073
VOC Emissions	25,993	107	820	7,847	595,361	468,491	0	468,491	68,697
Water Pollutant Emissions	1,061,926	190	1,300	6,850	247,853	311,650,000	0	311,650,000	16,562,201

Note: "1Q" refers to the 25th percentile value of the variable's distribution, "3Q" refers to the 75th percentile value of the variable's distribution, and SD refers to the variable's standard deviation. E&S scores are rounded off to 4 decimal points, while Emissions variables are rounded off to the nearest integer.

For components with a numeric value (eg, the level of CO_2 emissions), the same formula in equation (7) is applied to that component. Finally, sub-category scores (which are in turn used to calculate categorical scores as detailed above) are calculated based on an average of components within a sub-category, $subcatscore_f = \frac{1}{C}\sum_{c=1}^{C}[componentscore_{cf}]$ where C relates to the total number of components in that sub-category.[97] Refinitiv argues that the resultant scores are not very sensitive to outliers as they are based on a firm's relative rank.

Furthermore, as distinguished from its former ASSET4 counterpart, Refinitiv has generated a new 'controversies' category that attempts to discount the overall E&S performance score based on negative media stories by incorporating the impact of significant E&S controversies on the overall score. If an E&S scandal occurs pursuant to one of 23 controversy components (eg media reports linked to environmental impact on natural resources or customer health and safety), the firm involved is penalised with a discount factor ranging from 0 to 1 – what Refinitiv terms a 'controversies' score. Thus, a discounted E&S (Compensated) score may be generated by multiplying the E&S scores with the controversies score. As Table 2 shows, the E&S (Compensated) scores are generally lower than the E&S performance scores – the mean E&S performance score registers at 0.408 while its discounted counterpart registers at 0.299.

The distribution of E&S scores varies considerably across the sample firms – the lowest E&S score is observed at zero, while the highest score takes on a value of 0.965. The mean and median scores of the constituent category and sub-category scores also have a relatively large spread of values. Notably, perhaps due to the boolean components used to determine E&S performance, some of the sub-category scores have a large number of zero-valued (or near-zero-valued) observations. For example, the 25th percentile and median sub-category scores of the 'innovation' sub-category used in determining a firm's environmental score are both zero-valued. Similarly, the 'human rights' sub-category used in determining a firm's social score has zero-valued 25th percentile and median scores. Table 2 also provides summary statistics on granular greenhouse gas emissions data, a component which Refinitiv uses in determining the sub-category of a given firm's 'emissions' score.[98] Like the category and sub-category E&S scores, the distribution of greenhouse gas emissions is asymmetrically distributed – the 25th percentile firm in the sample emits 31,329 metric tons of carbon while the 75th percentile emits 2,078,600 tons of the same. As I will explain later, these stylised facts suggest that both the distributions of scores as well as the distributions of emissions are considerably skewed, motivating an estimation methodology distinct from the existing literature.

Figure 3 plots time series of the category and sub-category scores introduced in Table 2. Panel A of Figure 3 depicts a time series of E&S scores and E&S (Compensated) scores where the average score $\frac{1}{F}\sum_{f=1}^{F}[score_f]$ for a given time t is

---

[97] Refinitiv notes that about 186 components are used to calculate the 10 sub-category scores: Artikel Refinitiv (n 58 above).

[98] Refinitiv also examines other components such as the strength of a firm's environmental management systems, its biodiversity, and the amount of waste that it produces in determining the firm's 'emissions' reduction score: Artikel Refinitiv (n 58 above).

plotted against time. In contrast to Figure 1, the scores exhibit a declining trend that does not seem to accord with the rise in common ownership over time. Similarly, Panels B to D of Figure 3 depict time series of the various category and sub-category scores that constitute the E&S scores of firms. Again, the average category (and sub-category) score declines over time, with the average environmental score experiencing a sharper decline over time relative to the average social score.

Figure 3 E&S Scores over Time

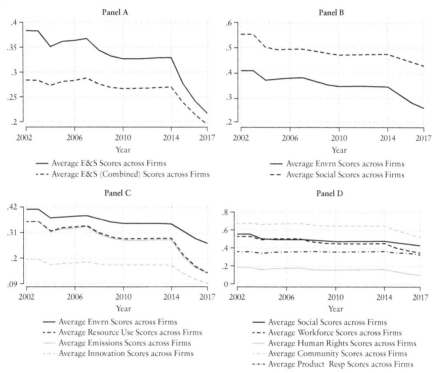

Note: All scores are bounded between 0 and 1.

Figure 4 plots kernel densities for the various (E&S) category and sub-category scores.[99] The various kernel densities in Panels A to D illustrate how many of these scores have right-skewed distributions with long right tails. Panels B and C show how the distributions of the 'environmental' score and its constituent scores (the 'resource use' score, 'emissions' score and 'innovation' score) are especially asymmetrical, with a large number of zero and near-zero-valued observations. Similarly, Figure 5 plots a histogram for CO_2 emissions. Again, the histogram illustrates the large density of zero and near-zero-valued observations in the dataset. In section IV.A, I explain some of the methodologies I use to address the pathologies arising from these distributions.

---

[99] An Epanechnikov Kernel bandwidth of 0.01 is used.

Figure 4 Distribution of E&S Scores (Kernel Density)

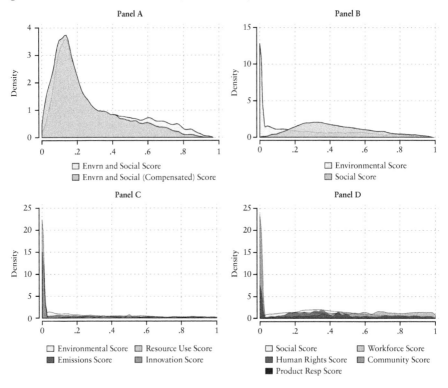

Figure 5 Distribution of CO$_2$ Emissions (Histogram)

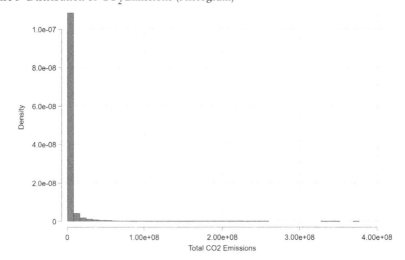

Table 3 Correlation Table for all Regressors

	Profit Weights (Equal Weights)	Log Total Assets	Log Mkt to Bk Ratio	Leverage	Return on Assets	Tangibility	Tobin's Q	Investor HHI	% owned by Inst Investors
Profit Weights (Equal Weights)	1.000								
Log Total Assets	0.404***	1.000							
Log Mkt to Bk Ratio	0.373***	0.555***	1.000						
Leverage	-0.011***	0.018***	0.088***	1.000					
Return on Assets	0.110***	0.048***	0.233***	-0.015***	1.000				
Tangibility	0.019***	0.020***	-0.027***	-0.005***	-0.023***	1.000			
Tobin's Q	0.010***	-0.331***	0.332***	-0.011***	0.199***	-0.140***	1.000		
Investor HHI	-0.325***	-0.228***	-0.282***	0.003***	0.007***	-0.093***	-0.021***	1.000	
% owned by Inst Investors	-0.090***	0.009***	-0.017***	-0.003***	0.152***	-0.108***	0.013***	0.860***	1.000

Note: ***p < 0.01, **p < 0.05, *p < 0.10.

iii. Financial Variables

Finally, portfolio firm financial characteristics are included as a set of controls in all empirical specifications to account for the effect of firm size, growth opportunities, historical performance, and firm debt which could potentially influence a firm's E&S performance. Although summary statistics for these variables are not included here, much of the literature suggests that the inclusion of these controls may be necessary to reduce omitted-variable bias.[100] For instance, 'Total Assets' is a proxy for firm size, which controls for the possibility that large firms face greater pressure over their environmental and social impact and the possibility that a firm's E&S performance scales with its volume of business activity. Similarly, 'Leverage' and 'Tangibility' measure a firm's credit constraints, which may impact its financing of environmentally or socially beneficial investments. In a similar vein, 'Return on Assets' is a common variable used to proxy for a firm's profitability, which may in turn influence its investments or actions that drive the firm's E&S performance. A detailed description of these control variables is provided in Table 13.

Table 3 shows the correlations between the regressors used in this chapter. To reduce problems associated with multicollinearity, I run empirical specifications with and without certain regressors which are highly correlated with each other. While some of these specifications do reduce the standard errors associated with the coefficients of interest, they do not significantly impact the robustness of my results.

IV. DOES COMMON OWNERSHIP DRIVE E&S PERFORMANCE?

A. Baseline Tests

As mentioned in section II above, a robust test of whether common ownership drives E&S performance would rely on a (truly) exogenous shock to common ownership. Once this exogenous shock is identified, the effect on E&S performance can be evaluated accordingly. Nevertheless, it is helpful to run a baseline test of the (naive) relationship between lagged measures of common ownership and firms' E&S performance. Following Dyck et al,[101] one could estimate the specification:

$$Log(Score_{fsjt}) = \alpha + \lambda \kappa_{fsjt-1}(\beta) + \gamma X_{fsjt-1} + \delta_f + \theta_s + \zeta_j + \eta_t + \varepsilon_{fsjt} \qquad (8)$$

where the dependent variable $Score_{fsjt}$ is a firm's category or sub-category score, f indexes a given portfolio firm, s indexes a given common owner, j indexes a given industry, and t indexes a given year. Thus, $\kappa_{fsjt-1}(\beta)$ is a measure of the common ownership (equal weight) profit weight as detailed in section III.A for a given firm f, common owner s, industry j, and year $t-1$.[102] Similarly, X_{fsjt-1} is a set of firm-level control variables for the same, and $\delta_f, \theta_s, \zeta_j,$ and η_t are firm, common owner, industry, and year fixed effects.

---

[100] Dyck et al (n 40 above); Azar et al (n 29 above); H Hong et al, 'Financial Constraints on Corporate Goodness' *Technical Report* (2012).

[101] Dyck et al (n 40 above).

[102] As mentioned in section III.A, I focus on the equal weight average to identify portfolio-wide externalities. Thus, I will henceforth refer to $\kappa_f^n(\beta)$ as $\kappa_f(\beta)$.

However, the specification in equation (8) is associated with several problems. First, because log[0] is undefined, estimating specification (8) would drop all zero-valued observations, removing important information and reducing the statistical power of the regression. As detailed in Figure 4, a substantial proportion of my dataset consists of zero-valued observations, militating against the use of specification (8). Second, Cohn et al[103] show that while the estimation of 'log1plus' regressions or inverse hyperbolic sine (IHS) transformations allow for the retention of observations with zero-valued outcomes, they do not give rise to economically-meaningful coefficients.[104] Furthermore, Cohn et al show that log1plus and IHS regressions require an implausible form of heteroskedasticity for consistent estimates, and that any non-linearities between the outcome variable and covariates or among covariates may result in biased estimates.[105] Indeed, the authors find that these regressions may even induce the wrong sign in expectation, making it difficult to infer even the direction of a relationship between two or more variables. Finally, Silva and Tenreyro[106] show that the log-linear specification in equation (8) results in biased estimates when heteroskedasticity in the underlying model is present – a feature present in my dataset.[107] Cohn et al extend the results in Silva and Tenreyro,[108] finding that the resulting bias can even cause the sign of a log-linear regression to be wrong in expectation, and that controlling for fixed effects can worsen this bias.[109]

To ameliorate the aforementioned problems, I follow Cohn et al, Silva and Tenreyro, and Blackburn[110] in estimating a generalised linear model (GLM) with a log-link function, often known as a 'GLM Poisson' model. Like the log-linear regressions used by Dyck et al and Azar et al,[111] a GLM Poisson regression assumes an underlying constant-elasticity structure where the regressors are assumed to have a multiplicative effect on the outcome variable.[112] However, unlike log-linear models, the GLM Poisson model is able to accomodate zero-valued outcomes and requires no assumption of homoskedasticity for consistent estimatation. Furthermore, the GLM Poisson model admits multiple levels of fixed effects, unlike competing non-linear models (eg Tobit/Probit/Negative Binomial models) which do not accomodate separable fixed effects. Methodological advancements by Gourieroux et al also allow the application of the GLM Poisson model to continuous data, with no restriction on the

---

[103] Cohn et al (n 37 above).

[104] Where the dependent variable is Y, a log1plus regression implements a $\log(1+Y)$ transformation while a IHS regression implements a $\log\left(Y+\sqrt{Y^2+1}\right)$ transformation.

[105] Cohn et al (n 37 above).

[106] MC Santos Silva and S Tenreyro, 'The Log of Gravity' (2006) 88(4) *The Review of Economics and Statistics* 641.

[107] I find that the null hypothesis in a Breush-Pagan test statistic (TS Breusch and AR Pagan, 'A Simple Test for Heteroscedasticity and Random Coefficient Variation' (1979) *Econometrica: Journal of the Econometric Society* 1287) is rejected at the 1% level.

[108] Santos Silva and Tenreyro (n 106 above).

[109] Cohn et al (n 37 above).

[110] ibid; JMC Santos Silva and S Tenreyro, 'Further Simulation Evidence on the Performance of the Poisson Pseudo-Maximum Likelihood Estimator' (2011) 112(2) *Economics Letters* 220–22; Santos Silva and Tenreyro (n 106 above); ML Blackburn, 'Estimating Wage Differentials without Logarithms' (2007) 14(1) *Labour Economics* 73.

[111] Dyck et al (n 40 above); Azar et al (n 29 above).

[112] E Ciani and P Fisher, 'Dif-in-dif Estimators of Multiplicative Treatment Effects' (2019) 8(1) *Journal of Econometric Methods*.

outcome variable's domain other than the requirement that no negative values are observed.[113]

To estimate the GLM Possion equivalent of specification (8), I consider the formulation:

$$\log(E\left[Score_{fsjt} \mid \mathbf{W}\right]) = \mathbf{W}\xi + \delta_f + \theta_s + \zeta_j + \eta_t \tag{9}$$

which is also equivalent to:

$$E\left[Score_{fsjt} \mid \mathbf{W}\right] = \exp\left(\mathbf{W}\xi + \delta_f + \theta_s + \zeta_j + \eta_t\right) \tag{10}$$

where $\mathbf{W}$ is the matrix of regressors:

$$\mathbf{W} = \kappa_{fsjt-1}(\beta) + X_{fsjt-1} \tag{11}$$

and the parameter of interest ξ is a vector of coefficients associated with the matrix $\mathbf{W}$. Like specification (8), f indexes a given portfolio firm, s indexes a given common owner, j indexes a given industry, and t indexes a given year; $\kappa_{fsjt-1}^n(\beta)$ is a measure of the common ownership (equal weight) profit weight as detailed in section III.A for a given firm f, common owner s, industry j, and year $t-1$; X_{fsjt-1} is a set of firm-level control variables for the same; and $\delta_f, \theta_s, \zeta_j$, and η_t are firm, common owner, industry, and year fixed effects. Meanwhile, the outcome variable $Score_{fsjt}$ is assumed to take on a Poisson distribution.[114] Denoting $Score_{fsjt} = y_{fsjt}$, the parameter ξ is estimated pursuant to the first order conditions that maximise the pseudo log-likelihood function:[115]

$$\sum_{fsjt=1}^{n} \left[y_{fsjt} - \exp(\mathbf{W}\xi + \delta_f + \theta_s + \zeta_j + \eta_t)\right]\mathbf{W} = 0 \tag{12}$$

where n relates to the total number of observations.

The coefficients from the estimated vector ξ are reported in Table 4. Following Abadie et al, all of the standard errors are clustered at the firm level.[116] In Regression (1),

---

[113] C Gourieroux et al, 'Pseudo Maximum Likelihood Methods: Theory' (1984) *Econometrica: Journal of the Econometric Society* 681; C Gourieroux et al, 'Pseudo Maximum Likelihood Methods: Applications to Poisson Models' (1984) *Econometrica: Journal of the Econometric Society* 701.

[114] Denoting $Score_i = y_i$ and including a single fixed effect α_i for parsimony, y is assumed to have the density $f(y|\mathbf{W}) = \frac{e^{-\mu(\mathbf{W})}\mu(\mathbf{W})^y}{y!}$ where $\mu(\mathbf{W}) = E[y|\mathbf{W}] = e^{\mathbf{W}\xi + \alpha_i}$. Accordingly, the likelihood function is $\prod_{i=1}^{n} \frac{e^{-e^{\mathbf{W}\xi+\alpha_i}}\left[e^{[\mathbf{W}\xi+\alpha_i]y}\right]}{y!}$ and the log-likelihood function is $\sum_{i=1}^{n}\left[y_i\left[\mathbf{W}\xi + \alpha_i\right] - \exp[\mathbf{W}\xi + \alpha_i] - \log[y_i!]\right]$. The first order condition of this function (assuming the existence of a solution) is $\sum_{i=1}^{n}\left[y_i\mathbf{W} - \exp[\mathbf{W}\xi + \alpha_f]\mathbf{W}\right] = 0$, similar to equation (9) as formulated by Gourieroux et al ('Pseudo Maximum Likelihood Methods: Applications to Poisson Models', n 113 above).

[115] Gourieroux et al ('Pseudo Maximum Likelihood Methods: Applications to Poisson Models', n 113 above).

[116] A Abadie et al, 'When Should You Adjust Standard Errors for Clustering?' *National Bureau of Economic Research Technical report* (2017).

E&S performance scores are regressed on a lagged common ownership profit weight $\kappa_{fsjt-1}(\beta)$ and a set of lagged control variables X_{fsjt-1}. The regression indicates a negative relationship between common ownership profit weights and a firm's E&S performance, with the coefficient significant at the 5 per cent level. The coefficient on $\kappa_{fsjt-1}(\beta)$, -0.202, indicates the multiplicative effect that common ownership has on a firm's E&S score. More specifically, a unit increase in the profit weight $\kappa_{fsjt-1}(\beta)$ is associated with an 18.3 per cent decrease in a firm's E&S score.[117] In other words, *ceterus paribus*, a 0.1 increase in $\kappa_{fsjt-1}(\beta)$ is associated with a 1.83 per cent decrease in E&S performance – a salient fact given that $\kappa_f(\beta)$ has risen by more than 0.2 over the course of 16 years. Similarly, in Regression (2), E&S performance scores are regressed on a lagged common ownership profit weight $\kappa_{fsjt-1}(\beta)$ and a set of lagged control variables X_{fsjt-1} but without regressors that are highly correlated with each other (see Table 3), reducing the potential for multicollinearity. The coefficient on $\kappa_{fsjt-1}(\beta)$ indicates that a unit increase in the profit weight $\kappa_{fsjt-1}(\beta)$ is associated with a slightly lower decrease of 18.0 per cent in a firm's E&S score. However, the coefficient is now significant at the 1 per cent level. In Regression (3), the dependent variable of E&S (Compensated) scores are used in place of E&S scores. The coefficient on $\kappa_{fsjt-1}(\beta)$ indicates a 21.2 per cent decrease in a firm's E &S score, but the coefficient is only significant at the 10 per cent level. Removing regressors that are highly correlated with each other in Regression (4) does not change the magnitude of the coefficient or its significance level (at 10 per cent).

Table 4 GLM Poisson Regressions of E & S Scores on Profit Weights

	(1) Envrn and Social Score	(2) Envrn and Social Score	(3) Envrn and Social Compensated Score	(4) Envrn and Social Compensated Score
Profit Weights (Equal Weights)	−0.202** (0.012)	−0.199*** (0.009)	−0.238* (0.099)	−0.238* (0.080)
Log Total Assets	0.110*** (0.000)	0.119*** (0.000)	0.027 (0.502)	0.029 (0.472)
Log Mkt to Bk Ratio	0.040** (0.020)		0.071*** (0.002)	
Leverage	−0.000 (0.375)	0.000 (0.213)	−0.000 (0.186)	0.000 (0.139)
Return on Assets	0.189** (0.015)	0.183** (0.014)	0.250** (0.032)	0.250** (0.022)
Tangibility	0.172 (0.217)	0.141 (0.319)	0.067 (0.702)	−0.006 (0.972)
Tobin's Q	−0.005 (0.618)	0.012 (0.190)	−0.005 (0.737)	0.018 (0.138)

(continued)

[117] To see why, note that the multiplicative effect may be calculated as $\exp(-0.202)-1 = -0.183$.

Table 4 *(Continued)*

	(1) Envrn and Social Score	(2) Envrn and Social Score	(3) Envrn and Social Compensated Score	(4) Envrn and Social Compensated Score
Investor HHI	−0.408 (0.912)		0.738 (0.906)	
% Owned by Inst Investors	0.238** (0.046)	0.257*** (0.001)	0.133 (0.447)	0.179* (0.091)
Observations	4236548	4530602	4236548	4530602
Common Owner FE	Yes	Yes	Yes	Yes
Firm FE	Yes	Yes	Yes	Yes
Industry FE	Yes	Yes	Yes	Yes
Year FE	Yes	Yes	Yes	Yes
Chi Square	43.974	42.672	16.845	12.911
Pseudo R Square	0.092	0.093	0.085	0.085

Note: ***p < 0.01, **p < 0.05, *p < 0.10. Standard Errors are Clustered at the Firm Level. All Regressors are lagged by one period w.r.t the Dependent Variable.

Table 5 reports the coefficients from the estimated vector ξ for the category score of 'environmental scores' and the sub-category scores of 'resource use' scores, 'emissions' scores, and 'innovation' scores. Like Table 4, the regressions collectively indicate a negative relationship between common ownership profit weights and a firm's environmental performance. Regression (1) suggests that a unit increase in the profit weight $\kappa_{fsjt-1}(\beta)$ is associated with a 28.9 per cent decrease in a firm's environmental performance, with the coefficient significant at the 1 per cent level. Regressions (2)–(5) examine the sub-category scores that constitute a firm's environmental score. Regression (2) indicates that a unit increase in the profit weight $\kappa_{fsjt-1}(\beta)$ is associated with a 34.3 per cent decrease in a firm's resource use score, with the coefficient significant at the 1 per cent level. Meanwhile, Regression (3) indicates that a unit increase in the profit weight $\kappa_{fsjt-1}(\beta)$ is associated with a 25.8 per cent decrease in a firm's emissions score, but the coefficient is only significant at the 10 per cent level. Removing regressors that are highly correlated with each other in Regression (4), however, reduces the standard errors associated with Regression (3). Here, a unit increase in the profit weight $\kappa_{fsjt-1}(\beta)$ is associated with a 28.0 per cent decrease in a firm's emissions score, with the coefficient significant at the 5 per cent level. Finally, Regression (5) finds a negative association between the profit weight $\kappa_{fsjt-1}(\beta)$ and a firm's innovation score. However, the coefficient on $\kappa_{fsjt-1}(\beta)$ is not significantly different from zero.

Table 5 GLM Poisson Regressions of Environmental Scores on Profit Weights

	Pillar Score	Sub–Pillar Scores			
	(1) Environmental Score	(2) Resource Use Score	(3) Emissions Score	(4) Emissions Score	(5) Innovation Score
Profit Weights (Equal Weights)	−0.341*** (0.006)	−0.420*** (0.004)	−0.298* (0.052)	−0.329** (0.031)	−0.345 (0.161)
Log Total Assets	0.149*** (0.006)	0.155** (0.011)	0.183*** (0.004)	0.191*** (0.001)	0.071 (0.334)
Log Mkt to Bk Ratio	0.056* (0.054)	0.070** (0.047)	0.073** (0.021)		−0.008 (0.866)
Leverage	−0.001 (0.261)	−0.001 (0.441)	−0.001* (0.086)	0.000 (0.506)	−0.000 (0.856)
Return on Assets	0.312** (0.014)	0.207 (0.161)	0.284*** (0.047)	0.244* (0.072)	0.704** (0.011)
Tangibility	0.261 (0.235)	0.254 (0.313)	0.009 (0.973)	−0.024 (0.930)	1.112** (0.031)
Tobin's Q	−0.016 (0.474)	−0.015 (0.581)	−0.041 (0.118)	−0.007 (0.748)	0.037 (0.273)
Investor HHI	1.970 (0.753)	2.616 (0.703)	12.106* (0.089)		−21.113* (0.090)
% Owned by Inst Investors	0.313 (0.131)	0.389* (0.078)	0.156 (0.510)	0.468*** (0.001)	0.562 (0.136)
Observations	3878790	3709652	3721274	3968331	2861654
Common Owner FE	Yes	Yes	Yes	Yes	Yes
Firm FE	Yes	Yes	Yes	Yes	Yes
Industry FE	Yes	Yes	Yes	Yes	Yes
Year FE	Yes	Yes	Yes	Yes	Yes
Chi Square	35.732	31.224	39.449	29.805	22.040
Pseudo R Square	0.132	0.129	0.133	0.135	0.150

Note: ***p < 0.01, **p < 0.05, *p < 0.10. Standard Errors are Clustered at the Firm Level. All Regressors are lagged by one period w.r.t the Dependent Variable.

Table 6 reports the coefficients from the estimated vector ξ for the category score of 'social scores' and the sub-category scores of 'workforce' scores, 'human rights' scores, 'community' scores, and 'product responsibility' scores. Unlike the environmental scores reported in Table 5, the coefficients of interests here are weaker in statistical significance, suggesting a less robust relationship between common ownership and social performance. Regression (1) suggests that a unit increase in the profit weight $\kappa_{fsjt-1}(\beta)$ is associated with a 10.9 per cent decrease in a firm's social performance, with the coefficient significant at the 10 per cent level. The removal of regressors that are highly correlated with each other in Regression (2) has a marginal effect on the magnitude of the coefficient reported in Regression (1), but does not change its significance level (at 10 per cent). Regression (3) finds a negative association between the profit weight $\kappa_{fsjt-1}(\beta)$ and a firm's workforce score, but fails to find that this relationship is statistically significant. However, Regression (4) indicates that a unit increase in the profit weight $\kappa_{fsjt-1}(\beta)$ is associated with a 54.7 per cent decrease in a firm's human rights score, and that the coefficient is significant at the 5 per cent level. Similarly, Regression (5) finds that a unit increase in the profit weight $\kappa_{fsjt-1}(\beta)$ is associated with a 13.4 per cent decrease in a firm's community score, and that the coefficient is significant at the 1 per cent level. Finally, Regression (6) finds a negative association between the profit weight $\kappa_{fsjt-1}(\beta)$ and a firm's product responsibility score, but fails to establish statistical significance for the relevant coefficient.

Table 6 GLM Poisson Regressions of Social Scores on Profit Weights

	Pillar Score		Sub-Pillar Scores			
	(1) Social Score	(2) Social Score	(3) Workforce Score	(4) Human Rights Score	(5) Community Score	(6) Product Resp Score
Profit Weights (Equal Weights)	−0.115* (0.076)	−0.116* (0.051)	−0.034 (0.684)	−0.791** (0.017)	−0.144*** (0.007)	−0.143 (0.417)
Log Total Assets	0.075*** (0.000)	0.082*** (0.000)	0.092*** (0.000)	0.154 (0.110)	0.044*** (0.009)	0.107** (0.025)
Log Mkt to Bk Ratio	0.031*** (0.009)		0.044*** (0.008)	0.045 (0.494)	0.019* (0.053)	0.051* (0.053)
Leverage	−0.000 (0.811)	0.000 (0.451)	−0.000 (0.870)	−0.000 (0.669)	0.000 (0.953)	−0.000 (0.501)
Return on Assets	0.099 (0.109)	0.105* (0.074)	0.148* (0.091)	0.381 (0.195)	−0.001 (0.990)	0.107 (0.394)
Tangibility	0.082 (0.440)	0.062 (0.558)	0.179 (0.170)	−0.358 (0.488)	0.167** (0.048)	0.142 (0.544)
Tobin's Q	−0.000 (0.950)	0.012* (0.066)	−0.002 (0.798)	−0.027 (0.559)	−0.000 (0.937)	0.008 (0.704)
Investor HHI	−1.807 (0.514)		−2.273 (0.550)	−8.019 (0.579)	−2.819 (0.295)	13.080* (0.060)
% Owned by Inst Investors	0.187** (0.028)	0.162*** (0.003)	0.228** (0.045)	1.103** (0.018)	0.148* (0.068)	−0.099 (0.657)

(continued)

Table 6 *(Continued)*

	Pillar Score		Sub-Pillar Scores			
	(1) Social Score	(2) Social Score	(3) Workforce Score	(4) Human Rights Score	(5) Community Score	(6) Product Resp Score
Observations	4236548	4530602	4236548	3008333	4236548	4146402
Common Owner FE	Yes	Yes	Yes	Yes	Yes	Yes
Firm FE	Yes	Yes	Yes	Yes	Yes	Yes
Industry FE	Yes	Yes	Yes	Yes	Yes	Yes
Year FE	Yes	Yes	Yes	Yes	Yes	Yes
Chi Square	37.527	38.596	39.610	31.835	26.937	19.638
Pseudo R Square	0.049	0.049	0.069	0.175	0.029	0.104

Note: ***$p < 0.01$, **$p < 0.05$, *$p < 0.10$. Standard Errors are Clustered at the Firm Level. All Regressors are lagged by one period w.r.t the Dependent Variable.

The results in Tables 4–6 challenge prevailing narratives in the existing literature. As mentioned in section II above, Dyck et al report their baseline tests (using specification (8)) for US domiciled firms, and find a positive but not always significant impact on E&S performance.[118] While my baseline regressions are also limited to US firms, I differ from Dyck et al in measuring common ownership as opposed to institutional ownership, and advance an estimation methodology (ie the GLM Poisson model) which is considerably distinct from theirs.[119] Here, I find a negative (and often significant) impact of common ownership on E&S performance, contradicting a popular narrative that diversified investors should be rationally motivated to internalise intra-portfolio negative externalities with a view to maximising portfolio returns.[120] Indeed, the results in Tables 5 and 6 suggest that this negative relationship is stronger for externalities that are associated with large and identifiable collective action problems (ie environmental externalities) – in line with Tallarita's findings that institutional investors invest in subsets of the economy that are relatively less vulnerable to climate risk.[121] In contrast, it may be much more difficult for institutional investors to invest in firms that are less vulnerable to 'social risks', except in relation to targeted events like the Russia-Ukraine war in 2022.[122]

While the use of lagged common ownership and control variables in specification (12) may ameliorate endogeneity concerns, they do not completely eliminate it so long

[118] Dyck et al (n 40 above).

[119] Unlike Dyck et al, my dataset is also limited to US institutional investors who are subject to 13F disclosures: Dyck et al (n 40 above).

[120] Condon (n 24 above); Coffee (n 25 above); Gordon (n 25 above).

[121] Tallarita (n 28 above).

[122] M Deng et al, 'Stock Prices and the Russia-Ukraine War: Sanctions, Energy and ESG' *Ideas* (2022), https://ideas.repec.org/p/chf/rpseri/rp2229.html.

as the lagged variables are strongly correlated with their unlagged counterparts.[123] In section IV.B.i, I attempt to address these problems by exploiting the BlackRock-BGI merger as an exogenous shock to common ownership.

B. Identification Strategy

i. Motivation

To identify an exogenous shock that varies common ownership without varying E&S performance, I follow much of the literature in harnessing a merger between institutional investors.[124] Intuitively, the merger of institutional investors should induce changes in common ownership, as the post-merger investor tends to preserve most of its holdings previously owned by its pre-merger institutions.[125] However, as Boller and Scott-Morton[126] have argued, some of these mergers do not affect certain measures of common ownership, making them a poor instrument for determining outcome variables of interest.[127] Hence, it is important to evaluate the effect of such mergers on *specific* measures of common ownership before employing them as a source of exogenous variation.

Much of the literature is divided on the appropriate *set* of mergers that would plausibly have an impact on common ownership. While papers like He and Huang, Bindal and Nordlund, and Lewellen and Lowry select for all mergers between two 13F institutions (or their parent firms) in the financial sector with SIC codes between 6000 and 6999 for a given time period (along with other selection criteria),[128] other papers like Azar et al[129] rely on a single merger – the BlackRock-BGImerger in 2009. However, Schmalz and Elhauge note that the use of multiple mergers may not actually create significant increases in common ownership, making them potentially weak instruments.[130] Indeed, mergers of institutional investors may fail to induce changes in common ownership where the merged investor fails to preserve its holdings previously owned by its pre-merger institutions. Furthermore, identification strategies which harness multiple mergers introduce complications associated with multiple time periods as standard DiD (difference-in-differences) models (used by He and Huang and Bindal and Nordlund[131]) are no longer robust to the heterogeneity of treatment effects.[132]

[123] WR Reed, 'On the Practice of Lagging Variables to Avoid Simultaneity' (2015) 77(6) *Oxford Bulletin of Economics and Statistics* 897.

[124] Azar et al (n 12 above); Anton et al (n 20 above); Bindal and Nordlund (n 27 above); He and Huang (n 48 above); He et al (n 23 above); Kini et al (n 49 above); Koch et al (n 6 above).

[125] He and Huang (n 48 above).

[126] Boller and Scott Morton (n 45 above).

[127] As Boller and Scott-Morton explain, the mergers that Koch et al exploit do not affect firm-level measures of common ownership (like $\kappa_{fsjt}(\beta)$), making them a poor instrument: Boller and Scott Morton (n 45 above); Koch et al (n 6 above).

[128] He and Huang (n 48 above); Bindal and Nordlund (n 27 above); Lewellen and Lowry (n 27 above).

[129] Azar et al (n 12 above).

[130] MC Schmalz, 'Recent Studies on Common Ownership, Firm Behavior, and Market Outcomes' (2021) 66(1) *The Antitrust Bulletin* 12; Elhauge (n 7 above).

[131] He and Huang (n 48 above); Bindal and Nordlund (n 27 above).

[132] Goodman-Bacon (n 57 above); Callaway and Sant'Anna (n 57 above).

Accordingly, I follow Azar et al and Xie and Gerakos in exploiting the BlackRock-BGI merger in 2009 as an exogenous shock to common ownership, where BlackRock agreed to pay US$13.5 billion to acquire the investment management business of Barclays, BGI.[133] The BlackRock-BGI merger is a particularly attractive instrument for my purposes as there is no reason to believe that the merger was led by E&S concerns or the E&S performance of their portfolio firms. Public sources suggest that the merger was motivated by BlackRock's desire to acquire a foothold in passive investing, as BGI was then a leader in exchange traded funds; alongside with the need for Barclays (BGI's parent company) to sell assets to shore up its balance sheet in light of the financial crisis.[134] Indeed, prior to the merger, BlackRock was seen as more of an active fund manager. As the CEO of BlackRock, Larry Fink, noted that at that time, 'there was a belief that the cultures of active and passive managers were so diametrically different that you could never have a firm have both'.[135] The BlackRock-BGI merger was also a merger that ostensibly induced very large changes in institutional ownership, given that it more than doubled its worldwide assets under management to about US$3.29 trillion from US$1.44 trillion. Indeed, in section IV.B.ii, I find evidence that the merger did induce changes in common ownership.

In a different context, Lewellen and Lowry argue that the use of index entries as an identification strategy creates a problem where associated changes in monitoring incentives (due to the fact that index entries are associated with significant declines in ownership by large (5 per cent or more) blockholders) may affect firm policies *independently* of any changes in common ownership.[136] However, similar concerns are associated with the use of institutional investor mergers as an identification strategy. To see why, consider the cosine decomposition of equation (6) as per Backus et al:[137]

$$\kappa_f^n(\beta) = \frac{1}{G} \sum_{\forall g \neq f} \frac{\sum_{\forall s} \beta_{fs}\beta_{gs}}{\sum_{\forall s} [\beta_{fs}]^2}$$

$$= \frac{1}{G} \sum_{\forall g \neq f} \left[\cos[\beta_f, \beta_g] \times \sqrt{\frac{\|\beta_g\|^2}{\|\beta_f\|^2}} \right] \quad (13)$$

where β_f and β_g are vectors defined over s and $\|\beta_f\|^2 = \sum_{s=1}^{S} \beta_{fs}^2$ (and likewise for β_g). Equation (13) reveals an important fact – given an exogenous increase in $\kappa_f^n(\beta)$, such an increase may be attributed to an increase in $\cos[\beta_f, \beta_g]$, a component of common ownership associated with overlapping ownership, *or* an increase in $\sqrt{\frac{\|\beta_g\|^2}{\|\beta_f\|^2}}$,

[133] Azar et al (n 12 above); J Xie and J Gerakos, 'The Anticompetitive Effects of Common Ownership: The Case of Paragraph IV Generic Entry' (2020) 110 *AEA Papers and Proceedings* 569.

[134] See https://www.ft.com/content/48e703d8-6d87-11e9-80c7-60ee53e6681d (Mr Diamond, executive chairman of BGI at the time, said: 'What the BGI deal gave BlackRock was a huge franchise in passive indexing and quantitative capabilities').

[135] See https://www.pionline.com/article/20190611/ONLINE/190619948/blackrock-s-acquisition-of-bgi-10-years-ago-fuels-breakneck-growth-of-investment-giant.

[136] Lewellen and Lowry (n 27 above).

[137] Backus et al (n 4 above).

a component of common ownership associated with the *relative* costs of exercising control rights over multiple firms – what Backus et al term a firm's 'Relative IHHI'. As $\sqrt{\frac{\|\beta_s\|^2}{\|\beta_f\|^2}}$ is a ratio of Investor HHIs, changes in $\sqrt{\frac{\|\beta_s\|^2}{\|\beta_f\|^2}}$ will affect a common owner's monitoring incentives regardless of the change in $\cos[\beta_f, \beta_g]$. As Backus et al note, however, the relationship between Investor HHI and $\sqrt{\frac{\|\beta_s\|^2}{\|\beta_f\|^2}}$ is ambiguous as Investor HHIs of firms f and g appear in both the numerator and denominator.[138] In section IV.B.iii, I find empirical evidence to suggest that the merger induced changes in the Investor HHI of treatment firms.

ii. Instrument Validity

To evaluate the impact of the BlackRock-BGI merger on common ownership, I follow the methodology of He and Huang in determining the selection of treatment and control firms.[139] I identify treatment firms as firms which are *either* block-owned by the acquirer, BlackRock, *or* the target investor, BGI in the year before the merger, 2008.[140] The aforementioned strategy seeks to identity the firms which are most likely to experience a change in firm-level common ownership post-merger. I identify control firms pursuant to three necessary conditions: (1) firms which are *neither* block-owned by the acquirer, BlackRock, *nor* the target investor, BGI in the year before the merger; or (2) firms which are *both* block-owned by the acquirer, BlackRock *and* the target investor, BGI in the year before the merger; and (3) firms which are not in treatment group.[141] Unlike He and Huang, Lewellen and Lowry, and Bindal and Nordlund, I do not require any additional condition(s) that either the acquirer or the target block-holds at least one of the same-industry rival firms prior to the merger, as my hypotheses evaluate portfolio-wide externalities, and do not depend on the existence of within-industry externalities (eg pecuniary externalities that ultimately increase product market prices).[142]

After identifying the treatment and control firms pursuant to the methodology I define above, I run a two-stage-least-squares (2SLS) test of my chosen instrument.[143] In the first stage, I run the specification:

$$Merger_{fsjt} = \alpha + \lambda \kappa_{fsjt}(\beta) + \rho EnScore_{fsjt} + \gamma X_{fsjt} + \theta_s + \zeta_j + \eta_t + \varepsilon_{fsjt} \qquad (14)$$

on the dataset prior to the merger year (ie 2008 and earlier years). In specification (14), f indexes a given portfolio firm, s indexes a given common owner, j indexes a

---

[138] Backus et al (n 4 above).

[139] He and Huang (n 48 above).

[140] Insofar as block-ownership is concerned, a threshold of 3% is used, in line with Dasgupta et al (2021), https://www.nowpublishers.com/article/Details/FIN-056.

[141] This possible due to the fact that control firms that fufil conditions (1) and (2) could subsequently merge with treated firms in the treatment group. Thus, condition (3) ensures that the treatment and control groups are mutually exclusive.

[142] He and Huang (n 48 above); Lewellen and Lowry (n 27 above); Bindal and Nordlund (n 27 above).

[143] Although the binary variable $Merger_{fsjt}$ is bounded between 0 and1, I do not run a probit or logit regression in the first stage as neither the conditional expectations operator nor the linear projection would

given industry, and t indexes a given year. $Merger_{fsjt}$ is a binary variable that is 1 if the firm is treated and 0 otherwise, $\kappa_{fsjt}(\beta)$ is the firm's common ownership profit weight, $EnScore_{fsjt}$ is the firm's E&S score, X_{fsjt} is a set of firm-level control variables, and θ_s, ζ_j, and η_t are common owner, industry, and year fixed effects.[144] The results from this regression are reported in Table 5, Regression (1). The coefficients on both $\kappa_{fsjt}^n(\beta)$ and $EnScore_{fsjt}$ are not statistically significant – suggesting that the merger was not driven by E&S or common ownership considerations.

In the second stage, the predicted values from specification (11), $\widehat{Merger_{fsjt}}$, are used as a regressor to identify the effects of the merger on a firm's common ownership profit weight $\kappa_{fsjt}^n(\beta)$. Thus, I run the specification:

$$\kappa_{fsjt}(\beta) = \alpha + \lambda \widehat{Merger_{fsjt}} + \gamma X_{fsjt} + \delta_f + \theta_s + \zeta_j + \eta_t + \varepsilon_{fsjt} \qquad (15)$$

on the dataset after the merger year (ie, 2010 and later years). In specification (15), f indexes a given portfolio firm, s indexes a given common owner, j indexes a given industry, t indexes a given year, X_{fsjt} is a set of firm-level control variables, while δ_f, θ_s, ζ_j, and η_t are firm, common owner, industry, and year fixed effects. These variables control for factors that may potentially influence a firm's common ownership but which are not captured by the first stage regression in equation (14). Standard errors are bootstrapped as per Freedman.[145]

The results from specification (11) are reported in Table 7, Regression (2). The coefficient of $\widehat{Merger_{fsjt}}$ is positive and highly significant at the 1 per cent level, indicating that treatment firms are likely to have a higher level of common ownership relative to control firms. Holding all else equal, Regression (2) suggests that a treated firm has, on average, a profit weight $\kappa_{fsjt}(\beta)$ that is (in the cross-section) 0.128 higher than a control firm.

The 2SLS methodology as expounded in specifications (14) and (15) assumes that the probability of treatment is driven by the observable variables in specification (14). However, as mentioned earlier, the BlackRock-BGI merger may not have been driven by firm-specific characteristics. For instance, the merger could have been motivated by BlackRock's wish to acquire the capabilities of BGI's fund managers as opposed to the composition of its portfolio firms. Furthermore, the 2SLS methodology does not account for the fact that common ownership is increasing over time for both treatment and control firms (see Figure 1). To consider the possibility that treatment is

---

carry through non-linear functions. As such, only an OLS regression in the first stage is guaranteed to produce predicted values that are uncorrelated with the residuals: WK Newey, 'Efficient Estimation of Limited Dependent Variable Models with Endogenous Explanatory Variables' (1987) 36(3) *Journal of Econometrics* 231.

[144] Firm fixed effects are not included as they are collinear with $Merger_{fsjt}$. Note that the firm-level control variables are not lagged as they are assumed to have a contemporaneous effect on common ownership (as opposed to E&S scores where the effects are assumed to take place over time).

[145] D Freedman, 'On Bootstrapping Two-stage Least-squares Estimates in Stationary Linear Models' (1984) 12(3) *The Annals of Statistics* 827.

driven by other unobservable factors and to account for time trends, I follow He and Huang and Bindal and Nordlund[146] in estimating the DiD regression:[147]

$$\kappa_{fsjt}(\beta) = \alpha + \lambda\left[Treated_f \times Post_t\right] + \gamma X_{fsjt} + \delta_f + \theta_s + \zeta_j + \eta_t + \varepsilon_{fsjt} \qquad (16)$$

where f indexes a given portfolio firm, s indexes a given common owner, j indexes a given industry, and t indexes a given year. $Treated_f \times Post_t$ is an interaction term that takes on the value 1 if a firm is treated and if the year is after the merger (ie 2010 and later years), but 0 otherwise. Meanwhile, X_{fsjt} is a set of firm-level control variables, while δ_f, θ_s, ζ_j, and η_t are firm, common owner, industry, and year fixed effects.[148] Following He and Huang and Azar et al, all of the standard errors in specification (16) are double clustered at the merger-firm level.[149]

The results from specification (16) are reported in Table 7. In Regression (3), specification (16) is run on a set of controls that excludes Investor HHI and Institutional Ownership. The coefficient of the interaction term, $Treated_f \times Post_t$, is positive and significant at the 5 per cent level. Holding all else equal, the coefficient on $Treated_f \times Post_t$ suggests that a treated firm has, on average, a profit weight $\kappa_{fsjt}(\beta)$ that is 0.019 higher relative to control firms post merger. In Regression (4), specification (16) is run on a set of controls that includes Investor HHI and Institutional Ownership. This variant of specification (16) (partially) controls for the component of common ownership associated with the *relative* costs of exercising control rights over multiple firms, $\sqrt{\dfrac{\|\beta_g\|^2}{\|\beta_f\|^2}}$.[150] The coefficient of the interaction term, $Treated_f \times Post_t$, takes on a value of 0.023 and is also positive and significant at the 5 per cent level. Regression (4) suggests that the increase in common ownership induced by the merger was led primarily by an increase in overlapping ownership, $\cos[\beta_f, \beta_g]$, as opposed to an increase in Relative IHHI, $\sqrt{\dfrac{\|\beta_g\|^2}{\|\beta_f\|^2}}$. Finally, in Regression (5), specification (16) is run on a set of controls that includes lagged values of Investor HHI and Institutional Ownership. The coefficient of the interaction term, $Treated_f \times Post_t$ here takes on a value of 0.021, and is positive and significant at the 5 per cent level. Collectively, Regressions (3)–(5) reinforce my findings that the BlackRock-BGI merger induced a positive and significant change in common ownership profit weights.

---

[146] He and Huang (n 48 above); Bindal and Nordlund (n 27 above).

[147] A GLM Poisson model is not implemented here given that the merger only has a additive but not multiplicative effect on the common ownership measure $\kappa_{fsjt}(\beta)$.

[148] Similarly, firm-level control variables in equation (13) are not lagged as they are assumed to have a contemporaneous effect on common ownership (as opposed to E&S scores where the effects are assumed to take place over time).

[149] He and Huang (n 48 above); Azar et al (n 12 above).

[150] This effect stems from the fact that relative HHI ($\sqrt{\dfrac{\|\beta_g\|^2}{\|\beta_f\|^2}}$) is a ratio of Investor HHIs in firms g and f.

Table 7 Determination of Instrument Validity

	2SLS		DiD CO		
	(1) Merger	(2) Profit Weights (Equal Weights)	(3) Profit Weights (Equal Weights)	(4) Profit Weights (Equal Weights)	(5) Profit Weights (Equal Weights)
$\widehat{Merger}$		0.128*** (0.000)			
Merger = 1 × Post = 1			0.019** (0.036)	0.023** (0.012)	0.021** (0.028)
Log Total Assets	0.008 (0.689)	0.030*** (0.000)	0.032*** (0.000)	0.019*** (0.004)	0.024*** (0.000)
Log Mkt to Bk Ratio	0.062*** (0.000)	−0.000 (0.922)	0.013*** (0.000)	0.011*** (0.002)	0.012*** (0.001)
Leverage	0.002 (0.518)	−0.000*** (0.002)	−0.000 (0.288)	−0.000 (0.176)	−0.000 (0.374)
Return on Assets	−0.160** (0.037)	0.091*** (0.000)	0.069*** (0.000)	0.022 (0.126)	0.070*** (0.000)
Tangibility	0.219* (0.086)	−0.024 (0.513)	0.053 (0.104)	0.061* (0.061)	0.054 (0.108)
Tobin's Q	−0.038*** (0.009)	0.013*** (0.000)	0.006*** (0.001)	0.004** (0.018)	0.005*** (0.004)
Investor HHI	0.000 (1.000)			−13.520*** (0.000)	
% Owned by Inst Investors	0.737*** (0.000)			0.513*** (0.000)	
Investor HHI (Lagged)					−7.734*** (0.000)
% Owned by Inst Investors (Lagged)					0.291*** (0.000)
Profit Weights (Equal Weights)	−0.112 (0.456)				
Envrn and Social Score	0.014 (0.816)				
Constant	−0.044 (0.793)	−0.069 (0.346)	−0.127* (0.052)	−0.174** (0.013)	−0.152** (0.030)

(continued)

Table 7   *(Continued)*

	2SLS		DiD CO		
	(1) Merger	(2) Profit Weights (Equal Weights)	(3) Profit Weights (Equal Weights)	(4) Profit Weights (Equal Weights)	(5) Profit Weights (Equal Weights)
Observations	1461287	3990573	4610905	4609611	3651816
Common Owner FE	Yes	Yes	Yes	Yes	Yes
Firm FE	No	Yes	Yes	Yes	Yes
Industry FE	Yes	Yes	Yes	Yes	Yes
Year FE	Yes	Yes	Yes	Yes	Yes
Adjusted R Square	0.464	0.888	0.831	0.850	0.845
F Statistic	6.536	13.904	14.467	41.972	23.385

Note: ***p < 0.01, **p < 0.05, *p < 0.10. Standard Errors are double-clustered at the Merger-Firm Level.

iii. Investor HHI and Total Institutional Ownership

As detailed in section IV.B.i, a given change in common ownership induced by an exogenous shock (regardless of whether it arises from a merger, index entry, or Russell re-composition) may lead to changes in Investor HHIs and Total Institutional Ownership for treated firms. Since both Investor HHIs and Total Institutional Ownership provide an indirect proxy for the costs of collective action in shareholder monitoring, I examine whether the merger induced a change in Investor HHIs and Total Institutional Ownership in Table 8.[151] In Regressions (1) and (2), I run the DiD specification:

$$y_{fsjt} = \alpha + \lambda\left[Treated_f \times Post_t\right] + \gamma X_{fsjt} + \delta_f + \theta_s + \zeta_j + \eta_t + \varepsilon_{fsjt} \qquad (17)$$

where y_{fsjt} is either a firm's Investor HHI or its Total Institutional Ownership, f indexes a given portfolio firm, s indexes a given common owner, j indexes a given industry, t indexes a given year, $Treated_f \times Post_t$ is an interaction term that takes on the value 1 if a firm is treated and if the year is after the merger (ie 2010 and later years), but 0 otherwise. Meanwhile, X_{fsjt} is a set of firm-level control variables, while δ_f, θ_s, ζ_j, and η_t are firm, common owner, industry, and year fixed effects. In Regressions (3) and (4), I run a similar specification where the outcome variable is log-transformed:

$$\log\left[y_{fsjt}\right] = \alpha + \lambda\left[Treated_f \times Post_t\right] + \gamma X_{fsjt} + \delta_f + \theta_s + \zeta_j + \eta_t + \varepsilon_{fsjt} \qquad (18)$$

and in Regressions (5) and (6), I run a GLM Poisson DiD specification[152] similar to equations (12) (with variables similar to specification (16)) where the parameter λ

---

[151] Admati et al (n 31 above); Doidge et al (n 89 above).
[152] Ciani and Fisher (n 112 above).

(a vector of coefficients) is estimated pursuant to the first order conditions that maximise the pseudo log-likelihood function:

$$\sum_{fsjt=1}^{n}\left[y_{fsjt}-\exp(\mathbf{W}\lambda+\delta_f+\theta_s+\zeta_j+\eta_t)\right]\mathbf{W}=0 \tag{19}$$

and $\mathbf{W}$ is the matrix of regressors:

$$\mathbf{W}=\left[Treated_f\times Post_t\right]+X_{fsjt} \tag{20}$$

All of the Regressions reported in Table 8 reveal that the BlackRock-BGI merger had a negative impact on both Investor HHI and its Total Institutional Ownership in treatment firms, with the coefficients of the interaction term significant at the 1 per cent level. Regression (6), for instance, suggests that treatment firms had a 9.6 per cent decrease in Investor HHI relative to control firms after the merger. These results are consistent with findings in Backus et al, who show that Total Institutional Ownership in BlackRock-BGI-owned portfolio firms remained constant at about 0.60 from 2010 to 2016.[153] In contrast, Total Institutional Ownership in Vanguard-owned portfolio firms increased from about 0.40 to 0.70 during the same period. In section V, I explain how these results provide a conceptual basis for the negative impact of the merger on E &S performance.

Table 8 DiD Regressions of Investor Concentration on Merger Treatment

	Linear		Log-Linear		GLM Poisson	
	(1) % owned by Inst Investors	(2) Investor HHI	(3) % owned by Inst Investors (Log)	(4) Investor HHI (Log)	(5) % owned by Inst Investors	(6) Investor HHI
Merger = 1 × Post = 1	−0.031*** (0.002)	−0.001*** (0.001)	−0.071*** (0.000)	−0.113*** (0.000)	−0.062*** (0.000)	−0.102*** (0.000)
Log Total Assets	0.022*** (0.000)	−0.000 (0.294)	0.043*** (0.000)	0.004 (0.820)	0.034*** (0.000)	−0.011 (0.443)
Log Mkt to Bk Ratio	−0.003 (0.357)	−0.000*** (0.004)	−0.003 (0.660)	−0.026*** (0.008)	−0.005 (0.373)	−0.027*** (0.002)
Leverage	0.000 (0.447)	0.000 (0.234)	0.000 (0.556)	0.000 (0.225)	0.000 (0.385)	0.000 (0.186)
Return on Assets	0.091*** (0.000)	−0.000 (0.939)	0.159*** (0.000)	0.033 (0.429)	0.144*** (0.000)	−0.001 (0.983)
Tangibility	0.004 (0.892)	0.001 (0.384)	0.031 (0.580)	0.104 (0.273)	0.011 (0.824)	0.077 (0.356)
Tobin's Q	0.003* (0.089)	−0.000 (0.809)	0.005* (0.100)	0.001 (0.865)	0.005* (0.080)	−0.001 (0.873)

(continued)

---

[153] Backus et al (n 4 above).

Table 8 *(Continued)*

	Linear		Log-Linear		GLM Poisson	
	(1) % owned by Inst Investors	(2) Investor HHI	(3) % owned by Inst Investors (Log)	(4) Investor HHI (Log)	(5) % owned by Inst Investors	(6) Investor HHI
Constant	0.447*** (0.000)	0.013*** (0.000)	−0.857*** (0.000)	−4.488*** (0.000)		
Observations	4609611	4609611	4609611	4609611	4609611	4609611
Common Owner FE	Yes	Yes	Yes	Yes	Yes	Yes
Firm FE	Yes	Yes	Yes	Yes	Yes	Yes
Industry FE	Yes	Yes	Yes	Yes	Yes	Yes
Year FE	Yes	Yes	Yes	Yes	Yes	Yes
Adjusted R Square	0.783	0.689	0.798	0.692		
F Statistic	9.644	3.358	11.111	3.014		
Chi Square					66.975	25.714
Pseudo R Square					0.013	0.007

Note: ***$p < 0.01$, **$p < 0.05$, *$p < 0.10$. Standard Errors are double-clustered at the Merger-Firm Level.

V. COMMON OWNERSHIP AND E&S PERFORMANCE

A. E&S Scores

Having established that the BlackRock-BGI merger provides an exogenous source of variation with regard to common ownership, I turn to the relationship between common ownership and E&S performance. As detailed in section I, large and diversified common owners who 'own most of the market' have been hypothesised to internalise broad externalities that apply across-the-board to their portfolio firms with a view to maximising portfolio returns.[154] However, as I have also elucidated in sections IV.B.i and IV.B.iii, an exogenous shock to common ownership may also induce changes in the monitoring incentives of institutional investors, *independent* of their interests in maximising their portfolio values pursuant to the profit weights implied by common ownership (section III.A).

In the usual instance where the outcome of interest relates to some type of externality imposed within a common industry, the selection of treatment firms and control firms must be conditioned on the existence of same-industry rival firms.[155]

---

[154] Condon (n 24 above); Coffee (n 25 above); Gordon (n 25 above).

[155] He and Huang (n 48 above); Lewellen and Lowry (n 27 above); Bindal and Nordlund (n 27 above).

Indeed, more sophisticated attempts at constructing treatment and control variables have extended beyond firms to that of firm-pairs, where each treatment pair consists of a firm owned by the acquirer and a firm owned by the target, and where the control pair consists of a firm owned by the acquirer and a firm *not* owned by the target.[156] However, as I have explained in section III.A, the measure of common ownership I use, $\kappa_{fsjt}(\beta)$, is very general and only depends on the assumption that the firm maximises a weighted sum of its shareholders' profits (ie in equations (1) and (2)), extending the applicability of the measure beyond industry-wide externalities to that of portfolio-wide externalities. Accordingly, I follow the strategy adopted in section IV.B.ii to identity the firms which are most likely to experience a change in firm-level common ownership post-merger. As explained earlier, treated firms are firms which were *either* block-owned by the acquirer, BlackRock, *or* the target investor, BGI in the year before the merger, 2008. These firms experienced an *increase* in their common ownership profit weights relative to control firms.

To evaluate the relationship between E&S performance and this exogenous increase in common ownership, I run a GLM Poisson DiD specification[157] similar to specification (19) where the parameter λ is estimated pursuant to the first order conditions that maximise the pseudo log-likelihood function:

$$\sum_{fsjt=1}^{n} \left[Score_{fsjt} - \exp(\mathbf{W}\lambda + \delta_f + \theta_s + \zeta_j + \eta_t) \right] \mathbf{W} = 0 \tag{21}$$

and $\mathbf{W}$ is the matrix of regressors:

$$\mathbf{W} = \left[Treated_f \times Post_t \right] + X_{fsjt-1} \tag{22}$$

where the dependent variable $Score_{fsjt}$ is a firm's category or sub-category score and the parameter of interest λ is a vector of coefficients associated with the matrix $\mathbf{W}$. Like specification (19), f indexes a given portfolio firm, s indexes a given common owner, j indexes a given industry, and t indexes a given year; X_{fsjt-1} is a set of firm-level control variables for a given firm f, common owner s, industry j, and year $t - 1$; and δ_f, θ_s, ζ_j, and η_t are firm, common owner, industry, and year fixed effects. Meanwhile, $Treated_f \times Post_t$ is an interaction term that takes on the value 1 if a firm is treated and if the year is after the merger (ie 2010 and later years), but 0 otherwise.

Coefficients from the estimated vector λ are reported in Table 9. Following He and Huang and Azar et al, all of the standard errors in specification (21) are double clustered at the merger-firm level.[158] In Regression (1), E&S scores are regressed on the interaction term $Treated_f \times Post_t$ and a set of lagged control variables X_{fsjt-1}. The regression indicates a negative relationship between the interaction term and a firm's E&S performance, with the coefficient significant at the 1 per cent level. The coefficient on $Treated_f \times Post_t$, -0.161, indicates the multiplicative effect of treatment

[156] Lewellen and Lowry (n 27 above).
[157] Ciani and Fisher (n 112 above).
[158] He and Huang (n 48 above); Azar et al (n 12 above).

on a firm's E&S score after the merger. In particular, a treated firm is associated with a 14.9 per cent decrease in its E&S score post-merger. In Regression (2), specification (17) is repeated with a slight modification to **W**, where W = [$Treated_f$ × $Post_t$] + $Post_t$ + X_{fsjt-1} but without year fixed effects η_t. Again, the regression indicates a negative relationship between the interaction term and a firm's E&S performance, with the coefficient on the interaction term $Treated_f$ × $Post_t$ significant at the 1 per cent level. Here, treatment is associated with a 12.9 per cent decrease in a firm's E&S score post-merger. Regression (3) repeats Regression (1) for a different dependent variable, E&S (Compensated) scores. The regression indicates a negative relationship between the interaction term and a firm's E&S (Compensated) score. Unlike Regression (3) in Table 4 where the coefficient on κ_{fsjt} (β) is significant only at the 10 per cent level, the coefficient here is now significant at the 1 per cent level. A treated firm is associated with a 21.2 per cent decrease in its E&S (Compensated) score post-merger. Finally, Regression (4) repeats Regression (2) for E&S (Compensated) scores. The results here are quantitatively similar to Regression (3). As treated firms are associated with an *increase* in common ownership (section IV.A.ii), the results in Table 9 collectively suggest an *inverse* relationship between common ownership and E&S performance.

Table 9 GLM Poisson DiD Regressions of E&S scores on Merger Treatment

	(1) Envrn and Social Score	(2) Envrn and Social Score	(3) Envrn and Social Compensated Score	(4) Envrn and Social Compensated Score
Merger = 1 × Post = 1	−0.161***	−0.138***	−0.200***	−0.175***
	(0.000)	(0.002)	(0.002)	(0.007)
Log Total Assets	0.102***	0.204***	0.016	0.204***
	(0.003)	(0.000)	(0.727)	(0.000)
Log Mkt to Bk Ratio	0.033*	0.062***	0.066**	0.118***
	(0.093)	(0.002)	(0.011)	(0.000)
Leverage	−0.000	−0.000	−0.000	−0.001**
	(0.513)	(0.154)	(0.237)	(0.021)
Return on Assets	0.221**	0.298***	0.271*	0.219
	(0.027)	(0.004)	(0.070)	(0.169)
Tangibility	0.109	0.062	0.095	0.158
	(0.469)	(0.674)	(0.621)	(0.411)
Tobin's Q	−0.005	−0.002	−0.009	0.016
	(0.688)	(0.900)	(0.559)	(0.288)
Investor HHI	0.042	−0.034	0.043	−0.099
	(0.267)	(0.352)	(0.581)	(0.226)
% owned by Inst Investors	0.032	0.245***	0.028	0.262**
	(0.665)	(0.001)	(0.817)	(0.039)

(continued)

Table 9 *(Continued)*

	(1) Envrn and Social Score	(2) Envrn and Social Score	(3) Envrn and Social Compensated Score	(4) Envrn and Social Compensated Score
Observations	3416471	3416471	3416471	3416471
Common Owner FE	Yes	Yes	Yes	Yes
Firm FE	Yes	Yes	Yes	Yes
Industry FE	Yes	Yes	Yes	Yes
Year FE	Yes	Yes	Yes	Yes
Chi Square	37.920	675.536	21.217	276.358
Pseudo R Square	0.088	0.085	0.081	0.078

Note: ***$p < 0.01$, **$p < 0.05$, *$p < 0.10$. Standard Errors are double-clustered at the Merger-Firm Level. All Regressors are lagged by one period w.r.t the Dependent Variable.

Table 10 reports the coefficients from the estimated vector λ for the category score of 'environmental scores' and the sub-category scores of 'resource use' scores, 'emissions' scores, and 'innovation' scores. Like Table 9, the regressions collectively indicate a negative relationship between common ownership and a firm's environmental performance. Regression (1) suggests that a treated firm is associated with a 25.2 per cent decrease in its environmental score post-merger, with the relevant coefficient significant at the 1 per cent level. Regressions (2)–(4) examine the sub-category scores that constitute a firm's environmental score. A treated firm is associated with a 23.9 per cent decrease in its resource use score post-merger, a 24.8 per cent decrease in its emissions score post-merger, and a 40.8 per cent decrease in its innovation score post-merger. All of the relevant coefficients are significant at the 1 per cent level. These results stand in stark contrast to the results in Table 5, where the coefficient on κ_{fsjt} (β) is negative but not always statistically significant.

Table 10 GLM Poisson DiD Regressions of Environmental scores on Merger Treatment

	Pillar Score	Sub-Pillar Scores		
	(1) Environmental Score	(2) Resource Use Score	(3) Emissions Score	(4) Innovation Score
Merger = 1 × Post = 1	−0.290*** (0.000)	−0.273*** (0.007)	−0.285*** (0.002)	−0.524*** (0.010)
Log Total Assets	0.139** (0.019)	0.142** (0.033)	0.179** (0.011)	0.050 (0.524)
Log Mkt to Bk Ratio	0.037 (0.246)	0.053 (0.173)	0.055 (0.120)	−0.042 (0.416)

(continued)

Table 10   *(Continued)*

	Pillar Score	Sub-Pillar Scores		
	(1) Environmental Score	(2) Resource Use Score	(3) Emissions Score	(4) Innovation Score
Leverage	−0.000 (0.390)	−0.000 (0.603)	−0.001 (0.143)	0.000 (0.834)
Return on Assets	0.351** (0.028)	0.235 (0.194)	0.335* (0.075)	0.705** (0.041)
Tangibility	0.164 (0.497)	0.167 (0.540)	−0.110 (0.711)	1.012* (0.053)
Tobin's Q	−0.010 (0.678)	−0.010 (0.722)	−0.033 (0.236)	0.049 (0.231)
Investor HHI	8.620 (0.190)	11.358 (0.124)	19.112** (0.014)	−18.395 (0.160)
% Owned by Inst Investors	0.106 (0.619)	0.135 (0.556)	−0.055 (0.830)	0.389 (0.308)
Observations	3233660	3094816	3113942	2441399
Common Owner FE	Yes	Yes	Yes	Yes
Firm FE	Yes	Yes	Yes	Yes
Industry FE	Yes	Yes	Yes	Yes
Year FE	Yes	Yes	Yes	Yes
Chi Square	32.431	25.077	39.661	23.706
Pseudo R Square	0.132	0.128	0.134	0.157

Note: ***$p < 0.01$, **$p < 0.05$, *$p < 0.10$. Standard Errors are double-clustered at the Merger-Firm Level. All Regressors are lagged by one period w.r.t the Dependent Variable.

Table 11 reports the coefficients from the estimated vector λ for the category score of 'social scores' and the sub-category scores of 'workforce' scores, 'human rights' scores, 'community' scores, and 'product responsibility' scores. Unlike the environmental scores reported in Table 10, the coefficients of interest here are weaker in statistical significance. While a negative relationship between common ownership a firm's (overall) social score is observed, the same relationship is not observed for all of its constituents. Regression (1) suggests that a treated firm is associated with a 7.8 per cent decrease in its social score post-merger, with the relevant coefficient significant at the 5 per cent level. Regressions (2)–(5) examine the sub-category scores that constitute a firm's environmental score. In Regressions (2) and (3), a treated firm is associated with a 9.1 per cent decrease in its workforce score post-merger and a 37.4 per cent decrease in its human rights score post-merger, but the relevant coefficients are only significant at the 10 per cent level. In Regressions (4) and (5), a treated firm is associated with a decrease in its community score and product responsibility score, but the relevant coefficients are not statistically significant from zero.[159] These results may be contrasted with Table 6 where some of the relevant coefficients (on $\kappa_{fsjt}(\beta)$) are statistically significant. Indeed, Tables 10 and 11 illustrate the importance of exogenous instruments, as the use of lagged variables in section IV.A are unlikely to completely eliminate endogeneity concerns.

Table 11 GLM Poisson DiD Regressions of Social scores on Merger Treatment

	Pillar Score	Sub-Pillar Scores			
	(1) Social Score	(2) Workforce Score	(3) Human Rights Score	(4) Community Score	(5) Product Resp Score
Merger = 1 × Post = 1	−0.081** (0.011)	−0.095* (0.060)	−0.468* (0.083)	−0.035 (0.284)	−0.118 (0.220)
Log Total Assets	0.067*** (0.003)	0.079*** (0.004)	0.118 (0.239)	0.041** (0.025)	0.101* (0.050)
Log Mkt to Bk Ratio	0.032** (0.018)	0.045** (0.015)	0.028 (0.698)	0.021* (0.060)	0.049 (0.107)
Leverage	−0.000 (0.839)	−0.000 (0.905)	−0.000 (0.894)	−0.000 (0.958)	−0.000 (0.509)
Return on Assets	0.115 (0.156)	0.165 (0.157)	0.448 (0.222)	−0.005 (0.924)	0.119 (0.460)
Tangibility	0.057 (0.619)	0.191 (0.167)	−0.619 (0.265)	0.173* (0.058)	0.037 (0.889)
Tobin's Q	−0.003 (0.746)	−0.004 (0.736)	−0.048 (0.360)	−0.002 (0.791)	0.008 (0.745)
Investor HHI	−0.150 (0.959)	−1.946 (0.626)	2.802 (0.853)	−1.453 (0.601)	16.313** (0.029)
% Owned by Inst Investors	0.126 (0.168)	0.234** (0.049)	0.610 (0.224)	0.090 (0.294)	−0.180 (0.431)
Observations	3462903	3462903	2516456	3462903	3397669
Common Owner FE	Yes	Yes	Yes	Yes	Yes
Firm FE	Yes	Yes	Yes	Yes	Yes
Industry FE	Yes	Yes	Yes	Yes	Yes
Year FE	Yes	Yes	Yes	Yes	Yes
Chi Square	33.156	36.295	22.833	16.071	17.215
Pseudo R Square	0.048	0.067	0.178	0.028	0.103

Note: ***p < 0.01, **p < 0.05, *p < 0.10. Standard Errors are double-clustered at the Merger-Firm Level. All Regressors are lagged by one period w.r.t the Dependent Variable.

[159] The removal of regressors that are highly correlated with each other pursuant to Table 3 does not change the significant levels of these results.

B. Emissions Data

To further explore the relationship between E&S performance and the exogenous increase in common ownership induced by the merger, I examine granular greenhouse gas emissions data used as a component in determining environmental scores. Greenhouse gas emissions are particularly salient in the context of portfolio-wide externalities as they: (1) are objectively easy to ascertain relative to other forms of E&S externalities; (2) give rise to direct (as opposed to indirect) effects on economic performance;[160] and (3) are associated with strong reputational consequences where a firm fails to comply with regulations which target emissions.[161] Indeed, in the field of economics the excess production of greenhouse gases is seen as a classic market failure, where individuals and firms benefit from activities that result in emissions but do not bear all the costs associated with these activities.[162] Accordingly, the reduction of greenhouse gas emissions has a strong potential to increase portfolio value.

To evaluate the relationship between greenhouse gas emissions and the exogenous increase in common ownership induced by the BlackRock-BGI merger, I run a GLM Poisson DiD specification[163] in specification (21) where the dependent variable $Score_{fsjt}$ is replaced with the dependent variable $Emissions_{fsjt}$. $Emissions_{fsjt}$ is a firm-level observation of the metric tons of greenhouse gases emitted by a given firm. I examine four types of greenhouse gas emissions: Carbon Dioxide Emissions, Nitrous Oxide Emissions, Sulfur Dioxide Emissions, and Volatile Organic Compound Emissions.[164] Coefficients from the estimated vector λ are reported in Table 12. I find no evidence that an exogenous increase in common ownership had an impact in reducing greenhouse gas emissions. While some of the relevant coefficients (on the interaction term $Treated_f \times Post_t$) are negative (in Regressions (1), (3) and (4)), all of the reported regressions are not statistically significant from zero. These results also suggest that components distinct from emissions are driving the negative relationship between common ownership and a firm's emission score (Regression (3) in Table (10)). For instance, a firm's emission scores are also dependent on components such as the firm's emissions trading policies, its waste recycling policies, its environmental reduction objectives, as well as its waste reduction initiatives.[165]

---

[160] M Wagner, 'The Role of Corporate Sustainability Performance for Economic Performance: A Firm-level Analysis of Moderation Effects' (2010) 69(7) *Ecological Economics* 1553.

[161] JP Shimshack and MB Ward, 'Regulator Reputation, Enforcement, and Environmental Compliance' (2005) 50(3) *Journal of Environmental Economics and Management* 519.

[162] NO Keohane and SM Olmstead, *Markets* and *the Environment* (Island Press, 2016).

[163] Ciani and Fisher (n 112 above).

[164] See https://www.epa.gov/ghgemissions/overview-greenhouse-gases.

[165] Artikel Refinitiv (n 58 above).

Table 12 GLM Poisson DiD Regressions of Environmental scores on Emissions

| | CO$_2$ Emissions | | | Other Emissions | | | |
	(1) CO$_2$ Emissions (Total)	(2) CO$_2$ Emissions (Direct)	(3) CO$_2$ Emissions (Indirect)	(4) NOx Emissions	(5) SOx Emissions	(6) VOC Emissions	(7) Water Pollutant Emissions
Merger = 1 × Post = 1	-0.226** (0.041)	-0.086 (0.186)	-0.324* (0.065)	0.254 (0.147)	-0.127 (0.518)	-0.574 (0.208)	-2.980*** (0.000)
Log Total Assets	0.429*** (0.000)	0.424*** (0.000)	0.693*** (0.000)	0.369** (0.026)	0.497 (0.201)	-0.214** (0.019)	-2.682 (0.175)
Log Mkt to Bk Ratio	-0.001 (0.992)	-0.000 (1.000)	0.049 (0.379)	-0.034 (0.652)	-0.551*** (0.001)	0.320*** (0.000)	-0.882 (0.536)
Leverage	0.000 (0.898)	-0.000 (0.917)	-0.005 (0.326)	-0.001 (0.935)	0.108** (0.035)	-0.012** (0.038)	-0.159 (0.756)
Return on Assets	-0.186 (0.342)	-0.318 (0.178)	0.547* (0.078)	-0.993 (0.245)	-0.674 (0.208)	-0.137 (0.736)	-17.041* (0.065)
Tangibility	0.034 (0.925)	-0.108 (0.777)	0.249 (0.674)	0.639 (0.523)	2.927** (0.012)	-1.698*** (0.000)	-26.484** (0.018)
Tobin's Q	-0.061 (0.325)	-0.031 (0.725)	-0.037 (0.553)	-0.138 (0.471)	0.083 (0.710)	-0.394*** (0.000)	0.822 (0.562)
Investor HHI	18.684* (0.097)	24.884* (0.090)	-24.944 (0.374)	56.078 (0.117)	-20.505 (0.570)	21.344 (0.378)	-46.639 (0.345)
% Owned by Inst Investors	-0.305 (0.372)	-0.562 (0.170)	1.076 (0.104)	-1.959*** (0.005)	0.800 (0.346)	1.668** (0.028)	-0.198 (0.831)
Observations	1857305	1592225	1547511	528049	495352	393113	169048
Common Owner FE	Yes	Yes	Yes	Yes	Yes	Yes	Yes
Firm FE	Yes	Yes	Yes	Yes	Yes	Yes	Yes
Industry FE	Yes	Yes	Yes	Yes	Yes	Yes	Yes
Year FE	Yes	Yes	Yes	Yes	Yes	Yes	Yes
Chi Square	62.149	36.189	50.527	56.087	41.569	256.200	746.925
Pseudo R Square	0.988	0.991	0.914	0.970	0.960	0.995	0.999

Note: ***p < 0.01, **p < 0.05, *p < 0.10. Standard Errors are double-clustered at the Merger-Firm Level. All Regressors are lagged by one period w.r.t the Dependent Variable.

As mentioned earlier, these findings challenge the results in Azar et al who find a strong and robust negative association between Big Three (institutional) ownership and subsequent carbon emissions among MSCI index constituents.[166] However, as distinguished from Azar et al, my study examines the relationship between common ownership (*cf* institutional ownership) and greenhouse gas emissions, draws on emissions data provided by a different data provider (Refinitiv), includes portfolio firms outside of the MSCI index constituents, and uses a different methodology (the Poisson GLM) to evaluate the aforementioned relationship. As detailed in section IV.A, the use of the Poisson GLM alone may drive differences in estimation results.

Table 13 Variable Definitions

Variables	Description
Log Total Assets	Logarithm of the firm's total assets.
Log Mkt to Bk Ratio	Logarithm of the book value of common equity (market capitalization) scaled by the market value of equity.
Leverage	Total debt scaled by total assets, where total debt is the sum of long-term debt and the debt in current liabilities.
Return on Assets	Net income scaled by total assets.
Tangibility	The firm's Property, Plant and Equipment (PPE) scaled by total assets.
Tobin's Q	The firm's market capitalization plus total debt scaled by total assets.
Investor HHI	The sum of the square of institutional investor's shares in a given firm for a given fiscal year.
% Owned by Inst Investors	The percentage of a firm's shares held by all institutional investors in a given fiscal year.

VI. CONCLUSION

In this chapter, I find a negative relationship between common ownership and E&S performance. This negative relationship is primarily driven by the relationship between common ownership and environmental scores, as opposed to the relationship between common ownership and social scores which is far less robust. These results are ostensibly counter-intuitive – while it is easy to understand why the common ownership hypothesis might not hold for portfolio-wide externalities,[167] it is much more challenging to understand why common ownership has an effect on E&S performance that actively *contradicts* a prior that common owners might be incentivised to internalise portfolio-wide externalities. However, these results are consistent with two distinct forms of collective-action problems where free-riding takes place.

---

[166] Azar et al (n 29 above).
[167] Bebchuk and Hirst (n 15 above); Morley (n 14 above).

The first type of collective action problem involves free-riding problems between common owners and other investors. Recall the discussion of equation (13) in section IV.B.i. A given exogenous increase in $\kappa_f^n(\beta)$ may be attributable to an increase in $\cos[\beta_f, \beta_g]$, a component of common ownership associated with overlapping owner-ship, *or* an increase in $\sqrt{\dfrac{\|\beta_g\|^2}{\|\beta_f\|^2}}$, a component of common ownership associated with the *relative* costs of exercising control rights over multiple firms. Importantly, an exogenous increase in $\kappa_f^n(\beta)$ may be entirely consistent with a *decrease* in a firm's Investor HHI $\|\beta_f\|^2$. If CSR is associated with fixed governance costs, an increase in the level of overlapping ownership without a corresponding increase in Investor HHI could possibly exacerbate collective action problems associated with shareholder monitoring, *reducing* the optimal level of investor engagement with portfolio firms.[168] Indeed, in section IV.B.iii, I find that the BlackRock-BGI merger induced a decrease in Investor HHI for treated firms. Intuitively, an increase in common ownership may lead to an associated *increase in the costs* of internalising portfolio-wide externalities by exacerbating free-riding problems amongst common owners. These problems are particularly salient where an increase in common ownership is largely attributable to an increase in overlapping ownership as opposed to an increase in investor concentration – a hallmark of increasing diversification.[169]

The second type of collective-action problem involves free-riding problems between common owners and other stakeholders who do not partake in ownership of their portfolio firms (eg consumers). This form of free-riding explains the stronger negative relationship between common ownership and environmental scores relative to social scores. Apart from the costs associated with collective action problems in shareholder monitoring, common owners also face many other costs associated with the internalisation of portfolio-wide externalities. However, common owners can also choose which firms to own so as to limit their exposure to these externalities – what Hirschman has termed the tension between 'voice' and 'exit'.[170] A rational common owner will compare the relative costs and benefits in exercising its control rights over portfolio firms (voice) with the same costs and benefits in exercising its rights to sell its shares (exit).[171]

The internalisation of portfolio-wide externalities is essentially a mechanism of voice – to influence the behaviour of its portfolio firms, a common owner will have to expend *some* governance costs to obtain a benefit, presumably in the form of increased portfolio returns. However, if most of the benefits from internalising E&S externalities are borne by consumers rather than portfolio firms (eg if environmental externalities have a higher impact on consumers relative to firms), a common owner might well find it rational to *not* exercise any of its control rights.[172] Intuitively, if the social benefits from exercising the mechanism of voice are much higher relative to the private benefits from doing the same, common owners will underinvest in the

---

[168] Admati et al (n 31 above).

[169] Backus et al (n 4 above).

[170] AO Hirschman, *Exit, Voice, and Loyalty: Responses to Decline in Firms, Organizations, and States* (Harvard University Press, 1970) 25.

[171] S Gehlbach, 'A Formal Model of Exit and Voice' (2006) 18(4) *Rationality and Society* 395.

[172] Khoo (n 17 above).

mechanism of voice relative to the socially optimal level of voice.[173] Here, consumers free-ride on investments by common owners to internalise E&S externalities, disincentivising these investments from being made in the first place.

In contrast, the mechanism of exit may involve far lower costs relative to the exercise of voice, especially in the liquid capital markets in which institutional investors operate. If exit is less costly than voice, one would expect common owners to respond to the presence of E&S externalities by investing in subsets of the economy that are less vulnerable to these externalities, which further reduces the incentives for common owners to intervene via the mechanism of voice (since there are less externalities to internalise in the first place). However, for exit to be a viable mechanism for common owners, common owners must be able to *identify* firms which are less vulnerable to E&S externalities. As this identification process for environmental externalities is considered to be much easier when compared to social externalities,[174] this explains why the negative relationship between common ownership and environmental scores is much stronger as compared to social scores. Indeed, Tallarita finds that common owners invest in subsets of the economy that are relatively less vulnerable to climate risk.[175] In contrast, it may be much more difficult for institutional investors to invest in firms that are less vulnerable to 'social risks', except in relation to targeted events like the Russia-Ukraine war in 2022.[176]

More generally, my results are consistent with a broader literature suggesting the rational passivity of institutional investors[177] and the possibility of 'greenwashing' where green marketing claims do not accurately match firms' conduct.[178] These results are also consistent with the empirical evidence suggesting that while ESG funds elect to invest in funds with strong E&S performance, they fail to induce firm-level changes in E&S conduct.[179] While I do not rule out the potential for the growing ESG movement to change firm behaviour, this chapter provides evidence that meaningful E&S reform does *not* occur through the mechanism of portfolio primacy. Rather, positive changes in E&S policies are likely to be led through other mechanisms which are consistent with shareholder primacy, such as the creation of norms induced by the ESG movement[180] or the adoption of 'E&S conscious' shareholder preferences.[181] Accordingly, policymakers should not rely on portfolio primacy as a panacea in targeting the spectre of climate change.

---

[173] To formalise the aforementioned intuition, consider a simple framework with a single common owner which owns all the firms in a given economy. The total gains from internalising E&S externalities in this stylised world amount to B_S where $B_S = \alpha B_S + (1 - \alpha)B_S$ and α defines the proportion of B_S captured by consumers who do not own any stakes in the institutional investor. Given a (collective) governance cost of G_v associated with the use of voice, a common owner will only engage in internalising portfolio-wide externalities if $G_v \leq (1 - \alpha)B_S$. As $\alpha \to 1$, however, $(1 - \alpha)B_S \to 0$, reducing the probability that voice would be exercised in equilibrium.

[174] P Söderholm and T Sundqvist, 'Pricing Environmental Externalities in the Power Sector: Ethical Limits and Implications for Social Choice' (2003) 46(3) *Ecological Economics* 333.

[175] Tallarita (n 28 above).

[176] Deng et al (n 122 above).

[177] Antón et al (n 32 above).

[178] S Szabo and J Webster, 'Perceived Greenwashing: The Effects of Green Marketing on Environmental and Product Perceptions' (2021) 171(4) *Journal of Business Ethics* 719.

[179] Heath et al (n 33 above).

[180] Katelouzou and Puchniak (n 34 above).

[181] Hart and Zingales (n 35 above).

Part II

Practical Reflections on Investment
Management Stewardship and
Sustainable Finance

9

Responsible Investing: The Status Quo and Remaining Challenges

ANDREW PARRY

I. INTRODUCTION

RECENT YEARS HAVE seen a dramatic surge of interest in the concept of 'responsible investing' and in organisations acting as good stewards of the assets entrusted to them. After many years as a specialist niche, strategies that fall under the broad responsible investing banner – socially responsible, environmental, social and governance (ESG), sustainable and impact being the main examples – have experienced record inflows.

While unprecedented levels of attention have been given to these strategies, there is still confusion over the distinction between each category, with practitioners using terms such as 'ESG' and 'sustainable' interchangeably and according to their own definitions. In this piece, 'responsible investing' is used as an overarching term that embraces the range of different investing approaches that explicitly incorporate environmental and social considerations and consequences, and how these issues are governed. A loose hierarchy can be summarised as ESG as an input, sustainable as the intent and impact as the consequences, with socially responsible investment using values-based exclusions that can be applicable across all these categories. Furthermore, to be truly responsible, investors should also actively cast the proxy votes granted to them and engage constructively with issuers on material environmental, social and governance issues as part of the long-term assessment of financial value.

Investors have found their voices, ushering in a new era of institutional activism across a wide spectrum of social and environmental issues, especially climate change. No longer are asset managers and asset owners absentee landlords. They are increasingly expected to assume greater responsibility for the underlying consequences of their investment decisions, going beyond purely financial returns, and acting as engaged and vocal stewards of client assets in support of their fiduciary duties. The growing demands of clients, financial services regulators and from government policy has spurred investors on and increasingly make it a commercial imperative. These pressures are imposing a broad social obligation on asset managers that has to be reconciled with their fiduciary duty for the production of appropriate risk-adjusted financial returns. The spotlight of responsibility has also been turned inwards, with investment firms now expected to hold themselves to the same – or higher – standards that they demand from the entities in which they invest.

Recognition of these broader responsibilities is not new. Most major religions of the world, as well as many indigenous cultures, have provided guidance, often for millennia, on avoiding usury, proscribing participation in certain business activities – a form of 'negative screening'[1] – and emphasising values associated with a particular faith when investing.[2] The first publicly-traded socially responsible mutual fund, Pax World Wide Fund, was launched in the US in 1971, in part as a reaction to the Vietnam War.

Pivotal in framing the thinking of the modern sustainability movement was the publication in 1987 of the report from the World Commission on Environment and Development, 'Our Common Future'.[3] It set out a pathway to ensure that (economic) development would be sustainable and meet 'the needs of the present without compromising the ability of future generations to meet their own'. But its release coincided with a paradigm shift in socioeconomic thinking: the rise of neo-classical economics, based heavily on the economic theories of Milton Friedman,[4] marked the 1980s as the beginning of the era of the shareholder's interest triumphant over that of stakeholders, and the unquestioned power of market forces. This atmosphere made it difficult for consideration of the World Commission's objectives to gain widespread traction.

Over the next three decades, the world entered a prolonged period of economic growth that helped lift over a billion people out of extreme poverty, increased life expectancy and reduced infant mortality globally, while literacy and access to education expanded, especially for girls. The percentage of people living in democracies also grew significantly.[5] This seemed, to many, to justify the new economic paradigm.

Success, however, can reinforce a belief system and turn it into a rigid dogma that fails to adapt in an increasingly complex and interconnected system. The confidence in market-based solutions solidified. An implicit mindset of growth at any cost pervaded. The shift emphasised the self-interest of the individual versus the collective needs of society, underscoring an increasingly extractive form of economics – not only the increasing assault on the natural world, but also financial extraction through weak antitrust enforcement and erosion of worker rights – that progressively became at odds with environmental and social science.

Early awareness of the dangers of anthropogenic climate change and the need for collective action were snuffed out by political inertia and short-termism, creating incentives in the system that still fail to value natural, human and social inputs equitably, if at all, alongside financial capital. The rewards for making nature and society invisible in economic value led to the increasing cost of the consequences of economic growth being labelled 'externalities': costs with no bearing on financial returns, and which could be therefore ignored.

---

[1] See https://www.unpri.org/an-introduction-to-responsible-investment/an-introduction-to-responsible-investment-screening/5834.article.

[2] See http://www.arcworld.org/downloads/ZUG_Guidelines_to_FCI_2017.pdf.

[3] See https://sustainabledevelopment.un.org/content/documents/5987our-common-future.pdf.

[4] *Capitalism and Freedom*, 40th anniversary edn (University of Chicago Press, 2002).

[5] Source: Our World in Data, https://ourworldindata.org.

It is no surprise that the nascent responsible investing movement that began to develop in earnest in the 1980s failed to get traction in the face of a system where there was little incentive to value anything beyond growth and profit. The lure of the returns to be made by turning a blind eye to the progressively increasing costs to human and natural systems was hard to resist, especially with central banks regularly underpinning growth (and asset prices) through the provision of abundant liquidity.

II. EMERGING SENSE OF PURPOSE

Yet, there appear to be signs of a fundamental shift in thinking about the system that we need to sustain financial, environmental and social well-being.

On 19 August 2019, the Business Roundtable, an association of the chief executive officers of America's largest companies, redefined the purpose of a corporation as being to promote 'an economy that serves all Americans',[6] committing to a move away from the primacy of the shareholder and to a model that included commitment to all stakeholders: customers, employees, suppliers, communities and shareholders. Many saw this as cynical marketing, which was understandable given the unwillingness of some of the signatories to spell out the steps they would take to demonstrate their commitment to a fairer and more balanced approach to business.

What is nonetheless increasingly apparent is the interconnectivity of social and environmental issues with other powerful forces, such as technological disruption, innovation and demographic shifts. The National Intelligence Council (NIC) of the US highlights this confluence in its 2021 Global Trends Report,[7] 'A More Contested World', wherein more traditional geopolitical concerns are set alongside the increasingly evident challenges of climate change and emerging social concerns. The complexity and interdependence of our system is a reminder that the economy does not operate in isolation from the society it is meant to serve and the planet that supports its functioning. The feedbacks loops between the different parts of the system are becoming more visible and disruption is a growing part of economic – and hence financial – life.

Partly as a consequence of these evolving perspectives, the last few years has seen a tsunami of interest in responsible investing. Climate change, once viewed as an externality to the fossil fuel industry, has progressively been internalised into business models, and the COVID crisis recalibrated the way that millions think of work and the value of labour. The breadth and depth of this movement has the potential to reshape the way that we think about the interplay between our economic, social and natural systems.

The investment industry acts as a mirror to the evolving values of civil society (as enacted through its economic wants and needs), and a potential agent for facilitating change. Companies are de facto social enterprises, whether they accept it or not, and increasingly rely on human inputs to maintain their franchise or social licence

---

[6] See https://www.businessroundtable.org/business-roundtable-redefines-the-purpose-of-a-corporation-to-promote-an-economy-that-serves-all-americans.

[7] See https://www.dni.gov/index.php/gt2040-home.

to operate. The reaction to the COVID-19 crisis highlighted divergent perspectives on economic needs, most notably through changing patterns of work.

Interest in sustainability (at the corporate and investor level) is leading to a gradual reappraisal of the concept of 'value', historically looked at through the sole dimension of financial assets. The stakeholder view implies that natural and social inputs, such as land and trees, and health and education – long considered as costs in our economic models – are in fact potential assets, with powerful shared societal-level value.[8] The closed loop nature of the financial system has immured it from the real world and the needs of its beneficiaries through the attractions of scale and the perceived power of markets to make the right choices. This was most vividly illustrated when the world was engulfed by the consequences of the global financial crisis in 2008. The changing dialogue offers hope that the investment industry can become re-attached to the world around it and puncture the gilded bubble in which it has happily dwelt for decades.

A. ESG in Investing

'ESG investing' refers to the inclusion of environmental, social and governance considerations in the investment process, often favouring those opportunities with the best metrics in each category, such as carbon footprint ('E'), labour conditions ('S'), and the proportion of women and minorities in executive positions ('G'). A popular notion in sustainable investment is that because it is oriented to the long term, attention to ESG matters is a proxy for good management, and that companies that do well by its metrics should outperform, on a purely financial level, those that do not.

But 'ESG investing' has always been something of a misnomer, as it suggests an approach that is distinct and divisible from 'normal' investing. At times, in the scramble to demonstrate sustainability virtue, the production of financial returns necessary to meet the saving or retirement needs of individuals is rendered subsidiary to reflection on wider societal goals, or viewed as an automatic outcome from good ESG practices. This subsumes the purpose of asset management and investment, threatening its effectiveness while diluting the effectiveness of responsible investment in attaining its goals. ESG in investing better reflects our role, which is first and foremost to be good investors of other people's money through fully appraising all salient risks and opportunities. ESG in investing, further, allows for a clearer distinction between the concepts of 'ESG integration', 'sustainable' and 'impact' (each discussed in more detail below) in investing: ESG represents a dynamic and nuanced range of inputs across all investment considerations; sustainable is the outcome being sought through the aligned and balanced application of capitals; and impact is the consequence of our actions, both the deliberate intention to contribute to solutions, as well as mitigating the environmental and social cost of our economic activities. ESG then becomes a part of traditional financial analysis, rather than a confusing label, and may even fade away as it just becomes good investment practice.

---

[8] See Trees as infrastructure: Part one (climate-kic.org), 23 March 2020.

B. Reappraisal of Value

A fuller and more consistent appraisal of the value of natural and social considerations, alongside financial capital, thereby creates a more logical framework that more appropriately integrates broader societal aspirations in investment decisions. But there is a caveat, as it requires wider society to value those same considerations in their own economic behaviours.

Smoking is a classic example of a potential disconnect. The well-documented dangers (and associated economic costs to society) of tobacco smoking have been known for decades and led to the exclusion of tobacco stocks in many portfolios. Yet smoking, while now in steady decline, continues and tobacco stocks historically delivered strong returns, in part helped by tax increases that masked underlying price increases. Reconciling the apparent contradiction between what society perceives as 'investing for good' with actual economic choices being made by society is not as straightforward as it is sometimes presented.

A well-known 'value/action gap problem' can also be created whereby investing in an ESG or sustainable investment fund may have the perverse outcome of increasing acceptance of environmentally or socially damaging activities by removing the moral burden of individual action. The promotion of climate indices and funds, as well as carbon offsetting, is a case in point. They may give the individual a warm glow of virtue, but if it is then used to justify the continuation of carbon intensive activities, such as flying (individuals) or oil extraction (companies), then the outcome is counter to the headline intention. If the lack of clear causal connection between the construction of an equity climate portfolio with real world carbon reduction outcomes is added into the mix, then the danger is amplified. Unwittingly it provides moral licence to continue with damaging behaviour in the mistaken belief that their investments or offsets are reducing actual emissions.

A common mistake is to mix up second order effects – what portfolio managers are changing – with the underlying activities of companies, which is where the actual environmental and social consequences of business choices occur. Simply buying shares in an equity fund, for example, has no direct causal effect on the carbon emitted by the underlying companies held in the portfolio, as few listed companies use share issuance to directly fund green growth. In 2021, abundant COVID-related monetary and fiscal stimulus led to a boom year for capital markets, with over US\$12 trillion of equity and debt financed raised and record fees for global investment banks.[9] While some of the fresh capital raised was linked to sustainable finance, the vast majority was used to fund growth, with soaring levels of merger and acquisition activity and company flotations.

C. Beyond the Hype

The danger is that 'ESG investing' has become a marketing buzzword, enabling some to cynically leverage the label to gather assets (with exaggerated claims of the real

[9] See https://www.ft.com/content/c656c3da-f5db-41f4-942b-1ed6de9c2d60?shareType=nongift.

world effects they can bring about), or – worse – implying that ESG investing alone will bring more favourable returns. Most individuals advocating responsible investing are passionate about delivering a better and more balanced world, but financial organisations have strong profit motives, through following the flow of money and scaling assets under management. Issue-driven activists push an agenda that is (often rightly) linked to important specific causes but they share no responsibility for the financial outcome born by investors and are at times at odds with financial activists focusing more squarely on financial outcomes.[10]

Over-emphasising poorly defined ESG characteristics alone at the expense of sound investment practices thereby risks shuffling the deckchairs on the Titanic while ending up with sub-optimal financial results for clients.

At the end of 2021 a public spat between Bloomberg and MSCI, two powerful firms in financial data provision, highlighted the increasingly vigorous debate on the purpose and benefits of ESG scores that have played such a central role in responsible investing thus far.[11] In an article published in December 2021 and titled 'The ESG Mirage', Bloomberg provocatively stated that ESG scores (as provided by MSCI and others) did not measure real world environmental or social impacts, but were a gauge of the potential bottom-line cost for companies. Reconciling normalised scoring methodologies for assessing 'best-in-class' corporate ESG performance with real world consequences lies at the heart of how the responsible investing industry will evolve from here. The fact that companies employ third-party consultants to optimise their self-disclosed ESG data to improve their ratings underscores the danger of emphasising methodology over purpose.[12]

The rise of sustainable and impact as emerging forms of responsible investing is part of a recognition that the industry needs to move beyond the use of ESG as an abstracted acronym and one-dimensional score. The development of new ways of understanding the economic value of social and natural capitals in a complex system is central to this aspiration. This entails shifting the perception of value away from a transactional force, based on competition and market share, to something more collaborative and open source. The willingness to share information and insights is a welcome part of sustainable and impact investing, and has fostered a deeper understanding of the issues, especially the necessity to operate on a smaller and more local scale than has been traditional. Collaboration should become the new growth paradigm for the next stage of responsible investing overall.

D. Reshaping the World

Powerful trends continue to be at work in the global economy, such as technology shifts, geopolitical tensions and the possible return of persistent inflation.

---

[10] See https://www.ft.com/content/0e5a0373-ee69-438a-9026-4588338f6ee4?shareType=nongift.

[11] See https://www.bloomberg.com/graphics/2021-what-is-esg-investing-msci-ratings-focus-on-corporate-bottom-line/.

[12] See https://www.responsible-investor.com/articles/adani-ports-and-its-cdp-score-the-problem-with-self-disclosure.

ESG considerations can only ever be part of understanding the fluid set of forces shaping future economic and financial outcomes, even if these are increasingly entangled with economic and political choices. Climate change is already a potent economic consideration, and deeply entangled in politics through the rise of competing green policies. Governments are keen to support innovation and a successful transition to a low carbon future, but they are conscious of countervailing pressures from wildly developing national incentives, especially in lower incomes countries or in fossil fuel backed states. Competition will dictate the pace and shape of the transition curve, reenforcing the need for global collaboration and the correct incentives in the system, if net zero ambitions are to be met.

Often what the critics (and even advocates) of the sustainable approach to investing fail to grasp is that it is not about agreeing a common taxonomy and crystal-clear definitions of still vague terms and a set of deterministic outcomes. There are no simple 'win-win' solutions; trade-offs and compromise are going to be part of the messy solution in the real world. Regulation will be needed alongside innovation and activism, and will form part of an evolving system. The strength of the interest in sustainability is in the plurality of its conception and that it is diffuse across economic sectors, social constructs and regional boundaries.

Even Milton Friedman knew that markets need boundaries and must reflect broader values of society. While his famous 1970 *New York Times* essay exhorted businesses 'to make as much money as possible', what is often omitted is the rest of the sentence: *'while conforming to the basic rules of the society, both those embodied in law and those embodied in ethical custom'* (emphasis added).[13] What was not fully appreciated at the time was how much Friedman's doctrine would shift thinking on those customs and define an age. Can the rise of sustainable finance mark a doctrinal shift that ushers in a new economic paradigm and is backed by guardrails of law and regulation that reflect the evolving values of society? Or is it merely a maintenance of the status quo?

For the investment world to make this metamorphosis will require going beyond the incrementalism of ESG labels and reducing harm, to regeneration and transformation, as seen through the conduit of business and economic models. In an industry that thrives (and is handsomely rewarded) on scale, methodology and efficiency, this is a daunting task. But given that it touches every part of the system and is an intimately embedded part of the society of people that is serves, the investment industry has the potential to act as a powerful enabler of change and adaptive regeneration.

Impact investing may still be a tiny proportion of the total invested assets in the world, but it is having an outsized influence in the thinking of the broader sustainable, and even traditional, investing world. Thinking is shifting away from inputs and outputs (associated with ESG) to real world outcomes and consequences. It is also introducing an emerging understanding of complex, integrated systems, that better informs the management of emergent risks, alongside the awareness of new opportunities in an adaptive and non-linear world.

---

[13] See https://www.nytimes.com/1970/09/13/archives/a-friedman-doctrine-the-social-responsibility-of-business-is-to.html.

E. Beyond ESG

A not untypical claim of major investment firms is that they have been doing ESG for 30 years, which is ironic as the term was coined in the materiality report of the UN Environment Programme Finance Initiative (UNEP FI) – published in 2004.[14] It was more formally adopted in 2006, when the UN launched the Principles for Responsible Investment (UN PRI), which, from a founding signatory list of 63 organisations, now boasts more than 4,000 signatories with collective assets under management of over US$121 trillion.[15]

No longer do investment managers have to justify why they consider ESG issues when making investment choices. Today, it is the opposite.

Yet, despite the recent successes, we are still at the start of a journey. The objective was never supposed to be inflow of new assets. Responsible investing had a broader objective: to be part of evolving the system to become more resilient, fairer and ultimately sustainable. Robust (but not necessarily better) long-term financial outcomes should follow because of the improved health and equity of the overall economic system.

Just as the industry appears to have finally started to embrace its wider social and ecological responsibilities, it has been challenged from within[16] and without[17] for potentially misleading claims on the real-world influence achieved by so called 'ESG investing'. Poor standards, inconsistencies and exaggerated claims have become foci of regulators in the US and UK.

In a way, this can be read as good news, as it indicates a growing maturity in the debate even with insatiable client demand for sustainable investment opportunities. But a dilution of standards may result from the need to meet rapidly increasing demand and threaten the entire enterprise. The emergence of so-called climate-orientated strategies that are crammed with fossil fuel stocks and have a correlation of nearly 1.0 with indices such as the S&P 500 are a case in point.

The financial system is a conduit for the flow of capital within the economy and the better outcomes implied remain highly conditional on what society itself wants and values. Finance is not the sole arbiter of those outcomes or a replacement for elected governments; it acts as an enabler and amplifier of collective values. The debate on sustainable investment, therefore, needs to moved beyond the aspirational and to be clearer in the boundaries between what can be delivered through investing responsibly and what needs to lie in the hands of policy makers. For major corporations, the governance of their social and environmental behaviours will become paramount.

---

[14] See https://www.euromoney.com/article/294dqz2h1pqywgbyh3zls/esg/the-united-nations-free-thinkers-who-coined-the-term-esg-and-changed-the-world.

[15] See UN, 'Secretary-General launches "Principles for Responsible Investment" backed by world's largest investors' (27 April 2006), https://press.un.org/en/2006/sg2111.doc.htm.

[16] See https://www.cnbc.com/2021/08/24/blackrocks-former-sustainable-investing-chief-says-esg-is-a-dangerous-placebo.html.

[17] See https://www.sec.gov/files/esg-risk-alert.pdf.

F. A Taxing Taxonomy

In a strange twist, the EU's laudable sustainable business and finance taxonomy (Taxonomy)[18] and associated Sustainable Finance Disclosure Regulation (SFDR)[19] threaten to encourage greenwashing. The Taxonomy was designed to support the transition to a more sustainable economic system through the acceleration of the allocation of capital to sustainable activities, and to help stamp out greenwashing through transparent and consistent disclosure.

It and the SFDR provide a strong conceptual framework for thinking about sustainable investing: identify eligible sustainable activities; demonstrate the degree of alignment with these activities; report any adverse impacts for balance; set minimum standards to do no significant harm; and act as good stewards through proxy voting and engagement with investee entities to ensure that good standards of social and governance practices are maintained. As a conceptual framework this works well.

The problem is that turning a framework into a prescriptive investment taxonomy involves a monumental volume of reporting of data that is not widely available, and creates inbuilt rigidity that will be slow to adapt to evolving best practices. Until the data challenge is solved, it can be seen as a great recipe but with no ingredients.

In-scope investment management firms will report their Principle Adverse Impacts at the entity level under the SFDR requirements for the first time on or before 30 June 2023 (for the reference period 1 January to 31 December 2022). It is proposed that the companies in which they invest will follow a year later. Part of the reporting regime is the self-determined disclosure of whether a fund falls into those that are deemed most sustainable. This puts fund managers in a dilemma: either miss out on new business or be accused of misrepresentation. Clients are demanding the higher classifications, Articles 8 and 9, but these are disclosures, not labels, and the definitions are subject to a wide and varied degree of interpretation, with limited available data to support claims. Reporting, therefore, has the potential to become an incentive for greenwashing and highlights some of the dangers of an overly prescriptive approach to sustainable investing before the information from the underlying entities is available. This potential pitfall is a symptom of clients' demand for more: The requirement for transparency and alignment with sustainable topics is growing, but the necessary data, especially related to causal outcomes, can be sparse and, when available, is often unaudited, estimated and opaque.

Despite the dearth of supporting data or the availability of new investment opportunities to build 'sustainable' funds significantly different to existing strategies, there is now a rush to repurpose existing funds or launch new funds to meet client demand. But launching additional sustainable funds does not magically expand the number of available investment opportunities, even in private markets, or immediately funnel a supply of new capital to green activities. As of July 2022, only one listed company in the EU, Acciona SA, was reporting non-financial information aligned to the EU taxonomy.

---

[18] See https://ec.europa.eu/info/business-economy-euro/banking-and-finance/sustainable-finance/eu-taxonomy-sustainable-activities_en.

[19] See https://eur-lex.europa.eu/legal-content/EN/TXT/?uri=celex%3A32019R2088.

According to the final report on the forthcoming taxonomy regulation from the European Securities and Markets Authority (ESMA), published in February 2021,[20] there is a marked mismatch between the available Taxonomy-aligned activities at the revenue level versus the scale of sustainable funds. ESMA found that only 2.5 per cent of the revenue in EU 27 countries reported under the Non-Financial Reporting Directive (NFRD) was aligned with the Taxonomy. While these figures are expected to grow, as the Taxonomy is designed to redirect capital flows, this takes time and leaves very few aligned activities through which investors can demonstrate material, tangible alignment with their sustainability goals. This challenge is particularly acute in public equities, which over the last 30 years have seen a marked fall in the number of listed stocks globally, and rarely do companies raise capital for investment through new share issuance.[21]

Claims that the EU has already watered down the environmental standards under pressure from individual member states and carbon-intensive industry bodies has brought another degree of uncertainty to the Taxonomy.[22] The European Parliament voted in July 2022 to allow the inclusion of specific nuclear and gas energy activities in the EU Taxonomy's list of environmentally sustainable economic activities despite the science being unequivocal that gas is nearly as harmful as coal when flaring, methane leaks and other greenhouse gases are taken into account.[23] Concerns have also been raised that intensive farming will be deemed sustainable.[24] Even in the sustainable space, lobbying remains a potent force.

However these issues are resolved, we need to ensure that a radical transparency transpires. We must highlight not just the benefits but also the costs of our collective actions. Marketing materials and investment reports freely highlight the positives (often poorly justified), but ignore the negatives that come with any human activity. We need more willingness to calculate and reveal the challenges of a pro-growth system and what that means for delivering a sustainable system. Sustainability impact reporting needs radical transparency based on honesty and clarity.

III. FROM SUSTAINABLE TO IMPACTFUL

The capacity and opportunity exist to create new models designed to finance and facilitate change, which is why the rise of impacting investing in recent years has potentially profound consequences. If ESG in investing was a niche activity a decade ago, impact investing – a term coined in 2007 to describe investments designed to

---

[20] See https://www.esma.europa.eu/sites/default/files/library/esma30-379-471_final_report_-_advice_on_article_8_of_the_taxonomy_regulation.pdf.

[21] See MarketWatch, 'The number of companies publicly traded in the US is shrinking' (30 October 2020), https://www.marketwatch.com/story/the-number-of-companies-publicly-traded-in-the-us-is-shrinkingor-is-it-2020-10-30#:~:text=Since%20peaking%20at%20around%208%2C000%20sometime%20in%20the,6%2C000%20companies%20trade%20on%20the%20NYSE%20and%20Nasdaq.

[22] See https://euobserver.com/climate/151437.

[23] See https://www.nationalgeographic.com/science/article/super-potent-methane-in-atmosphere-oil-gas-drilling-ice-cores.

[24] See https://www.fairr.org/article/investor-letter-eu-taxonomy/.

generate both financial and social returns – was a nascent network of innovators.[25] According to the 2020 Annual Impact Investor Survey from the Global Impact Investing Network (GIIN), the impact market has an estimated size of US$715 billion globally and is growing rapidly.[26] The lens of understanding the impact of our investment decisions – the costs to the world around us and the solutions to challenges – is simultaneously driving innovation and accountability. While impact investing had its origins in efforts to scale philanthropy by combining financial returns alongside delivering social benefits, its most powerful contribution has been to create a nascent network of social and environmental innovators.

The network effect that impact investing has created is having an outsized influence on the thinking of the broader sustainable, and even traditional, investing world. It is now permissible to discuss social and environmental consequences in investing.

Impact has opened up a range of innovative developments in finance and helped foster an historically unseen level of collaboration in the investment industry. The mainstream has benefited from growing interaction between social entrepreneurs, academics, non-government organisations, activists, development finance and UN agencies. Many of these have turned into new collaborative initiatives, such as the Institutional Investors Group on Climate Change (IIGCC),[27] Task Force on Nature-related Financial Disclosure (TNFD)[28] and Carbon Tracker.[29] These have generated shared learning and emerging awareness that have helped recalibrate the thinking of asset managers, asset owners and banks.

While the full scaling of impact has not yet occurred, this may prove to be a good thing. A wide chasm of real-world intent and practice still separates the philanthropist or social entrepreneur from the institutional asset manager. While 'sustainable' appears to be progressively replacing 'ESG' as a label in the mainstream world of investing, the adoption of 'impact' as fund title needs to be handled with more care.

Instead, the shared learning from the impact space has been more about an evolving understanding of the context of the complex web of influences, incentives and opportunities that the world has to offer investors. The Impact Management Project helped build a broad consensus on understanding the components of impact through the five dimensions of evaluation: the 'What', 'Who', 'How much', 'Contribution' and 'Risk' of a company's activities.[30] Trying to impose 'scale' on impact through a product lens misses the point that impact investing takes many different forms according to the context of the opportunity. Impact strategies that allocate new capital to projects that otherwise would not have happened – the 'additionality' that is the essential measure of successful impact investing – are inherently difficult to scale, even in private markets.

Impact investing has also shaped business' thinking of the cost of our actions. Markets typically apply cost-benefit analysis through the distorted lens of profits and

---

[25] See https://engage.rockefellerfoundation.org/story-sketch/the-rockefeller-foundation-weaving-ties-and-building-a-backbone-to-accelerate-impact-investing/.

[26] See https://thegiin.org/research/publication/impinv-survey-2020#charts.

[27] See https://www.iigcc.org.

[28] See https://www.fsb-tcfd.org.

[29] See https://carbontracker.org.

[30] See https://impactmanagementproject.com/impact-management/impact-management-norms/.

growth, which fails to capture the known costs of human activities on the environment or health. The general invisibility of nature and social consequences in financial accounting, however, is starting to change. Here, the investment industry has an important role to play and has been increasingly calling for mechanisms to remove the asymmetry in financial reporting to include the wider costs to the other considerations, such as the consequences for natural and social systems.

The asset management industry is increasingly exploring ways to build accountability for achieving net-zero system across the investment value chain, alongside a better understanding of the risks and opportunities in business models.[31] Task Force on Climate-related Financial Disclosure (TCFD),[32] for example, is becoming adopted globally as the top-down framework for climate risk scenario modelling, whereby companies assess which of their assets are at risk under various climate change projections, and to what degree. Importantly, in June 2021, the Board of the International Organization of Securities Commissions (IOSCO) published its vision for how the financial sector could 'support the transition to a more sustainable future' through the creation of an International Sustainability Standards Board under the auspices of the International Financial Reporting Standards (IFRS) Foundation.[33] In time, this will provide a consistent framework for understanding sustainability risks more fully in business models and remove the 'invisibility of nature' from financial disclosures. Whether 'accountants will save the world', only time will tell.[34]

Lawyers, however, may well be the emerging force providing substance to the sustainability movement. The significance of the changing legal interpretation of shifts in civil society's values are generally misunderstood and hence underestimated. The landmark victory in May 2021 of climate activists against Royal Dutch Shell is set to have profound implications for perceptions of risks in carbon intensive industries, and has triggered a wave of similar litigation.[35] Dutch lawyer, Roger Cox, based his case largely on the argument that the 1992 UN Framework Convention on Climate Change created a legal requirement for the 163 signatory countries to prevent 'dangerous anthropogenic interference with the climate'. As the science becomes more unequivocal about the human cause of climate change, this ruling has recalibrated the debate and provided a framework for other litigators to hold governments, companies and investors accountable for national commitments made at the COP26 climate conference.

New Zealand support of Maori beliefs has gone further and started to enshrine the rights of nature in law by giving giving legal personhoods status to natural features, such as rivers. This has been echoed elsewhere, in countries such as Ecuador and Bolivia, as well as by municipalities in the US. Acknowledging the legal status of nature is an important step towards being able to place tangible value on it that can be reported alongside traditional financial assets.

---

[31] See https://www.cfany.org/event/carbon-quotient-building-accountability-for-net-zero-across-the-investment-value-chain/.

[32] See https://www.fsb-tcfd.org.

[33] See https://www.iosco.org/library/pubdocs/pdf/IOSCOPD678.pdf.

[34] See https://www.ifac.org/knowledge-gateway/contributing-global-economy/discussion/can-public-sector-accountants-help-save-world-yes-we-can-and-here-s-why.

[35] See https://www.ft.com/content/c656c3da-f5db-41f4-942b-1ed6de9c2d60?shareType=nongift.

The EU too recognises the importance of financial reporting to include clear and verifiable information to support the sustainability objectives of its Taxonomy as an enabler of the European Green Deal. The simple removal of the inaccurate and somewhat derogatory term 'non-financial' from sustainability reporting is a welcome development, as the historic association of ESG-related issues as being financially immaterial has long needed dispelling. Financial and economic fundamentals still matter, if the savings and retirement objectives of clients are to be met. Any social or environmental benefit will prove short-lived if a corporation fails. If fossil fuels are to be eradicated from our system, as the Intergovernmental Panel on Climate Change and other multilateral organisations insist is a necessary condition for a sustainable system, does an investor – whether ESG-minded or not – want to invest in a company that is headed over a financial cliff? We must never forget that we are investors. Good business models still matter.

Another important development is the 'democratisation' of ESG-related data. A Global Climate Transition Centre from the Transition Pathway Initiative, a new, asset owner-led initiative, will provide free and publicly available data on the alignment of 10,000 companies with the net-zero pathway, and plans to add data on sovereign bonds and corporate debt issuers. The cost of ESG data (and its inconsistencies across providers[36]) has long been an issue for the widespread adoption of ESG-related considerations in investing. Even large pension funds struggle to afford the multiple sources of data needed to build robust insights that are not reliant on one third-party firm. Given the increasing power of ESG data providers, their regulation seems likely. The financial sector needs to be mindful of the lessons from other industries, where dominance by a small number of players has led to diminishing choice for consumers, higher prices and stalling innovation.

The developments in the provision of affordable and more consistent sustainability data is an important step in raising consciousness of the value of the full range of inputs deployed in the modern economic system. Formalising this information alongside traditional accounting numbers also allows the investment industry to take a step towards a more connected approach to managing and understanding the trade-offs in the system. Rather than aligning itself with a standardised methodology of what a normalised form of good looks like, the industry would be better served by balanced and open reporting of its exposure to the full range of risks and opportunities represented in the wider economy. Removing asymmetry in reporting helps breaks the log jam of inertia in the system.

IV. REMAINING CHALLENGES

The investment industry has still a lot of hurdles to surmount if it is to meet the ambitions of system change implicit in the sustainability movement. 'ESG investing', with an excessive focus on methodology, normalisation and labelling, encouraged stasis by being too disassociated from formative change. 'Best-in-class' in a degenerative system will never be enough. If it continues to pursue scale and look for normative

---

[36] See https://papers.ssrn.com/sol3/papers.cfm?abstract_id=3438533.

approaches to sustainable investing, then it will fail the commons that it ultimately serves. Blended finance, for example, can be a powerful tool for mobilising capital for good, but if it is simply a tool for asset managers to scale difficult to reach market opportunities by socialising losses through government guarantees, then it is merely self-serving.

Perhaps the biggest challenge for the investment industry is creating the right perspective for its ambitions and purpose. 'Maximising returns' still plays a role in a system that measures success by growth. Quality versus quantity of growth remains a difficult topic for investors to manage.

The investment industry is making progress and increasingly can lead by example through defining its own sense of purpose and the governance of its own business. More progress needs to be made on equity, inclusion and diversity, where the industry is a laggard. Improvements in practice can set examples to the entities in which we invest client assets that the goals and aspirations that we have for their behaviour are the ones we set for ourselves. On environmental issues too, especially climate, investment firms will need to set the standard by conducting TCFD reporting, integrated climate risk management, policies on use of renewable energy and curbing excess corporate travel.

Perhaps more telling will be the evolving nature of stewardship and stakeholder management, aligned with sustainable principles. Voting, engagement and public policy advocacy have seen the fastest area of growth in the investment industry and no longer are asset managers and asset owners the 'silent majority'. Indeed, they are now being urged to become loud advocates for change, expected to act as truly engaged owners of assets and recognise their broader societal responsibilities. One of the benefits of this approach is that it will encourage less short-termism. High levels of portfolio turnover have never been compatible with sustainable investing or with good stewardship, as aligned voting and engagement are difficult to achieve if a security is held for weeks or months. Index managers (and universal asset owners) are the ultimate long-term owners, which is why their increased involvement in engagement is major advance after years of passive (or absent) approaches to voting. The growing success of a number of important climate change-related proxy voting campaigns with major oil and gas companies in 2021, for example, is evidence of index managers' changing attitudes.

Yet, the 'own and engage' approach comes with caveats, as it favours scale and legitimises a passive approach to investing. If there is no sanction on the bad behaviour of a company from investors actively shunning or selling their securities, the effectiveness of engagement can be severely diminished. It is still, moreover, an open question whether investor engagement can really make a bad company good.

Still, the appetite for engaged stewardship by the investment industry is a signal to governments and regulators that they are pushing on an open door if they want to change social and environmental policy through the guardrails of regulation and law.

The developing arena of stewardship, in which virtually all investors are becoming activists, also raises a question of accountability and the role of collective bodies, versus individual managers, to effect change. If we wish to retain a rich ecosystem of investor perspectives, we need to ensure that the role of stewardship is set in the context of the role of individual firms and that we do not impose a monoculture that again favours scale and further consolidates the industry into the hands of ever fewer players.

Individual firms are increasingly being asked for the outcomes of their engagement activities and what they have specifically changed. But few engagements can be successful in isolation and might take many years to succeed. As the range of issues on which managers are expected to engage expands and becomes more specialist, the challenge of resources becomes a major factor.

There also needs to be more nuance of what is expected for the different classes of investors and the approach taken, including the role of divestment versus engagement. The marked difference in the approach of active versus passive managers is a case in point. The breadth and complexity of issues that many clients expect managers to tackle is ideally suited to the index business, given its breadth of exposure and fixed positions (beyond flows). For active managers, the situation is somewhat more complex. They have the added responsibility of delivering better returns than the index. ESG integration, sustainability intent or stewardship should be dynamic and not passive activities; the growing imperative for sustainable investing should therefore benefit active managers who can demonstrate clear intent.

Their challenge – especially smaller managers' – is to balance the competing needs between stewardship, reporting and investing (not that they are contradictory). For active managers, engagement should be a feedback loop that is an integrated part of the investment process, with the power to negate as well as reinforce the investment case. They should be in a strong position to understand and benefit from making selective and limited choices about the winners that will emerge as a consequence of the seismic forces reshaping our world. Increasingly, these will involve the environmental and social dimensions.

While it can be argued that the only true form of impact in public equity markets is engagement, we should not view it as a panacea for every societal ill. Outsourcing the responsibility for limiting emissions to the private sector alone is potentially fraught with consequences on accountability, governance and, more importantly, on effectiveness. The last 40 years has seen a progressive erosion of the developed world's guardrails (ie regulation and law) that limit the exploitation of society and nature. The US Federal Trade Commission has repeatedly ignored the consolidation of monopoly power, which is indeed now venerated; meanwhile, environmental and labour standards have been dismantled. Activists have turned to finance to punish companies that act in response to these developments in their immediate favour (and for which many of them lobbied and donated), but this indicates a misunderstanding of finance's role as a conduit of other people's money to gain financial returns – not to replace elected governments.

Many investors are ill-equipped to handle this burden, and it is not clear that – even if they are to shoulder it – their actions will precipitate the necessary changes. Governments more than anyone will dictate the shape of the energy transition curve and must ensure it is aligned with the best science available. If that curve is too shallow and back-end loaded to 2050, then the risks of a climate catastrophe rise dangerously.

Active managers do not divest; they simply avoid the majority of the names available in the market as they select the ones in which they see opportunities. Engagement, along with sustainability of business and economic models, will represent opportunities to step away from the consensus and recognise the powerful evolutionary forces at work, an approach that will work across asset classes and over time: in effect, putting ESG back into investing, rather than seeing ESG investing as a separate product line.

A. Adaptive Regeneration

The Royal Society of Arts in a 2021 report on sustainability in the fashion industry – a sector where the conflicts and need for balance are clear – used the analogy of a rain-forest for a better understanding of how complex system can build resilient futures.[37] Rainforests thrive on complexity and symbiotic relationships, from niche species on the forest flowers to the giant trees providing the canopy. Each has a role to play that evolves and adapts over time. So it should be with the investment world: a complex, adaptive system with symbiotic relationships forged on the understanding that there is no single approach or perspective that should dominate.

In an important report published in July 2021 jointly by the PRI, UNEP FI and The Generation Foundation and authored by Freshfields Bruckhaus Deringer, 'A Legal Framework for Impact',[38] the concept of sustainability impact in investor decision-making was introduced. From the organisations that introduced the acro-nym 'ESG' to the world, we now have the starting point for what comes 'beyond ESG'. The system is calling for change and the investment industry is a major agent for enabling that change, as long as it embraces a plurality of perspective and regenera-tion over the status quo.

B. Watershed

Responsible investing is at a watershed. After a long period in the wilderness it has come of age and the industry has been rewarded with a flood of money into a broadening array of responsible investing products. Systemically important matters, such as climate change, income inequality and antitrust abuses, regularly appear in discussions at trustee meetings and in stewardship reports. A growing, though not yet universal, social obligation, backed by increased regulatory imperatives, is ensuring that asset management firms are committing considerable resources to broadening and deepening their responsible investing activities. Veritably, billions are turning into trillions.[39]

But have those trillions provided the radical redirection of development finance to developing countries envisaged by the World Bank and International Monetary Fund in their 2015 report, 'From Billions to Trillions'? Launching new or relabelled sustain-able or ESG funds may align with client demand, and the 17 Sustainable Development

---

[37] See https://www.thersa.org/reports/regenerative-futures-from-sustaining-to-thriving-together.
[38] See https://www.unpri.org/policy/a-legal-framework-for-impact.
[39] See https://thedocs.worldbank.org/en/doc/622841485963735448–0270022017/original/DC20150002E FinancingforDevelopment.pdf.

Goals make for colourful marketing collateral, but the flow of new capital to pressing underserved or unmet social and environmental challenges remains pedestrian. System change is a complex endeavour and not automatically solved by fresh fund labels, taxonomies or standardised disclosures. To achieve the ambitions of sustainability impact, while delivering robust financial returns needs, the financial services industry has to move beyond scale for its own benefit – linear, incremental and mechanistic – to embrace a more collaborative, complex approach that recognises a plurality of approaches, with adaptation and regeneration at its heart.

The global financial crisis and the later COVID crisis saw economic and market recoveries fuelled by ambitious crisis-management policies. Yet those responses served to widen social divisions, solidify quasi-monopolies, and failed to grasp widely acknowledged environmental challenges; the inability to agree a coordinated response to climate change at COP26 in Glasgow was a case in point. The failure by policy makers to correctly align incentives in the system with rhetoric remains a frustration for delivering better sustainability impacts and a distorting influence on sustainable investing ambitions.

Despite these concerns, there are signs amidst the hyperbole that progress is being made and change is beginning: Collaboration across the actors in the sustainability movement – investors, academics, corporations, entrepreneurs and activists – is rising and contributing important shared learning and challenging entrenched dogma, even if there is still marked disagreement. Innovation, not only in the use of new forms of technology, but also through developments in financing techniques and social entrepreneurship, is expanding the areas of influence in which investors can operate and generate a real impact. Active stewardship has not only increased the accountability placed on corporations and governments for the consequences of their actions, it has forced investment management firms to look inwards, challenging their own practices and contribution to broader society. New thinking on the concept of 'value' is extending beyond financial capital to tentatively embrace natural and social assets, aided by accountants and lawyers, who are emerging as powerful contributors to sustainability impact.

While many think that system change can only come from the top down, that is rarely the case. Embedded actors in the system are coming together to create the groundswell of a collaborative movement that influences policy making. For investment firms, this must neither be a convenient marketing label nor an overlay divorced from their primary function of producing returns to support the saving and retirement needs of their client, if they are to fulfil their sustainability ambitions. They will need to look inwards first and determine their own intentional impact opportunities, and then look outwards to embrace the complexity of a highly interconnected and adaptive system. Only then can we go beyond the inertia of current approaches to ESG.

10

The Future of Stewardship: Time to Take a Step Back[1]

I. INTRODUCTION

ALONG WITH RESPONSIBLE investment, focused on the integration of environmental, social and governance (ESG) factors, stewardship of investors has become mainstream over the last few years. This has been driven by the development of best practice following the launch of the Principles for Responsible Investment (PRI) in 2006,[2] regulatory developments, such as the launch of the first Stewardship Code in the UK in 2010[3] and the coming into force of the revised Shareholder Rights Directive in 2017,[4] and the growing interest in ESG issues, most notably the climate crisis.

Historically, stewardship related to public equities has been considered as the activity that follows investment in a company, in the sense of 'active ownership', as defined in Principle 2 of the PRI. Active ownership can be defined as the use of the rights and the position gained from a shareholding to influence the governance, the activities or behaviours of investee companies. However, with the launch of the 2020 version of the UK Stewardship Code, the concept is defined much more broadly today, encompassing asset allocation and investment processes.

There is reasonable evidence to suggest that the practice of stewardship has improved over the last decade and many large asset owners and managers now employ stewardship professionals and produce a considerable amount of reporting.

[1] The author would like to thank Iris Chiu, Gary Greenberg and Marcel Jeucken for their extremely helpful comments on an early version of this chapter, which was completed in June 2022. The author bears responsibility for all errors and omissions. The views expressed in this chapter are personal opinions of the author and do not represent those of organisations he is affiliated with in a professional capacity.

[2] Principles for Responsible Investment (PRI), https://www.unpri.org/pri/what-are-the-principles-for-responsible-investment.

[3] FRC, 'The UK Stewardship Code' (July 2010), https://www.frc.org.uk/getattachment/e223e152-5515-4cdc-a951-da33e093eb28/UK-Stewardship-Code-July-2010.pdf.

[4] Directive (EU) 2017/828 of the European Parliament and of the Council of 17 May 2017 amending Directive 2007/36/EC as regards the encouragement of long-term shareholder engagement (Text with EEA relevance).

However, it is questionable whether more activity and reporting translate into effectiveness in practice in the form of stewardship-related outcomes, including the prevention of corporate governance failures and significant changes in the activities and behaviours of companies.

The sentiment about the status quo of stewardship practice in the UK was summarised in an unusually damning assessment of the impact of the original UK Stewardship Code published within a wider independent review of the Financial Reporting Council (FRC) in December 2018.[5] John Kingman, who led the review, described it as 'a major and well-intentioned intervention' but 'not effective in practice'[6] and concluded: 'If the Code remains simply a driver of boilerplate reporting, serious consideration should be given to its abolition'.[7] While floating the possibility of abolishing the Stewardship Code was an unexpected consideration, not least given the fact that it had been used as a blueprint around the world, the Kingman Review's assessment of stewardship reporting resonated with readers of stewardship disclosures.

The Kingman Review suggested that 'a fundamental shift in approach is needed to ensure that the revised Stewardship Code more clearly differentiates excellence in stewardship'.[8] Most importantly, it recommended: 'It should focus on outcomes and effectiveness, not on policy statements'.[9] Following extensive consultation by both the FRC and the Financial Conduct Authority (FCA) in 2019, a much-revised Stewardship Code was launched in the UK in 2020.[10]

The FRC's review of the first reporting under the UK Stewardship Code 2020[11] (SC 2020) confirms significant improvements in application by signatories, but there is still a long way to go in evidencing the effectiveness and impact of stewardship activities.

Against this backdrop, we argue in this chapter that to realise the full potential of investee company stewardship, it is time to take a step back. In support of this argument, it attempts to make the following main contributions. First, we highlight that the scope of the SC 2020 has expanded considerably and suggest that it has moved towards an expanded interpretation of materiality. We will argue that because of this expansion, it would be helpful to define and categorise different types of outcomes sought through engagement. This should include an explanation of the extent to which, and over what timeframes, outcomes are expected to have an impact on investment portfolio or market return. We suggest three distinct but overlapping and interdependent categories of outcomes and relevant ways to measure impacts.

---

[5] Independent Review of the Financial Reporting Council (December 2018) (Kingman Review), https://assets.publishing.service.gov.uk/government/uploads/system/uploads/attachment_data/file/767387/frc-independent-review-final-report.pdf.

[6] ibid 8.

[7] ibid 46.

[8] ibid 46.

[9] ibid 46.

[10] UK Stewardship Code 2020 (SC 2020), https://www.frc.org.uk/investors/uk-stewardship-code.

[11] FRC, 'Effective Stewardship Reporting – Examples from 2021 and expectations for 2022' (November 2021) (FRC Reporting), https://www.frc.org.uk/getattachment/42122e31-bc04-47ca-ad8c-23157e56c9a5/FRC-Effective-Stewardship-Reporting-Review_November-2021.pdf.

The proposed categorisation is useful in identifying and understanding potential trade-offs between engagement outcomes. Moreover, the categorisation of engagement outcomes can inform the organisation and resourcing of stewardship activities.

Second, we show that the reporting of stewardship outcomes and crucially the evidence of investment integration appears to remain largely anecdotal rather than being based on systematic stewardship practice. Moreover, we highlight that the question of causality or attribution, linking stewardship activities of an asset manager to engagement outcomes and investment integration of stewardship insights to investment performance, remains largely unaddressed.

Third, we outline the key building blocks of impactful engagement and suggest that asset managers should focus on them and their connection to achieve outcomes and obtain investment relevant stewardship insights. We argue that asset owners should have visibility about all aspects of the engagement process of asset managers, including around the setting of objectives, so they can assess whether it aligns with their interests and the outcomes they believe are most important.

Fourth, we suggest that asset managers who want to differentiate themselves based on their stewardship capability should aim to demonstrate how their stewardship activities contribute to engagement outcomes and whether, how significantly and when they affect investment returns and/or the real world. This, we argue, is important regarding outcomes addressing company specific investment opportunities or risks, which can contribute to the outperformance of specific investment portfolios, or alpha. We explain that it is also relevant regarding real world engagement outcomes, which can address systemic risks thus enhancing market returns, or contribute to progress on relevant sustainability indicators, such as the Sustainable Development Goals (SDG).

A. Chapter Structure

This chapter will proceed as follows. In section II, the SC 2020 is briefly introduced, and the most relevant Principles for the purposes of this chapter are highlighted. Section III looks at some key concepts and questions around engagement outcomes, ESG issues, materiality and fiduciary duty of asset owners and their managers. It also introduces a categorisation of engagement outcomes as a framework for later discussion. This is followed by a brief review in section IV of the principal findings of the FRC's review of 2021 stewardship reporting regarding relevant Principles. Section V identifies and provides an overview of the key building blocks of impactful engagement. Based on this, section VI discusses some of the largely missing links in current stewardship practice and explains how the gaps can be closed. Finally, section VII provides a summary and concludes.

B. Nomenclature and Scope of this Chapter

The chapter focuses on asset managers, principally active ones, and investment and stewardship in public equity. The focus is on direct engagement between investors and companies which itself has limitations that are expertly discussed elsewhere.[12] Such engagement could concern a range of strategic, operational, financial and ESG issues.

To keep the terminology simple and consistent we make a broad and somewhat simplistic distinction between asset owners, such as pension funds, and asset managers, who manage assets on behalf of them, and we refer to ultimate beneficiaries, end investors or savers as beneficiaries.

II. THE STEWARDSHIP CODE 2020

The UK SC 2020 was published in November 2019 following a series of consultations during which many of the significant changes were explained and feedback obtained. It took effect from 1 January 2020 with the first reporting at the end of March 2021.

Not surprisingly considering the fundamental criticism in the Kingman Review in 2018 and some of the feedback in the subsequent consultation, the SC 2020 is a very substantial revision of the 2012 Code, which was broadly like the original 2010 Stewardship Code,[13] demonstrating more ambition and significant change in important aspects.[14]

The SC 2020 consists of 12 'apply and explain' Principles for asset owners and asset managers that allow firms to meet the stewardship expectations in a manner that is aligned with their business model and strategy. There are also six Principles for service providers. The Principles are supported by reporting expectations which set out the information to be publicly reported to become a signatory.

The changes between the 2010/2012 and 2020 versions of the Stewardship Code are comprehensively analysed elsewhere.[15] For the purposes of this chapter, key changes to highlight include:

(1)   a much wider and ambitious definition of stewardship as 'the responsible allocation, management and oversight of capital to create long-term value for clients and beneficiaries leading to sustainable benefits for the economy, the environment and society';[16]

(2)   a strong focus throughout the Principles on activities, not least engagement (Principle 9) and, critically, outcomes of stewardship, evidenced through annual reporting, not just policy statements;

(3)   new expectations about how investment and stewardship are integrated, including regarding ESG issues (Principle 7).

---

[12] UN-convened Net-Zero Asset Owner Alliance, 'The Future of Investor Engagement: A Call for Systematic Stewardship to Address Systemic Climate Risk' (April 2022), https://www.unepfi.org/wordpress/wp-content/uploads/2022/03/NZAOA_The-future-of-investor-engagement.pdf.

[13] For a brief overview of the different versions, see FRC, https://www.frc.org.uk/investors/uk-stewardship-code/origins-of-the-uk-stewardship-code.

[14] For some excellent analysis, see P Davies, 'The UK Stewardship Code 2010–2020 – From Saving the Company to Saving the Planet?' in D Katelouzou and D Puchniak, *Global Shareholder Stewardship* (Cambridge University Press 2022) 44 and B Reddy, 'The Emperor's New Code? Time to Re-Evaluate the Nature of Stewardship Engagement under the UK's Stewardship Code' (2021) 84 *Modern Law Review* 842.

[15] See Davies (n 14 above).

[16] SC 2020 (n 10 above) 4.

Given the focus on both outcomes and investment integration, there seems an implicit recognition in the SC 2020 that stewardship by asset managers simultaneously serves two interrelated but quite different purposes, namely: changing the activities and behaviours of companies – and thus their real world impact; and gathering investment relevant information. These are in fact two different categories of stewardship delivery. This is important, as success in stewardship can be measured by looking through these different lenses. The two categories are also an illustration that stewardship has now firmly moved beyond the concept of 'active ownership' which implied actions after investment in a company.

Moreover, the SC 2020 now defines stewardship much more broadly and lists sustainable benefits for the economy as well as 'the environment and society' as its ultimate outcomes. For the first time, it also refers to and sets out expectations regarding ESG issues.

This chapter focuses on reported engagement outcomes and therefore on Principles 9–11 and to a lesser extent Principle 12 regarding the exercise of rights and responsibilities, including voting, which will only be considered as a component of engagement. It also considers reported progress on Principle 7 which requires the integration of stewardship insights into investment processes and decision-making.

Before looking at the FRC's review of reporting, let us briefly revisit the reporting expectations on key activities and outcomes highlighted in the SC 2020 regarding each of the principles we focus on in this chapter.

A. Principle 7: Systematic Integration of Stewardship and Investment

Principle 7 requires signatories to 'systematically integrate stewardship and investment'. Accordingly, asset managers should explain the processes they have used to 'integrate stewardship and investment, including material ESG issues, to align with the investment time horizons of clients and/or beneficiaries …'.[17] The expected outcome of Principle 7 should be an explanation of 'how information gathered through stewardship has informed acquisition, monitoring and exit decisions …'.[18]

B. Principle 9: Engagement to Maintain or Enhance Value of Assets

According to Principle 9, asset managers should explain how they have selected and prioritised engagement; how they have developed objectives for engagement; what methods of engagement and the extent to which they have been used and the reasons for their chosen approach.[19]

Reporting should describe the outcomes of engagement, for example, any action or change(s) made by the company; how outcomes of engagement have informed

---

[17] ibid 15.
[18] ibid 15.
[19] ibid 17.

investment decisions (buy, sell, hold) and how outcomes of engagement have informed escalation.[20]

Principle 9 is the main provision regarding engagement whereas Principles 10 and 11 on collaboration and escalation respectively can be seen as complementary.

Engagement

The concept of engagement is very important regarding the impact of stewardship. While it remains an integral part of stewardship in the SC 2020, it should not be used interchangeably with the broader concept. There is no explicit definition of engagement in the SC 2020. This is surprising as there has been much thinking about it in the industry, not least to differentiate it from purely information seeking activities of asset managers.[21] Definitions of engagement by the PRI,[22] the Global Sustainable Investment Alliance (GSIA)[23] and the UK's Investor Forum[24] make it clear that engagement involves active interactions to influence companies with the objective of affecting change. Such change could address strategic, operational, financial or ESG issues. We will use this definition of engagement in this chapter. The FRC should consider defining engagement in the SC 2020 along similar lines.

C. Principle 10: Collaboration where Necessary

Principle 10 requires asset managers to disclose 'what collaborative engagement they have participated in and why …'.[25] Reporting should describe the outcomes of collaborative engagement, for example: any action or change(s) made by the company; how outcomes of engagement have informed investment decisions (buy, sell, hold); and whether their stated objectives have been met.[26]

D. Principle 11: Escalation where Necessary

Principle 11 requires asset managers to explain how they have selected and prioritised issues and developed objectives for escalation; when they have chosen to escalate their engagement, including the issue(s), and the reasons for their chosen approach.[27]

Reporting should describe the outcomes of escalation including, for example, any action or change(s) made by the company; how outcomes of escalation have informed

---

[20] ibid 18.

[21] The FRC makes this distinction in its review of reporting, see section V.D, 'Effective Communication of Issue and Proposed Solution to Company'.

[22] PRI, 'Reporting Framework Glossary', https://www.unpri.org/reporting-and-assessment/reporting-framework-glossary/6937.article.

[23] GSIA, 'Global Sustainable Investment Review 2020', 7, http://www.gsi-alliance.org/wp-content/uploads/2021/08/GSIR-20201.pdf.

[24] The Investor Forum, 'Defining Stewardship and Engagement', https://www.investorforum.org.uk/wp-content/uploads/securepdfs/2019/04/Defining-Stewardship-Engagement-April-2019.pdf.

[25] SC 2020 (n 10 above) 19.

[26] ibid 19.

[27] ibid 20.

investment decisions (buy, sell, hold); and whether their stated objectives have been met.[28]

Finally, Principle 12 on the exercise of rights and responsibilities, including voting, requires asset managers to provide detailed contextual information on their approach to voting, including regarding their policies and processes.[29] Reporting regarding public equity should provide examples of the outcomes of resolutions.[30]

III. KEY CONCEPTS: ENGAGEMENT OUTCOMES, ESG ISSUES, MATERIALITY AND FIDUCIARY DUTY

A. Engagement Outcomes

There are 36 references to outcome or outcomes in the SC 2020 and for reporting purposes there are high level examples of relevant outcomes. While it is made clear that engagement outcomes principally means actions or changes made by the company, the lack of a definition of what type of outcome signatories should seek creates uncertainty. At the most fundamental level there is the question whether outcomes are defined in terms of their financial materiality for specific companies and investment portfolios or whether the definition is wider and comprises real world outcomes, namely the impact of business activities and investment decisions on environmental, social and financial systems. The definition of stewardship, which changed during the consultation process on the revised code,[31] suggests that both are within scope but that benefits to the economy, the environment and society will flow from the creation of long term value for investors, not independently of it.[32]

A helpful way to look at the concept of outcomes is to recognise that there is a continuous feedback cycle connecting investment-related outcomes affecting the real world and investment opportunities and risks, including those referred to as ESG issues, affecting specific companies and investment portfolios (see Figure 1).[33] The feedback cycle means that over time many real world outcomes caused by investments can feed back into the performance of investment portfolios, impact upon the resilience and sustainability of the financial system and affect market performance.[34] This is particularly true and important for universal owners, defined as large institutional investors that invest long term in broadly diversified holdings across geographies, asset classes and sectors so that they effectively hold a stake in the overall market.[35]

---

[28] ibid 20.

[29] ibid 21.

[30] ibid 22.

[31] See Davies (n 14 above) 60.

[32] ibid 60.

[33] PRI, 'Investing with SDG Outcomes: A Five-Part Framework' (June 2020), https://www.unpri.org/sustainable-development-goals/investing-with-sdg-outcomes-a-five-part-framework/5895.article.

[34] ibid 8.

[35] J Hawley and A Williams, *The Rise of Fiduciary Capitalism* (University of Pennsylvania Press, 2000). The seminal work by Hawley and Williams has inspired a significant amount of literature on various aspects of universal ownership. For an excellent literature overview and a practical framework for universal owners, see E Quigley, 'Universal Ownership in the Anthropocene' *Working Paper* (May 2019). https://ssrn.com/abstract=3457205.

Figure 1 Continuous Feedback Cycle Connecting Investment-related Outcomes Impacting the Real World and Company-specific Investment Opportunities and Risks Impacting Investment Portfolio Performance (Adapted from Investing with SDG Outcomes (2020))[36]

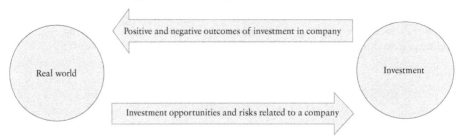

The implications of this feedback cycle for the investment industry and desirable activities of universal owners have been analysed by Lukomnik and Hawley in their book *Moving Beyond Modern Portfolio Theory – Investing That Matters*.[37] The authors describe the universal owner hypothesis as a way 'to look beyond the capital markets, to the real world'.[38] This is necessary, they argue, because universal owners will internalise a proportion of the economic externalities, both negative and positive, each company in their portfolios creates and therefore have an interest in minimising and mitigating negative and fostering positive externalities.[39] Lukomnik and Hawley highlight that market return, driven by systematic (non-diversifiable) risk, or beta,[40] rather than relative outperformance of a specific company or investment portfolio, alpha ('the residual performance that cannot be explained by systematic risk factors'[41]), determines the vast majority of the variability of return to an investor.[42]

This has important implications for universal owners and their stewardship activities. The key argument of the authors is that because the overall economic or market performance, driven by systematic risk, beta, will impact on the future value of the aggregate portfolios of universal owners more than alpha,[43] they should focus their engagement activities much more on systemic or systems risks, which are the risks to or arising from, environmental, social and financial systems.[44]

Put differently, the feedback cycle creates an economic incentive for universal owners and in turn their asset managers to pursue real world outcomes reducing company level externalities and systemic risks that can lead to economy-wide losses and enhancing those that create positive, economy-wide benefits.[45]

---

[36] PRI (n 33 above) 9.
[37] J Lukomnik and J Hawley, *Moving Beyond Modern Portfolio Theory – Investing That Matters* (Routledge, 2021).
[38] ibid 24.
[39] ibid 24.
[40] ibid 2.
[41] ibid 34.
[42] ibid 32.
[43] ibid 32–35.
[44] ibid Ch 5. See also J Gordon, 'Systematic Stewardship' European Corporate Governance Institute – *Law Working Paper 566/2021* (24 January 2022), https://ssrn.com/abstract=3782814.
[45] PRI (n 33 above) 9.

However, asset managers will find it hard to quantify the benefits of addressing systemic risks which will arise indirectly and over multiple decades for their clients and ultimate beneficiaries. In contrast, the cost of doing so is easy to ascertain. Thus, while asset owners and managers may agree that the focus on systemic risks and long-term market return is correct from a theoretical perspective, they are constrained by the legal framework, commercial realities and, critically, the timelines they are operating within. As such, without regulatory intervention, the argument that most ESG issues directly or indirectly and over the very long term will have some financial materiality is insufficient to align fully the interests of asset owners and commercially driven asset managers operating within the current legal framework. We will return to this issue in section VI.

The feedback cycle is also important in understanding the developing concept of materiality, to which we will return below.

The critical point for the purposes of this chapter is that engagament objectives of an asset manager can relate to outcomes that are very different in their nature and the benefit they deliver for different stakeholders and at the systems level. As such, different types of outcomes may be more or less aligned with the interests of asset owners.

B. Three Distinct but Overlapping and Interdependent Categories of Engagement Outcomes and their Measurement

i. Definition of Categories

We conclude from the discussion of the feedback cycle that for transparency and measurement of the effectiveness of stewardship, and ultimately accountability to asset owners, asset managers should be clear what type of engagement outcomes they are primarily seeking. The starting point is to explain whether an engagement primarily seeks to address investment opportunities or risks related to a specific company/investment portfolio within a typical holding period[46] (alpha enhancement) or to drive real world outcomes related to market performance over a long time horizon[47] (beta enhancement). Both types of engagement outcomes can over time, directly or indirectly, have an impact on investment returns and there can be significant overlap as well as trade-offs between the two objectives.

Consider, for example, engagement with a company on its response to climate change which was discussed in a recent report by the UN-convened Net-Zero Asset Owner Alliance.[48] Up to a certain point, asking a company to take action to decarbonise would target both a real world impact and address an investment opportunity or risk, as long as there is a 'business case' for taking 'no regret' actions.[49] Moreover, a company that fails to plan for a transition and starts to take meaningful action may

---

[46] For simplicity and illustration, we assume typical holding periods of three to five years in actively managed portfolios. The key point is that it is not several decades and as such the exact number does not matter for the purposes of this chapter.

[47] Long time horizon will be assumed to mean several decades.

[48] Net-Zero Asset Owner Alliance (n 12 above).

[49] ibid 10–11.

also suffer significant reputational damage which could impact on its share price. However, requesting decarbonisation beyond a certain point, where further action is 'impractical, uneconomic or uncertain', given the current regulatory context and state of technology,[50] would place the primary engagement outcome sought into the real world category focused on market return in the long term. It should be noted that during a typical holding period this may well have a negative performance effect at the company/portfolio level (and it is questionable whether in isolation the desired real world outcome would materialise).

There would seem to be a third outcome category also involving real world outcomes related to values held and norms adhered to by investors, which may or may not affect investment returns over time (or, at least, the impact on returns may be extremely difficult to measure or estimate). Such outcomes could relate to the Ten Principles of the UN Global Compact[51] or the OECD's Guidelines for Multinational Enterprises.[52]

However, again there is overlap between the outcome categories. For example, an issue that on the face of it falls squarely within the values and norms category, such as the right of freedom of association, could at the very minimum cause a reputational risk for a company, thus falling into the investment risk category.

If we disregard engagement outcomes that relate to disclosures of companies, for example regarding their carbon emissions or mitigation strategy,[53] rather than their governance, activities and behaviours, there seem to be three distinct but overlapping and interdependent outcomes categories:

(1) outcomes primarily addressing investment opportunities and risks relating to a specific company/investment portfolio and targetting investment returns in a typical holding period;
(2) real world outcomes focused primarily on systemic or systems risks impacting market return in the long term;
(3) real world outcomes focused primarily on values and norms.

Such categorisation is helpful in thinking about the measurement of the impact of engagement, as well as the organisation and resourcing of stewardship activities, and we will use it later in this chapter. It is also critical in deciding whether and to what extent engagement between asset managers and individual companies needs to be supplemented by sector and value chain and, critically, policy engagement. These questions are outside the scope of this chapter, but they have been expertly discussed in a recent publication by the UN-convened Net-Zero Asset Owner Alliance.[54]

The proposed categorisation is also useful in identifying and understanding potential trade-offs between engagement outcomes, for example, between company and portfolio investment returns (in the short term) and market return (in the long term).

---

[50] ibid 5.
[51] See https://www.unglobalcompact.org/what-is-gc/mission/principles.
[52] See http://mneguidelines.oecd.org/guidelines/.
[53] Such disclosure could be based on voluntary frameworks, such as the CDP (https://www.cdp.net/en), or the Task Force on Climate-Related Financial Disclosures (TCFD) (https://www.fsb-tcfd.org/).
[54] See Net-Zero Asset Owner Alliance (n 12 above).

A shareholder resolution presented at the shareholder meeting of BlackRock in 2022, which asked the asset manager to prioritise the financial performance of its clients' diversified portfolios over the financial performance of individual portfolio companies,[55] illustrates this issue and the industry will need to develop a coherent response as the topic comes into sharper focus.

Returning to the earlier example of company decarbonisation, regulators can influence in which category a particular engagement outcome principally falls, for example by forcing an internalisation of externalities, such as carbon emissions, through the introduction of a market price. In effect, they can make real world outcomes financially material in the short term.

Finally, it is important to note that governance outcomes in the first category, which may be critical in addressing investment oportunities and risks, may or may not have an immediate impact in the real world. Contrast, for example, significant Board composition changes and the implementation of an enhanced health and safety management system. We therefore use the term outcomes rather than real world outcomes for the first category.

ii. Measurement

Engagement outcomes addressing investment opportunities and risks, including those commonly referred to as material ESG issues, can directly impact the value of a specific company and by extension the performance of a specific investment portfolio and could be measurable as such.

In contrast, real world outcomes will need to be measured in a different way, for example in terms of their contribution to SDG targets and indicators,[56] or the Principal Adverse Impact (PAI) indicators under the EU's Sustainable Finance Disclosure Regulation (SFDR).[57] This is because their impact on the value of the company they relate to could be small (and in some cases might be negative), indirect or only occur over a long time horizon. While SDG related outcomes can fall into the first category, some will only benefit overall market performance, rather than the specific company engaged.

It is very difficult, if not impossible, to measure the economic impact of addressing real world outcomes. However, as argued above, mitigation of systematic risk, which is often created by systemic risks, including those relating to environmental, social and financial systems, should in the long term result in enhanced market performance and asset values.[58] This is an area where further research deriving at least estimates of the economic impact of achieving real world outcomes would be helpful in informing the debate.

---

[55] See the related SEC filing by the proponent of the resolution, https://www.sec.gov/Archives/edgar/data/1364742/000121465922005689/b422225px14a6g.htm.

[56] See https://sdgs.un.org/goals.

[57] Regulation (EU) 2019/2088 of the European Parliament and of the Council of 27 November 2019 on sustainability-related disclosures in the financial services sector (Text with EEA relevance).

[58] Lukomnik and Hawley (n 37 above) 107–109. The authors try to estimate the economic impact of what they call 'beta activism'.

We will return to the topic of measurement in section VI. For the purposes of this chapter, we will work on the basis that there are three distinct but overlapping and interdependent categories of engagement outcomes, as illustrated in Table 1.

Table 1 Different categories of engagement outcomes and their potential investment materiality

Outcome category	Outcomes primarily addressing investment opportunities and risks relating to a specific company/ investment portfolio	Real world outcomes focused primarily on systemic or systems risks impacting market returns	Real world outcomes focused primarily on values and norms
Time horizon	Typical holding period (three to five years)	Long term (multiple decades)	Both short and long term
Positive	Upside generation	Positive outcomes	Positive outcomes
Negative	Downside risk protection	Avoiding negative outcomes	Avoiding negative outcomes
Potential materiality for investment	'Alpha enhancement'	'Beta enhancement' (further research and better estimates required)	May not be financially material (or measurable)

Given the discussion of the different types of engagement outcomes, we also conclude that the SC 2020 would benefit from more discussion about this concept and definition of relevant categories.

C. ESG Issues, Materiality and Fiduciary Duty

The expanded definition of stewardship in the SC 2020, with its reference to ESG issues and related to this the concept of outcomes, raises the question whether all stewardship activities are within the scope of fiduciary duty as currently defined for asset owners and managers. This could be questionable where such activities target benefits for beneficiaries, which may not be readily quantifiable in financial terms and only arise indirectly because of better market returns and in the long term. This question is particularly pertinent considering the focus on the climate crisis but is equally relevant regarding other environmental and societal concerns, such as the loss of biodiversity and inequality.

This discussion relates to the ongoing debate about financial materiality defined as an accounting concept on the one hand and 'double materiality' on the other hand. The former focuses on the impact of ESG issues on the value of a specific company (and, by extension, specific investment portfolios in which the company is held); the latter adopts a broader scope covering real world outcomes, namely the impacts of business activities on the wider economy, including environmental, social and financial systems.[59]

[59] For background on double materiality, see European Commission, 'Guidelines on Reporting Climate-related Information' (2019) 6–8, https://ec.europa.eu/finance/docs/policy/190618-climate-related-information-reporting-guidelines_en.pdf.

As discussed earlier, real world outcomes can be financially material at the systems level, at least for universal owners, because of their long-term impact on market return. Moreover, given the ways we save for retirement via collective schemes managed by asset managers, or direct investments in their funds, often with significant passive or market exposure, it is arguable that today many citizens are universal owners.[60] If we accept these arguments, the boundaries between the conventional concept of materiality and double materiality become blurred at least when looking at the expected financial impact over time. Lukomnik and Hawley talk about an expansion of the definition of materiality to those issues that impact the environmental, social and financial systems.[61]

The concepts become even further blurred if we consider that what is regarded as financially material in practice can change over time. Looking at examples such as climate change and social factors during the COVID-19 pandemic, Lukomnik and Hawley describe materiality as a 'state of becoming' not a 'state of being'.[62] The main sustainability standard setters talk about 'dynamic materiality'.[63] Finally, as we discussed earlier, there are also real world outcomes in pursuit of widely accepted values and norms, that may or may not affect investment returns directly or indirectly.

Considering the ongoing work on sustainable finance regulation in Europe and elsewhere, the different concepts of materiality require clarification. The World Business Council for Sustainable Development (WBCSD) published *The Reality of Materiality*[64] in 2021, which identifies the challenges, synthesises current practice and makes recommendations. Edmans and Gosling have made a start regarding materiality in the investment and stewardship context in their important report *What does Stakeholder Capitalism Mean for Investors?*,[65] which was published in early 2022. They bring together various perspectives on materiality and set out a framework that comprises four dimensions of materiality, namely: conventional financial materiality; impact materiality (a company's impact on stakeholders); systemic materiality (market rather than company specific issues); and intrinsic materiality (non-financial goals of investors and society).[66]

For the purposes of this chapter, we will stick to the three categories of engagement outcomes identified above, which capture the key dimensions of materiality that are emerging. We note, however, that a different way of looking at the proposed categories is through the lens of materiality, where broadly issues falling into category 1 would be regarded as financially material using a conventional interpretation, whereas issues in categories 2 and 3 could be regarded as material regarding their impact on the real world ('double materiality').

---

[60] Quigley (n 35 above) 9–10.

[61] Lukomnik and Hawley (n 37 above) 88.

[62] ibid 63–67.

[63] 'Statement of intent to work together towards comprehensive corporate reporting' (September 2020) 4–5, https://impactmanagementproject.com/structured-network/statement-of-intent-to-work-together-towards-comprehensive-corporate-reporting/.

[64] See https://www.wbcsd.org/Programs/Redefining-Value/Redesigning-capital-market-engagement/Resources/The-reality-of-materiality-insights-from-real-world-applications-of-ESG-materiality-assessments.

[65] See https://www.investorforum.org.uk/wp-content/uploads/securepdfs/2022/01/Stakeholder-Capitalism_Report.pdf.

[66] ibid Part 3: Framework 2.

However, without clarity around the materiality nomenclature applied to engage-ment outcomes, it will be very difficult for asset owners to ensure that asset managers pursue outcomes that are aligned with their interests and objectives. The different ways to look at materiality are also important in the context of the boundaries fiduci-ary duty sets around stewardship activities.

D. Discretion on Financially Material ESG Issues under UK Fiduciary Law

At a global level, the conceptual debate about the compatibility of fiduciary duty and financially material ESG issues in the investment context seems over since the publica-tion of the UNEP FI/PRI report in 2019.[67] There is significant evidence demonstrating the financial materiality of a range of ESG issues, not least climate change, including for investment portfolios and ultimately returns to beneficiaries.[68] This allows asset owners and managers subject to fiduciary duty to consider and take decisions on ESG investment strategies as well as ESG stewardship on an informed basis supported by evidence. However, it is also clear that fiduciary duty does not currently require asset owners or managers to account for the real world outcomes and the sustainability impact of their investments beyond their effect on financial performance.[69]

In the UK, the law regarding ESG investment and by implication ESG stewardship activities for trust-based pension funds seems to be reasonably well settled.[70] If such asset owners have gone through a proper process considering relevant evidence and concluded in good faith that there are reasonable grounds to believe that addressing an ESG issue through stewardship activities will be in the long-term financial interest of their beneficiaries, they can and arguably should incur the costs of such activities.[71] At the very least, they are likely to have considerable discretion.[72] This is true despite considerable uncertainties about the timing and specific value of indirect benefits for beneficiaries given the nature and limitations of the empirical evidence available.

While the relevant duties will differ between the various types of institutional investors and their agents, it is reasonable to assume that the requirements in the SC 2020 are compatible with the legal rules that apply to the important asset owner group of trust-based pension funds.[73]

As discussed earlier, it is further arguable that at least some investment-related real world outcomes ultimately feed back into investment portfolios and therefore

---

[67] 'Fiduciary Duty in the 21st Century' (2019), https://www.unpri.org/policy/a-legal-framework-for-impact.

[68] ibid 17–18. For a leading study, see G Friede et al, 'ESG and Financial Performance: Aggregated Evidence from More than 2000 Empirical Studies' (2015) *Journal of Sustainable Finance & Investment* 210, https://ssrn.com/abstract=2699610.

[69] Fiduciary Duty (n 67 above) 23. The most recent instalment of the report series considering fiduciary duty did not significantly change this analysis: see 'A Legal Framework for Impact' (2021), https://www.unpri.org/policy/a-legal-framework-for-impact.

[70] Davies (n 14 above) 60–61 referring to work by the Law Commission (Law Commission, Fiduciary Duties of Investment Intermediaries, Law Com 350, 2014) later adopted by the Department of Work and Pension: The Pension Protection Fund (Pensionable Service) and Occupational Pension Schemes (Investment and Disclosure) (Amendment and Modification) Regulations 2018, SI 2018/988.

[71] ibid 60–61.

[72] ibid 61.

[73] ibid 61.

that they are financially material at least for universal owners, as they are likely to influence market return in the long term. However, as explained, not all real world outcomes fall into this category, which introduces uncertainty.

A discussion of the precise boundaries that fiduciary duty imposes regarding stewardship activities of asset owners and managers is beyond the scope of this chapter.[74] However, as there seems to be uncertainty regarding the compatibility of fiduciary duty with the concept of double materiality, this appears to be an area of the law that the Law Commission should revisit. ShareAction, a UK-based responsible investment advocacy organisation, has proposed a wholesale reform of the duties applying to institutional investors in its Responsible Investment Bill[75] and this seems something worth considering given the current uncertainties.

E. Interpretation for this Chapter

It is evident from a review of the stewardship reports of asset managers that they address ESG issues as investment opportunities and risks of specific companies as well as real world outcomes, both those that may over time have an impact on market returns and those where this may not be the case (or the impact may be impossible to measure or estimate).

This chapter therefore proceeds on the assumption that the FRC's definition of ESG issues and outcomes in the context of stewardship is broad enough to accommodate all three of the engagement outcomes categories we identified. Regarding real world outcomes that will or are likely to feed back into investment portfolios in the very long term, this interpretation is supported by the widened definition of stewardship in the SC 2020 and its Principle 4, which requires signatories to 'identify and respond to market-wide and systemic risks to promote a well-functioning financial system'. However, not all real world outcomes address systemic risks and there are questions therefore about whether seeking such outcomes is compatible with the definition of stewardship and more importantly fiduciary duty.

There has been much less reflection on the interpretation of fiduciary duty regarding ESG stewardship. This explains why it appears much looser than fiduciary duty regarding ESG investment, where there seems to be a clearer dividing line between ESG integration (focused on investment-related opportunities and risks at specific companies) and impact investing (focused on real world outcomes). There is no direct guidance in the SC 2020 and very little literature on the topic. This is perhaps not surprising given the different costs and potential benefits of investment and stewardship respectively to beneficiaries. However, as the compatibility of stewardship with fiduciary duty is a fundamental question, it would be beneficial for asset owners

---

[74] For the UK, see A Tilba and A Reisberg, 'Fiduciary Duty under the Microscope: Stewardship and the Spectrum of Pension Fund Engagement' (2019) 82 *Modern Law Review* 456. For a detailed US-focused analysis, see M Schanzenbach and R Sitkoff, 'Reconciling Fiduciary Duty and Social Conscience: The Law and Economics of ESG Investing by a Trustee (Environmental, Social, and Governance)' (2020) 72 *Stanford Law Review* 381.

[75] ShareAction, 'Responsible Investment Bill' (November 2020), https://shareaction.org/policies/responsible-investment-bill-the-change-we-need.

to understand what type of outcomes an asset manager is primarily pursuing when defining engagement objectives. We will return to this important point in section VI.

IV. FRC'S REVIEW OF STEWARDSHIP REPORTING

In the FRC's publication on effective stewardship reporting (FRC Reporting) published in November 2021, reporting on outcomes is highlighted as one of the areas that requires further improvement.[76] Moreover, the FRC emphasises that '[m]any organisations did not consistently report outcomes of their activities across all the Principles, and as a result did not achieve the standard expected by the Code'.[77]

In the FRC's view regarding engagement, 'effective reporting means clearly presenting data from the reporting period, using case studies that clearly set out objectives, methods, rationale and details of an investor's role, contribution and next steps'.[78]

Accordingly, there is much emphasis on this in Part 4 'Focus on Outcome Reporting' (across all Principles) and Part 5 of the publication which provides 'A Guide to Effective Engagement Reporting' covering broadly the Principles on engagement, escalation and collaboration and exercising rights and responsibilities (Principles 9–12).

A. Engagement Reporting: Principles 9–11

i. Guidance by the FRC

In the beginning of Part 5 of its report the FRC highlights an example showing how an asset manager can provide an overview of engagement activity.[79] It has also put together a useful checklist for engagement reporting that is based on and uses examples and case studies which includes eight points:[80]

- explain the issues that led to the engagement;
- state objectives for engagement;
- use representative examples;
- be specific about activities in the reporting year;
- give the rationale for the chosen engagement approach;
- explain the firm's role and contribution in collaborative engagements;
- explain the reasons for escalation;
- explain the outcomes of the engagement and identify next steps.

---

[76] FRC Reporting (n 11 above) 4 and 42.
[77] ibid 42.
[78] ibid 4.
[79] ibid 59 (J O Hambro Capital Management Ltd).
[80] ibid 59.

The FRC then goes through this checklist and provides explanations and examples illustrating what better reporting on each of the points looks like. Key observations include:

- The FRC emphasises the importance of clearly-stated objectives for engagement which explain what the asset manager likes the company to achieve.[81]
- The FRC highlights that asset managers should explain the reasons for their chosen engagement approach. They are encouraged to draw a link between their chosen engagement approach and their purpose, investment beliefs, strategy and their client base, assets under management and geographic spread.[82]
- The FRC encourages asset managers to explain when they have chosen to escalate their engagement, including the issue and the reasons for their chosen approach.[83]
- The FRC highlights that asset managers should clearly state whether an engagement has concluded or is ongoing and when reporting outcomes acknowledge setbacks experienced and lessons learned, as well as successes.[84]

As discussed in section III, while the FRC highlights the importance of clearly-stated objectives for engagement, it does not provide much guidance regarding the critical concept and different types of outcomes. We noted that there are three quite distinct categories of outcomes which require very different approaches regarding measurement.

It is also interesting to note that the FRC does not require or encourage asset managers to try to establish a link between their stewardship activities and outcomes. In other words, there is no guidance for asset managers to assess the contribution their engagement has made regarding the change that has occurred. While there is unlikely to be a solid causal relationship, one would expect asset managers to assess and have a view on the likelihood that their actions contributed in a meaningful way to change, thus showing a degree of causality. However, the FRC encourages asset managers to include narrative on the effectiveness of their activities.[85] We will come back to the concept of causality, or attribution, in section VI.

B. Review of Selected Reporting Examples and Assessment

A review of a selection of the stewardship reporting highlighted by the FRC in Parts 4 and 5 of its report suggests that at present effective engagement reporting practice of asset managers involves an explanation of what they have done, often in collaboration with other investors or stakeholders, along with a description of changes that the engaged company has made during the period.[86]

---

[81] ibid 60.
[82] ibid 62.
[83] ibid 64.
[84] ibid 65.
[85] ibid 54.
[86] For examples highlighted in the FRC's report, see FRC Reporting (n 11 above) 63–64 (Jupiter Fund Management), 64–65 (Lindsell Train Ltd) and 66 (Wellington Management Co).

Looking beyond reporting highlighted in the FRC's report, stronger stewardship reports go a step further and complement the action and change narrative with statements suggesting at least implicitly some link between their activities in the form of interactions with the company and outcomes. This is done, for example, by highlighting that changes at the company occurred on a topic that featured in dialogue or were made in line with feedback given or suggestions made.[87]

However, according to the author's review of selected stewardship reporting and knowledge of current market practice, there do not seem to be any mainstream asset managers that have and report on a systematic approach seeking to assess how much their stewardship activities have contributed to a specific outcome.

It is acknowledged that asset managers will only rarely be able to establish a solid causal link between their activities and change, for example, in the case of action requested in a shareholder resolution. Therefore, the objective could be to establish some likelihood or a degree of causality rather than a solid causal relationship. An asset manager could achieve this, for example, by providing clear evidence when and how a concern and a specific possible solution to deal with it, which was subsequently adopted, were raised with a company. Moreover, making this link could also be in the form of an acknowledgement of the asset manager's role by the company in an engagement case study.[88]

Both will help clients of asset managers, asset owners, and other interested parties to assess the link between stewardship activities of an asset manager and engagement outcomes and therefore the quality and effectiveness of the firm's stewardship capability. We will return to this important topic in section VI.

C. Stewardship Investment Integration Reporting: Principle 7

The SC 2020 significantly expanded the definition of stewardship making it clear that integration of engagement insights into investment processes and decision-making is a key requirement.

i. FRC's Discussion of Reporting

Given its significance, the FRC says surprisingly little about its assessment of outcome reporting regarding Principle 7, integration of stewardship and investment, in Part 4

---

[87] For examples, see Baillie Gifford, 'Our Investment Stewardship Activities – Year Ended 31 December 2020', 26, https://www.bailliegifford.com/jp/japan/professional-investor/literature-library/corporate-governance/baillie-gifford-investment-stewardship-activities-year-ended-31-december-2020/; EOS at Federated Hermes, 'Stewardship Report 2020', 9–11 and 15, https://www.hermes-investment.com/ukw/wp-content/uploads/2021/03/stewardship-report-2020-eos-at-federated-hermes-1.pdf; Federated Hermes International, 'Stewardship Report 2020', 59–60, https://www.hermes-investment.com/uki/wp-content/uploads/2021/03/ifh-corporate-stewardship-report-03-2020.pdf; JO Hambro Capital Management, 'Stewardship Report 2020', 17 and 19, https://www.johcm.com/uk/about-us/584/stewardship-report and Robeco, 'Stewardship Report 2020', 23 and 49, https://www.robeco.com/media/1/c/7/1c7b6a2c76f493509bbfc5200f0db79e_202104-robeco-stewardship-report-2020_tcm21-29518.pdf.

[88] See, for example, EOS at Federated Hermes case studies on PetroChina (March 2020), https://www.hermes-investment.com/uki/eos-insight/eos/petrochina-case-study/ and Centrica (February 2020), https://www.hermes-investment.com/uki/eos-insight/eos/centrica/.

of its report.[89] It highlights that when reporting on the outcomes of such integration, asset managers should provide 'examples of how stewardship considerations have been incorporated into an investment decision from the reporting period'.[90]

The FRC clarifies that '[r]eporting should state a clear cause and effect relationship'[91] between ESG research and tools, investment beliefs and company engagement, and the decision that was ultimately made to invest, monitor, or divest.

There is one example in the brief section focused on Principle 7 in Part 4, which highlights the work of asset manager Brewin Dolphin regarding its holdings in the controversial fashion company Boohoo, which culminated in its decision to remain invested.[92] There are other investment-related reporting examples in Part 5 of the FRC's report. These include the work of asset manager Jupiter Fund Management in collaboration with ShareAction with Barclays, which seems to have contributed to greater confidence in the investment,[93] and Majedie Asset Management's engagement with Orange, which resulted in a reduction of its overall holding in the company.[94]

Moreover, the stewardship report by Lindsell Train Limited, which is highlighted by the FRC in an earlier section of Part 4 of its report, seems to imply a link between investment returns and its stewardship activities ('… our stewardship activities have proved effective and we have been able to deliver good investment returns for our clients …').[95]

ii. Review of Selected Reporting Examples and Assessment

While insights from stewardship activities will rarely be the only or main driver behind any investment decision, when carefully integrated into fundamental analysis, they can inform investment decision-making and on occasions be a key factor in buy, hold or sell decisions.

The examples of stewardship reporting regarding investment integration discussed earlier show that the leading firms make general statements about the link between stewardship activities and investment, generally in company specific examples. However, the reporting remains anecdotal, is limited to a few case studies and lacks clarity regarding 'cause and effect relationship',[96] as required by the FRC. Review of selected reporting not highlighted by the FRC confirms that asset managers seem to remain high level and generic, observing, for example, that engagement dialogue with a company has enhanced confidence in their investment thesis.[97] There are very few examples where stewardship insights are directly linked to to investment decisions, typically divestment.[98]

---

[89] Principle 7 reporting is covered on one page. See FRC Reporting (n 11 above) 50.
[90] FRC Reporting (n 11 above) 50.
[91] ibid 50.
[92] ibid 50.
[93] ibid 64.
[94] ibid 66.
[95] ibid 43.
[96] ibid 50.
[97] See, for example, JO Hambro Capital Management, 'Stewardship Report 2020', 19.
[98] See, for example, Federated Hermes International, 'Stewardship Report 2020', 44 and Legal & General Investment Management, 'Active Ownership', 28–29, https://www.lgim.com/landg-assets/lgim/_document-library/capabilities/active-ownership-report-2020.pdf.

Critically, there is also no clear distinction between the different engagement outcomes categories we identified and discussed in section III, even though doing so would seem to be a prerequisite for the purposes of Principle 7. Some of the engagement examples highlighted seem to fall into the category of systems level real world outcomes (covered in Principle 4 of the SC 2020) rather than investment risks that can impact upon the performance of a specific company during a typical holding period and thus a specific investment portfolio in the relatively short term.

A review of selected stewardship reporting and the author's knowledge of current market practice suggest that there do not seem to be any mainstream asset managers that have and report on a systematic approach seeking to attribute investment performance to insights gained from or changes affected through stewardship activities.

Such approach and related reporting would go beyond the specific outcome sought under Principle 7 (an explanation of how information gathered through stewardship has informed acquisition, monitoring and exit decisions). But for asset managers who want to differentiate themselves based on the quality of their stewardship capability and benefit from it, such systematic approach at the investment portfolio level should be the ultimate objective.

Effectively integrating stewardship insights into investment processes and decision-making, and demonstrably linking it to investment performance, can be regarded as an important part of alpha focused engagement. As such, it is mostly relevant regarding outcomes addressing investment opportunities and risks relating to a specific company. If done effectively, the stewardship investment integration skill could allow asset managers to distinguish their offering from others and benefit from it financially, thus creating a competitive advantage in investment management. We will come back to this point in section VI.

The next section takes a step back and describes what systems, processes, strategies and policies an asset manager needs to put in place to facilitate impactful engagement.

V. KEY BUILDING BLOCKS OF IMPACTFUL ENGAGEMENT

In this section, key characteristics of a robust, transparent and ultimately credible approach to engagement will be outlined. The suggested approach works across a range of strategic, operational, financial and ESG issues. However, some of the elements, including escalation mechanisms and ultimate sanctions will differ depending on the nature of the issue. Moreover, the specific approach taken regarding the organisation and resourcing of stewardship activities will need to be informed by the nature of engagement outcomes sought. In this regard, the categorisation of outcomes introduced in section III will be important.

Throughout this section it will become apparent that the quality of engagement and consequently stewardship reporting will to a large degree depend on the systems and processes, strategies and policies on which an asset manager's systematic engagement is based. The related question of resourcing of stewardship activities, which is also closely related to the nature of engagement outcomes sought, is outside the scope of this chapter.

While the SC 2020 and the FRC's review of stewardship reporting provide useful guidance regarding outcomes and reporting, they are less helpful for asset managers regarding the internal infrastructure required for impactful engagement and reporting demonstrating the link between activities and outcomes and investment integration.

There are several key steps that an asset manager should go through regarding any systematic engagement which should be supported by detailed documentation evidencing the process, interactions with the company and related outcomes:

(1) identification of issues and concerns requiring change;
(2) setting relevant engagement objectives and categorising the types of outcomes sought;
(3) definition of an engagement strategy and related timelines, including clarity about ultimate sanctions where engagement proves unsuccessful;
(4) effective communication of issue and proposed solution to company;
(5) capturing activities and interactions and systematically tracking progress against objectives;
(6) implementation of an escalation strategy based on a framework setting out time-lines, including the use of systematic voting at shareholder meetings;
(7) measurement of progress and reporting.

Figure 2 Key Steps in Systematic Engagement

Asset owners should have visibility about all aspects of the engagement process of asset managers, including around objectives setting, so they can assess whether it aligns with their interests.

Let us look at each of these steps in turn.

A. Identification of Issues for Engagement

It is a prerequisite for impactful engagement that an asset manager properly under-stands an issue and its relevance for a specific company or at the systems level in sufficient depth and has a clear idea of the case for engagement and what the objec-tives of stewardship should be.

Today, many asset managers recognise that ESG issues, including climate change, loss of biodiversity and social inequality can be material for universal owners in the expanded definition introduced earlier, if not in the short term than in the medium to long term. As such there is a wide range of potential engagement issues beyond topics such as a company's business model, strategy and operational and financial performance.

With their desire for optimal impact and constrained by limited resources, asset managers will typically want to focus on companies where they have large positions in select markets and sectors. However, the selection of companies for engagements should be closely connected to the nature of the outcomes that an asset manager is focused on.

B. Setting Relevant Engagement Objectives and Categorising the Types of Outcomes Sought

There are three key requirements for credible engagement objectives. First, they must effectively address the specific underlying concern or issue within a reasonable time-frame; second, they should be achievable through engagement and third, they need to facilitate tracking of progress, allowing review and escalation at the right time. The latter can be facilitated by setting and tracking of milestones in achieving objectives set and be supported by dedicated engagement management systems. In short, engagement objectives should be SMART (specific, measurable, achievable, realistic, time-bound).

To facilitate appropriate accountability and relevant measurement of engagement progress, asset owners need to understand what types of outcomes an asset manager is primarily pursuing when defining engagement objectives. Therefore, asset managers should provide transparency around objectives and to the extent it is practically possible be clear whether an objective seeks to address investment opportunities or risks related to a specific company, or real world outcomes related to systemic risks or based on values and norms.

C. Definition of an Engagement Strategy and Ultimate Sanction where Stewardship Proves Unsuccessful

At present asset managers do not provide much public information regarding their overarching engagement strategy and how it applies in different sectors, across themes and regarding specific companies, even though Principle 9 of the SC 2020 requires a description of engagement methods. There is also little clarity about what happens if conventional engagement fails and the ultimate sanction where stewardship proves unsuccessful.

i. Engagement Strategy

The engagement strategy should include a plan to communicate with a company on a relevant issue and a proposed solution defined in an engagement objective. This should cover the means of communication, counterparts at the company, frequency of interactions and, critically, timelines. Asset managers should be explicit about how much time they give a company to resolve a concern that has been raised. The engagement plan should be regularly reviewed and updated. It is a critical element of a robust and credible escalation process.

While not every issue needs to go up to the Board, experience and some empirical evidence suggest that in person engagement at Board level including particularly the chair is more impactful than dialogue only with investor relations.[99] Clearly, such engagement will be more resource intensive than letter writing or listening into the CFO's quarterly results call. However, if stewardship is outcome-focused, then engagement on an issue that cannot be resolved reasonably quickly should be elevated via investor relations, subject specialists and management to the Board over time.

Such escalation has other advantages. Asset managers who make the investment in dialogue with senior company representatives, including the Board, are likely to get a better hearing and may become trusted partners of the directors. They may also find it easier to get some acknowledgement from companies for their role in driving change and securing outcomes.

ii. Ultimate Sanction

An engagement strategy should also be clear about the ultimate sanction when progress is not materialising within a reasonable time frame.

Asset owners are now expecting clarity on what the consequences of unsuccessful engagement are and question the credibility of asset managers who claim over many years that private engagement behind the scenes is leading to changes. This trend seems to be reflected in divestment policies and processes and, critically, announcements of both asset managers, such as LGIM[100] and Aviva,[101] and asset owners, such as Nest[102] and New York State.[103]

LGIM's climate impact pledge[104] combines very clearly structured engagement with companies selected based on proprietary public ratings following an escalation framework, which comprises voting against chairs, with the potential for divestment from some of its actively managed funds. It is a particularly good example of a clearly communicated ultimate sanction.

A discussion of the empirical evidence about the impact of divestment on both companies and investment returns is beyond the scope of this chapter. For the purposes of the present discussion, it is helpful to distinguish different motivations for divestment. Investors may pursue two primary objectives when opting for a divestment approach, which is not driven by a desire to optimise returns:

- taking a principles based or ethical position, which can influence public opinion and policy; and

[99] M Wolff et al, 'Talk is Not Cheap – The Role of Interpersonal Communication as a Success Factor of Engagements on ESG Matters' (September 2017), https://www.hermes-investment.com/uploads/2021/10/c0bf4fca7dbf219c12ea4a067df05fdc/hermes-eos-research-report-sep-17.pdf.

[100] C Hodgson, 'Britain's Largest Investor Blacklists AIG over Climate Risk Concerns – LGIM Drops US Insurer from £58bn Portfolio for Having No policy on Thermal Coal or Disclosure of Emissions' (*Financial Times*, 15 June 2021), https://www.ft.com/content/44245000-3167-46db-b9f7-8731ca925187.

[101] Attracta Mooney, 'Aviva Will Use Its "Ultimate Sanction" to Force Action on Global Warming – One of the UK's Largest Asset Managers Says it is Prepared to Fully Divest from 30 Oil, Gas and Mining Companies' (*Financial Times*, 31 January 2021), https://www.ft.com/content/596e8402-2dcb-45f9-915c-c5ecfabc7c7a.

[102] C Flood, 'Nest Dumps ExxonMobil over Climate Change Risks' (*Financial Times*, 20 December 2021), https://www.ft.com/content/b2205f72-fd11-4ac7-8f89-c34a4b00177a.

[103] B Nauman, 'New York State's $226bn Pension Fund Plans Rolling Fossil Fuel Divestments' (*Financial Times*, 9 December 2020), https://www.ft.com/content/67e87d22-f733-4914-8c6a-e447e61d9ea2.

[104] LGIM, 'LGIM's Climate Impact Pledge: the 2021 Results', https://www.lgim.com/landg-assets/lgim/_document-library/responsible-investing/climate-impact-pledge-brochure-uk-eu-2021.pdf.

- seeking to influence a sector's, or a company's, activities by increasing its cost of capital.

Moreover, it is important to consider whether divestment is complete or only partial, for example, in order to manage risks, which is best regarded as the integration of ESG risk factors in the investment process rather than divestment.

Research suggests that the direct impact of equity divestment on the targeted company is limited.[105] Moreover there is a real possibility that it may simply lead to ownership by investors that are less concerned about a specific issue, such as the climate crisis. Also, given the opportunity to influence companies through engagement, which is more effective when underpinned by an equity holding with associated voting rights,[106] complete divestment on a principles basis or to influence a sector or company, as opposed to the management of ESG investment risks, does not seem an approach that is likely to be adopted widely at this point.

However, while the focus of many asset managers is firmly on engagement, there is emerging evidence that combining elements of both approaches could be most effective in tackling issues such as the climate crisis.[107] This, of course, is what the SC 2020 seeks to encourage through the integration of stewardship insights into investment processes and decisions.

iii. Watch List and Engagement Escalation

An alternative consequence of lack of engagement progress could be to put a company on a high-risk internal or external watch list which could come with additional investment process, monitoring and reporting requirements. It could also involve doubling down on engagement with a final escalation push collaborating with others or filing of a shareholder resolution. These escalation techniques will be discussed below.

D. Effective Communication of Issue and Proposed Solution to Company

In its review of reporting, the FRC points out that there is a difference between information and change seeking engagement and encourages signatories to focus on the

---

[105] See for example D Blitz and L Swinkels, 'Is Exclusion Effective?' (2020) 46 *The Journal of Portfolio Management Ethical Investing* 42; S Braungardt et al, 'Fossil Fuel Divestment and Climate Change: Reviewing Contested Arguments' (2019) 50 *Energy Research & Social Science* 191; JF Kölbel et al, 'Can Sustainable Investing Save the World? Reviewing the Mechanisms of Investor Impact' (2020) 33 *Organization and Environment* 554.

[106] For a recent example, consider the successful engagement and voting campaign at Exxon, see D Brower, 'ExxonMobil Shareholders Hand Board Seats to Activist Nominees – Historic Vote Reflecting Climate Concerns Comes on Bruising Day for International Oil Companies' (*Financial Times*, 26 May 2021), https://www.ft.com/content/da6dec6a-6c58-427f-a012-9c1efb71fddf.

[107] See for example N Amenc et al, 'ESG Engagement and Divestment: Mutually Exclusive or Mutually Reinforcing?', *Scientific Beta Publication* (May 2020), https://www.scientificbeta.com/#/publicsurvey?slug=esg-engagement-and-divestment and V Atta-Darkua et al, 'Strategies for Responsible Investing: Emerging Academic Evidence' (2020) 46 *The Journal of Portfolio Management Ethical Investing* 26.

latter rather than the former.[108] As discussed in section II, the FRC should consider whether a definition of engagement in the SC 2020 would be helpful for signatories and the quality of reporting. Clearly, in practice, both types of interactions have their role in investment processes. However, one should be clear that most of the regular information-seeking interactions between companies and asset managers are very unlikely to lead to change and outcomes and should therefore not be called engagement.

Effective communication of an asset manager's concern or issue to the company along with a proposed solution is critical in quality engagement, and can require interactions with a range of company representatives of different seniorities including the Board.

E. Capturing Activities and Interactions and Systematically Tracking Progress against Objectives

Asset managers should invest in an engagement management system and processes that comprehensively capture their stewardship activities and interactions with companies and other stakeholders and systematically track progress against objectives along with evidence identifying when and how progress was achieved.

This should include, for example, when and how a concern and a proposed solution was first raised, when the company acknowledged the issue and when it committed to addressing this. Capturing this information is critical in substantiating claims that activities of an asset manager to some degree contributed to change (causation) rather than just occurred at the time when changes were being considered or made (correlation). This is an issue to which we will return in section VI. Dedicated systems and processes will be critical for systematic engagement programmes and addressing current weaknesses in reporting.

F. Definition of an Escalation Strategy, Including the Systematic Use of Voting

Many asset managers have now accepted that there are occasions where they are unable to achieve progress in engagement by working one-to-one with companies in private and where accordingly some escalation is required. Often this involves some public comment, for example around related voting decisions, or working together with other investors. Both are critical escalation techniques.

Asset managers should be clear about what escalation techniques they are willing to use and, critically, when they might do so. The FRC encourages signatories to explain the reasons for escalation.[109] That is why it is important to track progress against engagement objectives over time and have a well thought out engagement strategy, including regarding time allowed for companies to make necessary changes following dialogue.

---

[108] FRC Reporting (n 11 above) 58.
[109] ibid 64.

Given the perception that much stewardship has little impact, as evidenced in the 2018 Kingman Review[110] and some of the literature,[111] it has become critical for asset managers to be clear and ideally transparent about how much time will be allowed before escalation of engagement occurs. This is unlikely to be possible with any precision for all issues, including climate change across companies in different markets and sectors, however, asset managers should at least have a framework setting out estimated timings and providing an indication when escalation will occur and what form it will take. This framework could be captured in an internal document with a shorter version published as part of wider stewardship-related reporting.

The most common escalation techniques include:

- collaboration;
- public comment;
- voting against standard agenda items, such as directors, with or without public comment;
- annual general meetings interventions and questions;
- filing shareholder resolutions.

The exercise of voting rights including against management is of course a fundamental shareholder right and its use should not be limited to escalated engagement. A well thought out approach to voting based on tailored and communicated voting policies is a building block of good stewardship, as reflected in Principle 12 of the SC 2020. Similarly, collaboration which is covered in Principle 10 of the SC 2020 can be the starting point or the focus of an asset manager's engagement. However, both are also critical techniques in escalation and are included here on that basis.

As discussed above, in addition to the escalation techniques listed, complete or part divestment from a company can be used in combination with engagement and is therefore an important tool available for investors.

Shareholder litigation in general and claims against directors are beyond the scope of this chapter. While they can be useful tools in exceptional circumstances, they are not typically considered as part of a conventional engagement strategy.

i. Collaboration

Collaboration can be an efficient and effective way for asset managers to bring together resource and have more impact together partly because they are likely to represent a significant proportion of shareholdings in a company and partly because they can demonstrate to issuers that concerns are shared among other investors. It could take place within one of the thematic engagement frameworks, such as Climate Action 100+,[112] or one of the regional investor collaborations, such as the Investor Forum in the UK.[113] In practice, collaboration also happens on an ad hoc basis.

---

[110] See Kingman Review (n 5 above) and discussion in section I.
[111] See generally L Bebchuk et al, 'The Agency Problems of Institutional Investors' (2017) 31 *Journal of Economic Perspectives* 89 and focused on the UK Stewardship Code, Davies (n 14 above); Reddy (n 14 above).
[112] See https://www.climateaction100.org/.
[113] See https://www.investorforum.org.uk/.

Collaborations can bring many advantages and have proved their value in recent years, specifically around climate-related engagement. While they tend to cover a relatively small number of companies, need to be adequately supported and can suffer from collective action problems, they are an important escalation engagement technique.

Asset Managers should define in what circumstances they use collaboration as an escalation technique.

ii. Public Comment

Asset managers typically prefer conducting engagement privately, rather than taking a public route when seeking change at companies. They generally view working constructively with Boards and management in private as the most effective way to achieve positive change because such dialogue facilitates trusted relationships with companies, which results in more productive discussions. There is generally a reluctance to comment publicly, because of a fear that this could undermine the trust that would otherwise exist between a company and its owners.

However, perhaps reluctantly, many asset managers have now accepted that there are occasions when they are unable to achieve progress in engagement by working with companies in private and when, accordingly, some escalation involving public comment is required. This can be around the time of a shareholder meeting, for example, pre-disclosing voting decisions on key resolutions, or on an ad hoc basis. Moreover, it could be around a structured engagement escalation process highlighting concerns or specific objectives that an asset manager discusses with a company.

The purpose of public comment would typically be to alert other investors about a concern or an issue that could not be resolved in private dialogue. This is likely to result in other investors raising the same topic with the company, or adjusting their voting behaviours, which may unlock or accelerate the engagement. As such, it shares some functionality with collaboration.

Anecdotal evidence suggests that notification of companies in advance of objective public comment can strengthen rather than weaken relationships. As such, it is a tool that on occasion can be useful in advancing an engagement agenda.

iii. Voting

One of the most fundamental rights of an investor owning shares in a company is to vote at shareholder meetings. This includes regular election or re-election of the Board of directors, who should represent the interests of all key stakeholders, including shareholders. Given their role and responsibilities within corporate governance, directors should be both best informed and best placed to address issues facing their companies, including climate change, in an optimal way. As such, asset managers should focus on getting the right people onto Boards of directors.

Not a long time ago, voting against a resolution put forward by the management/ the Board or indeed against one of the directors at a company's shareholder meeting was considered a massive escalation step. Today, it is common to see mainstream asset managers vote against the Board's proposals regarding executive remuneration, financial statements/accounts and auditor reports, elections to the Board and increasingly environmental resolutions.[114]

Voting against is a natural escalation tool if an asset manager's engagement has consistently stalled and the firm has concluded that the company is not taking any action to address its concerns, or its progress in doing so is too slow.

If there is adequate communication around such voting with the company, for example by means of a dedicated call or meeting, this can send a strong signal to the company and can help progress in dialogue with it. Anecdotal evidence suggests that directors take even single digit percentage votes against their election or re-election at shareholder meetings very seriously. So, the exercise of voting rights is a sharp tool and should be viewed as an important asset to be deployed in support of achieving engagement outcomes.

Asset managers should integrate their voting policies into engagement strategies and use their voting rights systematically in the escalation of engagement within a pre-disclosed framework. Transparency and communication to companies in this regard is critical for optimal impact.

A good example of what such an approach could look like is LGIM's Climate Impact Pledge, which we discussed earlier. As an important part of the pledge, the asset manager has decided to vote against the chair of Boards when companies fail to demonstrate sufficient action over a pre-defined time in addressing shortcomings identified in its publicly available ranking.[115]

iv. Annual General Meetings Interventions and Questions

The pandemic-related switch to hybrid shareholder meetings makes it much easier and less resource intensive for asset managers to raise issues, ask questions and make proposals at annual general meetings. This effectively is a form of public comment underpinned by the exercise of shareholder rights. However, it has additional benefits of direct communications with management and typically some Board members who may otherwise not have direct exposure to the concerns and requests from asset managers. Moreover, in cases when it is possible to ask questions, additional information or clarification may be obtained.

Annual general meeting interventions by asset managers are a common feature in some European markets and can be an effective tool, not least in combination with other escalation techniques such as collaboration.

---

[114] See, for example, InfluenceMap, 'Asset Managers and Climate Change 2021' (January 2021). https://influencemap.org/report/Asset-Managers-and-Climate-Change-cf90d26dc312ebe02e97d2f f6079ed87; ShareAction, 'Voting Matter 2021 – Are Asset Managers Using Their Proxy Votes for Action on Environmental and Social Issues' (December 2021), https://api.shareaction.org/resources/reports/ ShareAction-Voting-Matters-2021.pdf; Ceres, 'As Climate Risks Skyrocket, Largest Asset Managers Vote for More Climate-related Shareholder Proposals, Tipping Support to Record Levels in 2021' (December 2021), https://www.ceres.org/news-center/blog/climate-risks-skyrocket-largest-asset-managers-vote-more-climate-related; Majority Action, 'Fulfilling the Promise: How Climate Action 100+ Investor-Signatories Can Mitigate Systemic Climate Risk' (March 2022), https://www.majorityaction.us/research.

[115] LGIM (n 104 above).

v. Filing or Co-filing of Shareholder Resolutions

Asset managers can also escalate engagement by the filing or co-filing of resolutions which support positive change. This practice has become increasingly common, especially regarding environmental and social issues.[116] Resolution filers now include specialised and mainstream asset managers as well as organisations, such as ShareAction[117] in the UK, Follow This[118] in the Netherlands and As You Sow[119] in the US, who often work or collaborate with asset owners and asset managers.

Generally, asset managers seek to exhaust more conventional engagement channels before resorting to the filing of resolutions. However, where engagement is refused by the company or progress is too slow, the filing of a resolution can be used by asset managers to force the company into dialogue or to make faster progress.

G. Measurement of Progress and Reporting

Capturing activities and interactions and systematically tracking progress against clearly defined and SMART objectives, as described earlier, facilitates escalation at an appropriate time and, critically, evidence-based reporting.

Asset manager reporting to clients should be both quantitative and qualitative. It should cover the number of companies engaged along with a definition of what counts as an engagement,[120] the number and nature of interactions with these companies, including corporate counterparts, the issues raised, and outcomes sought and, critically, progress. As discussed earlier, asset managers should categorise the types of engagement outcomes sought and explain how they align with the interests of asset owners. The quantitative information should be complemented by case studies describing and evidencing how engagement has led to or at least contributed to positive changes and, if applicable, what engagement escalation techniques were used. This should include information on when and how proposals to resolve concerns or issues were made.

It could be argued that private reporting to clients is sufficient. However, there are real benefits from public reporting, not least the transparency and accountability towards asset owners, beneficiaries and other relevant parties. Moreover, public reporting will signal to companies that there are consequences, if engagement does not lead to the changes sought by an asset manager, including in some cases divestment.

Furthermore, case studies of successful engagement can help the development of best corporate practice and facilitate learning in the asset management industry. Indeed, there are likely to be occasions where both companies and investors are interested in the publication of engagement case studies which can serve as a proof point of impactful engagement as well as corporate progress on sustainability. We will return to this point in section VI.

---

[116] See surveys referenced in n 114.

[117] ShareAction: https://shareaction.org/what-we-do/why-responsible-investment.

[118] Follow this: https://www.follow-this.org/.

[119] As You Sow: https://www.asyousow.org/.

[120] The FRC distinguished between information and change seeking engagement. See FRC Reporting (n 11 above) 58.

The FRC is very clear in its requirement to hear not just about successful engagements of asset managers but also cases in which dialogue with a company has not led to desired outcomes. It is therefore important for asset managers to be transparent about such cases. Examples could be presented in case studies[121] supplemented by quantitative reporting on stalled objectives across the universe of engagements.

In the next section we will outline the missing links in current stewardship practice along with suggestions of how to close these gaps. In doing so, it will become apparent why asset managers need to focus on the building blocks of impactful engagement described in this section.

VI. THE MISSING LINKS IN CURRENT STEWARDSHIP PRACTICE AND HOW TO CLOSE THE GAPS

In section IV we established that the reporting of engagement outcomes (Principle 9) and crucially the evidence of stewardship investment integration (Principle 7) appears anecdotal and not based on systematic practice. The question of causality or attribution, linking stewardship activities of an asset manager and engagement outcomes on the one hand and the integration of such outcomes or stewardship insights and investment performance on the other hand, remains largely unaddressed.

To move best practice forward, asset managers should focus on the key building blocks of impactful engagement and their connection, as explained in section V. Without these building blocks in place, including clarity about the types of outcomes sought, expecting significant change of the governance, activities and behaviours of companies and attributable outcomes involving some degree of causation rather than just correlation seems unrealistic.

In this section, we will argue that asset managers should aim to demonstrate how their stewardship activities contributed to outcomes and at least seek to quantify the real world or investment impact of such outcomes (or related insights). The quantification of real world outcomes is an area closely related to the practice of impact measurement where much work has already been done in this regard. In contrast, the question of how engagement outcomes or stewardship insights can contribute to the performance of specific investment portfolios or, in the long term, the market is largely new territory.

A. Different Approaches and Measurement for Different Types of Engagement Outcomes

Building on the categorisation introduced in section III when discussing different types of engagement outcomes, we will distinguish between outcomes that are primarily addressing investment opportunities and risks relating to a specific company/investment portfolio which may enhance alpha, real world outcomes primarily aimed at market return and outcomes primarily focused on values and norms that may or may not impact returns. This categorisation is captured in Table 2.

---

[121] For an example, see Federated Hermes International (n 87 above).

Table 2 Different Categories of Engagement Outcomes, Their Potential Investment Materiality and Measurement

Outcome category and measurement	Outcomes primarily addressing investment opportunities and risks relating to a specific company/investment portfolio		Real world outcomes focused primarily on systemic or systems risks impacting market return		Real world outcomes focused primarily on values and norms	
Time horizon	Typical holding period (three to five years)		Long term (multiple decades)		Both short and long term	
Positive	Upside generation	Portfolio level performance	Positive outcomes	SDG and PAI	Positive outcomes	SDG and PAI
Negative	Downside risk protection	Portfolio level performance	Avoiding negative outcomes	SDG and PAI	Avoiding negative outcomes	SDG and PAI
Potential materiality for investment	'Alpha enhancement'		'Beta enhancement' (further research and better estimates required)		May not be financially material (or measurable)	

As a first step, asset managers should be clearer about what type of engagement outcomes they are primarily targeting with their stewardship activities and for what purpose (see Table 2). This should include an explanation of the intended impact of outcomes on investment returns, directly or indirectly, short term or long term. It should also explain the overlap and interdependencies between the categories and how any trade-offs between different objectives are identified and addressed over different time horizons. This exercise would significantly enhance the credibility of stewardship and related activities by providing transparency, a starting point for measurement and ultimately client accountability. A categorisation of engagement outcomes will also inform the organisation and resourcing of stewardship activities.

Such categorisation of the outcomes of stewardship activities could conceptually follow the approach introduced for investment funds under the EU's SFDR. Under this regulation, asset managers are required to differentiate between funds that integrate ESG considerations with a focus on financial materiality and funds that have a specific, sustainability-related objective to achieve real world outcomes. Following the fund classification system, the categorisation of engagement outcomes and explanation around it could eventually form part of investment mandates. This would seem to be particularly important regarding real world outcomes related to values and norms that may not have an impact on returns.

B. Why is a Categorisation of Engagement Outcomes Important for Both Asset Managers and Owners?

Most asset managers are commercial entities and many of them are listed, or part of a listed company. Their key stakeholders include shareholders and employees.

They rely on how much they manage (assets under management) and for active managers, how successfully their funds perform relative to a benchmark in the short and medium term, as this attracts more funds and potentially generates performance fees. Staff costs are a main driver of profit margins in an increasingly competitive market environment for asset managers.

Putting credible engagement systems, processes, policies and strategies in place and running a systematic, global engagement programme will require significant resource. To justify this investment and differentiate their offering, asset managers will need to be able to demonstrate to their clients, asset owners, how systematic stewardship adds value to the main services they provide, namely investment management, and is aligned with clients' objectives.

As discussed in Section III, it has been argued that targeting real world outcomes that address systemic issues, thus enhancing long-term market return, will have a more significant benefit to universal owners (and, as such, clients of asset managers) than targeting alpha.

However, as explained in section III, while successfully addressing systemic risks, such as climate change, through engagement activities may be critical when looking at market return in the long term, neither the financial nor the non-financial benefits are likely to directly benefit the asset manager or the fund that incurs costs of doing so, unless there is overlap with company-specific risk.

Active asset managers may therefore want their stewardship activities to contribute also to enhanced relative performance of specific portfolios (alpha), which suggests a focus on outcomes addressing company-specific investment opportunities or risks.

Whether the focus is on real world outcomes or outcomes impacting investment opportunities or risks, asset managers will need to be able to quantify or measure what they achieve through their stewardship activities so that asset owners can make informed choices when awarding mandates and agreeing on management fees.

The FRC described differentiation between asset managers regarding stewardship and creation of demand for effective stewardship as an objective it was seeking with the revision of the SC 2020.[122] In effect, it was looking for asset managers to compete based on their stewardship capabilities.

To facilitate such competition, the clients of asset managers, asset owners, will need to be able to assess:

(1)   the link or causality between stewardship activities of an asset manager and engagement outcomes, and
(2)   the impact of such outcomes, or stewardship-related insights, on specific investment portfolios, market return or the real world over different time horizons.

Information facilitating such assessment will help asset owners to distinguish between firms based on the quality of their stewardship and the impact of related activities on investment returns and the real world. The challenge of doing this was identified by

---

[122] FRC, 'Feedback Statement – Consulting on a Revised UK Stewardship Code' (October 2019) 11–12, https://www.frc.org.uk/getattachment/2912476c-d183-46bd-a86e-dfb024f694ad/200206-Feedback-Statement-Consultation-on-revised-Stewardship-Code-FINAL-(amended-timetable).pdf.

the FCA as one of the remaining principal barriers to effective stewardship in its feedback statement during the stewardship code consultation.[123]

The SC 2020 explicitly recognises that investment and stewardship activities go hand in hand both in the definition of stewardship and in one of its key principles.[124] As such, the effective, portfolio performance enhancing stewardship integration into investment processes and decision-making is particularly important in the development of stewardship practice, at least for active managers.

Let us first look at the link between stewardship activities and engagement outcomes.

C. The Link between Stewardship Activities and Engagement Outcomes

Much of the current stewardship reporting does not allow an assessment of whether there is just a correlation between engagement and outcomes (there are outcomes after interactions between asset managers and companies) or causation (such interactions contributed to the outcomes). Asset managers must find ways to demonstrate that their stewardship activities contributed to engagement outcomes. The objective should be to establish a likelihood or a degree of causality rather than a solid causal relationship.

Causality for the purposes of stewardship will typically involve an acknowledgment of the influence an asset manager's activities have had in bringing about changes by the company that has been engaged. Building strong professional working relationships between investors and companies that allow such acknowledgement, even when there are potentially significant differences in opinions and robust discussions, will be critical in facilitating this.

There is evidence that getting a company's acknowledgment is possible. As demonstrated in some of the stewardship reporting reviewed in section IV, asset managers increasingly publish individual engagement case studies claiming at least implicitly to demonstrate a degree of causality between their stewardship activities and outcomes. Best practice amongst asset managers involves running these case studies past the engaged companies for approval and at least an implicit acknowledgement of their role in bringing about change. Most recently, Robeco has introduced an engagement impact attribution framework and started to seek systematic feedback from companies within its SDG Engagement fund that it engages in the form of a survey.[125]

Asset managers should be open in acknowledging that they will only very rarely, for example in the case of successful shareholder resolutions, take decisions for companies, thus establishing a direct link between engagement activity and outcome. However, high quality engagement may contribute to or accelerate changes and

---

[123] FCA, 'Building a Regulatory Framework for Effective Stewardship – Feedback Statement – FS 19/7' (October 2019) 29, https://www.fca.org.uk/publication/feedback/fs19-7.pdf.

[124] See, for example, SC 2020 (n 10 above) Principle 7.

[125] See Robeco, 'Robeco SAM Global SDG Engagement Equities, Impact Report 2021', https://on24static.akamaized.net/event/36/28/58/2/rt/1/documents/resourceList1650877002399/robecosamglobal sdgengagementequitiesimpactreport20211650876965939.pdf.

companies should be ready to acknowledge the role of asset managers who have worked constructively with them to achieve a specific outcome.

Again, the objective would be to establish a likelihood or a degree of causality rather than a solid causal relationship. An asset manager could build a supporting case by providing clear evidence when and how a concern and a specific potential solution to deal with it, which was subsequently adopted, were raised with a company. This is the reason why systems and processes to record objectives, capture interactions and track progress, as described in Section V, are critical.

Alternatively, or in addition, a regulator such as the FRC could reach out to companies for their assessment of the activities and effectiveness of asset manager engagement in contributing to changes. Furthermore, asset owners might play a role. The world's largest pension fund, Government Pension Investment Fund in Japan, has surveyed companies for six years seeking insights on the stewardship activities of its external asset managers and stewardship practice in general.[126] One drawback of this approach is of course that the feedback could be compromised where companies feel that asset managers pushed too hard, or made unreasonable requests.

If there is an engagement outcome at a specific company and a degree of causality linking it to an asset manager's stewardship activity, the final step is to quantify and ideally measure the effect of the outcome on the performance of a specific investment portfolio, market returns or the real world.

D. The Impact of Outcomes on Specific Investment Portfolios, Market Returns or the Real World

Let us start with the impact of engagement outcomes, or stewardship-generated insights, related to company-specific investment opportunities or risks on the performance of investment portfolios during a typical holding period.

i. Measurement of Impact on Specific Investment Portfolios

a. Stewardship Performance Attribution

The ultimate objective should be attribution of the impact of stewardship activities and related insights on investment performance. Performance attribution is a key part of investment performance evaluation, which analyses a portfolio's results in the context of the investment management process. It decomposes returns into all the components that are consistent with the investment decision-making process and explains the active choices that made the portfolio outperform or underperform its benchmark.[127] Performance attribution is a technique used to determine the additional return or alpha of a portfolio. As such, it is a key tool in assessing the quality and

---

[126] Government Pension Investment Fund, 'Report of the 6th Survey of Listed Companies Regarding Institutional Investors' Stewardship Activities' (May 2021), https://www.gpif.go.jp/en/investment/summary_report_of_the_6th_survey.pdf.

[127] K Koedijk et al, *Achieving Investment Excellence – A Practical Guide for Trustees of Pension Funds, Endowments and Foundations* (Wiley, 2019) 104–105.

success of investment decision-making of a fund manager. If stewardship outcomes or investment relevant insights can influence the performance of a portfolio, attribution analysis seeks to quantify their impact.

b. The Impact of Engagement Outcomes and Insights on Investment Portfolio Performance

While stewardship performance attribution should be the ultimate objective, there are intermediate steps asset managers can take to estimate the impact of engagement on investment portfolio performance. A growing body of studies of the stewardship activities of mainstream asset managers[128] suggests that the engagement outcomes at companies they contribute towards can have a significant positive effect on an investment portfolio's risk/reward profile and thus performance.[129] Moreover, the stewardship reporting reviewed in section IV implies that asset managers believe that their activities are contributing to engagement outcomes and that the integration of related insights into investment processes and decision-making can add investment value.

An important recent academic study by Becht, Franks and Wagner goes further and illustrates how investment performance could be attributed to stewardship insights.[130] It looks at the stewardship activities of an active UK asset manager, which include high level private meetings with company representatives, including management and Board members, and then analyses how its monitoring and engagement work influences trading decisions. The research provides a detailed picture of how the decisions of fund managers are influenced by stewardship activities which include putting companies on watch lists when there are concerns and systematic escalation, including votes against. These monitoring and engagement signals generated by both fund managers and engagement specialists are picked up in rating changes of internal analysts which, the research finds, contribute to trading decisions. The study provides evidence that stewardship can generate investment-relevant insights and its results suggest that in the case of the asset manager studied they contributed to performance and alpha generation. As such, the findings highlight how fund managers and stewardship specialists working together as a team can generate advantages in active asset management.[131]

The study breaks new ground as no prior research has been able to make the link between private stewardship activities and investment decisions of an

---

[128] This term is used to distinguish them from shareholder activists, such as hedge funds, which should be considered as a separate discipline in practice and the literature.

[129] See for example, E Dimson et al, 'Active Ownership' (2015) 28 *The Review of Financial Studies* 3225; A Hoepner et al, 'ESG Shareholder Engagement and Downside Risk' *AFA 2018 paper, European Corporate Governance Institute – Finance Working Paper 671/2020* (30 April 2021), https://ssrn.com/abstract=2874252. For a leading study on a European activist fund, see M Becht et al, 'Returns to Shareholder Activism: Evidence from a Clinical Study of the Hermes U.K. Focus Fund', *ECGI Finance Working Paper No 138/2006, London Business School Finance Working Paper No FIN462* (April 2008), https://ssrn.com/abstract=934712.

[130] M Becht et al, 'The Benefits of Access: Evidence from Private Meetings with Portfolio Firms' *ECGI Finance Working Paper No 751/2021* (27 March 2021), https://ssrn.com/abstract=3813948; Becht et al, ibid.

[131] ibid 33.

asset manager.[132] It also raises the question whether the asset manager might have benefited from insider information, as regulations do not permit selective disclosure of price-sensitive information. The authors highlight the internal rules and compliance function of the asset manager studied[133] and explain why, even when adhering to relevant regulations, information from meetings could still have value: First, fund managers may be able to combine non-material information obtained in stewardship interactions with other information they have collected in their research process; second, personal interactions with management and Boards may be valuable in judging individuals, including their character and ability, thus providing insights that generate an information advantage.[134] As such, the informational asymmetry can be a perfectly legal source of alpha; however, there can be a fine line between stewardship generated, investment enhancing non-material information and insider information.

c. Towards Stewardship Performance Attribution

The boundaries between stewardship-generated investment insights on the one hand and engagement outcomes addressing investment opportunities or risks on the other hand can be fluid and overlap, for example regarding anticipated changes. It is helpful to look at them separately, as operationalising stewardship attribution will significantly differ between the two categories. Assuming an actively managed investment portfolio with holding periods of three to five years, it is critical in both cases to focus on insights and outcomes that are likely to be financially material for the specific company rather than at a systems level.

d. Performance Attribution Related to Stewardship Generated Investment Insights

Stewardship can benefit investment performance in the absence of specific outcomes, namely through investment relevant insights that are gained in interactions between an asset manager and a company. This is recognised in Principle 7 of the SC 2020 and the related stewardship outcome, namely examples of how information gathered through stewardship has informed acquisition, monitoring and exit decisions.

To attribute the impact of stewardship activities and insights in investment performance evaluation represents multiple challenges, not least the fact that there are often several factors influencing an investment decision. Moreover, stewardship insights related to investment opportunities or risks may or may not materialise within a portfolio relevant timeframe. Having said this, based on academic work, at least where stewardship insights are the only or a main factor in investment decisions, it should in theory be possible to attribute performance. Further challenges for an asset manager will be documenting, internally communicating and then causally linking

---

[132] ibid 6.
[133] ibid 5.
[134] ibid 5.

the stewardship insights with buy, hold or sell decisions. The systematic translation of qualitative stewardship insights into investment signals is likely to involve an intermediate step in the form of a rating that changes because of information obtained.[135] Experienced practitioners point out that attribution analysis is much less precise in practice than it seems when considered as a theoretical concept and there are significant operational challenges in implementing it, not least because of the interrelation of factors.[136]

However, while it may remain an imprecise science, the study by Becht et al discussed earlier suggests that at least for some stewardship insights, it should be possible to undertake some stewardship performance attribution on a more systematic basis. In the meantime, the case studies included in some of the stewardship reporting reviewed in section IV making a qualitative link between engagement activities and investment decision-making are a first step in this direction.

e. Performance Attribution Related to Engagement Related Outcomes Addressing Investment Opportunities or Risks

There are even more significant challenges and limitations to stewardship performance attribution if they relate to engagement-related outcomes. As discussed, companies may be ready to acknowledge that they were influenced even on major issues by an asset manager. However, it will be very hard – and in many cases impossible – to make a robust link between a stewardship-driven outcome and the performance of an investee company and subsequently a portfolio, given the direct and indirect benefits of engagement outcomes which often occur over long time horizons. Much will depend on the nature of the issue addressed, when the specific outcome will materialise and how it will impact investment opportunities or risks related to a specific company.[137]

However, the academic studies referenced earlier[138] suggest that at least an estimation of the impact of engagement on the performance of investment portfolios is feasible regarding robustly measured outcomes that address investment opportunities or risks likely to be material for a specific, targeted company within the holding period of the relevant investment portfolio.

Systematic stewardship performance attribution could and arguably should be the ultimate objective and achievable to some extent regarding some issues, at least regarding stewardship-generated investment insights. However, qualitative and quantitative descriptions and estimations of the impact of engagement outcomes and insights on the performance of investment portfolios are important first steps that asset managers should take while more sophisticated methods are developed and tested.

---

[135] For an example of what this can look like, see Becht et al (n 130 above).

[136] Feedback from Gary Greenberg, Head of Global Emerging Markets at Federated Hermes Ltd, on an early draft of this chapter (on file with the author).

[137] A McKinsey study suggests that there are five ways in which companies that are high performing in terms of their management of ESG issues create value. See Witold Henisz et al, 'Five Ways that ESG Creates Value' *McKinsey Quarterly* (2019), https://www.mckinsey.com/business-functions/strategy-and-corporate-finance/our-insights/five-ways-that-esg-creates-value#.

[138] See n 129 above.

ii. Measurement of Real World Outcomes, Including their Impact on Market Return

We established that engagement outcomes addressing investment opportunities and risks related to a specific company, including those commonly referred to as material ESG issues, can impact the performance of investment portfolios and can be measurable as such.

In contrast, real world outcomes are unlikely to be measurable in terms of their impact on the performance of specific investment portfolios. As highlighted in Table 2, they need to be measured in a different way, for example in terms of their contribution to SDG or PAI targets and indicators, as their impact on the value of a specific company or portfolio could be small (and in some cases might be negative), indirect or only occur over a long time horizon.

This does not mean that all or most real world outcomes are financially *immaterial*. The feedback cycle described in section III means that over time some real world outcomes can feed back into the performance of investment portfolios, impact upon environmental, social and financial systems and affect market performance. For universal owners, it has been shown that in the long term the overall market return will impact on the value of their aggregate portfolios more than the performance of specific companies or portfolios in the short to medium term. Asset owners should ask their asset managers to provide them with estimates of how their stewardship activities contribute to protect or enhance long-term market return. Such estimates will need to be based on an understanding and measurement of the real world impact of stewardship activities using the SDGs and other relevant frameworks.

The 17 SDGs and the underlying targets and indicators provide a comprehensive, globally agreed framework for the measurement of sustainability-related real world outcomes of investments which is already widely used in the financial industry.[139] The SDGs cover many systemic risks relating to or stemming from environmental, social and financial systems and as such seem well placed to serve as a basis and common language between asset owners, asset managers and companies. They are particularly relevant for universal owners.

Moreover, there is a wide range of impact measurement frameworks,[140] including the Global Impact Investing Network's IRIS+, a system for measuring social, environmental, and financial success of impact investing.[141]

Finally, the EU's PAI framework introduced by the SFDR, will provide a regulatory measurement system specifically targeted at asset managers. The PAI define indicators that asset managers will need to track covering a wide range of company related real world sustainability outcomes, including on greenhouse gas emissions, biodiversity, water, waste, social and norms based indicators.

Going forward, asset managers should seek to demonstrate that their stewardship activities contribute to real world outcomes measured under an appropriate and robust framework using recognised indicators. And, wherever possible, they should

---

[139] See PRI, https://www.unpri.org/sustainability-issues/sustainable-development-goals.

[140] For a list of frameworks and tools, see the PRI's website: https://www.unpri.org/sustainable-development-goals/investing-with-sdg-outcomes-a-five-part-framework-appendix-1-3-tools-and-investor-examples/5907. article.

[141] See https://thegiin.org/tools/.

attempt to estimate the impact of their activities addressing systemic risks on market return in the long term.

VII. SUMMARY AND CONCLUSION

A. Scope and Definitions of the SC 2020

The SC 2020 has a much expanded definition of stewardship, bringing together investment, engagement and ESG, and focuses throughout on outcomes. Surprisingly, in our brief review we found that it lacks a definition of engagement and does not attempt to define and differentiate between different types of outcomes. Therefore, the boundaries of the outcomes of engagement the SC 2020 requires signatories to seek are unclear. This is an important omission given the ongoing debate about the materiality of ESG issues and the different nature and benefits of potential engagement outcomes.

Based on the wider definition of stewardship and particularly Principle 4 of the SC 2020, we concluded that real world outcomes that are not necessarily financially material for a specific company or investment portfolio during a typical holding period seem to be within the scope of outcomes sought under the SC 2020. As such, the new code seems to have moved towards an expanded interpretation of materiality.

B. Categorisation of Engagement Outcomes

Given the developing definition of materiality, which has important implications for the measurement of the impacts of stewardship, we recommended a categorisation of the primary outcomes that are being sought through engagement activities and identified different types of outcomes. We suggested three distinct but overlapping and interdependent categories of outcomes and relevant ways to measure impacts. The proposed categorisation is useful in identifying and understanding potential trade-offs between engagement outcomes.

Asset managers should indicate to what extent and over what time frames outcomes sought are expected to have an impact on a specific company/investment portfolio or whether they are expected to address systemic issues and enhance market return. We concluded that there would be a third category which would capture outcomes related to values held and norms adhered to by investors, which may or may not contribute to returns over time (or may be impossible to measure or estimate).

A categorisation of engagement outcomes would enhance the credibility of stewardship, accountability to clients and inform the measurement of its impacts. It can also inform the organisation and resourcing of stewardship activities.

C. Improved but Anecdotal Reporting Failing to Demonstrate Causality of Outcomes

The SC 2020 has led to considerable improvements in stewardship reporting which reflect better implementation and practice by asset managers investing in relevant resources. However, the reporting of engagement outcomes (Principle 9) and, crucially, the evidence of stewardship investment integration (Principle 7) remains largely anecdotal rather than being based on systematic practice. Without a clearer definition of engagement outcomes and a categorisation, this should not be surprising.

Moreover, the question of causality or attribution, as defined in this chapter for stewardship purposes, linking stewardship activities of asset managers to engagement outcomes, both those addressing investment opportunities and risks and real world, remains under-explored and requires attention of the industry.

D. Building Blocks of Impactful Engagement

Having argued that there are missing links in current stewardship practice, we went through the key building blocks of impactful engagement and their connection and suggested that asset managers should focus on them to achieve outcomes and obtain investment relevant stewardship insights. Without these building blocks in place, expecting significant attributable change at companies and engagement outcomes involving some degree of causation rather than just correlation appears unrealistic.

Asset owners should have visibility about all aspects of the engagement process of asset managers, including around the setting of objectives, which should provide clarity about the nature of outcomes sought, so they can assess whether they align with their interests.

E. Measurement of the Impact of Engagement Outcomes

We argued that asset managers who want to differentiate themselves based on their stewardship capability should aim to demonstrate how their stewardship activities contribute to engagement outcomes and whether, how significantly and when they affect investment returns and/or the real world. This is important regarding outcomes addressing company-specific investment opportunities or risks (or related stewardship insights), which can contribute to the outperformance of specific investment portfolios, or alpha. It is equally relevant regarding real world engagement outcomes, which can address systemic risks thus enhancing market return, or contribute to progress on relevant sustainability indicators, such as the SDGs.

F. The Future of Stewardship: Taking a Step Back Regarding Corporate Engagement

Until the asset management industry starts to recognise and address the challenges with engagement and investment practices identified in this chapter, the full potential of investee company stewardship in securing returns for asset owners and their beneficiaries with due regard to real world outcomes will remain untapped. As such, it is time to take a step back for the investment industry.

11

Responsible Investment

DAVID HICKEY*

I. A NEW SPECIALISM

THE FIELD OF responsible investment has grown rapidly in recent years, driven by increasing stakeholder interest and rapidly deployed new legislation and regulation. This has led firms in all parts of the investment industry to build out capability. While the field of responsible investment has been around for decades (under the guises of stewardship, ESG, sustainability etc), the number of specialists has been small, and the depth of talent not enough to suddenly supply the entire industry with the headcount necessary for the explosion in roles being experienced at the time of writing.

Given the clear mismatch in supply and demand for talented and experienced resource in responsible investment, employers have often been forced to repurpose existing investment staff into responsibility-focused roles, or else hire individuals with backgrounds in sustainability into roles with a high degree of investment. Your author is one of these individuals, coming from a pure investment background and having to rapidly re-skill in the sustainability arena, and re-educate on an ongoing basis following sweeping regulatory changes.

The difficulty of operating within the responsible investment landscape is high due to the twin lenses through which a practitioner must view any investment strategy: both responsible *and* investment. While this may sound obvious to many readers, it is remarkable how many newcomers (and more seasoned veterans) of this arena still misunderstand the interplay between the two. It is possible to learn the basics of finance in a few months: the UK CFA Investment Management Certificate will provide a good grounding in basic concepts. Learning the intricacies of finance, across many different market conditions, takes a lifetime. This is one of the key reasons longevity is held in such high regard in investment management in particular, and why it is so highly rewarded. Likewise, the dizzying array of different competing issues within the responsibility/sustainability/stewardship arena across

* The views expressed in this chapter are personal opinions of the author and do not represent those of organisations he is affiliated with in a professional capacity.

the traditional environmental, social and governance (ESG) pillars are so broad and interlinked, with positive and negative feedback cycles from issue to issue, it is arguably impossible for one person to have more than a working knowledge of more than three or four areas. An individual who perhaps possesses an MSc in Environmental Management and has completed the full Chartered Financial Analyst (CFA) qualification is in a good place to *start* a career, but the expertise in both responsible *and* investment will need to be built up over time. Becoming doubly-expert is very difficult.

In recognition of the doubly difficult nature of mastery during this time of transition, below are presented some musings on key points of misunderstanding, and some critical points that need to be understood by all market players. Individuals from either a traditional investing background or from a sustainability background should be able to increase their empathy towards those in the other camp. Those just starting out in their careers, like the individual mentioned in the previous paragraph sporting a sustainability-focused MSc and holding the CFA charter at the outset of their career, will likely roll their eyes at much of this. They will be 'sustainability natives' that understand all sides of the discussion from the outset, but even these individuals will have much to learn from those deemed 'industry veterans'.

II. LOST IN TRANSLATION

'The British and the Americans are two great peoples divided by a common tongue'

George Bernard Shaw, November 1942

The above quote, usually attributed to playwright George Bernard Shaw, could quite easily be paraphrased to describe the collision of sustainability focus into the world of traditional asset management.

'Investment managers and sustainability specialists are two great professions divided by a common lexicon'

David Hickey, January 2022

One of the key issues the investment management industry is currently facing is in communicating the new field of sustainable or responsible investment. Many will attempt to gloss over this difficulty by simply describing everything as 'ESG'. With this shortcut, the industry has been bombarded with lazy product marketing, lazy editorial, and lazy analysis, with the term ESG being attached to anything that may have an environmental tilt (often accompanied by the equally cringe-inducing photo of a sapling growing from a pile of coins, or from dirt held in cupped hands).

Given the likelihood of confusion with all these different terms, it is worth introducing some definitions of terms that will be repeatedly used throughout this chapter, followed by a guide to use, misuse and misunderstanding of these terms. Terms in the investment lexicon are generally well understood because the nomenclature has been developed over decades, and the industry is mature. This is not the case for what will be referred to throughout the remainder of this chapter as responsible investment.

III. WHAT I TALK ABOUT WHEN I TALK ABOUT RESPONSIBLE INVESTMENT

The PRI[1] defines responsible investment as a strategy and practice to incorporate ESG factors in investment decisions and active ownership. This is a neat and accurate definition that immediately highlights that the term responsible investment is dominant to the terms ESG and active ownership. This in turn suggests that more nebulous terms such as 'green', 'impact', 'sustainability' and a host of other terms are sub-sets of responsible investment. Responsible investment encompasses the whole gamut of this new(ish) field. It is important to think about where the various terms sit within the framework that makes up responsible investment, so that as writers it is possible to convey accurate, unambiguous communication about the field, and as readers it is possible to easily detect misinformation and deception from those writers aiming to take advantage of ambiguity in this area of the market. As such, it is worth outlining some of these terms and considering how they might be used best, as well as how they may be most commonly misused.

The most recognisable term in the field of responsible investment is the acronym ESG. It is so ubiquitous that it is taken by many to be easily interchangeable with responsible investment as shorthand to describe the field of study. It is the latest in a series of acronyms misused as shorthand in this way, following on from CSR (corporate social responsibility) and SRI (socially responsible investing), which, like ESG, do represent approaches that are useful subsets within the responsible investment field, but do not capture all the nuance required to paint a full picture. The acronym ESG was first coined by Ivo Knoepfel in a report for the UN Global Compact called 'Who Cares Wins',[2] published in 2005, where the authors suggested that the 'analysts are asked to better incorporate … ESG factors in their research as appropriate, and to further develop the necessary investment know-how, models and tools in a creative and thoughtful way'.

ESG factors are best described as being concerns or opportunities that can have an impact on an investment which can affect the financial outcomes of that investment (otherwise known as a financially material factor). Analysis of such factors becomes part of the investment process, through incorporation during stock analysis and/or screening. So, while the list of inputs that could be considered as having a financially material impact on an investment is very long, the correct incorporation of those inputs is well defined, and arguably a narrow process.

---

[1] 'What is Responsible Investment?', www.unpri.org/an-introduction-to-responsible-investment/what-is-responsible-investment/4780.article.

[2] The Global Compact, 'Who Cares Wins' (2004) 6, https://d306pr3pise04h.cloudfront.net/docs/issues_doc%2FFinancial_markets%2Fwho_cares_who_wins.pdf.

For a term originally coined by Dr Knoepfel to describe three classes of information for input into investment analysis, ESG has been misused for years by market participants, and in many cases has become meaningless shorthand for something 'green' (another grossly overused, overly ambiguous term). Market participants will often refer to individual funds, or even entire suites of funds, as being 'ESG funds'. Given the definition presented, this terminology is clearly meaningless. Often funds will try to target opportunities presented by risks in ESG factors, in which case 'ESG thematic fund' would be a suitably descriptive term. Funds may try and overweight or underweight exposure to particular factors in a portfolio, producing an 'ESG factor' or 'ESG tilted' fund, with many examples available of funds using carbon data to reduce exposure to high carbon industries in 'carbon tilted' funds. This is also usefully descriptive. As a general rule, the term ESG should be used as an adjective, or better still, use a more specific phrase.

The second term to consider is 'sustainable investing' (often used interchangeably with 'sustainability' in the investment industry). The issue with this term is twofold. The first is that sustainable investing was a term that existed prior to the growth in mainstream responsible investment and referred to something quite different. Whereas the term 'responsible' inherently implies a duty of care, 'sustainable' simply describes the likelihood of something being able to continue. Sustainable growth, sustainable dividends, sustainable franchises – all are terms used within the lexicon of traditional investing. Second, there is often a challenge that comes with the use of sustainable investment. When allocating investments to mandates that support sustainability, there is the implication, using the strict definition of the word so commonly used in traditional investment circles, that those mandates that are not in the sustainable investment allocation are therefore deemed unsustainable. Whilst many professionals in responsible investment may roll their eyes at the predictability of such a response, it is a fair challenge. Investing uses the language of investing, and the terminology for sustainability in the responsible investment sense comes from the world of economic development. As such it is perfectly normal for the use of the word 'sustainable' to be challenged by traditional investors, no matter how frustrating or churlish this may seem.

When using the term 'sustainability' in a responsible investment context, the definition is taken from the UN Bruntland Commission's report on sustainable development, where it is taken to mean 'meeting the needs of the present without compromising the ability of future generations to meet their own needs'.[3] This is an excellent concise definition that is exceptionally useful in an investment context. This definition does away with the prior issue mentioned, that the opposite of sustainable is unsustainable. Instead, it would be fair to describe those investments outside of any sustainability allocation as having traits that may compromise the ability of future generations to meet their own needs. Some may read this last sentence and suggest that it simply sounds like a synonym for 'unsustainable'. While on one level that may be accurate, the subtle difference in messaging and delivery is important, for reasons that will be discussed later in this text.

---

[3] United Nations Academic Impact, 'Sustainability', https://www.un.org/en/academic-impact/sustainability.

The final term to consider is 'green'. Green is arguably the most easily recognisable term in the field of responsible investment. It is a catch-all term meaning 'environmentally friendly' and is now ubiquitous in all walks of life, making it easily recognisable and understandable. This ubiquity is both a blessing and a curse. Green as used in a phrase is evocative and paints a picture of clear streams and summer meadows, images that have in the past often gone unchallenged. New words have recently entered the lexicon, first 'greenwashing' (the claim that something is environmentally positive when it likely is not) and then 'greenwishing' (the painting of actions and approaches as having a more positive environmental impact in the future than they are likely to have). The existence of these two newly minted words implies much about issues with the term green, which may be easily extended to the term ESG as before: these terms suffer from a lack of specificity which in turn devalues them in the eyes of professionals who want more than a vague overview of what an investment opportunity may be.

A. Words Have Power

It would be easy to question the challenges made above. Does it really matter what ESG or green mean if everyone takes them to mean something broadly positive for the environment and/or society? The answer to that lies in intention, both the intention of the writer of those terms, and the intention of the consumer of them. How one presents phrases, in word usage, context and delivery, can have enormous impact on interpretation, as wordsmiths throughout the centuries can attest. To reflect on this, it is worth considering a single line from a single piece of literature:

> To be or not to be, that is the question.[4]

Ten words spoken by the character Hamlet, in Shakespeare's play by the same name, the start of a much longer soliloquy and arguably the most famous line in all of English literature. For over 400 years it has beguiled audiences. Whether someone has ever read or seen a performance of Hamlet, they are likely to know this line. Aye, there's the rub. Familiarity with a term or piece of text can lead to a false sense of understanding, or an honest misunderstanding.

Going back to the famous line above, those familiar with the full text will be aware it is a speech questioning whether the eponymous Hamlet should make the choice to continue living, or to bring about his own death. Despite their age, audiences understand these words, this phrase, as easily as if it were uttered in a modern pop song. It would seem that musing on the nature of human existence is a pastime that resonates across the ages. Ten words spoken countless times by innumerable actors over centuries, it is simple to assume that those words tell an audience all they need to know of the situation. There is, of course, far more to it than that. Subtle alterations to the delivery of this line, emphasis on different words, changes in pacing, all

---

[4] W Shakespeare, *Hamlet* (Penguin, 2005) Act 3 Scene 1.

reveal depths to Hamlet's character, what his mental state is when delivering the lines. Feeling, context and subtext is all.

It is reasonable to ask what any of this has to do with responsible investment. The answer is: quite a lot. Part of the beauty of Shakespeare is in a theatre company's ability to reinterpret the exact same text in myriad ways to keep audiences interested. Meaning can shift with delivery, a line here and there upended through alteration of the set, or the physical acting, providing differing context to words. Reinvention is what keeps audiences returning to these texts, it is their imprecise nature that gives them their longevity and wonder.

Musing on imprecision in wording is important when considering this chapter's central theme of the language being used to describe responsible investment. Whereas audiences in theatres will delight at the twists and turns of the latest interpretation of the Prince of Denmark, financial literature should contain no such ambiguity of meaning. The lack of deliberate and precise usage of terminology used in the field of responsible investing represents a failure of the financial industry and the professionals within it (despite the best efforts of many to prevent such failure). This has created a situation where terms like 'ESG' can be warped to fit any approach to investment, where fund managers can cynically relabel funds as 'ESG' despite there having been no change to the fund's investment approach for many years, and where individuals seemingly become experts in 'ESG' because it is reasonably easy to be expert in something with no real definition.

Wherever a Wild West-like situation appears, a Sheriff soon follows, and the field of responsible investment is no different. In the absence of sensible self-regulation, many regulators have now stepped in to try to bring order to some of the chaos currently being experienced in the market.

The EU is currently the most advanced body in introducing regulation, with the Sustainable Finance Disclosure Regulation (SFDR)[5] coming into force in March 2021 and the EU Taxonomy for Sustainable Activities (EU Taxonomy)[6] coming into force in July 2020 (though the final wording of what activities are and are not considered sustainable is being agreed in 2022). The CFA Institute, home of the internationally recognised Chartered Financial Analyst designation, has also introduced Global ESG Disclosure Standards for Investment Products[7] and is promoting these standards through its extensive network of over 160,000 charter holders across the globe. Finally, the formation of the International Sustainability Standards Board (ISSB)[8] will bring much-needed standardisation to sustainability data presented in company accounts, in turn allowing common approaches for investors. These attempts at the

---

[5] Commission, 'Sustainability-related Disclosure in the Financial Services Sector', https://ec.europa.eu/info/business-economy-euro/banking-and-finance/sustainable-finance/sustainability-related-disclosure-financial-services-sector_en.

[6] Commission, 'EU Taxonomy for Sustainable Activities', https://ec.europa.eu/info/business-economy-euro/banking-and-finance/sustainable-finance/eu-taxonomy-sustainable-activities_en.

[7] CFA Institute, 'Global ESG Disclosure Standards for Investment Products' (2021), www.cfainstitute.org/en/ethics-standards/codes/esg-standards.

[8] IFRS, 'International Sustainability Standards Board', www.ifrs.org/groups/international-sustainability-standards-board/.

standardisation of language and disclosure are absolutely vital to the future credibility of any efforts in responsible investment and will bring a new era of professionalisation to the space.

B. Why is This Important?

There are two key reasons why precision is vital to credibility in responsible investment. The first is down to client expectations. Whether the term client is taken to mean an individual investor making a small regular payment into pension fund, or a sovereign wealth fund with billions of dollars to invest, the message is similar: clients have a right to know what they are investing in, and that it matches their expectations on an ongoing basis. This point alone requires deliberate, unequivocal language throughout the investment value chain; from product designers, investment managers, marketing teams, brokers or wealth managers, each part needs to be clear what the investment opportunity presented offers and what it does not. Where language is vague and left open to interpretation it is easy to envisage a situation where a provider sells a product that the client is convinced offers something beyond what it really does. The lack of a clear definition around the term ESG and green is partly responsible for this. It is clear there will be examples where a seller may classify a product as 'ESG friendly' whereas in reality the client would not see it as such.

Clear and unambiguous language will help here. It should not be incumbent upon clients to have to dig right down into the small print of a product, or take many hours of meetings with a manager to understand the crux of what they mean by 'ESG'. While it may indeed be possible for a large institutional buyer to do this, it is not possible for a small retail investor to have this level of access. There is a real danger of a huge mis-selling scandal to develop due to this gap in interpretation. There is no accusation here that the industry is maliciously misleading investors, but accidentally misleading investors will often be viewed in a similar light by regulators. Trust is a key issue in the financial markets, and the sheer number of past financial scandals present in the minds of the general public mean that caution needs to be exercised in this area. The conflation of the terms ESG, green, responsible and the word 'ethical' mean that the field of responsible investment will always be held to a much higher standard than the likes of high-risk venture capital or speculative areas like crypto currencies. The industry must strive to do better in the eyes of the general public.

Linked to this last point is the second reason precision will garner credibility for responsible investment. There are many in the finance industry who have become successful through managing investments using traditional approaches and have no interest in moving towards running sustainable mandates. These individuals and their associated firms are the incumbents that are in the throes of being disrupted by the sustainable investment wave and will do all they can to disparage the modern, multi-stakeholder approach. Traditional investors will seize on the vague interpretations offered by terminology in responsible investment, often twist it and use strawman arguments to present it as folly, and journalists will further sensationalise the arguments as 'liberal' and 'woke'. While proponents of responsible investments should welcome this as it is indicative of a strong move into the mainstream, it also shows the need for the industry to mature to the point where these arguments can no longer be formed, and when accusations are thrown, are more easily extinguished. Clear, unambiguous terminology agreed throughout the industry would be a major step in this direction.

So far this chapter has been focused on developing the language needed to make a success of the responsible investment field, and has been targeted at all practitioners of all backgrounds. The next section is primarily aimed at those practitioners that have entered responsible investment from a sustainability background.

IV. CAPITAL

This chapter opened on the difficulties of becoming doubly expert. Unfortunately, experience shows that there are many professionals working in the area of responsible investment who lack the financial literacy required to be fully effective in the roles they are doing. While it may not be necessary to spend years qualifying for the Chartered Financial Analyst designation, a strong background in the mechanics of markets and the basics of stock and bond analysis provide a distinct advantage to anyone coming from a sustainability background, and nowhere is this more significant than in the origination of, and the uses of, capital.

A good definition of capital comes from Investopedia:

> Capital is a broad term that can describe any thing that confers value or benefit to its owner, such as a factory and its machinery, intellectual property like patents, or the financial assets of a business or an individual. While money itself may be construed as capital is, capital is more often associated with cash that is being put to work for productive or investment purposes.[9]

Capital is essentially all the things that allow a business to operate as a going concern.

Capital has a source. That source can supply capital to a company on a permanent basis (equity capital) or on a term basis (debt capital). These injections of capital are made through swapping cash for an ownership share in the company (in the case of equity) or through providing cash via a repayable loan for a fixed term, and receiving interest payments in the interim (in the case of debt). Companies can also inject capital into themselves through reinvesting profits made through business activities (retained earnings).

Capital has a cost. This cost is easy to discover in terms of debt financing, and largely impossible to discover in terms of equity financing (both from equity capital injections and retained earnings). There are many mathematical models that point towards the cost of equity, including the dividend growth model[10] and the capital

---

[9] M Hargrave, 'Capital' (*Investopedia*, March 2021), www.investopedia.com/terms/c/capital.asp.
[10] W Kenton, 'Cost of Equity' (*Investopedia*, August 2021), www.investopedia.com/terms/c/costofequity.asp.

asset pricing model.[11] Both of these models have big flaws when calculating the cost of equity to a company. Investors exhibit lots of behavioural factors that are not captured by these models. Furthermore, any investors that use these models will use different assumptions, so when an equity offering is subscribed to at a fixed price, the cost of equity assumed by the investors is hidden as the market can only guess at their future cashflow assumptions. Add to this the fact that the majority of companies (particularly large cash generative companies) simply do not raise new equity capital, often choosing instead to de-equitise their companies through market buy-backs, and it is simple to come to a stark conclusion: for the vast majority of listed equity, the cost of equity is a market derived guesstimate, and it is impossible to claim what factors do and do not drive it. For companies and projects outside that classification, the cost of equity is simply the return expected to make the investment worthwhile on a risk adjusted basis.

The cost of debt is set by the market and is based on a company's ability to pay that debt. The more obvious a company's ability to generate cashflow with which to pay debt, the cheaper its debt will be. Companies use the financial markets to raise debt capital on a constant basis, and as such the cost of debt for companies is very transparent. The fixed term nature of debt agreements makes it very easy to calculate fully the assumptions made by market participants in pricing debt.

The role of debt markets is critical to the financing of thousands of companies across the world, in particular those companies with large capital requirements, such as companies in the utilities, mining and energy sectors. These are the same types of companies that are unlikely to raise capital on the equity markets. They are also the same types of companies that are often the subject of divestment campaigns. As divestment campaigns involve the disposal of existing equity, there is no change to a company's capital position as a result. The right to a dividend and the right to vote at the AGM simply transfer to a new owner, which may be taken as a positive by incalcitrant management where the new owners place less importance on sustainability issues than the divestors. While some make the argument that depressing share prices increase the cost of equity, in reality this is meaningless because companies in this situation do not issue new equity. As such the cost of equity and the weighted average cost of (overall) capital are poor measures of the ongoing cost of financing this type of company, with the cost of debt being the key measure.

A key method for impacting the cost of debt of companies is a remarkably simple approach: don't buy it. Where a firm engages in activity that does not meet the sustainability standards of a particular investor, then that investor should withhold funding from that company. While equity investors are able to use their votes to impact company behaviour, debt investors are able to make business as usual more expensive through debt denial. A large shift in demand for a company's debt will lead to a shift in price, partly as a result of simple supply/demand shifts, and partly because an element of the risk of bonds is in the repayment of capital at the end of a

[11] W Kenton, 'Capital Asset Pricing Model (CAPM)' (*Investopedia*, January 2022), www.investopedia.com/terms/c/capm.asp.

bond's term. Any inability to 'roll' capital from one bond to a subsequent bond raises the risk, and thereby raises the cost. Debt denial at scale has the potential to be one of the biggest levers that asset owners can collectively pull to influence company change. It is an obvious next step for any asset owners with strong approaches to equity voting and engagement. Engage your equity, deny your debt.

Understanding capital structures is what allows a practitioner to tie language to action. When discussing the need for precision in language above it is important to understand the mechanisms for turning that language into impactful action. The actions of engagement and voting are inherently actions of directing capital allocation. Debt denial is an action directing capital allocation. Through the mechanism of capital allocation away from activities that have been precisely defined (as above) as being unsuitable for the client base, and towards similarly well-defined activities that are deemed suitable for the client base. The expression of client will can only come through capital allocation, meaning that an understanding of the sources and flows of capital is the single most important financial concept a responsible investment practitioner can learn.

V. RECOMMENDATIONS FOR BEING A BETTER RESPONSIBLE INVESTMENT PROFESSIONAL

This chapter lays out a series of issues as identified by an asset owner who is both an experienced investment manager and an experienced responsible investment strategist. There are other important issues outstanding in the field of responsible investment, but it is the author's belief that addressing some of the shortcomings set out above will go a long way to help solve structural issues in the industry. As such, it is appropriate to close out this chapter with some recommendations for individuals and managers in the responsible investment space.

A. Education

Individuals enter responsible investment either from an investment background, or from outside the finance industry (often coming from a sustainability or non-governmental organisation background). It is vital for individuals to get a basic education in the 'other side' of this responsible – investment duality. The UK CFA Investment Management Certificate is a fantastic qualification that should be considered a must-study for anyone entering the investment industry. Likewise the UK CFA Certificate in ESG Investing is a brilliant conversion qualification for anyone familiar with financial markets. These qualifications should be thought of as similar to a driving test, giving an individual enough to start travelling on their own, but by no means producing the finished product.

B. Empathy

It is important to develop a sense of why people are for and against various aspects of responsible investment, what it means for them as individuals, and what clients expect from their products. Only through understanding the motivations of others can professionals be effective in their arguments. There is a great deal of ineffective virtue signalling involved in some areas of responsible investment, and many individuals involved in the space think that simply having 'purpose' is enough to drive change in the broader finance industry. An understanding of the issues is only one factor, and needs to be joined by an understanding of the wider landscaper (see previous paragraph) and an understanding of individual psychology.

C. Precision

Be unambiguous with language. Call out others for lacking precision in their own use of language. This is of particular importance for those involved in product development, sales and marketing. Investment managers that use so-called ESG overlays as part of their process should be able to understand and explain precisely how they work. Seniors should know both what their policies are, and what this means in a practical sense. There is no room for error, as promises made in financial products come with heavy regulatory consequences when not delivered.

D. Collaboration

A successful shift from traditional, transaction-based finance to a more holistic multi-stakeholder model that successfully incorporates externalities requires a new way of thinking throughout the industry, one which cannot be achieved through the individual actions of unconnected parties. Collaborative engagement, collaborative standards setting, and collaborative framework creation are all critically important initiatives being spearheaded by well-informed and driven individuals throughout the industry. As a responsible investment practitioner it is important to know how this works, and where possible to use any resources at the practitioner's disposal to get involved in these initiatives wherever they align with the expected outcomes of the client. The skillset required to work effectively and within the confines of the law in a collaborative setting are subtly different from working alongside colleagues within the same employer. Echoing the above point on education, it is vital for practitioners to learn this skillset.

It is time to professionalise responsible investment throughout the industry. The shift towards sustainability in finance is vital for delivering a bright future, and therefore it is vital that the industry, and the individuals within it, succeed.

12

Investment, Sustainability and Stewardship: Perspectives of a Sovereign Wealth Fund

OLA PETER K GJESSING*

I. INTRODUCTION: RIGHTS AND RESPONSIBILITIES

WHEN THE NORWEGIAN Petroleum Fund hired its first dedicated ownership team back in 2005 it was headed by philosopher and peace researcher Henrik Syse. The team's first job was to formulate a strategy for an emerging ownership role. The view was that the long-term financial return on the fund was a genuinely ethical concern in itself, because a key motivation behind the fund is to preserve wealth from natural resources for future generations.

Also in a narrower sense, ethics and financial interests were seen as complementary to a large extent. Thoughtful ownership to protect financial interests would in the first instance focus on good corporate governance. If successful, that would leave companies less conflicted, more transparent, and more conscious of the world around them – in other words, better citizens. Extending the ownership work to efforts at improved market practices followed a similar logic. Well-functioning markets would better fulfil their social purpose while at the same time providing a good basis for long-term returns on a diversified equity portfolio.[1]

* Ola Peter K Gjessing is Lead Investment Stewardship Manager in the Corporate Governance team at Norges Bank Investment Management. Gjessing is a Certified European Financial Analyst (CEFA) and has been involved in the ownership and corporate governance efforts of NBIM since 2005. NBIM manages the Government Pension Fund Global, originally known as the Petroleum Fund, on a mandate from the Ministry of Finance of Norway.

[1] H Syse, 'Hvorfor vi gjør det … Om etikk og eierskapsutøvelse i Statens pensjonsfond – Utland' (unofficial translation: 'Why We Are Doing It … On Ethics and the Exercise of Ownership in the Government Pension Fund Global') (Oslo, 6 December 2007), *Penger og Kreditt* 4/2007 (volume 35) 128–32, https://norges-bank.brage.unit.no/norges-bank-xmlui/handle/11250/2502260. Note: All expectation documents, position papers and discussion notes examined in this chapter are available at www.nbim.no and for practical reasons not included as separate sources in the bibliography.

As with everything else, the fund has evolved with time, but to this day, four features characterise the fund:

- *It is a generational fund.* We have to take a long-term perspective on the profitability of our investments, the risks of our portfolio and the functioning of the financial markets.
- *It is a fund owned by the people.* We must respect and support the demand for legitimacy of our investment management, and we must report transparently to allow democratic control.
- *It is a fund with one, well-informed principal: the Norwegian state.* The three involved branches – Norges Bank (the central bank), the Ministry of Finance, and the Storting (the parliament) – have distinct roles and a clear understanding of them.
- *It is an international fund with no domestic investments.* We have no home market, we prioritise stewardship globally, and we are benchmarked against best practices.

Ownership comes with both rights and responsibilities. The fund's investments are held up against Norwegian values and the country's international obligations. We assess how companies impact on the environment and society. There are companies that Norges Bank or the authorities choose not to hold, for sustainability or ethical reasons.

Today, the corporate governance team has grown into a diverse group of 20 economists, engineers, scientists, lawyers, philologists, IT specialists and finance professionals with deep expertise in key sustainability challenges facing companies and societies. We have extensive corporate governance skills coupled with specific sector and market knowledge. Other parts of the investment management organisation – from risk to securities selection – are closely involved alongside the governance team.

This chapter is organised in four substantive sections. Section II explains the investment framework, and how return over the long haul is the single management objective. While the investment strategy is built on global diversification, the Ministry of Finance transparently restricts the investment universe – on an explicitly ethical basis – to ensure legitimacy in the population.

Section III explains how the fund sees value in helping improve market practices. Being invested outside Norway only, the investment organisation is always looking outwards and is not allowed the natural inclination to emphasise a home market when stewarding investment, unlike so many institutional investors. Corporate governance is seen as an instrument to protect financial interests and contribute to the enduring vitality in the companies where we invest.

Section IV is the story about how we monitor the portfolio, divest from certain business models and selectively invest in assets that might benefit as authorities globally emphasise emissions reductions and the environment.

In section V, we discuss the value of investor stewardship, how we already 15 years ago focussed on the rights of children and the responsibility of companies when engaging authorities on climate policies. We explain how principles of corporate governance commit us, as a large shareholder, to both the responsibility and the self-interest of doing our part.

We conclude by revisiting our role as the operational manager in the governance framework for the fund, and the importance of each actor having a clear perspective of the objective of the fund.[2]

II. SOVEREIGN WEALTH FUND IN NORWAY – THE INVESTMENT FRAMEWORK

The Government Pension Fund Global (GPFG)[3] is different from most institutional investors and even from most sovereign wealth funds (SWFs). It has just one owner, and that owner is an open democracy with strong institutions. The Norwegian government, represented by the Ministry of Finance, acts as the owner on behalf of the country's 5.4 million people.

Being owned by the people requires the management to be transparent. Each year, the government presents a thorough report to the Storting. The report analyses management results. In most years it would also lay out selected aspects of the investment strategy for further research and improvement.[4]

By law, the operational management of the fund is delegated to Norges Bank, the central bank of Norway. This is the job of Norges Bank Investment Management (NBIM). Our mission is to safeguard and build financial wealth for future generations.

A. Objective: Return for Future Generations

The Ministry of Finance sets an investment mandate that is very clear:

> The Bank shall seek to generate the highest possible return, net of costs, measured in the currency basket of the investment portfolio [...] within the applicable investment management framework.

And furthermore:

> Responsible management shall form an integral part of the management of the investment portfolio [...] A good long-term return is considered to depend on sustainable economic, environmental and social development, as well as on well-functioning, legitimate and efficient markets.[5]

---

[2] This chapter is in part a shortened and updated version of the book *Investing Responsibly. The 20-Year History* (Norges Bank Investment Management, 28 August 2020). Together with six other 'historic management reviews', this book is freely available for download at NBIM's website, https://www.nbim.no/en/publications/.

[3] In 2006, the name was changed from the Government Petroleum Fund to the Government Pension Fund Global. The name change was meant to signal that the fund, to a large extent, would cover the costs of an ageing population. The investment framework did not change as a result.

[4] Ministry of Finance, *The Government Pension Fund 2021* (White Paper, Meld St 24 / 2020–2021, Oslo, 9 April 2021), https://www.regjeringen.no/en/topics/the-economy/the-government-pension-fund/arlig-melding-til-stortinget/id2357436/.

[5] Ministry of Finance, *Management Mandate for the Government Pension Fund Global* (as of 24 August 2021), https://www.regjeringen.no/contentassets/9d68c55c272c41e99f0bf45d24397d8c/gpfg_mandate_2021.08.24.pdf.

The clear management objective builds on thinking that materialised at the outset. 'Any investments for which performance is measured on the basis of criteria other than the direct financial return, taking risk into account, should therefore be separated from the Petroleum Fund', Norges Bank stated in a letter of advice to the Ministry of Finance back in 1997. In other words, the government will pursue its general policy objectives outside of the fund and not blur the role of the fund management.

The governance of the fund is built around this return objective and provides a clear division of responsibilities between the Ministry as owner and Norges Bank as operational manager. The Ministry defines the investment universe and sets a clear and easily identifiable benchmark for measuring the fund's performance in a transparent manner. These commandments are reflected in the mandate.

B. Strategy: Global Diversification

When the Storting passed the law to establish the Government Petroleum Fund in 1990, and the first capital transfer from the Ministry of Finance was made in 1996, it was to help finance the Norwegian welfare state for future generations. To achieve this, the fund invests the state's net revenue from domestic petroleum production into the global securities market. In later years, real estate and infrastructure have been added as asset classes. Investments are spread widely across markets, sectors and issuers to reduce risk and capture global growth.

The fund is invested abroad only. This was a natural choice since the petroleum revenues originated in foreign energy markets. Norway's economy was small relative to the petroleum revenues. Today, the market value of the fund is more than three times the gross domestic product of the country. Even as a long-held fiscal rule limits annual spending to a long-term real-return estimate of 3 per cent, this injection boosts the government's budget by about 25 per cent. No matter how you measure, the fund is big relative to the economy.

The fund's equity and bond investments largely mirror the benchmark indices defined by the Ministry. Property purchases are funded through the sale of equities and bonds. Investments in renewable energy infrastructure are part of the fund's environmental mandates, which are subject to an upper limit of 120 billion crowns (US$14 billion). Unlisted renewable energy infrastructure was added to the mandate in November 2019, and the first investment was announced in 2021.

The fund holds shares in more than 9,000 companies globally and the value of the equity portfolio stood at $1.01 trillion at the end of 2021 out of total assets under management of $1.40 trillion. The strategic allocation to equity is 70 per cent. The majority of assets are managed by NBIM internally, with less than 5 per cent of assets managed by external managers appointed by us.

The portfolio means that the fund – and by extension the Norwegian population – owns a slice of most of the largest listed companies in the world. Today, it is the single largest owner in the world's stock markets with an average stake of 1.4 per cent in every listed company. In Europe, that figure is 2.6 per cent. Equally important, even if holdings in each company vary over time, the fund is expected to be a significant owner in most companies for a long time.

Our fundamental strategies aim to achieve the highest possible return after costs. Investments are made based on a strong understanding of individual companies and their long-term prospects.

Our market exposure strategies seek to cost-efficiently manage our large, global exposures and to trade efficiently. We use portfolio construction and trading strategies to reduce turnover and market impact. We avoid costly mechanical benchmark replication and utilise securities lending and positioning around corporate actions and capital markets events to enhance returns.[6]

Our stewardship strategy supports the fund's return objective. Through the integration of environmental, social and governance issues into the management of the fund, we seek to improve the long-term economic performance of our investments and reduce financial risks. This will be discussed from several angles throughout the chapter.

C. Universe Restrictions: Ensuring Legitimacy

Successive governments, with broad parliamentary support in the Storting, have maintained that the fund is a tool for the state's financial saving and that it should have only one, financial, goal. At the same time, the government has recognised that there are limits to what the fund should own and has laid down ethical guidelines. A formal mechanism for exclusion ensures that the fund is not invested in companies whose products or behaviour are considered grossly unethical.

Companies producing weapons that violate fundamental humanitarian principles through their normal use are excluded from the Fund. This includes nuclear weapons, cluster munitions and antipersonnel landmines. The production of tobacco is also a criterion for exclusion. The same goes for mining companies and power producers dependent on thermal coal. Exclusions related to companies' behaviour are also based on formal criteria centred on serious or systematic human rights violations, severe environmental damage and gross corruption. Any assessment for exclusion is forward-looking as the guidelines ask whether the risk is unacceptable. Exclusions are not intended to sanction past incidents.[7]

An independent Council on Ethics examines the portfolio to identify companies that might be in breach of the formal ethical criteria. Recommendations for exclusion, or observation, are sent to Norges Bank for decision by the Executive Board.

---

[6] Securities lending and asset positioning contributed to a relative return of 0.05 and 0.07 percentage points respectively per year over the 2013–2021 period, ie almost half of the total relative return of 0.25 percentage points produced by Norges Bank over the period. When stocks are lent out over the record date for a general meeting of shareholders, the lender will not be able to vote for those stocks. However, the economic exposure to the return on the stock, and thereby the value of stewardship, are not affected. See Norges Bank Investment Management, *Government Pension Fund Global Annual Report 2021*, table 31, p 55, https://www.nbim.no/en/publications/reports/2021/annual-report-2021/.

[7] Ministry of Finance, *Guidelines for Observation and Exclusion from the Government Pension Fund Global* (19 November 2021), unofficial English version, https://files.nettsteder.regjeringen.no/wpuploads01/sites/275/2021/11/Guidelines-for-Observation-and-Exclusion-GPFG-29-November-2021.pdf.

As of 2021, 152 companies and two countries under UN sanctions, Syria and North Korea, had been excluded from investment. Since the start of the current exclusion regime in 2006, the net impact on fund return has been zero in dollar terms, but the effect has varied substantially through this period.[8]

In addition, since 2012 the fund has on its own account divested from 366 companies whose business models we do not consider sustainable in the long term. These risk-based divestments will be discussed in more detail later in the chapter. Taken together, the restrictions are intended to ensure that the fund can enjoy broad legitimacy among the Norwegian population and remain aligned with Norway's international obligations. The cost of restricting ownership has been accepted as necessary to maintain this legitimacy.

III. IN IT FOR FUTURE GENERATIONS – THE VALUE OF IMPROVING MARKET PRACTICES

The long-term return on the fund is inherently linked to the long-term performance of the global economy. We are exposed to global risks and opportunities, and to companies' handling of these, all of which benefit from global standards. For corporate governance, these standards help create a level playing field for companies and an efficient division of responsibility between shareholders and Boards.

Sustainability and financial returns often go hand in hand. Companies that do not care about the world around them could lose customers, face lawsuits and harm their reputation. And this can obviously have financial consequences. We support standards for corporate sustainability reporting and responsible business conduct which serve the interests of the fund but typically are also likely to improve outcomes for people and the planet over time.

A. Looking Outwards

Our authorities decided early on to build on international standards, rather than simply export Norwegian values abroad. The 2004 edition of the ethical guidelines were based on the OECD Principles of Corporate Governance, the UN Global Compact and the OECD Guidelines for Multinational Enterprises. Since 2017, our principles also refer to the UN Guiding Principles on Business and Human Rights.

The first example of international participation was in 2005, when the then UN Secretary-General Kofi Annan invited Norges Bank and a group of other large institutional investors to develop the Principles for Responsible Investment. We were an active participant in this work, which resulted in six principles which we adopted in November that year.

---

[8] Table 12, Norges Bank Investment Management, *Responsible Investment Government Pension Fund Global 2021* (3 March 2022), https://www.nbim.no/en/publications/reports/2021/responsible-investment-2021/.

Over two decades, we have provided input to regulators and other market-standard setters on a wide range of issues ranging from governance and protection of minority shareholders to corporate reporting and responsible business conduct. Through constructive engagement, we believe the fund has contributed to better corporate governance and responsible business standards.

We realised early on, however, that we could have more impact when international principles were mirrored in more targeted views developed within our own investment and ownership context. When we decided to publicly express expectations of companies, we did something fundamentally new at the time.

In 2008, we published our first expectation document, on children's rights. Although child labour was recognised as a risk, companies had limited awareness of other ways they might be infringing upon children's rights. The expectations were developed in dialogue with experts in the field representing organisations such as UNICEF, Save the Children and the ILO.

Today, NBIM maintains eight different expectation documents. The latest addition is the 2021 expectations on biodiversity and ecosystems.[9] In essence, NBIM expects companies to integrate the topic into corporate strategy and risk management, disclose dependencies, metrics and targets, and engage stakeholders.

Information asked for in the expectation documents was rarely available, however. We therefore made the choice to start gathering information systematically.

The first of the compliance assessments, as they were called at the time, were published in 2008: 430 companies were systematically analysed on the basis of the criteria set out in our Investor Expectations on Children's Rights. We entered into dialogue with 135 companies that did not report adequately. When we reassessed these companies a year later, 33 per cent of them had improved their reporting on these topics. Transparency improved in all sectors, but the improvements were most apparent in the cocoa and apparel retail sectors. The mining and steel companies also had an increased number of policies on child labour. These encouraging early results emphasised the benefits of the assessments as a systematically deployable analytical tool.[10]

B. Corporate Governance to Protect Financial Interests and Ensure Enduring Vitality

The fund has often been associated with its positions on ethics and sustainability. However, corporate governance was emphasised from the outset. Governance was seen as overlapping with ethical concerns. Protecting financial interests through good governance was an imperative in its own right.

As early as 2006 we engaged with the US Securities and Exchange Commission to make it easier for shareholders to propose alternative Board candidates in the US

---

[9] See https://www.nbim.no/contentassets/f1fa22a3a6c54ed88cf18607f75953c0/nbim_biodiversity_2021_web.pdf.

[10] Norges Bank Investment Management, *Government Pension Fund Global Annual Report 2009*, 52, https://www.nbim.no/globalassets/reports/2009/nbim_annualreport09.pdf.

market. We proposed giving shareholders proxy access as a cheaper and less confrontational alternative to proxy fights. In 2012 and 2013, we filed shareholder proposals seeking bylaw changes at US companies to give shareholders this right, as the first major institutional investor and the only non-US one.

The proposals received 30–40 per cent support and significant public attention.[11] This was a strong showing for shareholder proposals in the US on a new topic. Other shareholders later filed similar proposals to strengthen the role of the Board and protect shareholder rights. In 2019, 76 per cent of US companies in the S&P 500 index had implemented proxy access.[12]

In 2012, we published our first corporate governance expectations in the form of a discussion note setting out our views on Board accountability and equal treatment of shareholders. In developing the expectations, we had consulted 20 company chairpersons. They advised that there should be clear expectations on the integrity, behaviour, motivation and character of directors.

Taking a principled view on management incentives in 2017, we sought to strengthen alignment of CEO and shareholder interests through simplification of remuneration plans, emphasising transparency and long-term shareholding. In 2018, we argued our position on the time commitment and industry expertise of Board members and on the separation of chairperson and CEO. In 2020, we further clarified our views on Board independence, share issuances, multiple voting rights, related-party transactions, corporate sustainability reporting and shareholder proposals on sustainability issues. Our 11 position papers serve as a starting point for our discussions with company Boards and explain our voting.[13]

In some of the positions, we have decided to take a principled view quite far from market practice at the time, and subsequently observed market practice moving closer to our position. Few companies fully comply with our position that CEO pay should be dominated by shares mandatorily held for 5–10 years, but since 2017 we have encountered growing support for the direction that the document lays out, towards simple, transparent and long-term deferred shares rather than complex and highly leveraged incentive plans.

Nearly 1 in 10 leading UK companies now use a deferred share model in place of traditional 'long-term incentive plans'.[14] Companies are now expected to require that some incentive shares are kept for one or two years after the CEO has left the company, significantly extending the true time horizon of the stock incentive for any CEO. In the US, the Council of Institutional Investors now advocates simple, long-dated equity as an alternative to options and 'performance share units'. 'Performance-based compensation plans are a major source of today's complexity and confusion in executive pay',

---

[11] Norges Bank Investment Management, *2013 Annual Report for the Government Pension Fund Global* (28 February 2014), https://www.nbim.no/globalassets/reports/2013/annual-report/annual-report_2013_web.pdf.

[12] Sidley, *Proxy Access: A Five-Year Review* (16 January 2020), https://www.sidley.com/en/insights/newsupdates/2020/01/proxy-access-a-five-year-review.

[13] All position papers are available at https://www.nbim.no/en/the-fund/responsible-investment/our-voting-records/position-papers/.

[14] *The Purposeful Company Study on Deferred Shares Progress Review* (September 2020), https://thepurposefulcompany.org/wp-content/uploads/2021/01/tpc-deferred-shares-progress-review-2020-200930-2.pdf.

says the Council of Institutional Investors' updated Corporate Governance Policies.[15] This is significant because US institutional investors used to argue that awards should be 'performance based' rather than 'time based'. Among US companies, the time horizon of equity awards is increasing. Incentive equity awards are trending towards three-year 'cliff vesting' from three-year 'ratable vesting', where the first third vests already after one year and only a third stays for three years. The German corporate governance commission in 2018 proposed a simple 1+4 year deferred-shares scheme as a substitution for popular and complex cash-settled incentives, but this was withdrawn after corporate opposition.[16]

IV. RETURN AND RISK FOR FUTURE GENERATIONS –
THE VALUE OF PORTFOLIO MONITORING AND ADJUSTMENT

The objective for the management of the fund is to ensure that future generations will benefit from Norway's petroleum wealth. By maximising the return on its investments, the fund further increases the amount of wealth available to later generations. A narrow return focus, however, may ignore any negative externalities associated with companies' operations. This is particularly relevant for a generational challenge like greenhouse gas emissions and the impact on climate change. Failure to adequately address climate change now would increase the burden on future governments to remedy the damage, further diverting returns from the fund.

A. Carbon Footprint

We analyse greenhouse gas emissions in our investee companies. The analysis captures scope 1 and 2 emissions, but we also analyse emissions along the value chain, so-called scope 3 information. Many companies still do not report emissions, and this makes estimations necessary.

Emissions from companies in the portfolio fell in 2021. This was largely a result of the decision by the Ministry of Finance, as usual after consultation with the Storting, to remove upstream oil and gas companies from the fund's benchmark. However, our management under the environmental mandates contributed too. We funded these investments by reducing our holdings in companies that are not part of the investment universe for the environment-related mandates. This reduced our positions in large emitters.

We have estimated that the exclusions under the ethical guidelines have cut the emissions in the benchmark index by 18 per cent, largely due to the coal criterion.

Following the adoption of the Paris Agreement in December 2015, governments had to report their nationally determined contributions and set plans for reducing emissions. Earlier that year, the Storting decided to remove coal companies from the

---

[15] CII, *Corporate Governance Policies*, section 5 Executive Compensation (updated as of 22 September 2021), https://www.cii.org/files/09_22_21_corp_gov_policies.pdf.

[16] Deutscher Corporate Governance Kodex, *181106 Draft amended GCGC* and *181106 Press release* (6 November 2018), https://www.dcgk.de/en/consultations/archive/consultation-2018/19.html.

fund, arguing that extracting and burning coal was an ethical issue. The Storting decided that mining companies and power producers could be excluded if they derived 30 per cent or more of their revenues or based 30 per cent or more of their operations on thermal coal. Criteria have since been tightened. As of September 2021, 72 coal-related companies were excluded from the fund.

B. Risk-based Divestments

In addition to the exclusion of coal-related companies, NBIM has of its own accord divested from companies on the basis of risk assessments. In contrast to exclusions under the ethical guidelines, where each announcement is backed up by specific documentation of the facts leading to concern, these divestments do not imply any publication of findings at the company level. In 2021, for instance, we divested from four companies where data on coal were sparse, but where indications were that exposure was unacceptably high.

NBIM has even divested from companies contributing to climate change through large-scale deforestation. Starting in 2011, the fund became increasingly aware of the risks of palm oil production, which often involves the clearing, or even burning, of rainforest. The Council on Ethics had already recommended the exclusion of Samling Global Ltd due to its logging activities in the rainforests of Malaysia and Guyana. After logging, areas might end up as palm oil plantations.

In March 2012, a report published by the Rainforest Foundation Norway and Friends of the Earth Norway criticised the fund's investments in activities resulting in deforestation, including palm oil production. At the same time, the Norwegian government was providing funds for the preservation of the rainforest in the same countries. At the global climate conference in Bali in 2007, the Norwegian government pledged to contribute up to 3 billion crowns a year (US$540m) to help avoid deforestation. In 2008, the government announced it would contribute 1 billion dollars to preserve the rainforests in Brazil.

This was an instance where the fund's investments were considered not to be in alignment with Norway's international obligations. In the annual report for 2012, the fund announced that 23 palm oil producers had been removed from the equity portfolio in the first quarter of the year 'because their long-term business model was deemed unsustainable'.

In the 2012–2021 period, risk-based divestments increased the cumulative return on the equity reference portfolio by around 0.44 percentage points, or 0.02 percentage points annually. Divestments linked to climate change and human rights increased the cumulative return on the equity reference portfolio by 0.28 and 0.08 percentage points respectively. Divestments linked to anti-corruption decreased the cumulative return on the equity reference portfolio by 0.03 percentage points and those relating to water management had a negligible impact.[17]

---

[17] Norges Bank Investment Management, *Responsible Investment Government Pension Fund Global 2021*, Table 9, 49 (3 March 2022), https://www.nbim.no/contentassets/950222269756407898cadb999926c16c/gpfg-responsible-investment-2021-web.pdf.

C. Targeted Investment

On three occasions, the government has mandated special allocations to environment-related investments. Those mandates have had the same risk and return requirements as the overall fund.

The current mandates are not earmarked by the Ministry as a separate portfolio with its own universe and benchmark. Instead, they were established as actively managed sub-portfolios. Norges Bank must define which sectors and companies are considered to be environment related.

Our approach is based on a belief that there are opportunities for investing in companies and technologies that enable more environmentally friendly economic activity. These investments are likely to have positive externalities that will benefit society, such as more efficient resource use, less pollution and lower energy costs. Over the long term, there is an expectation that companies that develop technological solutions will benefit economically from the ongoing shift towards lower pollution and greater natural resource efficiency.

The annualised return on the environment-related equity mandates from 2010 until 2021 was 10.4 per cent, compared to 10.6 per cent for the fund's equity benchmark.[18] In 2019, the government decided to add renewable energy infrastructure to the fund's investment mandate. The first investment in offshore wind assets was made in 2021.

The return has been more volatile than the return on the equity benchmark. This is only to be expected, as the environment-related mandates are invested in fewer stocks. Because the mandates make up less than one per cent of the fund, these investments have had little impact on the fund's overall return or risk.[19]

V. MAKING THE BEST VERSION OF THE COMPANY –
THE VALUE OF INVESTOR STEWARDSHIP

Large, multinational companies tend to have dispersed ownership. Some of the largest shareholders are institutional investors, like us, who own a relatively small slice of thousands of companies. We cannot know each company in our portfolio in detail, but the future value of the fund depends on the value they create.

Ownership can be split into hard and soft power. Hard power includes the legal right to take part in shareholder meetings to elect the Board and approve other fundamental decisions at the company. Soft power covers a broader set of informal interactions to influence the company. Investors can ask to meet the Board and management and communicate their priorities to the company. Our active position taking in the stocks in individual companies communicates conviction, or the lack

---

[18] ibid, Table 5, 40.

[19] The environment-related mandates made up 108 billion Norwegian crowns (US$12 billion), compared to the total fund value of 12,340 billion (US$1,400 billion) at the end of 2021. In the spring of 2022, the Storting approved a government proposal to remove the mandate requirement for environment-related investments.

of it. The questions we ask when meeting companies convey beliefs, concerns, and information needs.

The fund started out as a reluctant owner. Exercising ownership rights was seen as problematic, given the resources required, our limited influence, and our status as a sovereign fund.

Two different considerations gradually persuaded us to make more active use of voting rights and the opportunity for dialogue: promoting ethical behaviour in companies and protecting the investments of the fund.

Today, we vote at more than 11,000 shareholder meetings annually. We aim to be principled and transparent when we use our voting rights and interact with companies. Starting in 2021 we announce our vote intentions five days ahead of each shareholder meeting, with a rationale pointing to the relevant section of a public voting guideline.

A. Human Rights. Starting with the Next Generation

The objective of the fund is the welfare of future generations. Inspired by this, children's rights have always been seen as a natural focus. In our current programme, we discuss the marketing of breast milk substitute in China and experience that companies enhance their policies. We expect telecoms to consider how their services impact children. We have expanded our dialogues with firms having exposure to war and conflict zones.

Dialogue on social issues was on the agenda from the outset. We engaged with close to 60 companies on child labour and children's rights back in 2007. The target companies were exposed to child labour risks in agriculture and metals. In response to the dialogue, all companies acknowledged the importance of the issue and committed to continue interacting with us.

A notable early example of an industry initiative focussed on seed production in India. In 2009 this brought together four companies – Monsanto, Bayer, Syngenta and DuPont – which committed to work together to address the challenge of child labour in their supply chains. The resulting industry standard – CropLife Position on Child Labor in the Seed Supply Chain – described the joint effort these companies committed to make to eliminate the use of child labour by suppliers and other partners in the seed sector.[20]

Another example of an industry initiative is the Network on Children's Rights in the Garment and Footwear Sector established by UNICEF and the fund in 2017. Well-known companies participated in network activities and contributed to the development of a guidance tool on the integration of children's rights into sustainability strategies and responsible sourcing frameworks, including adidas AG, Carrefour SA, The Walt Disney Co, Hennes & Mauritz AB, Kering SA, Li & Fung Ltd, Next, Tesco plc and VF Corporation. Having published our human rights expectations in 2016, we started to raise human rights more systematically in company dialogues.[21]

---

[20] *Government Pension Fund Global Annual Report 2009* (n 10 above) 50.

[21] Norges Bank Investment Management, *Responsible Investment 2017 Government Pension Fund Global* (13 February 2018) 47, https://www.nbim.no/contentassets/67c692a171fa450ca6e3e1e3a7793311/responsible-investment-2017---government-pension-fund-global.pdf.

Following the publication of our tax transparency expectations in 2017, we wrote for the first time to the largest 500 companies in our portfolio about their approach to tax. Subsequent interactions have focused on publication of corporate tax policies and country-by-country reporting of taxes paid, providing us with data that we could use to enhance our financial and risk analysis.[22]

B. Climate Concerns and the Environment. The Role of the Company

Climate change was identified as an ownership focus area in 2006, then with an emphasis on companies' interaction with authorities regarding public policy. Today, the risks and opportunities of climate change policies take centre stage as we develop our stewardship strategies in dialogue with the fund owner.

In current thematic dialogues we discuss with consumer goods firms using palm oil, soya and beef and expect transparency on their management of the risk of deforestation. We discuss with cement producers how they plan for the transition to a low-carbon society. We ask banks how they manage climate risk in their loan portfolios. We talk to iron and steel companies to understand how they manage risks and opportunities in the transition. As of the end of 2021, for instance, we reported that seven of the cement companies we engaged with had set more ambitious emission reduction targets.

To support our work with companies on climate, we have recently clarified our expectation that companies set a target for emissions reduction. Targets and strategies should be aligned with the Paris Agreement. We stepped up the focus on biodiversity and ecosystems with a separate expectation document in the summer of 2021. An increasing loss of species and weakening of ecosystems may impact on the long-term ability of companies to create value for investors.

During the first decade of the fund's operations, international norms as well as the thinking on the responsibility of companies to address social and environmental impacts of their operations were still relatively immature and often confused with more philanthropic activities. Some issues proved controversial. Our early interaction on climate lobbying[23] was perceived by some to interfere with national policy agendas on energy security. We also learnt that it was a difficult issue to raise with some sectors, for example oil and gas, given our nature as a sovereign investor in many companies operating on the Norwegian Continental Shelf. However, such issues are now a regular feature of most investor interaction with companies, including our own.

Our first environment-related dialogues on ethical criteria commenced in 2013. We raised the risk of severe environmental damage due to oil spills in the Niger Delta with Eni SpA and Royal Dutch Shell plc. We also raised the risk of severe environmental damage and gross human rights breaches with AngloGold Ashanti Ltd with respect to the company's two gold mines in Ghana. These dialogues are still ongoing.

---

[22] ibid 23.
[23] Norges Bank Investment Management, *Annual Report 2007, Feature Article: The environment and lobbying* (4 March 2008) 95, https://www.nbim.no/globalassets/reports/2007/nbim_07_eng.pdf.

C. Good Corporate Governance: for Sustained Profitability

The fund has come a long way since it initially avoided using its voting rights for fear of getting involved in difficult decisions. Today, the fund actively uses its voting rights at nearly all shareholder meetings. NBIM has a principled approach and publishes all votes five days before the shareholder meeting.

Portfolio managers are involved in voting decisions. Each portfolio manager with an active mandate selects a set of companies where he or she will get involved in considering the voting items. The involvement of portfolio managers in the process has improved our analysis and given each manager a deeper understanding of the companies' governance. Since portfolio managers concentrate on many of the largest companies in the portfolio, their voting input relates to about 50 per cent of the value of the equity portfolio.

D. Governance Dialogue

We have always maintained that company dialogue contributes to the protection of shareholder interests and supports the fund's objective of achieving the highest possible return. Following the adoption of the 2004 ethical guidelines, we concluded that there could also be an ethical dimension to the exercise of ownership rights. We found that poor corporate governance was sometimes a result of a fundamental lack of ethics. Corporate priorities were sometimes driven by individual interests rather than the interests of shareholders and the common good. At the same time, we noted that it would not be appropriate to use our ownership rights to address ethical concerns that could not be justified based on financial considerations.

Holding Boards of directors to account was crucial for us as a financial investor. This naturally centres around Board accountability for company strategy, but also extends to the environmental and social consequences of company operations. Without well-functioning Boards, we lose out as investors.

Therefore we decided in 2005 that direct contact with individual companies for stewardship purposes should primarily be with Board members and avoid micromanagement. We noted the experience of institutional investors with a reputation for effective ownership, that attempts by single shareholders to micromanage a company are likely to frustrate and undermine management, disturb strategy processes and blur lines of responsibility.

Since 2013, we have chosen to participate in the shareholder-led nomination committees of selected Swedish companies to support well-qualified and balanced Boards. This interaction has at the same time enabled us to gather invaluable information about effective nomination processes and Board evaluation.

VI. CONCLUSION – UNDERSTANDING OUR SPECIAL ROLE

This chapter has emphasised that throughout the history of the fund, Norges Bank and the authorities have consistently maintained that the fund should act exclusively as a financial investor. The Ministry defines the investment universe and sets a clear and easily identifiable benchmark for measuring the fund's performance in a transparent manner. These commandments are well reflected in a public mandate.

Furthermore, we show that while the fund is invested abroad only, it is not an instrument of foreign policy. The international character of the portfolio has had implications for our ownership policies. Unlike many institutional investors we have no home market that can receive special attention. Instead, we have been challenged to make global priorities and obtain a global perspective. As a sovereign investor, we have been careful not to take positions that could be confused with foreign policy. We have even avoided engaging companies in collaboration with other investors, for fear that we may not have full control over how the agenda was perceived. Company meetings have generally been conducted in one of our foreign offices or at other venues abroad, rather than in Oslo, in order to emphasise how we are a global investor with operational separation from Norwegian public policy.

We have an ethical obligation to use our ownership to improve company practices. We are focussed on outcomes, even if the results of dialogue are difficult to measure. It is hard to establish whether a change in business practice at a company is due to interaction with its shareholders or would have occurred independently of investor outreach. Ownership through dialogue takes time, but we believe that results emerge over the long term.

Even if the key principles of ownership are still recognisable from the start 20 years ago, our global policies, and actions, are constantly evolving. Climate change has been with us as a focus area for 15 years, but the sense of urgency of this generational problem has deservedly increased. Implications are abundant, for ecosystems, public policy, consumer preferences, corporate strategy, and fund risk. Our long-term owner is expecting more from its investment manager in terms of risk management. A thorough understanding of our role, garnered through the experiences of our first decades, is helpful in this complex challenge, as it is for other strands of responsible investment management.

13

Evolution of Sustainable Investing: A US Perspective

KEN BERTSCH

I. INTRODUCTION

WHILE THE US has the largest capital markets in the world, it has been slower to embrace certain approaches to sustainable investment than Europe and some other financial centres. The US has even been portrayed outside the mainstream on investing practices that emphasise environmental, social and governance (ESG) factors.[1] However, 'ESG investing' involves a complex and diverse set of understandings and issues, and comparisons are complicated. And what arguably is the most important current development in sustainable finance – development and consolidation of sustainability reporting standards – currently has strong support in the US, including through private standard-setting (now being rolled up into the International Sustainability Standards Board (ISSB)) that has substantial US participation, and the Biden-era US Securities and Exchange Commission (SEC), which appears to be looking to international standards as it sets new requirements for climate-related corporate disclosure.

There clearly is some validity to the commonplace view that European and other markets in recent years have embraced proactive roles on climate change investing initiatives ahead of US market actors. The US was much later than many other markets in developing a stewardship code.[2] US-based asset managers overall have been later to sign onto the Principles for Responsible Investment (PRI), and many US asset owners have continuing reluctance to embrace PRI.

A 2021 study by Rajni Gibson Brandon and others found an 'ESG disconnect between the US and the rest of the world'.[3] While focused only on investment in

---

[1] See eg R Gibson Brandon et al, 'Do Responsible Investors Invest Responsibly?' *Swiss Finance Institute Research Paper Series No 20-13* (May 2021) (also published as European Corporate Governance Network (ECGI), *Working Paper Series in Finance No 712/2020*).

[2] See the Investor Stewardship Group Stewardship Principles for Institutional Investors, launched in 2017, at https://isgframework.org/stewardship-principles/.

[3] Gibson Brandon et al (n 1 above) 30.

publicly listed companies, and using flat and not fully satisfactory proxies for approaches to ESG (and not giving real weight to engagement and stewardship activities), the Gibson Brandon study does provide some evidence of a more limited embrace of aspects of ESG investing in the US for the period studied. The study analysed PRI survey responses and portfolio holdings for the years 2013–2017. The authors write that this disconnect 'appears to be driven by a more business-oriented approach to ESG, as opposed to ESG investing that is intrinsically motivated by social norms more prevalent in other parts of the world'.[4]

I would argue that the Gibson Brandon findings are entirely unsurprising considering US fiduciary rules, and, to a lesser extent, shareholder primacy enshrined in corporate law in Delaware and other states. While the structure of the asset management industry also may play a role (accounting for at least some of the 'more business-oriented approach' in the US), differences in fiduciary rules and company law appear to me to be more fundamental drivers of US difference.

While the term 'shareholder primacy' is sometimes invoked in a rhetorical and misleading fashion (including by some who wish to limit shareholder rights to protect senior executives and Board members from accountability), it is clear that US law, as well as business and investment culture, have and continue to place shareholders at the centre of corporate governance, albeit with increasing emphasis on 'long-term' shareholder interest, as opposed to short-term 'share price' primacy, and more nods to non-shareholder stakeholders than in the past. 'Stakeholder' capitalism has stronger buy-in in Europe.

Still, there appears to be significant change in the US since the period covered in the Gibson Brandon study. Moreover, the US over several earlier decades pioneered aspects of ESG in investment, particularly on certain social issues (such as diversity, equality and inclusion) and governance matters and mechanisms (for example the shareholder proposal, and various improvements in accountability that grew out of the Enron and WorldCom scandals early in this century).

In fact, one could argue that, longer term, the US often has been at the forefront of ESG in investment. Since the 1930s, US publicly listed companies have been required to provide investor-useful public disclosure, including on material risks. Beginning in the 1960s, certain US non-governmental organisations, institutional religious investors and their allies led the way in expression of shareholder voice for corporate social responsibility. And they were joined in the 1980s by social investment fund managers that pioneered sustainable investment as an investment category, supported by certain large public pension funds. Finally, the US has vigorous and meaningful shareholder activism that has effectively challenged incumbent Board members at poorly performing companies and some that have been unresponsive to shareholders. The 2021 headline for this was the stunning victory of dissident candidates nominated for the ExxonMobil Board of directors by shareholder Engine #1.[5]

---

[4] ibid 30.
[5] See M Phillips, 'Exxon's Board Defeat Signals the Rise of Social-Good Activists' (*The New York Times*, 9 June 2021).

Why is the US different? What are the distinctive elements of US practice? And what are the most prominent ESG matters at present for US institutional investors? This chapter seeks to provide answers to these questions.

II. AT THE ROOT: LEGAL FACTORS DIFFERENTIATING THE US ON SUSTAINABLE INVESTING

While investing may be global, local factors shape key aspects of investment. Factors that differentiate the US include fiduciary law, company law, political environment, the structure of asset management industry and broad cultural elements.

Of particular importance in the US legal realm are: (1) fiduciary standards for fund trustees and investors more generally; (2) company director duties under corporate law; and (3) disclosure rules for companies.

The US features fiduciary obligations in managing 'other people's money' that constrain funds and investment managers from pursuing ends other than financial returns for those who entrust them with assets. In an authoritative recent discussion on trustee fiduciary duties and consideration for ESG factors in investment, law professors Max M Schanzenbach and Robert H Sitkoff write that American pension fund and other trustees 'continue to resist explicit use of ESG factors on the grounds that to do so would entail consideration of collateral benefits to third parties in breach of the sole interest rule imposed by the trust law fiduciary duty of loyalty'.[6] Fund trustees owe a fiduciary duty of loyalty that could be questioned if investments are used for collateral purposes.

Investor fiduciary standards are founded mainly in common law in the US, as in the UK and Commonwealth nations.[7] That said, statutes also play an important role. The discussion below centres on the US Employment Retirement Income Security Act of 1974 (ERISA), overseen by the US Department of Labor's Employee Benefits Security Administration (EBSA).[8] It should be noted that, strictly speaking, ERISA applies only to private retirement and health plans. This excludes, for example, public entity retirement plans. But its rules and adjudication have had a cascading effect, including on norms for public pension funds and for investment managers (particularly, for the latter, regarding investment management for ERISA plans).

Fiduciary law has diverged between markets. Schanzenbach and Sitkoff write, 'The exclusive and mandatory focus under ERISA on financial benefits distinguishes American pension law from that in the UK, which is more tolerant of nonfinancial

---

[6] MM Schanzenbach and RH Sitkoff, 'Reconciling Fiduciary Duty and Social Conscience: The Law and Economics of ESG Investing by a Trustee' (2020) *Stanford Law Review* 381, 385. Schanzenbach and Sitkoff write that the 'sole interest rule ... requires a trustee to consider only the interests of the beneficiary without regard to the interests of anyone else, whether the fiduciary personally or a third party': ibid 388.

[7] For discussion of common law and statutory foundations of fiduciary duty in different markets, see Principles for Responsible Investment, *Fiduciary Duty in the 21st Century: Final Report* (2019) 12.

[8] 29 United States Code Chapter 18. ERISA in important respects points back to common law. See Schanzenbach and Sitkoff 399–400 ('For the most part, trust law supplies the relevant fiduciary principles, not only for trusts, but also for pensions and charitable endowments .... [ERISA] imposes a mandatory trust structure on most private pension and retirement accounts as a matter of federal law'.).

investment factors'.[9] The US Supreme Court has ruled that ERISA's sole interest rule provides that the exclusive purpose for an ERISA trustee must be 'financial benefits (such as retirement income)'.[10] This interpretation of ERISA seems to rule out consideration for other benefits for beneficiaries, which further mitigates against certain approaches to ESG investing.

Schanzenbach and Sitkoff make a distinction that is useful from the standpoint of US fiduciary law, between 'collateral benefits ESG' that is motivated by providing a benefit to a third party, and 'risk-return ESG' that is aimed only at improving risk-adjusted returns.[11] In real life, this distinction may blur, but it is nonetheless useful, and pertinent to reluctance by US pension funds and their investment managers to incorporate ESG considerations that may reduce risk-adjusted returns.

Over the years, Democratic and Republican administrations have regularly used 'interpretations' of ERISA (as opposed to formal regulations) to nudge understandings at the margin, with Democratic governments shading guidance to seem more supportive of consideration of ESG factors in investment and engagement with portfolio companies, and Republican governments shifting in the other direction. These changes can be seen as tinkering at the edges (at most), notwithstanding that the actions each time provoked loud opposition.

However, in 2020, the Trump administration rushed through regulations (as opposed to lesser interpretive bulletins or letters used in previous decades by EBSA) that did appear to move the needle in a manner hostile to both ESG in investing and engagement, along with considered proxy voting, by funds.[12] As EBSA later characterised sentiment of many comment letters, stakeholders 'have indicated that the rules have been interpreted as putting a thumb on the scale against the consideration of ESG factors, even when those factors are financially material'.[13]

Then, in October 2021, EBSA under President Biden published for comment new regulation that largely reversed the Trump-era language.[14] In doing so, EBSA stated that it was concerned that:

> uncertainty with respect to the current regulation may deter fiduciaries from taking steps that other marketplace investors would take in enhancing investment value and performance, or improving investment portfolio resilience against the potential financial risks and impacts often associated with climate change and other ESG factors.[15]

EBSA also expressed concern that the Trump-era regulation had 'created a perception that fiduciaries are at risk if they include any ESG factors in the financial evaluation

---

[9] Schanzenbach and Sitkoff (n 6 above) 404.
[10] *Fifth Third Bancorp v Dudenhoeffer* [2014] 134 S Ct 2459, 2468.
[11] Schanzenbach and Sitkoff (n 6 above) 397–399.
[12] US Department of Labor Employee Benefits Security Administration (EBSA), Financial Factors in Selecting Plan Investments, 85 Federal Register 72,856 (12 November 2020); and EBSA, Fiduciary Duties Regarding Proxy Voting and Shareholder Rights, 85 Federal Register 81,658 (15 December 2020).
[13] EBSA, Prudence and Loyalty in Selecting Plan Investments and Exercising Shareholder Rights, 86 Federal Register 52,272 (13 October 2021) 57,275. By 13 December 2021, deadline for comments, EBSA had received 894 comment letters: https://www.dol.gov/agencies/ebsa/laws-and-regulations/rules-and-regulations/public-comments/1210-AC03.
[14] ibid.
[15] ibid 275.

of plan investments, and that they may need to have special justifications for even ordinary exercises of shareholder rights'.[16]

Notwithstanding considerable noise and controversy, the October 2021 EBSA proposal would do little more than restore the status quo ante before the Trump-era regulations, although on a firmer footing than with past interpretive letters. The better footing is because the proposal is incorporated into formal regulation, and because of clarity of language on certain issues.[17] The October 2021 proposal still is pending; the US Department has indicated that it aims to finalize the rule sometime in 2022.[18] In my view, adoption of the rule as proposed would not open the door to the type of ESG investing that the Gibson Brandon study says is missing in the US.

Using the Schanzenbach/Sitkoff language, the EBSA proposal would protect risk/return ESG, not collateral benefits ESG, although the fact that there are collateral benefits would not be used as evidence that fiduciary rules are being flouted. Essentially, the new rule would re-commit EBSA to what it describes as its long-standing policies:

> that ERISA fiduciaries may not sacrifice investment returns or assume greater investment risks as a means of promoting collateral social policy goals …. [and] that the fiduciary act of managing plan assets that involve shares of corporate stock includes making decisions about voting proxies and exercising shareholder rights.[19]

EBSA states that proscription on sacrifice of returns or increased risk based on collateral social policy goals 'flow directly from ERISA's stringent standards of prudence and loyalty under section 404(a) of the statute'. It seems highly unlikely that the underlying statute will be changed in the foreseeable future. This leaves US fiduciary law, as it applies to private pension funds, in a different place than fiduciary law in the UK, Europe and elsewhere.

The second critical legal aspect for ESG investing is company law. Board member duties and accountability create the context for investors and other company stakeholders in influencing portfolio corporate policies and practices.

A key element of this relates to shareholder rights. Both state and federal rules in the US have fostered an active market for corporate control, and a large role for investor activism to challenge corporate Board members. While activists sometimes complain about lack of an even playing field, there is no doubt that shareholder activism is lively in the US, and on the minds of Board members even where they

---

[16] ibid.

[17] As an example of clarity of language, the October 2021 EBSA proposal would specify that a tie-breaking decision to make an ESG investment may be made if the fiduciary prudently concludes between competing choices or investment courses of action 'equally serve the financial interests of the plan'. The concept of tie-break was a subject of the back-and-forth between different administrations. The Trump EBSA regulations defined the tie-break situation as only involving choices 'indistinguishable' based on 'pecuniary factors', terminology that at best was confusing, and could lead fiduciaries away from selecting an ESG choice: ibid 57,278–57,279.

[18] See US Office of Management and Budget, "Agency Rule List," Spring 2022, DOL/EBSA, "Prudence and Loyalty in Selecting Plan Investments and Exercising Shareholder Rights (RIN 1210-AC03 at https://www.reginfo.gov/public/do/eAgendaViewRule?pubId=202204&RIN=1210-AC03.

[19] ibid 57,273.

have not (yet) been challenged.[20] Aside from proxy contests to elect Board members (and activist investor influence through the threat to nominate Board candidates), the shareholder-sponsored resolution for decades has played an important role in the US market in raising environmental, social and governance issues. The shareholder proposal process, which is robust in the US, is governed by a combination of state law and Rule 14a-8 of the Securities Exchange Act of 1934.[21] Rule 14a-8 spells out grounds for company exclusion of shareholder proposals, which can be subject to political influence, but which for the most part has functioned in a manner acceptable to leading proponents of shareholder proposals.[22]

Stepping back, company law in the US – primarily the responsibility of states rather than the federal (national) government[23] – places the central obligation of Boards and officers to shareholders, albeit with substantial freedom of judgement under the 'business judgment rule' and with clear obligations to the entity itself. In the dominant US view, company Board member and officer actions must relate to creation of shareholder value.[24] This sometimes is called 'shareholder primacy'.

In 2019, the Business Roundtable (BRT), an association of large-company CEOs, kicked off renewed debate in the US when it released a new 'Statement on the Purpose

---

[20] For a useful discussion of the range of current shareholder activism in the United States, see M Castanon Moats et al, Pricewaterhouse Coopers LLC, 'The Director's Guide to Shareholder Activism', *Harvard Law School Forum on Corporate Governance* (11 June 2021), https://corpgov.law.harvard.edu/2021/06/11/the-directors-guide-to-shareholder-activism/. We should note that in the absence of a formal dissident challenge to Board members, the US director election mechanism is weak in the absence of company policies to provide for a 'majority voting' standard in election of Board members. The default standard under the laws of Delaware and other states provides for plurality voting, and votes 'against' or 'withheld' from a Board member do not count at all. Each year, a number of Board members are 're-elected' to their Board despite receiving more votes 'against' than 'for'. For information, see Council of Institutional Investors, 'Director Elections', https://www.cii.org/director_elections.

[21] ibid.

[22] See eg letter from Josh Zinner, CEO of the Interfaith Center on Corporate Responsibility, a leading coordinator of shareholder proposal activity, to SEC Secretary Vanessa Countryman (27 July 2020) ('For decades, the shareholder proposal process has served as a cost-effective way for corporate management and Boards to gain a better understanding of shareholder priorities and concerns'): https://www.sec.gov/comments/s7-23-19/s72319–6702907-206070.pdf.

[23] Under the US federal system, powers are divided between the national and state governments. Corporate law historically has been a matter for the states, which to some extent compete between themselves in attracting company incorporations. The state of Delaware has been the leading state for incorporation for more than a century. Currently, some 67% of Fortune 500 companies are incorporated in Delaware, and 93% of initial public offerings in 2020 were by Delaware companies. See State of Delaware, Division of Corporations, 'Annual Report Statistics', https://corp.delaware.gov/stats/. Most other states to one extent or another incorporate guidelines set forth by the Model Business Corporation Act, promulgated by the American Bar Association. See https://www.americanbar.org/groups/business_law/publications/the_business_lawyer/find_by_subject/buslaw_tbl_mci_mbca/. Both Delaware law and the MBCA provide for considerable latitude to Boards and executives under the business judgement rule.

[24] Fiduciary duties also are held by company Board members, to the company and (in the dominant view) to shareholders, but the practical application of this to debates over stakeholder obligations may be limited. See eg J Povilani, 'The Use and Misuse of Fiduciary Duties: Why Corporate Fiduciary Duties Aren't Worth Fighting For' (2021) 13(1) *William & Mary Business and Law Review* 1 at 13 ('… while fiduciary duties remain a powerful tool for preventing [corporate] directors' improper pursuit of their own self-interests, these duties have almost no impact on their decisions regarding the distribution of resources among various corporate constituencies. As such, even if directors were to owe fiduciary duties to stakeholders like employees or customers, this would not protect them from the negative distributive effects of corporate decision-making …').

of the Corporation'.[25] The BRT said it was rejecting shareholder primacy, and committing its CEO members to serve all stakeholders. The BRT statement received substantial criticism, including that it was little more than public relations spin.[26] Of course, the BRT does not set corporate law, but the seeming commitment of CEOs to stakeholder governance set off furious debate in corporate law circles as well as elsewhere.[27]

That debate has taken place amidst an already-started American Law Institute (ALI) Project for a Restatement of the Law of Corporate Governance.[28] Despite the BRT statement, there has been little change in shareholder-centric thinking in the law of Delaware and other important venues for company incorporation. A Restatement section that was approved by the ALI membership in May 2022 indicates that in 'common-law jurisdictions', including Delaware, 'the objective of a business corporation is to promote the economic value of the corporation, within the boundaries of the law ... for the benefit of the corporation's shareholders'.[29] ALI uses broad language on how Delaware and other common-law jurisdiction companies may consider stakeholders, but it is within the context of long-term benefit of shareholders.[30]

The new Restatement language does state a different objective for 'stakeholder jurisdictions', referencing some states that have multi-stakeholder constituency

---

[25] See Business Roundtable, 'Business Roundtable Redefines the Purpose of a Corporation to Promote "An Economy That Serves All Americans": Updated Statement Moves Away from Shareholder Primacy, Includes Commitments to All Stakeholders' (19 August 2019), https://www.businessroundtable.org/business-roundtable-redefines-the-purpose-of-a-corporation-to-promote-an-economy-that-serves-all-americans.

[26] See eg Council of Institutional Investors, 'Council of Institutional Investors Responds to Business Roundtable Statement on Corporate Purpose' (19 August 2019), https://www.cii.org/aug19_brt_response ('CII believes Boards and managers need to sustain a focus on long-term shareholder value. To achieve long-term shareholder value, it is critical to respect stakeholders, but also to have clear accountability to company owners ....BRT has articulated its new commitment to stakeholder governance ... while (1) working to diminish shareholder rights; and (2) proposing no new mechanisms to create Board and management accountability to any other stakeholder group'); N Minow, 'Six Reasons We Don't Trust the New "Stakeholder" Promise from the Business Roundtable', Harvard Law School Forum (2 September 2019), https://corpgov.law.harvard.edu/2019/09/02/six-reasons-we-dont-trust-the-new-stakeholder-promise-from-the-business-roundtable/ (reason six: 'Corporations are not designed for making public policy').

[27] See eg L Bebchuk and R Tallarita, 'The Illusory Promise of Stakeholder Governance' (2020) 106 *Cornell Law Review* 91; and Bebchuk and Tallarita, 'Will Corporations Deliver Value to All Shareholders?' (forthcoming) 75 *Vanderbilt Law Review*, December 2021 draft ('Overall, our findings support the view that the BRT Statement was mostly for show and that BRT Companies joining it did not intend or expect it to bring about any material changes in how they treat stakeholders. These findings support the view that pledges by corporate leaders to serve stakeholders would not materially benefit stakeholders, and that their main effect could be to insulate corporate leaders from shareholder oversight and deflect pressures for stakeholder-protecting regulation. Stakeholder governance that relies on the discretion of corporate leaders would not represent an effective way to address growing concerns about the effects corporations have on stakeholders').

[28] See 'Restatement of the Law: Corporate Governance', https://www.ali.org/projects/show/corporate-governance/.

[29] American Law Institute, 'Restatement of the Law, Corporate Governance, Tentative Draft No 1 (April 2022). For ALI report on approval of certain sections of the Restatement, see https://www.ali.org/projects/show/corporate-governance/.

[30] ibid (in promoting value for shareholders, according to the ALI revision, a common-law-jurisdiction corporation may have regard to '(a) the interests of the corporation's employees, (b) the desirability of fostering the corporation's business relationships with suppliers, customers, and others, and (c) the impact of the corporation's operations on the community and the environment', as well as ethical considerations related to the responsible conduct of business).

statutes. The new Restatement language suggests that in these jurisdictions, where a minority of US public companies are incorporated, the corporation should enhance the economic value of the corporation 'for the benefit of the corporation's share-holders and/or, to the extent permitted by state law, for the benefit of employees, suppliers, customers, communities, or any other constituencies'. But the constituency statutes, mostly dating from the 1980s, affect a limited minority of US public compa-nies and have not changed lately,[31] and there is little or no evidence that they have significantly affected behaviour of companies in a manner to protect non-shareholder stakeholders.[32] A further clause that would apply to US companies incorporated in both types of jurisdiction indicates that a corporation 'may devote a reasonable amount of resources to public welfare, humanitarian, educational, and philanthropic purposes, whether or not doing so enhances the economic value of the corporation'. Again, this codifies existing practice, and is not likely to lead away from shareholder primacy.

Like fiduciary law, current developments underline the status quo in US corporate law, with shareholder value the central objective of corporations. That said, both investors and company officials (executives and Board members) have shown greater regard over the last several years for stakeholder interests, and the strength of society more generally, but in the context of pursuing long-term shareholder value.

This is reflected in the third prong of law that is central to ESG investing: disclo-sure rules. Disclosure is the most important element of US federal securities laws, which are predicated on the view that investors should have access to key financial and other company-specific information to make investment decisions. The founda-tional laws for US federal securities regulation, enforced by the SEC, are the Securities Act of 1933 and the Securities Exchange Act of 1934. As the SEC indicates:

The main purposes of these laws can be reduced to two common-sense notions:

- Companies offering securities for sale to the public must tell the truth about their business, the securities they are selling, and the risks involved in investing in those securities.

- Those who sell and trade securities – brokers, dealers, and exchanges – must treat investors fairly and honestly.[33]

---

[31] Constituency statutes sometimes were put in place to protect particular politically influential compa-nies from takeovers, tending to entrench management of those companies without serving broad public purpose.

[32] See Bebchuk and Tallarita (2020) (n 26 above) 136 ('even companies incorporated in states with a constituency statute have corporate governance guidelines with strong shareholder-centric principles'), 156 (studying private equity acquisitions for the period 2000 through 2019, the authors find that lead-ers of corporations in constituency statute states 'generally did not use their negotiating power to secure any constraints on the power of the private equity buyer to make choices that would adversely impact stakeholders. Despite the risk of significant post-sale layoffs and reduction in employment, we found that in almost all cases corporate leaders did not negotiate for any restrictions on the freedom of the private equity buyers to fire employees. Also, in the rare cases in which such restrictions were found, the deal terms denied employees any power to enforce these constraints. Furthermore, we found that corporate leaders did not negotiate any constraints on buyers' post-deal choices that could pose risks to several other notable stakeholder groups – consumers, suppliers, creditors, or the environment').

[33] SEC, 'The Role of the SEC', https://www.investor.gov/introduction-investing/investing-basics/role-sec.

In pursuit of the first purpose, the SEC requires issuers to provide investors with 'material' information on securities when they are first offered on public markets, and on a continuing basis. The framework seeks to be comprehensive. 'Materiality', wrote the US Supreme Court, involves 'the significance of an omitted or misrepresented fact to a reasonable investor', in making and continuing an investment (or selling), and in voting.[34] The SEC requires issuers of securities to file not only a prospectus, but periodic and material event reports.

This legal framework creates a paradox for those who seek to ensure that a range of environmental and social matters be disclosed under SEC rules. On the one hand, if a matter is material, its disclosure always has been mandated under US securities laws. If it is not material, the SEC has limited authority (at best) to require its disclosure, absent explicit legislative requirements. The SEC provides guidance from time to time for various areas of disclosure, importantly including on risk factors, and also comments to issuers on specific filings.

An important milestone for SEC guidance on climate-related disclosures came in 2010, when the commission reminded issuers of their obligations in describing risk factors and other elements of disclosure to consider the impact of legislation and regulation and of international agreements; indirect consequences of regulation or business trends; and physical impacts of climate change.[35] In doing this, the SEC was sensitive to the potential for criticism that it was exceeding its mandate.[36] Some studies since then have found that while US company financial report disclosures on climate change may have improved following the guidance, it often was perfunctory. While stand-alone sustainability reports were increasingly prevalent, they lacked sufficient comparability and rigour.[37]

As discussed below, the SEC is working on new projects to enhance disclosures on climate change and on human capital management.Regarding climate change, at least, the SEC has looked to international developments that have had strong participation from US actors, including the Task Force on Climate-related Financial Disclosures (TCFD). But there is significant opposition to additional disclosure requirements, often on the view that the SEC risks exceeding its mandate by promoting general policy goals not firmly tied to material risk at particular companies.[38] On the other hand, proponents of sustainable investing fear that often, in the US

---

[34] US Supreme Court, *TSC Industries, Inc, et al, Petitioners, v Northway, Inc*, 426 US 438 445 (1976).

[35] SEC, 'SEC Issues Interpretive Guidance on Disclosure Related to Business or Legal Developments Regarding Climate Change' (27 January 2010), https://www.sec.gov/news/press/2010/2010-15.htm.

[36] Then SEC Chair Mary Schapiro said, 'We are not opining on whether the world's climate is changing, at what pace it might be changing, or due to what causes': ibid.

[37] See for example H Welsh and S Kwon, 'State of Sustainability and Integrated Reporting 2018', Investor Responsibility Research Center Institute (2018), https://www.weinberg.udel.edu/IIRCiResearchDocuments/2018/11/2018-SP-500-Integrated-Reporting-FINAL-November-2018-1.pdf.

[38] See for example PG Mahoney and JD Mahoney, 'The New Separation of Ownership and Control: Institutional Investors and ESG' (2021) 2 *Columbia Business Law Review*, https://ssrn.com/abstract=3809914 ('The adoption of ESG disclosure mandates in order to serve environmental or social goals is not well-aligned with the SEC's stated mission of protecting Main Street investors and maintaining fair, orderly, and efficient markets. Accordingly, the SEC should decline to act absent a showing that ESG disclosures will serve the financial interests of the households for whom institutional investors are fiduciaries and whose retirement and other savings they manage').

political context, regulators, companies and investors fear disclosure around matters in areas of political controversy, leading them to limit disclosure of ESG material risk factors.

One additional note: among SEC disclosure rules are those regarding corporate governance, with particular relevance for company shareholder meeting proxy statements. The SEC has relatively robust disclosure requirements with regard to Board members and senior executives, executive and Board member compensation and Board structures and processes, among other matters. After significant enhancements in disclosures following the Enron and WorldCom scandals, and perceived governance challenges in the 2008 financial crisis, US investors are not seeking much further governance disclosure enhancement in the US. This is not to say that US governance disclosure is completely satisfactory. Investor associations seek better disclosure around potential insider trading, for example, and while not subjects of much attention, US disclosure on some other governance matters lags other markets (for example, US Board disclosure on Board member attendance at Board meetings is notably vague in comparison with the UK and many other markets).

III. OTHER FACTORS DIFFERENTIATE THE US ON ESG

While this chapter has focused on legal factors as the most salient factors that differentiate the US from European and some other markets, we should acknowledge that other elements are important, including investor and Boardroom culture, political pressures, the structure of the asset management industry and antitrust and SEC 'group formation' rules that, while vague, can discourage asset managers from collectively engaging shared portfolio companies.

Clearly political pressures play a significant role. For example, I do not believe that other markets have such a sizable and politically potent faction that denies the reality of climate change altogether. Even trade groups that on some level acknowledge human-caused climate change can be antagonists to institutional investors seeking to push substantive action on climate change issues.

Another difference: collective investor engagement with companies can be a particularly effective and efficient approach to dialogue between companies and investors, and is encouraged in the UK and elsewhere. But collective engagement is effectively discouraged in the US by both SEC and antitrust rules. Working in concert with other investors can subject a shareholder to onerous SEC disclosure rules depending on subjective factors that can be difficult to determine in advance.[39] Cautious investor lawyers may urge clients to avoid potentially hazardous situations that later could be seen as elements in the formation of a 'group' as defined by the SEC.

Danger of being caught up in antitrust considerations can be even more potent for large asset managers, and not just related to working with other shareholders.

---

[39] SEC rule 13d-5 defines a 'group' as 'two or more'.

Again, the law is vague, but investors fear actions that could be viewed retro-actively as requiring onerous reporting and trading restrictions, including under what are called Hart-Scott-Rodino provisions of US antitrust law.[40] And this risk appears to have increased recently, following academic suggestions that investor corporate governance activity could contribute to collusive behaviour between competitors.

Finally, culture is important in its own right. To be clear, it is difficult (and prob-ably pointless) – notwithstanding the previous section of this chapter – to totally separate law from culture. They are ineluctably intertwined. But fiduciary and legal standards and norms are only part of the picture informing views and culture, and it is quite possible that asset management sales culture (for example) is stronger in the US than Europe, as Gibson Brandon et al suggest, leading to greenwashing.[41]

There is little question that at least some versions of ESG investing have been viewed sceptically by many US-based portfolio managers and investment analysts. I assert this from conversations I have had over the last 25 years with a good number of investors. Without endorsing all his conclusions, I believe Tariq Fancy, formerly CIO of Sustainable Investing at BlackRock, accurately captures this scepticism in his controversial three-part essay, 'The Secret Diary of a "Sustainable Investor"'.[42] Fancy described his own disillusionment with much ESG investing, and with references to

---

[40] Hart-Scott-Rodino (HSR) refers to 1976 amendments to US antitrust law that, among other things, require pre-notification to the Federal Trade Commission (FTC) of certain mergers, tender offers and major stock acquisitions. The trigger for the latter was raised in February 2022 to ownership of securi-ties in a company totaling $102 million. The FTC provides an 'investment-only' (or 'passive investment') exemption, but the commission has not been clear on what constitutes 'investment-only', and has not aligned the definition with SEC rules. See Proskauer, 'A Practical Guide to the Regulation of Hedge Fund Trading Activites' (3 April 2019) 10, https://prfirmpwwwcdn0001.azureedge.net/prfirmstgacctp-wwwcdncont0001/uploads/a2267a8c377ce6a9deae3818e1efa1b8.pdf ('An investor that does no more than simply hold shares for investment purposes may rely on the exception, but any activities beyond that – other than merely casting routine votes – could invite scrutiny'). Filing involves substantial fees and trading restrictions, and violations can incur very substantial costs. See BlackRock letter to the FTC (1 February 2021) 2, https://www.blackrock.com/corporate/literature/publication/ftc-hsr-coverage-exemption-transmittal-rules-020121.pdf, p 2 ('A notification filing initiates an initial review period of up to 30 days, during which the filer may not purchase additional shares. Each filing incurs a fee ranging from $45,000 to $280,000, depending on the size of the proposed transaction'). Recent academic work in the US has raised further questions about governance engagement by large investors and antitrust consid-erations. For a discussion, see EB Rock and DL Rubinfeld, 'Antitrust for Institutional Investors' (2018) 1 *Antitrust Law Journal* 221. The FTC in December 2020 proposed changes that could provide additional clarity, but due to technical definition in how the FTC aggregates share holdings of large investors, ESG engagement by the largest shareholders could be even more discouraged. See D Lim, 'Investment Giants Lobby to Avoid Antitrust Scrutiny' (*The Wall Street Journal*, 8 April 2021), https://www.wsj.com/articles/investment-giants-lobby-to-avoid-antitrust-scrutiny-11617883203.

[41] Gibson Brandon et al use the term 'greenwashing' in particular with reference to a subset of US PRI signatories that the authors contend fail to show any incorporation of ESG factors in investment, p 21 ('[W]e identified that a group of US PRI signatories who do not report any ESG incorporation actually exhibit significantly worse ESG scores than non-PRI investors. These results suggest "greenwashing" by some US PRI signatories given that their equity investments are not aligned with the responsible investment goals set by the PRI').

[42] T Fancy, 'The Secret Diary of a Sustainable Investor', Medium.com, 20 August 2021; see Part I, and a link to a pdf that combines the three essays: https://medium.com/@sosofancy/the-secret-diary-of-a-sustainable-investor-part-1-70b6987fa139.

views of investors, such as venture capitalist Marc Andreessen (impact investing 'is like a houseboat – not a very good house, not a very good boat') and Warren Buffett, who said:

> If people want us to junk our coal plants, either our shareholders or the consumer is going to pay for it …. So, there's a cost to somebody … the question is how it gets absorbed, but overwhelmingly that has to be a governmental activity.[43]

Fancy also heard similar comments from less prominent investors, and characterises views of BlackRock PMs more generally:

> The marketing and sales people at BlackRock were all about ESG – they couldn't get enough of it. The portfolio managers were often the opposite: many of them wanted to pass the 'ESG test' and be left alone. In one chat with a portfolio manager of stocks, I noticed that his subtle dismissal of the latest research declaring *ESG-data-is a-godsend!* had a 'thou doth protest too much' air to it. It wasn't hard to guess why: besides a few specific areas such as risk, they generally didn't have other parts of the firm politely insisting that they please consider this important data set they hadn't considered all that much before. The portfolio manager's view was that they're already focused on performance since it usually determines their compensation, so if ESG information was truly useful they'd use it without being asked.

While this reference is to BlackRock, I think the attitude described can be generalised much more broadly – including the assertion that an investor was always responsible for understanding risks of all kinds, including ESG risk. And while Fancy lives in Toronto, I think he is capturing views that are fairly pervasive in the US, where he worked for BlackRock.

IV. WHERE DIFFERENCES MAY BE OVER-EMPHASISED

The discussion above risks over-emphasising the differences between the US and Europe. As mentioned, the extensive Gibson Brandon study that finds large divergence between the US and other markets, at least as of 2017, provides some useful evidence as far as it goes. But the study is limited. Most importantly, it does not really measure investor/company engagement, clearly a key element of ESG investing, and arguably the efforts that have the greatest impact on company behaviour. As with European investors – though more recently – major US-domiciled firms have geared up substantial efforts to engage with companies on ESG matters, albeit going solo in doing so (rather than doing so with other institutional investors).

Second, like any study, the Gibson Brandon research (and other earlier research) is time-bound. Much has happened since 2017 in the US that has led to greater focus on ESG, including often-negative reaction to policies of the Trump administration; the peak impact of the 'me-too' movement and a focus on sexual harassment; much greater attention to racial justice issues after the murder of George Floyd, and growth

[43] R Armstrong, 'Warren Buffett on Why Companies Cannot Be Moral Arbiters' (*Financial Times*, 29 December 2019).

of the Black Lives Matter movement; the initial shock of COVID-19, and the focus of many investors on worker safety and health and related matters during the pandemic; an unprecedented wave of weather crises and costs to companies from fires and other events that appear to have become more frequent and severe due to anthropogenic climate change; and the advent of the Biden administration, with new officials, including in securities regulation and pension oversight, who in response to investor views are seeking regulations that will better equip investors for issues related to climate change.

Still, it is clear that there continue to be significant differences in practices between Europe and the US, shaped especially by legal and fiduciary rules, but also by divergent political context, differences in culture and other factors. Given these differences, the challenges for sustainable investment in the US may differ somewhat from those in Europe. That said, the most important current challenge, in my view, is largely the same: improving sustainability measurement and disclosure. And there is some hope that there will be a global approach, at least on climate change. Below I suggest what I see are some key US challenges, including those that are perhaps unique to the US market.

V. KEY SUSTAINABLE INVESTMENT CHALLENGES FOR THE US

This section briefly touches on a few key challenges facing ESG investing in the US.

Some observers might put change in fiduciary and company law at or near the top of the list. This could include some combination of: (1) loosened fiduciary rules that permit greater freedom from narrow financial interests of a fund plan and its participants; (2) the shift away from shareholder primacy to legal obligation to stakeholders generally (or to certain specific non-shareholder stakeholders). I do not share in that view. While rhetoric against shareholder primacy has made a big splash in the last several years, it has not moved the ball and is unlikely to do so. Similarly, for all the attention on ERISA fiduciary standards over the last five or more years, the net effect is no real change. Moreover, discipline and accountability around fiduciary obligations and on company Board duties are critical underpinnings for successful and dynamic US capitalism, which is of great importance for general welfare and also to innovate and address problems.

The following are briefly discussed below:

(1) sustainability measurement and disclosure, particularly related to climate change and human capital management;
(2) private company disclosure, and mechanisms to make private companies more accountable to the public;
(3) improved universal owner focus on and understanding of systemic risk;
(4) better focus and understanding on the necessary role of government, with corrective to laissez faire myths that undercut the capability of government to respond to crises, including climate change;
(5) improvement to regulatory structures, particularly to address the gap generated by lack of alignment between stock exchanges and shareholders generally.

A. Measurement and Disclosure

There is substantial global momentum behind meaningful, comparable sustainability disclosure, which is critical not only for ESG investing, but more generally for the public to see progress in addressing climate change. On this topic, US investors, regulators and public interest advocates should be in tune with global developments. Global 'convergence' eluded accounting regulators a decade ago, but progress over the last two years towards integrating the various sustainability/integrated reporting organisations has been truly impressive. This is particularly true of the announcement in November 2021 by the IFRS Foundation of a new, truly global ISSB, with plans to consolidate the Value Reporting Foundation (itself now the tent for the Integrated Reporting Framework and SASB Standards) and the Climate Disclosure Standards Board into the new ISSB.

The challenges in reaching agreement on detailed standards is formidable, but progress is encouraging.

Meanwhile, the US SEC in March 2022 proposed mandatory, extensive climate disclosure standards for SEC-registered companies.[44] Among disclosures that would be required by the massive proposal are direct greenhouse gas (GHG) emissions (Scope 1) and indirect emissions (Scope 2). Emissions from upstream and downstream activities in a company's value chain (Scope 3) must be disclosed 'if material or if the registrant has set a GHG emissions target or goal that includes Scope 3 emissions'.[45] The proposal is hotly contested, and the SEC has received thousands of public comments on it.[46] It appears to me highly likely the SEC will approve the proposal, although very possibly with some significant modifications, in 2022.

B. Private Company Disclosure

Public disclosure on private companies in the US is largely channelled through securities laws, focused on publicly held companies (including those listed on exchanges as well as, since the 1960s, companies traded over the counter with enough shareholders and amount of assets). With the growth of private companies – many of which can achieve high valuations with less need for capital than earlier generations of companies – there is a large and growing information gap on corporate governance and activities.

Former SEC Commissioner Allison Herren Lee focused attention on this while she was at the Commission. Unicorns – private companies with valuations of $1 billion or more:

> are not just big, but also consequential, making significant positive contributions to innovation .... they have a dramatic and lasting impact on our economy, at the local, state, and

---

[44] Press Release, 'SEC Proposes Rules to Enhance and Standardize Climate-Related Disclosures for Investors', 21 March 2022, US Securities and Exchange Commission, at https://www.sec.gov/news/press-release/2022-46.

[45] ibid.

[46] https://www.sec.gov/comments/s7-10-22/s71022.htm.

even national level. But investors, policymakers, and the public know relatively little about them compared to their public counterparts.[47]

There are a variety of mechanisms to improve private company disclosure, not least through examining how the SEC defines the 'number' of shareholders in a company, which does not break out beneficial owners, but counts at the level of brokers and banks. Consideration could be given to basic disclosure requirements for sizable companies outside the securities law framework. More generally, pension funds and other clients of private equity and venture capital firms could seek more transparency and better policy from the companies backed by PE and VC funding.

C. Universal Owners and Systemic Risk

A few groups and individuals recently have discussed whether universal owners can better address systemic risk, which a company-by-company focus can sometimes obscure. A notable initiative in this regard is The Shareholder Commons, which indicates that:

> By harnessing the power of universal owners – large institutional investors with diversified portfolios that have a financial interest in the well-being of the economy as a whole – we are working to ensure our capital markets give priority to long term systemic health over individual company profits.[48]

The Shareholder Commons was founded in 2019 by Frederick Alexander, a leading Delaware corporate attorney who has been a pioneer of the benefit corporation model. A benefit corporation (or the B-Corp) now is specifically authorised under the law of Delaware and many other states, and has a specific commitment to stakeholders generally rather than only shareholders. The Shareholder Commons project, which is supported by the Ford Foundation, the Omidyar Network and the Tipping Point Fund on Impact Investment, seeks to encourage 'profit maximizing behaviour within pre-competitive guardrails established to protect the global commons'. On my read, this fits within 'risk/return ESG', and could be a promising approach.

D. Understanding the Necessary Role of Government

The 2019 BRT statement on the purpose of the corporation was received poorly by many, in part because it seemed unrealistic for corporate executives to shape and lead the solutions to such social problems as inequality, climate change and pollution. This is not to say there is not a critical role for companies, as major employers (in fair and equitable treatment of employees) and operators (that can cause terrible pollution, but also innovate and create better alternatives). Similarly, some advocates

---

[47] Commissioner Allison Herren Lee, 'Going Dark: The Growth of Private Markets and the Impact on Investors and the Economy', remarks at SEC Speaks (12 October 2021), https://www.sec.gov/news/speech/lee-sec-speaks-2021-10-12.

[48] See https://theshareholdercommons.com/.

for dual class shares at founder-led companies posit such share structures as enabling those founders to solve society's problems, unfettered by pesky shareholders. (Dual class shares with special voting rights in recent decades have enabled founders like Mark Zuckerberg at Meta, parent of Facebook, to continue to control their companies without owning anywhere near a majority of shares.) It is naïve to believe that founders and top executives, marshalling their companies, have the interests, aptitude or inclination to substantively address many social problems, particularly where they may be on the benefit side of current dysfunction (eg inequality, and externalising of pollution cost).

Martin Lipton, founding partner of the prominent US corporate law firm Wachtell, Lipton, Rosen & Katz, strongly defended the BRT statement rejecting shareholder primacy, writing that 'the argument that protection of stakeholders other than shareholders should be left to government regulation ... would lead to state corporatism or socialism'.[49]

This seems to me to be a category mistake. Only government can fully address key systemic problems, by setting rules of the road that align market participants with public interest. Tariq Fancy, the former BlackRock ESG CIO, wrote that 'we've built private firms from the ground up to do one thing really well: extract profits'. He writes that:

> if you want to change the behaviour of all the players in the game, you have to change the rules of the game for everyone ... Fixing the rules of this system so that it produces better societal outcomes is not 'intervening in the free market' – especially as there *is* no such thing as a 'free market' in the first place. A market economy is at its core a collection of rules. No rules, no market.

Fancy goes further and says that ESG in investment diverts attention from what government needs to be doing. Perhaps that can be true at times, but sustainable investment can and does call attention to what government should do. The investor focus on climate change has played a role in putting climate change at the forefront of the agenda for major government players, even if a carbon tax, the solution favoured by Fancy and many active in ESG investment, has not gained traction yet in the US. More specifically, US investor activism raising questions about corporate political contributions and lobbying influence has helped pinpoint a major point of failure, with companies lobbying for narrow interests on key matters in ways that harm the broader possibility for progress.[50]

---

[49] M Lipton, 'Stakeholder Corporate Governance, Business Roundtable and Council of Institutional Investors' Harvard Law School Forum on Corporate Governance (21 August 2019), https://corpgov. law.harvard.edu/2019/08/21/stakeholder-corporate-governance-business-roundtable-and-council-of-institutional-investors/.

[50] For an example of useful commentary on corporate political contributions, see DS Lund and LE Strine, 'Corporate Political Spending is Bad Business' (2022) *Harvard Business Review*, January/February ('most investors hold a broad portfolio of stocks reflecting the whole economy. They don't want their dollars to be spent on political rent-seeking by a specific company, which helps one company but causes externalities for other companies, taxpayers, and consumers like themselves, and therefore is likely to slow real overall economic and portfolio growth. It is more likely to entail at best a transfer of value from one company to another and at worst an increase in externalities borne by society in general').

E. Strengthening Regulation and Market Structure

There are significant lacunae in US market regulation because of insufficient clear SEC authority over stock exchanges. The balance of power between the SEC and stock exchanges has shifted by several court decisions in recent decades, most recently in 1990, when The Business Roundtable in lower court won a lawsuit against an SEC rule that would have barred national securities exchanges from listing stocks that violated the one-share, one-vote principle.[51] This has become more of a problem in recent decades, as stock exchanges have moved to ownership by for-profit public companies. Ironically, while leading exchanges are very effective at serving their shareholders, they sometimes do so at the expense of shareholders generally.

This has been evident in long-running trends on dual-class shares where there are differential voting rights. While the New York Stock Exchange, as a non-profit near-monopoly, led in shutting down dual-class structures common in the 1920s (as well as establishing key financial reporting, audits of financial statements and Board audit committees), competition between US exchanges has led a global race to the bottom regarding stock exchange requirements on share voting. This was why the SEC sought to regulate in this area before it encountered judicial push-back. The Council of Institutional Investors and others have advocated for legislation that would more clearly establish SEC authority over stock exchanges on dual-class shares, although arguably the problem of SEC power relative to the stock exchanges is much broader than the voting rights issue.

VI. CONCLUSION

Approaches to sustainable (or ESG) investing in the US must wrestle with the particular force of US law, particularly around institutional investor fiduciary duties and the legal purpose of the corporation under the law of Delaware and other states. Other legal differences (including those related to antitrust concerns) as well as cultural divergence also must be taken into account. That said, the most urgent need of investors engaged in a range of types of ESG investing, at least at the moment, is the same in the US as in other markets – better, more comparable and agreed standards for measurement, particularly around climate change matters.

---

[51] *The Business Roundtable v SEC, United States Court of Appeals*, District of Columbia Circuit, 12 June 1990, 905 F2d 406 (DC Cir 1990).

14

The Model Mandate: Hardwiring Stewardship into Investment Management

GEORGE DALLAS AND CHRIS HODGE

I. INTRODUCTION

INVESTMENT MANDATES CONTAIN the instructions on how the funds of an asset owner or investment beneficiary should be invested by an asset manager. They are used as contractual elements to guide the actions and choices of the fund's manager. Mandates may also set out the level of risk that the beneficial owner of the funds will permit and the type of investments to be prioritised. Without an agreed mandate and an investment management agreement (IMA) to underpin it, asset owners have limited understanding of how their assets are allocated and overseen – which would impact their ability to hold their managers to account.

Asset owners increasingly expect the managers they appoint actively to exercise stewardship over their assets, and to do so in a way that is consistent with their own long-term investment objectives.

This chapter focuses on the 'Model Mandate' as a practical tool for embedding stewardship in the investment process, which provides a framework of issues and contract language to guide and include in IMAs between asset owners and asset managers.

We begin with a discussion of what stewardship is and what it seeks to achieve. We make use of a globally recognised framework for stewardship, the Global Stewardship Principles (GSP) published by the International Corporate Governance Network (ICGN), an investor-led membership organisation of governance and stewardship professionals.[1] The GSP break down stewardship into individual principles, actions and reporting practices. Our discussion of the Model Mandate concept takes this one step further and articulates how these practices can be codified and built into the process of investment management.

The Model Mandate can be applied in different ways as a tool for asset owners. It can be used in the asset manager selection process to highlight asset owner

---

[1] ICGN was founded in 1995 and its members come from over 40 countries globally. As of 2022 ICGN's investor members managed assets around $70 trillion: https://www.icgn.org.

expectations in requests for proposals (RFPs), the awarding of investment mandates, as well as in IMAs – the contract that defines the services to be provided by the asset manager. The underlying goal behind the Model Mandate is to 'hardwire' steward-ship practices into the process of investment management.

For many asset owners, stewardship includes consideration of sustainability issues, including environmental, social and governance (ESG) factors and how these link to systemic risks and broader frameworks such as the United Nations (UN) Sustainable Development Goals (SDGs). In some jurisdictions asset owners and/or managers are now expected to be accountable for how they have done so, for example in the EU through the Sustainable Finance Disclosure Regulation.[2] In this context, the Model Mandate can help to serve the purpose of institutionalising the integration of these sustainability issues into investment analysis and decision making.

In this chapter we will review the 'history' of the Model Mandate and present it in the broader context of the asset manager selection and monitoring processes. We will explore how this mandate might enhance the alignment of interests between the asset owner and asset manager. We will also consider how the Model Mandate might reinforce accountability by the asset manager to the asset owner, as well as the accountability of the asset owner to its ultimate beneficiaries.

II. HISTORICAL CONTEXT

Investment management has been an established profession for decades. However, the concept of investor 'stewardship' is relatively new. ICGN, for example, published its statement on Institutional Shareholder Responsibilities in 2003,[3] recognising that investors have not only rights but responsibilities as well. But it was not until 2010, when the UK Financial Reporting Council published the UK Stewardship Code, that the term stewardship became more widely adopted in capital markets globally. At present there are over 20 stewardship codes in place around the world in jurisdictions that include developed, emerging and frontier markets.[4]

To accompany, and support, the acceptance and implementation of stewardship ICGN pioneered the first 'Model Mandate Initiative'[5] in 2012 to help asset owners express what they expected of the asset managers that they engaged, and to reflect those expectations in investment contracts and mandates. Its particular, focus was on the parts of the mandate relating to the investment approach, stewardship, ESG and the manager's accountability to their clients.

The environment in which asset owners and managers operate, and the expecta-tions and obligations placed on them, has changed considerably since then. There

---

[2] European Union (2019), Regulation on sustainability-related disclosure in the financial services sector: https://ec.europa.eu/info/business-economy-euro/banking-and-finance/sustainable-finance/sustainability-related-disclosure-financial-services-sector_en.

[3] ICGN Statement on Institutional Shareholder Responsibilities (12 December 2003).

[4] G Dallas and M Lubrano, *Governance, Stewardship and Sustainability: Theory, Practice and Evidence* (International Corporate Governance Network, 2021) Ch 1.

[5] International Corporate Governance Network, *ICGN Model Mandate Initiative: Model contract language between asset owners and their fund managers* (2012).

have been significant changes in capital allocation both between and within asset classes and exponential growth in the value of assets allocated to sustainable and responsible investing, which are predicted to exceed US\$50 trillion – more than one-third of global assets under management – by 2025.[6]

ICGN's Model Mandate has also been followed by similar initiatives from other organisations, developing approaches to mandates reflecting their own strategic priorities. For example, the Principles for Responsible Investment (PRI) has created a framework for mandate requirements to promote ESG integration by investors.[7] The advocacy group FCLT Global also published a report on institutional investor mandates, outlining key elements and contract provisions with the goal of reinforcing long-term investment perspectives.[8]

Ten years on from its 2012 launch, ICGN updated the original Model Mandate guidance and the revised version was published in 2022.[9] ICGN undertook this revision in partnership with the Global Investors in Sustainable Development (GISD) Alliance,[10] an international coalition of investors and companies supported by the UN whose mission is to encourage long-term investment in sustainable development.

The formation of the GISD Alliance initiative reflects an increased public and political expectation that investors should contribute to long-term sustainable value creation, including through addressing the UN SDGs. ICGN's partnership with the GISD Alliance has brought a clearer focus on the sustainability dimension to the revised Model Mandate guidance.

III. PURPOSE OF THE MODEL MANDATE

The Model Mandate is addressed to asset owners and managers, as well as to those who provide advice to them and who set the regulatory and reporting frameworks in which they operate.

While intended to be relevant to all mandates irrespective of the owner's investment strategy, the updated guidance also contains specific advice on how to reflect sustainable investment objectives in mandates and contracts alongside the more generally applicable guidance.

From our discussions with asset owners and managers it is clear that there is a demand for some assistance on this topic. Many asset owners we spoke to are only

---

[6] Bloomberg Intelligence, 'ESG 2021 Midyear Outlook' (2021), https://www.bloomberg.com/company/press/esg-assets-rising-to-50-trillion-will-reshape-140-5-trillion-of-global-aum-by-2025-finds-bloomberg-intelligence/.

[7] Principles for Responsible Investment, *Mandate Requirements and RFPs* (2019), https://www.unpri.org/investment-tools/asset-owner-resources/mandate-requirements-and-rfps.

[8] FCLT Global, *Institutional Mandates: Anchors for Long-term Performance* (2020), https://www.fcltglobal.org/wp-content/uploads/Institutional-Investment-Mandates-Anchors-for-Long-term-Performance_FCLTGlobal.pdf.

[9] ICGN and GISD Alliance, *Model Mandate* (2022), https://www.icgn.org/icgn-gisd-alliance-model-mandate-guidance.

[10] The GISD Alliance was founded in 2019 and seeks to deliver concrete solutions to scale-up long-term finance and investment in sustainable development: see GISD Joint Statement. The Alliance consists of 30 leaders of major financial institutions and corporations spanning all the regions of the world: https://www.gisdalliance.org.

starting to think through how in practice to reflect such objectives in their investment approach, while asset managers reported receiving often conflicting requests from existing and potential clients.

If the Model Mandate can help to provide some clarity about the issues to be covered in mandates and IMAs then it will serve a useful purpose. The other primary purpose of the guidance is to provide common 'rules of engagement' between asset owners and managers, both when agreeing the terms of the mandate and when reporting on how it has been implemented.

The primary audience for the guidance is asset owners. It aims to help them ensure that their investment strategy and their own fiduciary obligations to clients and beneficiaries are properly reflected in the terms agreed with asset managers, and that they have the ability to monitor whether their objectives and interests are being met.

It does so by working systematically through the different issues related to stewardship and sustainability that should be addressed in their mandates, and by providing model contract clauses. In addition, the guidance identifies information that owners should seek to obtain through the tendering and due diligence process that could help them identify managers whose investment approach best meets their own expectations. The guidance does not, however, try to tell asset owners what their stewardship and sustainability objectives should be.

The guidance may also be valuable to asset managers, as it potentially provides a common framework for discussing with existing and potential clients how issues relating to sustainability and stewardship can be incorporated into their mandates and common metrics for reporting to clients. Asset managers are encouraged to incorporate some of the model clauses in their own standard contract terms or offer them as options for those clients that request them.

The benefits of such a common framework increase the more widely it is adopted. For that reason, ICGN's guidance has been designed to be capable of being used for different asset classes and in different markets. By addressing the range of stewardship and sustainability issues that should be covered in contracts at a relatively high level, this framework can be adapted or built on to work alongside local requirements.

The guidance may therefore also be of interest to advisers to asset owners and managers such as investment consultants, and to organisations that aim to promote long-term sustainable value creation through the investment chain such as standard-setters, regulators and industry associations. By endorsing and encouraging the use of the guidance they can contribute to providing that common framework.

One example of how regulators might use the Model Mandate to strengthen their local framework can be found in South Africa, where the Financial Sector Conduct Authority has incorporated some of the draft contract terms in the 2012 Model Mandate in its standard template for IMAs.

IV. CORE CONCEPTS

Before we consider how to structure mandates it is important to have a grounding in core concepts of stewardship, fiduciary duty, sustainable investing and systemic risk to guide the mandate process.

A. Stewardship

Starting with a generic definition, stewardship can be described as *the proper use of entrusted power*. Implicit in this concept is one person (a 'steward') acting as an agent on behalf of another person or underlying beneficiary. Translating this into an investment management context, stewardship is the application of the fiduciary duty of care and loyalty that institutional investors owe to their underlying clients and beneficiaries in the provision of professional investment services. Investors assume that the role of stewards is to preserve and enhance long-term value on behalf of their beneficiaries. In the first instance the beneficiaries are the individual savers or pension fund beneficiaries whose funds are being managed.

The ICGN's Global Stewardship Principles consist of seven key components:[11]

(1)   internal governance: foundations of effective stewardship;
(2)   developing and implementing stewardship policies;
(3)   monitoring and assessing investee companies;
(4)   engaging companies and investor collaboration;
(5)   exercising and protecting voting rights;
(6)   promoting long-term value creation and integration of ESG;
(7)   meaningful transparency, disclosure and reporting.

These ICGN Global Stewardship Principles are broken down into further subcomponents that can be articulated in the contract language of IMAs. The ICGN Principles represent a globally accepted framework recognised by asset owners, asset managers and regulators around the world. They are the end-product of extensive ICGN member consultation and have been ratified in ICGN's AGMs. As such, these ICGN Stewardship Principles provide a legitimate foundation for negotiating asset management mandates.

It is noteworthy that Principle 6 focuses on ESG integration as a critical component of stewardship. When the ICGN Stewardship Principles were first published in 2016 ESG was not a common reference in many prominent stewardship codes globally, including the UK Stewardship Code – the world's first formal stewardship code. However, since that time ESG integration has now become part of the UK Code and many other stewardship codes around the world, with South Africa and Malaysia having led the way in this respect.

A similar trend can be observed in corporate governance codes and regulation to which listed companies and their directors are subject. The lines between 'traditional' governance considerations and ESG are increasingly blurred, and we are seeing a broader interpretation of the fiduciary duties of both directors and investors.

B. Fiduciary Duty

Fiduciary duty is at the core of investor stewardship. Fiduciary duties exist to safeguard the current and future interests of beneficiaries and are fundamental to the

---

[11] ICGN, *Global Stewardship Principles* (2020), https://www.icgn.org/icgn-global-stewardship-principles.

development of stewardship policies and practices. It is vital that the asset owner adopts an investment strategy and stewardship practices which allow them to meet their fiduciary obligations.

Asset owners may have to balance potentially competing interests across different beneficiary groups, particularly when managing assets to cover long-term liabilities with different maturities. By their very nature, certain asset owners such as pension funds and insurers are more likely to have a long-term approach for their investments.

Asset owners cannot discharge their fiduciary obligations to their end beneficiaries simply by hiring an asset manager or an investment consultant to advise in the choice of asset managers. They may delegate investment tasks to asset managers, but fiduciary duty itself is a core governance concept that cannot be delegated. It is therefore essential that owners take steps to ensure that their managers act in a way that is consistent with the owner's fiduciary obligations – including in the design and monitoring of their mandates.

A primary obligation of investor fiduciaries with long-term liabilities is to align investment practices with the creation of long-term, sustainable value – for example, by identifying investment opportunities arising from the SDGs – while minimising risks that could impact future returns.

ICGN's 2018 'Guidance on Investor Fiduciary Duties'[12] provides general guidance to investors on how fiduciary duty relates to a range of factors, including investor governance, systemic risks and fiduciary duty in the investment chain. The 2019 UNEP/PRI 'Fiduciary Duty in the 21st Century: Final Report' is focused in particular on the linkage between investor fiduciary duty and ESG integration.[13]

C. Sustainable Investing

Sustainability is an important concept and its application in business and finance continues to develop. Sustainability was defined in the 1987 World Commission on Environment and Development's Brundtland Report as 'meeting the needs of the present without compromising the ability of future generations to meet their own needs'.[14] From an economic and financial perspective sustainability has been defined by the EU's High Level Expert Group as 'making economic prosperity long-lasting, more socially inclusive and less dependent on exploitation of finite resources and the natural environment'.[15]

Taken this way, sustainability is a natural ally to the stewardship agenda, particularly with its intrinsic focus on long-term performance. Many institutional investors are either long-term asset owners, such as pension funds, or asset managers serving long-term asset owners and their beneficiaries. This implies – or at least should

---

[12] ICGN, *Guidance on Investor Fiduciary Duties* (2018).

[13] UNEP/PRI, *Fiduciary Duty in the 21st Century: Final Report* (2019), https://www.unpri.org/fiduciary-duty/fiduciary-duty-in-the-21st-century-final-report/4998.article.

[14] World Commission on Environment and Development, *Brundtland Report* (1987).

[15] High Level Expert Group, *Financing a Sustainable European Economy*, European Commission (2018), https://ec.europa.eu/info/sites/default/files/180131-sustainable-finance-final-report_en.pdf.

imply – for many investors a long-term investment horizon and an emphasis on sustainable value creation. This long-term perspective has relevance not only for individual companies but also for markets and economies.

The 2022 revisions to the ICGN/GISD Model Mandate place particular emphasis on the term 'sustainable development investing' which has specific focus on linking the Model Mandate to the 17 UN SDGs.[16]

D. Systemic Risks

As well as the specific sustainability risks affecting their individual investments, asset owners need to be aware of risks which can affect the investment value of their overall portfolio – as well as the health of financial markets and wider economies. As with ESG generally, this subject is now beginning to feature in national stewardship codes, including the UK Code.

This includes not only risks which affect the immediate volatility of their portfolio, but also those systemic risks which can affect value over a longer period or a broader spread of investments, markets and economies. These systemic risks include, but are not limited to, climate change, biodiversity, human rights, income inequality and financial system stability. These include the systemic risks to long-term sustainability that the UN SDGs aim to address.

An investor's choice of investment approach can itself contribute to systemic risk. Asset owners are exposed to financial markets generally and so are unlikely to benefit over the long run from investment strategies which produce returns by generating systemic risks and/or jeopardising the efficient functioning and stability of one or more markets.

The choice of investments and active engagement with investee companies are ways in which investors can contribute to addressing systemic risks, preserving market stability and promoting the SDGs, but they are not the only ones. An increasing number of asset owners and managers are actively engaging in public policy debates. Many are also participating in sectoral or regional initiatives, such as Climate Action 100+ and the FAIRR Initiative which focuses on ESG risks in the global food sector, in order to have a greater impact than they could achieve on their own. Owners may wish to make use of their mandates to encourage their managers to be active participants in such activities if doing so will support the achievement of the owners' sustainability objectives and/or specific SDGs.

V. BEFORE NEGOTIATING MANDATES

Developing the terms of the investment mandate itself is a multi-stage process, beginning with an understanding of the asset owner's fiduciary duties to its beneficiaries and extending through the formation of investment strategies, policies and

---

[16] United Nations, *Sustainable Development Goals* (2015), https://sdgs.un.org/goals.

procedures, mandate design and manager selection. From a sustainability perspective the consideration of ESG factors should also be regarded by asset owners as a fiduciary duty – when these factors are considered through the financial lens of risk and not only if the ultimate beneficiary is also looking to support positive social outcomes (or at least avoid negative ones).

A. Investment Strategy

In many respects the investment strategy is the most important stage in the mandate process, as the strategy will subsequently determine the investments that are made and how they are overseen. It should set out the asset owner's investment beliefs, the desired outcomes and, in broad terms, how they will be achieved. From the perspective of sustainable investment, including investment specifically focused on SDGs, it is at this stage of the process that decisions should be taken about the overarching sustainability outcomes that the investor is seeking to achieve, for example identifying which individual SDGs or sustainability themes to prioritise.

Financial elements of a typical investment strategy include:

- investment beliefs;
- expected return on assets;
- time horizon;
- material sustainability considerations;
- type of investments to be held;
- balance between different types of investments;
- realisation of investments, cashflow, liquidity management;
- risk appetite, capacity and management;
- investment constraints and limitations linked to scale or duration of liabilities.

Integrating stewardship and sustainability factors into the investment strategy brings further considerations that link to both policy formation ultimate implementation and integration to the investment process. These can include:

- how sustainability and ESG are integrated in investment decision-making (including risk assessment, valuations);
- sustainability priorities and their materiality to the portfolio – for example, by reference to specific SDGs;
- exclusions and divestments (if any);
- what will be delegated to external managers and how they will be monitored;
- monitoring of and engagement on investments – methods, selection criteria and priority issues;
- exercising voting rights – covering management and shareholder resolutions;
- stock lending policy;

- participation in collaborative engagement and industry initiatives;
- how the owner will report publicly and to clients.

All these factors can be articulated in language that can be included in IMAs.

Asset owners will typically have an investment policy or policies which set out how the principles in the strategy should inform individual investment decisions and how investments will be managed and monitored. These will generally address, for example, asset allocation, investment parameters, the use of benchmarks and counterparties and other topics.

Some owners will include in this general policy the other sustainability and stewardship issues addressed in this guidance, while others prefer to address them in separate responsible investment and/or stewardship policies. These typically include not only how investments are selected but how the owner – or manager where activities are delegated – will exercise stewardship over their investments.

There is no preferred practice; the important thing is that the owner's policies on these issues should be clearly set out in writing so that they can be shared with current and prospective asset managers, and with the owner's clients and beneficiaries.

VI. MANDATE DESIGN, NEGOTIATION, MANAGER SELECTION AND MANAGER MONITORING

For each individual mandate, asset owners will need to develop a detailed specification that fits their requirements, and which clearly describes their expectations for the way in which investment decisions are made and how the manager exercises stewardship on the owner's behalf. They will also need to ensure during the selection process that they obtain the information they need to assess whether a manager is capable of meeting those requirements.

As well as the tailored specifications for individual mandates, some owners have developed asset manager assessment processes that are applied to all mandates of a certain type, for example setting minimum criteria related to sustainability that managers must meet to be considered for sustainable or impact investing mandates.

Key to successfully matching a manager to the mandate is the request for proposals (RFP) and the accompanying due diligence process. While all RFPs will have some elements in common, the content will need to be tailored to each specific mandate to take account of factors such as asset class, investment horizon and the weight to be given to sustainability and ESG considerations.

Asset owners need to be clear about their ability to negotiate the exact terms to be included in the investment management terms. Asset managers will typically have standard terms for their investment products, and while many are willing to vary these terms to a degree or agree to additional terms in an appendix or side letter, this will not always be the case (for example, if the product is a pooled fund).

Asset owners also need to be clear about whether the sustainability and stewardship services that they require are part of the standard terms, and therefore covered by the fee for managing the mandate, or whether the asset manager considers them to be optional extras which will require additional fees. This information should be sought during the RFP process.

A. Keeping the Mandate and Manager's Performance under Review

Manager selection, appointment, monitoring and evaluation is an ongoing process, and sustainability and stewardship issues should be integrated in all parts of this process.

This process applies to existing mandates as much as it does to the awarding of new ones. These issues should be assessed when evaluating a possible extension or renewal of a contract with an asset manager. In addition, if the owner's own sustainability objectives and policies have been updated since the mandate was awarded, they may wish to consider discussing with the manager at this stage in the process whether there is scope to adjust the mandate or issuing formal guidelines and/or reporting expectations to them.

VII. ALIGNMENT BETWEEN ASSET MANAGERS AND ASSET OWNERS

The IMA should seek to ensure that asset managers act in alignment with the objectives of the asset owner. Asset owners should agree with their managers a commitment to long-term value creation and consideration of sustainability in the investment process that appropriately reflects the asset owner's investment strategy and policies. Owners should expect that managers will be able to explain how this has been reflected in their investment approach and decision making. For most mandates the onus will be on the owner to ensure that their needs and expectations are clearly set out in the IMA.

Sometimes this could be in the form of a statement of commitment from the asset manager to apply recognised standards written by third parties; this is the most likely approach if investing in pooled funds. In many cases though, and in particular in segregated mandates, asset owners will wish to ensure that their own investment strategy, targets and policies will be applied when investment decisions are taken and will inform the way in which the asset manager oversees the investments.

Some asset owners will also have screening criteria or exclusion lists which are intended to be used to exclude investment in certain industries, products or services and/or in companies whose activities may undermine the achievement of the SDGs or raise other ESG concerns such as human rights and corruption.

Whichever is the case, the expected standards or principles are more likely to be carried into practice if they are either incorporated in or appended to the agreement with the asset manager or contained in a side letter agreed by the two parties. Depending on how they are written, this might be done by requiring adherence to the policies in some form or requiring the asset manager to be aware of the standards in carrying forward their investments. For example, in the case of exercising voting rights or stock lending, the asset owner should seek to ensure that the asset manager acts in alignment with the asset owner's policies and priorities.

Where the asset owner has its own responsible investment policy or equivalent and/or exclusion lists or screening criteria, it is good practice for these to be appended to and referenced in the IMA. With this foundation the IMA can then turn to more granular considerations, including asset allocation, portfolio turnover, fee structures and manager remuneration.

VIII. ACCOUNTABILITY

An asset manager's structure, resources, governance and control systems can influence its capacity, ability and willingness to promote their clients' investment objectives and represent their interests effectively. Asset owners are advised to seek reassurance about a manager's culture and capabilities as part of the due diligence process before making an appointment.

Many asset owners may will seek reassurance about, for example: the size and nature of the resources dedicated to stewardship; the effectiveness of its Board and other governance structures; the effectiveness of its risk management and internal control systems; and its commitment to professional standards. Accordingly, the IMA might address the asset manager's professionalism and accountability to the asset owner in the context of its approach to risk management, conflicts of interest commissions and counterparties.

IX. ASSET MANAGER REPORTING TO THE CLIENT

Asset owners have a fiduciary duty to be accountable to their clients and beneficiaries for how their investments have been managed, including those investments that are managed on their behalf by asset managers. Asset owners should report to their clients and beneficiaries on a regular basis, and some owners are subject to detailed regulatory requirements to do so.

As well as obtaining from their managers the information that they in turn will report to their clients or beneficiaries, asset owners should also aim to obtain information that will enable them to assess the performance of the manager and assure themselves that the agreed investment management and stewardship policies are being applied.

It is therefore important that the IMA sets out clearly what information the manager will provide to the client, and the frequency and format in which it will do.

Many asset owners may also seek additional information that is relevant to their investment objectives and stewardship expectations. The exact nature of this information will depend on factors such as the agreed performance measures, the asset owner's responsible investment policy, recognised third party standards and their own reporting obligations.

Additional information that is neither covered by the clauses in this guidance nor contained in the manager's standard periodic reports to clients should either be specified in the IMA or – where that is not possible, for example because the mandate is for a pooled fund – in an appendix or side letter agreed with the manager.

X. CONCLUSION

The motivation behind the Model Mandate is to provide a practical tool to articulate and codify critical elements of stewardship and sustainable investing to guide the investment manager selection process, IMAs between asset owners and asset managers and monitoring of asset managers by asset owners. It is a tactic to motivate specific behaviours and outcomes, breaking stewardship down into discrete pieces subject for inclusion on RFPs and IMAs. In their partnership, ICGN and the GISD Alliance encourage:

- asset owners to use the Model Mandate as the basis for negotiating mandates with their asset managers, and to disclose to their own clients and beneficiaries the extent to which it has been used in their contracts with asset managers;

- asset managers to review their own standard contract terms and reporting to clients against the Model Mandate, and to be willing to use clauses from the Model Mandate when requested by clients;

- investment consultants and other advisers to raise awareness of the Model Mandate among their clients, and to reflect it in the advice that they provide;

- relevant regulators, standard-setters and investor bodies to consider how the Model Mandate could be adopted or adapted for use in their markets.

APPENDIX: SAMPLE CONTRACT PROVISIONS

The 2012 ICGN Model Mandate Initiative, and the revised 2022 ICGN/GISD Model Mandate, should be read on their own, as these documents will place specific sample IMA provisions into greater context. However, for purposes of illustration, we provide a few examples of draft mandate provisions to give a sense of their structure and content.

Example 1: Fiduciary duty: ensuring the fund manager undertakes to abide by investment principles agreed with the client:

> The Manager shall carry out its duties under this Agreement in accordance with the Client's responsible investment policy, which may be amended from time to time, the most recent version of which is attached. The Manager shall also manage the portfolio in accordance with the ICGN Global Stewardship Principles and other relevant standards and industry best practice as specified.

Example 2: Systemic risks: aligning the manager and client understanding what the key risks are to achieving the client's portfolio goals:

> The Manager acknowledges the need to consider long-term and systemic risk factors and market failures in order to manage risks which are relevant to the Client's long-term investment horizon and to the Client's fiduciary responsibilities.

The Manager shall have a process for monitoring current or potential investments in relation to relevant long-term and systemic factors. The Manager shall ensure that its staff exercise due care and diligence when complying with this monitoring process, including considering the extent to which such long-term factors generate investment risks or opportunities.

Example 3: Voting: setting out the basis on which the underlying shares are to be voted, where this has been delegated to the manager:

The Manager shall procure the exercise of any voting rights attaching to the Portfolio investments in accordance with the Client's expressed voting guidelines, as attached.

The Manager shall report to the Client on how they have voted on the Client's behalf in the previous reporting period, including ... an analysis of votes cast for and against, details of any controversial votes at significant holdings, and details of any resolutions on which they voted contrary to the Client's voting policy and the reasons why.

15

Corporate Purpose: Narrowing the Gap between Corporates and Investors on Sustainability Issues

BRIAN TOMLINSON

I. INTRODUCTION

T HE IDEA THAT corporations in the US should have purpose beyond profits is far from new. The earliest incorporated entities in the US were chartered to perform specific functions considered to have public value: operating a steamship route on the Hudson; or taking fares on a bridge across the Charles River in Boston.[1] Tight specificity in the purpose of the corporate form was abandoned with the advent of general incorporation laws in the nineteenth century, providing the corporate form flexibility to respond to the changing needs of a rapidly developing market society.[2]

The contemporary debate is a case of going 'back to the future', raising the prospect of requiring corporations to engage in work of identifiable public value. Driving this debate are a widely shared set of concerns that collective corporate practice has, in the act of generating products and services, undermined, impaired and distorted aspects of our societies and environment – from the climate crisis to the effectiveness of our political institutions.

II. CORPORATE PURPOSE: NEW PARADIGM OR NEW LABEL

Corporations are run in the interests of shareholders.[3] Legal scholars and corporate practitioners seem in broad agreement on this simple sounding objective.[4] The only

---

[1] A Berle and G Means, *The Modern Corporation and Private Property* (1932).

[2] General incorporation provides that rather than existing to perform a specific function – such as taking tolls at a particular turnpike – corporations could pursue an unlimited range of activities. Specific incorporation laws were often regarded as prone to corruption and, by inhibiting competition, abridged the exercise of entrepreneurial energies.

[3] Taking Delaware as the primary jurisdiction of interest. In the US, corporate incorporation law is a creature of State law and the majority of large US listed companies are incorporated in Delaware – making its legal code and case law of singular importance in the US.

'stakeholders' that have a formal accountability framework over corporations are its shareholders. They have the power to elect the Board, receive the residual interest in bankruptcy, and sue through derivative suits.[5] Salutary case law also indicates the limits of corporations pursuing non-shareholder interests as a stated goal.[6] Corporations are, of course, afforded extremely broad latitude in how they can pursue shareholder interests; almost anything is permitted provided there is a rational connection to shareholder value. Through the business judgement rule, the courts (in the absence of formal conflicts of interest) simply will not second guess the commercial judgement of management.

Pursuing shareholder value is not, however, synonymous with short-term profit maximisation – or profits at any price. You won't find 'short-term profit maximisation' as a stated objective in state incorporation statutes. However, for quite some time, short-term profit maximisation took on the form of corporate ideology, acquiring a name 'The Friedman Paradigm', named after its most effective propagandist. This paradigm was interpreted as setting out a simple-to-explain, aphoristic approach to the management of corporations: 'The social responsibility of business is to increase its profits'.[7] The Friedman Paradigm identified the consideration of other objectives beyond profit as misguided and self-defeating. Short-term profit taking became the prime objective, elevated above all others, in all circumstances.[8]

The contemporary corporate purpose debate is, in a sense, a reaction to that paradigm and its consequences. The emerging paradigm has been commonly labelled 'stakeholder capitalism', drawing a simple rhetorical contrast with 'shareholder capitalism'. This also establishes a convenient, though largely misleading, appearance of a binary choice between organising approaches to the corporate form.

The statement of this seemingly contesting paradigm that has received the most attention was, perhaps ironically, issued by the Business Roundtable (BRT) and signed by over 180 CEOs in 2019. This stated that 'While each of our individual companies serves its own corporate purpose, we share a fundamental commitment to all of our stakeholders'. The statement enumerates a laundry list of stakeholders, each of which is described as 'essential', and includes customers, employees, suppliers, communities and shareholders. The statement makes no claims to primacy among the enumerated stakeholder groups. Such language is not new.

Several US jurisdictions (though not Delaware) have constituency statutes, which expressly enable corporations to consider the interests of corporate stakeholders beyond shareholders. Those statutes were largely a reaction to corporate raiders in

---

[4] L Strine, 'The Dangers of Denial: The Need for a Clear-Eyed Understanding of the Power and Accountability Structure Established by the Delaware General Corporation Law' (2015) 50 *Wake Forest Law Review* 761, U of Penn, Inst for Law & Econ Research Paper No 15-08, https://ssrn.com/abstract=2576389.
[5] ibid.
[6] ibid.
[7] 'A Friedman Doctrine – The Social Responsibility of Business is to Increase its Profits' (*New York Times*, 13 September 1970), https://www.nytimes.com/1970/09/13/archives/a-friedman-doctrine-the-social-responsibility-of-business-is-to.html.
[8] EB Rock, 'For Whom is the Corporation Managed in 2020?: The Debate over Corporate Purpose' (1 May 2020), *European Corporate Governance Institute – Law Working Paper No 515/2020*, https://papers.ssrn.com/sol3/papers.cfm?abstract_id=3589951.

the 1980s, where M&A activity often resulted in closures and layoffs (with negative social consequences in the affected geographies).[9] Additionally, several State incorporation laws (including Delaware) now enable incorporation as, or conversion to, a benefit corporation which bakes a particular stakeholder objective into the governance of the corporation.

The language the BRT used in 2019 was not totally new to the BRT either. In 1982, the BRT had issued a rather more expansive statement which seemed to set out something of a stakeholder-centric view:

> A corporation's responsibilities include how the whole business is conducted every day. It must be a thoughtful institution which rises above the bottom line to consider the impact of its action on all, from shareholders to the society at large. Its business activities must make social sense just as its social activities must make business sense.[10]

I will leave readers to consider whether the 1980s was a decade characterised by 'stakeholder capitalism'.

Nonetheless, rhetorical shifts can be the advance party of practical change. Unfortunately, rhetorical signalling can also be an effective strategy for inhibiting real change. That has, in fact, become a core critique of the failings of the way mainstream sustainability practice has developed. Nonetheless, the language, the signatories, and the context in which the most recent BRT statement was made suggest that it ought to have practical significance. But what are the practical implications? Is this a statement of existing practice or is it more prospective, indicative of future developments?

III. A SAMPLE OF SCEPTICISM

We can unpack some of the implications of corporate purpose by examining the scepticism expressed in relation to it.

A. Shareholder Rights

Institutional investors expressed concern that a stakeholder approach may merely be an excuse for pursuing a policy agenda that seeks to erode shareholder rights.[11] Corporate lobby groups have long pursued a policy agenda which has sought to reduce shareholder access to independent advice and narrow the shareholder proposal process; a set of anti-shareholder policy priorities vigorously pursued by the leadership of the Securities and Exchange Commission under the prior Presidential Administration. Elevating 'stakeholders' as an express objective of management

---

[9] For similar language, see s 172 of the Companies Act 2006 (UK), enabling the consideration of non-shareholder constituencies in corporate decision-making.

[10] K Bresnahan, 'Back to the '80s: Business Roundtable's "Purpose" Statement Redux' (Directors and Boards, 2021).

[11] Council of Institutional Investors, 'Council of Institutional Investors Responds to Business Roundtable Statement on Corporate Purpose' (August 2019), https://www.cii.org/aug19_brt_response.

could be strategically used to seek further restrictions on shareholder power, leading to further management entrenchment.

B. Limited Meaning

Underlying corporate law seems to limit the significance of adopting a stakeholder centric view. Even given the flexibility afforded by the business judgement rule, there are limits to the extent to which corporations can expressly pursue non-shareholder interests.[12] Stakeholder capitalism may be more akin to 'enlightened shareholder capitalism' or 'shareholder capitalism lite'; where stakeholder interests can be pursued within the confines of decisions that must have a 'rational connection to shareholder value'. This means that shareholder interests will prevail in the event of clear trade-offs with stakeholder interests (whether employees, suppliers, communities). This clearly severely limits the promise of stakeholder capitalism. At the company level, a recent analysis identified that the BRT signatory companies had not adjusted corporate governance documents to reflect the stakeholder outlook set out in the BRT statement.[13] As such, in terms of underlying law and corporate governance, there are questions about the real-world impact that 'stakeholder capitalism' may have.

IV. RETHINKING VALUE: THE RISE OF ESG

The rise of ESG – incorporating environmental, social, and governance themes, considerations, and metrics – into mainstream investment practice shares a similar root with the contemporary debate on corporate purpose.

ESG represents an acknowledgement that our capital markets have failed to account for the broad set of issues and dependencies that underpin performance (particularly over the long term). Such selective vision has caused manifold cascading failures in the way our capital markets function, including mispricing, capital misallocation and a systematic failure to accurately identify, mitigate and manage risk – at both company and portfolio levels of analysis.

In the journey of ESG to the mainstream of investment practice, it has encountered many misconceptions, confusions, and obstacles. For a significant period, it was broadly thought that the fiduciary duties that investors owe to their clients essentially forbade the consideration of ESG factors in investment decisions. A few frustrating and sticky assumptions regarding ESG seemed to underlie these misconceptions, namely that ESG *necessarily* means:

- narrowing the investment universe;
- accepting concessionary returns; and
- imposing personal moral or social preferences into the investment process.

---

[12] ibid, Strine 3.
[13] LA Bebchuk and R Tallarita, 'The Illusory Promise of Stakeholder Governance' (2020) 106 *Cornell Law Review* 91, *Harvard Law School John M Olin Center Discussion Paper No 1052*, https://ssrn.com/abstract=.

These misconceptions seemed to derive part of their hold through conceiving of ESG as a *product* rather than a *process* and by failing to disaggregate the wide variety of objectives and strategies that may deploy themes from the ESG spectrum.

The nature of investment practice changes over time. We see that reflected in the ways in which the SEC's continuous disclosure framework has expanded to require disclosure of information previously not subject to a disclosure mandate (recall that there was a time, pre-SEC, when GAAP had not yet been codified). ESG in the investment process is part of that meta phenomenon which responds to technological change, analytical awareness, and normative pressure to change the way investors seek to perform the complex task of assessing the performance and prospects of portfolio companies.

At its heart, building ESG themes into investment analysis seeks to derive deeper insights and understandings into the sources of risks and opportunities both in portfolio companies and at the level of the portfolio as a whole.

ESG *does not* necessarily entail a narrowing of the investment universe – which would otherwise involve concomitant worries regarding under-diversification. There are certainly strategies that apply negative screens to exclude certain sectors or products. However, negative screening is just one partial and historic strategy not representative of ESG investment strategies as a whole. Screening in fact started its life as a feature of ethical investing, where ethically-minded and religious investors sought investment strategies that allowed them to avoid investing in products they abhorred (whether tobacco, firearms or cluster bombs). Negative screening should be carefully distinguished from ESG integration and certainly should not be allowed to appear as a dominant or defining strategy.

ESG *does not* entail concessionary returns. ESG in fact provides critical insights into sources of risk that conventional investment management may miss. For example, analysis of a portfolio company's management of employee health and safety, mitigation of environmental impacts, or the effectiveness of its corporate governance arrangements can enable an ESG-engaged investor to see and assess sources of value at risk and reputational damage to which other investors may be functionally blind. ESG strategies do not always deliver out-performance; it would be foolish to suggest that they do (just as anyone claiming that any investment management technique *always* delivers out-performance should be treated with great scepticism). However, there are numerous studies which suggest that companies which demonstrate strong performance on their material ESG issues tend to outperform firms with poor performance on those same factors.[14]

ESG *does not* involve the imposition of personal social preferences into the investment process. Fiduciaries cannot turn investment decisions into a forum for expressing personal moral judgements: those are not relevant fiduciary considerations. The responsibility of a fiduciary is the delivery of an appropriate financial return. ESG simply seeks to expand and deepen the elements that fiduciaries consider in the task

---

[14] M Khan et al, 'Corporate Sustainability: First Evidence on Materiality' (2016) 91(6) *The Accounting Review* 1697, https://ssrn.com/abstract=2575912; U Atz et al, 'The Return on Sustainability Investment (ROSI): Monetizing Financial Benefits of Sustainability Actions in Companies' (2019) 39(2) *Review of Business: Interdisciplinary Journal on Risk and Society* 1, https://ssrn.com/abstract=3465637.

of delivering that financial return and the context in which that financial return will be delivered. In that sense, ESG is an imperative to see more and know more about the dependencies and impacts of delivering a financial return. ESG is additive to the conventional elements of investment management. It seeks to infuse a numbers game with structured analysis of people, places, and things.

To illustrate this concept, consider the qualitative and legally significant difference illustrated by a simple example: a fiduciary wishes to divest from tobacco because she morally disfavours tobacco; another fiduciary wishes to divest from tobacco because she considers that the associated litigation risk, increasing scope and effectiveness of anti-tobacco regulation, and decline of tobacco users makes tobacco a high-risk asset likely to underperform over the long term. The latter fiduciary is conducting an ESG analysis wholly appropriate to her role; the former fiduciary needs to take better advice.

Through the breadth of its themes and the topics they encompass, ESG *does* necessarily entail consideration of the stakeholders of portfolio companies. For example, investors have begun to focus on human capital as a key ESG theme. As corporate value increasingly rests on intangibles, corporate culture and the skill sets of employees, investors have sought more disclosure to understand corporate approaches to their workers, including through shareholder engagements on specific themes[15] and rule-making petitions;[16] a demand recognised to an extent by the SEC's recent modernisation of aspects of Regulation S-K and future rulemaking on the same topic.[17] Investor interest on employees can encompass pay and conditions, worker safety, training, attrition, collective bargaining, and diversity (at all levels of the firm). As such, in pursuit of stable financial returns, ESG-aligned investors think about stakeholders in a structured fashion – and consequently expect corporations to do be able to do so too.

V. PURPOSEFUL STEPS – JOINING THE DOTS WITH ESG

Corporations have for some time been building out their capacity to speak about ESG. The majority of large US listed companies now issue a 'sustainability report', have developed policies on ESG themes, and have a function with responsibility for 'sustainability' issues.[18]

Yet sustainability and ESG have often been relegated to a silo – not connected to strategy, financial disclosures, or the main decision-making forums within firms.

---

[15] Board Accountability Project (NYC City Comptroller), https://comptroller.nyc.gov/services/financial-matters/boardroom-accountability-project/boardroom-accountability-project-3-0/.

[16] Rulemaking Petition to Securities and Exchange Commission (Human Capital Management Coalition, 2017), https://www.sec.gov/rules/petitions/2017/petn4-711.pdf.

[17] 'SEC Adopts Rule Amendments to Modernize Disclosures of Business, Legal Proceedings, and Risk Factors Under Regulation S-K' (Securities and Exchange Commission, 2020), https://www.sec.gov/news/press-release/2020-192.

[18] AA Shah et al, 'ESG & Long-Term Disclosures: The State of Play in Biopharma' (CECP, June 2021), https://ssrn.com/abstract=3859214.

That is changing for the better, driven by the capital markets and normative pressures to demonstrate ESG awareness and performance – and the availability of disclosure infrastructure.[19]

Corporate purpose can play a role in stiffening corporate resolve around ESG adoption, creating structured accountability and buy-in, ensuring that ESG is treated as a core business issue like any other. So how can corporations respond to purpose to help them on their ESG journey? From my work with companies, I suggest a few practical steps.

A. Say What Your Purpose Is

Companies should clearly identify a distinctive corporate purpose. Many companies issue high-level statements which are essentially for marketing purposes or a statement of the obvious. However, more is needed from a statement of corporate purpose. For example, a Board-issued purpose statement provides a structured means for the Board to identify the key stakeholders that it holds in view, how it expects to oversee them, and the time-horizon over which the company sets strategy and manages the business.[20] It should be clear that the established purpose is intended to be outcome determinative in the event of critical choices; for example, returns will be left on the table if they require activities regarded as at odds with stated purpose. Without this, purpose statements will remain fuzzy aspirational statements unconnected to real-world managerial decision-making.

B. Structuring for Materiality

Stakeholders are at the core of corporate purpose, so corporations need to have readily applied frameworks to help them navigate the stakeholder landscape, and crucially make choices between stakeholder groups. A materiality assessment provides multiple outputs useful for stakeholder awareness – from the process to create it, to the outcomes it generates, including having a framework that can be disclosed to provide capital markets and stakeholder groups with an explanatory rationale for how stakeholder concerns are being addressed.[21] The outcomes of a sufficiently rigorous materiality process must be connected to risk, finance, and Board oversight to ensure that the insights it can deliver are built into strategy, business model structure and capital allocation decisions.

---

[19] 'Materiality Map' (Sustainable Accounting Standards Board, 2020), https://www.sasb.org/standards/materiality-map/.

[20] R Eccles, 'Moving beyond Shareholders-come-first Thinking: Why Boards Should Have a Statement of Purpose' (Said Business School, Oxford University, 2019), https://www.sbs.ox.ac.uk/oxford-answers/moving-beyond-shareholders-come-first-thinking-why-boards-should-have-statement.

[21] B Tomlinson and MP Krzus, 'Method of Production of Long-Term Plans', *CECP: Strategic Investor Initiative White Paper No 3*, https://ssrn.com/abstract=3332342.

C. Teachable Moments

Purpose ought to be a whole-firm, living concept. As such, companies need to find ways of giving it life. One technique is for companies to feature teachable moments from its corporate purpose in management training and development programmes – including at the highest levels (including Board induction processes) – identifying how the firm's distinctive purpose led certain decisions to be taken one way rather than another (illustrating with salient examples). This communicates that purpose is real and is an expected feature of the firm's day-to-day practice. There is, though, reasoned scepticism about the connection between purposeful 'phrases' and business practice, meaning that corporations must indicate real-world structures through which purpose will credibly flow.

D. Tie to Financial Value

Purpose can be associated with strong financial performance – though it is not necessarily the case that firms without purpose will perform poorly.[22] Many firms have business models that have a degree of stakeholder harm as a necessary condition of their current operations (from the tobacco industry to oil and gas). We also know that corporate purpose is not about back-slapping camaraderie or 'good vibes' among employees. It is more about clarity – giving decision makers throughout the firm a clear roadmap and guide for decision-making.[23] Clarity can enable focus on a range of key themes and metrics that are critical to delivering a firm's stated purpose, providing management with a basis for talking about how purpose and financial value relate. A firm can then use a variety of different channels for talking about its purpose and ESG performance beyond just the sustainability report, including the quarterly earnings call.[24]

E. Purpose, Compensation Alignment and the Long-term

Purpose may also help push back against managerial short-termism. We know that short-termism is a problem in our capital markets. The seminal example would be cutting R&D or other long-term value investments in order to hit a short-term earnings target. Such actions may be rational in the short term, particularly where

---

[22] GV Milano et al, 'The Return on Purpose: Before and During a Crisis' (21 October 2020), https://ssrn.com/abstract=3715573.

[23] C Gartenberg et al, 'Corporate Purpose and Financial Performance' *Harvard Business School Working Paper*, No 17-023 (September 2016), http://nrs.harvard.edu/urn-3:HUL.InstRepos:30903237.

[24] K Eckerle et al, 'ESG and the Earnings Call: Communicating Sustainable Value Creation Quarter by Quarter' (27 May 2020), NYU Stern Center for Sustainable Business; and CEO Investor Forum at CECP, https://ssrn.com/abstract=3607921.

executives have short-term stock-price-linked compensation – but are value destructive in the long term. At a minimum, executives should have long-term compensation packages, avoiding the incentives that make short-term value-destructive moves attractive. Incentives matter.

Purpose – in combination with ESG – may assist management in shifting its focus to a long-term time horizon, helping to countervail the customary market forces that tend to be focused on the quarter as the critical unit of analysis. Stakeholder concerns can take years to work through and deliver promised value, whether that comes from environmental investments or enhancements in workforce development and training. A short-term lens provides little guide for effective purpose and ESG-based investments.

F. Limits to Purpose and ESG

These practical measures are only the start of the ESG journey. This mainstream practice of ESG attracts increasing scepticism, informed by concerns that it has delivered the rhetoric of impact without the impact;[25] essentially, business as usual with a little sugar.[26] To respond to the scale of challenges we collectively face, the emerging paradigm must enhance its ambition and coherence and in doing so adopt a systemic stance. I highlight a selection of areas for attention that illustrate the limits of the current iteration of the corporate purpose and ESG paradigm.

VI. THE POLITICS OF PURPOSE

Corporations and corporate lobby groups are highly engaged and systemically significant actors in the political process. Since the late 1970s, under the prompting of former Supreme Court Justice Lewis Powell and his famous memorandum (usually referred to as the Powell Memo), business has taken an assertive (some might suggest outcome determinative) stance toward the political process, especially through industry associations such as the Chamber of Commerce.[27] As corporate lobby groups expanded, other sources of countervailing political engagement have shrunk in significance; most notable being the policy-driven decline of America's private sector unions (a once-formidable source of lobbying heft).

As corporations make well publicised policy statements on ESG themes – such as climate change and diversity – institutional investors and other stakeholders are asking whether corporate political activities (who they fund and their policy positions) are

---

[25] K Pucker, 'Overselling Sustainability Reporting' (*Harvard Business Review*, May–June 2021), https://hbr.org/2021/05/overselling-sustainability-reporting.

[26] A Schendler, 'The Complicity of Corporate Sustainability' (2021) *Stanford Social Innovation Review*, https://ssir.org/articles/entry/the_complicity_of_corporate_sustainability.

[27] LF Powell Jnr, 'Attack on American Free Enterprise System' (August 1971), https://law2.wlu.edu/deptimages/Powell%20Archives/PowellMemorandumTypescript.pdf.

aligned with the policy statements they have made; on the theme of climate, such efforts have become increasingly focused and assertive.[28]

This has all been given elevated significance by the ruling in *Citizens United*, which removed many of the restraints on corporate political activity.[29] To illustrate that, since *Citizens United* the volume of corporate money flowing through the American political system has significantly increased. In turn, public awareness of this issue has risen commensurately. Indicative of that heightened focus, a Rulemaking Petition to the SEC seeking disclosure on corporate political spending attracted a record number of public comments in favour.[30]

The high-profile adoption of a 'stakeholder approach' can be interpreted in itself as a political act – an attempt to forestall regulation at a time when corporate practice is under scrutiny. The BRT statement was made at a time when leading politicians were issuing policy proposals to restructure corporate governance arrangements and adjust the objectives of corporations (including workers on Boards, and public benefit corporation conversion). A broad pro-social statement such as that made by BRT members could be interpreted as a response to discontent seeking to avoid regulatory intervention: 'no need to regulate, we already have social objectives in mind'.

In this analysis, I am suggesting that a corporation's political activity can be regarded as a highly indicative measure of its true approach to corporate purpose. This is the case even though corporations themselves may be silent on the matter. Corporations have vigorously opposed all initiatives that seek disclosure of corporate political spending. For example, for several years the SEC has been prohibited, through a budget appropriations rider, from rulemaking in relation to corporate political spending. Additionally, corporates are able to use third party lobby groups, such as the Chamber, to vociferously advocate for policy positions that they would be unlikely to want to advocate for in their own name. Even best-practice voluntary disclosure of political spending leaves significant gaps, requiring detective work to understand the recipients and impact of the money given.[31]

If corporations have LGBTQ policy positions and commitments to diversity, is it consistent to then support politicians who seek to disadvantage segments of those communities?[32] Additionally, is it appropriate for corporations to sign statements of support of voting rights, while the trade associations they fund vigorously oppose specific legislation to protect voting rights? Is it plausible to expect businesses to pursue the type of pro-social practice implied by stakeholder capitalism? Political contributions do not appear to align with the promise of stakeholder capitalism, and

---

[28] Climate Action 100+, 'NetZero Benchmark', https://www.climateaction100.org/progress/net-zero-company-benchmark/.

[29] *Citizens United v FEC*, case summary: https://www.fec.gov/legal-resources/court-cases/citizens-united-v-fec/.

[30] 'Committee on Disclosure of Corporate Political Spending Petition for Rulemaking' (3 August 2011), https://www.sec.gov/rules/petitions/2011/petn4-637.pdf.

[31] Track your company, 'How Companies Rank in the CPA-Zicklin Index' (Centre for Political Accountability), https://www.trackyourcompany.org/cpa-zicklin-index/.

[32] 'Conflicted Consequences' (Centre for Political Accountability), https://politicalaccountability.net/hifi/files/Conflicted-Consequences.pdf.

corporations themselves seem to not want us to be able to join the dots between statements and contributions.

At a minimum, this situation calls for comprehensive mandatory disclosure of corporate political spending. The inconsistencies and risks associated with such spending demonstrate that it is a high priority corporate governance issue requiring informed shareholder oversight – and perhaps periodic shareholder approval. In such disclosure, corporations must also demonstrate that a thorough assessment has been made of the relationship between the firm's policy positions and those of the politicians and third-party groups they have chosen to fund.

A. The Inevitability of Trade-offs

One of the flaws in the advocacy discourse in relation to both corporate purpose and ESG has been to present these concepts as if defined necessarily by a set of win-win scenarios. Such scenarios do perhaps exist, but at the margins. We should resist magical thinking which suggests that win-win scenarios are a defining feature of corporate practice. After all, trade-offs are an inevitable feature of complex situations between actors with diverse and often conflicting interests. Trade-offs are also not static; their characteristics adjust depending on the time frame used to assess them. For example, better pay for employees may result in marginally higher prices for consumers (if the increased wage costs are passed on). Yet, increased wage costs may over time yield benefits in terms of productivity, retention, improved customer satisfaction, and more prosperous communities in which those employees live – as well as being a first order good for the employees (and their families) receiving better pay. In the context of the COVID-19 pandemic, trade-offs were often binary and stark. Prominent companies continued to pay out regular dividends and implement scheduled share repurchase programmes at the same time they furloughed staff – arguably an obvious example of shareholder interests being treated as primary.

Corporate purpose and ESG, where meaningfully incorporated into strategy and decision-making, can help provide a prioritisation and decision matrix for navigating the complexities of corporate decision-making. This is a situation not absent trade-offs, but where trade-offs have been critically assessed, with an analysis that extends beyond the corporation's own value chain out into the stakeholders meaningfully impacted. An indicator of these concepts being operationally significant would be where analysis reveals that proposed activities entail significant harm (beyond the bottom line) in a way that seems inconsistent with stated purpose such that the corporation chooses not to proceed – essentially, 'our purpose says we can't'.

B. Taking a System-level View

An analysis of trade-offs can be built on an understanding of the impact and dependencies of the business model and proposed strategies. Corporations exist in a real world of people, places and ecosystems, often with identifiably finite carrying capacities. For an understanding of the risk the business model is exposed to, corporations must have an understanding of its ecosystem and the impact corporate practice has on it across the value-chain. These are the beginnings of a context-based, system-level of view of corporate practice. At its heart is a simple question: 'are we damaging the things we depend on'?

The ESG space has rapidly sought to develop metrics by which a corporation's practice on ESG themes material to its financial prospects can be assessed – in addition to metrics which seek to understand a corporation's impacts on the world around it. The next phase for this work is context. The pursuit of science-based targets is an indicative example: namely, how can we keep emissions of greenhouse gases within planetary boundaries? Ultimately, every target set on an environmental or social theme ought to have a context-based rationale which explains the basis on which the context was assessed – that is a judgement that will involve significant discretion and sophistication, especially in the highly contested and quasi-political theme of 'social' issues. Such targets should also be ambitiously prospective, reflecting the time horizon over which negative impacts can arise. Disclosing such analysis can enable stakeholders and shareholders to assess management's approach to the impact of the corporation on the world around it; in turn, this allows financial performance to be weighed against social impact.[33] Such disclosures would provide ESG-aware shareholders with information to enable them to formulate engagement strategies on the basis of the balance of those context-based impacts, whether positive or negative. That can help amplify the pressures to focus investment towards business-models that, ideally, do no significant harm.

C. Limited Impact without Policy Advocacy

A danger in the considerable activity and attention around purpose and ESG is to lull us into complacency; we conclude that the activity and attention *simply must* be indicative of real change and impact. That is unfortunately not necessarily the case – and a chorus of sceptical commentary has begun to ask whether the positive social impacts of ESG and corporate purpose are real – and if they are real, are they even close to sufficient?

It does not appear plausible that marginal adjustments to corporate and investment practice can overcome our manifold systemic problems, including the climate crisis, systematic tax avoidance, the rise of authoritarianism.[34] As such, corporate purpose and ESG players have to embrace a supporting policy agenda to ensure that private ordering at the corporate level and regulatory intervention are aligned. We need both: it is not an either or.[35] That means more than just alignment of policy positions and political spending – it means an assertive attempt to enable policy change using all the levers available.

---

[33] For examples of approaches to impact measurement see Impact Weighted Accounts Initiative; and Value Balancing Alliance.

[34] J Mayer, *Dark Money* (Scribe Publications, 2016).

[35] R Finighan and A Schwartz, 'Why Sustainable Investment Means Investing in Advocacy' (September 2021) *Stanford Social Innovation Review*, https://ssir.org/articles/entry/why_sustainable_investment_means_investing_in_advocacy.

VII. PARTING THOUGHTS

For corporations, alignment of purpose and politics will increasingly be expected, and is increasingly urgent for sustaining the system on which firms depend. The structural disparities that exist between corporate policy positions and the stance of the corporate lobby groups and politicians they fund are often glaring. Such missteps may be deliberate obfuscation, or they may be failures of governance and oversight; both can have reputational impacts on a significant scale. Absent a context-based approach, corporations' claims to be creating value will consistently be contrasted with the ways in which their activities cause harm, often irreparable. The adjustments I suggest in this chapter, among many others that will be recommended, can help ESG and corporate purpose evolve beyond accusations of being business as usual with a little sugar.

.

16

Targeting Net Zero: Embedding Accountability for Portfolio Decarbonisation and Resilience in the Asset Owner – Asset Manager Relationship

FAITH WARD

I. INTRODUCTION

S TEEP REDUCTIONS IN greenhouse gas emissions will be needed during the remainder of this decade if the hope of safeguarding a temperature rise of no more than 1.5°C by the end of the century is to remain in sight. Over 130 of the 191 parties to the Paris Agreement have committed to achieving net-zero by the middle of this century.[1] They are joined by companies, cities, and financial institutions across the globe.

Climate change will, due to the scale and longevity of the impacts, have profound implications for investors, particularly those with, or who support, long-term liabilities.[2] Action is needed to reduce and mitigate emissions, to adapt to the physical changes already underway as well as to make portfolios more resilient to minimising the potentially devastating financial impacts of climate change. Investors have critical role to play in enabling and supporting the low carbon transition, and can benefit substantially – through reducing risks in their portfolios and through accessing investment opportunities – from doing so.

Responding to these risks, delivering on fiduciary duties as well as societal expectations, is complex, and it requires action from a multitude of other actors, not

---

[1] UNFCC, *NDC Registry* (March 2022).
[2] IPPC, *First to Sixth Assessment Reports* (1990–2022).

just investors. These include policymakers, regulators, other financial institutions, companies and individuals.

The key challenges for asset owners include finding enough of the right asset managers and products that align with progressive beliefs and an innovative investment strategy; and ensuring risk processes, investment time horizons and incentives structures are designed to deliver the desired outcomes. These challenges are not new or unique to portfolio decarbonisation but are the more pressing to overcome given the timelines the scientific community have made clear.[3] With global assets under management calculated to be in excess of US$100 trillion,[4] the scale of both the challenge and the opportunity of getting accountability for portfolio decarbonisation and resilience embedded through the investment chain is essential. To be clear, it is vital that the expectation set by asset owners is that the asset managers not only consider all the risks and opportunity arising from climate risk but change their processes to take climate into account. This should result in different outcomes from investment decision making. The corollary of this is that asset owners need to support managers in changing their processes by being mindful of the parameters set, but also that they change manager monitoring to hold them to account.

This chapter aims to cover the context of the challenge, the risks and the frameworks set out to guide investors embarking on net-zero. It draws on specific case studies from the direct experience and practices of Brunel Pension Partnership Limited (Brunel). These case studies seek to illustrate how that company has gone about setting expectations, challenged, and changed processes and delivered different outcomes – ones we hope get us a lot closer to net-zero.

A. About Brunel

Founded in 2017, the Brunel Pension Partnership is one of eight UK Local Government Pension Scheme pools and the Partnership brings together more than £35 billion of investments of ten likeminded pension funds.[5] Our approach to climate is strongly influenced by our clients' demands and expectations. Whilst addressing climate change is important to all our clients, they also have different risk appetites, which means we need to provide a range of products to reflect their specific ambitions.

In March 2021, Brunel committed to achieving net-zero by no later than 2050. We made the commitment through the Paris Aligned Net Zero Asset Owner Commitment,[6] originally developed by the Institutional Investor Group for Climate Change (IIGCC)[7] and now part of a global investor collaboration.

---

[3] ibid.

[4] Investment Association, *Investment Management in the UK 2020–2021* (2021).

[5] Avon, Buckinghamshire, Cornwall, Devon, Dorset, the Environment Agency, Gloucestershire, Oxfordshire, Somerset and Wiltshire. Brunel is authorised and regulated by the FCA as a full-service MiFID firm.

[6] Paris Aligned Investment Initiative, *Asset Owner Net Zero Commitment* (2021), https://www.paris-alignedinvestment.org/.

[7] See https://www.iigcc.org/.

Figure 1 Brunel Pension Partnership

Our priority is to manage our fiduciary duties to our clients. Our partnership has also made major commitments on Climate Change and Responsible Investment, in line with our shared values. In this way, **we aim to help our clients provide not only for their members' retirement, but for the world they will retire into**.

We believe that:

- Climate change presents a **systemic and material risk** to the ecological, societal and financial stability of every economy and country on the planet, and therefore will impact our clients, their beneficiaries and **all portfolios' holdings.**

- Investing to support the **Paris goals that deliver a below 2C°** temperature increase is entirely consistent with **securing long-term financial returns** and is aligned with the best long-term interests of our clients.

- For society to achieve a net-zero carbon future by 2050 (or before) requires **systemic change in the investment industry and equipping and empowering our clients** (and other investors) is central to this change.

Given our strengths and our position in the market, we therefore believe that the key objective of our climate policy is to systematically change the investment industry so that it is fit for purpose for a world where temperature rise needs to be kept to well below 2°C compared to pre-industrial levels.

The 5 P's of Brunel's Climate Policy

Policy	Encourage policy makers to establish comprehensive and robust climate change policy frameworks.
Products	Increase the number and range of products available to our clients and the wider investment market that deliver substantial climate change benefits and sustainable investment returns
Portfolios	Ensure our investment portfolios are resilient under a range of climate change scenarios (both mitigation and adaptation) by adopting best practices on climate risk management and working with our managers to further improve and develop our processes.
Positive Impact	Enable investments in activities that directly support the low carbon transition and that enable effective adaptation to the unavoidable impacts of climate change.
Persuasion	Challenge and encourage companies and other entities in which we invest and contract with to support the transition to the low carbon economy, and to ensure that they are resilient to the unavoidable impacts of climate change.

Source: Brunel Pension Partnership.

All (100 per cent) of Brunel's mandates are outsourced to asset managers, so it essential that we genuinely work in partnership with these managers to achieve the investment outcomes that we desire. In establishing Brunel's 17 listed markets portfolios between 2018 and 2021, our team engaged with over 200 asset managers, reviewed over 200,000 pages of tender information covering over 530 different investment strategy proposals. This chapter highlights case studies from that experience. Whilst we have similar approaches in our private markets' portfolios (infrastructure, real estate, private equity and debt), these are at an earlier stage and harder to replicate but we actively share our work and publish case studies in our annual Responsible Investment and Stewardship Outcomes report.[8]

II. CLIMATE-RELATED FINANCIAL RISK AND THE ROAD TO NET-ZERO

The financial services industry's understanding of the nature of climate change has developed significantly over the last few years, with most participants regarding it as a foreseeable and materially significant financial risk. A pivotal moment was Mark Carney's speech 'Breaking the tragedy of the horizon – climate change and financial stability' at Lloyd's of London in 2015.[9] In his speech, Carney clearly set out why this is a matter for everyone in the financial services, as 'climate change will threaten financial resilience and longer-term prosperity'.

Helpfully, Carney also sets out the principal sources of risks to financial stability, which were further developed and enshrined in the recommendations of the Task Force for Climate-related Financial Disclosures (TCFD), initiated by Mark Carney in his role as Chair of the Financial Stability Board in 2015 and first published in 2017:[10]

> Climate change and financial stability. There are three broad channels through which climate change can affect financial stability:
>
> First, physical risks: the impacts today on insurance liabilities and the value of financial assets that arise from climate- and weather-related events, such as floods and storms that damage property or disrupt trade;
>
> Second, liability risks: the impacts that could arise tomorrow if parties who have suffered loss or damage from the effects of climate change seek compensation from those they hold responsible. Such claims could come decades in the future, but have the potential to hit carbon extractors and emitters – and, if they have liability cover, their insurers – the hardest;

---

[8] Brunel, *Responsible Investment and Stewardship Outcomes Report* (2020–2022).
[9] M Carney, 'Breaking the Tragedy of the Horizon Climate Change and Financial Stability' (Mansion House speech, Bank of England, 2015).
[10] *Recommendations of the Task Force on Climate-related Financial Disclosures* (Task Force on Climate-related Financial Disclosures, 2017).

Finally, transition risks: the financial risks which could result from the process of adjustment towards a lower-carbon economy. Changes in policy, technology and physical risks could prompt a reassessment of the value of a large range of assets as costs and opportunities become apparent. The speed at which such re-pricing occurs is uncertain and could be decisive for financial stability. There have already been a few high-profile examples of jump-to-distress pricing because of shifts in environmental policy or performance.

Brunel believes that addressing climate risk is an essential component of fulfilling its fiduciary duty to its client partner funds and their beneficiaries. Brunel signed up to report to the recommendations of the TCFD in 2017, the same year that Brunel was formed as a business. This was a clear acknowledgement of the importance of not only managing climate risks but being transparent about steps taken and outcomes progressed.

Asset owners and managers are increasingly being asked to evidence that climate risk, as well other sustainable issues, are being effectively managed. The TCFD recommendations often form the basis of the climate change disclosure requirements.[11] The TCFD starts by requiring organisations to be clear on their climate governance and to describe the board's oversight of climate-related risks and opportunities.

Brunel took its climate beliefs and translated them into the strategic risk management of the organisation, embedding them into the terms of reference of committees managing the risk and the objectives of key personnel. For example, Brunel's Chief Executive Officer (CEO) has overall responsibility for the delivery of Brunel's climate policy and owns 'climate' as a strategic risk to the organisation. Additionally, the Chief Operating Officer is accountable for the organisation's own resilience and business continuity that might arise from the impact of physical climate risk. This principle of ensuring that the whole organisation, starting with our most senior managers, stands behind the decision to decarbonise the portfolios and strive for net-zero is essential. When appointing asset managers, Brunel seeks to identify whether there are similar levels of accountability. This can act as an indicator of the manager's own maturity in dealing with the issue. A red flag would be an asset manager identifying climate risk management being led (as opposed to being supported by) by the responsible investment and/or stewardship team without further reference to higher level of governance and accountability.

III. DESIGN AND DELIVERY OF CLIMATE RESILIENT INVESTMENTS

The design and delivery of net-zero investment mandates will be considerably more effective when emanating from strong climate governance. The road to a net-zero

---

[11] The Occupational Pension Schemes (Climate Change Governance and Reporting) Regulations 2021, SI 2021/839, introduce new requirements relating to reporting in line with the TCFD recommendations.

economy is going to be complex and bumpy and there are a lot of areas where approaches are still being developed; setbacks and mistakes are inevitable, and so strong board and senior executive buy-in is essential.

Direct capital investment in solutions, engaging policy makers and changing the operations and behaviours of the companies we invest in are all part of how we will deliver real world decarbonisation needed to achieve net-zero. It is important to recognise that the outcomes of embedding accountability for decarbonisation must support real economy emission reductions. To genuinely reduce climate risk requires a net-zero economy, not net-zero portfolios. This nuance means that the task of stewarding assets through the transition is incredibly complex.

The evaluation of the investment risk in the context of climate change, including the direct physical impacts but also those arising from policy, technology and other market risks is far from straightforward. Climate change is a complex, multifaceted, long-term issue and as such views on how it will manifest as an investment risk will vary enormously. For example, there will be multiple views on which countries, sectors and companies will be affected and to what extent and when.

This is challenging for an asset owner with these views arising not only from their own internal teams and internal research but from their asset managers as well as their data and research providers. In these circumstances it is useful to use authoritative sources to ask questions of asset managers and how they have considered this viewpoint. We use a range of tools and sources which include the IPCC and UNFCC reports which have already been referenced extensively. To this, add the International Energy Agency's research, most particularly its *Net Zero by 2050, A Roadmap for the Global Energy Sector*,[12] as well extensive academic research.

The work of the London School of Economics, Grantham Research Institute on Climate Change and the Environment, is a go-to resource for Brunel. Highlights include research on policy, regulations, the 'Just Transition', as well as being the academic partner to the asset owner-led Transition Pathway Initiative (TPI). Brunel co-leads and financially supports TPI. Its application in supporting investment decisions is highlighted in case studies later in the chapter. TPI assessments are also used to guide Brunel stewardship, for example engagement and voting.[13]

Brunel has also utilised the Principles for Responsible Investment's research on the Inevitable Policy Response (IPR),[14] particularly the summary of key policy levers in training, stakeholder outreach, and as a ready list of questions to ask asset managers,

---

[12] IEA, *Net Zero by 2050, A Roadmap for the Global Energy Sector* (May 2021).

[13] 'Brunel Pension Partnership Ltd Stewardship Policy' (Brunel Pension Partnership, 2021).

[14] UNPRI and Vivid Economics, *What is the Inevitable Policy Response (IPR)* (PRI, 2021). The IPR aims to prepare institutional investors for the portfolio risks and opportunities associated with a forecast acceleration of policy responses to climate change. IPR contends that governments will be forced to act more decisively than they have thus far, leaving financial portfolios exposed to significant transition risk.

both current and prospective. These can include: How does the investment process consider such risks? What assumptions has the portfolio manager made in relation to these risks? What, if any, climate stress testing has been undertaken and did the stress testing consider these risks?

Brunel uses these resources to form its climate policy, to identify relevant climate-related investment risks which are used to engage with managers and set expectations which flow into the monitoring of asset managers.

Table 1 IPR 2021 (IPR forecasts higher policy ambition across eight key policy levers)

Carbon pricing	Coal phase-out	100% clean power	Zero emissions vehicles
• Carbon taxes • Emissions trading systems • Border carbon adjustments	• Prohibiting regulations • Emissions performance standards • Electricity market reforms	• 100% clean power targets • Renewables capacity auctions and other support policies	• 100% zero emission vehicles (ZEV) sale legislations • Manufacturer ZEV obligations • ZEV consumer subsidies
Low-carbon buildings	**Clean industry**	**Low-emissions agriculture**	**Forestry**
• Prohibiting regulations for fossil fuel heating systems • Purchase subsidies for low-carbon heating systems • Thermal efficiency regulations for new build and retrofit • Minimum energy performance standards for new appliances	• Emissions performance standards for industrial plant • Subsidy for new or retrofit clean industrial processes	• Methane or nitrous oxide emissions tax or cap-and-trade system • Subsidy for low-emissions agricultural practices and technologies • Farmer education and technical assistance programmes	• Strong policy actions against deforestation, such as monitoring and penalties, supported by consumer pressure • Incentives for reforestation and afforestation via domestic action and carbon markets

Source: UNPRI, IPR, Vivid Economics (2021).

Figure 2 Paris Agreement and Net-Zero

The term Paris alignment is widely used, and in general captures the wider aims and objectives of the legally binding international treaty on climate change adopted in Paris, at COP21. The term net-zero is also thrown around somewhat casually and used in many different contexts. There are many variations and interpretations, which causes confusion. In this section, we provide practical definitions of both terms to provide a context for our work. It is a high-level starting point, but the International Panel on Climate Change (IPPC) website provides a superb glossary which can be confidently used as an authoritative source.

The **Paris Agreement** under the United Nations Framework Convention on Climate Change was adopted in 2015 at COP21 and replaced previous international treaties designed to limit the release of greenhouse gases. The Paris Agreement set the ambition to achieve emissions reductions that would limit mean global temperature increases to well below 2 degrees, preferably 1.5 degrees Celsius (by 2100) above pre-industrial levels. It is understood that to limit this temperature increase by the end of the century, emissions need to be reduced to net-zero by no later than 2050. It also means that GHGs emissions beyond 2050 also need to stay at or below zero.[1]

The Paris Agreement also established the comprehensive oversight and implementation mechanisms for countries in of setting and reviewing the targets and plans proposed by countries (nationally determined contributions – NDCs) as well as commitments relating to the 'just transition', climate finance, adaptation and resilience.

The term 'Paris Aligned' by investors is used to capture these broader ambitions that seek to ensure that the transition is equitable (between and within countries and communities); that the physical risks (extreme weather events, sea level rise, drought, etc) associated with climate change amongst other matters are considered as part of the investment process.

Net-Zero

In its simplest terms Net-Zero is achieved when emissions of man-made GHGs are balanced out by removals – natural (forests, oceans, etc) and artificial (carbon storage and capture). A credible net zero strategy must address contributions to warming made by other anthropogenic greenhouse gases. Most particularly methane (CH^4) and nitrous oxide (N_2O) are very potent and problematic in their own right and relevant to the investors, particularly those with exposure directly or via the supply chain to agriculture, chemicals, transportation and waste treatment.

Net-Zero from an investment perspective is still evolving and Net-Zero Investment Frameworks outlined in the chapter aims to translate into tangible actions and targets.

[1] United Nations Environment Programme (2019). Emissions Gap Report 2019. UNEP, Nairobi.

IV. WHAT DOES IT MEAN TO BE A NET-ZERO INVESTOR?

The setting of climate beliefs and developing climate governance supports the integration of climate risks into investment decision-making. This section provides insights into requirements, frameworks and practical actions that support investors progressing net-zero, with examples of what Brunel has done in the next section.

Translating the Paris Agreement – which was designed for world governments – into tangible definitions and requirements for businesses, cities, investors and other 'non-state actors' is critical if the objectives are to be achieved. To this end, the

UNFCCC's Climate Ambition Alliance launched the 'Race to Zero' campaign on 5 June 2020. The initiative, led by Chile and the UK, sought to 'bring together the leadership and support of businesses, cities, regions and investors for a healthy, resilient and carbon-free recovery that prevents future threats, creates decent jobs, and enables inclusive and sustainable growth'.[15]

The initiative sets out minimum criteria, or 4P's (pledge, plan, proceed and publish) that are required of initiatives to be deemed Race to Zero compliant. There are three investor initiatives that are accredited for the financial sector:[16]

- the Paris Aligned Investment Initiative (PAII);[17]
- the Net-Zero Asset Managers Initiative (NZAM);[18] and
- the UN-convened Net-Zero Asset Owner Alliance (NZAOA).[19]

A key challenge for asset owners in working with asset managers is aligning expectations, investment objectives and processes when tackling long-term challenges such as climate change. Investors do not have to be part of one of these initiatives to commit to being a net-zero investor, but what the initiatives do provide is a consistency of expectations across the investment chain.

IIGCC, who initiated the PAII, are also part of the Investor Agenda endorsing the NZAM Initiative. The coordination between the initiatives provides a supportive environment to improve alignment. The list below summarises the translation of the Race to Zero 4P's into the respective commitments for both asset owners (PAII) and asset managers (NZAM), including the overlapping shared objectives.

A. PAII and NZAM

Shared objectives of these initiatives include:

- set 'fair-share' interim targets toward 50 per cent emissions reduction by 2030;
- consider material scope 3 emissions;
- increase investment in climate solutions;
- prioritise real economy emissions reductions;
- implement a net-zero stewardship and engagement strategy, with clear escalation and voting policy;
- limitations on use of offsets.

The NZAM commitment asks managers to:

- increase the proportion of AUM to be managed in line with net-zero;
- work with clients to achieve net zero, offering information and analytics;

---

[15] UNFCC, *Race to Zero Climate Ambition Alliance* (UNFCC, 2020).
[16] As at April 2022.
[17] See https://www.parisalignedinvestment.org/.
[18] See https://www.netzeroassetmanagers.org/.
[19] See https://www.unepfi.org/net-zero-alliance/.

- create investment products in line with net zero;
- support science-based policy on investment in coal and other fossil fuels.

Just one year after launch, NZAM has 273 signatories, with US$61.3 trillion in AUM,[20] clearly illustrating the commitment of many asset managers to align with net-zero objectives.

Alignment has been further advanced by the development of the Net-Zero Investment Framework (NZIF), codeveloped by both asset owners and asset manager as part of the PAII. To clarify the alphabet soup of initiatives, the PAII and NZAM are commitments to what organisations are signing up to. The NZIF, first published in March 2021, provides a common set of recommended actions, metrics and methodologies through which investors can maximise their contribution to achieving global net zero global emissions by 2050 or sooner.[21]

Figure 3 Net-Zero Investment Framework

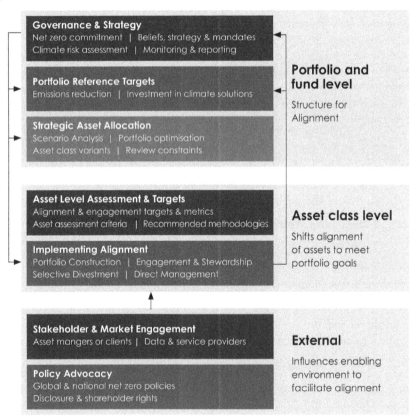

Source: IIGCC (2021).

[20] As at 31 May 2022.
[21] PAII, 'Net Zero Investment Framework Implementation Guide' (Paris Aligned Investment Initiative, March 2021).

The NZIF methodology recognises that different legal structures and applications in different jurisdictions will require flexibility in implementation. The first edition of the framework sets out the steps for investors in relation to strategic asset allocation, setting high-level and portfolio specific targets; stewardship and specific guidance on listed equities, corporate bonds, real estate and sovereign debt.

The framework also signposts to resources that have been evaluated by investors and can support implementation. The NZIF continues to develop asset class implementation methodologies, eg private equity, infrastructure, together with guidance on key issues such as use of offsets, derivatives and benchmarks.

Asking managers to use the framework and – even better – to formally commit to NZAM, will break down many of the barriers identified in the introduction, as the frameworks help to align the outcomes, the expectations and even the mechanisms that can be used to analyse and discuss individual assets. The contribution NZIF has made to aligning asset owners with their asset managers in delivering portfolio decarbonisation cannot be underestimated.

V. BRUNEL CASE STUDIES

Our Climate Policy was published in 2020. The heart of the Policy is the belief that we need to use our position in the investment chain to be a stimulus for system-wide change. Brunel can exercise power in many parts of the financial system, with policymakers and with companies although, due to our size, this is generally most productive when done in collaboration with peers. More significantly, we have considerable power through the selection, appointment, monitoring and ultimately retention of asset managers.

Brunel made it very clear in its climate policy what it expected of its asset managers and was also clear that it would, if alignment did not seem evident, terminate mandates. Whilst we have not used specific climate-linked incentive structures in asset manager fees structures as we believe building it into how managers are appointed, assessed and retained, acts as an incentive in itself.

Brunel's 2020 Climate Policy contains the following text:[22]

> We will rigorously, assertively and continuously challenge our investment managers on their analysis and assessment of change-related risks in their investment practices and processes. We will expect them to continually improve these practices and processes, and will explicitly consider these improvements in our monitoring, management, selection, appointment and reappointment of our investment managers.

A. Brunel Position on Divestment is Key to Manager Accountability

Brunel supports divestment from specific fossil fuel and other carbon-intense companies, if these companies are considered to present material investment risks to our

---

[22] 'Brunel Climate Policy' (Brunel Pension Partnership, 2020).

portfolios. An example might be companies who face the risk of having a significant number of 'stranded assets'. These decisions are based on analysis by our investment managers. We expect managers to take these decisions independently (ie based on their assessment of the risks and opportunities presented by companies). That said, there is an increasing availability of data and analysis that can aid the asset managers' decisions and also equip the asset owner to challenge the assumptions made by the manager. The use of frameworks such as NZIF by both asset manager and owners will aid harmonisation of approaches to divestment and engagement.

We chose not to use exclusion lists with our active managers. Instead, we require them to analyse the companies and other entities they invest in, and to justify their investments in any companies who have higher greenhouse gas emissions. We do not issue exclusion lists because, in our view, what is most needed is change in the way investment managers work. Simply enforcing exclusions, or requiring divestment from specific stocks or sectors, will not compel investment managers to develop their capacity on climate change or to drive change in the companies they hold. In a world of exclusion lists, climate change inevitably becomes a technical operational matter, not an investment priority.

Driving changes in company behaviour is a complex process and is much more nuanced than what is often reduced to an 'engagement versus divestment' debate. What Brunel is seeking to do is embed the accountability for what is held – or indeed not held – in our portfolios with those who are employed to select those assets. To ensure that we are accountable for the outcomes of these processes, we not only publish all our holdings but also a comprehensive carbon metrics report that demonstrates the outcomes, such as exposure to fossil fuels and future fossil fuel emissions, for these portfolios. That said, we also recognise that we may want to selectively exclude certain stocks or activities, particularly in the context of passive or quantitative products, and will review these options as part of the climate stocktake process that begins in 2022. Brunel has published a statement outlining its approach to engagement versus divestment,[23] which explores the issue more deeply.

B. Manager Selection

Brunel's policy is to embed climate into all its mandates. We do have some specialist products – sustainable equities, for example – where the requirements are more specific, but in the main there are very few differences in our approach. We do acknowledge that managers focusing on smaller companies and emerging markets will have constraints on data availability and we do take these constraints into account. However, all managers in the context of their mandate have the same expectations shaped around our policy which is to limit warming arising from emissions,

---

[23] Brunel Pension Partnership (2021), https://www.brunelpensionpartnership.org/climate-change/our-approach-to-engagement-and-divestment/.

and to positively invest in climate solutions and companies that are aligned and more resilient than their peers.

New mandates provide an exciting opportunity to test market participants and put them through their paces in relation to climate risk and opportunity. Brunel had the advantage of building all its portfolios since 2018, in a time where the investment management industry has been more aware of climate risk. That said, there remains a wide disparity in managers' technical understanding and the maturity of their approaches, even within the same asset class.

i. Tender Questionnaires

Brunel uses questionnaires as part of the initial tender process for its listed markets portfolios. Climate risk questions have been used in all of them at one point or another. One example is our multi-asset credit (MAC) manager search in 2021. There was clear client demand to find MAC managers who would need to have capability to support our climate policy and commitment to net-zero. The word capability is used specifically, as our market research suggested there was little evidence of current provision for such strategies in the market at the time.

Brunel often used both an Expression of Interest questionnaire (EOI, first stage screen) and Invitation to Tender (ITT, second stage); ESG questions, including climate, would be in both.

The ITT climate questions, in combination with those relating to stewardship and engagement, represented over half the score relating to quality and service. We would recommend ensuring sufficient weight is applied to these areas, in order to send the message to asset managers that climate policy alignment and accountability are genuinely important.

The questions explored not only the managers' current approach but also how they expected it to evolve considering Brunel's climate requirements. The focus on the future was vital as climate integration into this asset class was not well developed and the interest and capacity to be innovative – recognising the fast-moving nature of climate research, tools and available data – is essential. Manager selection is a resource-intensive process and one Brunel does not seek to do more than necessary. We believe long-term asset manager relationships increase alignment and increased probability of better long-term performance.

Brunel's approach to tender evaluation across all searches is for several members of the team to score each answer. To assist in consistency the lead portfolio manager will provide guidance as to what makes for a good answer. What stood out in this process was that the best answers (ie the investment managers who scored the highest) were those which clearly demonstrated some of the challenges with integration and where the managers were very honest about what they did and did not do, and where they faced specific challenges (eg the challenges of conducting climate risk assessments of some credit types such as asset backed securities and other derivative based instruments due to the lack of data and methodologies).

Figure 4 Brunel's Multi-Asset Credit Invitation

Extract – Climate questions

a) How do you think about climate change in the context of ESG?
b) What climate change integration already exists within your proposed strategy;
c) What is currently in the process of being implemented (with anticipated completion timescales) and;
d) What are your more ambitious long-term goals.

Please note that your answers to the questions above should be specific to your proposal for this mandate, not fixed income in general.

Please provide an overview of your approach to Climate Change analysis for the Multi Asset Credit portfolio, with reference to the following:

- How and why do you integrate Climate Change factors into the Multi Asset Credit investment process? To what extent does Climate Change data impact investment decisions for this portfolio?
- If you have developed proprietary Climate Change ratings, please explain how these are created and monitored.
- How do you overcome the challenge of limited carbon data in the Multi Asset Credit universe?
- If you utilise any third-party Climate Change data, please specify the data providers and how this data is incorporated.
- What Climate Change parameters do you impose on this portfolio and why?

Please provide an example or report you will be able to provide.

Source: Brunel Pension Partnership.

The questionnaires also explored the managers' approach to engagement. Engaging with the underlying assets to positively impact operations and behaviours in the real economy is what will deliver the real world decarbonisation needed to achieve net-zero. This is a core area of manager monitoring. Carbon footprinting alongside asset level net-zero alignment are key metrics in manager monitoring.

All the managers selected committed to a set of actions, to be delivered over time, that will support aligning the portfolio with net-zero. The evidence emerging from early manager monitoring is very positive with increased resources allocated to climate analysis and numerous examples of where the analysis has had a direct impact on the portfolio construction, reducing climate risk with no impact on return expectations.

ii. Using Carbon Footprinting Data to Support Selection of Asset Managers

In 2019, we were searching for investment managers for a global equity strategy. Essentially this involved finding a blend of asset managers whose approaches were different, eg highly concentrated with a focus in high growth, to a strategy that held a much larger number of holdings focusing on value (stocks which trade at a significant discount to their intrinsic value), allowing us to balance risk through using a mix of styles.

Figure 5 illustrates the carbon intensity for each of the short-listed managers grouped by the investment characteristics of their approach. The carbon intensity, but more importantly the managers' ability to explain it, formed part of the due diligence process. It was not a case of only choosing the managers with the lowest intensity but selecting who we thought were the best managers in each group. One part of determining what 'best' was included a good understanding of the portfolio's climate and carbon risks. The managers we selected are circled.

As can be seen, the carbon footprint of most was significantly below the reference benchmark. The exception was in the value category, a particularly challenging category from a climate change perspective. This is because many carbon intensive sectors have the financial characteristics sought by value managers and so value portfolios tend to have higher than standard market benchmark carbon intensities.

When we analysed one of the prospective manager's holdings, we found that 70 per cent of the carbon intensity was attributable to a single holding – LafargeHolcim, now Holcim Group, one of the world's largest cement producers. We discussed this holding with the manager and were reassured that they had a good understanding of the climate related risks associated with Holcim and with the cement sector as a whole, and were also aware of Holcim's strategy for managing these risks.

When looking at carbon intense companies we use the data provided by the Transition Pathway Initiative.[24] The TPI analysis suggested that while the company was not net-zero aligned at the time, it had a strategy that would see it aligned with Paris in the long term. Holcim was a Level 4 performer on management quality, which means it was publicly reporting the majority of key information investors require, which is also a Brunel Climate policy target.

This case study also shows the usefulness and the limitations of using carbon intensity metrics as a sole data point. Carbon intensity does not convey the whole story and using it in insolation can lead to perverse outcomes. For example, it may result in the managers avoiding investments in businesses, that whilst still high climate impact, are needed by the economy and can be aligned to net-zero over time. The TPI analysis is useful to investors to provide a more rounded and forward-looking assessment of companies compared to their peers on a like for like basis. We find the combination of the two tools very useful indeed.

Figure 5 The carbon footprint (weighted average carbon intensity) of the short-listed managers groups by style factor

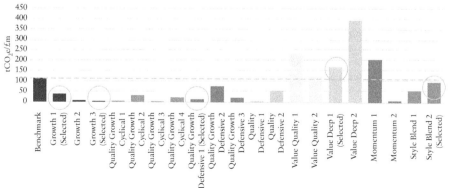

[24] The TPI is a global, asset-owner led initiative which assesses companies' preparedness for the transition to a low carbon economy: https://www.transitionpathwayinitiative.org/.

C. Manager Appointment

Brunel includes the requirement to adhere to our Climate Policy, provide climate data (eg carbon footprint) and regular stewardship reporting in our investment management agreements (IMAs) for segregated mandates. Even in pooled vehicles we seek to get side letters agreed that enhance our expectation of managers. However, what we need to support our approach to climate change is evolving rapidly and there is a risk of the requirements in an IMA becoming quickly obsolete. In assets or geographies where climate risk is less developed, asset managers can also be wary of legally committing to requirements that are broadly defined (as we know they will need to evolve) and therefore difficult to capture in formal legal negotiations. This can lead to protracted and resource intensive conversations.

To solve the problem of ensuring that Brunel's expectations are clear but do not require detailed explanation, Brunel developed a principles-based approach documented in the Brunel Asset Management Accord.[25] The Accord is intended to help clarify understanding and shape expectations in the implementation of the investment mandate that Brunel has awarded. It is not intended to create legal obligations on either party; in all matters of contract the investment management agreement takes precedence. However, the Accord captures the spirit of the relationship and a partnership approach that Brunel is seeking to establish. It is a two-way commitment, with Brunel committing to being long term and to acting to support the manager, particularly in periods of under-performance.

Its purpose is to focus on establishing 'long-term investment' relationships and therefore touches on matters much broader than those specifically relating to climate change. However, given the need to evolve investment approaches to deal with the long-term nature of climate risk, it is a key component of the toolkit. Extracts that are particularly relevant to dealing with climate risk are presented below.

> (2) Brunel takes a long-term view of its fiduciary duties and expects the Manager to act as if it were a fiduciary investing for the long term when operating this mandate
>
> (8) Brunel demands high standards of transparency from the companies and organisations it works with, so likewise places a high priority on being transparent itself and providing high standards of reporting and communication. Brunel will expect the Managers' reporting to facilitate its ability to deliver this commitment.
>
> (14) Brunel are prepared to be innovative and demonstrate thought leadership in collective investment, within the requirement of prudence and joint fiduciary duty. Brunel welcomes open dialogue to explore ways to meet both its own and our clients' evolving investment needs. The Manager will keep Brunel informed of the evolution of its business and its investment process so that Brunel can ensure the mandate remains fit for purpose.

---

[25] 'Brunel Asset Management Accord' (Brunel Pension Partnership, 2018).

The Brunel Asset Management Accord has been well received by asset managers and has been signed by managers with whom we have a direct relationship across both public and private markets.

D. Manager Monitoring, Working in Partnership

As outlined above, the Accord sets out clearly the commitment to the integration of ESG risk, the need to collaborate and to innovate. The Accord recognises that investment processes will need to evolve it they are to remain fit for purpose. We view this evolution as eminently preferable to needing to design new mandates and undertake the lengthy, costly and time-consuming exercise of retendering and transition. By extension, therefore, given the multidecadal challenge of climate change, ongoing manager monitoring is going to be the most important part of the investment process.

In the spirit of the Accord, Brunel prioritises its time in working in partnership with our managers, seeking to be pragmatic, patient and collegiate in resolving issues. The example below is just one of many examples and the work will always continue, especially in the context of achieving net-zero. We believe this style of working with our managers will be critical if we are to succeed.

Over a period of 18 months, starting in January 2020, we worked closely with Invesco, one of our UK managers, in order to decarbonise our UK Active Equity Portfolio. Invesco uses an approach called quantitative investing, also known as systematic investing. This approach uses proprietary modelling and data analysis to deliver the investment objectives. The solution to looking at the climate risk, therefore, had to follow the same quantitative approach, rather than using tools such as engagement with the companies.

Over the 18 months we experimented using different parameters and there was a lot of back and forth and sharing research and outcomes. Working together, we developed a bespoke low-carbon solution through integrating carbon data into the existing multi-factor strategy. Along with Invesco, we identified several project objectives, including: stable and predictable carbon emission reductions over time; minimal impact on expected investment performance; and the ability to quantify the low-carbon impact on portfolio risk and return. Exposures to quality, momentum and value factors were maintained, which was important because they represent the targeted factors of the strategy.

The outcome from this work has been a significant reduction in the carbon intensity of the Brunel UK Active Portfolio. When it was first measured in March 2019 it was 362 tCO2e/mGBP), but, by December 2020, had reduced to 199 tCO2e/mGBP – a reduction in intensity of 45 per cent over the 21-month time period.

Figure 6 Carbon Intensity of Brunel's UK Active Equity Portfolio (March 2019–December 2020)

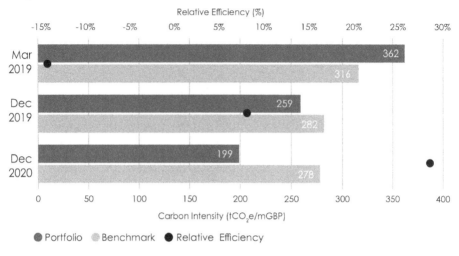

Brunel requires its managers to observe our climate policy and undertake carbon footprinting, at least annually. Analysis of the holdings, supported by the footprint and other data, is used in regular manager monitoring meetings. In addition to manager monitoring, climate change is embedded into product governance, risk and reporting. For example, carbon metrics such as emissions intensity and fossil fuel exposure are included in quarterly and annual client reports and investment risk reports.

Another important aspect was the work in 2021 to develop and launch the Paris Aligned Benchmarks series with FTSE-Russell. These benchmarks enabled us to provide net-zero index products and will support our next steps in setting out climate policy and work with asset managers.

VI. DISCUSSION

It is vital that the expectation set by asset owners is that the asset managers are not only considering all the risks and opportunity arising from climate risk but changing their processes to take it into account. This should result in different outcomes from investment decision making. Although Brunel's mandates are all relatively new, and engaging managers is an ongoing and evolving activity, we believe we have different portfolios as an outcome from the interventions and many managers are using the principles of work with us in other product areas. Whilst we recognise weighted average carbon intensity is only one metric for gauging changes in portfolio outcomes, it does provide supporting evidence for the outcomes from our approach.

Table 2 Brunel Pension Partnership Weighted Average Carbon Intensity for a Sample of Brunel's Portfolios[26]

Portfolio	Reduction %	Carbon Intensity (£m invested)	
		2021 Portfolio	2019 Baseline
Active Portfolios			
Brunel UK Active Portfolio	25.90%	209.0	282
Brunel Global High Alpha Portfolio	50.41%	149.3	301
Brunel Emerging Markets Portfolio	32.86%	382.7	570
Brunel Active Low Volatility	35.72%	214.7	334
Brunel Global Sustainable Portfolio	15.47%	282.3	334
Brunel Climate Transition Benchmark UK Equity Index	18.39%	229.3	281
Brunel Paris Aligned World Developed Equity Index	43.41%	171.5	303
Brunel Climate Transition Benchmark Developed Market Equity Index	22.48%	234.9	303

Source: Brunel Pension Partnership (2022).
Note: Carbon intensity is a weighted average carbon (equivalent) intensity per million pounds invested. The baseline was the investable universe (performance benchmark) for each product as at 31 December 2019, although many were launched in 2020 and 2021.

Brunel does not have all the answers to embedding manager accountability to achieve net-zero, but we have made a good start. We shared a selection of case studies that aim to share tools and techniques that have enabled progress and are evidenced in portfolio outcomes.

The key component has been to build strong relationship-based partnerships with asset managers, moving away from a more traditional transactional approach. A practical example of the shift in behaviour we want to see would involve asset managers moving from doing what has been asked (ie following, to the letter, the investment agreement), to thinking about the outcome that is being sought, asking whether there are better ways of achieving that goal and, if needed, proposing adjustments to the investment agreement that would enable that to be achieved, eg widening risk tolerances. This would be reciprocated with us – Brunel – acknowledging that contribution as part of our ongoing assessment and retention of the manager. This shift feels essential to deal with the challenges, such as climate change, that investment industry faces in the 2020s.

VII. CONCLUSION

Becoming Paris-aligned and hitting the net-zero target is the challenge of our generation, especially as the remaining years of this decade are going to be some of the

[26] 'Responsible Investment and Stewardship Outcomes Report' (Brunel Pension Partnership, 2022).

most critical in human history. For investors, particularly asset owners, who carry the responsibility of managing assets on behalf of others, the challenge is incredibly complex. There are still a lot of unknowns and we still need to make judgements on incomplete information, but we know enough to start taking action and as new information arises, we review and adapt those actions.

Drawing on the experience of Brunel we would summarises our critical components of achieving asset manager accountability as:

- senior level commitment and robust governance on your own climate policy, objectives and outcomes;
- being clear on how those policy objectives translate to expectations on asset managers and actively monitor the managers against them;
- not being overly prescriptive on how those outcomes are to be achieved. The manager will know their process best and therefore is best placed to adapt it. They are also therefore accountable for the outcomes;
- welcoming a variety of approaches to managing climate risks and targeting net-zero, as this will help avoid creating other risks, eg factor and concentration risks;
- prioritising those portfolios which present the highest risk and take time to work out the optimal solution. Brunel's portfolio projects have generally taken between 12–18 months to implement;
- being supportive and being prepared to back managers who experiment with changes designed to meet your needs – they will not all work, but failure is an essential component of innovation;
- regularly reviewing and agreeing amendments where necessary. It is expected that portfolios will need to evolve over time;
- ensuring good flow of communication, with climate risk issues integrated into the regular touchpoints;
- ensuring that your other climate policy objectives (policy advocacy, corporate engagement, etc) are consistent and support the expectations on asset managers and the portfolio outcomes.

Our starting point was recognising that that the finance system itself is not fit for purpose in dealing with climate change and placing improving the financial system at the centre of our policy and at the heart of our approach. Our approach recognises that addressing systemic risk needs all those in the system to work together, and that addressing climate change requires a change of mindset and a willingness to push at the boundaries of the conventional wisdom that has shaped the investment industry for generations.

We have learned that to embed accountability to achieve decarbonisation and build resilience into investment strategies, we need to be explicit and persistent in setting the expectations of asset managers and ensuring that climate change is built into each and every process to convey the seriousness of the pursuit. The commitment to do so must therefore come from the top and flow down to everyone in the organisation.

The best innovations come from teamwork, and the challenges of integrating new research into investment processes, in light of the scientific evidence of climate change, will best be done working collaboratively across the industry. There is now a huge amount of guidance and support – possibly too much in some areas and not enough in others – but as an industry we have made huge strides and continue to do so. Sharing our experiences with others is crucial to enable all of us to learn from both successes and failures, and Brunel will continue to do so as part of its mission to work towards a world worth living in.

17

Net-Zero Asset Owner Alliance Climate Voting Transparency and Benchmarking

THEODOR F COJOIANU, ANDREAS GF HOEPNER, YANAN LIN,
KATE VAN DER MERVE AND ANH VU*

I. INTRODUCTION

A. Asset Owners' Role in Limiting Global Warming to 1.5°C: Asset Allocations and Active Ownership

I N THIS CHAPTER, asset owners discussed are mostly insurance firms and pension funds which are members of either the United Nations Principles for Responsible Investment (UNPRI) or of the Net-Zero Asset Owner Alliance (NZAOA). Those asset owners usually entrust their assets to asset managers, which may or may not belong to asset owners' own asset management arms. The unique position of asset owners in responsible investment stems not only from their considerable assets under management (AUM) but also from their role as long-term fiduciaries to a large body of beneficiaries. Asset owners' asset allocation decisions play an instrumental role in responsible investment since their assets under management represent on average 34 per cent of GDP in OECD countries.[1] For example, according to an estimate in 2012, pension funds were the largest type of institutional investors with an AUM of US$33.9 trillion.[2] With the enormous assets, pension funds own more than a quarter of global listed equities in organisations that are accountable for sustainability issues such as environmental externalities. Moreover, with the advent of state pension auto-enrolment in the UK, the role of pension funds and asset owners in the financial industry is expected to increase.[3] As such, asset owners can be drivers in limiting

---

*The authors are grateful to the Sunrise Project for commissioning the analysis and to Jane Chu, Minyoung Shin and Alex Wilks for their invaluable input, editorial assistance and case study preparation.
[1] R Sievänen et al, 'The Drivers of Responsible Investment: The Case of European Pension Funds' (2013) 117(1) *Journal of Business Ethics* 137.
[2] H Létourneau, 'The Responsible Investment Practices of the World's Largest Government-Sponsored Investment Funds' in *The Routledge Handbook of Responsible Investment* (Routledge, 2015).
[3] S Vitols, 'European Pension Funds and Socially Responsible Investment' (2011) 17(1) *Transfer: European Review of Labour and Research* 29.

global warming to 1.5°C by allocating assets to more sustainable investments and corporate practices.

From the real economy's perspective, if we consider finance as 'the grease of the economy'[4] and as controller and monitor of capital flows, then a more sustainable finance would mean a more sustainable economy.[5] In that sense, asset owners, which are at the top of the institutional investors food chain,[6] play a key role in building and promoting a sustainable economy.[7] It is widely accepted in the industry that asset owners create demand for responsible investing. Researchers hypothesise that there is a transmission mechanism between the financial industry and the broader economy in the context of responsible investing. Specifically, asset owners take leadership, prompting asset managers, financial intermediaries, and finally the broader economy to follow suit. There are empirical studies confirming this argument.[8]

Apart from being one of the largest types of investors, asset owners also act as fiduciaries to beneficiaries that are large enough in size to be deemed representative of a society in general. Asset owners' characteristics fit well with the universal owner hypothesis which proposes that the largest institutional investors invested in the total market will stand to benefit from an economy that grows sustainably rather than from particular stocks that earn profits by causing or taking advantage of negative externalities such as damages on the environment or on communities they operate in. Hence, integrating Environmental, Social, and Governance (ESG) factors into investment decisions will be beneficial in the long term for asset owner.[9] Indeed, several asset owners have assumed leadership in responsible investing, such as the Norway Government's Pension Fund Global,[10] the Swedish AP Funds, or the California Public Employees' Retirement System (CalPERS).[11]

B. Asset Owners and Climate Voting

Prior research has focused on the consistency of ESG commitment and the votes of asset managers[12] and specific characteristics that influence ESG voting patterns, the

---

[4] B Scholtens, 'Finance as a Driver of Corporate Social Responsibility' (2006) 68(1) *Journal of Business Ethics* 19.

[5] AGF Hoepner et al, 'Does an Asset Owner's Institutional Setting Influence its Decision to Sign the Principles for Responsible Investment?' (2021) 168(2) *Journal of Business Ethics* 389.

[6] RA Monks, *The New Global Investors: How Shareowners Can Unlock Sustainable Prosperity Worldwide* (Capstone, 2001).

[7] T Busch et al, 'Sustainable Development and Financial Markets: Old Paths and New Avenues' (2016) 55(3) *Business & Society* 303.

[8] ibid; Scholtens (n 4 above); B Scholtens and R Sievänen, 'Drivers of Socially Responsible Investing: A Case Study of Four Nordic Countries' (2013) 115(3) *Journal of Business Ethics* 605.

[9] M Kiernan, 'Universal Owners and ESG: Leaving Money on the Table?' (2007) 15(3) *Corporate Governance: An International Review* 478; S Lydenberg, 'Universal Investors and Socially Responsible Investors: A Tale of Emerging Affinities' (2007) 15(3) *Corporate Governance: An International Review* 467; R Thamotheram and H Wildsmith, 'Increasing Long-Term Market Returns: Realising the Potential of Collective Pension Fund Action' (2007) 15(3) *Corporate Governance: An International Review* 438.

[10] AGF Hoepner and L Schopohl, 'On the Price of Morals in Markets: An Empirical Study of the Swedish AP-Funds and the Norwegian Government Pension Fund' (2018) 151(3) *Journal of Business Ethics* 665. See also Ch 12 above.

[11] G Clark and A Monk, 'The Legitimacy and Governance of Norway's Sovereign Wealth Fund: the Ethics of Global Investment' (2010) 42(7) *Environment and Planning A* 1723; O Gjessing and H Syse,

incentives of investors to vote for ES proposals,[13] the comparison of ESG funds and other funds on voting patterns.[14] These studies offer contradictory conclusions on the ESG voting of investors who are dedicated to integrating ESG factors into their investment. For example, Curtis et al[15] investigate whether ESG funds vote the shares in their portfolio companies differently from non-ESG funds, using the Voting Analytics database from ISS for 2018–2019. They find that ESG funds are substantially more likely to oppose management by supporting shareholder proposals, particularly when shareholder proposals address environmental issues, 'E' funds are far more likely than other funds to oppose management. Similarly, Michaely et al[16] find that ES funds are approximately 30 per cent more supportive of ES proposals compared to non-ES funds. Dikolli et al[17] report that ESG funds are more likely than non-ESG funds to vote for ES proposals: 32.03 per cent of votes by ESG funds on ES proposals are in favour of the proposals, compared to only 21.38 per cent for non-ESG funds.

However, other studies present the opposite evidence, showing that the ESG dedication is not reflected in the voting records of investors. In particular, He et al[18] look at the mutual funds voting across 2004 to 2016 on ES proposals, and conclude that mutual funds are less likely to vote for ES issues supported by ISS, compared to other shareholder proposals that are similarly receive ISS support, and the tendencies to disagree with ISS for recommendations on ES proposals has increased over time. CN Griffin[19] even more directly focuses on the three largest asset managers only (Vanguard, BlackRock, and State Street), and concludes that they support far less ES proposals than some of their competitors. A more recent study identifies the contradiction of increased interest in sustainable investing and lower level of support on ESG issues with a more extensive sample. Specifically, W de Groot et al[20] investigate how the largest US asset managers vote on ESG related issues, using over 20 million voting records filed in Form N-PX with the US Securities and Exchange Commission (SEC) from 2009 until 2018. They find that despite the increasing absolute number of votes on environmental and social issues over the recent decade, the relative number of these proposals are put forward by shareholders. Furthermore, asset managers vote against the majority of all environmental and social proposals. Large and passive asset managers vote significantly less in favour of environmental and social proposals

'Norwegian Petroleum Wealth and Universal Ownership' (2007) 15(3) *Corporate Governance: An International Review* 427; J Hawley and A Williams, *The Rise of Fiduciary Capitalism: How Institutional Investors Can Make Corporate America More Democratic* (University of Pennsylvania Press, 2007).

[12] W De Groot et al, 'Sustainable Voting Behavior of Asset Managers: Do They Walk the Walk?' (2021) *SSRN Electronic Journal*; CN Griffin, 'Environmental & Social Voting at Index Funds' (2020) 44(2–3) *Delaware Journal of Corporate Law* 167.

[13] Y He et al, 'Mutual Fund Voting on Environmental and Social Proposals' (2018) *SSRN Electronic Journal*.

[14] Q Curtis et al, 'Do ESG Mutual Funds Deliver on Their Promises?' (2021) 21(17) *University of Pennsylvania Institute for Law & Economics Research Paper*; S Dikolli et al, 'Walk the Talk: ESG Mutual Fund Voting on Shareholder Proposals' (2021) *SSRN Electronic Journal*.

[15] Curtis et al, ibid.

[16] R Michaely et al, 'ES Votes That Matter' *ECGI Working Paper No 774/2021* (2021), https://ecgi.global/sites/default/files/working_papers/documents/michaelyordonezcalafirubiofinal.pdf.

[17] See n 14 above.

[18] See n 13 above.

[19] See n 12 above.

[20] See n 12 above.

compared to medium-sized and active managers. Members of PRI do not vote in favour of ESG proposals more often than non-members, and asset managers with a longer membership tenure have no better voting records than more recent members.

Below we focus on NZAOA members with AUM as of early 2022 of US$10.4 trillion (UNEPFI, 2022) and bold commitments to transitioning their investment portfolios to net-zero emissions by 2050.

C. About the NZAOA

Launched in September 2019, the UN-convened NZAOA represents 60 institutional investors with US$10 trillion assets under management.[21] The Alliance describes itself as 'an international group of institutional investors delivering on a bold commitment to transition our investment portfolios to net-zero greenhouse gas (GHG) emissions by 2050'.

As a collaborative initiative, the NZAOA recommends that its members seek to align their portfolios with the Paris Agreement by contributing to a number of tracks, which include setting engagement targets, sector targets, sub-portfolio emission targets and financing transition targets. Among these tracks, the engagement target is the only mandatory track.[22]

The NZAOA has also underlined the importance of climate voting in a report it released in April 2021, 'Elevating Climate Diligence on Proxy Voting Approaches: A Foundation for Asset Owner Engagement of Asset Managers'. This position paper outlines a set of principles that serve as a tool for asset managers to use when conducting climate-related proxy voting, such as governance, long-term interest, merit-based evaluation of climate relevant votes, and transparency and accessibility of voting records. In particular, the report states that climate votes should 'be evaluated based on merit of the proposal and not current status of engagement or other engagement considerations'.[23] The Alliance also specifies that the alignment between asset owners and asset managers in climate stewardship activities, such as proxy voting, is crucial to support reaching the commitment to NZAOA's goal of net-zero portfolio emissions by 2050.

II. A QUANTITATIVE ANALYSIS OF NZAOA MEMBERS' RECORDS

A. Climate Votes

For analysing the climate voting behaviour of NZAOA members and other PRI members that are not members of the NZAOA, we used data extracted from

---

[21] NZAOA, https://www.unepfi.org/net-zero-alliance/.

[22] NZAOA, *Inaugural 2025 Target Setting Protocol* (January 2021), https://www.unepfi.org/publications/aoapublication/inaugural-2025-target-setting-protocol/.

[23] NZAOA and PRI, 'Elevating Climate Diligence on Proxy Voting Approaches: A Foundation for Asset Owner Engagement of Asset Managers' (April 2021), https://www.unepfi.org/wordpress/wp-content/uploads/2021/04/16-Elevating-Climate-Diligence-2.pdf.

ProxyInsight in September 2021. Proxy Insight frequently uses Freedom of Information Requests, which provides them with better global coverage for asset owners than alternative data sources. Since all NZAOA members that appear in the Proxy Insight data are PRI members, when the report mentions PRI members, it means PRI members that are non-NZAOA.

The dependent variable in the climate votes analysis is proxy votes in favour of the climate. We use data on climate-related votes for the period from April 2009 to September 2021 provided by ProxyInsight. And through a series of steps illustrated in Figure 1, we were able to observe climate votes directly cast by asset owners.

Figure 1 Filtering Process of Asset Owners from Proxy Insight

Only 'for' votes on climate resolutions were counted towards voting in favour of climate resolution. The text of the resolution was also reviewed to ensure the vote cast 'for' would truly be a vote in favour of the climate. For example, in the case of a resolution text that reads 'Approve Lobbying Inconsistent with the Goals of the Paris Agreement', the 'for' votes were re-classified as an 'against' vote. We also assigned several exploratory variables to observe and analyse the climate voting patterns of NZAOA members and its non-member peer group including 'NZAOA membership', 'votes after NZAOA member signs up to the Alliance' and 'company's industry in the fossil fuel industry'. The control variable in this study was AUM. The research also analysed the voting pattern on ambitious climate resolutions, such as those that require companies to change their business model and to align their business strategy with the Paris Climate Agreement. Finally, the study also compared a subsample of nine NZAOA members with climate voting records before and after joining the Alliance against nine non-NZAOA peers. The peer group was determined based on country, AUM,[24] and voting patterns before the NZAOA membership date.

[24] For all asset owners, we use IPE website for AUM (https://www.top1000funds.com/asset-owner/). In case of Allianz Global Investors, Ilmarinen Mutual Pension Insurance Company, and Achmea where IPE directory does not have their AUM records, we refer to their 2020 PRI public reports. For Mercy Investments, we refer to its website report (https://www.mercyinvestmentservices.org/VivaMercy_2020.01_10%20 Years%20of%20Investing%20with%20Values%20and%20Vision.pdf) since neither IPE directory nor its PRI public report has its AUM.

Table 1 Subsample of NZAOA and non-NZAOA group

NZAOA member	PRI member
Allianz Global Investors	**Ilmarinen Mutual Pension Insurance Company**
Country: Germany	*Country: Finland*
AUM: US$562,943m	*AUM: US$55,696m*
Type: Insurance Company & Asset Manager	*Type: Insurance Company*
California Public Employees' Retirement System (CalPERS)	**California State Teachers' Retirement System (CalSTRS)**
Country: USA	*Country: USA*
AUM: US$373,000m	*AUM: US$238,861m*
Type: Pension Fund	*Type: Pension Fund*
AMF	**Fjarde Ap-Fonden**
Country: Sweden	*Country: Sweden*
AUM: US$80,760m	*AUM: US$50,160m*
Type: Pension Fund	*Type: Pension Fund*
Storebrand Asset Management	**KLP Kapitalforvaltning**
Country: Norway	*Country: Norway*
AUM: US$90,378m	*AUM: US$67,680m*
Type: Insurance Company & Pension Fund	*Type: Pension Fund*
Aviva Investors	**Brunel Pension Partnership**
Country: UK	*Country: UK*
AUM: US$23,426m	*AUM: US$40,000m*
Type: Insurance Company & Asset Manager	*Type: Pension Fund*
AXA Investment Managers	**Achmea**
Country: France	*Country: Netherlands*
AUM: US$634,925m	*AUM: US$48,868m*
Type: Insurance Company & Asset Manager	*Type: Insurance Company*
Wespath Investment Management	**Mercy Investments**
Country: USA	*Country: USA*
AUM: US$19,970m	*AUM: US$35,000m*
Type: Faith-based pension fund	*Type: Faith-related investment company*
Pensionskassernes Administration (PKA)	**PenSam**
Country: Denmark	*Country: Denmark*
AUM: US$53,500m	*AUM: US$22,626m*
Type: Pension Fund	*Type: Pension Fund*

(continued)

Table 1 *(Continued)*

NZAOA member	PRI member
P+ (DIP/JOEP)	AP Pension
Country: Denmark	*Country: Denmark*
AUM: US$19,917m	*AUM: US$18,000m*
Type: Pension Fund	*Type: Pension Fund*

After selecting the variables, the study conducted: (i) a logistic regression for the whole sample and for each resolution; (ii) a difference-in-differences (DiD) regression for the whole dataset; (iii) a DiD regression for the subsample; (iv) DiD regression for the whole dataset and subsample for ambitious climate resolutions, such as those that require companies to change their business model.

B. Voting Transparency

The research also reviewed the voting patterns of NZAOA members on ESG voting from data provided in the 2020 reporting year of the PRI Transparency reports to understand how the rest of the NZAOA members were voting on climate. All NZAOA members studied in this report are members of the PRI and are required to publicly disclose their responsible investment and stewardship activities annually. We analysed the PRI Transparency reports to understand the voting pattern of NZAOA members, including how NZAOA members make decisions, evaluate external adviser's recommendations and use voting as an escalation strategy. In October 2021, the Alliance published its first Progress Report to highlight its commitments and achievements over the two years. Although the Progress Report provides few examples highlighting improvements in proxy voting policies of some members and its expectations of asset managers in aligning proxy voting with net-zero commitments, it does not provide a comprehensive overview of how its net-zero aligned proxy voting guideline is impacting the voting outcomes on climate resolutions.[25] Therefore, we concluded that the latest PRI Transparency is the most comprehensive publicly available information for this part of the analysis.

C. Analysis Results

Our study has unveiled the following key findings. In terms of climate voting practice, voting data from ProxyInsight revealed that out of 46 asset owners who are part of the NZAOA (the number of members as of the start of the study – September 2021), only 13 asset owners directly exercise their share voting rights on climate-related

---

[25] Net Zero Asset Owner Alliance and PRI, 'Credible Ambition, Immediate Action: The first progress report of the UN-convened Net-Zero Asset Owner Alliance' (October 2021), https://www.unepfi.org/wordpress/wp-content/uploads/2021/10/AOA-Progress-Report-2021.pdf.

shareholder proposals. Although NZAOA members were early adopters of strong climate stewardship, joining the NZAOA does not result in asset owners improving their voting in favour of climate resolutions more than peers in the non-NZAOA group.

Our research reveals that between April 2009 to September 2021, asset owners that are now members of the NZAOA were more likely to vote in favour of climate action at company Annual General Meetings (AGMs) than the non-NZAOA peer group. This is an indicator that investors that joined the NZAOA in its first two years were early adopters of strong climate voting policies. However, when we analysed the voting pattern of NZAOA members and their non-member peer group, we found that after becoming an NZAOA member, the NZAOA group's increase in pro-climate voting is not statistically different to the increase of the non-NZAOA peer group during the same time period. This is an indicator that joining the Alliance may be a recognition of existing voting practice, not an accelerator of that practice.

Asset owners (both NZAOA and non-NZAOA group) are more likely to vote in favour of climate resolutions at fossil fuel companies. However, this voting behaviour does not apply to ambitious climate resolutions that call for Paris-aligned strategies at major oil and gas companies. We find that asset owners (both NZAOA and non-NZAOA group) are more likely to vote in favour of climate resolutions if the company whose shares are voted is a fossil fuel company. On the other hand, our case studies suggest inconsistent voting behaviour by NZAOA members when it comes to supporting ambitious climate resolutions that call for Paris-aligned strategies. For example, during the 2021 AGM at Royal Dutch Shell, only three out of the nine observed NZAOA members voted for the independent shareholder resolution that required Shell to set quantitative targets to reduce its emissions in line with the Paris Agreement's goal of limiting global warming to 1.5°C, while voting against management's Say on Climate proposal.

Figure 2 How Matched NZAOA and PRI Members Vote on Climate-related Issues over Time

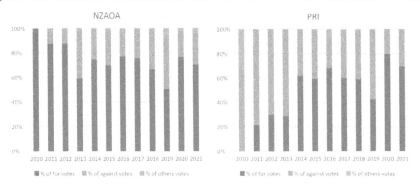

(9 NZAOA members and their 9 PRI counterparts)

Regarding voting transparency, according to the PRI Transparency reports, we find that a large proportion of NZAOA members have little insight into how their voting mandates are being exercised by service providers: 39 per cent of NZAOA members do not make public how voting decisions are typically being made; among

NZAOA members who report that they hire service providers, 75 per cent do not disclose publicly whether they review their advisors' voting recommendations; 78 per cent of NZAOA members do not disclose if they (co)filed any shareholder resolutions; 63 per cent of NZAOA members either do not make public or do not have a formal escalation strategy after unsuccessful voting; 72 per cent of NZAOA members do not disclose whether they have a securities lending programme.

III. CASE STUDIES

In this section, we present case studies to demonstrate whether NZAOA members are practising merit-based climate voting to support ambitious climate resolutions in line with the Paris Climate Agreement.[26]

A. Case Study 1: Royal Dutch Shell Climate Resolutions

The 2021 AGM of British-Dutch oil and gas major Royal Dutch Shell serves as an example of how NZAOA members evaluated two contrasting climate votes. In the spring of 2021, the shareholder advocacy groups Follow This and ACCR filed a climate resolution that would require Shell to set quantitative targets to reduce its emissions in line with the Paris Agreement's goal of limiting global warming to 1.5°C. The resolution further specified that these targets should cover the short-, mid- and long-term emissions of the company's operations and its energy use (scope 1, 2 and 3).[27]

Shell then tabled its own resolution, asking investors to vote to approve its transition plan. The oil and gas major's transition plan was identified by NGOs and some investors as falling short of what is needed to limit global warming to 1.5°C.[28] Instead, Shell's plan allows the company to continue to invest billions of dollars in upstream oil and gas and to exclude petrochemicals from its targets, while implementing very large amounts of offsets this decade. In the lead up to the company's AGM, a group of six NGOs – Greenpeace, ShareAction, Follow This, Reclaim Finance, ACCR and Oil Change International – wrote an open letter to investors urging them to reject Shell's transition plan.

---

[26] Since this study focuses on establishing the causality of NZAOA membership and ambitious climate voting, for the case studies, we only analysed the votes of asset owners that were NZAOA members at the time of the AGM. And for select asset owners we referred to the voting records of the asset owner's asset management wing.

[27] Follow This, '2021 Royal Dutch Shell Resolution', https://www.follow-this.org/wp-content/uploads/2021/01/CR2102-Shell-Climate-Targets-Resolution-2021.pdf.

[28] Reclaim Finance, 'Open Letter to Investors Engaging Shell on Climate Strategy' (26 February 2021), https://reclaimfinance.org/site/en/2021/04/13/open-letter-to-investors-engaging-shell-on-climate-strategy/; 'Advisory Firm PIRC Slams Shell on Climate Stragety before AGM' (*Reuters*, 11 May 2021), https://www.reuters.com/world/uk/leading-advisory-urges-shareholders-oppose-shells-climate-resolution-2021-05-11/; 'Methodist Church Dumps Shell over "Inadequate" Climate Plans' (*Financial Times*, 30 April 2021), https://www.ft.com/content/9c8195ac-2203-428d-b6c3-91cb717eb084.

At the AGM:

- 30 per cent of investor votes cast backed the independent climate targets resolution;
- 88 per cent of investor votes cast backed Shell's transition plan.

Nine NZAOA members' votes at Shell's 2021 AGM are available in ProxyInsight. There is inconsistency in how individual NZAOA members vote on ambitious climate resolutions that call for Paris-aligned strategies. Specifically, in the context of ProxyInsight data, we define ambitious climate resolutions as those that would force companies to transform their business models to align with the Paris Agreement, for example, adopting quantitative GHG goals for operations, adopting quantitative renewable energy goals, and ceasing to make new investments in non-renewable energy and scale down existing investments.

- three NZAOA members voted in favour of the independent shareholder resolution and voted against Shell's energy transition plan;
- five Alliance members supported management by voting in favour of Shell's energy transition plan, while one abstained;
- finally, one Alliance investor voted in favour of both the independent shareholder resolution and Shell's own proposed energy transition plan.

The votes of the remaining NZAOA members who may hold shares at that time are, however, not publicly available.

Table 2 NZAOA Vote Cast on Independent Shareholder Resolution That Requests Shell to Set and Publish Targets for GHG Emissions during Shell's 2021 AGM

Resolution: Request Shell to Set and Publish Targets for Greenhouse Gas (GHG) Emissions (Proposal #21) **Proponent:** Shareholder	
Asset Owner	**Vote Cast**
Allianz Global Investors	Against
Aviva Investors	For
AXA Asset Management	Against
BNP Paribas Asset Management	Against
CalPERS	Against
Nordea Investment Management	For
PKA	For
Storebrand Asset Management	For
Wespath Investment Management	Against

Source: ProxyInsight, accessed November 2021.

Table 3 NZAOA Vote Cast on Management Proposed Resolution that Request to Approve Shell's Energy Transition Strategy during Shell's 2021 AGM

Resolution: Approve Shell's Energy Transition Strategy (Proposal #20) **Proponent:** Management	
Asset Owner	**Vote Cast**
Allianz Global Investors	For
Aviva Investors	Against
AXA Asset Management	For
BNP Paribas Asset Management	For
CalPERS	Abstain
Nordea Investment Management	For
PKA	Against
Storebrand Asset Management	Against
Wespath Investment Management	For

Source: ProxyInsight, accessed November 2021.

Despite the emphasis on the importance of merit-based climate voting, this inconsistency among members on how they vote on ambitious climate resolutions raises queries about whether NZAOA members have a sufficiently consistent view of what a strong corporate climate plan needs to contain, or are walking the talk on their climate voting mandates. It also illustrates how being a member of the Alliance does not automatically improve a member's ability to see through and reject a heavy emitter's plans to continue expanding fossil supply.

Just ten days after Shell's AGM, a Dutch judge ordered the company to cut its emissions sharply, finding that the climate plans the company had presented to its AGM 'largely amount to rather intangible, undefined and non-binding plans for the long term'.[29]

B. Case Study 2: Sempra Energy Climate Lobby Alignment Resolution

A resolution at US-based power utility Sempra Energy provides insights into how Alliance members approached the issue of climate lobbying alignment.

Independent shareholder advocacy organisation As You Sow tabled a resolution calling on Sempra Energy's board of directors to:

> evaluate and issue a report at reasonable cost omitting proprietary information describing
> if and how Sempras lobbying activities direct and through trade associations align with the

---

[29] Editorial, 'Big Oil is in the Dock' (*Guardian*, 28 May 2021), https://www.theguardian.com/business/commentisfree/2021/may/28/the-guardian-view-on-climate-change-lawsuits-big-oil-is-in-the-dock.

Paris Agreements goal to limit temperature rise to 1.5 degrees and how Sempra plans to mitigate risks presented by any misalignment.[30]

Sempra's concerted anti-climate lobbying has received sustained negative attention in recent years. Federal legislators have also taken note and sent a public letter condemning Sempra's efforts to 'systematically undermine greenhouse gas reduction targets in California'.[31]

Sempra subsidiary Southern California Gas (SoCalGas) stands accused of establishing and funding a consumer front group to promote 'renewable gas' and 'balanced energy solutions', including through mobilising Latino leaders.[32]

The California Public Utilities Commission's Public Advocate's Office investigated SoCalGas for its use of ratepayer funds to promote natural gas.[33] Then, in April, a few weeks before Sempra's 2021 AGM, regulators at the California Public Utilities Commission ruled that SoCalGas misused customer money to lobby against energy-efficiency standards for buildings, and ordered the utility to refund those amounts to ratepayers.[34]

In addition to its lobbying directly and via its subsidiaries, Sempra Energy provides very limited transparency on lobbying via industry associations of which it is a member. It makes very significant financial contributions to the American Gas Association and the US Chamber of Commerce.[35] Both organisations have been found by Influence Map – an independent think tank providing analysis on how businesses affect the climate crisis – to back significant lobbying against climate-friendly legislation.

At Sempra Energy's AGM the lobby alignment resolution was backed by just 37 per cent of investors. Eleven NZAOA members' votes on this resolution are available in ProxyInsight and all voted in favour of this resolution. The votes of the remaining NZAOA members who may hold shares at that time are, however, not publicly available.

---

[30] 'Proxy Memo, Sempra Energy Shareholder Proposal on Climate Lobbying', https://static1.squarespace.com/static/59a706d4f5e2319b70240ef9/t/60a7e82dc167506808613839/1621616686377/21.SRE.1+Sempra_ClimateLobbying_ProxyMemo_20210323+-+WEB.pdf.

[31] 'California Federal Legislators Press SoCalGas on Reported Efforts to "Undermine" California's Climate Goals', (*Utility Dive*, 2 November 2020), https://www.utilitydive.com/news/california-federal-legislators-press-socalgas-on-reported-efforts-to-under/588174/.

[32] 'US Gas Utility Funds "Front" Consumer Group to Fight Natural Gas Bans' (*Guardian*, 26 July 2019), https://www.theguardian.com/us-news/2019/jul/26/us-natural-gas-ban-socalgas-berkeley.

[33] 'Is America's Biggest Gas Utility Abusing Customer Money? A California Watchdog Demands Answers (*LA Times*, 23 July 2020), https://www.latimes.com/environment/story/2020-07-23/is-americas-biggest-gas-utility-fighting-climate-action-california-demands-answers.

[34] 'CPUC Judge Orders SoCalGas to Return Ratepayer Funds but Stops Short of Imposing Financial Penalty (*Utility Dive*, 27 April 2021), https://www.utilitydive.com/news/cpuc-judge-socalgas-return-ratepayer-funds/599048/.

[35] Sempra Energy: Climate Policy Engagement Overview (*Influence Map*, April 2021), https://ca100.influencemap.org/site//data/000/009/Sempra-Energy-Resolution-Briefing-April21.pdf.

Table 4 NZAOA Vote Cast on Independent Shareholder Resolution that Requests Report on Lobbying Payments and Policy with the Paris Agreement during Sempra Energy's 2021 AGM

Resolution: Report on Lobbying Payments and Policy with the Paris Agreement (Proposal #5) **Proponent:** Shareholder	
Asset Owner	**Vote Cast**
Allianz Global Investors	For
AMF	For
Aviva Investors	For
AXA Asset Management	For
BNP Paribas Asset Management	For
CalPERS	For
Cbus Super Fund	For
Nordea Investment Management	For
PKA	For
Storebrand Asset Management	For
Wespath Investment Management	For

Source: ProxyInsight, accessed November 2021.

This lack of data limits the Alliance's ability to fulfil its objective to 'be reliably transparent and proactive in explaining our role, views and how we are addressing key issues and limitations of portfolio decarbonisation beyond our control [and] to learn from and build on external feedback received through public dialogue'.[36]

The aggregated data in the Alliance's Progress Report describing its first two years of activity also fails to bring sufficient transparency to Alliance member voting.[37]

IV. RECOMMENDATIONS

Based on our specific quantitative and case studies above, we would like to put forward the following brief recommendations related to NZAOA signatories and their climate proxy voting activities. First, asset owners in the NZAOA and similar initiatives should align their proxy voting with the goal of limiting global warming to 1.5°C in alignment with the International Energy Agency Net Zero pathway. Second, asset owners should develop and publicly disclose escalation policies, and make transparent in a timely manner, all elements of their voting outcomes. The third recommendation is that asset owners should track, monitor and disclose how votes are exercised on their

---

[36] Net-Zero Asset Owner Alliance, 'Inaugural 2025 Target Setting Protocol' (January 2021), 13, https://www.unepfi.org/wordpress/wp-content/uploads/2021/01/Alliance-Target-Setting-Protocol-2021.pdf.

[37] Net-Zero Asset Owner Alliance, 'Credible Ambition, Immediate Action' (October 2021), https://www.unepfi.org/publications/credible-ambition-immediate-action/.

behalf. Fourth, asset owners should commit to holding asset managers accountable if the asset manager fails to represent their climate voting values and commitments. This includes finding alternative asset managers if necessary. Finally, future versions of NZAOA's Progress Report should provide more detail on the issues covered by the aforementioned analysis.

However, there are critical challenges that need to be addressed. In fact, although asset owners as investors would like to engage with and push companies to reduce GHG emissions, it remains to be seen what it means for companies in terms of operations and strategies, especially those in the oil and gas sector, to be aligned with the net-zero goal. Until we have a clearer definition of such alignment, it is difficult for all asset owners as investors to reach an agreement on their voting decisions regarding climate resolutions put forward at annual general meetings. In addition, certain aspects of transition strategies depend on technological progress, whereby hindering companies' transition to be aligned with the goal of limiting global warming to 1.5°C. The Institutional Investors Group on Climate Change are working with other investor networks to build an oil and gas net-zero standard that can support companies in the transition and outline clearly measures needed to increase the credibility of the transition from investors' perspective.[38]

V. CONCLUSIONS

Using data from ProxyInsight and the PRI, we unveil that out of the 46 NZAOAs analysed, only 13 have at least one observable climate vote which the asset owners have cast themselves. Comparing the pro-climate voting performance of these 13 asset owners with their non-NZAOA PRI peers, we find that after signing on to the NZAOA, these asset owners have not increased their pro-climate voting more than their peers. In addition, by examining the PRI Transparency reports of the entire NZAOA cohort, the evidence suggests that NZAOAs do not systematically track or disclose how (climate) votes are exercised on their behalf.

This points to two important areas of improvement for NZAOAs and any asset owner that looks to positively impact the climate and ultimately seeks to claim climate investing leadership. First, it would require complete and timely transparency on how each climate related vote was cast, either by asset owners directly or on their behalf. Second, for those votes which were voted against climate change mitigation actions, asset owners should disclose the rationale for doing so, either as a result of their own analysis or the rationale of the proxy advisers that they choose to follow. This would allow for a comprehensive benchmarking exercise across the climate voting record of asset owners whose investments are either managed in-house, are fully outsourced or are a mix of the two. Such level of transparency would also allow for an accurate

---

[38] Adam Matthews, '"The Goal is Clear and Unambiguous, and Shell is Accountable for Delivering" CoE Pension Board's Adam Matthews on Shell's Transition Strategy' (*Responsible Investor*, 27 April 2021), https://www.responsible-investor.com/the-goal-is-clear-and-unambiguous-and-shell-is-accountable-for-delivering-coe-pensions-board-s-adam-matthews-on-shell-s-transition-strategy/.

assessment of whether the NZAOA initiative is indeed a leading initiative. The level of transparency of the NZAOA members does not allow for such a comprehensive assessment and thus, the NZAOA initiative cannot claim global climate voting leadership. As a follow-up, climate voting research would benefit from further insights into the recommendations of proxy advisors and what determines whether asset owners follow or diverge from the recommendation, particularly if it is against the advancement of climate change mitigation. Follow-on research could also address the impacts of signing-up to the PRI and how the PRI's transparency report data on voting relates to the actual voting performance of asset owners.

Index

Lightning Source UK Ltd.
Milton Keynes UK
UKHW021353180223
417080UK00005B/85

9 781509 953752